The SPIRITUAL HERITAGE *of the* HUMAN RACE

The SPIRITUAL HERITAGE of the HUMAN RACE

An Introduction to the World's Religions

Suheil Bushrui • Mehrdad Massoudi
In collaboration with James Madaio,
Michael Dravis, and Michael Russo

ONEWORLD
OXFORD

A Oneworld Book

First published by Oneworld Publications 2010

A CIP record for this title is available
from the British Library

ISBN 978–1–85168–574–5

Typeset by Jayvee, Trivandrum, India
Cover design by www.fatfacedesign.com
Printed and bound in India for Imprint Digital

The publishers would like to thank Mr Hassan and Mrs Tahereh Saadat
for their generous financial support for this publication

Oneworld Publications
UK: 185 Banbury Road, Oxford OX2 7AR, England
USA: 38 Greene Street, 4th Floor, New York, NY 10013, USA
www.oneworld-publications.com

The Spiritual Heritage of the Human Race is an essential component to the methodology of the study of religion developed at the University of Maryland at College Park under the auspices of the Honors Program and the Center for International Development and Conflict Management. The course was the recipient of the first Temple of Understanding Interfaith Education Award for outstanding work in the field of interfaith education.

Learn more about Oneworld. Join our mailing list to
find out about our latest titles and special offers at:

www.oneworld-publications.com

To
Anna Harper
in grateful recollection
of her generosity and many kindnesses,
her luminous example of love and service,
and her unshakable faith in the Good, the True, and the Beautiful

Mehrdad Massoudi dedicates his share of the work
to his wife Huda Jarrah
and
to the memory of her parents, Hayat and Yusuf Jarrah

CONTENTS

3 THE RELIGIOUS TRADITIONS OF ANCIENT EGYPT

4 THE RELIGIOUS TRADITIONS OF ANCIENT GREECE

5 THE ZOROASTRIAN FAITH

6 THE HINDU TRADITION

7 THE BUDDHIST TRADITION

12 THE JEWISH FAITH

13 THE CHRISTIAN FAITH

ILLUSTRATIONS

A NOTE ON THE TEXT

In transliterating into the Roman alphabet from the languages of the various spiritual and religious traditions, the authors of this book have adopted simple forms without diacritical signs, except where it is essential. All other transliterations in quoted passages are retained as they appear in the text from which they are extracted. In addition, since the authors have endeavored to place emphasis on interfaith understanding throughout this book, and to present all the religious traditions in a spirit of unity and mutual respect, they have tried to maintain consistency across all the chapters by omitting the honorific titles before the names of founders of religions.

FOREWORD

ALISON VAN DYK

The Spiritual Heritage of the Human Race is a work developed out of a lifetime of scholarship and teaching about the great religions of humanity. Using the history of the evolution of civilization as a framework, the authors seek to follow a parallel evolution, that of man's "universal yearning for transcendence." We are given a profound view of humankind's search for ultimate reality, both through the diversity of form and the unity of aspiration for the divine. One of the implications that can be drawn from this epic approach is that religions have evolved one out of the other throughout history. Out of the ancient Hindu religion, for instance, grew Buddhism, Jainism, Sikhism. Out of the Jewish religion grew Christianity and Islam. Out of ancient Chinese religious thought grew the teachings of Lao Tzu and Confucius. This perspective creates a flow and movement that can be likened to one great eternal river of religious inspiration. The reader is conscious of both the uniqueness of each religion and of the vast heritage of religious thought from the earliest "First Peoples" to the great traditions of today. *The Spiritual Heritage of the Human Race* creates for us a passage of initiation into the heart of each of the world's great religions from the standpoints of their relationship to each other as well as their independence from one another. In this way, this book creates a unique contribution to interfaith understanding.

Another gem that comes from such a complex study of religious thinking throughout the ages is the discovery of the universality of symbols. Images such as the Yin and Yang of Taoism are reflected throughout many traditions as duality and non-duality (Buddhism) and the many aspects of the Divine and the oneness of Ultimate Reality (Hinduism). I believe these universal images are helpful in encouraging a new ethic of interfaith dialogue and a paradigm shift of embracing "the other." This movement towards a new openness that dispels hatred, fear, and prejudice is critical for what the authors see as necessary because "a shift in the thinking of humankind brought about by a global ethos offers hope that the patterns of the past, the cycles of tribal and international conflict, can be transcended."[1]

In 2005 the Temple of Understanding, a non-profit interfaith grassroots organization based in the United States, celebrated its forty-fifth anniversary. We asked British artist Thetis Blacker to make us an interfaith banner that would express the concepts of the interfaith movement. As executive director of the organization I was privileged to witness the remarkable process of the birth of the universal image that she created. She describes her painting thus:

> The Tree bears 12 multi-colored fruits which hang from the branches in the shape of a heart. These represent the different faiths, each with its own doctrine, different but linked here in harmony. The leaves of the Tree are olive leaves and symbolize hope. Four roots grow from the four directions of the world, while four rivers of vital water flow outwards to all parts of the earth. Above the Tree hovers a dove, symbol of peace and love. It brings divine blessing upon all in unity.

As I read through the many religions represented in this book, I have thought back to my discussions with Ms. Blacker as she described her process of dreams and revelations to find a universal image for this banner. It is in this context that I was struck by the description of the Mayan symbol of the World Tree. "The three regions of the World Tree – roots, trunk, and branches – reflect the cosmic regions of the underworld, the terrestrial world and the heavens. The World Tree is the cosmic pillar or central axis joining these regions and enabling communications among them."[2] Many parallels are obvious: almost all indigenous religions; the Bodhi Tree of the Buddha; the Kabbalah of Judaism; and the Christmas Tree of Christianity, etc. This interfaith banner, I believe, carries the message of both the uniqueness of each faith tradition and the potential for harmony among them symbolized by the dove of peace. We need these images today to evoke in us a universal consciousness of our oneness as much as we need a new emphasis on interfaith study and dialogue.

In 2004 the Temple of Understanding was given a grant in the name of our founder, Juliet Hollister, for a Temple of Understanding Interfaith Education Award. We looked for a professor or teacher who exemplified the ideals of interfaith education that our organization had tried to uphold over its long history. One such person came immediately to mind: Dr. Suheil Bushrui, the creator of the outstanding interfaith education course taught at the University of Maryland's Center for International Development and Conflict Management. *The Spiritual Heritage of the Human Race* is the culmination of Dr. Bushrui's extensive and cutting-edge work in interfaith education. This book will, I believe, transform the way the study of religions is taught in universities. In setting the history of religions against the background of the evolution of humanity's spiritual heritage, Dr. Suheil Bushrui, Dr. Mehrdad Massoudi, and their colleagues have given us a masterful and unique window into both the essence of each religion and its relationship to the whole of humankind's search for transcendence.

Alison Van Dyk
Chair of the Board
Temple of Understanding
Leaders in Cross-Cultural and Interfaith Education

PREFACE

"The Spiritual Heritage of the Human Race" is the title of a long-standing project initiated by myself in 1993 and conducted under my direction at the University of Maryland. It began as an undergraduate course, of the same title, offered to students in the University of Maryland's Honors Program, with the aim of developing a religious studies curriculum appropriate for today's world of global interdependence and interfaith dialogue.

The intention from the start had been to publish a book that might offer a new, integrative approach to the understanding of religion both to students and to the general reader. Over the last fifteen years, the manuscript was revised and expanded in response to comments furnished by students, colleagues, and learned practitioners and scholars from the various religions represented. The manuscript underwent a significant transformation when Dr. Mehrdad Massoudi, who made major, substantive contributions to the evolution of the book's approach and content, joined the project in 2001. In addition to being a full-time researcher at the Department of Energy, and an adjunct professor at the Biomedical Engineering Department at Carnegie-Mellon University in Pittsburgh, Dr. Massoudi has published many articles on both spirituality and Eastern religions. He also delivered numerous lectures in the "Spiritual Heritage of the Human Race" course on topics related to world religions, dialogue, and pluralism, as well as on issues of science and spirituality. Notably, his many contributions to this book are found in the chapters pertaining to religions originating in India and China, the Zoroastrian and Abrahamic religions, as well as the Introduction. It is no exaggeration to say that Dr. Massoudi has helped greatly to define the *raison d'être* of the book as a whole.

The Spiritual Heritage of the Human Race should be understood as a collaborative effort. The text as it stands today was finalized, in large measure, by myself together with my former student and current colleague, James Madaio. For the past three years Mr. Madaio has been co-lecturer of the "Spiritual Heritage of the Human Race" course, and he has made important contributions throughout the book, while also helping to shape its content and methodology. Michael Russo, lecturer in the Philosophy Department at George Washington University, has also played an important role in bringing this book to fruition. Mr. Russo offered significant, substantive contributions to numerous chapters and has been a guest lecturer in the Spiritual Heritage course on Greek religious philosophy. Michael Dravis, faculty research associate at the Center for International Development and Conflict Management, was an early contributor to and, especially, editor of the text. In the latter capacity, he helped ensure consistency of style and content across the various chapters. Profound gratitude is also due to the students of the "Spiritual Heritage of the Human Race" course, whose interest and responsiveness enriched our understanding, and justified and rewarded all our efforts.

My greatest debt is to Hassan and Tahereh Saadat without whose inspiration, support, and encouragement this book would not have seen the light. Finally, I would like to pay special tribute to Juliet Mabey and the team at Oneworld Publications for the selection of photographs and illustrations, and the general artistic layout of the book.

Suheil Bushrui

The cross of the Russian Orthodox Church of St. Mary Magdalene
on the Mount of Olives is silhouetted against the golden dome of the
Dome of the Rock, Jerusalem

INTRODUCTION

WHAT IS RELIGION?

What is the meaning of human life, or, for that matter, of the life of any creature? To know an answer to this question means to be religious. You ask: Does it make any sense, then, to pose this question? I answer: The man who regards his own life and that of his fellow creatures as meaningless is not merely unhappy but hardly fit for life.[1]

– Albert Einstein

As societies around the world become more interconnected, the question of how we engage and understand cultural and religious diversity is increasingly important. As part of a growing effort to allow human beings to live together peacefully in a global society – embracing our cultural diversity while respecting our common humanity – this book presents a variety of religious paths that have linked human beings with the sacred. From the perspective adopted in this text, one can observe across cultural boundaries a universal yearning for transcendence. This yearning has found its most complete expression, in different times and places, within the religious and spiritual traditions of the world. In that sense, religious diversity is in fact a form of unity – sharing in a common aspiration or religious quest.

Religious diversity is a form of unity – sharing in a common aspiration or religious quest

This introduction presents a discussion of some salient aspects of religious thinking over the ages. The considerations put forward here are starting points for reflection. They are intended to help the reader grasp and appreciate not only the complexity and diversity of religion, but also those essential commonalities and goals that religions share.

An important feature of religious ways of life is that they involve sustained attention to what can be called "ultimate questions," questions of permanently vital relevance to our deepest concerns as human beings. For example, "What is the purpose of life?"; "Is there a God or Ultimate Reality?"; "What makes some actions morally right and others morally wrong?" Such questions have a persistent presence in the human heart and mind, and express our need to live authentically in relation to meaning, truth, and value. In endeavoring to live in this way, biological survival and material prosperity are understood within a wider context that is primarily concerned with the significance of life and how we ought to live as human beings. By nature, human beings of all times and places have been driven to pose ultimate questions. Different peoples are culturally educated to respond to them in different ways (or to ignore them altogether). Religious ways of life aim at maintaining an enduring awareness of ultimate questions and the issues they raise.

No matter how they are formulated, beliefs about such fundamental issues form the basis of our worldviews. In that sense, such beliefs help to determine not only the substance of one's life but also the quality of the world in which we live. Worldviews influence how human beings treat each other, the environment, and all living creatures; what we value individually and, in turn, as societies; how we interpret human suffering; whether or not we view history as directed toward an ordained culmination; and what we believe about the nature of our own humanity. The theologian Paul Tillich suggests that religion pertains to humanity's ultimate concerns and is the all-determining ground, or dimension of depth, that informs the direction of our lives.[2] In many cases, this dimension of depth contains the unexamined premises of our thinking, and these premises, in turn, determine our worldview. They are, so to speak, the filters that color our field of vision. A meaningful study of the spiritual heritage of the human race requires that we honestly examine our own personal, fundamental ideas and ultimate concerns in light of the great religious awakenings and spiritual teachings preserved in the world's wisdom traditions.

Religious perspectives have long been associated with awareness of the sacredness of life and of the profound mysteries of existence. Many of our ancestors lived in awe of these mysteries. Today many people believe that scientific achievements are explaining the mysteries away. But as the philosopher Ludwig Wittgenstein observed, "[empirical or scientific] facts all contribute only to setting the problem, not to its solution. It is not *how* things are in the world that is mystical, but *that* it exists."[3] From this perspective, even a complete description of how the physical universe is constituted would not diminish its mystery. In a sense, the increase of empirical knowledge brought about by scientific investigation serves only to amplify our wonder. The sheer immensity of the cosmos and the stunning order manifest in the cycles of nature have been enduring sources of astonishment, forever giving rise to new questions to consider and new beauties to behold. As the poet Edwin Markham stated:

> [The poetic and the scientific] modes of approaching the world will continue forever — as long as [human beings] have minds to be enlightened and hearts to be awakened. It is true that the poetic imagination needs mystery for a background, but mystery will always remain. The unknown will surround us, however deep we may delve into the universe. Science only increases the mystery of life: every new pioneering opens up a new frontier.[4]

In other words, the mystery of being cannot be exhausted through an increase of empirical data. Therefore, alongside the continued development of scientific knowledge there remains a state of wonder and awe at the mystery that will forever encompass the totality of what we can know. Religion serves in part to keep us aware of this mystery. In this context, the recognition of genuine mystery is not a form of ignorance, but a form of wisdom that is higher than ordinary knowledge. As the scholar Abraham Heschel has concluded, wonder is a way of thinking that "goes beyond knowledge" and "does not come to an end when knowledge is acquired; it is [not mere curiosity but] an *attitude* that never ceases."[5] Albert Einstein, the most renowned scientist of the twentieth century, expressed a similar sentiment when he stated that knowledge is rooted in an awareness of "something we cannot penetrate, of the manifestations of the profoundest rea- son and the most radiant beauty, which are accessible to our reason in their most elementary forms."[6] Einstein also asserted that "one cannot help but be in awe when [one] contemplates the mysteries of eternity, of life, of the marvelous structure of

> **That religion has served an essential function in the lives of human beings is demonstrated by its continuous and ubiquitous existence**

reality … Never lose a holy curiosity."[7] In light of the foregoing observations, it should be noted that adopting a religious point of view does not entail sacrificing intellectual acuity, curtailing rational contemplation, or abandoning scientific investigation. The fact that sem- inal figures in the history of science – such as Pythagoras, Aristotle, Francis Bacon, Galileo Galilei, Isaac Newton, and Albert Einstein – were motivated by religious convictions is a testament to this fact.

Humanity's search for the sacred can be viewed as an innate yearning for wholeness, transcendence, and unity. This impulse expresses a reaching toward something that is more complete than anything the material world can provide. The Indian thinker Sri Aurobindo captured the essence of religion's upward-looking gaze – which is often contrasted with the mundane concerns of material existence – when he asserted that "our true complete- ness comes not by describing wider circles on the plane where we began, but by tran- scendence."[8] In this sense, the religions of the world suggest that spiritual fulfillment cannot be attained by satisfying material aims and desires alone; rather, we must ultimately transcend those aims and desires in order to achieve a higher mode of being.

The fact that concern with the sacred has been a feature of human life since the begin- ning of recorded history strongly suggests that spirituality is essential to human nature.[9] This point was well expressed by the historian of religion Wilfred Cantwell Smith: "there is a transcendent dimension to human life – so far as I can see, there has always been, from paleolithic times. Most human beings on earth over the centuries have been aware of this and have lived their lives less or more vividly, less or more effectively, in terms of it."[10] Archeologists have demonstrated that religious expression has been integral to every known traditional culture. Émile Durkheim, regarded by many as the founder of modern sociology, concluded that religion gives birth to "all that is essential to society," including great endeavors such as science.[11] Sociological research demonstrates that if an institution fails to serve an important function in society over the long term, it fades away. That religion has served an essential function in the lives of human beings is demonstrated by its continuous and ubiquitous existence from prehistory to the present. Although sociological investigations may help us to discover, from the outside, that religion serves an essential function, it is only from within a religious point of view that we can fully understand just what that function is; in other words, the aims and purposes of religion should not be identified with the sociological effects of religious worldviews and practices.

ULTIMATE REALITY

The world's religions share important elements that scholars have identified as forming a general worldview – sometimes referred to as the traditional worldview (since all traditional cultures were religious). A prominent feature of the traditional worldview is the notion that ultimate power and goodness converge in a transcendent, Ultimate Reality (exceeding, but not excluding, the material world). The scholar John Hick describes various understandings of Ultimate Reality as follows:

> Each of the great religious traditions affirms that in addition to the social and natural world of our ordinary human experience there is a limitlessly greater and higher Reality beyond or within us, in relation to which or to whom is our highest good. The ultimately real and the ultimately valuable are one, and to give oneself freely and totally to this One is our final salvation/liberation/enlightenment/fulfillment. Further, each tradition is conscious that the divine Reality exceeds the reach of our earthly concepts. It is infinite, eternal, limitlessly rich beyond the scope of our finite conceiving or experiencing. Let us then both avoid the particular names used within the particular traditions and yet use a term which is consonant with the faith of each of them – Ultimate Reality, or the Real.[12]

The world religions conceive of Ultimate Reality in two general ways: either in theistic or non-theistic terms. The theistic perspective envisions Ultimate Reality with personal attributes (such as that of being the beneficent Creator who is active in the unfoldment of history). Non-theistic perspectives view Ultimate Reality without personal attributes, such as the Transcendent, Absolute, divine Principle or Power (for example, the notions of *nirguna brahman* or *satchitananda* of the Hindu tradition, uncompounded *sunyata* or Emptiness of the Buddhist tradition, the Transcendent Tao of the philosophical Taoist tradition, the Form of the Good in Platonic philosophy, or the Divine Mind posited in Aristotelian philosophy). It should be noted that both the personal and non-personal ways of thinking about Ultimate Reality can be complementary; in fact, different thinkers within the same religion have articulated and emphasized both viewpoints.[13]

Ultimate Reality is distinguished from "conditioned reality" – the world of appearances perceived by our physical senses.[14] Ultimate Reality – the general notion for both God (theistically stated) and the Transcendent (non-theistically stated) – is understood to be more real than conditioned reality in the sense that conditioned reality depends upon Ultimate Reality, while the reverse is not the case. Ultimate Reality may be considered as a reality of unlimited potential and infinite possibility. It informs or vitalizes conditioned reality (which is finite, dependent, and limited).[15] Ultimate Reality is held to possess greater actuality and being, meaning that it has greater power (it is omnipotent), duration (it is everlasting), unity (it is without division), presence (it is omnipresent), importance (it is absolute), and worth (it is perfect).[16] A religion's view of Ultimate Reality is the apex of its metaphysics, and it is in relation to this that all things are given their place and worth. The affirmation that Ultimate Reality is divine is the life-directing principle that differentiates spiritual or religious perspectives from secular worldviews.[17]

> **A feature of the traditional worldview is the notion that ultimate power and goodness converge in a transcendent, Ultimate Reality**

RELIGION AS A WAY OR PATH

The scholar of religion Frederick Streng noted that "when one has 'visited' (seen) a wide range of religious life, from all parts of the world and throughout human history, it becomes apparent that religion is a way of life that involves many processes – all of which, in different ways, are directed to a common end. The goal is to reach a state of being that is conceived to be the highest possible state or condition."[18] As Streng suggests, this goal is brought forth by way of different processes that form a holistic system or way of life. The scholar Ninian Smart identified seven processes, or dimensions, which can be understood as the foundational features of a religion. These seven dimensions are the mythic or narrative dimension (sacred stories about the lives of religious founders as well as sacred literature that conveys how the cosmos came into being "in the beginning"); the doctrinal and philosophical dimension (dogma and religious teachings that specify the nature of Reality and humanity's predicament, purpose, and aim); the ritual or practical dimension (sacramental rites, prayer, devotional worship, pilgrimage, meditative practices, etc.); the ethical or legal dimension (moral codes, ethical imperatives, and laws of personal conduct that structure daily life); the organized or social movement (structures that perpetuate religion through time, such as organized religious communities, groups, and orders that perform ceremonies, meetings, communal worship, etc.); the materialistic and artistic

Offering to the Giant Buddha on Lantau Island, Hong Kong

dimension (buildings and shrines associated with worship and congregation, as well as other aspects of religiously inspired artistry and architecture); and the experiential dimension (transformative experiences associated with the presence of the sacred).

Any single aspect, or dimension, of a religion is not an end in itself. Taken as a whole, then, a religion is a path, way, or vehicle which structures one's life in accord with a certain vision of the supreme good – the ultimate aim or goal of life variously formulated among the world religions, such as enlightenment, deliverance, salvation, liberation, and realization. The view of religion as a "way" or "path" is, in fact, intrinsic to the religions themselves. In the Hindu tradition, for example, the major ways (*margas* or *yogas*) to the supreme good include the paths of *jñana* (attainment of metaphysical knowledge or gnosis), *bhakti* (worship of, and devotion to, the divine), and *karma* (selfless service). In the Buddhist tradition the way is conceived as the Eightfold Path set forth by the Buddha (the fourth truth, as it were, in the Buddha's Four Noble Truths). In the traditions native to China, Taoists adhere to, literally, "the Way" (*Tao*) and Confucians to "the Way of Heaven" (*T'ien-Tao*). The path of the Orthodox Jewish tradition is the disciplined observance of the *Halakhah* or Jewish legal system (which includes the inner aspect of *Aggadah*). Early Christians were referred to as followers of "the Way" (*Hodos* in Greek), namely, the path exemplified by Jesus Christ, including the practice of universal love, devotion, service, and sacrifice. Within Islam the way entails the practice of the Five Pillars and the observance of the divine law or *shari'ah* (which for Sufis includes the inner path or *tariqah*).[19]

> **A religion is a path, way, or vehicle which structures one's life in accord with a certain vision of the supreme good**

A religious path, or way, provides a disciplined and structured lifestyle. The parameters of this lifestyle are identified in the rules or laws upheld by each religion. The practice of spiritual disciplines, given the requisite foundation of virtuous character, is understood as having the potential to transform consciousness. The scholar James Duerlinger observed the important relationship between spiritual discipline and Ultimate Reality as follows:

> Religion is to be found … in man's organized pursuit of the divine life, one in which he perpetually enjoys an eternal blissful state of consciousness of ultimate reality, a reality whose nature has been differently conceived by different traditions and even within the same traditions, but which transcends things as they originally appear and which frees him when he perceives it from all sufferings. What is ultimate about this reality, these religions seem to agree, is that it is what is experienced by man at the acme of his spiritual quest and is more permanent than what he once took to be real. Spiritual discipline, accordingly, may be defined as activity which is believed to be an effective way, when performed properly and regularly, to attain the divine life.[20]

A wide variety of spiritual or contemplative disciplines have been developed, tested, and utilized by the world's religions.[21] Contemplative disciplines – representing what might be called a "pan-human technology of human spiritual development"[22] – are, in a real way, the engine of any religious path. The scholar Philip Novak noted that:

> contemplatives universally presuppose the psyche is malleable. Consciousness and the structures which determine it thus comprise the pivot point between whoever we think we are and ultimate reality. Contemplative discipline aims at nothing less than the transformation of the undergirding structures of our consciousness so that their new formation allows us to awaken from the sleep of bondage and to stay awake – both for our own welfare and for that of the human community.[23]

What is sought after in contemplative practice, therefore, is not the passing attraction of altered states of consciousness but, rather, permanently altered traits of consciousness – a new state of being. In relation to these disciplines, there are important categorical similarities among all religions. For example, prayer, in its various forms and methods, is a prevalent spiritual practice. Meditation, whether aimed at concentration, probing the nature of identity and reality, or the refinement of attention, is also a well-developed and widespread practice (or "inner technology"). Different forms of chanting, including the repetitive invocation of the name of God, the recitation of holy scripture, or sacred formulas (sometimes called mantras), are also found in all religions; chanting, it is believed, can help orient a practitioner's perception toward the sacred. Many religions have also developed practices that forge an integration of spirit, mind, and body through somatic exercises or movements (such as *hatha yoga*, *t'ai chi*, or religious dance) and traditional systems of healing (based on "first-person physiology"), as well as methods of cultivating inner energies. Other widespread religious practices include retreats in solitude, ablution or purification rites, fasting, contemplation, and the study of scripture.

The experiential dimension of religion is particularly important because most religious traditions began as a result of a powerful illuminating experience. By their very nature, religious experiences are difficult, perhaps even impossible, to describe. Some scholars refer to these experiences as "numinous," suggesting that they reveal the presence of the sacred.[24] Such moments of illumination are profoundly different from the occurrences of everyday life, which are sometimes referred to as "profane" by contrast.[25] According to the scholar Hendrik Vroon, "in religious experience, concrete reality is experienced in relation to transcendence (regardless of how this might be further interpreted)."[26] One might imagine what the historical Buddha experienced as he

Most religious traditions began as a result of a powerful illuminating experience

sat under the Bodhi Tree and attained enlightenment; one might wonder about the intense experiences of Jesus during his forty-day desert retreat; the life-changing and physically overwhelming event Muhammad experienced while he received the Qur'an in the cave of Hira; or the intense revelations of Baha'u'llah during his captivity in a Tehran dungeon. In general, these luminaries are believed to have attained a higher, or purified, state of consciousness that allowed them to gain a deeper insight into reality.[27] Some of these great spiritual figures are said to have received a revelation from God, while others underwent an inner illumination or realization. However such religious awakenings are described, the experiences, and the subsequent teachings they catalyzed, helped shape the world as viewed by human beings. The spiritual traditions that began with these prophets and teachers dramatically altered the course of human history by transforming the quality of human consciousness, by organizing societies, and by raising moral standards. In many cases, the experiences and awakenings of great prophets and teachers became the impetus of entire civilizations and thereby inspired culture and art, including poetry, sculpture, crafts, music, and architecture.

THE STUDY OF RELIGION

I hold that it is the duty of every cultured man or woman to read sympathetically the scriptures of the world. If we are to respect others' religions as we would have them to respect our own, a friendly study of the world's religions is a sacred duty.[28]

— Mahatma Gandhi

The study of religion naturally leads to encounters with various concepts and ideas about religion and spirituality. In order to come to terms with religion, it is helpful to begin with a general picture of how it has been studied in the past. In the case of religion, and spirituality in general, this is especially important because many past theories and understandings regarding the meaning and origin of religion have come to permeate modern thinking on the subject.

Traditional Studies of Religion

Religious studies, of course, originated with religious practitioners and not academics. Learned aspirants functioned as authoritative guides within their respective religious communities. The views of such thinkers were, in fact, formative in shaping the outlook of their religions as a whole. In some cases they provided important elaborations and commentaries on, as well as codifications of, Holy Scripture. Those who fall into this category include, but are not limited to, the *acharyas* of the Hindu tradition such as Shankara; Buddhaghosa and Nagarjuna of the Buddhist tradition; Maimonides of the Jewish faith; Thomas Aquinas and Meister Eckhart of Christianity; and al-Ghazali and Ibn al-'Arabi of Islam. Contemplative thinkers such as these embarked on advanced studies of scripture, metaphysics, and ethics, and also on experiential practices intended to verify and confirm doctrinal beliefs. Such aspirants, in a general way, studied religion from within; that is, they were motivated by spiritual concerns and sought to transform their consciousness in accord with Ultimate Reality.

Similar to the notion that one must attain likeness to that which one aims to understand, those who embark on traditional religious studies do not view religion as an abstract, historical, sociological, or cultural concept but, rather, as a way of life. This fact should be remembered when studying religion as a scholarly endeavor. The thinker Raimon Panikkar observed: "Only those who cultivate a religious dimension in their own lives can really dare to enter the excruciating task of trying to understand what religion is all about. The study of religion is not the classification of 'religious' data, but the study of the religious dimension of the human being."[29] There is an important distinction to be made between a removed, scholarly viewpoint of religion and the perspective of a practitioner. Religious people seek not only knowledge, but also transformation through spiritual practice. To be sure, religious teachings have many levels of meaning and thus our examination, which is confined to a single book, should be guided by humility.

The writings and teachings of contemporary and traditional contemplatives and philosophers remain an important and integral part of religious expression and exegesis to this day; however, this type of religious study is distinguished from academic "religious studies." The modern discipline of "comparative religious studies," sometimes referred to as the "history of religion" or the "science of religion," is a discipline of Western origin. This field of study developed during the important changes that occurred in Europe from the sixteenth to twentieth centuries. The following short historical survey highlights some important events that shaped European thinking about religion; the discussion should not, however, be understood as exhausting the complex cultural realities and philosophical thought of the period.

The Historical Development of Religious Studies

The Reformation

The sixteenth century of the Common Era bore witness to a variety of reform movements within Christianity, referred to as the Protestant Reformation. The Reformation saw vast areas of Europe breaking away from the religious and political authority of the Roman Catholic Church. The Reformation consisted of many different movements, but in general it challenged Catholic theological interpretations and clerical authority in a way that had not previously occurred during the medieval period (*c*.400–1400 C.E.). In general, these reform movements rejected the authority of the papacy and what they saw as its corruption and abuses of power, such as the Inquisition. The Inquisition, a term which refers to a variety of different Catholic tribunals from the twelfth to nineteenth centuries, sought to eradicate and persecute heresy, both in terms of variant Christian views and those who held other religious perspectives. Similarly motivated reform movements as those of the Protestant Reformation were also occurring within the Catholic Church that later came to be labeled, somewhat misleadingly, as the Counter-Reformation.

This period of European history led to strife and dissention throughout the Christian world. Christian communities split into hostile and competitive groups. From within Europe the reality of war brought to bear new questions concerning the purpose of religion while explorations outside Europe led to contact with thriving societies in India, China, and the Americas – all of which held systems of morality and advanced religious beliefs that were not of Judeo-Christian origin. These encounters led Christian thinkers to question the centrism of the Judeo-Christian worldview and to consider the deeper implications of religious diversity.

The European Enlightenment

During the seventeenth century a major intellectual movement began, referred to as the European Enlightenment. The advocates of this movement held that rational inquiry and empirical observation are the determining factors in discovering truth. Thus, appeal to religious authority was replaced by experimentation, observation, and reasoning from "self-evident" truths. Among the many important figures of the period were the English philosopher John Locke (1632–1704) and the English scientist Isaac Newton (1642–1727). Notably, the political philosophy of Locke influenced attitudes toward tolerance, democracy, and human rights that were significant in the following centuries. Similarly, Isaac Newton's theory of a deterministic universe based on laws of gravity, motion, and orbital dynamics was formative in shaping Western thinking. In many ways, the Newtonian model led to the demystification of the universe, and many people came to believe that the world had been thoroughly explained. These changes in Europe occurred only a short time after the Italian philosopher Giordano

During the Enlightenment, appeal to religious authority was replaced by experimentation, observation, and reasoning from "self-evident" truths

Temple at Abu Simbel, Egypt

Bruno (1548–1600), who posited an infinite universe that contains an indefinite number of worlds, was imprisoned and burned at the stake for heresy.

The general acceptance of the Newtonian view of the universe as a closed-causal system led many people to infer the impossibility of divine intervention or miracles, a prominent aspect of the Judeo-Christian religious perspective. This view developed, in part, because the Newtonian worldview held that unalterable laws regulated the universe. This, alongside the championing of reason over revelation, contributed to the rise of deism, a religious perspective that posits the existence of one God knowable through reason without need of revelation. Deists believe that God does not intervene in the world, but rather created the world and set it in motion based on "natural laws." Deism, a religious perspective that had been proposed before the advent of Newtonian science, became popular among many intellectuals of the period, including the French philosopher Voltaire (1694–1778) and prominent early American figures such as Benjamin Franklin (1706–1790) and Thomas Jefferson (1743–1826). In general, deism put forward a belief in the existence of a universal, or natural, religion. This loosely defined theological viewpoint consists of only a few basic beliefs – namely, that a Supreme Being is the creator of humanity and the world and endows the former with souls and the latter with natural laws. Deism also upheld the existence of a positive afterlife, contingent on doing good and avoiding evil. In general, the deist perspective denied a privileged position to any single religion over another, and promoted a tolerant viewpoint that sought universal fellowship. Significantly, deism, and other religious perspectives that emerged during this period, sparked debates regarding the nature of truth and religion which had previously not occurred during the ascendancy of the Roman Catholic Church. European thinkers now struggled with realities of religious and ideological diversity, among which emerged not only variant theological positions but non-religious philosophies as well.

Naturalism and Reductionism

Among the changes occurring in Europe during the Enlightenment was the emergence of a new sense of uncertainty with respect to religious doctrines, and philosophical movements such as skepticism, empiricism, and materialism began to displace the traditional (or religious) worldview. Informed by the methodology of empirical science, many thinkers of this period believed the universe to be an intricately complicated mechanism, comprehensible through quantitative measurement and natural laws. The underpinnings of this worldview are present in the work of French philosopher René Descartes (1596–1650). Although not a materialist, Descartes postulated that the essential property of material existence is "extension." Furthermore, he argued, the qualities of any material thing (e.g. its color, taste, or the degree of its heat) are explicable in terms of its quantifiable features – more specifically, the motion, size, shape, and situation of its parts relative to one another.

This led Descartes to envision the workings of the material world – including those of human and animal bodies – as completely mechanical. These ideas played a profound role in developing the worldview that came to dominate the European Enlightenment.

Alongside these changes in worldview, a critical interpretation of religion arose. For example, French thinker Bernard de Fontenelle (1657–1757) suggested that religious narratives were mistaken attempts at explaining natural, or material, occurrences. Other thinkers came to study religion as a strictly historical or social institution. One scholar suggests that the paradigm shift in understanding religion as a human element of culture rather than from within a religious worldview occurred in the works of the Scottish philosopher David Hume.[30] Hume dismissed traditional metaphysics and suggested that religion represents humanity's attempt "to cope" with the unknown.

Within the framework of a naturalistic worldview, secular theorists attempted to identify an origin from which religion evolved. Underlying this perspective was the view that human history was the history of "progress." Notably, the view of history as progress was understood, in many cases, within the context of the evolutionary philosophy of the British naturalist Charles Darwin (1809–1882) – who posited the theory of biological evolution by means of "natural selection." It should be noted, however, that the general theories of religion that emerged during this period were significantly limited to the Judeo-Christian context. Western social scientists, many of whom were hostile to Christianity, had yet to penetrate into the religious worldviews of Asia or other regions.

Social scientists of the period attempted to explain religion with ideas of cultural evolution; namely, they sought to identify the origin of religion in non-religious causes. A variety of thinkers used this approach, including the French philosopher Auguste Comte (1798–1857), the German political theorist Karl Marx (1818–1883), the Austrian psychiatrist Sigmund Freud (1856–1939), and the French social scientist Émile Durkheim (1858–1917). The aforementioned thinkers were some of the most influential social scientists of the nineteenth century, and from their work entire academic fields of study emerged, including modern psychology and sociology. Theories attributable to these thinkers include: the projectionist theory (religion reduced to illusory psychological projections); the functionalist theory (religion viewed as having no validity beyond a mere functional task in the development and perpetuation of society); and the evolutionist theory (religion reduced to a stage in human development that is to be outgrown).[31] Other theorists such as the English anthropologists E. B. Tylor (1832–1917) and James G. Frazer (1854–1941) believed religion to be a remnant of the faulty reasoning of primitive "savage philosophers." Tylor and Frazer, who were influential in the emerging disciplines of anthropology and comparative religious studies, approached religion under the assumption that only empirical explanations of phenomena were valid, and thus religion, which appeals to "spiritual beings" (to use Tylor's phrase), was a primitive science that so-called civilized peoples had, with the advent of modern science, eclipsed.[32]

The theorists discussed here offered important insights into certain aspects of religion, especially its social dimension. Their premises, however, did not allow for the ultimate validity of religion. Thus, their methodology and conclusions – derived from their premises – explained religion away as if it were a mere epiphenomenon or side-effect of a non-religious cause. This view of religion prevents one from fully understanding the meaning of any religious doctrine or insight. The scholar Mircea Eliade explained the problem of this approach as follows:

> A religious phenomenon will only be recognized as such if it is grasped at its own level, that is to say, if it is studied as something religious. To try to grasp the essence of such a phenomenon by means of physiology, psychology, sociology, economics, linguistics, art or any other study is false; it misses the one unique and irreducible element in it – the element of the sacred.[33]

Comparative Religious Studies

Reductionist tendencies in the study of religion were partly absorbed and superseded by comparative religious studies. The comparative approach was an important step forward in understanding similarities and differences among the religions. The advancement afforded by the field of comparative religion, essentially rooted in the work of the scholar Max Müller (1823–1900), made available detailed accounts of religious practices and numerous translations of the sacred texts and mythologies of the religions of the world, both tribal and historical. Much of the early scholarship in this field was, however, adversely affected by biases that prevented an accurate and fair portrayal of world religions. In some cases, these biases were derived from materialistic worldviews, as discussed above, and in other cases from ethnocentric and theological prejudices. In the case of the latter, comparative studies developed within a European Christian context. Thus, the approach drew upon Christian categories of thought, as demonstrated in the many early translations of sacred texts from Asia that employ Christian theological terminology for non-Christian concepts. Non-Christian religions interpreted in terms of a Christian template were, in most cases, considered inferior to Christianity. There was also a general lack of ability, or inclination, on the part of early comparative scholars to empathetically penetrate into contemplative practices and philosophical viewpoints outside the Judeo-Christian context. Rather, scholars tended to focus on the sociological and ritualistic dimensions of religion; such an unbalanced approach led to superficial conclusions and, in general, an incomplete picture of the religions.

The information that comparative historians, researchers, and ethnographers have gathered has played an important role in heightening modern sensitivities to differences between disparate cultures and languages. Scholars have also brought to light the lack of attention paid to the role of women in religious history. In some cases, scholarship has identified the oppression of women, and other societal ills, that have been committed in the name of religion. These investigations and approaches have been complemented by research that has recognized the universality of fundamental cultural structures and categories of thought. In light of these uniting factors, scholars have demonstrated recurrent themes, symbols, archetypes, and motifs that occur in religions, mythologies, and sacred literature across time and cultures. The phenomenological approach to religion, which is a descriptive exploration of religious consciousness, studies the quality of religious experience. Some scholars who identify with this approach view religious experience in relation to a common essence among all religions. For example, the scholar and theologian Friedrich Schleiermacher concluded: "The more you progress in the understanding of religion, the more the whole religious world will appear to you as one indivisible whole."[34] The existence of modern comparative religious studies has not only increased awareness of religious diversity, but also has offered a clearer understanding of the underlying unity of which that diversity is an expression.

Religious Studies in the Global Age

In this global age, education in religion is increasingly considered to be essential for obtaining an understanding of the world and its diverse peoples. Thus, scholar Ninian Smart asserts: "To understand human history and human life it is necessary to understand religion, and in the contemporary world one must understand nations' ideologies and faiths in order to grasp the meaning of life as seen from perspectives often very different from our own."[35] The scholarly study of comparative religion has advanced a view of the world religions that is not based on prejudice and ethnocentrism. Itself a product of the Western humanist spirit of research and investigation, this scholarship has not entirely transcended its Western origins, but it has awakened many to the richness and diversity of the world's spiritual traditions. In devising concepts that could be used to describe quite disparate religions, an increasing number of scholars have developed pluralistic and dialogical approaches to the study of religion that provide a framework for understanding religion and "the other." The scholar Wilfred Cantwell Smith has observed:

> **In this global age, education in religion is considered to be essential for obtaining an understanding of the world**

> The traditional form of Western scholarship in the study of the other was that of an impersonal presentation of an "it." The first great innovation in recent times has been the personalization of the faiths observed, so that one finds a discussion of a "they." Presently the observer becomes personally involved, so that the situation is one of a "we" talking about a "they." The next step is a dialogue where "we" talk to "you." If there is listening and mutuality, this may become that "we" talk with "you." The culmination of the process is then "we all" are talking with each other about "us."[36]

This book has been written from a perspective that recognizes the fundamental need to establish mutual understanding and dialogical patterns of thought among the religions.

A GLOBAL ETHOS

During the last few centuries, advances in technology have collapsed the divide between the vast expanses of the earth. Far-off peoples, who were once the stock of legends, are now neighbors, classmates, and business partners. Spectacular changes in international travel, immigration, commerce, and communications have redefined the social reality of human life. The world can no longer be understood as a conglomeration of homogeneous cultures or as self-contained tribes or nation-states; rather, in a significant sense it is now a single, interdependent society. The scholar Masao Abe has observed that "the term 'world' should now be grasped qualitatively rather than quantitatively – that is, not as a mere gathering of various nations, but as one single human community participating in a common life and sharing in the same fate. The nation is no longer the basic unit for understanding the world; the world itself is the basic unit."[37] From economy to ecology, all sectors of human life can best be understood if a new global perspective is adopted. At the basis of this paradigm shift is the need to develop a consciousness capable of widening the nationalistic, ethnocentric, and individualistic patterns of the past into a planetary outlook and responsibility capable of sustaining a truly global society. It is through the emergence of a global ethos, on both the individual and collective levels, that the opportunity for a peaceful and sustainable future can be enhanced.

The scientist and systems theorist Ervin Laszlo has defined a planetary consciousness as "knowing, as well as feeling, the vital interdependence and essential oneness of humankind. It is the conscious adoption of the ethic and the ethos that this entails." He adds that the "evolution [of planetary consciousness] is the basic imperative of human survival on this planet."[38] In other words, Laszlo argues that in the global age personal identity must be broadened to a more universal and fundamental level – requiring the cultivation of a consciousness that brings to the forefront of one's thinking the essential oneness of humanity.

Top: *Jain temple in Pawapuri, Bihar, India*
Bottom: *Sistine Chapel ceiling, painted by Michelangelo between 1508 and 1512*

It was the American civil rights leader Martin Luther King, Jr. who observed "every nation must now develop an overriding loyalty to mankind as a whole in order to preserve the best in their individual societies. This call for a worldwide fellowship that lifts neighborly concern beyond one's tribe, race, class, and nation is in reality a call for an all-embracing and unconditional love for all mankind."[39] Laszlo's concept of planetary consciousness posits that interdependence is a fundamental reality of human life. Every action, whether performed by individuals or groups, affects everything and everyone else. Similarly, the Buddhist monk Thich Nhat Hanh suggested that living

> **Humanity is interdependent – in Thich Nhat Hanh's words, we "inter-be" with our surrounding environment**

beings do not, and cannot, exist independently from the world around them. Humanity is interdependent – in Thich Nhat Hanh's words, we "inter-be" with our surrounding environment.[40] A global ethos recognizes that living beings are not islands unto themselves; neither are governments, industries, technologies, or religions. Abraham Heschel, a leading religious thinker of the twentieth century, noted that the world religions:

are no more self-sufficient, no more independent, and no more isolated than individuals or nations. Energies, experiences, and ideas that come to life outside the boundaries of a particular religion or all religions continue to challenge and to affect every religion … No religion is an island. We are all involved with one another. Spiritual betrayal on the part of one of us affects the faith of all of us.[41]

Scholars of religion have observed that in the global age – which they see as a period of human history defined by the convergence of the peoples of the world – "the religions must meet each other in center-to-center unions, discovering what is most authentic in each other, thereby releasing creative energy toward a more complexified form of religious consciousness."[42] The order of consciousness needed to peacefully and positively respond to the religious diversity of a connected world necessitates the ability to rise above ego and in-group habits while developing dialogical patterns of life reflective of an age of global interdependency.[43]

A shift in the thinking of humankind brought about by a global ethos offers hope that the patterns of the past, the cycles of tribal and international conflict, can be transcended. It is in this sense that interfaith studies and interreligious dialogue, two central themes of this book, must be a hallmark of humanity's next phase of development. "There will be no lasting peace on earth," observed Mahatma Gandhi, "unless we learn not merely to tolerate but even to respect the other faiths as our own."[44] The achievement of mutual respect and understanding among the world religions will depend, in large part, on the development of a multicultural approach to education. In particular, a new curriculum must entail an interfaith program that encourages cooperation and friendship rather than competition among the diverse religious traditions. Such an approach will facilitate the attainment of the kind of tolerant, pluralist societies that are a necessity in today's global environment.

RELIGIOUS EXCLUSIVISM

One way to highlight the advantages of the pluralist response to diversity is to consider an opposing view, namely exclusivism. A religious exclusivist believes that his or her religion embodies the Absolute Truth in its totality. Therefore, the exclusivist concludes that the supreme good (deliverance, salvation, liberation, etc.) is the privileged possession of a particular religious group and that it is only available by adherence to the religion of that group. From this perspective, other religions are deemed incomplete, misguided, inferior, or even sinful ways of life. The scholar Diana Eck described the dynamics of personal identity within an exclusivist worldview as follows:

> The exclusivist affirms identity in a complex world of plurality by a return to the firm foundations of his or her own tradition and an emphasis on the distinctive identity provided by that tradition. This identity is in part what social theorists call an "oppositional identity," built up over and against who we are not. Exclusivism is more than simply a conviction about the transformative power of the particular vision one has; it is a conviction about its finality and its absolute priority over competing views. Exclusivism may therefore be the ideological foundation for isolationism. The exclusivist response to diversity, whether theological, social, or political, is to mark ever more clearly the boundaries and borders separating "us" from "them." It is little wonder that exclusivism has been one of the tools of racism and ethnocentrism.[45]

Exclusivists do not seek real dialogue with those outside their tradition because they believe that there is nothing of ultimate import that can be learned or discovered from so-called "non-believers." The theologian Hans Küng observed that such a narrow viewpoint is representative of "a self-opinionated theological apologetic which is incapable of learning and causes more problems than it solves."[46] In an age of multicultural and religious diversity, the inability to respect and learn from viewpoints other than one's own is a major hurdle in the pursuit of mutual understanding and peaceful coexistence.

RELIGIOUS PLURALISM

An increasing number of religious thinkers are drawing on internal resources within their respective religions to demonstrate universal patterns of religious thinking that embrace other religions as valid, transformative, and meaningful.[47] A study of each religion demonstrates a rich tradition of teachings and interpretations that provide perspectives which move beyond exclusivist and literalistic views.[48] These traditions are typically associated with the philosophic and contemplative component of each religion. In fact, scholars have observed that those who move toward the inner dimension of their tradition – that is, embody the spiritual message at the heart of their religion – are less likely to emphasize the differences between the various religions.[49] Conversely, however, the more that religious adherents emphasize the outer form of a religion and do not internalize the inner transformative message, then the differences between the religions are cited as justification for exclusivism or divisive competition.[50] Teachers from all religions have affirmed that authentic religious attitudes are based in humility; they extend universal love, compassion, and service to others. In a global age, it can be dangerous for believers of a particular religion to claim superiority over others and to establish barriers between peoples. The observance of humility, especially in relation to other religious traditions, is a necessity in a globalized world. As the thinker Hasan Askari stated: "Who knows that one whom we condemn today because of his or her different belief may be found tomorrow among the friends of God. Let us leave all things wherein we differ for another day, and as far as this day is concerned, ask forgiveness of each other, treat each other in patience and humility; and if ever we speak of God, we should hear and use speech as though in his Presence."[51]

A pluralist approach to religion offers a response to religious diversity that can help secure a peaceful future. Within a framework of pluralism, the world religions can work cooperatively to uplift humanity to the high values and ideals that each religion strives to achieve. The essential principles of the pluralist perspective are defined by the scholar Diana Eck as follows:

First, pluralism is not the sheer fact of diversity alone, but is active engagement with plurality.
Second, pluralism is not simply tolerance, but also the seeking of understanding.
Third, pluralism is not simply relativism, but assumes real commitment.
Fourth, pluralism is not syncretism, but is based on respect for difference.
Fifth, pluralism is based on interreligious dialogue.[52]

A pluralist does not view religious diversity as grounds for competition or isolationism; rather, he or she understands diversity as an opportunity to gain a greater understanding of reality through dialogue. A religious pluralist is rooted within a particular religion but remains open to the possibility that other faiths are equally valid ways of living meaningful lives that lead to, or are in harmony with, the supreme good.

The philosopher John Hick offered the following commentary:

> The great world faiths embody different responses to the Real or the Ultimate from within the major variant cultural ways of being human; and that within each of them the transformation of human existence from self-centredness to Reality-centredness is manifestly taking place – and taking place, so far as human observation can tell, to much the same extent. Thus the great religious traditions are to be regarded as alternative soteriological "spaces" within which, or "ways" along which, men and women can find salvation/liberation/enlightenment/fulfillment.[53]

From this perspective, religions are not abstract "things." In other words, religious traditions should not be reified as if they are fixed concepts with rigid boundaries that are mutually exclusive (a viewpoint that is, notably, a relatively recent notion of Western origin and one not held by other cultures). Religions are, rather, cumulative traditions that have undergone change, in both structure and form, while moving through history.[54] In fact, the religions of today, although referred to by their traditional names such as "Christianity" or "Judaism," are no longer in their original state. The diverse streams of religious life, known as "religions," can be understood as varying responses to the same Ultimate Reality, with

Authentic religious attitudes are based in humility; they extend universal love, compassion, and service to others

each spiritual path offering the aspirant a way to move from a negative self-centered way of life to a positive Reality-centered way of life. John Hick calls this form of transformation "a positive openness to the Divine [whether beyond us or in the depths of our own being] which gradually transforms us and which is called salvation or liberation or enlightenment."[55] In this sense "faith" is a descriptive term that does not represent belief in a particular doctrine or thought content but rather in a way of life – it is the quality of a person's living in terms of transcendence.[56]

It should be emphasized that a pluralist view of diversity does not entail nihilistic relativism, which is a perspective that denies the existence of any Absolute or Ultimate Reality. Rather, a pluralist religious perspective categorically affirms the existence of a divine Ultimate Reality, while acknowledging that the totality of Ultimate Reality is beyond the finite understanding of human minds.[57] As the scholar Raimon Panikkar has stated, "Pluralism is not the mere justification of opinions, but the realization that the real is more than the sum of all possible opinions."[58] The pluralist viewpoint is, therefore, fully attuned to the "relativity" of the human perspective.[59] Relativity is understood to mean that ultimate truth-claims are about the Absolute Truth, but are not absolutely true themselves (just as a poem can be about a person without being that person). Ideas about

Ultimate Reality are, however, limited to humanity's finite, and hence fallible, cognitive capacities. Thus, human understanding, which is imperfect, can never exhaust all the ways of seeing or understanding Ultimate Reality.[60] In this sense, Diana Eck argues that "pluralism is not ... radical openness to anything and everything that drains meaning from particularity." Rather, according to Eck it is "radical openness to Truth – God – that seeks to enlarge understanding through dialogue."[61]

THE INTERFAITH MOVEMENT AND INTERRELIGIOUS DIALOGUE

Religion and the Pursuit of Peace

The history of humanity testifies to the darkness and confusion spread by those who have appropriated the symbols and rhetoric of religion for their own selfish purposes. Those who have asserted that they, and they alone, are the sole possessors of Truth bear a heavy responsibility for the chaos and disorder that blights the earth.[62] Thus the invocation of religion in contemporary conflicts fits within a historical pattern. Although religion has been misused throughout history as a mobilizing force in ethno-political conflicts, the contribution of religion towards the establishment of peace has for too long been undervalued. Cardinal Francis Arinze, President of the Vatican's Pontifical Council for Interreligious Dialogue, concluded: "In my seventeen years of engagement in the promotion of inter-religious dialogue, I have not come into contact with the follower of any religion who does not regard his or her religion as in favor of peace."[63] All religions embody worldviews promoting peace, and therefore have the potential to play a positive role in the cause of peace. In an age when global threats – such as international terrorism, weapons of mass destruction, overpopulation, poverty, disease, environmental degradation, and corrupt moral standards – call for coordinated action, it is incumbent on the world religions to work to help insure a peaceful and sustainable future for all humankind. The spiritual and virtue-centered worldview inherent to all religions, alongside their common concern for compassion, service, and peace, offers a strong foundation on which the religions can collaborate rather than compete in working toward peace. As the theologian Hans Küng observed: "Peace among the religions is a precondition for peace among the nations."[64]

> **The spiritual worldview inherent to all religions offers a strong foundation on which the religions can collaborate in working toward peace**

A landmark event in the effort to establish mutual understanding among the world religions occurred at the first meeting of the Parliament of World Religions in 1893 in Chicago.[65] Notably, Max Müller – the father of comparative religious studies and editor of a series of scriptural translations entitled Sacred Books of the East, which played a major

An Orthodox Jew prays at the Western or Wailing Wall, Jerusalem

role in opening the European–American consciousness to a global awareness – took keen notice of the historic significance of the Parliament. In a lecture delivered in Oxford in 1894, Müller referred to the meeting in Chicago as "one of the most memorable events in the history of the world." He described the importance of the event as follows:

> That meeting was not intended … for elaborating a new religion, but it established a fact of the greatest significance, namely, that there exists an ancient and universal religion, and that the highest dignitaries and representatives of all the religions of the world can meet as members of one common brotherhood, can listen respectfully to what each religion had to say for itself, nay, can join in a common prayer and accept a common blessing, one day from the hands of a Christian archbishop, another day from a Jewish rabbi, and again another day from a Buddhist priest (Dharmapâla). Another fact, also, was established once for all, namely, that the points on which the great religions differ are far less numerous, and certainly far less important, than are the points on which they agree …
>
> Whoever knows what human nature is will not feel surprised that every one present at the religious parliament looked on his own religion as the best … Yet that predilection did not interfere with a hearty appreciation of what seemed good and excellent in other religions.[66]

Scholars and interfaith proponents regard the Parliament of World Religions as the inception of the modern interfaith movement. The adherents of the major world religions who gathered in Chicago in 1893 were motivated by a general sense of universality that acknowledged that Truth was not the sole monopoly of any one religion. In his opening remarks at the Parliament, Swami Vivekananda, representing the Hindu tradition, declared his hope that the gathering would mark the end of religious intolerance:

> Sectarianism, bigotry and its horrible descendant, fanaticism, have long possessed this beautiful earth. They have filled the earth with violence, drenched it often with human blood, destroyed civilisations and sent whole nations to despair. Had it not been for these horrible demons, human society would be far more advanced than it is now. But their time has come; and I fervently hope that the bell that tolled this morning in honor of this convention may be the death-knell of all fanaticism, of all persecutions with the sword or with the pen, and of all uncharitable feelings between persons wending their way to the same goal.[67]

A growing number of interfaith initiatives, including prayer events and collaborative community building, have served as important venues for increasing friendship and cooperation across religious boundaries. In general, the interfaith movement, represented by numerous non-profit organizations worldwide, has concentrated on the facilitation of education initiatives and interreligious dialogues designed to promote mutual understanding, identification of common ground and shared goals, and the elimination of ignorance and prejudice.[68] The interfaith movement can, therefore, be understood within the greater context of humanity's search for peace – a value central to all religions.

Essential to peace-building is recognition of the universal nature of human morality. As one scholar has stated: "The basis of our morality is in our obligation as human beings – as individuals and in our societies – to allow and help one another to flourish as human beings. And since the human essence is universal, requirements for human flourishing are universal, obligations to promote such flourishing are universal, and therefore, so is human morality."[69] The recognition of universal religious values and ethical religious standards can allow each religion to flourish by protecting the security of all communities. An assertion of common values was made during the World Conference on Religion and Peace held in Kyoto, Japan, in 1970. In Kyoto, representatives of the various traditions concluded:

As we sat down together facing the overriding issues of peace we discovered that the things which unite us are more important than those things which divide us. We found that we share:

A conviction of the fundamental unity of the human family, and the equality and dignity of all human beings;

A sense of the sacredness of the individual person and his conscience;

A sense of value of human community;

A realization that might is not right; that human power is not self-sufficient and absolute;

A belief that love, compassion, selflessness, and the force of inner truthfulness and of the spirit have ultimately greater power than hate, enmity and self-interest;

A sense of obligation to stand on the side of the poor and the oppressed as against the rich and the oppressors; and

A profound hope that good will finally prevail.[70]

The reflections of the World Conference on Religion and Peace in Kyoto were echoed at the 1993 Parliament of World Religions. That gathering endorsed a proposal entitled Declaration Toward a Global Ethic.[71] This watershed declaration identified "a minimal *fundamental consensus* concerning binding *values*, irrevocable *standards*, and *fundamental moral attitudes*" rooted in the common values and ethics of the religious and spiritual traditions of humankind.[72] The bedrock principle of this declaration is that "Every human being must be treated humanely." From this principle four directives ensue: commitment to a culture of non-violence and respect for life; commitment to a culture of solidarity and a just economic order; commitment to a culture of tolerance and a life of truthfulness; and commitment to a culture of equal rights and partnership between men and women. The 1993 declaration has, in fact, opened the way to continued dialogue about a moral foundation for a diverse religious and multicultural global society based on dignity, justice, peace, and fellowship. It is within such a society that, as specified in Article 18 of the United Nations' Declaration of Human Rights, "Everyone has the right to freedom of thought, conscience and religion; this right includes freedom to change his religion or belief, and freedom, either alone or in community with others and in public or private, to manifest religion or belief in teaching, practice, worship and observance."[73]

The Age of Dialogue

The multicultural, interdependent, and pluralist societies that have emerged in some parts of the world require dialogue in order to flourish. Without dialogue among the peoples of the world, ignorance and prejudice cannot be overcome and mutual understanding will not be achieved. In short, without mutual understanding there can be no peace. Some scholars have suggested that human survival depends on humanity's ability to transition successfully from the old age of monologue (defined by isolated tribes and nation-states) to a new age of global, interdependent dialogue. These scholars have explained this critical turning point in human civilization as follows:

> Today nuclear or ecological, or other, catastrophic devastation lies just a little further down the path of monologue. It is only by struggling out of the self-centered mono-logic mindset into dialogue with "the others" as they really are, and not what we have projected them in our monologues, that we can avoid such cataclysmic disasters. In brief: we must move from the Age of Monologue to the Age of Dialogue.[74]

When applied on a universal basis, the teaching that we should treat others as we ourselves wish to be treated, an ethic variously repeated in all the world religions, clearly demonstrates the principle that should guide interreligious and intercultural exchanges. As a universally acknowledged moral standard, the Golden Rule serves as an ethical norm rooted in all traditional cultures. A sample of various renditions of the Golden Rule, as formulated by some of the major religious and spiritual traditions of the world, is represented below:

The Baha'i Faith: "And if thine eyes be turned towards justice, choose thou for thy neighbour that which thou choosest for thyself."

Baha'u'llah, *Lawh'i 'Ibn'i 'Dhib* (Epistle to the Son of the Wolf), 30

The Buddhist Tradition: "Hurt not others in ways you yourself would find hurtful."

Udana-Varga, 5:18

The Christian Faith: "In everything do to others as you would have them do to you; for this is the law and the prophets."

Matthew 7.12

The Confucian Tradition: "Do not unto others what you do not want them to do to you."

Analects, 15.13

The Hindu Tradition: "This is the sum of duty: do naught unto others which would cause you pain if done to you."

Mahabharata, 5:1517

The Faith of Islam: "Not one of you is a believer until he loves for his brother what he loves for himself."

Fortieth Hadith of an-Nawawi, 13

The Jain Tradition: "A man should wander about treating all creatures as he himself would be treated."

Sutrakritanga, 1.11.33

The Jewish Faith: "What is hateful to you, do not do to your neighbor: that is the whole of the Torah; all the rest of it is commentary."

Talmud, *Shabbat* 31a

The Native American Tradition: "Respect for all life is the foundation."

The Great Law of Peace

The Sikh Faith: "Treat others as thou wouldst be treated thyself."

Adi Granth

The Taoist Tradition: "Regard your neighbor's gain as your own gain and your neighbor's loss as your own loss."

T'ai Shang Kan Ying P'ien

The Zoroastrian Faith: "That nature alone is good which refrains from doing unto another whatsoever is not good for itself."

Dadistan-i-Dinik, 94:5[75]

The success of any interreligious dialogue greatly depends on fostering an atmosphere of genuine mutual respect – an attitude which goes far beyond mere "tolerance."[76] It was the poet Johann Wolfgang von Goethe (1749–1832) who rightly observed that "tolerance should really only be a passing attitude: it should lead to appreciation. To tolerate is to offend."[77] In fact, no useful interreligious encounter can occur in a spirit of discourtesy, mistrust, or prejudice. In order to dialogue with another, one must develop the ability to see from different perspectives.[78] The scholar Huston Smith explains that "we need to see ... adherents [of religions other than our own] as men and women who faced problems much like our own ... If we lay aside our preconceptions about these religions, seeing each as forged by people who were struggling to see something that would give help and meaning to their lives; and if we then try without prejudice to see ourselves what they saw – if we do these things, the veil that separates us from them can turn to gauze."[79] It is, therefore, critical to approach a dialogue with openness, honesty, humility, and courage. Under favorable conditions, interreligious dialogue can be a transformative experience, one which could lead to a sense of unity with "the other."[80]

An interreligious dialogue is neither a debate nor an empty exchange of platitudes; rather, an authentic dialogical encounter must be motivated by the desire to learn. The success of a dialogue should, therefore, not be judged by whether it achieves some sort of final concurrence; instead, the process of dialoging, if undertaken properly, is an end in itself that can lead to mutual understanding and even to transformation.[81] According to the thinker J. A. Buehrens:

> The secret to dialogue is passing over and then returning. We pass over into an appreciative attempt to understand the experience and insight of another person or tradition. When we return to ourselves, as we inevitably do in one way or another, we are no longer precisely the same person we were before. We are changed by the experience, in some way transformed and enlarged. This pattern may be a paradigm for spiritual growth in our pluralistic world.[82]

In this sense, dialogues can develop into a spiritual practice – for they enrich our search for Truth and play a significant role in providing the means by which we can expand our own vision of reality.[83] To be sure, a dialogue is not only a way of coming to know "the other's" religious perspective but also of coming to know, in greater depth, one's own. Since one cannot see oneself, or one's religion, from the outside looking in, there are inevitably perspectives and insights that are subjectively transparent, and therefore unrecognized. In light of this fact, the scholar Raimon Panikkar concluded:

Top: *The Wheel of Dharma, Lhasa, Tibet. The eight spokes*
represent the Noble Eightfold Path of Buddhism

Bottom: *Bas-relief sculptures of Apsara dancers, or Hindu guardian deities, on the*
exterior of the twelfth-century temple of Angkor Wat, Cambodia

Dialogue is a way of knowing myself and of disentangling my own point of view from other viewpoints and from me, because it is grounded so deeply in my own roots as to be utterly hidden from me. It is the other who through our encounter awakens this human depth latent in me in an endeavor that surpasses both of us. In authentic dialogue this process is reciprocal. Dialogue sees the other not as an extrinsic, accidental aid, but as the indispensable, personal element in our search for truth, because I am not a self-sufficient, autonomous individual. In this sense, dialogue is a religious act par excellence because it recognizes my religatio to another, my individual poverty, the need to get out of myself, transcend myself, in order to save myself.[84]

One technique is for each dialogue partner to present not only their own viewpoint but also the perspective (they have understood) as being communicated to them by "the other." The viewpoint of "the other" – a representative of a perspective that engages reality from a different set of premises – can provide insights into one's own worldview. Such insights may, in fact, not be noticed or realizable from a first-person perspective or from exchanges with others who echo and reaffirm likeminded views. In this way, "dialogue partners serve as mirrors" that can, under the right circumstances, act as catalysts for self-knowledge.[85]

When participating in a dialogue, two states of mind are essential for developing a positive and deep connection with a representative of another tradition. Those two qualities of mind are openness and wonder – both are opposed to the inclination to label, categorize, compare, and judge. Such labeling and judging often occurs at a level of subtlety that barely registers in one's conscious field of awareness. Such a tendency can interfere with one's ability to remain in a sense of awe – a vital quality of mind for anyone hoping to learn, let alone to experience, a transformative encounter.[86] Without a sense of wonder and awe, the mind becomes rigid and closed to authentic experience. "If your mind is empty," noted the Zen Master Suzuki Roshi, "it is always ready for anything; it is open to everything. In the beginner's mind there are many possibilities; in the expert's mind there are few."[87] An "expert," in this context, is someone who believes he or she knows all there is to know about a given subject; that is, one who holds to his or her beliefs inflexibly, leaving little possibility for growth and the emergence of new perspectives, insights, and understanding. If a participant enters a dialogue with entrenched opinions or immediately judges and categorizes other participants, it is unlikely that such a person will learn and respond creatively and, if needed, change a previously held opinion.

The physicists David Bohm and David Peat note that in the dynamics of a successful dialogue, "what is essential … is the presence of the *spirit* of dialogue, which is, in short, the ability to hold many points of view in suspension, along with a primary interest in the creation of a common meaning."[88] If a person is unable to suspend judgment, he or she distorts present experience with previous experiences and beliefs; thus, he or she fails to fully understand all aspects of what is being communicated in the present moment. Only a participant who suspends his or her own viewpoint and listens attentively, rather than conjuring old points of contention or future counterpoints, is fully able to contribute to a fruitful dialogue. The inability to suspend one's own point of view prevents spontaneity and inhibits engaging "the other" non-judgmentally. An ideal dialogical disposition, therefore, requires at least some detachment from one's own ideas and views.

Dialogues on sensitive political and socio-economic issues may arouse a variety of emotions that cluster around particular ideas and images. Some of these may entail long-standing points of contention between communities. When topics arise that elicit anger, revenge, or the like, one's mind gives way to afflictive emotions that distort the perception of reality and "the other." Adherents of closely related religions, who might be expected to conduct dialogues in a relaxed manner, can discover that their very related-ness causes heated emotions. Emotions, in fact, play a significant role in shaping human reality and influencing modes of communication; it is, therefore, unrealistic to expect participants in a dialogue to remain entirely "rational" at all times. In fact, we cannot always provide sound reasons for our actions or beliefs, nor is it always appropriate or possible to demand logical explanations for certain fundamental human realities, such as love. Although a rational approach to dialogue works well in impersonal discussions, when the dialogue is about religion, or any ultimate concern, exclusive appeal to reason is a sure path to contention. Mahatma Gandhi observed that a "mere appeal to reason does not answer where prejudices are agelong and based on supposed religious authority. Reason has to be strengthened by suffering and suffering opens the eyes of the understanding."[89] Dialogues must, therefore, supplement appeal to reason with a certain quality of heart, namely the ability to feel another's suffering.

If an interreligious dialogue is to be effective, it must be carefully organized and clearly structured so that the categories of discussion – such as doctrinal or institutional issues – do not become mixed and convoluted. A dialogue must also be guided by clear rules which are agreed upon and studied by both parties before the dialogue begins. Specific terms of conduct can help insure the effectiveness of a dialogue by setting clear boundaries. The following ten rules of dialogue are suggested by the scholar Leonard Swidler, co-founder of the *Journal of Ecumenical Studies* and the Global Dialogue Institute. They provide solid guidelines for communication and conduct within interreligious settings. Swidler's ten "Rules of Dialogue" are reproduced on the following pages.

FIRST COMMANDMENT: The primary purpose of dialogue is to learn, that is, to change and grow in the perception and understanding of reality, and then to act accordingly. Minimally, the very fact that I learn that my dialogue partner believes "this" rather than "that" proportionally changes my attitude toward her; and a change in my attitude is a significant change in me. We enter into dialogue so that we can learn, change, and grow, not so we can force change on the other, as one hopes to do in debate – a hope realized in inverse proportion to the frequency and ferocity with which debate is entered into. On the other hand, because in dialogue each partner comes with the intention of learning and changing herself, one's partner in fact will also change. Thus the goal of debate, and much more, is accomplished far more effectively by dialogue.

SECOND COMMANDMENT: Interreligious, interideological dialogue must be a two-sided project – within each religious or ideological community and between religious or ideological communities. Because of the "corporate" nature of interreligious dialogue, and since the primary goal of dialogue is that each partner learn and change himself, it is also necessary that each participant enter into dialogue not only with his partner across the faith line – the Lutheran with the Anglican, for example – but also with his coreligionists, with his fellow Lutherans, to share with them the fruits of the interreligious dialogue. Only thus can the whole community eventually learn and change, moving toward an ever more perceptive insight into reality.

THIRD COMMANDMENT: Each participant must come to the dialogue with complete honesty and sincerity. It should be made clear in what direction the major and minor thrusts of the tradition move, what the future shifts might be, and, if necessary, where the participant has difficulties with her own tradition. No false fronts have any place in dialogue.

Conversely – each participant must assume a similar complete honesty and sincerity in the other partners. Not only will the absence of sincerity prevent dialogue from happening, but the absence of the assumption of the partner's sincerity will do so as well. In brief: no trust, no dialogue

FOURTH COMMANDMENT: In interreligious, interideological dialogue we must not compare our ideals with our partner's practice, but rather our ideals with our partner's ideals, our practice with our partner's practice.

FIFTH COMMANDMENT: Each participant must define himself. Only the Jew, for example, can define what it means to be a Jew. The rest can only describe what it looks like from the outside. Moreover, because dialogue is a dynamic medium, as each participant learns, he will change and hence continually deepen, expand, and modify his self-definition as a Jew – being careful to remain in constant dialogue with fellow Jews.

Thus it is mandatory that each dialogue partner define what it means to be an authentic member of his own tradition.

Conversely – the one interpreted must be able to recognize herself in the interpretation. This is the golden rule of interreligious hermeneutics, as has been often reiterated by the "apostle of interreligious dialogue," Raimundo Panikkar. For the sake of understanding, each dialogue participant will naturally attempt to express for herself what she thinks is the meaning of the partner's statement; the partner must be able to recognize herself in that expression. The advocate of "a world theology," Wilfred Cantwell Smith, would add that the expression must also be verifiable by critical observers who are not involved.

SIXTH COMMANDMENT: Each participant must come to the dialogue with no hard-and-fast assumptions as to where the points of disagreement are. Rather, each partner should not only listen to the other partner with openness and sympathy but also attempt to agree with the dialogue partner as far as is possible while still maintaining integrity with his own tradition; where he absolutely can agree no further without violating his own integrity, precisely there is the real point of disagreement – which most often turns out to be different from the point of disagreement that was falsely assumed ahead of time.

SEVENTH COMMANDMENT: Dialogue can take place only between equals, or par cum pari as the Second Vatican Council put it. Both must come to learn from each other. Therefore, if, for example, the Muslim views Hinduism as inferior, or if the Hindu views Islam as inferior, there will be no dialogue. If authentic interreligious, interideological dialogue between Muslims and Hindus is to occur, then both the Muslim and the Hindu must come mainly to learn from each other; only then will it be "equal with equal," par cum pari. This rule also indicates that there can be no such thing as a one-way dialogue. For example, Jewish–Christian discussions begun in the 1960s were mainly only prolegomena to interreligious dialogue. Understandably and properly, the Jews came to these exchanges only to teach Christians, although the Christians came mainly to learn. But, if authentic interreligious dialogue between Christians and Jews is to occur, then the Jews must also come mainly to learn; only then will it too be par cum pari.

EIGHTH COMMANDMENT: Dialogue can take place only on the basis of mutual trust. Although interreligious, interideological dialogue must occur with some kind of "corporate" dimension, that is, the participants must be involved as members of a religious or ideological community – for instance, as Marxists or Taoists – it is also fundamentally true that it is only persons who can enter into dialogue. But a dialogue among persons can be built only on personal trust. Hence it is wise not to tackle the most difficult problems in the beginning, but rather to approach first those issues most likely to provide some common ground, thereby establishing the basis of human trust. Then, gradually, as this personal trust deepens and expands, the more thorny matters can be undertaken. Thus, as in learning we move from the known to the unknown, so in dialogue we proceed from commonly held matters – which, given our mutual ignorance resulting from centuries of hostility, will take us quite some time to discover fully – to discuss matters of disagreement.

NINTH COMMANDMENT: Persons entering into interreligious, interideological dialogue must be at least minimally self-critical of both themselves and their own religious or ideological traditions. A lack of such self-criticism implies that one's own tradition already has all the correct answers. Such an attitude makes dialogue not only unnecessary, but even impossible, since we enter into dialogue primarily so we can learn – which obviously is impossible if our tradition has never made a misstep, if it has all the right answers. To be sure, in interreligious, interideological dialogue one must stand within a religious or ideological tradition with integrity and conviction, but such integrity and conviction must include, not exclude, a healthy self-criticism. Without it there can be no dialogue – and, indeed, no integrity.

TENTH COMMANDMENT: Each participant eventually must attempt to experience the partner's religion or ideology "from within"; for a religion or ideology is not merely something of the head, but also of the spirit, heart, and "whole being," individual and communal. John Dunne here speaks of "passing over" into another's religious or ideological experience and then coming back enlightened, broadened, and deepened.[90]

Swidler's "Rules of Dialogue" are useful because they help insure a polite and respectful atmosphere under which learning, communication, and mutual understanding can be achieved. Any dialogue that is not orderly and courteous quickly degenerates into unease, and even argumentative competition.

The trend toward interreligious dialogue in pluralist societies offers a positive example of how disparate communities can work together toward collective goals such as justice, peace, and unity. Exploration of the shared values of the world religions can, in fact, lead to the creation of universal moral standards. Such standards, in the words of the Indian philosopher Radhakrishnan, "give a soul to the growing world consciousness."[91] It is only by working together that the various religions can foster mutual respect, fellowship, love, and trust across religious boundaries. The emergence of a just global society depends in large measure on achieving interreligious harmony.[92]

Moai at Rano Raraku, Easter Island

CHAPTER 1
THE RELIGIOUS TRADITIONS OF THE FIRST PEOPLES

I looked ahead and saw the mountains there with rocks and forests on them, and from the mountains flashed all colors upward to the heavens. Then I was standing on the highest mountain of them all, and round about beneath me was the whole hoop of the world. And while I stood there I saw more than I can tell and I understood more than I saw; for I was seeing in a sacred manner the shapes of all things in the spirit, and the shape of all shapes as they must live together like one being. And I saw that the sacred hoop of my people was one of many hoops that made one circle, wide as daylight and as starlight, and in the center grew one mighty flowering tree to shelter all the children of one mother and one father. And I saw that it was holy.[1]

– Black Elk of the Oglala Sioux

INTRODUCTION

The major religions of today are often referred to as the "great religions" or "world religions." The world religions are, however, comparatively new when seen in light of the spiritual traditions of the first peoples, which have existed for tens of thousands of years. "First peoples" is a general term that is used to refer to our primal ancestors. In many places around the world – such as North and South America, the Pacific Islands, Africa, Siberia, New Zealand, Australia, and the Arctic – there are communities that retain a lifestyle and culture similar to that of the primal peoples. The religious beliefs and practices of these communities are often classified as "tribal religions" because they developed among small social units called tribes. Scholars distinguish the non-literate, oral-based traditions of tribal societies from "civilizational religions" that developed within city-states and utilized a form of written language. Examples of civilizational religions include those of ancient Egypt, Greece, and among the Maya and Aztecs of Pre-Colombian Mesoamerica.

One going to take a pointed stick to pinch a baby bird should first try it on himself to feel how it hurts *Yoruba Proverb from Nigeria* THE GOLDEN RULE

It is important to note that the world religions developed within particular historical and social contexts. Religious teachings are conveyed utilizing the imagery, motifs, and symbols relevant to a time and place. It is in this sense that the world religions are, in fact, intimately related to their predecessors – both tribal traditions and civilizational religions. For no religion represents a complete break with all previous organizational models, rites of passage, religious symbols, mythic narratives, beliefs and practices; rather, religious movements inherit, absorb, and reform many beliefs and practices that are embedded within the preexisting cultural milieu. Some scholars suggest that this is not only true for religions and social institutions, but also for the human psyche in general. The psychologist C. G. Jung noted that "*Primordial* means 'first' or 'original'; therefore a primordial image refers to the earliest development of the psyche. Man inherits these images from his ancestral past, a past that includes all of his human ancestors."[2] From many perspectives, then, it can be determined how the primal way of life serves as the foundation of humanity's spiritual heritage.

Describing in detail the vast and intricate beliefs and practices of the primal religions is a far greater task than one book chapter can achieve. Therefore, the discussion that follows is a thematic approach aimed at illustrating the general worldview of many of the world's first peoples. In some cases, the presentation draws distinctions between the views of modernity (perspectives rooted in the intellectual, industrial, and technological revolutions of the modern West) and that of the primal worldview. Conceding that there is no single primal or tribal religion, this chapter synthesizes a wide range of cross-cultural traditions.

MODERNITY AND TRIBAL TRADITIONS

Contemporary tribal peoples represent the closest link to humanity's prehistoric ancestors. Surviving tribal cultures have, however, been influenced by contact with modern societies, often under hostile conditions. In many cases, invading colonizers and modern industry have severely challenged the tribal way of life, which is based on land, communal living, and occupations such as farming, fishing, and hunting. In certain tribes charismatic seers have arisen with prophetic visions and teachings in response to outside challenges; such seers have offered new ways of sustaining tradition, responding to modernity, and grasping meaning and purpose within a rapidly changing world. One example of a religious movement that has emerged partly in response to modernity is the Ghost Dance Movement prevalent among Native North Americans.

The world religions, particularly Christian missionary activity, have also influenced tribal traditions. This influence has led to a variety of syncretic movements that have synthesized aspects of certain world religions with traditional tribal practices. Amalgamative movements among tribal peoples in North America, influenced by Christianity, include the Peyote Religion or Native American Church and the Longhouse Religion. In Africa, and elsewhere, many tribal peoples have adopted modern religions, at least on the surface, while maintaining traditional beliefs and practices. New religious movements in Africa, influenced by Christian missionaries but with distinctive teachings and, in some cases, new prophets, include the Zionist Churches and the Nazareth Baptist Church of characteristically Zulu heritage. Other small-scale movements, influenced by modernity and modern religions but with strong ties to tribal practices, have surfaced in South America, Melanesia, Fiji, Jamaica, New Zealand, Siberia, India, Korea, Japan, Vietnam, Burma, Indonesia, and the Philippines, among other places.

APPROACHING THE PRIMAL WORLDVIEW

As members of societies we are born into cultures that have particular worldviews. In that sense, we have inherent assumptions, embedded in those worldviews, that influence what we believe constitutes knowledge (epistemology) and reality (ontology). The study of tribal societies and religious worldviews in general is especially important because it enables students to envision radically different ways of understanding existence. For example, unlike modern societies, in which secularism has become widespread, "religion," as it is called today, permeated all aspects of life for the primal peoples. It was something that had no distinct name, nor was it relegated to a certain domain of life; rather, simply being alive was "religious".

Much of the early European–American scholarship on tribal cultures assumed that the worldviews of industrialized societies that wield the powers of empirical science were fundamentally superior to traditional worldviews. The bias that influenced early scholarship regarding tribal peoples was best described by Mircea Eliade, one of the foremost authorities on tribal traditions:

> The image that our nineteenth century created of "inferior societies" was largely derived from the positivistic, antireligious, and ametaphysical attitude entertained by a number of worthy explorers and ethnologists who had approached the "savages" with the ideology of a contemporary of Comte, Darwin, or Spencer. Among the "primitives" they everywhere discovered "fetishism" and "religious infantilism" – simply because they could see nothing else. Only the resurgence of European metaphysical thought at the beginning of the present century, the religious renaissance, the many and various gains by depth psychology, by poetry, by microphysics, have made [it] possible to understand the spiritual horizon of "primitives," the structure of their symbols, the function of their myths, the maturity of their mysticisms.[3]

As students of religion, it is important to resist the idea that advancements in technology and industry indicate advances in spiritual or religious insight. In fact, the predicaments that afflict modern "civilized" society – such as war, nationalistic competition, tyranny, poverty, and the mistreatment of the environment – could be viewed as "barbaric" or "savage" when viewed from a different vantage point.

THE HIGH GOD

Popular terms employed for the classification of religious worldviews include "polytheism" (belief in many gods) and "monotheism" (belief in one God). These terms, however, can cause more confusion than clarity, more prejudice than understanding. For example, many modern people view themselves as holding the religious perspective of "monotheism" while simultaneously believing in the existence of souls, spirits, and angels. However, one finds similar underlying beliefs in primal traditions under the label of "polytheism," even though most tribal religions feature a belief in one ultimate God. For example, the scholar E. Bolaji Idowu concluded:

> I do not know of any place in Africa where the ultimacy is not accorded to God … I conclude that the religion can only be adequately described as monotheistic. I modify this "monotheism" by the adjective "diffused," because here we have a monotheism in which there exist other powers which derive from Deity such being and authority that they can be treated, for practical purposes, almost as ends in themselves.[4]

Among African tribes, the divine presence is made apparent via lesser spirits and powers that inhabit the world. A popular dictum in the northern regions of Ghana and Nigeria decrees: "the sun falls in the evening, but he [God] is always there."[5] For many African tribal peoples, belief in a High God is implicit. In some cases, the High God is rarely prayed to unless an individual is experiencing dire circumstances. The notion of a distant High God, especially in terms of African tribes, arises from the belief that God is not directly involved in the happenings of human life. Many early scholars and outside observers were ignorant of the prevalent tribal belief in one Supreme Being because they did not see people directly worshiping a supreme Creator. In many cases, the Supreme Being is not invoked because the main concerns of daily life are directed by lesser spirits and gods.

A popular dictum decrees: "the sun falls in the evening, but he [God] is always there"

The anthropologist E. E. Evans–Pritchard, during fieldwork in Sudan, documented the religious beliefs and practices of the Nuer tribe. Evans–Pritchard, having learned the language of the Nuer, observed that they believe in one High God, called Kwoth nhiali, as well as a variety of lesser spirits that exist in minor spheres of influence. The Nuer view

God as the unseen, all-knowing creator and sustainer of life. According to Evans-Pritchard the relationship between the one God and the lesser spirits, such as air spirits, is as follows:

> The spirits of the air are, nevertheless, being Spirit, also God. They are many but also one, God is manifested in, and in a sense is, each of them. I received the impression that in sacrificing or in singing hymns to an air-spirit Nuer do not think that they are communicating with the spirit and not with God. They are … addressing God in a particular spiritual figure or manifestation … They do not see a contradiction here, and there is no reason why they should see one. God is not a particular air-spirit but the spirit is a figure of God … Nuer pass without difficulty or hesitation from a more general and comprehensive way of conceiving of God or Spirit to a more particular and limited way … and back again.[6]

Due to the linguistic diversity of Africa, the High God is called a different name by various tribes: to the Ibo (in present-day Nigeria), Chukwu; to the Zulu (in present-day South Africa), Inkosi Yezulu or Umvelingqangi; to the Yoruba (in present-day Nigeria), Oloruw; to the Baila (in present-day Zambia), Leza; to the Dinka (in present-day Sudan), Temaukel; to the Luo (in present-day Kenya), Nyasi; to the Mende (in present-day Sierre Leone), Ngewo.

The Great Mysterious

Practically all Native North American tribes believe in a High God or Great Spirit. Among some tribes, the Great Spirit is viewed as the underlying principle of unity that manifests in a multiplicity of spiritual forms. Among the tribes of the Great Plains, this divine unity is called Wakan-Tanka or the "Great Mysterious." The modern visionary Black Elk of the Ogala (Sioux) tribe explained that "peace … comes within the souls of men when they realize their relationship, their oneness with the universe and all its powers, and when they realise that at the centre of the Universe dwells *Wakan-Tanka*, and that this centre is really everywhere, it is within each of us."[7] The Wakan-Tanka is manifested within a chain of hierarchical divine, or *wakan*, beings. A member of the Dakota (Sioux) tribe asserted that "every object in the world has a spirit and that spirit is wakan … they are all as if one."[8] The many spirits are thus collectively conceived as one unified, divine power.

ORAL TRADITIONS AND MYTHIC NARRATIVES

Unlike many of today's most prominent world religions, tribal religions have no discernible beginning or authoritative scripture. Rather, tribal religious life is based in a continually renewed tradition preserved through oral teachings handed down from generation to generation. Oral traditions are, in fact, the repository of a tribe's cultural and spiritual values – the very fabric that holds a tribe together. Since primal cultures did not develop systems of writing, emphasis is placed on human relationships in the process of transmitting sacred teachings.

In tribal cultures, sacred teachings and mythic narratives are preserved by the elders, who are the embodiment of a tribe's wisdom and thus highly respected and honored. The elders are, as it were, living and breathing scriptures that personally pass down the teachings of a tribe by spoken word and through other creative mediums, such as dance, song, and drama. The use of spoken language is closely associated with the life-breath among many tribal peoples. The use of words and speech thus entails responsibility, particularly in the process of naming objects and people, and is believed to wield power and consequences.

The oral nature of tribal teachings, as opposed to written scriptures, is also important because religious myths were not codified, and could undergo change in form while retaining their function. It was, therefore, possible for new symbols to emerge that would facilitate enduring contact with the sacred. The mythologist Joseph Campbell, who stressed the non-literal and metaphorical nature of religious myth, noted that:

> the first and most important effect of a living mythological symbol is to waken and give guidance to the energies of life. It is an energy-releasing and [energy]-directing sign ... one conducive to your participation in the life and purposes of a functioning social group ... When the vital symbols of any given social group evoke in all its members responses of this kind, a sort of magical cord unites them as one spiritual organism, functioning through members who, though separate in space, are yet one in being and belief.[9]

As such, religious myths are not "falsehoods"; rather, they offer ways of grasping realities beyond human understanding and provide values, orientation, and meaning – all of which are not quantifiable or attainable through conceptual analysis alone. Thus sacred narratives contain clues to meaningful ways of life that not only structure the basic roles and functions of society but also nurture a mystical awareness of transcendence. The scholar Ananda Coomaraswamy describes myth as follows: "The Myth [is] the penultimate truth, of which all experience is the temporal reflection. The mythical narrative is of timeless and placeless validity, true nowever and everywhere ... Myth embodies the nearest approach to absolute truth that can be stated in words."[10]

A Zulu shaman performs a traditional healing ritual

For example, origin stories are important mythic narratives because they provide the framework from which reality is experienced as an ordered cosmos rather than random chaos. Such narratives are rarely concerned with historical events. Rather, they relate the entire succession of historical events to mythic happenings that occurred "in the beginning" – in timelessness. These archetypal events are eternal principles made manifest within the ordering and coming-into-being of the here and now. Some myths depict the emergence of the cosmos at a specific location (such as a tree, pole, cave, mountain, or island) – referred to by scholars as a sacred space. Such a sacred space may function as the center or pivot of all existence, providing direction and orientation within a world that may otherwise seem bereft of meaning. It is not merely indicative of a physical locality but also other metaphysical planes – it is an *axis mundi* that links heaven, earth, and the underworld.

> **Religious myths are not "falsehoods"; rather, they offer ways of grasping realities beyond human understanding and provide values, orientation, and meaning**

Many mythic narratives contain a story about a lost Golden Age, a period closest to the origin of all things. During this primordial epoch, humanity is typically believed to have enjoyed immortality or the presence of the divine. Many myths claim that this paradisal state was brought to an end by a calamity of some sort that befell humankind. In the region of Africa formed by the countries of Nigeria, Ghana, and the Ivory Coast, narratives teach that humanity was isolated from the Creator because of an arrogant desire to achieve his standing. The Vugusu of Africa believe that a powerful semi-divine chameleon, with whom they would not share sustenance, cursed humans with a temporal existence. The Hopi tribe (North America) believes that our world is the fourth of its kind – the previous versions were destroyed by the Creator because the inhabitants forgot their origin and brought conflict and war to the land. A Haida myth (North America) tells of a great flood that dispersed the peoples of the earth. Myths from the Cheyenne tribe (North America) speak of a time when all of the Great Mystery's creations, such as humans and animals, lived together in peace while observing a vegetarian diet.

MYTHIC TIME AND RITUAL

Modern societies are firmly rooted in a linear conception of time that suggests a reality that is moving irreversibly, like an arrow, in one direction – from the past, through the present, to the future. In most tribal languages, however, there are no tenses corresponding to what we call past, present, and future. The scholar Frithjof Schuon concluded:

> traditions having a prehistoric origin are, symbolically speaking, made for "space" and not for "time"; that is to say, they saw the light in a primordial epoch when time was still but a rhythm in a spatial and static beatitude, and when space or simultaneity still predominated over the experience of duration and change. The historical traditions on the other hand must take the experience of "time" into account and must foresee instability and decadence, since they were born in periods when time had become like a fast-flowing river and ever more devouring.[11]

Primal people were not unaware of time as it is understood by most people today; they experienced duration and change in relation to what they saw as ultimately real – timelessness (or eternality). In that sense, primal peoples were aware of two "times," or modes of experience. On the one hand, there are events that come and go with the passage of time; on the other, there is "sacred time" which is actualized through mythically imbued ritual and ceremony. The Eternal Now of sacred time is always present and is participated in when sacred rituals are performed. In light of eternality, primal peoples viewed ordinary time as a mere shadow of what is real; thus ordinary time is understood as secondary, profane, and only marginally real.

Concepts such as individualism are foreign to tribal societies. It can be said that many tribal peoples do not conceive of themselves as fully "real," or actualized, unless they are participating in mythic archetypal patterns, or models of behavior, that were established "in the beginning." The primal acts that occurred in the beginning, such as the actions of heroic ancestors, establish the patterns of daily life. These stories are conveyed and preserved through myth.[12] In this way, the actions of daily life are ritualized and thus infused with cosmic significance. The scholar Evan Zuesse suggested that:

> The transcendental center of symbolic action is the heart of ritual. Ritual mediates between the real and ideal, flesh and mind, material and spiritual, giving each a shape which is that of the other. "Centeredness" … is the real action of ritual, through which Being is translated into Becoming.
>
> … Every [ritual] action on its deepest level seeks to sustain the divine order and its continual self-regeneration; in this sense every ritual enactment … is utterly selfless.[13]

In many tribal cultures, daily routines such as hunting are sacred. Each step of the hunting process entails an inspired, and often intricate, ritual. In reference to Australian Aborigines, the scholar Huston Smith has observed:

> We are inclined to say that when the Arunta go hunting they mime the exploits of the
> first and archetypal hunter, but this distinguishes them from their archetype too sharply.
> It is better to say that they enter the mold of their archetype so completely that each
> becomes the First Hunter; no distinction remains. Similarly for other activities, from
> basket weaving to lovemaking. Only while they are conforming their actions to the
> model of some archetypal hero do the Arunta feel that they are truly alive, for in those
> roles they are immortal.[14]

When a primal person "merges" with a mythic event or heroic figure, that person embodies, or partakes in, Eternity. On such an occasion it is believed that Eternity and Being are present in the ritual act.

THE ANIMISTIC UNIVERSE

The rendering of philosophical treatises regarding the nature of Ultimate Reality is a prevalent and important form of religious expression (exemplified by, for example, the religiously motivated philosophers of ancient Greece). However, when studying tribal peoples it is important to recognize, as the scholar Rudolf Otto did, "that religion is not exclusively contained and exhaustively comprised in any series of 'rational' assertions; and it is well worth while to attempt to bring the relation of the different 'moments' of religion to one another clearly before the mind, so that its nature may become more manifest."[15] According to Otto, "moments of religion" are numinous experiences (derived from the Latin *numen*, meaning "spirit" or "divine being"). These are irreducible and transcend rationality; they are meaningful in and of themselves. Numinous experiences correspond to a variety of emotions – such as terror and unspeakable bliss – typified in Otto's phrase *mysterium tremendum fascinans* ("something unknown which is both awesome and enchanting"). To incur such experiences is to encounter the sacred. The scholar Mircea Eliade suggested that "the sacred is equivalent to a power, and, in the last analysis, to reality. The sacred is saturated with being. Sacred power means reality and at the same time enduringness and efficacity … Thus it is easy to understand that religious man deeply desires to be, to participate in reality, to be saturated with power."[16]

In approaching the primal view of the universe, it is important to appreciate the experiential dimension of religion and how awe-inducing experiences are central within a worldview that engages the universe as something enlivened with soul (*anima*) and teeming with life. This view of reality is classified by scholars as "animism."

Animism, a word etymologically derived from the Latin *anima*, meaning "soul," was first coined to indicate belief in spiritual beings. Today, animism is associated with the worldview that all things are endowed with a soul and, in some cases, that all things taken as a whole have one Soul. The animistic perspective is best understood as a belief that everything is alive; in that way, nothing is "dead matter," "inanimate," or "insentient." Rather, all things are understood as animated by a spiritual essence or power (sometimes referred to by scholars as soul, spirit, vital energy, or spiritual force). For example, the Melanesians of the Pacific Coast islands use the term *mana* to signify the divine power inherent in all things. The archeologist R. H. Codrington, who pioneered the study of the Melanesian religion, noted:

> There is a belief [amongst the Melanesians] in a force altogether distinct from physical power, which acts in all kinds of ways for good and evil … and which it is of the greatest advantage to possess or control … It is a power or influence, not physical, and in a way supernatural; but it shews itself in physical force, or in any kind of power or excellence which a man possesses. This Mana is not fixed in anything, and can be conveyed in almost anything; but spirits, whether disembodied souls or supernatural beings, have it and can impart it.[17]

In that sense, tribal peoples view the power inherent in nature – the waves in the ocean, the growth of crops, the heat of the sun, or the motion of animals – as manifesting spiritual power that is not reducible to materiality or the causality of a deterministic universe. Many African tribes hold a belief in a spiritual force termed *nyama*, which is similar to the Melanesian concept of *mana*. According to the contemporary scholar of religion Geoffrey Parrinder:

> From the western Sudan down to the Guinea Coast one finds variants of this word, sometimes used as a title for God, sometimes for human or animal strength, or again as the mysterious force in medicines. Nyama is often conceived of as impersonal, unconscious energy, found in men, animals, gods, nature and things. *Nyama is not the outward appearance, but the inner essence.*[18]

Belief in a spiritual force, such as *nyama*, exists throughout tribal societies under different names. For example, Native North Americans believe in a fundamental spirit or vital force that enlivens all things. To the Iroquois tribe this life force is known as *orenda*; to the Dakota, *wakanda*; and to the Algonquin, *manito*.

Taboos

This spiritual force can, however, be dangerous, especially if an individual's relationship with reality is unbalanced. Thus, tribal peoples are generally concerned to maintain a harmonious relationship with the environment. This entails an underlying belief in the interdependency and reciprocity of all actions, including words and thoughts. From the tribal perspective, equilibrium can be assured when certain purifications and behavioral restrictions are upheld. Actions that might disturb a harmonious relationship between all things, especially the relationship between the seen (gross) and the unseen (subtle), are considered harmful and might, therefore, be designated as taboo. The word "taboo" is etymologically derived from the Polynesian word *tapu*, meaning "marked off". Taboos ensure a proper relationship with the spiritual forces of the universe and thus help to maintain the health, fecundity, and prosperity of the tribe. Among many tribes, menstruating women are separated from the community because they are believed to possess unusually strong spiritual powers which can be dangerous to others. Other common taboos guard against impurities, such as people nearing death and corpses.

> **The word "taboo" is etymologically derived from the Polynesian word *tapu*, meaning "marked off"**

SACRED MODES OF PERCEPTION

In their belief that reality is essentially spiritual, tribal peoples perceive phenomena quite differently than most modern people. For example, a modern person typically sees a tree or animal as a fundamentally "material" or "organic" object. Thunderous rainstorms and howling winds are seen as "natural" occurrences, often implying something rarely described as "spiritual." The materialistic worldview, an attribute of modernity, explains the universe in terms of empirical data, often in conjunction with impersonal concepts such as natural law, causality, and linear time. A tribal person, however, has a different mode of perception – he or she sees "natural" objects and occurrences as manifesting something spiritual, mysterious, and divine. Mircea Eliade observed:

> [The modern person] finds it difficult to accept the fact that, for many human beings, the sacred can be manifested in stones or trees, for example … The sacred tree, the sacred stone are not adored as stone or tree; they are worshipped precisely because they are hierophanies [manifestations of the sacred], because they show something that is no longer stone or tree but the sacred, the ganz andere.
>
> By manifesting the sacred, any object becomes something else, yet it continues to remain itself, for it continues to participate in its surrounding cosmic milieu. A sacred stone remains a stone; apparently (or, more precisely, from the profane point of view), nothing distinguishes it from all other stones. But for those to whom a stone reveals itself as sacred, its immediate reality is transmuted into a supernatural reality. In other words, for those who have a religious experience all nature is capable of revealing itself as a cosmic sacrality. The cosmos in its entirety can become a hierophany.[19]

From this perspective, tribal peoples see things in relation to their essence – understood intuitively to be Spirit. In this way, trees and stones may be seen as symbols that manifest Spirit. The scholar Joseph Epes Brown, in relation to the Plains Indians of North America, suggested that "the material form … is not thought of as representing some *other* and higher reality, but *is* that reality in an image. The power or quality, therefore, which a particular form reflects may be transferred directly to the person in contact with it."[20] From this perspective, the symbolic seeing of nature as a sacred reality is both perceptual – that is, the seeing of the divine in a multiplicity of manifest forms – and interactive – meaning, engaging these luminous forms and acquiring the powers intrinsic to them.

The cosmos in its entirety can become a hierophany

The act of reading serves as an analogy that helps to illustrate "symbolic seeing." When reading a poem, one not only "sees" the printed word on the page (the appearance) but one also envisions the meaning (the essence) that the words, as symbols, connote. Similarly, primal peoples do not tend to see reality as literal, neither do they understand reality to be "more real" when it is reduced to its physical constituent parts (such as cells, atoms, or, to stay with the current analogy, the letters that make up the words of the poem). Rather, from this point of view, material appearance is seen as symbolic of spiritual reality. This "symbolic seeing" is not achieved through discursive reasoning but by seeing through appearances to their source. As Frithjof Schuon describes, "the symbolist vision of the cosmos is a priori a spontaneous perspective that bases itself on the essential nature – or the metaphysical transparency – of phenomena."[21] In this way, certain tribal peoples – for example, the tribes of the Great Plains in North America – see nature as translucent to Spirit. Nature, therefore, when seen in light of its source, is experienced as divine.

RITES OF PASSAGE

In modern society, transitional stages of life such as birth, puberty, and death are often understood as personal events divorced from both religious and communal significance. One scholar has noted that within the modern world's growing individualism, many people encounter discomfort because "an increasing number of individuals are forced to accomplish their transitions alone and with private symbols."[22] Tribal peoples, however, mark transitional periods as thresholds to new stages of life. These transitions, or initiations, are intertwined with communally recognized ceremonial rituals rooted in religious myth and meaning. The basic motif of transitional rites of passage is that of death and rebirth: death to a previous state of being, or stage in life, and rebirth to a new state of being, or

Top left: Totem pole found in Victoria, British Columbia, Canada

Top right: Stonehenge, England. Archaeologists still fiercely debate the purpose and method of construction of this prehistoric monument

Bottom: Ayers Rock, Australia. Also known as Uluru, this colossal rock formation is sacred to many local tribes

stage in life. The function of initiations and rites of passage is not merely societal but religious and cultural, for initiations are the means by which individuals are introduced to spiritual values.

The ethnographer Arnold van Gennep suggested that, to some extent, life consists of a succession of stages (or initiations), and each stage has its accompanying rites and rituals.[23] According to van Gennep, there are three main stages in ritual or ceremonial initiation which occur in progression. He states that these transitional stages are liminal[24] periods of both physiological and psychological growth. The first stage is the pre-liminal period, associated with rites of separation; the second stage is the liminal period, associated with rites of transition; and the final stage is the post-liminal period, associated with rites of re-integration or reincorporation. During the separation or pre-liminal stage the initiate is estranged from society and thus removed from his or her societal status, normative attitudes, and patterns of daily life. In effect, the separation stage represents the death of the initiate's old status and way of being. Having been drastically severed from society, the initiate enters a liminal period that entails no societal status whatsoever. The liminal period is considered an ambiguous and dangerous realm of marginality associated with death. It is, therefore, regarded as a period in which contact with the divine is more readily available, especially by way of visions and dreams. After the completion of a physically and spiritually strenuous ordeal the initiate is reincorporated into the tribe and recognized with a new status and even, in some cases, a new name. This stage is representative of the symbolic rebirth of the initiate. Many rites of passage, such as those concerned with puberty, help individuals to cross thresholds of transformation while strengthening the bond of the tribe as a whole.

> **The basic motif of transitional rites of passage is that of death and rebirth**

The model van Gennep has suggested does not necessarily correspond to all rites and rituals in all tribal cultures; however, it elucidates a prevalent and important underlying structure that appears in practices across cultures. Van Gennep's model also sheds light on various aspects of modern cultural institutions that are similarly structured.

Spiritual Maturity through Disenchantment

The scholar Sam Gill has documented a rite of passage that utilizes disenchantment to bring about spiritual maturity.[25] Gill identified instances of "initiation by disenchantment" among Native North Americans, Africans, as well as aboriginal Australians. The "*kachina* cult" of the Native North American Hopi tribe is particularly illustrative of the phenomenon described by Gill.[26] The children of the Hopi tribe are raised to believe in spirit beings known as *kachina*s. These spirit beings, who are really men of the tribe elaborately costumed with intricately designed masks, descend from nearby mountains and perform various religious dances and ceremonies of symbolic significance. The children of the tribe are taught that the *kachina*s are real spirit beings, that they are the source of Hopi culture, exemplars of divine virtues, and that they sustain the welfare of the tribe. At around the age of ten, the children, who have been meticulously shielded from participation in and knowledge of adult religious life, are initiated into the "*kachina* cult." The initiation, which represents entrance into adult life, is viewed as the pinnacle of childhood.

In Hopi culture, which is inseparable from Hopi religion, great emphasis is placed on the initiation rite. Initiates, for example, are forbidden to reveal the mysteries to the uninitiated. The *kachina* cult initiation, which coincides with a major seasonal ceremony, lasts for over a week. During this time, the children are taught spiritual lessons, and even ritually whipped, to impress upon them the importance of never revealing the secrets of initiation. At the culmination of this ceremonial initiation process, the children are allowed to watch a special dance of the *kachina*s, which of course they have never seen before. With great anticipation the children are led to a *kiva*, a partly underground chamber that houses the ceremonial dance. With a reverent awe, they approach this most sacred dance, only to see unmasked *kachina*s dancing. The children, in a state of shock and utter dejection, recognize that the *kachina*s are not really spiritual beings but the men of the tribe, their neighbors, fathers, brothers, and uncles. All that they had clung to as embodying the truth, represented in the *kachina*s, is destroyed in the culminating moment of the initiation. Gill explains the dynamics of initiation by disenchantment, of which the *kachina* cult is one instance, as follows:

> The whole initiatory process reinforces [the] sense that the fullness of the religious reality is invested in these figures and objects [in this case, the *kachina*s]. Then in the concluding moments, upon the threshold of a new life, the illusion is dissolved, and the shock of disenchantment shatters all that went before. The experience makes a return to the previous state of life impossible. The naïve realism of the uninitiated perspective has been exploded. The rites have demonstrated irreversibly that things are not simply what they appear to be, that one-dimensional literalism is a childish faith that one has to grow beyond or else despair of a life rich in meaning and worth. Surely, being thus forced to abandon one's ingrained notion of reality is to experience a true death of the former self.[27]

Initiation by disenchantment serves to deepen contemplative religious thinking; it heightens appreciation of mystery and shifts an initiate's perspective to essence rather than form. In fact, children undergo a depressing state of disillusionment from which emerges a widening of spiritual perspective – a symbolic death and rebirth. After realizing that the *kachina*s are not spiritual beings, as Gill describes, the Hopi initiate is presented with a choice:

> He may see the world as meaningless, or he may undertake a quest for a fuller under-standing of the world. This is scarcely a choice. The experience of disenchantment ini-tiates the world-creating and world-discovering human and cultural processes we know as religion. It stimulates inquiry, thought, creativity, wonderment, and the eventual for-mation of the sense of the religious world.[28]

The child–initiate thus endures the growing-pains of entering a mature religious life, which entails entering a new world of spiritual possibilities. Initiates come to see their for-mer literalist beliefs, associated with the non-contemplative life of a child, as a develop-mental stage in a greater process of spiritual growth. After initiation, children enter the adult religious life of the Hopi and participate in future *kachina* festivities. Thus, Hopi reli-gious practice does not end with *kachina* initiation, but rather it begins in earnest. Deeper religious pursuits associated with esoteric teachings are available to those Hopi who have undergone initiation. In short, the *kachina* initiation by way of disenchantment does not lead to irreligion but, rather, to an even deeper religious life.

The Vision Quest

One of the most important rites of passage is the vision quest, fundamental to many tribal peoples, especially those recognized as shamans (see below). The nature and meaning of the vision quest differs among various tribes. It is, however, generally regarded as one of the major transitional rites of passage incurred by a young adult entering formal religious life. Vision quests are also commonly performed as part of initiations into esoteric societies and by adult aspirants during periods of struggle and spiritual yearning. In short, vision quests are the pursuit of a spiritual vision that has the potential to impart power and inform life with direction and purpose. The experience incurred on a vision quest serves as a pil-lar of spiritual support and strength during the entire life of an individual. Vision quests are particularly important among Native North Americans. Thus, Native American traditions are examined in the following general description of the vision quest. Aspects of the Native American vision quest are manifested in other traditions and may therefore be archetypal in nature.

A vision quest is not something undertaken hastily; rather, it requires guidance from elders and preparatory training, including the ability to discriminate between spiritually authentic and inauthentic visions and dreams. A vision quest is preceded by preparatory rituals, including an intense purification rite designed to expunge impurities, promote harmonious integration of the inner and outer world, and heighten awareness of the sacred. After preparatory rituals are completed, an aspirant begins a solitary retreat entailing prayer and meditative disciplines. During this retreat an aspirant fasts from food and drink while directing his or her attention and aspiration solely toward the attainment of a spiritual vision, a revelatory dream, or a communication with a benevolent or guardian spirit (often such spirits take the form of animals). The scholar Joseph Epes Brown explained that "it is through the vision quest, participated in with physical sacrifice and the utmost humility, that the individual opens himself up in the most direct manner to contact with the spiritual essences underlying the forms of the manifested world."[29] A quest does not usually end until a vision has occurred; in fact, an aspirant may go days without food or drink, wearing only the barest coverings, alone on a mountain or in a cave awaiting a vision or spiritual communication. If the seeker of a vision feels that it is necessary in order to demonstrate greater commitment to the quest, he or she might sacrificially sever a finger or cut pieces of flesh from his or her arm.

After the attainment of a vision, an individual returns to the tribe and shares the experience attained. Conveying one's vision experience, whether by word, dance, song, or dramatic reenactment, is the seal of the spiritual act that contributes to the vitality and sustenance of the tribe as a whole. Among some tribes, elders are consulted to decipher and interpret an aspirant's experiences. For example, a member of the Brule (Sioux) tribe of Native North America tells of an elder who consoled a youth who believed he did not have a true vision. The elder responded: "A vision comes as a gift born of humility, of wisdom, and of patience. If from your vision quest you have learned nothing but this, then you have already learned much."[30]

SHAMANS

Among many tribes around the world – both in the distant past and today – there is a religious practice loosely termed "shamanism." The word "shaman" (*saman*) is borrowed from the Tungu tribe in Siberia, who are known for their shamanic practices. Shamanism is a sacred vocation that is available only to a few inspired individuals called shamans. Shamanism is not a religion, but rather a component of many tribal cultures; some scholars consider it to be the "prototype of mysticism."[31] Mircea Eliade defines shamanism as a "technique of ecstasy." He suggests that "the shaman specializes in a trance during which his soul is believed to leave his body and ascend to the sky or descend to the underworld."[32] In fact, it is a commonly held belief among tribal peoples that shamans have the ability to converse with spirits and to invoke ecstatic states and visions. Shamans are also thought to travel to different levels of reality by way of out-of-body psychic excursions. In that way, shamans are considered to be mediators between ordinary reality and the spiritual realm.

Scholars have shown that there is a pattern common among shamans – many have undergone a crisis at a young age. Often this crisis is related to psychological abnormality and even physical seizures. If the individual overcomes the crisis and, in so doing, achieves a faculty of visionary perception or healing powers, it is likely that he or she will be recognized as a shaman by fellow tribe members. Thus, some scholars view shamans as embodying the motif of the "wounded healer." In that sense, a shaman is one who, having endured a state of bewilderment or psychological dismemberment, plunges into the transpersonal depth of the psyche.[33] Through spiritual struggles, trials, and tribulations, the shaman is able to heal him- or herself and attain psychic integration.[34] This entails a series of inner confrontations that bring forth a transformation of consciousness and the attainment of spiritual powers. A shaman, therefore, experiences a symbolic death of his or her former state of being and incurs a spiritual rebirth into a new state. After this symbolic rebirth, the shaman returns to society with new powers and societal status to help and heal others. Shamans of this kind often decree that they were called to take up the shamanic path, either by spiritual beings or from within. Some would-be shamans seek initiation from an existing guild of shamanic masters, or they inherit the role through family lineage. Those shamans that enter an apprenticeship must pass through severe, sometimes tortuous, ordeals and vision quests.

Shamans, often referred to as "medicine men," are widely known for their ability to heal. A society's healing techniques and categories of diagnosis are informed by its dominant worldview. Modern societies have developed very powerful methods of healing the body. Shamans, however, do not see the body as fundamental; rather, they believe spiritual reality to be the organizing principle of material reality. Within this general worldview is the belief in various spirit entities, some of which are harmful to humanity, and thereby drain the energy and vitality of people or cause obstructions in the personality. Shamans, often by way of dramatic and elaborate techniques, intervene in the spiritual world on behalf of the ill to expunge the spirits that hinder the sick.

CHAPTER SUMMARY

One may ask, "What is the relevance of tribal religions today?" The answer to this question might very well be found in the mystical dimension of religious life – the perception of sacredness. Technological advancement does not necessarily equate to a progression in spiritual awareness. Due to the rapid expansion of industry and technology, the future of the tribal way of life, however, appears bleak. Nevertheless, tribal religions are a living tradition. As humanity moves further away from experiencing the environment as sacred, nature has become less invested with religious meaning. In fact, the religious symbol of Mother Earth, and the chthonic energies of renewal associated with it (archetypically associated with the feminine), has progressively lost its numinous resonance among many modern peoples.

According to the scholar Francois Petitpierre all primordial peoples "saw the 'more' in the 'less,' in the sense that the landscape was for them a reflection of a superior reality which 'contained' the physical reality; they added, may one say, to the latter, a 'spiritual dimension' which escapes modern man."[35] Situated within a universe animated by Spirit, many tribal peoples see the sacred manifested through the sun, the moon, the sky, the trees, the rocks, the stones, and the mountains. As one scholar has noted, for many indigenous Africans, the spiritual forces of the world are so engulfed within the visible world that African tribes are forced "to reckon with 'things invisible to mortal sight'."[36] In modern times, appreciation of the subtleties of life – and

Shamans are considered to be mediators between ordinary reality and the spiritual realm

accordingly the awareness of spiritual reality – is increasingly filtered out amid fast-paced and materialistically dominated societies. Reflecting on the contribution and the understanding of tribal cultures raises an awareness of the sacredness of all life, and particularly of nature, and can thereby contribute to a more balanced and harmonious relationship with the environment. The following advice, offered by a Native North American, is paradigmatic of tribal spirituality:

"You must learn to look at the world twice," he told me as I sat on the floor of his immaculately swept adobe room. "First you must bring your eyes together in front so you can see each droplet of rain on the grass, so you can see the smoke rising from an anthill in the sunshine. Nothing should escape your notice. But you must learn to look again, with your eyes at the very edge of what is visible. Now you must see dimly if you wish to see things that are dim – visions, mist, and cloud-people … animals which hurry past you in the dark. You must learn to look at the world twice if you wish to see all that there is to see."[37]

Mayan Pyramid of Kukulkan, Chichen Itza, Mexico

CHAPTER 2
THE RELIGIOUS TRADITIONS OF MESOAMERICA

Truly earth is not the place of reality.
Indeed one must go elsewhere;
beyond, happiness exists.
Or is it that we come to earth in vain?
Certainly some other place is the abode of life
    ...

No, O Lord of the Close Vicinity [the Omni-
    present],
it is beyond, with those who dwell in Your house,
that I will sing songs to You, in the innermost
    heaven.
My heart rises;
I fix my eyes upon You,
next to You, beside You,
O Giver of Life![1]

    – an Aztec sage

INTRODUCTION

The term "Mesoamerica" (or "Middle America") refers to
regions of Central America and southern North America
(roughly from central Mexico to Honduras). It is believed
that, as early as 30,000 B.C.E., hunter-gatherers from northeast Asia migrated into the Americas through the Bering
Straits, which connect Siberia and Alaska. By around
20,000 B.C.E. they had reached the Basin of Mexico. The
worldview of these tribal peoples was shamanic in nature
and had a lasting influence on the religious traditions of
subsequent Mesoamerican civilizations.[2] With the onset
of agricultural lifestyles and urban development, city-states
gradually emerged. By around 1500 B.C.E., the Olmec civilization, the so-called "Mother Culture" of Mesoamerica,
had laid the groundwork for later Mesoamerican societies.
Over the next three thousand years, a variety of indigenous
traditions flourished in Middle America, some of them

Timeline

20,000 B.C.E.
Hunter-gatherers reach
    Basin of Mexico
*c.*2000 B.C.E.
Formative or Pre-Classic
    Period: Settlements
    established
1500 B.C.E.
Olmec civilization takes
    root
*c.*250 C.E.
Classic Period begins:
    Maya civilization
    develops and flourishes
*c.*500 C.E.
Teotihuacan reaches
    height of influence
*c.*900 C.E.
Post-Classic Period:
    Toltecs predominant
*c.*1325 C.E.
Tenochtitlan founded
1519 C.E.
Spanish arrive at
    Tenochtitlan
1522 C.E.
Aztec Empire falls

continuing in this region today (such as the traditions of the Maya in the Yucatan Peninsula).

Scholars have divided Mesoamerica's cultural history into at least three periods: the Formative or Pre-Classic Period (*c.*2000 B.C.E.–250 C.E.); the Classic Period (*c.*250–900 C.E.); and the Post-Classic Period (*c.*900–1521 C.E.). Most scholars agree that Mesoamerica's high culture emerged independently of the cultural developments in other regions of the world, although there are many parallels with these traditions. For example, creation stories from many cultures, including Mesoamerican narratives such as the Maya creation myth found in the Popol Vuh, describe the world as originating out of a primordial water and formless darkness through the agency of a divine entity. This creation narrative reflects a deeply rooted aspect of early civilizations across the globe – a common sense that the origin of the world and the source of life is divine.

Another significant feature that is common to both Mesoamerican religious traditions and those of other regions is the intentional alignment of temples and architectural monuments with astronomical bodies that were believed to be divine. This practice is exemplified by a variety of Mesoamerican temples and pyramids (described below), by the Egyptian Pyramids, and by Stonehenge (a site in present-day England where religious rituals were once performed), in addition to monuments in other regions. Given that these shared practices and beliefs arose independently of one another, they seem to reflect an innate yearning to reshape the world in which the activities of human life are carried out so that those activities are imbued with divine significance and harmonized with the cycles of the cosmos. Indeed, the traces of innate spirituality can be seen in the simple fact that religious beliefs and practices have naturally emerged in cultures of all times and places.

However, spiritual impulses express themselves in various ways, according to the specific geographical, socio-political, and cultural conditions of a given time and place. Thus, while the Mesoamericans shared many central beliefs and practices with distant peoples, they expressed their worldview through a religious symbolism tailored to their own particular conditions. Accordingly, the interpretation of Mesoamerican religious beliefs requires mastery of this unique symbolism, a challenge that is intensified by the fact that the authentic traces of Mesoamerican religious beliefs have become increasingly faint with the passage of time. Thus, the student of Mesoamerica's religious traditions is faced with a vast array of beliefs and practices, many of which are not completely understood and have received conflicting interpretations by scholars. Nevertheless, it is possible to discern the outlines of Mesoamerican religious worldviews. This chapter presents an overview intended to familiarize the reader with important religious traditions of Mesoamerica's Formative Period (exemplified by the Olmecs), Classic

> **The Mesoamericans shared many central beliefs and practices with distant peoples**

Period (represented by the city of Teotihuacan and the Maya), and Post-Classic Period (illustrated by the Toltecs and the Aztecs).

THE OLMECS: MOTHER CULTURE OF MESOAMERICA

Mesoamerica's Formative Period (*c.*2000 B.C.E.–250 C.E.) witnessed the birth of an advanced civilization, which took place through the construction of ceremonial centers, the emergence of hieroglyphic writing, and the formulation of complex methods of chronology, among many other things. For the most part, the achievements of this period resulted from the flourishing of the Olmec civilization, which rose up around 1500 B.C.E. along the Gulf of Mexico in Veracruz and Tabasco. Often referred to as the "Mother Culture" of Mesoamerica, Olmec traditions eventually spread westward and served as the foundation for later Mesoamerican societies. Today, the existent Olmec remains include massive basalt sculptures of the heads of Olmec rulers and gods (the so-called "Colossal Heads" of San Lorenzo), the remnants of ancient pyramids (the earliest known example being at La Venta), cave paintings, stone carvings, and other art objects. These vestiges of Olmec society reveal a faint glimpse of their creators, who remain veiled behind many uncertainties wrought by the passage of time.

Symbology was instrumental in the establishment of Olmec religion and culture, for it enabled the community to absorb a shared worldview

Scholars generally agree that the Olmecs developed a codified religious symbology, meaning that icons signifying specific gods or supernatural aspects of the cosmos were presented in a standardized way. This symbology was instrumental in the establishment of Olmec religion and culture, for it was through these images that priests and shamans passed religious insights to others, enabling the community to absorb a shared worldview. From these iconographic beginnings, a hieroglyphic form of writing emerged, which went on to serve as a medium through which Olmec religion and culture were preserved and transmitted to future generations, thereby transforming the Olmec society from a tribal, oral-based society to a literate civilization.

Similar to the hieroglyphic script that developed in ancient Egypt, many of the Olmec icons include extraordinary combinations of human and animal forms. For example, one common form is part human, part jaguar. Sometimes referred to as a "were-jaguar," this image is believed by some scholars to represent a rain-god that served as the central deity of the Olmec pantheon (seemingly reflecting their agricultural way of life). There is also speculation that, rather than representing particular gods, these mixtures of human and animal forms refer to the content of shamanic experiences. In such experiences shamans are thought to embody animal powers. In addition to human–animal hybrids, Olmec art displays many combinations of animal forms.

Although scholars recognize the existence of an Olmec iconography, the images that comprise this iconography lend themselves to conflicting interpretations. Complexities of interpretation notwithstanding, the elaborate rearrangements of natural forms found in these images may connote divinities that are both immanent (within the natural world) and transcendent (beyond the natural world). On the one hand, transcendence is suggested insofar as these deities are represented by hybrid animal forms that have no physical existence. On the other hand, immanence is displayed in that these rearranged natural forms are the vehicles through which divinities are made manifest.

TEOTIHUACAN: THE PLACE WHERE THE GODS WERE BORN

One of the many cultural–religious practices that later peoples of Mesoamerica inherited from the Olmecs was the construction of ceremonial centers. Such construction was particularly widespread during the Classic Period (*c.*250–900 C.E.). This era saw the establishment of large cities with complex political structures. Such cities often included massive pyramid temples and ceremonial centers where religious narratives were publicly enacted and rituals were performed. Monuments of this kind served as the organizing principle of the city, both physically, in terms of the city's spatial layout, and symbolically, by representing the spiritual center of gravity of the populace.

A paradigm urban center of the Classic Period was Teotihuacan, a city in central Mexico that reached the height of its influence around 500 C.E. and may have had a population of up to 200,000 people. Like other Mesoamerican cities (and sacred cities of other cultures), Teotihuacan was designed to be a microcosmic image of the universe and to symbolically harmonize human society with the cosmos as a whole. For instance, features of the natural landscape were altered so that two main avenues divided the city into quadrants symbolizing the four cardinal directions of the cosmos (north, south, east, and west), which were important elements of all Mesoamerican cosmologies from at least the time of the Olmecs. Palaces and dwellings, as well as ceremonial sites, were strategically placed within these quadrants. The most significant structures in Teotihuacan were the Pyramid of the Sun, the Pyramid of the Moon, and the Pyramid of Quetzalcoatl (the Feathered Serpent). Built above subterranean ritual caves, the Pyramid of the Sun directly faces the Pleiades star cluster as it makes its appearance on the horizon in late April (when the new agricultural season begins). Fascination and speculation regarding the cosmological alignment of these pyramid structures continues to this day.

Another important deity that was represented at Teotihuacan was Tlaloc, a rain-god usually depicted with goggle eyes and large fangs. This god was important to later Mesoamerican cultures such as the Aztecs (*fl.* 1325–1521 C.E.), who made offerings to Tlaloc on certain days of their calendar year that were considered unlucky. In addition to honoring the gods of Teotihuacan, the Aztecs and other Mesoamerican cultures attached both historical and mythological significance to the city as a whole. Teotihuacan received its name from the Aztecs hundreds of years after being abandoned by its original inhabitants. In Nahuatl (the Aztec language), "Teotihuacan" means "Place Where the Gods were Born," a reference to the Aztecs' mythological identification of Teotihuacan as the place from which the gods created the present age, and perhaps as the place where the gods themselves were created. A second way of interpreting this Aztec word is "Place Where One Becomes a God." This meaning may be associated with the fact that Teotihuacan was the end-point of religious pilgrimages undertaken by many Aztec priests and rulers (including Motecuhzoma II, ruler of the Aztec Empire at the time of the Spanish Conquest). Thus, in addition to being of profound importance for other Mesoamerican civilizations, Teotihuacan represented both a divine origin and a sacred destination for the Aztecs. One contemporaneous civilization that was in direct contact with the peoples of Teotihuacan and deeply influenced by their traditions was that of the Maya.

THE CLASSIC MAYA

Although it had already been in existence for two millennia, the Maya civilization attained its greatest creative flourishing during the Classic Period (*c.*250–900 C.E.). Geographically, this civilization was spread across the region encompassing present-day Guatemala and the Yucatan Peninsula (where indigenous Maya peoples still live). Those who inhabited this area during the Classic Period spoke a number of different languages but shared a relatively unified worldview. Modern scholars speculate about the Classic Period worldview through the few authentic remains of that era: ancient architectural ruins and fragmented art objects that are difficult to interpret; accounts of Maya belief orally preserved in Mayan languages and phonetically transcribed into the Roman alphabet long after the Classic Period, indeed after the Spanish Conquest (such as the Book of Council or Popol Vuh); and only four original Maya hieroglyphic codices (presently called the Dresden Codex, the Madrid Codex, the Paris Codex, and the Grolier Codex).[3]

Among other elements, the Popol Vuh contains a Maya creation myth. As in many other traditions, the Maya account begins in a formless darkness consisting of sea and sky. The gods create through their thoughts and words, and as things are created they are said to move out of shadow and into light. Interestingly, the creation of human beings is particularly important to the gods. They say, "There will be no high day and no bright praise

Top left: Incan statue; Top right: Peruvian deity; Bottom: Aztec eagle deity

for our work, our design, until the rise of the human work, the human design."[4] The initial attempt at a human design fails to satisfy the gods and they report, "It hasn't turned out well, they haven't spoken … It hasn't turned out that our names have been named. Since we are their mason and sculptor, this will not do."[5] And later they state, "our recompense is in words."[6] According to the scholar Dennis Tedlock, "What [the gods] want is beings who will walk, work, and talk in an articulate and measured way, visiting shrines, giving offerings, and calling upon their makers by name, all according to the rhythms of a calendar."[7]

The Maya hieroglyphic codices are not completely understood, although scholars have translated a significant portion of them and have determined that they include astronomical information, prophetic and/or historical narratives, and details regarding the sequence of certain religious rituals within the complex Maya calendar. In fact, all Mesoamerican cultures had an intense interest in time and its measurement according to intricate calendar cycles. In the Maya cosmos, the very passage of time was seen as an attribute of the gods – "they carry [time] on their backs."[8] Additionally, the five spatial directions within the cosmos (the four quadrants and the central axis) were all recognized as being governed by time, so that time was described as "a road in five directions."[9] Indeed, nearly all Maya concerns were related to their calendar in one way or another. For instance, agricultural matters were clearly of great importance because it was through replenishing plant life (particularly maize or corn) that the Maya sustained their civilization and prospered. Accordingly, they envisioned maize in many deified forms and considered agriculture to be a sacred art involving cycles of birth, death, and rebirth, which were reflected in their calendar. Regarding the prevalence of agricultural symbols and motifs in Maya mythology, the scholar Davíd Carrasco writes:

> [The] cosmic sowing and dawning provides the model for all subsequent creations, innovations, and changes. In Maya mythology seeds are sown in the earth to dawn as plants; celestial bodies are sown beneath the earth to dawn in their rising; humans are sown in mothers' wombs to dawn into life; and the dead are sown in the underworld to dawn as sparks of light in the darkness [i.e. stars].[10]

One of the most potent agricultural symbols used by the Maya, and other Mesoamerican cultures, was the World Tree. The three regions of the World Tree – roots, trunk, and branches – reflect the cosmic regions of the underworld, the terrestrial world, and the heavens. The World Tree is the cosmic pillar or central axis joining these regions and enabling communication among them.[11] Overseeing this connection between the realms was one function of the Maya kings. Although they shared a common worldview, no single political ruler governed all the Maya people. Rather, a number of rulers controlled different regions from their respective seats of power in cities such as Tikal, Palenque, and Copan (some of these regional groups even went to war against one another). The Maya kings possessed immense political and religious power. To signify this power, they were adorned in elaborate ceremonial costumes covered with depictions of gods, animal spirits, the World Tree, and other symbols of cosmological significance. Recalling their shamanic roots, Maya rulers performed self-administered bloodletting rituals. It was believed that the resulting wounds, usually inflicted with obsidian instruments, allowed the kings to absorb the animal and divine powers depicted on their robes. Additionally, human sacrifice was performed in order to renew the agricultural cycle. Interestingly, it was also believed that these practices helped sustain the lives of the gods, particularly the sun, by releasing and offering to them the most potent of all material substances – human blood. Human sacrifice was a time-honored tradition throughout pre-Columbian Mesoamerica. The victims of this practice were often (but not always) enemy warriors captured in battle. During the Post-Classic Period (c.900–1521 C.E.), a renowned Mesoamerican ruler and spiritual teacher, Topiltzin Quetzalcoatl, attempted to break with this and other religious traditions, which may have led to his downfall.

TOPILTZIN QUETZALCOATL: TOLTEC WARRIOR-PRIEST-KING

The Toltec warrior-priest-king Topiltzin Quetzalcoatl ("Our Prince of the Feathered Serpent") was named after the ancient Mesoamerican god Quetzalcoatl. The story of Topiltzin Quetzalcoatl's life accrued legendary aspects and served as a mythological pattern for later warrior-priests and artists. Said to have been conceived when his mother swallowed a precious jewel, he underwent seven years of intense ascetic spiritual practice in preparation for priesthood. However, in contrast with the Maya tradition of authority derived from royal lineage, Topiltzin Quetzalcoatl rose to power as a warrior and priest. Under his rule the Toltec culture attained extraordinary achievements in metallurgy, medical knowledge, and art.

Among the spiritual practices adopted by Topiltzin Quetzalcoatl were fasting, bathing in ice-cold water, and ritual bloodletting. Through these means, he is said to have attained communion with Ometéotl (the Dual God or God of Duality, discussed below). Topiltzin Quetzalcoatl's spiritual practices were imitated by Aztec warrior-priests. Evidence suggests that his discontinuance of human sacrifice provoked his enemies, who were led by a sorcerer named Tezcatlipoca ("Smoking Mirror"). Through deceptive means, Tezcatlipoca caused Topiltzin Quetzalcoatl to become intoxicated, which led him to dishonor himself and break certain ritual vows. According to some accounts, Topiltzin Quetzalcoatl was then banished from the community and traveled to the sea coast, where he started a bonfire into which he threw himself, whereupon his heart rose up and became the morning star. An alternative description is found in the Florentine Codex (which was compiled after the Spanish Conquest by Fray Bernardino de Sahagún based on the testimony of Aztec informants). In the Florentine Codex, it is claimed that, upon succumbing to Tezcatlipoca's temptation, Topiltzin Quetzalcoatl acknowledged his dishonor and fled of his own accord in repentance. Following his departure, he encountered various adventures on his way to the coast. Sahagún's informants explain what happened when Topiltzin Quetzalcoatl reached his destination:

> And when this was done, when he went to reach the sea coast, thereupon he made a raft of serpents. When he had arranged the raft, there he sat as if it were his boat. Thereupon he went off; he went swept off by the water. No one knows how he went to arrive there at Tlapallan, "The Place of Light and Wisdom."[12]

Topiltzin Quetzalcoatl's legacy was especially influential on the Aztec tradition, in which he was deified and credited with the invention of arts and sciences. In short, he was considered a "culture bearer." Under Topiltzin Quetzalcoatl's guidance, the Aztecs believed, the Toltecs had experienced a golden age of natural plentitude (of things such as cotton, maize, and squash) and human accomplishments (in technology and artistic genius). As one Aztec report explains, "Nothing was difficult when [the Toltecs] did it."[13] The flourishing Toltec capital city, Tula or Tollan, thus served as a model toward which the Aztecs aspired in their own capital city of Tenochtitlan.

THE AZTECS: FOUNDERS OF TENOCHTITLAN

The city of Tenochtitlan was founded some time around 1325 C.E. Its founders are now referred to as the Aztecs, although they are more properly designated as the Mexica.[14] The term "Aztec" derives from "Aztlán," the name of the Mexica's place of origin (translated as "the place of herons"). The location of Aztlán is uncertain, but it may have been near the present-day regions of Lake Chapala in Mexico or the Colorado River in the United States of America. The Mexica were one among seven groups of people that inhabited this region, but they eventually migrated from their homeland. Some accounts claim that they departed because their patron deity, Huitzilopochtli, prophesied through his priests that a promised land would be found. With exceptional perseverance, and after eight years of hardship and searching, the Mexica reached Lake Texcoco. According to tradition, at Lake Texcoco they encountered the sign that Huitzilopochtli (sun-god and god of war) had said would be revealed at their destination: an eagle perched on a prickly-pear cactus. On an island in the middle of the lake, the Mexica established their capital, Tenochtitlan.

In Tenochtitlan, the Aztecs built the Hueteocalli ("Great God House"), referred to as the Great Temple or Templo Mayor. Located at the very center of Tenochtitlan, the Templo Mayor consisted of a dual pyramid symbolically identified as the center of the cosmos. This dual pyramid had two shrines upon its summit that were accessible by two separate staircases along the face of the pyramid. The northern shrine was dedicated to Huitzilopochtli and the southern one to Tlaloc (god of water, rain, and fertility). The duality embodied in the Templo Mayor reflected the widespread and deeply rooted Mesoamerican belief that duality is at the core of everything. Indeed, in their theology and metaphysics, the Aztecs postulated Ometéotl (the Dual God or God of Duality) as the creator god and the ultimate reality. According to some scholars all, or nearly all, Aztec gods were seen as facets of Ometéotl. Aztec gods were composed of dual aspects, and each was also paired with a counterpart god, thus becoming components within greater dualities. Consequently, it was believed that duality permeates the entire realm of divinities, and this omnipresent duality is Ometéotl – the Divinity within all divinities.

For example, Quetzalcoatl was imagined as a combination of the Quetzal bird and the rattlesnake, which inhabit the dual regions of the sky and the earth. As scholar Enrique Florescano explains, "In Mesoamerica, the bird and the serpent are symbolic representations of two regions significant to religious and cosmological thought: heaven and earth … [Quetzalcoatl, the Feathered Serpent] is a synthesis of opposites: it conjugates the destructive and germinal powers of the earth (the serpent) with the fertile and ordering forces of the heavens (the bird)."[15]

Tezcatlipoca, who had a number of interactions with Quetzalcoatl, was even more explicitly associated with duality. The god of rulers, sorcerers, and warriors, Tezcatlipoca was the source of all forms of conflict and discord. Accordingly, he was fond of mocking human beings – but, as one scholar explains, "these 'mockeries' became related to ordeals through which mortals would foresee their destiny."[16] Thus, on one level Tezcatlipoca thwarted human progress, but on a deeper level he was its guide. More abstractly, Tezcatlipoca was characterized by a number of pairs of complementary properties. To cite two examples, the pair Tloque–Nahuaque (the lord of being close–the lord of being near) made him the lord who is everywhere, and the pair Yohualli–Ehecatl (night–wind) made him invisible and intangible. In this sense, Tezcatlipoca was composed of dualities. Gods comprising dual pairs of this kind were often depicted in semi-anthropomorphic form as two gods joined at the back. Moreover, Tezcatlipoca was also an element in a greater duality, involving himself and his counterpart, Tezcatlanextia ("Illuminating Mirror"). The scholar Miguel León-Portilla summarizes the Aztec view of the gods as dualities in the following manner:

> In the popular religious belief all the gods are [Ometéotl's] children. But the Nahuatl texts and the ancient codices also reveal that, in the thought of the sages, the teteo ["gods"], appearing in parts or at times even androgynous, are regarded as just as many presences of the supreme dual god. Is not the ultimate reality our mother, our father, who give life everywhere and everywhen, indeed a beautiful form of approaching the mystery — that which is beyond the wind and the night?[17]

Tragically, the beautiful forms through which the Aztecs approached the mystery — the religious symbolism through which they perceived the meaning of their lives, the precious wisdom that was passed down for centuries from one generation to the next, the religious way of life by which they honored their gods — were all shattered by the arrival of the Spanish conquistadores. On 8 November 1519 C.E., Hernán Cortés and his Spanish soldiers arrived at the Aztec capital, Tenochtitlan. Ironically, the Aztec rulers believed that Cortés was their own "culture bearer," Topiltzin Quetzalcoatl, returning to destroy them. Topiltzin Quetzalcoatl was born in a year called *ce acatl* (One Reed). He left or was exiled from Tula fifty-two years later, when the cycle of calendar years had once again come around to One Reed. Before he left Tula, he vowed to return. As fate would have it, centuries later the year One Reed coincided with 1519, the year that Cortés arrived. Within three years the great Aztec Empire had fallen. "In their final appearance before Cortés," León-Portilla describes, "the [Aztec sages], bringing the drama of their dying culture to its climax, exclaimed, 'If, as you say, our gods are dead, it is better that you allow us to die too.'"[18]

> **Tragically, the beautiful forms through which the Aztecs approached the mystery were shattered by the arrival of the Spanish conquistadores**

CHAPTER SUMMARY

Numerous civilizations prospered over the course of Mesoamerica's pre-Columbian history. In many ways, the Olmec civilization was the precursor to later civilizations of Mesoamerica such as the Maya, the Teotihuacanos, the Toltecs, and the Aztecs. At the core of these civilizations was a vast array of religious worldviews and spiritual practices. Independently of similar achievements in Africa, Asia, and Europe, the Mesoamerican people developed advanced hieroglyphic writing and a complex calendar, and built elaborate architectural monuments. All three of these features of their culture served to enrich the spiritual depth of their lives.

The development of hieroglyphic writing enabled Mesoamerican priests and sages to preserve their ancestral wisdom in painted codices, temple inscriptions, and other art objects. The temporal cycles reflected in their calendar made it possible for Mesoamericans to regulate their activities in accordance with the patterns of change observed in the cosmos (including astronomical and agricultural cycles of change). Mesoamerica's architectural monuments were both symbols of spiritual significance and seats of political power. In fact, in pre-Columbian Mesoamerica, exercising political power was a religious function. Thus, seats of political power were primarily religious ceremonial centers, which were built in the heart of their respective cities and served to represent the center of the cosmos. In these ways, among others, Mesoamerican peoples sought to relate their lives to the divine.

One of the central themes of interfaith studies in general, and this book in particular, is that many religious traditions share similar spiritual values and ultimate concerns, and hold parallel worldviews. Nevertheless, it was suggested earlier in this chapter, spiritual values, ultimate concerns, and religious worldviews are expressed through different symbolisms in different traditions. Each tradition's symbolism is influenced by the particular conditions of life in which that tradition flourishes. In this way, a symbology that serves to give meaning to the lives of people at one time and place may not be effective in this regard for other people. Thus, when the Spanish conquistadores transplanted their religion into the hearts of the Aztec people, the initial consequences were devastating. The old gods were dead and the new gods were meaningless to the Aztecs. Perhaps the Aztec priests witnessing these events would have seen them as the fulfillment of the following Mayan prophecies:

> **At the core of these civilizations was a vast array of religious worldviews and spiritual practices**

> In the [next era]
> heads will bow to foreign priests,
> to alien gods,
> to barbarous rulers.
> Those who live
> will live as half men,
> their heads locked in stocks.
> It will be a time of evil,
> of constant thunder,
> an era when tame beasts bite,
> the wise become dunces,
> the prophets blind...[19]
> It is the era

of the conqueror
and the conquered
of pillage and ruin and waste,
the gods driven underground
and buried
in the minds
of a few old men gone mad.[20]

One of four small gold mummiform coffins from the tomb of the pharaoh Tutankhamun

CHAPTER 3

THE RELIGIOUS TRADITIONS OF ANCIENT EGYPT

The Word came into being.

All things were mine when I was alone.

I was Rê in [all] his manifestations:

I was the great one who came into being of
himself,

who created all his names as the Companies of the
[lesser] gods.[1]

– The Book of the Dead

INTRODUCTION

The transition from tribe to city-state depends, in part, on the ability to produce large amounts of food, which allows people to devote themselves to activities other than farming and hunting. In general, the movement away from a nomadic lifestyle and toward the raising of animals and the cultivation of agriculture enabled societies such as that of the Egyptians to sustain large congregations of people in the same location without the need to follow migrating animal herds. Along with a city-state lifestyle, systems of commerce, travel, trading, and written languages emerged. Advanced forms of science and mathematics also developed to serve the needs of agriculture and irrigation. Reflecting the importance of this activity, agricultural symbols played a major role in the religious lives of many ancient peoples, especially the Egyptians.

> **Do for one who may do for you, that you may cause him thus to do**
> *The Tale of the Eloquent Peasant*
> **THE GOLDEN RULE**

The culture of ancient Egypt is one of the world's greatest legacies. Originating from humble beginnings in the Nile Valley, it developed and flourished for some 3,200 years. The great Egyptian monuments, such as the Pyramids and the Sphinx, recognized worldwide, never cease to intrigue and amaze. The Egyptians were a complex people,

Timeline

***c.*3000 B.C.E.**
Emergence of Egyptian
    civilization and religion
***c.*3000–2686 B.C.E.**
Early Dynastic Period:
    Menes unites Egypt
    under one polity
***c.*2686–2125 B.C.E.**
The Old Kingdom:
    Great pyramids built
    under direction of
    pharaohs Djoser,
    Sneferu, and Khufu
***c.*2160–2055 B.C.E.**
First Intermediate Period
***c.*2055–1650 B.C.E.**
The Middle Kingdom:
    New philosophical
    awakening occurs with
    emphasis on god
    Osiris
***c.*1650–1550 B.C.E.**
Second Intermediate
    Period: Hyksos invasion
    and occupation of Egypt
***c.*1550–1069 B.C.E.**
The New Kingdom:
    Amon-Ra increasingly
    viewed as creator god
1352–1336 B.C.E.
Pharaoh Amenhotep IV
    (Akhenaton) institutes
    revolutionary changes
    toward monotheistic
    worship of god Aten
    (known as Amarna
    Religion)

deeply concerned with an afterlife and endowed with creative abilities of the imagination. Egypt's location in the Nile Valley provided its inhabitants with a high level of physical security; this environmental buffer offered protection from unwanted external influences for centuries.

The emergence of the Egyptian religion and the creation of a unified Egyptian kingdom occurred simultaneously around 3000 B.C.E. In ancient Egypt, the political, social, and religious spheres constituted a unified worldview that sustained the development of a great culture. In fact, the modern notion of separate "spheres" of life would not even be intelligible to an ancient Egyptian. There was no word for "religion" in Egypt, because religion permeated all aspects of life. Egyptian city-states united under the rulership of successive pharaohs, or kings, to form one state. Only in the early Common Era, when Egypt was converted to Christianity, did the social–religious system of Egypt undergo a radical transformation.

> **There was no word for "religion" in Egypt, because religion permeated all aspects of life**

*c.*664–332 B.C.E.
Late Period
*c.*332 B.C.E.
Egypt conquered by Alexander III of Macedonia
*c.*332–30 B.C.E.
Greek/ Ptolemaic Period
*c.*30 B.C.E.–395 C.E.
Roman period in Egypt and spread of Christianity
*c.*641 C.E.
Egypt conquered by Arab Muslims

APPROACHING EGYPTIAN RELIGION: ATEMPORAL VS. TEMPORAL

It is easy to become lost in the long and varied history of the Egyptians. Local Egyptians had their own gods and cosmogonies (mythical accounts of the emergence of the universe); and with the rise of a new pharaoh, or a new dynasty of pharaohs, certain religious myths gained prominence over others. These shifts, however, did not reflect an essential change in the underlying religious worldview of the Egyptians. The Egyptian religion was firmly rooted in a non-historical, atemporal realm called the "First Time" (Tep Zepi). It is important to understand the unchanging backdrop of Egyptian religious belief before attempting to survey the vast historical changes that Egyptian civilization endured over time.

According to Egyptian belief, the First Time, or Tep Zepi, was a Golden Age – a perfect and divinely ordained period of cosmic order. The happenings of the Primordial Epoch were relayed through religious myths, which were the source of authority in Egyptian culture. The myths of the First Time explained the origin of existence, the origin of the gods, and the establishment of divine kingship. These events, although conveyed differently through a variety of myths, were all grounded in the timeless Beginning that was constantly being re-actualized and followed as a divine model. The basis of religious practice and ritual in Egypt centered on reestablishing the equilibrium and order found at the Beginning – this was a sacred tradition invested with cosmic significance. As the scholar Frithjof Schuon observed, "to conform to tradition is to keep faith with the Origin, and for that very reason it is also to be situated at the Center; it is to dwell in the primordial Purity and in the universal Norm."[2]

MYTHS OF THE FIRST TIME

The Primeval Mound and Serpent

According to Egyptian myth, in the beginning primeval waters covered the entire world. This infinite span of water was a formless, dark void. Order, life, and light arose from these waters, usually taking the imagery of a primeval mound or hill.[3] In addition to signifying chaos, the image of water is also an image of monistic unity, where all opposites are united and have no distinct form. Some scholars suggest that the emergence of life from the primordial waters symbolizes the emergence of consciousness from unconsciousness.

Some of the Egyptian myths purport that an egg, lotus, or serpent, rather than a mound, took form. The Creator God was believed to have appeared above the mound, or to have been the mound. In some texts the Creator God is identified with the serpent or the lotus. In one pyramid text, the primordial serpent decrees:

> I extended everywhere, in accordance with what was to
> come into existence,
> I knew, as the One, alone, majestic, the Indwelling Soul,
> the most potent of the gods.
> He [the Indwelling Soul] it was who made the universe
> in that he copulated with his fist and took the pleasure of
> emission.
> I bent right around myself, I was enriched in my coils,
> one who made a place for himself in the midst of his coils.
> His utterance was what came forth from his own mouth.[4]

Although the Egyptians used a variety of mythic symbols, the central meaning of the myths often remained the same – existence began with the emergence of light out of darkness, order out of chaos, all of which was co-emergent with, or by the decree of, a Divine Mind or command.

The Memphite Theology

Another explanation of the origin of existence is found within one of the oldest Egyptian cosmogonies – in fact, one of the oldest known to all humanity – the Memphite Theology. The Memphite Theology is so called because it arose in the ancient city of Memphis. In the Memphite Theology, Ptah, also known as the "Lord of Truth," is depicted as the Creator of all existence and the source of all moral imperatives in the world. It was believed that Ptah created the universe through his thought – which formed in his heart and was made manifest through his tongue or word. This process included the creation of lesser gods that infused themselves into the physical world. Ptah was also considered the first king of Egypt. As one scholar has declared: "The whole universe was a monarchy, and the king of the world had been the first king of Egypt."[5] The importance of a divine king, grounded within the First Time, is a recurring theme in Egyptian myth. The explanation of creation as stemming from the thought (or word) of one God (in this case, Ptah) existed for some two millennia before Hebrew and Greek texts, among others, propound similar ideas.

The Heliopolitan Cosmogony

One of the predominant cosmogonies of Egypt developed in the city of Heliopolis and spread throughout Egypt. The Heliopolitan cosmogony consisted of an ennead of gods: Atum, Shu, Tefnut, Geb, Nut, Osiris, Isis, Seth, and Nephthys. The cosmogony places Atum ("The Complete One") as the androgynous Creator God. Atum was equated with the mound that rose from the primordial water. Atum was also identified with Ra, the sun-god, and is sometimes referred to as Ra–Atum. This sort of syncretic identification is common throughout the Egyptian religion. In some cases, as a particular conception of the High God rose to the forefront; that god was usually identified with the sun-god Ra (also referred to as Rê). In some sense, whereas Atum was the Hidden God (*deus absconditus*) – the transcendent and unknowable – Ra, in the form of the sun, was the god in manifest form.

The Heliopolitan cosmogony posited that out of Itself, Atum created all the other gods. Through this self-generating action, Tefnut (moisture) and Shu (air or atmosphere) were brought forth, which in turn bore Nut (sky) and Geb (earth). Shu separated the union of Geb and Nut; subsequently, Nut bore the next generation of gods, or the "Children of Nut." These gods included Osiris, Isis, Seth, and Nephthys.

The Myth of Osiris

The Myth of Osiris, also called the Passion of Osiris, provided the mythic foundation that established an accessible linkage back to the Golden Age through the personage of the pharaoh. According to the myth, Osiris was the first king of Egypt. Pristine order and justice characterized his reign as king. Osiris married his sister, Isis. Osiris' brother Seth

(Set) – who seems to symbolically represent the forces of disintegration, chaos, and even evil – plotted to overthrow Osiris' kingship. Seth, through a wicked plot of deception, killed Osiris and disposed of his body in the Nile River. Isis, a possessor of great magical powers, recovered the body of Osiris, only to have Seth defiantly cut it into pieces. Isis gathered the pieces of Osiris' body, lamented, and gave Osiris a proper burial. Through her magical powers, she was able to impregnate herself with the child of the dead Osiris – Horus.

Isis gave birth to Horus and kept him hidden from Seth. When Horus came of age, he avenged the murder of his father by defeating Seth in battle. Before a great council, Horus was praised and named king of Egypt. Horus' kingship represented a return to order and the end of the chaotic reign of Seth. During their battle, however, Seth was able to gouge out one of Horus' eyes. Horus took his disembodied eye to the unconscious Osiris in the Underworld. Osiris, now as a formless spirit, awakened. Horus' good eye became identified with the sun-god Ra, which was indicative of the close link established between Osiris and the cult of Ra in later periods.

Osiris became the "King of the Underworld" and was fully imbued with the powers typical of a chthonic god, such as fertility, renewal, and the generative powers of the earth. The pharaoh – the king of Egypt – was identified with Horus. According to the scholar John Wilson, when an ancient Egyptian surmised "that the king [pharaoh] was Horus, he did not mean that the king was playing the part of Horus, he meant that the king *was* Horus, that the god was effectively present in the king's body during the particular activity in question."[6] After the pharaoh died, he was identified with Osiris in the Underworld. Thereby, above ground, Horus (the pharaoh) upheld the ethical, social, and religious order; while underground, Osiris (the dead pharaoh) maintained the fecundity of the earth. The risen or resurrected Osiris was identified, after a heavenly ascension, with the sun-god Ra. Therefore, the pharaoh was thought to have been an incarnated god who served as king on earth. The pharaoh never really died; he incurred a physical death, descended into the Underworld, and awakened. He was then identified with Ra, the High God. Each successive pharaoh continued the tradition of incarnation and resurrection – a pattern following the model of Osiris.

The pharaoh was thought to have been an incarnated god who served as king on earth

The Pharaoh and Ma'at

"*Ma'at*" is a word that cannot be directly translated without divesting it of some portion of its original meaning. For Egyptians, *ma'at* entailed the interrelationship of the physical and metaphysical realities, which in turn determined the social, political, and ethical order of society. In its ethical connotation *ma'at* encompassed truth, justice, and peace. It was based on the initial order established by the Creator (under whichever form or name the

Top: Pyramid at Giza, Egypt
Bottom: Hieroglyphs at the Temple of Isis, Philae Island, Egypt

Creator took in any given myth). *Ma'at* was also the perfect, paradigmatic state established during Osiris' mythic reign as king of Egypt.

Through religious myth, the Egyptians were well aware of the destruction that ensued from injustice and chaos. The world plunged into chaos when the paradisal order came to an end after Seth killed Osiris. The pharaoh, however, was the incarnation of Horus (the son of Osiris) who could maintain order and prosperity through a kingship that resembled Osiris' perfect dispensation of *ma'at*. Some scholars have placed *ma'at* at the center of all Egyptian religion; the Egyptologist Jan Assmann, for example, concluded:

> Turning their historical perspective backward, [the Egyptians] strove with all their might to keep the original plenitude of meaning in view and to bring it into force through constant activity … With the result that virtually all had a share in the work of realizing Maat … Thus, in a very general sense the Egyptian concept of religion can be defined as the realization of Maat, which can be specified, according to the Egyptian fomulation, as the tasks of
>
> > speaking justice for humankind
> > satisfying the gods
> > giving offerings to the gods
> > and mortuary offerings to the deceased.[7]

The pharaoh was the paradigm for all Egyptians. It was under his divinely inspired rulership that Egyptian society could participate in and remain closely aligned with *ma'at* – in this context understood as the cosmic equilibrium.

As there was no division between religion and government, the pharaoh was the High Priest. As god incarnate, he was the point through which the infinitude of the divine light could shine into the finite world. The mythical realm of the First Time justified the pharaoh's authority. Challenging the pharaoh was equivalent to challenging order – thereby embodying chaos – which could only lead to destruction. Transgression from the pharaonic rulership meant deviating from the original divine model; it was believed that such folly would cause chaos and disintegration.

Ritual, Time, and Renewal

One of the pharaoh's titles was the "Lord of the Ritual," implying not only supremacy in such matters, but also the authority to perform rituals associated with certain temples and festivals. The performance of rituals insured stability against degeneration from the Original Order. Rituals also focused religious activity on pleasing the gods and thereby living in accord with *ma'at*. The Sed festival, one of the most long-standing and popular festivals of ancient Egypt, occurred thirty years into a pharaoh's reign to renew his energy and power so that he could continue to rule with *ma'at*. However, the most important ritual was the coronation of a new pharaoh.

The Egyptians upheld a cyclical conception of time rather than the linear model that is prevalent today. The cyclic model was based on the pharaoh's ability to re-actualize the mythic realm. Each new pharaoh brought forth a new era of *ma'at* that was modeled on the divine prototype. One scholar concluded: "For the Egyptians, the reign of each new king represented a new beginning, not merely philosophically but practically … This means that there would probably have been a psychological tendency to regard each new reign as a fresh point of origin: every king was, therefore, essentially reworking the same universal myths of kingship within the events of his own time."[8] The Egyptians documented "time" by recording how

> **The pharaoh was the point through which the infinitude of the divine light could shine into the finite world**

many days had elapsed from the current pharaoh's accession to the crown. When a new pharaoh was crowned, "time" would essentially start anew, and all dates from that point forward would begin again. Egyptian society consisted of cycles initiated by each new pharaoh's coronation; these cycles were renewed through festivals such as the New Year celebration and the Sed festival. The overarching idea was to mirror a divine archetypal plan by upholding order and justice (*ma'at*) through the inspired leadership of the pharaoh.

The notion of cyclical time was also extended, in certain Egyptian philosophical–religious texts, to the cosmos as a whole. Such a concept emerged within the so-called "coffin texts." One such text depicted a conversation between Osiris, who was relegated to the status of "emergent" deity, and Atum, who was considered the "transcendent" deity. The scholar R. T. Rundle Clark paraphrases and comments upon one such text, which specifically invokes the Egyptian idea of a cyclical view of creation:

Darkly, Atum replies that he is not to be forgotten; for, one day, millions of years hence, he will bring the present dispensation to an end. Then creation will be reversed and all things return to the Primeval Waters. When all differences have disappeared he and Osiris, the transcendent and the emergent forms of deity, will be reunited in the universal primordial form of life, the original Serpent, the form in which divinity existed before the coming of gods or men. The final fate, then, is to return to the primordial unity. Here we see Egyptian thought reaching out to a concept very like that of the [Hindu] Upanishads.[9]

This highly lofty and philosophical text suggests the notion of a cyclical creation in which all things will eventually return to the Primordial Waters and, apparently, emerge once again through the divine consciousness depicted in the form of the Serpent.

RELIGIOUS BELIEFS

The Gods

A notable feature of the Egyptian religion was the variety of pictorial representations ascribed to its gods. In fact, the ancient Egyptian script, the hieroglyphs, was pictorial in nature. Some thinkers suggest that the Egyptian mode of perception was part and parcel of a mythically infused vision of reality – a living landscape of symbols; from this point of view, the ancient Egyptians conceived of the world in a radically different way than the analytic mode of thinking common to contemporary societies. The influential Neoplatonist philosopher Plotinus[10] (205–270 C.E.), who was born and studied in Alexandria, Egypt, explained:

> In the case of those things which they, in their wisdom, wanted to designate, the Egyptian sages did not use written characters, literally representing arguments and premises and imitating meaningful sounds and utterances of axioms. Rather, they wrote in pictures, and engraved on their temples one picture corresponding to each reality … Thus, each picture is a knowledge, wisdom … perceived all at once, and not discursive thought nor deliberation.[11]

Some of the pictorial representations of the gods included animal forms, such as jackals (Anubis, the god of embalming), bulls (Apis, the Memphite god), vultures (Mut, the goddess of Karnak), and falcons (Horus, god incarnate as pharaoh). The images of the gods could also take human form or be hybrids – such as the Sphinx – although human bodies with animal heads were far more common than the reverse. Human form was generally given to those gods associated with nature, including the earth-god Geb, the sky-goddess Nut, the sun-god Ra, and the moon-gods Khons and Thoth. The god Thoth was considered a patron of civilization, and was believed to have bestowed science and language upon the Egyptians. The Greeks identified Thoth, sometimes called "the scribe of the gods," with the Greek god Hermes (also known as Hermes Trismegistus).[12]

A notable feature of the Egyptian religion was the variety of pictorial representations ascribed to its gods

The gods Osiris and Isis were considered divine educators who taught humanity methods of agricultural cultivation. During later historical periods, Isis, a goddess of magic, became a universal goddess; Isis, for example, was worshiped by a mystery cult across the Roman Empire.[13] Osiris was especially connected with agriculture. The "death" of the grain in the winter and its "rise" in the spring was linked with the death and resurrection of Osiris; so too was the rise and fall of the Nile River, which flooded every year.

Alongside the sun-god Ra, Osiris was the most enduring and central figure in all of Egyptian myth.

The Egyptian god Ra, often identified as the Creator, was a solar god depicted with a human body and the head of a falcon. Ma'at, the goddess of cosmic equilibrium, was depicted in an early period of Egyptian history as the daughter of Ra. She had a temple in Karnak devoted to her, was subsequently divested of her human form, and became associated solely with the abstract concept of order.

Temples and Oracles

Many of the gods were assigned temples, with associated plots of land to insure the perpetual well-being of the places of worship. In the temples, religious officials conducted daily rituals that closely followed those of the pharaoh, in whose name they would open the shrines and lay provisions before statues. Offerings were also made during services, and hymns were recited to the god whose nature they depicted.

Apart from appearances in festival processions, the temple cult was exclusive – detached from the general population. The populace had to be content with images of gods and other divine symbols when they were displayed outside the temple. Especially revered were oracles or priestly figures endowed with divine wisdom that was shared with worshipers. In addition, the burial places of those among the dead who deserved special respect were distinguished by statues or fine tombs erected in their honor.

Magic

The power of magic, so important to ancient Egyptians, was invoked by appealing to the name and image of a god and by uttering prescribed incantations. The exemplar of magical use was the goddess Isis. Magic served to ensure purity or fecundity, or to cure the sick. Physicians used a variety of spells to cure ailments, such as scorpion bites. The power of magic was a sort of cosmic energy available to those who were adept in its use. The best-known collection of magical rites and spells of ancient Egypt are contained in the Book of Going Forth by Day (also known as the Book of the Dead).[14] This famed book consists of a variety of "coffin texts" that were placed in the tombs of the deceased. These texts consisted of a variety of esoteric spells and mystical formulae.

The "Soul" and the Afterlife

Scholars disagree about the exact details of ancient Egyptian beliefs concerning the afterlife and the constitution of the human soul. Furthermore, there existed multiple views about these subjects at different times and places in ancient Egypt. According to one formulation, each human being consists of a physical body (referred to as the *khat*) and six spiritual aspects or souls (the *ba, ka, khu, khaibit, sekhem,* and *ren*).

For the ancient Egyptians, the most significant characteristic of the physical body was its liability to decay (which is why it was referred to as the *khat*, the central meaning of which is "something inherently prone to decay"). This was important, because in order to secure one's afterlife, they believed it was necessary to prevent the body's total decomposition. This was achieved through the process of mummification. By preserving the physical body, this highly advanced embalming technique enabled one's spiritual aspects (particularly the *ba* and *ka*) to recognize the body after physical death and to return to it.[15] If this occurred, the deceased could incur a resurrection in the next world.

The *ba* was identified as the personality of the deceased person, and it was represented pictorially as a two-headed bird or a human-headed hawk. There are some suggestions that the *ba* formed after physical death, although scholars disagree on this point. Whatever the case may be about its formation, it was believed that the *ba* could enter the heavens and rejoin the gods after death and that it could return to the mummified body. However, it required guidance to find its way. It received this guidance from the *ka*, which was remotely similar to a "guardian angel" and was considered to be superior to both the *ba* and the physical body. Pictorially represented by a pair of open arms reaching upward, the *ka* was one's spiritual double and existed alongside the physical body in astral form. Identified with the inner conscience, the *ka* was sent from the High God and was part of the High God's essence.

The function of the remaining soul-parts is equally difficult to uncover. Very briefly, they can be described as follows. The *khu* was a luminous and intangible entity that took the shape of the physical body and apparently corresponded to intelligence. Similar to the *ka*, this aspect of the soul was in danger of being imprisoned in the tomb, and therefore, various incantations were uttered to prevent this from taking place. In contrast to the *khu* (sometimes translated the "shining one"), the *khaibit* is the "shadow." Next, the *sekhem* is strength or "vital power." With reference to this meaning, the god Ra was sometimes referred to as the "Great Sekhem." Lastly, *ren* indicated one's name. As with other ancient peoples, the Egyptians placed an important significance on the immortality of names. Names were also considered important because if one knew and could properly pronounce a thing's name, one would gain power over it. The journey through the Underworld experienced after death was sometimes described as passing through a number of gates. It was believed that one was required to utter the names of the guardians who kept watch over those gates.

> **By preserving the body, mummification enabled one's spiritual aspects to recognize the body after death and return to it**

THE EARLY DYNASTIC PERIOD AND THE OLD KINGDOM

The period of early Egyptian history is conventionally divided into the Early Dynastic Period (*c.*3000–2686 B.C.E.) and the Old Kingdom (2686–2125 B.C.E.). During the Early Dynastic Period, a unified polity came into being under the kingship of Menes, who founded the first capital of an integrated Upper and Lower Egypt at Memphis. Menes' accession to the crown at Memphis marked the beginning of the long-standing Memphis coronation tradition.

During the First Dynastic Period, the pharaohs were buried at the royal cemetery at Abydos. These tombs were elaborately decorated with remarkable art. Such exquisite burial sites for the pharaoh, his queen, and high court are indicative of the special status that the pharaoh and his court held within the Egyptian social order. The pharaoh, of course, was given the most elaborate burial plot. The tombs of this period were rectangular structures that were low to the ground and called mastabas. The pharaohs were buried with many of the possessions that they had enjoyed in life and items that they might need in the next life. During the First Dynastic Period it seems this practice may have been at its extreme. Archeological findings suggest that court personnel and pets were killed in order to be buried with the pharaoh and thereby accompany and serve him in the afterlife. After this period, small statues were used instead of actual people and animals.

Fueled by religious devotion, Egyptians made unparalleled advances in architecture and large-scale building projects. During the Old Kingdom (2686–2125 B.C.E.), increased time and effort went into the construction of the pharaoh's tomb. In fact, it is believed that the first large-scale stone building was constructed as part of the pharaoh Djoser's (2661–2648 B.C.E.) funerary complex. This stone structure is called the Step Pyramid, and it represents a taller and more complex version of the mastaba tomb – a forerunner to the Pyramid. Funerary complexes such as these were elaborate and complicated, and often included various underground passages, chambers, and galleries. One of Djoser's top officials was his architect, Imhotep. Imhotep was a high priest at Heliopolis, who was eventually deified and was honored with a cult. Imhotep was viewed as the inventor of Egyptian architecture, and was a patron of scribes and physicians. The Greeks identified Imhotep with their heroic figure Asklepios, who was also deified.[16]

During the Fourth Dynasty (2613–2498 B.C.E.) of the Old Kingdom, the pharaoh Sneferu (2613–2589 B.C.E.) commissioned unprecedented state and social projects. He funded the building of both the Bent Pyramid and the Red Pyramid at Dahshur. The Red Pyramid served as his tomb. The largest and most famous Pyramid, the Great Pyramid at Giza, was built by Sneferu's successor, the pharaoh Khufu (2589–2566 B.C.E.), as part of his funerary complex. A son of Khufu, the pharaoh Khafra (2558–2532 B.C.E.), built his

Statue of Anubis, or Inpu, the Egyptian jackal-headed god of the dead

funerary complex with an immense custodian statue of a human-headed lion, known as the Great Sphinx. The funerary complexes of the pharaohs had their own royal funerary cults. These cults were paid for by the state and included a host of priests who gave offerings to the dead pharaohs and honored the gods in the names of the pharaohs. The pharaohs intended these cults to remain active forever. The Pyramids built during the Fourth Dynasty astonish architects and scholars today. Their immense size, precise mathematical measurements, and their alignment with certain stellar constellations continue to spark debate about their true origin and purpose. Most scholars are convinced, however, that the Pyramids served as tombs for the all-important pharaohs.

During the Fifth Dynasty of the Old Kingdom (2494–2345 B.C.E.), the sun-god Ra became what some scholars have called "the state god." Temples were built all over Egypt in his honor. These temples, called sun-temples, had an open-air design so that the sun could be visible. Their obelisks were symbols of the sun-god. Although Ra was recognized as the High God, the worship of local gods continued throughout Egypt.

At the end of the Old Kingdom, the pharaohs began to lose power to local administrators. The pharaoh's declining power, which culminated in a period without centralized power, undercut the entire system of belief in Egypt. This period is called the First Intermediate Period (2160–2055 B.C.E.). The events of this period remain in dispute, but it is known that prosperity declined across Egypt. Although an apparent breakdown of the pharaonic system occurred during the First Intermediate Period, centralized power, including a reaffirmation of the pharaoh as god incarnate, would again emerge in the Middle Kingdom (2055–1650 B.C.E.). The Middle Kingdom gained ascendancy from its base in the city of Thebes.

> **The pharaohs intended these funerary cults to remain active forever**

THE RELIGIOUS REVOLUTIONS OF THE MIDDLE KINGDOM

Numerous texts from the Middle Kingdom demonstrate new philosophical–religious skepticism among a growing intellectual community. Rather than a materialistic conception of the afterlife – which was partly the motive for placing material objects in the pharaoh's tomb – a more immaterial, or metaphysical, outlook developed. These new attitudes entailed a more personal approach toward the gods, including a belief that direct contact with them through prayer or ritual was available to everyone. Previously, the pharaoh and cultic priests had been deemed the only intermediaries to the divine realm. Now, however, the pharaoh was held responsible for his actions. Thus, while the pharaoh remained a god incarnate, he had become fallible in the eyes of the people, and was considered accountable for any decline in prosperity or ethics.

The religious privileges newly available to the whole populace included the availability of an afterlife, the existence of a personal "soul," the right to mummification (an important aspect of securing an afterlife), and a new emphasis on a Last Judgment after death. The god Osiris also rose to the forefront during the Middle Kingdom, and his myth became the most popular religious theme in Egypt.

The Osiris Mysteries

During the Middle Kingdom, annual ceremonies were held in honor of Osiris (the "Osiris Mysteries") at the city of Abydos. Osiris' life, death, and rebirth (a rite previously identified only with the pharaoh) became the paradigmatic example of the life–afterlife for the entire populace. As the popularity of the Osiris cult at Abydos continued to grow, and as the sun-god Ra became identified with him, the worship of Osiris became universalized. The Osiris Mysteries included a dramatic reenactment of the myth of Osiris. This drama, imbued with mythical symbols and metaphysical connotations, emphasized the life, death, and resurrection of Osiris, and included a procession that carried the statue of Osiris past onlookers, who paid homage. During the Mysteries, devotees divided themselves into two groups – the "Followers of Seth" and the "Followers of Horus" – in order to reenact the mythic battle between the two gods. The scholar Mircea Eliade, commenting on such a perennial motif, remarks as follows: "The battle between two groups of actors *repeated the passage from chaos to cosmos*, actualized the cosmogony. The mythical event became present once again."[17] Such festivals provided a linkage back to the First Time, and allowed Egyptians to participate in that mythic reality in the present moment.

The Last Judgment

The idea of a Last Judgment after physical death became a prominent belief during the Middle Kingdom. It was a particularly important theme within the Book of Going Forth by Day (which is dated to the Middle Kingdom but represents a synthesis of old and new religious beliefs). The judgment of the dead was presided over by a panel of forty-two judges and the god Osiris in the Hall of Ma'ati. During this procedure the deceased would express his or her righteousness in negative terms, denying that they had lived a sinful life. This process was called a Negative Confession, or a Declaration of Innocence. Such a declaration is recorded in the Papyrus of Ani:

> I have come unto thee, O my Lord, and I have brought myself hither that I may behold thy beauties. I know thee, I know thy name, I know the names of the Forty-two Gods who live with thee in this Hall of Maati, who live by keeping ward over sinners, and who feed upon their blood on the day when the consciences of men are reckoned up in the presence of the god … In truth I have come unto thee, I have brought Maati [Truth] to thee. I have done away sin for thee. I have not committed sins against men. I have not opposed my family and kinsfolk. I have not acted fraudulently [or, deceitfully] in the Seat of Truth. I have not known men who were of no account. I have not wrought evil.[18]

After the Declaration of Innocence the deceased's heart was weighed on the "scales of judgment" against a feather – a symbol for Truth, or *ma'at*. If the person's heart was heavier than the feather, they were not permitted entrance into the realm of the gods.

THE NEW KINGDOM

After the fall of the Middle Kingdom, power passed into the hands of the foreign invaders known as the Hyksos. This era is known as the Second Intermediate Period (1650–1550 B.C.E.). The Hyksos occupation brought an end to the isolationist mentality to which Egyptians were accustomed. It also seems to have greatly affected the idea that Egypt was the center of the world and the Egyptian people were divinely privileged. The rule of the Hyksos was eventually overthrown, and the period called the New Kingdom (1550–1069 B.C.E.) began.

During the New Kingdom, the god Amon (or Amon-Ra) became associated with the sun-god Ra and, in a process known as "solarization," was worshiped as the High God, or Creator of all other gods. Amon, represented by the sun, was recognized as a universal God who shines on all peoples, not only the Egyptians. The worship of many gods, however, did not cease, nor would it until well into the Roman period (see below). As temples and cults in honor of Amon increased, the priestly class accrued great power over religious rites and practices. However, the power of the cultic priests was curtailed by the religious revolution of the pharaoh Amenhotep IV, who turned all religious attention towards the one universal and only God – Aten (or Aton).

THE AMARNA RELIGION

The pharaoh Amenhotep IV (1352–1336 B.C.E.) attempted to turn the religious minds of the Egyptians away from the belief in many gods and toward the belief in one great God. He vanquished religious cults, closed and destroyed various temples, and divested the priestly class of their power. Amenhotep IV changed his name to Akhenaton ("The Spirit of Aten") and his wife, Nefertiti, changed her name to Nefernefruaten ("Beautiful in beauty is Aten"). They moved the capital to the city of Amarna and formed what is called the Amarna Religion. In the following hymn to Aten, Akhenaton expresses his fervent faith in the one and only universal God:

> Splendid you rise in heaven's lightland,
> O living Aten, creator of life!
> When you have dawned in eastern lightland,
> You fill every land with your beauty.
> You are beauteous, great, radiant,
> High over every land;
> Your rays embrace the lands …
> How many are your deeds,
> Though hidden from sight,
> O sole God beside whom there is none!
> You made the earth as you wished, you alone,
> All peoples, herds, and flocks;
> All upon earth that walk on legs,
> All on high that fly on wings,
> The lands of Khor and Kush,
> The land of Egypt.
> You set every man in his place,
> You supply their needs;
> Everyone has his food,
> His lifetime is counted.
> Their tongues differ in speech,
> Their characters likewise;
> Their skins are distinct,
> For you distinguished the peoples.[19]

Although the official Egyptian religion became centered on Aten during the life of Akhenaton, the belief in a one-and-only God did not gather a widespread following amongst the populace. After Akhenaton's death, the Amarna religion was quickly overturned in favor of the traditional pantheon of gods.

The New Kingdom was also distinguished by the pharaoh Rameses II (1279–1213 B.C.E.), during whose reign the so-called Amon hymns appear to have been written. One of the central messages of the Amon hymns is that the Creator is mysterious, transcendent, and beyond the comprehension of humans or other gods. It is also thought that a major religious event of historical interest occurred during the New Kingdom. According to the biblical account, around 1280 B.C.E., the Jewish prophet Moses led the Jewish people out of slavery in Egypt in an occurrence known as the Exodus.

The era following the New Kingdom was marked by political unrest that helped precipitate the decline of an independent Egyptian civilization. This period is known as the Late Period (664–332 B.C.E.). During this period, Egypt fell to a succession of foreign rulers, including the Persian Empire, which incorporated Egypt as a satrapy (or province). However, the Persians did not abolish the Egyptian religion or the pharaonic system of rulership. In 332 B.C.E., Egypt was conquered by Alexander III of Macedonia (336–323 B.C.E.), also known as "Alexander the Great." This era brought a great influx of Greek culture into Egypt.

THE HELLENISTIC AGE

After Alexander died, his empire was divided into three major monarchies, centered in Macedonia, Syria, and Egypt. Ptolemy I Soter of Macedonia took control of Egypt. The Ptolemy line of rulers were accepted as pharaohs; and their reign in Egypt is called the Ptolemaic Period (332 B.C.E.–30 B.C.E.). During this period, new cities were built to accommodate vast numbers of settlers, particularly from Greece. Remarkably, much of the internal religious and political structure of Egypt remained intact. The city that Alexander founded, Alexandria, developed into one of the premier centers of learning in the world. The city contained the Library of Alexandria, which, through an ambitious campaign to gather the most important texts in the world, became the most prominent library and cultural center of its time. Neoplatonists and other Greek philosophers were active in Alexandria; there was also a Jewish community, with scholars such as Philo (c.20 B.C.E.–50 C.E.).

It is believed by most scholars that the second ruler of the Ptolemaic dynasty, Ptolemy II Philadelphus (282–246 B.C.E.), commissioned Jewish scholars from Jerusalem to translate Jewish scriptures from Hebrew into Greek so that they could be added to the Library of Alexandria. This translation is known as the Septuagint, and it was the standard form of the "Old Testament" in the early Christian Church. Today, the text remains the authoritative version of the Eastern Orthodox Church.

In general, during the Hellenistic Age, there arose an appreciation of the universality of the human race. This worldview seems to have stemmed from Alexander's short-lived unification of the "East and West" under one polity, his openness to certain qualities of different cultures, his adoption of some non-Greek political practices, and his encouragement of ethnically mixed marriages. During this period, the phenomenon of overt religious syncretism – the synthesis of various religious ideals from different cultures – was extremely common. Greeks who migrated to Egypt identified gods of the Egyptian pantheon with gods of their native land (and vice versa); for example, Horus was identified with the Greek god Apollo, Thoth with Hermes, and Amon-Ra with Zeus.[20]

A new god called Serapis took form in Egypt at the beginning of the fourth century before the Common Era. Worship of Serapis may have developed under the political initiative of the Ptolemys in order to create a common god between Egyptians and Greeks. Serapis, whose name was derived from a combination of the Egyptian gods Osiris and Apis, synthesized the aspects of the Greek gods Zeus, Dionysus, and Hades into one god, which took the visual image of Zeus. The cult of Serapis became very popular, especially in Memphis and Alexandria, and it eventually spread to Rome.

THE ROMAN PERIOD

The Ptolemaic Kingdom ended when Ptolemy XV (44 B.C.E.–30 C.E.) and his mother, the co-regent Cleopatra (69–30 B.C.E.), were defeated by Roman forces under the command of Octavius, also known as Caesar Augustus (63 B.C.E.–14 C.E.). This begins the Roman period in Egypt (30 B.C.E.–395 C.E.), during which time Egypt was under the control of Roman emperors and was eventually converted to Christianity. In Egypt, Christianity enjoyed early popularity in Alexandria, which bore witness to impressive Christian metaphysicians such as Origen (185–254 C.E.). Gnostic Christian communities flourished in Egypt, and it was in the deserts of Egypt that the first Christian hermits took up monasticism.[21] In 641 C.E., Egypt was conquered by Arab Muslims, which brought the religion of Islam to the country. Today Islam is the majority religion of Egypt.

CHAPTER SUMMARY

The ancient Egyptian people upheld the ideals of peace, justice, and order (*ma'at*) as their guiding lights in public and private morality. In the ancient Egyptian religious tradition, we see the development of some key features exhibited by later religious movements: the turn toward monotheism; the importance of the soul and the afterlife; the vision of a judgment after death; and the belief that religious practice is a guarantor of the political, social, and spiritual order. The archetypical forms of such order were believed to exist eternally in the realm of the First Time. The mythic theology of the ancient Egyptians enabled them to see the events of the world they inhabited as repetitions of mythical events of the First Time, and their rituals were designed as reenactments of such primordial happenings. It was hoped that through these means, conditions in Egyptian society would approach the

The Egyptians upheld the ideals of peace, justice, and order as their guiding lights in public and private morality

perfection of the First Time. The many achievements of the ancient Egyptians were thus rooted in a deep, imaginative insight, reflected in their mythic symbolism and hieroglyphic language, both of which served as the metaphysical instruments with which they built the whole of their culture. The modern scholar R. T. Rundle Clark concluded:

> For the Egyptians, mythology was not a collection of texts but a language. This is fundamental. It explains why the doings of the gods could be altered, be expanded and even reappear with other protagonists without apparent inconsistency. But myths do not have to be consistent. They belong to a way of thinking in which consistency in the logical sense is irrelevant. The myth was a way, and before the emergence of lay philosophy with the Greeks, the only way, to express ideas about the cosmos or the needs of the human soul. This is why Egyptian mythology is so simple, so absurd, and sometimes so profound. It is dream, metaphysics and poetry, all at once.[22]

The Parthenon on the Acropolis in Athens, Greece

CHAPTER 4

THE RELIGIOUS TRADITIONS
OF ANCIENT GREECE

Thou deep Base of the World, and thou high
   Throne
Above the World, whoe'er thou art, unknown
And hard of surmise, Chain of Things that be,
Or Reason of our Reason; God, to thee
I lift my praise, seeing the silent road
That bringeth justice ere the end be trod
To all that breathes and dies.[1]

                    – Euripides

INTRODUCTION

Today, many think of the world and its diverse peoples as constituting one civilization – human civilization. In the past, however, the word "civilization" was often applied to particular empires or states. In that sense, the term "civilization" denoted a distinct line between the way of life of tribal or nomadic peoples and the way of life of "civilized" peoples or members of city-state communities. The historian Arnold Toynbee observed: "Interpreted literally, the word ['civilization'] ought to mean an attempt to attain the kind of culture that had been attained by citizens of a Graeco-Roman (in my terminology, Hellenic) city-state."[2] The concept of the city-state (*polis*) was profoundly important to the ancient Greeks. In fact, they developed the notion that human beings are essentially political or social beings. This view was expressed by Aristotle, who wrote "[A] human being is by nature meant for a [city-state]."[3]

In accordance with this view, human fulfillment was closely associated with active and direct engagement in the processes of a self-sufficient, organized society. In fact, the ancient Greeks, and especially their Roman successors, developed a view of citizenship that incorporated peoples beyond a single ethnicity. Greek culture was, in fact, often-times a model for European–American cultural and social

Timeline

*c.*1200 B.C.E.
Legendary time of
   Trojan War
800–700 B.C.E.
Oral tradition prevails
*c.*570–500 B.C.E.
Pythagoras
500–323 B.C.E. Classical
   Age
*c.*500 B.C.E.
Heraclitus
*c.*492–432 B.C.E.
Empedocles
*c.*475 B.C.E.
Parmenides
*c.*470–399 B.C.E.
Socrates
*c.*427–347 B.C.E.
Plato
384–322 B.C.E.
Aristotle
336 B.C.E.
Alexander III of
   Macedonia launches
   great military conquests
323–146 B.C.E.
Hellenistic Age
146 B.C.E.
Greece and Macedonia fall
   to Romans
106–43 B.C.E.
Cicero
*c.*55–135 C.E.
Epictetus
121–180 C.E.
Marcus Aurelius

achievements. In regard to the study of Greek religious ideas, the historian of religion Wilfred Cantwell Smith concluded: "it is legitimate and helpful to consider … the Greek tradition in Western civilization, rationalist-idealist-humanist, within the generic context of various [other] religious traditions of mankind. It is neither absurd, nor trite, to reinterpret it as one of our planet's major religious traditions."[4]

Geographically, ancient Greek culture encompassed not only modern Greece and its neighboring islands, but also portions of modern Italy and Turkey, among other places. Although often spoken of as one common country, ancient Greece was never a politically united nation for any sustained interval. The Greeks were divided into often rivaling, self-sufficient city-states. The successors of the Greeks, such as the Romans, absorbed much of the Greek worldview; the Greeks, in turn, had absorbed foreign ideas from bordering peoples and precursor traditions. In fact, the Indo-Aryans are believed to have conquered the region of modern Greece around the twentieth century B.C.E., and the Dorians are thought to have occupied the area in the twelfth century B.C.E. Thus, preexisting and neighboring cultures, including the peoples of Mesopotamia, the Minoans in Crete, Mycenaeans, Phoenicians, Persians, and Egyptians, influenced the development of Greek culture.

> **Do not do to others that which would anger you if others did it to you**
> *Socrates*
> **THE GOLDEN RULE**

204–270 C.E.
Plotinus
306–337 C.E.
Roman emperor Constantine converts to Christianity
*c.***335–263 C.E.**
Stoic philosophy founded by Zeno of Citium
379–395 C.E.
Christianity becomes state religion of Roman Empire
411–85 C.E.
Proclus
527–65 C.E.
Reign of Emperor Justinian, under whom the last Platonic schools of philosophy closed

THE OLYMPIAN RELIGION

Ancient Greek culture featured a somewhat unified code of ethics and religious ideals that were accepted, at least to some degree, throughout the region. The common meeting point for much of the Greek world was found within the epic works of the eighth-century B.C.E. bards referred to as Homer and Hesiod.[5] The epic myths and cosmologies attributed to Homer and Hesiod developed within an oral tradition carried on by professional poets and storytellers, referred to as *rhapsodes*. Although the works attributed to Homer and Hesiod were the crowning achievements of this long-standing tradition of Greek poetry, they did not function as inerrant revelations; they often differed with each other in their explanations and genealogies of the gods. There were also other accounts of the gods, including a variety of Orphic interpretations, which did not conform to Homeric or Hesiodic versions. Oftentimes, individual Greek city-states had their own myths, interpretations, religious cults (i.e., minority religious groups), and rituals which were geared toward local concerns and traditions. A city-state's patron deity (for example, the goddess Athena in her namesake city of Athens) assumed a more prominent role in local religious life than did other gods. Although there was considerable diversity of religious beliefs, the Homeric and Hesiodic myths – the foundation of the Olympian Mythology (or Mythical Theology) – were authoritative as political and moral reference points within the Greek world. The writings of Homer and Hesiod were also the standard curriculum of Greek education, and therefore helped to form a common moral standard and cultural heritage familiar to all Greeks. Scholars have suggested that the Homeric and Hesiodic worldview evolved from an older substratum of religious beliefs that was mainly concerned with *daimones*, or spirits. If this is true, the religiosity of Homer and Hesiod represents an evolution of Greek thought, namely the deification of inner (psychic) and outer (natural) powers into a pantheon of gods.[6]

Hesiod, especially in his *Works and Days*, tempered the minds of the Greeks through ethical teachings that invoked reverence for the godly virtues of justice, hard work, fellowship, friendship, and honesty. However, it should be noted that Hesiod and Homer told their tales from within the context of a patriarchical society; therefore, their stories overtly championed male superiority. Hesiod also offered advice on techniques for prosperous harvesting. In his *Theogony*, Hesiod set forth the origin, generation, and genealogy of the immortal gods that manipulate and intervene in the affairs of humanity. According to the *Theogony*, the first of all things to come into being was the god Chaos – a gaping void or primeval abyss (with no suggestion of "disorder," as this term carries in modern English). At some point, the gods Gaia (Earth), Tartarus (the Underworld), and Eros (sexual desire) came into existence. Through the force of Eros, Gaia and Tartaros divided Chaos. These primal gods produced a generation of immortals called the Titans. Subsequently, the Titans bore the gods known as the Olympians. Through a spectacle of tumultuous fighting, tyrannies, and revolts, the mighty Olympian Zeus came to power in a divine kingship by overthrowing his oppressive father, a Titan by the name of Kronos.

According to Greek myth, Zeus established order and became the ruler of all gods and humans, albeit with a good portion of defiance, back-talking, and mischief from his divine relatives and children. As a divine monarch, the sky-god Zeus was often depicted as a judge and dispenser of justice who could intervene in human affairs. Hesiod declared:

> **The writings of Homer and Hesiod helped to form a common moral standard and cultural heritage familiar to all Greeks**

> When it comes down to it
> Justice beats out Violence. A fool learns this the hard way …
> But for those who live for violence and vice,
> Zeus, Son of Kronos, broad-browed god, decrees
> A just penalty, and often a whole city suffers.[7]

Zeus is depicted as possessing supreme knowledge and power, but even his decrees were sometimes subject to the impersonal principle of Fate (Moira). For example, in the fifth century B.C.E. the Greek historian Herodotus recorded, "not God himself could escape destiny."[8] Zeus is not without a family; his two brothers, Poseidon (god of the seas) and Hades (god of the Underworld), and three sisters, Hestia (goddess of the hearth and the household), Demeter (goddess of the harvest), and Hera (goddess of marriage), all supported him in his battle against the Titans. Zeus married his sister Hera, who became queen of the Olympians. The marriage of Zeus and Hera ordained the institution of marriage within Greek society. Zeus' marriage to Hera, however, did not prevent him from taking both other goddesses and mortal women as his consorts. To the jealous rage of Hera, Zeus had numerous children outside his marriage. Other important Olympian gods and goddesses include Aphrodite (goddess of love and beauty), Apollo (the sun-god who later represented prophecy, order, and the arts), Ares (god of war), Artemis (goddess of the hunt and protector of children), Athena (goddess of wisdom, war, and crafts), and Hermes (the divine messenger of Zeus). The Olympian gods made their home at Mount Olympus, a large mountain in central Greece, which served as an *axis mundi* (or cosmic pillar or center) which connects earth to the realm of the gods.

> **Zeus is depicted as possessing supreme knowledge and power, but even his decrees were subject to impersonal Fate**

The great bard Homer, who is said to have been blind, seems to embody the motif of the "blind seer." Heavily quoted throughout ancient Greek literature, Homer is regarded by legend as the first and greatest Greek poet. His remarkable works are often cited as the foundation of the European literary tradition. The characters, stories, images, and themes contained in Homer's works, like other traditional Greek myths preserved by the Roman poet Ovid (43 B.C.E–17 C.E.), remain in the imagination of many modern Westerners.[9] In general, Homer's writings are representative of a value system based on the acquisition of honor and fame, which were most readily attainable through glory in battle. Homer's epic poems, entitled *Iliad* and *Odyssey*, both speak of the legendary time period of the Trojan War, which is dated to around 1200 B.C.E. Historians debate whether the Trojan War was an actual historical event.

In Homer's works, the soul (*psyche*) is depicted as a shade or spiritless shadow that is carried by the god Hermes into the Underworld after death. In the desolate Underworld, these shadows (or phantoms) are presided over by the god Hades ("Hades" was also the name of the Underworld itself). According to traditional myth, the Underworld – a dark place surrounded by five rivers, most notably the river Styx – can only be reached by paying Charon, the mythical ferryman, a coin to cross the river. Hence, it became customary for the Greeks to bury their dead with a coin so they could pay Charon to enter the Underworld. Homer's *Odyssey*, a less historically oriented recitation than his *Iliad*, is a didactic adventure – a hero's quest. It tells of the adventures and transformations that Odysseus endures on his pilgrimage home to his wife and son after the Trojan War.

RELIGIOUS BELIEFS AND PRACTICES

Mortals and Immortals

Homer depicted many interactions between gods and humans, the former being represented through anthropomorphic imagery. Although the poets conceived the gods in ways that were peculiarly human, the gods were viewed as immortals of far superior worth and power than human beings. Herodotus lamented, "human life is like a revolving wheel and never allows the same people to continue long in prosperity."[10] It was considered an excessive display of pride or overestimation of one's worth, referred to as "hubris," for a mortal to believe himself or herself to exist on the same level as the gods. The ancient Greeks believed that the gods punish those who transgress the ordained order, including those who demonstrate hubris or fail to honor the gods. Diseases and plagues were often attributed to an unappeased god, and journeys by land and sea began with pleas for divine protection. The Greeks sought to appease the gods or to win their favor through prayers, offerings, sacrifices, rituals, and hymns. Purity ordinances were also a central concern for the Greeks, especially before entering a temple or making an offering to a god. The Greeks believed that impurity was infectious and that contact with a dead person was the highest form of unholiness. Accordingly, they placed great emphasis on the need for proper burial of the dead. The Greek playwright Sophocles (*c*.496–406 B.C.E.), through the character Antigone, decreed that such observances were part of "the great unwritten, unshakable traditions."[11] Undoubtedly one aspect of those unshakable traditions was the honoring of the gods, especially through animal sacrifice, which served as the centerpiece of the city-state's communal observances. Animal sacrifices to the gods had strict preceding and succeeding rituals to ensure the purity and effectiveness of the rite.

Providence and Divination

For the ancient Greeks, life was saturated with an awful and inspiring presence of divinity. The ubiquity of spiritual forces naturally extended their concern for spiritual matters into all spheres of life. Believing that the gods found excellence and beauty pleasing, rhetorical speeches, dramatic plays, musical productions, and athletic games (such as the Olympic

Games) all had religious overtones. The performance of dramatic plays, particularly tragedies and comedies, was often tied to religious ceremonies. Notably, the Greeks believed that a sort of reciprocal pathway existed between the terrestrial and celestial realms. This allowed access to revelation and divination through the medium of inspired poets, prophets, and diviners. According to the Roman philosopher Cicero (106–43 B.C.E.):

> [Divination] is an ancient belief, going back to heroic times but since confirmed by the unanimous opinion of the Roman people and of every other nation, that there exists within mankind an undeniable faculty of divination. The Greeks called it mantike, that is the capacity to foresee, to know future events, a sublime and salutary act that raises human nature most nearly to the level of divine power. In this respect, as in many others, we have improved upon the Greeks by giving this faculty a name derived from the word god, divinatio, whereas according to Plato's explanation the Greek word comes from furor (mania from which mantike is derived). What cannot be gainsaid is that there is no nation, whether the most learned and enlightened or the most grossly barbarous, that does not believe that the future can be revealed and does not recognize in certain people the power of foretelling it.[12]

The belief in a "prophetic faculty" to which Cicero alludes was clearly evident in the Greek oracles. The most important oracle in ancient Greece was the Oracle at Delphi. Central to the operation of the Oracle was the Pythia, the priestess and attendant to the god Apollo. The Pythia devoted herself to Apollo, the god of artistry and prophecy, and was viewed as his "bride." Individual visitors or delegations went to the Oracle at Delphi seeking revelation from Apollo. Seekers believed that the Pythia was possessed by Apollo and thereby acted as a medium. Specifically, a visitor to the Oracle posed a question and the Pythia, in a trance-like state, replied with an enigmatic response which "signified" rather than explicitly answered. The Pythia's prophetic utterance was recorded by male attendants who edited and interpreted the prophecy. Recognized as a pan-Hellenic site, the Oracle at Delphi played a central role in Greek society, especially in political decision making and during wartime.

A sudden burst of insight, panic, inspiration, or lust might be attributed to a god

Greeks openly embraced the divine presence not only at religious places such as oracles, temples, and shrines, but in qualitative experiences. A sudden burst of insight, panic, inspiration, or lust might be attributed to a god; a person in the grip of such experiences was thought to be possessed by the particular god personifying that experience. Although mundane explanations for strange occurrences might be discernible, the Greeks were open to the possibility that bizarre and numinous events were signs from Providence. Diviners were an important class of religious figures in Greek society; they were thought to possess the ability to interpret certain phenomena as omens. For example, Greek diviners, utilizing a subtle and complicated system, revealed the will of the gods by interpreting the activity and flight pattern of birds. Diviners inspected and interpreted the remains of animal sacrifices to ascertain whether a proposed action, such as a political decision or military maneuver, enjoyed the favor of the gods. The Greeks also interpreted meaningful coincidences, or synchronistic events, as religiously significant. Another kind of omen included peculiar, involuntary movements, such as seizures.

The Greeks assigned special religious significance to sleep and dreams. Some dreams were interpreted as divinely inspired and were probed for hidden meanings. Dreams were a central aspect of the cult of Asklepios. His followers believed that Asklepios, son of Apollo, had mastered the art of healing and could raise the dead. If a person became ill, they could go to the temple of Asklepios and pray to the god. After performing an intricate and sometimes exhausting series of rites and rituals, the devotee slept in the temple of Asklepios in the hope that the god would provide healing or indicate a cure during a dream.

THE MYSTERY RELIGIONS

Scholars often classify Greek gods into two categories: the Olympian gods, who dwell in the heavens above, and the Cthonioi, the gods of the earth below. The mystery religions, or elective cults, were centered on the deities that personified chthonic powers – such as Hades, Demeter, Persephone, and Dionysus. These gods were often connected with the themes of renewal and fertility. Accordingly, the rituals of initiation associated with these gods were designed to produce a transformation akin to spiritual renewal or rebirth. As Aristotle states, the initiate does not simply learn something from this process, but undergoes an experience that transforms the condition of his or her very being.[13] In contrast to Olympian sacrifices and proceedings, the chthonic traditions were very emotional, and often included dramatic expressions of grief and joy. Elective cults, such as the Eleusian Mysteries, along with later movements during the Hellenistic period and the Roman era, developed symbolic religious rituals for the transformation of consciousness, the stirring up of numinous emotions, removal of sin or purging of psychological pollution, and union with the divine. Regarding the Greek and Roman mystery cults, the scholar Walter Burkert wrote:

> Ancient mysteries … are not puberty rites on a tribal level; they do not constitute secret societies with strong mutual ties … admission is largely independent of either sex or age; and there is no visible change of outward status for those who undergo these initiations. From the perspective of the participant, the change of status affects his relation to a god or a goddess; the agnostic, in his view from outside, has to acknowledge not so much a social as a personal change, a new state of mind through experience of the sacred.[14]

The Mysteries at Eleusis

Believed by some scholars to have been influenced by Egyptian myths surrounding the goddess Isis, the Mysteries at Eleusis became one of the most widespread initiatory rituals in ancient Greece. They were performed annually on the outskirts of Athens. The ritual was explained in a variety of hymns addressed to Demeter, many of which describe the abduction of the daughter of Zeus and Demeter, Persephone, into the Underworld by the god Hades. According to some versions of the myth, when Demeter (the mother of corn) realized that her daughter was missing, she was bereaved and became spiteful toward Zeus for allowing Hades to take her. Demeter, suffering from the loss of her daughter, refused to allow vegetation to grow. She assumed the form of an old hag and took refuge in the city of Eleusis. When she revealed her true identity to the Eleusinians, she demanded that the city build her a temple; in return, she would reveal her secret mysteries. Eventually, after the intervention of Zeus, Persephone was allowed to return to her mother for a portion of the year. However, she was forced to spend the remainder of the year as Hades' wife in the Underworld. In the end, Demeter told the Eleusinians her mysteries and gave them a rite which allowed humanity to ascend to her hallowed state. However, she prevented vegetation from growing during the period of the year when Persephone was in Hades (the winter season).

Those seeking initiation into the Mysteries at Eleusis were required to undergo a two-stage process. Each aspirant was first introduced to the Lesser Mysteries before returning another year for full initiation into the Greater Mysteries. The Mysteries at Eleusis were a pan-Hellenic phenomenon that brought seekers from all over the Greek world. In general, the mystery religions maintained that those who had not been "initiated" were excluded from the blessing of a positive afterlife. Thus, attainment of liberation, salvation, or a joyful afterlife depended upon initiation. Initiation was available during nine-day festivals. During such a festival, the initiates, called *mystes*, went through an exhaustive program, including a night of sleep-deprived dancing. It is believed that the initiation sequence involved a visually stimulating and emotional dramatization of the Demeter myth. Some scholars believe that emphasis was placed upon Persephone's descent into the Underworld (her "death"), Demeter's sorrows, and Persephone's return to her mother (her "rebirth"). Accordingly, during the initiation the *mystes* descended into a dark cave illuminated by torches and were shown sacred objects, one of which is thought to have been a grain of wheat or an ear of corn. The Eleusinian Mysteries used such agricultural symbols to indicate the generative and renewal powers of the earth. When such symbols were applied to the human soul,

> **During such a festival, the initiates went through an exhaustive program, including a night of sleep-deprived dancing**

they suggested the continuation of life after a physical death. Apparently, such teachings were designed to help the initiate live a joyful life with a hopeful perspective on death. However, the exact teachings and dramatic events orchestrated by the hierophant, the high priest of the Eleusinian Mysteries, remain unknown. Like other mystery religions, the Eleusinian Mysteries had a strict and honored vow of secrecy. As the Homeric Hymn to Demeter describes them, the rites that Demeter revealed to the Eleusinians are "sacred things not to be transgressed, asked about, or uttered: great awe of the gods stops the voice."[15]

The Cult of Dionysus

Dionysus was a chthonic god associated with wine, ecstasy, madness, and vegetation. He was also closely linked to procreative power, creativity, and the image of the phallus. Stark contrasts are often drawn between the frenzied and orgiastic energy associated with Dionysus (the Dionysian principle) and the structured, measured, and balanced energy associated with the god Apollo (the Apollonian principle). Dionysus was the centerpiece of a variety of theogonies that differed from the Hesiodic version. One such theogony was an essential doctrine of the Orphic movement (see below). Members of the Dionysian cults (or Bacchic cults) sought union with the god through ecstatic experiences (*ekstasis*). The ecstatic experience was thought to allow a momentary "stepping out" of oneself. In so doing, practitioners hoped to move beyond reason and experience the drunken "madness" of the gods (in particular, Dionysus). The nineteenth-century philosopher Friedrich Nietzsche, who was greatly influenced by Greek thought, captured the essence of this Dionysian mystical experience when he wrote:

Under the charm of the Dionysian not only is the union between man and man re-affirmed, but Nature which has become estranged, hostile, or subjugated, celebrates once more her reconciliation with her prodigal son, man. Freely earth proffers her gifts, and peacefully the beasts of prey approach from desert to mountain. The chariot of Dionysus is bedecked with flowers and garlands; panthers and tigers pass beneath his yoke. Transform Beethoven's "Hymn to Joy" into a painting; let your imagination conceive the multitudes bowing to the dust, awestruck – then you will be able to appreciate the Dionysian. Now the slave is free; now all the stubborn, hostile barriers, which necessity, caprice or "shameless fashion" have erected between man and man, are broken down. Now, with the gospel of universal harmony, each one feels himself not only united, reconciled, blended with his neighbor, but as one with him; he feels as if the veil of Mâyâ [illusion] had been torn aside and were now merely fluttering in tatters before the mysterious Primordial Unity.[16]

Seeking frenzied states of divine possession, worshipers of Dionysus often used wine, music, and dancing as methods to achieve ecstasy. An important group associated with the worship of Dionysus was the Maenads. The Maenads were an all-female secretive cult of Dionysus. In its extreme form, as immortalized by the Greek playwright Euripides in his *Bacchae*, the maenadic women left their societal roles and retreated into the wilderness to honor the god Dionysus through orgies, dancing, and the violent tearing and eating of uncooked animal flesh. Raw animal flesh, usually from a bull, was associated with the

Worshipers of Dionysus often used wine, music, and dancing to achieve ecstasy

god Dionysus and was eaten to achieve a sacramental union with the god. In a less extreme form, the honoring of Dionysus seems to have provided a release from the constraints of societal norms.

THE ORPHIC MOVEMENT

It is believed that Orpheus was from Thrace, and that he lived before the time of Homer. According to one interpretation, Orpheus was a religious teacher and reformer who, influenced by the cult of Dionysus, established a new religious order later called Orphism. Historians and scholars remain divided on the nature of Orphism, and some have suggested that Orpheus was not a real person but a mythological figure. It is unclear who Orpheus was; also unclear is the relationship between the historical Orpheus (if there was one) and the movement that took his name. Legend speaks of Orpheus as a musician of divine caliber. He was credited with mitigating the savagery of past ages, including the practice of cannibalism, through his agricultural and religious teachings. In various pictorial representations, whether in art or pottery, Orpheus is often depicted with a lyre and as a worker of miracles. It is said that Orpheus enjoyed the power of prophecy and that he could tame wild animals, including the animalistic side of humans, with his celestial music. He seems to have been a shaman, and is often described as the founder of religious "initiations."

The teachings attributed to Orpheus were accepted as revelation by his followers. The communities founded by his disciples fostered the first fraternal religious movement in Greece. Orphic communities were removed from the normal ebb and flow of the polity. They also abstained from eating or sacrificing animals. The Orphics placed great importance on rites of initiation and on upholding an ascetic lifestyle based on strict rules that insured purity. The Orphics were influenced by the ecstatic experiences of the Dionysiac cults, and believed that such experiences allowed the soul to momentarily exit the body. Orphics viewed the soul as imprisoned, not only in the "tomb" of the body,[17] but in the "wheel of life" where it endured rebirths based on merits accrued in previous lives.

A central Orphic myth proclaimed that Dionysus was fathered by Zeus, who, having transformed himself into a serpent, impregnated his daughter Persephone. Zeus declared that the son born from this union, Dionysus, also known as Zagreus, would be the heir to his throne – the next ruler of gods and men. Some of the ancient gods, known as the Titans, became jealous, took the baby Dionysus, tore him to pieces, and ate him. Furious at the killing of his son, Zeus unleashed his mighty thunderbolts, which burnt the Titans to ashes. Athena procured the heart of Dionysus from the pile of ashes and brought it back to life with her divine breath. Zeus swallowed the heart and then impregnated a woman named Semele so that Dionysus could be reborn – this time to a mortal woman. Like Persephone and the Egyptian god Osiris, the "twice-born" Dionysus embodies the motif of a god who suffers, dies, and is resurrected.

> **The "twice-born" Dionysus embodies the motif of a god who suffers, dies, and is resurrected**

According to the Orphic tradition, humanity was derived from the ashes of the Titans, which contained both the evil inherent in the Titans and the divinity of Dionysus. From this perspective, humanity had a polluted nature from birth, stemming from its inherent Titanic element, which obscured the latent Dionysiac, or divine, essence. It is believed that Orphic initiates sought to recreate the suffering of Dionysus in order to achieve salvation. By practicing an ascetic lifestyle, the initiate tried to achieve a transformation of consciousness and to free the soul from the body, i.e. to actualize the divine nature within. Eventually, Orphics hoped that through reincarnation they could be transformed from sinful mortals into immortal gods.

PYTHAGORAS AND THE PYTHAGOREANS

Pythagoras of Samos (c.570–500 B.C.E.) was an inspired philosopher, a charismatic teacher, and the founder of an esoteric religious order. For the members of this school philosophy was a way of life and a spiritual discipline. Pythagorean philosophy shaped the course of ancient thought and was rejuvenated periodically throughout antiquity – notably, according to ancient accounts, by Plato.

Over time, as lore was mingled with historical fact, Pythagoras became an icon for all things philosophical and esoteric. According to his ancient biographers, he traveled widely and gathered wisdom from every possible source: he reportedly studied with the Milesian philosophers Thales and Anaximander; he is said to have imbibed traditional wisdom from Egyptian priests, Chaldean priests, Hebrew prophets, and Indian ascetics. The philosopher Iamblichus states that in Egypt Pythagoras spent twenty-two years diligently frequenting the temples, studying astronomy and geometry, and becoming initiated into the mysteries of the gods. In Babylonia he spent twelve years steeped in Chaldean wisdom and studied arithmetic, music, and "all other sciences," while amongst the Hebrews he acquired expertise in the interpretation of dreams. Some accounts link Pythagoras with religious teachers and miracle workers such as Abaris, Aristeas, Hermotimus, Epimenides, and Pherecydes. These figures (reminiscent of the shamans of Siberia) were known for their psychic powers, out-of-body excursions, powers of healing and prophecy, postmortem reappearances, belief in reincarnation, direct perception of the spiritual world, solitary retreats, fasting, spirit possession, and other extraordinary faculties. Some accounts suggested that Pythagoras was a reincarnation of a previous shaman, possibly Orpheus. Other sources state that he was purified from the pollutions of his past lives and taught the nature of virtue by the Persian prophet Zoroaster.

No treatises written by the hand of Pythagoras have survived, but many important philosophical perspectives are attributed to him, suggesting his authoritative status. An important distinction exists between what Pythagoras actually taught and what "Pythagoreans" – those who formed communities based on teachings attributed to Pythagoras – propounded. Pythagoreans placed great importance on the study of music, geometry, astronomy, and mathematics. They gathered insights from the study of harmonics and applied them in relation to ratios and proportions. An admirer, the pioneer of quantum physics Werner Heisenberg, asserted:

> Pythagoras is said to have made the famous discovery that vibrating strings under equal tension sound together in harmony if their lengths are in a simple numerical ratio. The mathematical structure, namely the numerical ratio as a source of harmony, was certainly one of the most momentous discoveries in the history of mankind. The harmonious concord of two strings yields a beautiful sound. Owing to the discomfort caused by beat-effects, the human ear finds dissonance disturbing, but consonance, the peace of harmony, it finds beautiful. Thus the mathematical relation was also the source of beauty.[18]

The concept of musical and mathematical balance was generalized to encompass the Pythagorean idea of a healthy human life, that is, a life based on balance between extremes (an insight reached by later Greek philosophers, generally referred to as the Doctrine of the Mean). It has been suggested that Pythagoras' ability to translate music into mathematical representation led him to believe that all things were numbers, and that the cosmos (kosmos) – the universe understood as a rational and harmoniously ordered totality – could ultimately be understood and described by means of numbers. Pythagoreans likened the heavens to a musical scale. They also asserted that the world was the byproduct of a relationship between the bounded (limited) and the unbounded (unlimited).

Pythagoreans believed that the physical body was a temporary vessel for the journey of the soul. Accordingly, the soul endures many incarnations through a process of

Top: *1876 steel engraving of Jacques-Louis David's* The Death of Socrates
Bottom: *(Left) head of the god Apollo at Nemrut Dagi, Turkey. Apollo was worshiped in both the ancient Greek and Roman religions*

transmigration until it becomes purified enough to achieve union with the divine. The Pythagoreans practiced memory training exercises as well as spiritual and meditative practices. They observed many social taboos and upheld strict rules of conduct. They believed that an essential kinship existed between all living creatures, and they held steadfastly to a vegetarian diet. They also abstained from animal sacrifices, a traditional Greek communal norm, which made them outcasts in the eyes of Greek traditionalists. Nestled within small communities, especially the Greek colonies in Italy, the Pythagorean approach to understanding reality was holistic in nature and

> **Pythagoreans believed that the physical body was a temporary vessel for the journey of the soul**

honored philosophy as a way of life. Pythagoreans formed small-scale societies, engaged in politics, and developed an integrated system of education. They viewed mathematics, geometry, and science as sacred instruments for attaining knowledge of the divine. The Pythagoreans exercised great influence on later religious, scientific, astronomical, mathematical, philosophical, and occult movements.[19] Pythagoras' influence is clearly discernible in the philosophy of Plato, who is believed to have undertaken serious Pythagorean studies. Interestingly, the Italian scientist Galileo Galilei's (1564–1642 C.E.) scientific and astronomical inquiries were viewed, at the time, as a Pythagorean revival.

PRE-SOCRATIC PHILOSOPHY

The use of philosophy as a means of gaining insight into the divine is one of the most important aspects of Greek religious history and of religious thinking in general. One scholar has concluded:

> To anyone who has tried to live in sympathy with the Greek philosophers, the suggestion that they were "intellectualists" must seem ludicrous. On the contrary, Greek philosophy is based on the faith that reality is divine, and that the one thing needful is for the soul, which is akin to the divine, to enter into communion with it. It was in truth an effort to satisfy what we call the religious instinct … [Ancient Greek philosophy] includes most of what we should now call religion.[20]

A way of categorizing the various religious viewpoints of ancient Greece was proposed by the Roman thinker M. Teventius Varro (116–127 B.C.E.) and the Catholic philosopher St. Augustine (354–430 C.E.). Both Varro and Augustine classified Greek religion according to three categories: mythical theology; political theology; and natural theology.[21] Commenting on this tripartite categorization, the modern scholar Werner Jaeger noted that "Mythical theology had for its domain the world of the gods as described by the poets; political theology included the official State religion and its institutions and cults; natural theology was a field for the philosophers – the theory of the nature of the divine as revealed in the nature of reality."[22]

During the sixth century B.C.E., in the Greek city of Miletus in Ionia (modern Turkey), three thinkers named Thales, Anaximander, and Anaxamenes developed natural theology. These Ionian teachers, or "pre-Socratic" philosophers (i.e. philosophers before the advent of Socrates), believed the universe to be intelligently ordered, and appealed to natural law as the ruling principle. The Ionian thinkers, in general, identified a first cause of existence – that from which all things emerge and to which all things return – and then imbued this one substance, cause, or principle with divine significance. For Thales, the first cause was water; for Anaximander, it was the eternal Boundless (*aperion*) – an indeterminate thing which encompasses all and governs all through retributive justice (*dike*); and for Anaxamenes, it was air, from which all arose and perished through a process of condensation and rarefaction. Because they were concerned with producing a rational account of the natural cosmos, these Ionian thinkers were referred to as "physicists" (from the ancient Greek term *phusis*, meaning "nature"), and were hailed as the first Greek philosophers.

The Milesian or Ionian approach resulted in an impersonal conception of a divine principle immersed throughout the material universe. This approach utilized a methodology of argumentation, empirical investigation, and experimentation. Rather than invoking the Muses, the nine daughters of Zeus who symbolized inspiration, the Milesian school appealed to the human senses and the faculty of reason. However, these growing rationalist inclinations did not drive the ancient Greeks to reject traditional religious viewpoints or practices such as divination, oracles, and prophecy. On the one hand, the rationalist movement represented a small minority of thinkers distinct from the majority of Greek traditionalists. On the other hand, although the rationalist methodology has often been employed in the absence of, and even in opposition to, a religious viewpoint, this methodology itself does not reject spirituality. In fact, the Milesian methodology was integral to the perennial quest of the Greek philosophers to uncover the Divine Unity that binds together the apparent multiplicity of the Cosmos. This issue is also known as the problem of "the One and the many."

The philosophical problem of "the One and the many" is concerned with rectifying the manifest plurality of existence (the many things apparent to our senses) with the intuitive insight, or numinous sense, that there is ultimately a single underlying unity. The Milesian thinkers, presented above, propounded a view referred to as material monism – namely, that all things are derived from one original (divine) substance (or in the case of Anaximander, the Boundless). Pre-Socratic philosophy is demonstrative of how

Greek religion was broadened from mythological origins to the study of Being (ontology). The problem of the "One and the many" was of central concern to other Pre-Socratic religious thinkers, such as Heraclitus (*c.*500 B.C.E.), Parmenides (*c.*475 B.C.E.), and Empedocles (*c.*450 B.C.E.). These three philosophers were inspired religious poets and shamanic figures.

Heraclitus of Ephesus, a mystical and enigmatic poet, is often described as a prophet. Most of his poetry is in the form of paradoxical riddles which reveal a new way of seeing reality; they force a simultaneous apprehension of opposites. Heraclitus believed that everything is arranged by the Logos, the divine and universal intelligence that orders the cosmos (the Greek term *logos* also means "word," "account," and "reason," among other things). The nature of reality, as dictated by the Logos, is an unseen tension between opposites (a process sometimes called "Strife," "Fire," "Wisdom," or "Justice"). The key point for Heraclitus was that underneath the incessant process of exchange between opposites is a single, unchanging principle (namely, the Logos). What appears to be a constantly changing reality of "warring" opposites is, in reality, a harmonious process: namely, the opposites ultimately complement each other and form a sort of cosmic continuum. For example, a human consciousness that is aware only of the parts might interpret two elements of a certain whole, one which pulls and another which pushes, as being in opposition. When viewed from the perspective of the whole, however, these two parts really complement each other and form a reciprocal unity.

According to Heraclitus, perception must include not only the parts, or the ever-changing flux of opposites, but the underlying divine unity that those opposites comprise. For Heraclitus, being is an ever-changing but unified reality; manifestly a plurality but essentially a unity (ultimately represented, as in the Zoroastrian tradition, by the symbol of fire; fire is always changing but maintains an integral unity as fire). If one hopes to attain wisdom and virtue, Heraclitus argued, then one must gain insight into the unitive cosmic process, and structure one's life according to that insight. In summarizing Heraclitus' realization, one scholar commented:

> [The] double process of analysis and synthesis will be required if we are to discover the full significance of the world and our place in it. We must come to appreciate how each quality contributes to the work of its opposite, and to the effective operation of the cosmos as a whole. This may involve understanding how the same thing can have opposite qualities from different points of view.[23]

Parmenides of Elea (*c.*475 B.C.E.) is best known for his shamanic poem in which he is taken by chariot to meet a goddess. The goddess bestows upon Parmenides a revelation of the

Way of Truth (as opposed to the Way of Opinion). The Way of Truth is the road to true knowledge and unity with being: it decrees the existence of a single, eternal, unchangeable Being (that which is). On the other hand, the Way of Opinion – common among mortals – is the worldview serviced by the senses. It is deceptive and leads one to believe in a multiplicity of things ("the many") which arise, perish, and constantly change. A traveler on the Way of Truth, however, leaves the illusory world of the senses in favor of the Mystery of Being, which is grasped by means of inspired intellection. The seeker ascends from the dark (opinion) to the light (knowledge) by attaining the mystical insight that reality is One and has no independent parts. A contemporary scholar has commented, "Parmenides' poem is concerned with a unique inner experience, the encounter of one's mind with Being and the realization that they are the same. The road that leads to this experience is therefore a 'Way,' a spiritual path rather than a logical route or an analytical method."[24] According to Parmenides, the experience of Being, the Existent, is a transformative religious experience bestowed by the divine.

Empedocles of Akragas (c.492–432 B.C.E.) was a remarkable poet and a charismatic figure, regarded by some of his followers as a god. He posited that there is an inherent plurality in what exists. He suggested that there are four primal elements (Air, Earth, Fire, and Water), and he referred to them as gods. He believed that all things ("the many") consist of these four elements. For Empedocles, the original substances are at the sway of two opposing cosmic forces, namely Love and Strife (also symbolized as gods). According to Empedocles' perspective, all change in the universe is dictated by the attracting force of Love or the averting force (or repulsion) of Strife. Empedocles posited the existence of cosmic cycles in which Love (or harmony) and Strife (or discord) gradually alternate in their dominance over all things. These cycles eternally move through stages; when the cycle of Love is fully attained, at its height, all things become united in Love, described as the cosmic Sphere. Eventually, the Love uniting this Sphere falls to its contrary, Strife, and the cycle begins anew. Unity and multiplicity therefore alternate in cycles.

Empedocles viewed the human soul as a microcosm of the cyclical cosmic process; thus the human soul also vacillates between Love and Strife. Seemingly drawing from Orphic myths, he proposed that humanity collectively fell from an original state of bliss, probably by way of meat-eating, into the "wheel of birth." He suggested that the soul endures transmigration in the mineral, animal, and human kingdoms, and can ultimately reunite with the divine source. Viewing his own lifetime as occurring during a stage of cosmic Strife, Empedocles spoke passionately about the ancients who practiced vegetarianism; he reports that during this Golden Age, a spiritual kinship existed between humans and animals; he also spoke of an ancient prophetic figure, resembling a god, who lived among humans and was a master of all facets of reality.

It should be emphasized that scholars remain divided on many aspects of pre-Socratic philosophy, especially since pre-Socratic writings have only survived in fragments. It is clear, however, that pre-Socratic philosophers represent a shift in Greek religious thinking. Although it would be incorrect to assume that all Greek philosophers dismissed the mythological and poetic modes of thinking, their mythic imagination became distinctly more philosophical; the gods became allegorical representations of impersonal divine powers – a view already found in seed form in Hesiod's *Theogony*. It is clear that within the Greek tradition, there existed a diversity of religious–philosophical perspectives. Oftentimes, this diversity encouraged new ways of thinking as Greek thinkers built on previous theories.[25] For example, the philosophy of Heraclitus influenced philosophers known as the Stoics. Stoic philosophy was founded by Zeno of Citium (*c*.335–263 C.E.), who established a school in Athens. The Stoic worldview continued into the Roman period and was championed, and transmitted to posterity, by way of the Roman thinkers Seneca (*c*.4 B.C.E.–65 C.E.), Epictetus (*c*.55–135 C.E.), and Marcus Aurelius (121–180 C.E.). Pre-Socratic philosophy also served as the foundation for the better-known Greek thinkers Plato and Aristotle.[26]

HERODOTUS IN EGYPT

Herodotus (425–485 B.C.E.), often regarded as the "father of history," is one of the most important of the ancient Greeks. Well known for his romantic account of the Persian invasion of Greece, Herodotus' method of historical writing, which contained vivid stories and entertaining digressions, represented a different genre of literature from that of Homer's epic style. The epic poets were traditional bards – that is, they recited imaginative and poetic mythologies. The aim of mythology is to impart archetypal or universal truths concerning perennial human experiences, questions, and aspirations. For the mythological poets, unlike the historians, time and historical events are irrelevant. On the other hand, Herodotus' style of writing, and even more so that of the Athenian Thucydides (*c*.460–404 B.C.E.), was a written, factual account which recorded events and probed their historical causes. During Herodotus' career as a historian and explorer, he visited many places, including Egypt. He later proclaimed that the Greeks had derived many aspects of their religion from ancient Egypt. Herodotus also asserted that the Greeks had learned the names of the gods from the Egyptians.[27]

Within the Greek tradition, there existed a diversity of religious – philosophical perspectives

PHILOSOPHY IN ATHENS: SOCRATES, PLATO, AND ARISTOTLE

Socrates

Socrates of Athens is one of the most influential thinkers in all of Western philosophy. He is noted for developing the method of inquiry now referred to as the Socratic Method. The Socratic Method is a process of examination (*elenchus*) through which the meaning of a given concept is clearly articulated and an eternal Form comes into view. For instance, in Plato's dialogue *Euthyphro*, the investigation is aimed at answering the question "What is piety?" by explicitly identifying that "one single characteristic" which all and only pious actions share. This process is meant to culminate in defining or understanding the essence of piety, establishing an absolute standard or model according to which individual actions can be (correctly) judged and perceived as pious or impious. Through this form of progressive clarification, one approaches a pure vision of the essence of piety.

The Socratic Method advances toward its goal in discursive steps in which a question is posed (such as "what is knowledge?"; "what is justice?"; or "what is virtue?"), and the interlocutor (the person involved in the discussion) will then try to articulate his understanding of the concept in question. The interlocutor's answers will then be refined through the use of counterexamples. In practicing this method, Socrates often exposed his interlocutor's claims of knowledge as essentially unfounded. Socrates himself declared that he possessed no expert knowledge of the kind the Socratic Method aims at attaining. Like other well-known spiritual masters, he never wrote anything. Our portrait of Socrates is almost entirely derived from the favorable depiction left by his most notable follower, Plato, especially in Plato's works *Euthyphro*, *Apology*, and *Crito*.

When he was approximately seventy years old, Socrates was brought to trial in Athens. He was accused of not believing in the gods of the Athenian state, inventing new gods, and corrupting the youth. He was found guilty and sentenced to death.

While he was on trial, Socrates gave a famous and stirring speech that was conveyed by Plato in a work called the *Apology*, or "defense speech." Socrates declared that in practicing the art of philosophy he was acting in loyalty to the dictates of his *daimon* – his inner conscience of divine origin – which he valued over any worldly concern. According to Plato, Socrates referred to this inner voice as a "prophetic power," a "divine sign," and a "spiritual manifestation." Socrates believed that his philosophical activity was just and beneficial for his fellow citizens. While in prison, Socrates had a chance to escape but he chose to remain and abide by the decree of the court; he chose to die rather than to commit injustice. He refused to compromise his religious convictions or to express regret for a lifestyle that he believed was virtuous and in accord with the will of the gods.

> **For Socrates, the ultimate criterion for judging if a life was truly happy and worth living was whether it was just and virtuous**

Socrates challenged his fellow Athenians to reconsider their beliefs and implored them to value wisdom, truth, and the condition of their souls above such ephemeral concerns as wealth and power. For Socrates, the ultimate criterion for judging if a life was truly happy and worth living was whether it was just and virtuous. He held virtue as the most admirable of all attributes, as objective, and as non-relative. Socrates had "good hope" about the chances for a positive afterlife and considered death to be a "blessing." Regardless of the majority opinion, Socrates declared that "one must not even do wrong when one is wronged."[28] He was confident that good and virtuous actions brought merit, not only here but in the afterlife. According to Socrates, "a good man cannot be harmed either in life or in death, and ... his affairs are not neglected by the gods."[29]

Plato

Plato (*c*.427–347 B.C.E.) founded a school in Athens called the Academy. As an educator, he instructed his students in a process of character development through philosophical contemplation. Plato's enormous influence on Western philosophy is undeniable; the twentieth-century philosopher Alfred Whitehead concluded: "The safest general characterization of the European philosophical tradition is that it consists of a series of footnotes to Plato."[30] Plato was not only an astute discursive thinker, he was also a genius of the imagination. His writings represent a synthesis of the mythic–poetic way of thinking (mythical theology) and rational discernment (natural theology). Plato's treatises utilize symbols, allegories, myths, and other literary devices as vehicles to express philosophical and religious insights. The English poet Percy Bysshe Shelley concurred: "Plato was essentially a poet – the truth and splendour of his imagery and the melody of his language is the most intense that it is possible to conceive."[31] Plato's works are written in the form of dialogues, in which his master, Socrates, was often the lead character. Plato was not dogmatic in his beliefs; in fact, he may have been the first philosopher to offer criticisms of his own theoretical ideas. Thus, he did not simply put forward completed doctrines, but drew his audience into a learning process. As the poet Samuel Coleridge put it, Plato's aim was "not to assist in storing the passive mind with the various sorts of knowledge ... as if the human soul were a mere repository or banqueting room, but to place it in such relations of circumstance as should gradually excite the germinal power that craves no knowledge but what it can take up into itself, what it can appropriate, and reproduce in fruits of its own."[32]

Plato's dialogues critiqued stories attributed to Homer that depict the gods as possessing non-virtuous, malevolent qualities. By distinguishing himself from the epic poets, Plato was forging his own theological philosophy which posited the existence of a supreme Good. The classicist Werner Jaeger traced the origins of the word "theology" to Plato:

> Theology is a mental attitude which is characteristically Greek, and has something to do with the great importance which the Greek thinkers attribute to the *logos*, for the word *theologia* means the approach to God or the gods (*theoi*) by means of the *logos* ...
>
> Plato was the first who used the word "theology" ... and he evidently was the creator of the idea. He introduced it in his *Republic*, where he wanted to set up certain philosophical standards and criteria for poetry ... Thus, when Plato set forth ... "outlines of theology," in the *Republic*, the creation of that new word sprang from the conflict between the mythical tradition and the natural (rationalist) approach to the problem of God. Both in the *Republic* and the *Laws* Plato's philosophy appears, at its highest level, as theology in this sense. Thereafter every system of Greek philosophy (save only the Sceptic) culminated in theology, and we can distinguish a Platonic, Aristotelian, Epicurean, Stoic, Neopythagorean, and Neoplatonic theology.[33]

Accordingly, Greek philosophy has been described as "Divine Philosophy," and Plato has been referred to as a "Divine Philosopher." In fact, many religious and philosophical concepts later developed by Jewish, Christian, and Islamic thinkers originated from the Greek tradition. Plato's orientation toward the divine (and his mastery of poetic images) is exemplified in the following passage from the dialogue *Timaeus*:

> As concerning the most sovereign form of soul in us we must conceive that heaven has given it to each man as a guiding genius – that part which dwells in the summit of our body and lifts us from earth toward our celestial affinity, like a plant whose roots are not in earth, but in the heavens ... [If a man's] heart is set on the love of learning and true wisdom and he has exercised that part of himself above all, he is surely bound to have thoughts immortal and divine, if he shall lay hold upon truth, nor can he fail to possess immortality in the fullest measure that human nature admits; and because he is always devoutly cherishing the divine part and maintaining the guardian genius that dwells within him in good estate, he must needs be happy above all.[34]

Elsewhere in *Timaeus* Plato presents a myth that describes God as a perfectly good and benevolent craftsman. According to *Timaeus*, God is not an anthropomorphic being but a Divine Mind, a generative Reason, who uses mathematics to fashion order out of pre-existing chaos. In other dialogues, Plato suggests that each individual is endowed with an immortal soul that is distinct from its body. In general, his dialogues purport that the soul is immaterial and that it ultimately constitutes the essential identity of a person. In his work *Phaedo*, Plato's idea of the soul is closely aligned to Orphic and Pythagorean concepts. The dialogue suggests that philosophy helps to free the soul from association with the body because its object of study is wisdom. Accordingly, the acquisition of wisdom, through the embodiment of courage, moderation, and justice, purges the impurities that arise from the soul's submergence in a physical body. The soul is regarded as a simple entity (meaning not a "compound"), and thus it is exempt from disintegration into parts. In *Meno*, Plato asserts: "As the soul is immortal, has been born often and has seen all things here and in the underworld, there is nothing which it has not learned; so it is in no way surprising that it can recollect the things it knew before, both about virtue and other things."[35] The position implied in the previous statement suggests that all knowledge is innate within the soul; from this perspective, when a person "acquires" knowledge, it is actually a process of remembering (*anamnēsis*). Plato suggested that after the body perishes in physical death, the soul forgets the knowledge attained through contemplation of the eternal Forms and therefore is reborn in the physical world. However, through the spiritual practice of philosophy (which for Plato is the love of wisdom and an awareness of the Divine) one can recollect forgotten knowledge learned in previous lives and thereby avoid reincarnation.

According to Plato, the sensible world, which constitutes what we perceive, is always in a state of becoming and consists of essentially unreal, transitory images. The physical human senses, then, are not reliable instruments for grasping Reality as it truly is. Plato suggested that sensible objects were mere reflections, or semblances, of Ultimate Reality – a Reality constituted by what he called the Forms. From this perspective, everything that exists participates in an archetypal Form or Idea which resides in an eternal, universal, intelligible realm. For example, every just action participates in the unchanging eternal Form, or Archetype, of Justice. Accordingly, every beautiful object participates in the Form of Beauty. Plato therefore distinguished between beautiful things and Beauty itself (the Form of Beauty). He believed these universal Forms to be eternal and unchangeable, representing a Reality of more being and worth than the reality detectable by our physical senses.

In the dialogue entitled *Symposium*, Plato explored the powers of the god Eros (the god of love, and attendant of Aphrodite, called Cupid by the Romans). The work presents a variety of perspectives on love, each of which is argued by a different character. At the summit of the dialogue, Socrates relays a mythic story about love, which, he reports, was told to him by the priestess Diotima. The allegorical story explains the different hierarchical levels on the ascending path of love. As love advances, it expands from the personal and particular to the general and universal, and then into realms of higher contemplative order such as poetry, politics (the study of law and the best organization of society), and science.

Plato describes the zenith of this upward path as the sudden apprehension of "the essence of beauty" or "Beauty Itself." The ascent to Beauty begins with one's attraction to things of the body and then evolves into an attraction for abstract matters of the mind. Later philosophers, including Neoplatonists and Christians, understood Plato's *Symposium* as an allegory representing the spiritual path to God and as purporting a hierarchy of ontological realities.

Aristotle

Plato's most notable student was Aristotle (384–322 B.C.E.). After Plato's death, Aristotle founded a school in Athens called the Lyceum. Although Aristotle disagreed with certain arguments advanced by Plato, such as the nature of Forms, he essentially continued his teacher's approach, and refined many of Plato's concepts. According to Aristotle, "the human good turns out to be activity of soul in accordance with virtue, and if there are more than one virtue, in accordance with the best and most complete."[36] More specifically, Aristotle argued that happiness (*eudaimonia*) for a human being is a life in which rational intelligence is active in accordance with virtue or excellence. He drew this conclusion from his beliefs that rational intelligence is humanity's most distinctive capacity and "the good" for any given thing is to exercise its distinctive capacity with excellence. Following in the tradition of Socrates and Plato, who exemplified philosophy as a way of life inextricably linked to the acquisition of virtue, Aristotle asserted that the true philosopher does not merely theorize about virtue but lives in such a way as to become virtuous.

In addition to his insightfulness in ethical philosophy, Aristotle was one of the greatest scientists of antiquity. His research and methodology served as the Western world's authoritative standard for centuries after his death. Aristotle made unprecedented advancements in many areas of research, particularly in logic and biology. However, he was no less interested in theology. He interpreted all natural processes, including the motion of the planets, as striving toward God. Specifically, as Werner Jaeger explicated, "[Aristotle] understands by 'theology' that fundamental branch of philosophical science which he also calls 'first philosophy' or 'science of first principles' – the branch which later acquires the name 'metaphysics' or 'science of the first principles' among his followers. In this sense theology is the ultimate and highest goal of all philosophical study of Being."[37] Jaeger states that Aristotle used the term "theology" in different ways. Sometimes, especially in historical contexts, theology for Aristotle meant the mythical theology of the poets, which he critiques; in other instances, it referred to what has been called natural theology, or metaphysics, which, according to Aristotle, is a superior way of thinking about the divine.[38]

> **Aristotle believed that the best human activity is the contemplation of God**

Aristotle described God as Nous – the divine Mind or Intellect. Concerning God, Aristotle concluded: "It must be of itself that the divine thought thinks (since it is the most excellent of things), and its thinking is a thinking on thinking."[39] For Aristotle, God is perfect actuality and the first principle of all motion and existence. What this means is that, ultimately, all change in the cosmos originates from this one unchanging source. Thus, God is eternal and considered the "Primal Mover" or "Unmoved Mover." God causes change without undergoing change, as an object of love moves and affects the lover. Ultimately, the whole cosmos is set in motion by the love for this complete actuality, which is God. Aristotle believed that the best human activity is the contemplation of God. Aristotle wrote:

> Whatever mode of choosing and of acquiring things good by nature – whether goods of body or wealth or friends or the other goods – will best promote contemplation of God, that is the best mode, and that standard is the finest; and any mode of choice and acquisition that either through deficiency or excess hinders us from serving and from contemplating God – that is a bad one.[40]

THE HELLENISTIC AGE AND THE ROMAN PERIOD

By means of ambitious diplomacy and military force, the Macedonian king Philip II (382–336 B.C.E.) united the Greeks and the Macedonians (who later considered themselves to be Greek). Later, Philip's creation was known as the League of Corinth. As of 338 B.C.E., when all the Greek states came under the control of Philip, individual Greek cities would never again be fully sovereign polities. In 336 B.C.E., Philip's son, Alexander III of Macedonia, who had once been a student of Aristotle, inherited a remarkably strong army and a substantial kingdom from his father. Alexander soon launched one of the greatest military conquests in history, which eventually reached as far east as India. Alexander conquered Asia Minor, Syria, Lebanon, Egypt, Babylonia, and Persia. In Egypt, where he founded the city of Alexandria, he was crowned and honored as pharaoh. It is believed that he visited and honored the oracle of the Egyptian god Amon (identified by the Greeks as Zeus). Historians hold various views of Alexander; however, all scholars agree that he was driven by a vision of creating a world monarchy. His reign marked the beginning of the Hellenistic Age (323 B.C.E.–146 B.C.E.), in which Greek culture, including Greek language and educational standards, were infused across his vast conquests.[41]

The Isis Mysteries

By 146 B.C.E., all of Greece and Macedonia had fallen under Roman domination. During this period, the Egyptian goddess Isis became a universal deity among many Greeks and

Romans. Isis was particularly popular among women, and the worship of Isis extended as far as Spain. The cult of Isis held various religious services, including great festivals in which devotees took part in a dramatic play which demonstrated the story of Osiris and the sorrows of Isis. During the second century C.E., the Roman writer Apuleius, in his work entitled *The Golden Ass* (also known as *Transformations*), penned an allegorical story about the spiritual transformation available to worshipers of Isis. The depiction of Isis as the one universal God is clearly asserted. In Apuleius' story, Isis declares:

> I am Nature, the universal Mother, mistress of all the elements, primordial child of time, sovereign of all things spiritual, queen of the dead, queen also of the immortals, the single manifestation of all gods and goddesses that are … I am worshipped in many aspects, known by countless names, and propitiated with all manner of different rites, yet the whole round earth venerates me.[42]

Apuleius described his initiation experience into the cult of Isis as a symbolic death and spiritual rebirth. A large temple of Isis was built in Rome during the rule of Emperor Caligula (37–41 C.E.).

Plotinus and the Neoplatonic Tradition

A profound contribution to Western philosophy and mysticism stems from Plotinus (204–270 C.E.), who was the father of the Neoplatonist tradition. Neoplatonism, often referred to as the "Religion of Platonism," included such spiritual and philosophical teachers as Plotinus, Porphyry (*c*.233–309 C.E.), Iamblichus (*c*.242–327 C.E.), and the last great Neoplatonist, Proclus (411–85 C.E.). Neoplatonists, in general, conceived of Plato as "the master," and they interpreted his works with particular emphasis on his mystical tendencies. In general, they endorsed Plato's assertion that philosophy was a transformative discipline that can make a person "like the gods,"[43] and that philosophy was ultimately "practice for death and dying."[44]

> The Neoplatonists endorsed Plato's assertion that philosophy was a transformative discipline that can make a person "like the gods"

Plotinus was from Alexandria (in Egypt), and he eventually moved to Rome, where he established a school of philosophy. He was a student of Ammonius Saccas (*c*.175–242 C.E.) and considered himself an expounder, or commentator, on Plato. Plotinus' philosophy, like that of later Neoplatonists, is a synthesis of Greek philosophical thought – especially that of Plato, Aristotle, and the Stoics. Revered as a spiritual leader by his students, Plotinus is generally regarded as one of the greatest metaphysicians in all of Western philosophy. Porphyry, Plotinus' student, claimed that "the god who has neither shape nor form, and is set above intellect and all that is intelligible, appeared to this daemonic man [Plotinus] as time after time he drove himself on towards the first and transcendent god, with his own reflections and according to the ways set forth by Plato in the *Symposium* [Plato's dialogue on love]."[45] According to the scholar E. R. Dodds, Plotinus' philosophical system has two goals: "first, to furnish a rational account of the Reality implied in experience; secondly, to place the individual in direct contact with this Reality."[46] Plotinus' system, which forms the basis of the entire Neoplatonic tradition, is a rational pursuit of God that, at its summit, aims at achieving union with the Divine through philosophical contemplation. Plotinus' work, *The Enneads*, consists of treatises arranged and edited by his disciple Porphyry; the work remains the greatest legacy of Neoplatonic philosophy.

Plotinus referred to God as the self-sufficient "One" or as "the Good." For Plotinus, the One is non-spatial, unchangeable, eternal, and ultimately beyond all human conception. Plotinus' metaphysics is based on a hypostatic trinity (or three levels of existence) in which the One takes precedence as the Ultimate Reality and is known as the first hypostasis (or underlying reality) from which emanates all else. The second hypostasis is the Intellect or Intelligence (*nous*), and the third is the Soul (*psyche*). According to Plotinus, the One (*to hen*), the first hypostasis, turns inwards upon Itself and effortlessly emanates Intelligence (*nous*). For Plotinus, Plato's Forms – those archetypal and unchanging realities – are the thoughts of the divine Intellect (*nous*), the second hypostasis. In some sense, the Forms, such as Justice and Beauty, are the thoughts of God. Apart from emanating the platonic Forms, the Intellect (*nous*) also emanates the Cosmic Soul (*psyche*). This Cosmic Soul, the third hypostasis, is the creative force that forms the sensible realm and supplies the power of life to all things. The Cosmic Soul, or World Soul, mysteriously individuates Itself into human souls.

The human soul's pilgrimage, or ascent, through the three hypostases, or levels of reality, is identified by Plotinus as the spiritual path to salvation – the flight of the alone to the Alone. In the words of E. R. Dodds, the mystical journey of Plotinus' Neoplatonist philosophy posits that "man's centre and God's centre are identical, and the individual finds salvation by an ascent which is no barren process of abstraction but a conversion or reversion to God and at the same time an inversion upon his own deepest self."[47] According to Plotinus, the human soul has a higher or divine aspect, which, if actualized, can contemplate the higher orders and therefore detach itself from the material realm by means of a spiritual and contemplative process of purification. However, the soul also has a lower base-side, which, without the cultivation of philosophy and ascetic purity, can entrap itself within the sensual realm. Later, some Neoplatonists incorporated spiritual disciplines, such as theurgy (religiously inspired rituals and magical sacraments which were thought to influence cosmic harmony and invoke the presence of spirits), alongside an ascetic lifestyle centered on the practice of philosophy. It is recorded that like Pythagoras, Socrates, and Plato, the Neoplatonists Plotinus, Porphyry, and Proclus all observed a vegetarian diet and were highly concerned with moral imperatives toward all living beings.

The Advent of Christianity

The Roman emperor Constantine (r. 306–337 C.E.) eventually converted to Christianity, and it was during his reign that the persecution of Christians under Roman authorities ceased. During the reign of the emperor Theodosius (r. 379–395 C.E.), Christianity became the official state religion of the Roman Empire; eventually it was the only accepted religion. Hostile to "pagan" religions, Roman Christian authorities slowly wiped out the mystery religions (in Rome, Egypt, and Greece) and propagated a practice of forced conversions throughout the area. During the rule of the emperor Justinian (r. 527–65), the last Platonic philosophy schools were destroyed. Greek views concerning the availability of Providence, prophecy, and divination (by way of shamanic trances, oracles, mantic speech, ecstatic communion, and dreams) were at odds with the Christian Church. These traditional practices and beliefs were seen by Christian authorities as demonic (of, or belonging to, the devil or demons), as opposed to the Greek view that they were daimonic practices (of, or relating to, divinity or the spirit world).

CHAPTER SUMMARY

The ancient Greeks cultivated many different modes of religious thinking, each of which made important contributions to the religious diversity of Greek culture. The eighteenth-century German playwright Friedrich Schiller was impressed by the refined culture of the Greeks, and wrote: "In fullness of form no less than of content, at once philosophic and creative, sensitive and energetic, the Greeks combined the first youth of imagination with the manhood of reason in a glorious manifestation of humanity."[48] For the Greeks, the divine presence, abstracted in many ways, was available in daily life through oracles and divination. They embraced the divine in both the aesthetic and the physical; they also participated in esoteric religious mysteries which facilitated profound religious experiences and communion with the divine. The plethora of religious and philosophical paths within ancient Greece was not exclusionary. A Greek could participate in communal sacrifices to Zeus, recite Homeric poetry, study Greek philosophy, visit the Oracle at Delphi, and participate in initiation rites at the Eleusian Mysteries. In other words,

> **The ancient Greeks cultivated many different modes of religious thinking**

participation in one movement did not entail exclusion from another (although there were moments and places, such as in fifth-century Athens, when it was difficult to engage in philosophy without running afoul of the religious authorities).

The most distinctive legacy of the ancient Greeks, however, lies in their philosophical achievements. In fact, they are the pillars on which the entire tradition of Western philosophy (and, in some sense, theology) rests. The poet W. H. Auden concluded:

> I can think of no better way of indicating what we owe to Greece than *drawing distinctions*, for of all intellectual acts, that is perhaps the most characteristically Greek. It is they who have taught us, not to think – that all human beings have always done – but to think about our thinking, to ask such questions as "What do I think?", "What do this and that other person or people think?", "On what do we agree and disagree, and why?"[49]

A keen ability for discernment enabled the Greeks to attain extraordinary achievements in philosophy, psychology, science, and theology – all of which were one system of inquiry – *philosophia* – the love of wisdom. Greek philosophers, such as those discussed in this chapter, did not specialize in particular fields of knowledge, but developed holistic worldviews. For the Pythagoreans and Platonists, for example, mathematics and science were sacred methods for acquiring insight into the divine. Most trends of Greek philosophy, although rigorously logical and rational, culminated in theology and, in some cases, ecstasy. In general, Greek philosophy was, therefore, a spiritual way of life which was closely linked with maieutics (the process of inner knowing through introspection) and the acquisition of virtue.

Zoroastrian fire temple

CHAPTER 5

THE ZOROASTRIAN FAITH

In this world may obedience triumph over dis-
    obedience,

May peace triumph over discord,

May generosity triumph over niggardliness,

May love triumph over contempt,

May the true-spoken word triumph over the
    false-spoken word,

May truth triumph over falsehood.[1]

                – Yasna 60.5

INTRODUCTION

Zoroastrians (or Zarathushtis) believe that Zoroaster (Zarathustra) was a prophet of God who reinvigorated and transformed ancient Persia into a disciplined, spiritual society rooted in ethical principles.

Although Zoroastrians, who often refer to their religion simply as *veh-din* ("the Good Religion"), can be found worldwide, the majority live in Iran and India. The contemporary population of Zoroastrians is comparatively small, yet the influence of Zoroastrian ideas on the development of reli-

> **That nature alone is good that refrains from doing unto another whatsoever is not good for itself** *Dadistan-i-Dinik 94.5*
>
> **THE GOLDEN RULE**

gious thought has been profound. The scholar Mary Boyce notes that the Zoroastrian tradition gave rise to the first recorded "doctrines of an individual judgment, Heaven and Hell, the future resurrection of the body, the general Last Judgment, and life everlasting for the reunited soul and body."[2] These ideas, some of which are similar to those of ancient Egypt, spread throughout Central Asia, the Middle East, and the Mediterranean, due in part to the expansive influence of the classical Persian Empire(s).

    The Zoroastrian religion emerged during what some

Timeline

*c.*2000–1000 B.C.E.
Aryan migration into
    Iranian plateau

*c.*1200 B.C.E.
Life of prophet Zoroaster
    (dates are contested)

549–330 B.C.E.
Achaemenid Empire

*c.*580–529 B.C.E.
Persian Emperor Cyrus II

*c.*549–486 B.C.E.
Darius I

334 B.C.E.
Alexander III of
    Macedonia defeats
    Persian Empire

247 B.C.E.–30 C.E.
Parthian Empire

226–651 C.E.
Sassanian Empire

276 C.E.
Manichaean prophet
    Mani put on trial,
    condemned to prison,
    and killed

651 C.E.
Last Sassanian king
    captured by Arabian
    army

7–8th centuries C.E.
A number of
    Zoroastrians flee from
    persecution in Islamic
    Persia to India (where
    they become known as
    Parsees)

scholars see as a transitional period in human development. The philosopher Karl Jaspers, for example, describes this period in history as the Axial Age (*c.*800–200 B.C.E.), a time that ushered forth a revolution in the structure of both human civilization and consciousness. Jaspers suggests that it was during this epoch that "the spiritual foundations of humanity were laid, simultaneously and independently … And these are the foundations upon which humanity still subsists today."[3] Jaspers cites the importance of Axial teachers in triggering this change, including Zoroaster, the Jewish prophets, the luminaries of India (the mystics of the Upanishads and the Buddha) and China (such as Confucius and Lao Tzu), as well as the philosopher-mystics of ancient Greece (see the previous chapter for examples). Continuing Jasper's line of interpretation, Karen Armstrong described the paradigm shift of the Axial Age in her book *The Great Transformation*:

> Before the Axial Age, ritual and animal sacrifice had been central to the religious quest. You experienced the divine in sacred dramas that, like a great theatrical experience today, introduced you to another level of existence. The Axial sages changed this … Their objective was to create an entirely different kind of human being. All the sages preached a spirituality of empathy and compassion; they insisted that people must abandon their egotism and greed, their violence and unkindness. Not only was it wrong to kill another human being; you must not even speak a hostile word or make an irritable gesture. Further, nearly all the Axial sages realized that you could not confine your benevolence to your own people: your concern must somehow extend to the whole world.[4]

Armstrong asserts that the vision taught by Axial teachers "was so radical that later generations tended to dilute it. In the process, they often produced exactly the kind of religiosity that the Axial reformers wanted to get rid of."[5] Determining whether later generations failed to live up to the initial, liberating impulses of these teachings exceeds our purpose here; it is sufficient to note, however, that the spiritual outpouring of the Axial Age forms the bedrock of contemporary religious thought.

Concepts identified with the Axial period include the idea of a transcendent center of the self; the development of systematic methods for training the heart and mind; a general realization of causality and independent laws of nature; and an overall sense of moral responsibility and justice. Along with these issues, Zoroaster was particularly influential in the development of monotheistic thought and other important concepts, such as the role of free will in religious soteriology (the process of salvation) and the understanding of history as teleological (moving toward a specific end or culmination). These concepts, like others found in the Zoroastrian faith, were of particular importance to the theologies that emerged later among the Semitic peoples of the Middle East (as witnessed in the Jewish, Christian, and Islamic faiths).

THE INDO-ARYANS

Scholars believe that an ancient group of tribes, who called themselves Aryans (or "nobles"), migrated from the Russian steppes into Eastern Europe, Central Asia, and northern India sometime around the second millennium B.C.E. This wave of migration may have been fueled by a newfound power informed by the domestication of animals (such as horse transportation) and metallurgy (which allowed high-quality swords to be produced). Scholars believe this conglomeration of tribes, referred to as the Proto-Indo-Aryans, shared a common culture and religion. It is therefore not surprising that the pre-Zoroastrian religion of Persia and the Vedic–Hindu religion of India (discussed in the next chapter) run parallel in many regards, including a shared pantheon of gods, rituals, sacrifices, priestly caste and social hierarchy. Remnants of the Indo-Aryan tradition are, for example, clearly visible in the oldest of the Hindu sacred texts, the *Rig Veda*.

The Indo-Aryan is thought to have "regarded … [any] natural phenomenon not as 'it' but as 'thou', as a fellow living entity."[6] This implied belief in a plurality of spiritual forces, known as *mainyu*s, identified with animate and inanimate elements, as well as emotions and abstract principles. Central to this spiritual universe were the gods, known as *ahura*s (Sanskrit, *asura*s) or "lords," and the "shining ones" or *daeva*s (Sanskrit, *deva*s). Different gods were identified with different spheres of cosmic and earthly influence, and it seems that different segments of society (such as priests, warriors, and workers) revered the god considered to enjoy the greatest influence over their social and occupational life. All such gods, however, were understood as subordinate to an overriding principle of cosmic order and truth, known as *asha* (Sanskrit, *rta*). In fact, to the Avestan-speaking Aryans the most important *ahura*s – Mitra, Varuna, and Mazda – were viewed as guardians of *asha*. Like the concept of *ma'at* in Egyptian civilization, *asha* was, in this way, the centerpiece of civilization – it was that which placed humanity in right relationship with the divine. To fall away from this principle was to come under the influence of the opposing force in the universe, or *druj* (Sanskrit, *druh*), a condition associated with chaos.

As the Indo-Aryan peoples developed new technologies, such as weapons and the horse-cart, it appears that many Aryan tribes transitioned from a peaceful, pastoral culture into a violent, marauding warrior society. From the viewpoint of those that strove to maintain *asha* – a way of life that sought peace, respected animals, honored the gods, and valued self-sacrifice as intrinsic to the life-process – these changes must have been attributed to the power of *druj*. As the heroic warrior mentality rose to prominence, so too did worship of Indra, who at that time was viewed as a god of war, as well as the seemingly morally ambiguous *daeva*s. The prophet Zoroaster, who was born during this tumultuous period, seems to have turned his ardent meditations instead on Lord Mazda, who was identified with wisdom and justice. Zoroaster, unlike his counterparts in India, came to the view the *daeva*s as evil;[7] his realization, however, went further than simple negation – he expounded a new monotheistic theology that would change the world.

THE PROPHET ZOROASTER

There is not enough factual information to date Zoroaster's life with any certainty, and many traditional accounts are of the mythic type and include stories of miraculous events. Many dates have been suggested for his birth, all of which are highly contested; some scholars, however, propose that Zoroaster was born around 1200 B.C.E. It is believed that he was the son of a Persian landowner and that he later assumed the occupation of priest (*zaotar*). Zoroaster was, in that way, trained in the practices of the prevailing Indo-Aryan religion, including rituals, sacred chants, and contemplative disciplines. For example, the scholar Mary Boyce points out that Zoroaster "is the only founder of a credal religion who was both priest and prophet."[8] In fact, Zoroaster refers to himself as a *mantram* (one who speaks inspired utterances) and can be likened to an *ereshi* (or mystic seer, known as *rishi* in Vedic India). His revelations – which were originally retained in oral tradition by chanting – are prophetic utterances or *manthra*s.

By the time he was a young adult, Zoroaster was disheartened by the prevalence of corruption and moral decadence among his people. As noted, the peaceful, pastoral way of life of the elder Indo-Iranians had been rejected by warlike tribes that attacked other groups and mistreated animals as part of the brutal raids they enjoyed conducting. This general disregard for morality, including honesty in word and deed, may have been part of Zoroaster's deep antipathy for the status quo and his reason for embarking on a spiritual quest. The scholar Joseph Campbell identified common themes in the lives of many mystics, prophets, and mythic heroes which exemplify Zoroaster's journey to prophethood: departure from society; enduring of ordeals, temptations, trials, and tribulations; attainment of a definitive spiritual transformation; and subsequent return to society with a new realization, message, or boon.[9]

In the case of Zoroaster, he had become acutely aware that the world around him was infected with a spiritual malady. Just as a physician would seek a cure for a bodily ailment, Zoroaster sought an understanding capable of bringing individuals and society back into accord with the true nature of reality. His search led him to abandon societal life and to inhabit a cave in a remote mountainous region; there, he spent numerous years in ascetic solitude, overcoming various challenges while devoting himself to moral uprightness, prayer, chanting, contemplation, and meditation. Juxtaposed to the social chaos that had engulfed his society, he sought realities that transcend decay, corruption, and change. In the elements of nature and the celestial bodies he discovered elements that appeared constant and demonstrated cyclic regularity. He affirmed, as his ancestors did, that all things were regulated by an overarching cosmic principle called *asha* (known as *rta* in Sanskrit and later termed *dharma* by Hindus). Zoroaster, however, came to see that this regulatory law – the basis of cosmic and civilizational order – is the will of God, the Creator of all things, whom he called Ahura Mazda, or "the Wise Lord":

> **Zoroaster had become acutely aware that the world around him was infected with a spiritual malady**

> When I conceived of Thee, O Mazda,
> As the very First and the Last
> As the Most Adorable One,
> As the Father of Good Thought,
> As the Creator of the Eternal Law of Truth and Right,
> As the Lord Judge of our actions in Life,
> Then I made a place for Thee in my eyes.[10]

With the advent of his revelation – and his quest to realign society with truth, justice, and order – Zoroaster set forth on a sacred mission to teach; in doing so, he expunged what he saw as corrupt practices, including forms of animal sacrifice and irreverent use of hallucinogens (or *hoama*, the Vedic *soma* discussed in the next chapter). Understood in context, Zoroaster's teachings were revolutionary because they challenged the self-serving habits of his day, and he frequently chastised and provoked the priestly establishment. This situation may help explain why Zoroaster, like other prophets, was initially rejected by his own people.

HISTORY

In Afghanistan (which was part of the Persian Empire), Zoroaster's teachings came to the attention of a local ruler, Prince Vishtaspa. Vishtaspa's wife converted to the new faith, and it was she who led the way for Vishtaspa himself to embrace the prophet's teachings. As a new believer, Prince Vishtaspa became thoroughly devoted to his adopted faith. Committed to proclaiming the new religion throughout his land and beyond, Vishtaspa began by spreading relevant teachings to his senior advisors and officials, who, because of their status and high offices, were highly influential. As Zoroaster's message spread across ancient Persia by way of missionary movements, significant opposition to the new religion arose. Amid continuing hostilities, the followers of Zoroaster were eventually compelled to fight in defense of their religion. In his late seventies, Zoroaster himself fell prey to violence in the city of Balkh (in modern Afghanistan), where he was killed by marauding chieftains.

Zoroaster may have been killed while performing a rite of the faith he proclaimed, but his teachings concerning Ahura Mazda survived his death and spread within the Iranian cultural continent − a vast area that includes Afghanistan, Armenia, Azerbaijan, Bahrain, Georgia, Iran, Iraq, Tajikistan, Uzbekistan, Western China, and greater Kurdistan. An important aspect in the growth and influence of Zoroastrian teachings − including the legendary lore of Zoroaster that reached non-Persians, such as the Greeks and Romans − was the rise of the Persian Empire. For example, Zoroaster's basic religious disposition (i.e. worship of Ahura Mazda) seems to have been upheld by the Persian emperor Cyrus II (d. 529 B.C.E.), though whether Cyrus the Great held allegiance specifically to Zoroaster's teachings remains a subject of scholarly debate. Cyrus, who conquered most of Central Asia, South Asia, and Egypt, among other places, founded the Achaemenid dynasty, which bore witness to Persia's most famed and powerful period. Cyrus is widely noted for his sense of cultural and religious tolerance. He allowed conquered regions to govern themselves (as provinces) and to worship freely − a notion in step with the Zoroastrian emphasis on choice and free will as determining factors in the trajectory of one's life. When Cyrus conquered Babylonia, he freed the Jewish people who were held in captivity there, and allowed them to return to Jerusalem. For this act, Cyrus was hailed as a messiah in the Jewish Bible (Isaiah 45:1). Also significant was Cyrus' uniting of Greater Persia with conquered regions inhabited by the Medians. The priestly clan of the Medes, the Magi, adopted Zoroastrian ideals and became influential in development of the Zoroastrian faith.

Another important figure of the Achaemenid dynasty was Darius I (d. 486 B.C.E.), who facilitated the development of the Persian Empire through great building projects − including the library at the city of Persepolis. Inscriptions from the period bear witness to Darius' allegiance to, and worship of, Ahura Mazda.[11] Eventually, the Achaemenid dynasty launched two invasions of Greece that resulted in a series of decisive land and sea battles, including at Marathon (492 B.C.E.) and off the island of Salamis (480 B.C.E.). The temporarily united Greek city-states, however, defeated both Persian incursions by the slimmest of margins. In 334 B.C.E., Alexander III of Macedon (known to history as Alexander the Great), citing the need to avenge the Persian invasions, attacked Persia, defeated the empire, and ended the Achaemenid dynasty. During Alexander's invasion, his forces destroyed Persepolis − and, with it, possibly, Avestan texts. A period of Greek rule in Persia ensued under the Seleucids, a dynasty named after a Greek general who inherited a portion of Alexander's empire when it was partitioned after his death in 323 B.C.E. In the late third century B.C.E., an indigenous tribe called the Parni overthrew Seleucid rule and established the Parthian Empire. The powerful Parthians (or Arsacids) conquered both Syria and Jerusalem, and repeatedly opposed with force Roman attempts to expand their empire in the east.

The Sassanians, from the southern region of Iran, overthrew the Parthian dynasty in the third century of the Common Era. In some ways, the Zoroastrian religion, as it is known today institutionally, took shape during the Sassanian era (226–651 C.E.). Scholars, for example, suggest that Zoroastrian religious practice before this period differed region to region in accord with local traditions, although the worship of Ahura Mazda was widespread during the Achaemenid dynasty. In light of its status as the official state religion of the Sassanian emperors, a canon of Zoroastrian scriptures was solidified, epic traditions redacted, and efforts were made to unify a set of beliefs for all Zoroastrian communities. It was also during this period that the Zoroastrian faith was politicized, leading in some cases to priestly rigidity, ethnocentrism, and intolerance. This period witnessed persecution of adherents of other religions as well as newly formed ones, including followers of Manichaeism (see below).

The Sassanian period, however, would be the last in which the Zoroastrian religion was a majority religion in any land. In the seventh century of the Common Era, the Arabs conquered Persia, toppled the Sassanian Empire, and established Islam as the official religion of the state. Many of these Arab migrants, and later converts to Islam, were hostile to Zoroastrians and their practices. Later invasions of Persia by the Turks and Mongols led to periods of severe persecution that further reduced the size of the Zoroastrian community. During the long history of Islamic Persia, the Zoroastrians have been victims of social ostracism, forced conversions, and even genocide. Because of such persecution, some Zoroastrians fled their native Persia and took refuge in India, where they eventually came to be called "Parsees" (or "those who came from Persia").[12] In India, the Parsees have enjoyed religious freedom and prosperity amongst a people who regard spiritual diversity as a natural aspect of their culture.

> **The Zoroastrians have been victims of social ostracism, forced conversions, and even genocide**

SCRIPTURES

The language of the Proto-Indo-Aryans, before their migratory dispersion, is thought by linguists to be the source of the Indo-European family of languages, a linguistic grouping

Top: Zoroastrian priests perform a hand clasp ritual
Bottom: A head priest offers a prayer at a fire temple, Bombay

which includes the Celtic, Germanic, Italic, Balto-Slavic, Hellenic, Albanian, Armenian, and Indo-Iranian tongues. Notably, within the Indo-Iranian branch there are two important related languages: Sanskrit, the sacred language of the Hindus, and the Gathic Avestan, or Old Persian language. Gathic Avestan was the language of the prophet Zoroaster; similarly, the corpus of Zoroastrian scriptures also bears the name Avesta. The central and most important holy book within the Avesta is the liturgy text known as the Yasna; contained within the Yasna are the five Gathas – the only writings attributed to the prophet Zoroaster (except for Yasna 51).[13] Though a considerable amount of Zoroastrian writings were lost or destroyed during periods of subjugation or persecution, there are also other texts in a later dialect of Avestan (or Younger Avestan), such as the Yasht, containing epic literature; the Vivevdad, containing purificatory laws; and the Visparad, containing litanies. In later periods of Zoroastrian history a number of other writings were produced in the language of Pahlavi, or Middle Persian, such as the Dinkard and Bundahishn, among others.

ZOROASTRIAN THEOLOGY

Zoroaster's monotheistic perspective, similar to the proclamations of early biblical writings and the Egyptian pharaoh Akhenaton, does not deny the existence of lesser gods – rather, Zoroaster proclaimed that there is one self-existent, self-effulgent God from which all things, lesser gods included, originate. This kind of metaphysics – a position sometimes referred to as the great "chain of being" – implies that reality is manifested in a series of levels or degrees – at the apex of which is the Godhead (or God beyond knowable attributes). In accord with this notion, Zoroastrians hold that Ahura Mazda is

> **Zoroaster proclaimed that there is one self-existent, self-effulgent God**

both independent and beyond His creation (or transcendent) as well as present (or immanent) throughout the entirety of creation. The Zoroastrian scholar Farhang Mehr explains how:

> [Ahura Mazda] … manifests himself in the entire creation. He is present everywhere in the cosmos: in the grains of sands, in the seeds of the plants, in the being of animals, and in the spirit of man. He is in and with, as well as out and beyond, all creations. He is beyond time and space, though time and space are with and in him. All creations exist in the presence of God.[14]

Meditation on the divine presence in the here and now can invoke a sense of awe, mystery, paradox, and unity, and is a practice utilized by many mystical traditions. Later Iranian mystics, utilizing Zoroastrian symbols, referred to God as the Light of lights (*nur al-answar*) whose radiant luminosity, in various degrees, can be known through a type of spiritual insight called "knowledge by presence" (*al-ʿilm al-huduri*).

An important mystical teaching in the Gathas connects the origin of all things with the thought of God; in other words, this complex, multi-tiered reality, consisting of celestial (*manahya*) and terrestrial (*gaethya*) worlds, bodies (*tanu*), and souls (*urvan*), is understood to emanate from the thought of the Living Lord:

> Ahura Mazda's First Thought
> blazed into myriads of sparks of light
> and filled the entire heavens.
> He Himself, in His Wisdom,
> is the Creator of Truth which
> upholds His Supreme Mind.
> O Ahura Mazda,
> You who are eternally the same...[15]

From this perspective, it is from the mind of God that the phenomenal world bursts forth, infusing all things with "sparks of light," as well as the attributes of God. The most important attributes include Vohu Manah (good mind), Asha[16] (truth, order, and righteousness), Shathra (good power), Armaiti (devotion and goodwill), Haurvatat (perfection), and Ameretat (immortality). These attributes, which are also understood as subordinate entities or spirits (the Amesha Spentas or Bountiful Immortals), are powers that affect the cosmos and which are capable of entering into a worthy aspirant. A seeker may "participate in or conform his life to the first four of these qualities of God [the Amesha Spentas listed above]. The last two, Perfection [or Haurvatat] and Immortality [or Ameretat], cannot be won by man; they are bestowed as gifts to those who seek the other qualities."[17] In other words, the Amesha Spentas are objective spirits – extensions of Ahura Mazda – that are honored and revered by practitioners; subjectively speaking, however, they can be embodied, and represent, in an esoteric way, spiritual qualities developed from within.

The Zoroastrian way can be characterized as a path that aims to actualize Good Mind (Vohu Manah) and other divine qualities by living in accord with spiritual principles and acquiring the virtues that reflect those principles. Evil (or ignorance), however, inhibits an individual from realizing their spiritual nature. Committing evil acts means going astray from the path of Truth (Asha), thereby obscuring one's innate (divine) potential. Theologically, evil is not understood as an aspect or attribute of God: Ahura Mazda is believed to transcend all opposites, including good and evil. It is, however, the very duality of good and evil – symbolically, light and dark – that Zoroastrians see as defining the human predicament. This (ethical) dualism between what is good and what is not is explained in Zoroastrian scriptures with reference to two opposing *mainyu*s ("spirits" or "mentalities") – Spenta Mainyu, the Holy Spirit, and Angra Mainyu, the Evil Spirit.

It is important to note, however, that the following explication of the Holy (or Benevolent) Sprit and the Evil (or Malevolent) Spirit utilizes the Gathas as the preeminent exegetical (or interpretive) authority. Some later developments proposed two ultimate principles – called Ohrmazd and Ahriman in Middle Persian – indicating a type of cosmic dualism that seemingly compromises the monotheistic doctrine explained above. These later developments (aspects of which can be seen in some Younger Avestan and Pahlavi texts) are, by and large, viewed as deviations or heresies by Zoroastrian traditionalists; they also appear to contradict both the ancient Gathic viewpoint (attributed to Zoroaster himself) and the contemporary self-representation of Zoroastrians.

According to the Gathas, Angra Mainyu and Spenta Mainyu are twin, primordial Spirits. Angra Mainyu (the Evil Spirit) acted in opposition to Spenta Mainyu (the Holy Spirit or creative principle of God) and chose a path contrary to Asha (cosmic order, truth, righteousness, etc.). In the Gathas this apparently archetypal happening is described as follows: "Of these two Spirits the Wicked One chose achieving the worst things. The Most Holy Spirit … chose right, and (so do those) who satisfy Lord Mazda continually with rightful acts."[18] In that sense, those who follow the path of Angra Mainyu, the Deceiver (Dregvant), are followers of the great lie or falsehood (*druj*); on the other hand, those who are led by Spenta Mainyu are followers of truth (*asha*), and are just (*ashavan*). The scholar Mircea Eliade elaborates the implications of this view as follows:

> Zarathustra's theology is not dualistic in the strict sense of the term, since Ahura Mazdā is not confronted by an anti-god; in the beginning, the opposition breaks out between the two Spirits. On the other hand, the unity between Ahura Mazdā and the Holy Spirit is several times implied (see Yasna 43.3, etc.). In short, Good and Evil, the holy one and the destroying demon, proceed from Ahura Mazdā; but since Angra Mainyu freely chose his mode of being and his maleficent vocation, the Wise Lord cannot be considered responsible for the appearance of Evil. On the other hand, Ahura Mazdā, in his omniscience, knew from the beginning what choice the Destroying Spirit would make and nevertheless did not prevent it; this may mean either that God transcends all kinds of contradictions or that the existence of evil constitutes the preliminary condition for human freedom.[19]

Parallel to the primordial choice made by Spenta Mainyu and Angra Mainyu, i.e. whether to choose good or evil, Zoroastrians believe that humans are volitional beings, endowed with a conscience (*daena*) and the freedom to choose (free will). From this perspective, there is no coercion in religion, or any other aspect of life. It is left to each individual to find the path of Truth, and not for others, god or human, to impose by wrath or guilt. In the Gathas it is proclaimed:

> With your penetrating mind discriminate
> between these twin mentalities,
> man by man, each one for his own self.[20]

Similarly, Zoroastrian teachings posit that an individual's character and destiny are the direct result of their actions: "words and deeds bear fruit, evil comes to the evil, a good reward to the good."[21] "Reward," in this context, is the natural result of a system of cause and effect; for just as the law of *asha* – which emanates from God – regulates and orders a coherent universe, so does it regulate moral causality – in this life and the next.[22]

Choosing goodness over evil, and upholding truth in opposition to falsehood, not only has soteriological value (relating to salvation), but eschatological implications (relating to last, or final, issues, such as the end of time). Those who endeavor in the cause of truth – by way of good thoughts, words, and deeds – ultimately play a role in cleansing the world of evil and bringing about the great restoration (*frashokereti*) at the end of days. In doing so, one becomes a *saoshyant*, a deliverer or savior, as Zoroaster was himself. In fact, humanity is bestowed with the exalted position of being a fellow-worker, or *hamkar*, in the cause of truth; a cause which aims at the spiritual transformation of life, the renewal of existence, the restoration of the blissful primordial perfection. Accordingly, Zoroaster in the Gathas passionately asks:

Zoroastrians believe that humans are volitional beings, endowed with a conscience and free will

> When will the just overcome the wicked, O Mazdā?
> Then indeed
> will come about the wondrous renewal of life.[23]

In later Pahlavi (or Middle Persian) texts, the term *saoshyant* is rendered as *soshyos*, and also refers to the coming of three messianic saviors, miraculously born from the seed of Zoroaster by virgins. It is prophesied that these messianic figures will perform miracles and greatly advance humanity toward the great restoration or *frashokereti*. The tradition surrounding these saviors was explained by the scholar Farhang Mehr as follows:

> Pahlavi writers assert that the three Saoshyants will come in the last millennia before the end of the world, at regular intervals, each at the end of a millennium. The first millennium belongs to Hoshidar, which is the Persian word for the Avestan Ukhshyat-ereta. The second millennium is that of Hoshidar mah, the Persian rendering of the Avestan Ukhshyat-nemah. The third or the last one is Soshyos, or Saoshyant proper.[24]

Also found in Pahlavi texts are the concepts of a final judgment, an apocalyptic end of time, and a bodily resurrection. One tradition holds that an individual who exemplifies goodness throughout his or her lifetime will successfully cross the Bridge of Separation (or Chinvat Bridge) and enter paradise. On the other hand, one whose actions are characterized by evil will be cast off from the bridge into the fires of hell. Hell is described as the "Abode of the Lie" (Drujo-Demana), a place of intense suffering, darkness, and despair. The righteous, by contrast, attain the "Abode of Song" (Garo Demana), a heavenly realm of light, joy, and spiritual fulfillment. Many Zoroastrians, however, do not interpret matters of heaven and hell literally; instead, they understand such concepts as connoting "mentalities."

MITHRA AND MANICHAEISM

The changes of habit that Zoroaster's teachings demanded of old Iranian society were not easily attained, and it seems that in the process of adapting to the new teachings, his disciples absorbed various elements of local religions. For example, the prevalent Indo-Aryan god Mithra, who features prominently in the Vedic religion of ancient India and who is mentioned in the Avesta, assumes, at times, an ambiguous role in Zoroastrian history. Mithra, for example, was highly revered but technically held as a subordinate deity to Ahura Mazda (though this distinction may have not always been clear). Eventually, the fame of Mithra, who was later identified with the sun, spread beyond Central Asia and into a religious cult known as the "mysteries of Mithra" in ancient Rome.[25]

Certain issues concerning the Zoroastrian religion remain obscure and hotly debated. This situation arises, in part, because over time Zoroastrian communities upheld varied interpretations of their faith. There have also been a variety of internal modifications, challenges, and revivals, such as Zurvanism and Mazdakism. New religions also arose, such as the one taught by the prophet Mani (*c.*216–276 C.E.), who established a movement based on revelations that he received through his celestial "twin" (identified with the

Paraclete or *logos*). Although Mani's religion, or Manichaeism, is no longer practiced today, it was once widely adhered to, with followers in Europe, the Middle East, Central Asia, North Africa, northern India, Tibet, and western China. As an Iranian gnostic religion,[26] Manichaeism is mostly associated with the concept of dualism, for it characterized life in terms of the opposition of good and evil, spirit and matter, and, especially, light and dark. Mani's teachings were deemed heretical by Zoroastrians, Christians, and Muslims alike, and his followers were often persecuted. Although his detractors commonly labeled his teachings as pessimistic, Mircea Eliade points out that in the Manichean worldview the principle of Light is judged to be stronger than Darkness, for no matter how painful the "embrace of Darkness was, Light nevertheless shone in every blade of grass."[27]

> **Certain issues concerning the Zoroastrian religion remain obscure and hotly debated**

Mani saw himself as a prophet in the same line of messengers that included Zoroaster, Buddha, and Jesus. His ecumenical and syncretic religion consciously welcomed previous religions into its fold, offering salvation to all humanity. He consciously explained his teachings with reference to ideas from earlier religions – adopting, for example, Zoroastrian, Buddhist, and Christian terminology. The historian of religion Wilfred Cantwell Smith held Mani to be "the first person in human history ever to have consciously played a role of a world prophet."[28] During Sassanian rule in Persia, Mani presented his teachings to King Shapur I (d. 272 C.E.); though Shapur was initially favorable to the new religion, Mani was later exiled. After long teaching expeditions, which took him to India, among other places, Mani returned to Persia. After achieving initial inroads in terms of gaining adherents, he fell from favor and was viewed as a threat to the existing political–religious establishment. In 276 C.E. he was put on trial, condemned to prison, confined in chains, and killed. With a missionary zeal and a strong church organization, his religion, however, spread rapidly; it influenced many gnostics and other thinkers, including the Catholic St. Augustine, who was an adherent of the Manichean religion for about a decade.

RITUALS AND PRACTICES

In the Zoroastrian faith, worship is conducted only in conditions of cleanliness. Cleanliness is a prerequisite for prayer and all rituals, and in general it is considered an essential aspect of a believer's daily life. Before praying, believers must perform ritual ablutions (cleansing procedures). Prayer is typically offered five times daily, and is often performed in a temple or any clean area in front of sacred fire. Misinterpreted by many outsiders, the Zoroastrians are not "fire-worshipers." The fire, still used in Zoroastrian rituals and temples today, is a religious symbol that represents the attributes of Ahura Mazda, such as power, light, and purity. While praying, a Zoroastrian remains standing while tying and untying a sacred cord, known as a *kusti*. A temple fire burns perpetually within a metal vessel, a stone pillar, or a structure similar to an altar. Temple fires are regarded as particularly sacred, and young children are taken to view them so that they develop a sense of reverence. Although there are ceremonies specifically performed only within temples, others, known as "outer ceremonies," may be conducted in any ritually clean location.

Spiritual beings called *yazata*s, or angels, play many roles in Zoroastrian beliefs. For example, they protect children and youth. During a special ceremonial rite of passage, Zoroastrian children enter into communion with a *yazata* which, from that time onwards, acts as a protector and guardian. The large number of shrines dedicated to *yazata*s are a good indication of how much their intercession is valued by believers. Interestingly, the hierarchy of angels that is posited in Zoroastrian belief is also indicative of a sacral cosmology; for example, "concerning the ritual of the 28th day of the month, the sacred scripture of Zoroastrianism asserts, 'We are celebrating this liturgy in honor of the Earth, which is an Angel.'"[29]

> **Spiritual beings called *yazata*s, or angels, play many roles in Zoroastrian beliefs**

Children who are initiated into the Zoroastrian faith undergo a rite called the "donning of the sacred shirt," or Sedra-pushun. The ceremony takes place between the ages of seven and fifteen, depending on local custom. Before being brought to the location where the rite is conducted, the initiate is cleansed outwardly in a bath and inwardly by means of a special drink. During the ceremony, the youth dons a sacred shirt (*sudreh*) and a Zoroastrian priest presents the initiate with a *kusti*. The newest member of the Zoroastrian community is then presented with gifts by family and friends.

The Zoroastrian calendar has twelve months, with each month consisting of thirty days. In order to correspond to the solar year of 365 days, five or six days are added to the final month of the year. The most important holy day for Zoroastrians is known as Naw-Ruz, meaning "new day." On Naw-Ruz, Zoroastrians anticipate the final triumph of good over evil.

THE INFLUENCE OF THE ZOROASTRIAN TRADITION

The historian of religion Mircea Eliade notes that the Zoroastrian faith has made a variety of important contributions to the development of religion in the Western world. For example, Eliade credits the Zoroastrian tradition with "the articulation of several dualistic systems … the myth of the savior; the elaboration of an optimistic eschatology, proclaiming the final triumph of Good and universal salvation; the doctrine of the resurrection of bodies; very probably, certain Gnostic myths; finally, the mythology of the Magus, elaborated during the Renaissance."[30] Scholars posit that Jewish thinkers absorbed Zoroastrian ideas during their captivity in Babylonia, such as angelology (or belief in the existence of angels) – a general notion not found in earlier Jewish writings but one that would play an important role in subsequent Abrahamic faiths. According to the scholar Richard Foltz,

> The apocalypticism of biblical prophets such as Daniel dates from the post-Babylonian period after Israelites had come into contact with Iranian ideas. The concept of a messiah (literally, 'anointed one') who will come to save the righteous at the end of time would seem to derive from the Iranian [or Persian] belief in the Saoshyant. The figure of ha-Satan, literally 'the accuser,' appears no earlier than in the Book of Job, which was composed in the post-exilic period as well. Thus, the Satan reviled by Christians and Muslims alike clearly evolved from the Zoroastrian evil deity, Ahriman [or Angra Mainyu], a notion most likely transmitted to the Semitic world by the Jews of Iran.[31]

Zoroaster is mentioned by numerous early Christian writers (such as Clement of Alexandria and St. Augustine) and there is a direct biblical linkage between Christianity and the Zoroastrian tradition in the form of the Zoroastrian astronomer-priests known as the magi. According to the biblical story, the magi foretold the birth of Jesus through the stars and offered the infant gifts of gold, frankincense, and myrrh (Matthew 2:1–12).

To the ancient Greeks, Zoroaster was a highly regarded sage, a supreme philosopher (or Magus). His authority and prestige, like that of the ancient Egyptians, was well known and respected within the Greek philosophical tradition. The Neoplatonic philosopher Porphyry (c.233–309 C.E.), a student of the philosopher Plotinus, alleges that the Greek sage Pythagoras studied under Zoroastrian priests (or the magi): "[Pythagoras advised] … above all things to speak the truth, for this alone deifies men. For as he had learned from the Magi, who call God Horomazda, God's body is like light, and his soul is like truth."[32] Zoroastrian ideas are also thought to have influenced Mahayana Buddhism (which flourished in

The Zoroastrian faith has made a variety of important contributions to the development of religion in the Western world

places such as the northeastern parts of Iran – including present-day Afghanistan) and Gnostic movements which were, along with the Jewish and Christian religions, in close proximity in Central Asia during the early period of the Common Era. Zoroastrian mystical teachings, such as those dealing with light (*xvarnah*) and angelology, were also absorbed by one of Persia's most important Islamic mystics, Suhrawardi (1155–1191 C.E.), as witnessed in his *The Philosophy of Illumination*. In fact, Persia's Zoroastrian heritage, as well as Persian epic literature and traditional poetry (such as the poet Ferdowsi's opus *Shanameh* or "The Book of Kings"), remains a significant aspect of present-day Iranian cultural identity.

CHAPTER SUMMARY

Zoroaster delivered his teachings from within the Indo-Aryan milieu, and his universal message brought forth a new standard of spiritual discipline, ethical conscientiousness, and personal responsibility. Extending justice to the poor and protection to animals, he stripped away excessive ritualism and provided a path to spiritual enlightenment (*baodha*). Rabindranath Tagore, one of the great poetic and religious minds of modern India, hailed him as "the greatest of all the pioneer prophets who showed the path of freedom to man, the freedom of moral choice, the freedom from the blind obedience to unmeaning injunction, the freedom from the multiplicity of shrines which draw our worship away from the single-minded chastity of devotion."[33]

By following a deep calling from within, Zoroaster set forth on a spiritual journey that attained fruition with divine visions and discourses with God. It was through these revelations that Zoroaster realized the true reality, Ahura Mazda – the One, the Creator, the Sustainer, the Unconquerable, the Understanding, the Knowledge, the Perfection.[34] He came to know that all things were derived from God, and it was by way of His manifest attributes that humanity can recognize and serve Him. According to Zoroaster, humanity has been given a purposeful mission on earth – to uplift the world and eliminate evil through steadfast effort in spiritual life. Blessed with faculties of discernment, Zoroastrians are thereby called to become co-workers in the cause of truth, ever mindful of the Adversary, Angra Mainyu (later known as Shaytan or Satan).

A sadhu reading the Upanishads, Haridwar, India

CHAPTER 6
THE HINDU TRADITION

May my speech be one with my mind, and may
my mind be one with my speech.
O thou self-luminous Brahman, remove the veil
of ignorance from before me, that I may behold
thy light.
Do thou reveal to me the spirit of the scriptures.
May the truth of the scriptures be ever present to me.
May I seek day and night to realize what I learn
from the sages.
May I speak the truth of Brahman.
May I speak the truth.
May it protect me.
May it protect my teacher.[1]
Om … Peace – peace – peace

– Rig Veda

INTRODUCTION

As the birthplace of numerous religions, India has been an
object of fascination and spiritual pilgrimage for many
people across the globe. Enjoying one of the most ancient
cultures on earth, many aspects of India's religious heritage
remain interwoven within its contemporary religious practices. This mixture makes for a rich diversity of practices
and beliefs. Visitors to India are often struck by a culture
that incorporates an array of apparent contradictions.
Octavio Paz, a recipient of the Nobel Prize for literature,
lived in India for many years and wrote in his memoirs:

> The first thing that surprised me about India, as it has sur-
> prised so many others, was the diversity created by
> extreme contrast: modernity and antiquity, luxury and
> poverty, sensuality and asceticism, carelessness and effi-
> ciency, gentleness and violence; a multiplicity of castes
> and languages, gods and rites, customs and ideas, rivers

Timeline

***c.*1500 B.C.E.**
Dravidian peoples inhabit
 Indian subcontinent
***c.*1500–1200 B.C.E.**
Older substratum of the
 Vedas date to this period
9–6th centuries B.C.E.
Sramana, or wandering
 ascetic, movement, and
 emergence of Buddhist
 and Jain traditions
***c.*700–300 B.C.E.**
Composition of Upanishads
***c.*600 B.C.E.**
Classical Period of Hindu
 religion begins
***c.*300 B.C.E.–1200 C.E.**
Early part of Middle
 Period, often called
 the Scholastic Period
***c.*250 C.E.**
Life of sage Patañjali who
 systematized *Yoga Sutras*
***c.*788–820 C.E.**
 Shankara, founder of
 Advaita Vedanta
1017–1137 C.E.
Ramanuja
1199–1278 C.E.
Madhva
1200–1700 C.E.
Later part of Middle Period:
 India dominated by
 Islamic powers
1206 C.E. Delhi sultanate
 established

and deserts, plains and mountains, cities and villages, rural and industrial life, centuries apart in time and neighbors in space. But the most remarkable aspect of India, and the one that defines it, is neither political nor economic, but religious: the coexistence of Hinduism and Islam.[2]

According to many scholars, the roots of the Hindu religion are among the oldest of any living religion. The tradition as a whole is also, perhaps, the most difficult religion to grasp in its entirety. Without a unified dogma or specific founder, it eludes strict categorization and classification. A single chapter cannot possibly do justice to all of the Hindu tradition's varied practices, rituals, and systems of interpretation. This is especially true because the Hindu tradition is the parent religion of three other spiritual traditions: the Buddhist, the Jain, and the Sikh. Unlike another parent religion – the Jewish religion – the Hindu tradition has no historical beginning and little emphasis on historical events.

> **One should not behave toward others in a way that is disagreeable to oneself. This is the essence of morality. All other activities are due to selfish desire**
> *Mahabharata, Anusasana Parva 113.8*
> **THE GOLDEN RULE**

It should be noted that the term "Hindu" did not actually derive from within the Hindu religion. It was the ancient Persians who referred to the expanse beyond the Indus River Valley as "Sindhu," which over time became "Hindu." The words "Hindu" and "Hinduism" transited into the English language by way of Islamic scholars and travelers. Generally, natives of India refer to what outsiders might call the Hindu religion as *sanatana-dharma*, meaning "Eternal Truth" or the "Eternal Reality," or *vaidika-dharma*, which means "the religion of the Vedas" (the central scriptures of the Hindu tradition). Scholars distinguish between the modern Hindu religion and the Vedic religion; the latter refers to the ancient religion of Indo-Aryan origin and the former to a conglomerate of traditions that incorporates not only the original Vedas, but also sacred epics and philosophical texts from various Indian sages. As such, the Hindu religion entails great diversity,

1440–1518 C.E. Life of mystic and poet Kabir

1772–1883 C.E. Ram Mohan Roy

1823–1883 C.E. Dayananda Sarasvati

1834–1886 C.E. Hindu saint Ramakrishna

1858 C.E. British monarchic rule officially established over India

1863–1902 C.E. Swami Vivekananda

1869–1948 C.E. Mahatma Gandhi

1876 C.E. Queen Victoria adopts title 'Empress of India'

1893 C.E. Vivekananda represents Hindu religion at 1893 Parliament of World Religions in Chicago, USA

1947 C.E. India attains independence from Britain

and can be characterized as many religious paths united by a common framework. It is common, therefore, to find two people, both Hindus, who have two different ways of practicing their religion, both of which are equally "Hindu."

THE RELIGIOUS DIVERSITY OF THE HINDU TRADITION

A central question that must be asked about the Hindu religion is, "how has it been able to absorb and accept communities of Jews, Christians, Zoroastrians (known as Parsees, or 'those who came from Persia') and others, allowing each of them to flourish alongside its own forms of spirituality?" In fact, history attests to the Hindu tradition's ability to dynamically and positively accommodate foreign ideas that have entered India's borders, some of them brought by invading armies. To name just a few examples, Indian cultural and spiritual life has responded creatively to occupation by ancient Greeks, Muslim Turks, Moguls, and the British. India has also provided a peaceful refuge for religious groups fleeing persecution, such as Zoroastrians and Tibetan Buddhists. Hindus have demonstrated the ability to reach within the depths of their own tradition, even to the extent of revising traditional viewpoints, in order to accommodate and make sense of foreign religious concepts. Additionally, skeptical and reformist movements from within the Hindu tradition have also been accommodated.

> The *Rig Veda* is an excellent starting point for understanding the essential concepts of the Hindu worldview

The *Rig Veda*, one of the four Vedas, is an excellent starting point for understanding the essential concepts of the Hindu worldview. One scholar remarked that the *Rig Veda* is a hymn that is "particularly striking for its cosmic vision, its imaginative picture of a universe evolving out of a primal condition that was neither being nor nonbeing, neither cosmos nor chaos."[3] The ancient and intellectually demanding view of creation in the *Rig Veda* includes the following pertinent section:

> Then even nothingness was not, nor existence.
> There was no air then, nor the heavens beyond it.
> What covered it? Where was it? In whose keeping?
> Was there then cosmic water, in depths unfathomed?
> Then there was neither death nor immortality,
> nor was there then the touch of night and day.
> The One breathed windlessly and self-sustaining.
> There was that One then, and there was no other.
> At first there was only darkness wrapped in darkness.

All this was only unilluminated water.
That One which came to be, enclosed in nothing,
arose at last, born of the power of heat.
In the beginning desire descended on it –
that was the primal seed, born of the mind.
The sages who have searched their hearts with wisdom
know that which is is kin to that which is not.
And they have stretched their cord across the void,
and know what was above, and what below.
Seminal powers made fertile mighty forces.
Below was strength, and over it was impulse.
But, after all, who knows, and who can say
whence it all came, and how creation happened?
The gods themselves are later than creation,
so who knows truly whence it has arisen?
Whence all creation had its origin,
he, whether he fashioned it or whether he did not,
he who surveys it all from highest heaven,
he knows – or maybe even he does not know.[4]

The last line of the hymn can be interpreted as a disavowal of human knowledge, and per-haps of all possible knowledge; it even appears to question the divine. This can be seen as a seed of non-exclusiveness that has flowered in the form of religious diversity. Within the creation myth there is no certainty or concrete dogma concerning creation; this flexibility allowed the Hindu religion to adapt and respond to other spiritual movements and to develop different philosophical interpretations from within. The *Rig Veda*'s openness toward Ultimate Reality may partially explain why the Hindu religion was well suited to become a parent religion without provoking conflicts between its progeny.

THE SUPREME BEING

Hindu interpretations of the nature of God, the Supreme Being, are diverse. This diver-sity has permitted variations in forms of worship and views of the divine, all of which are equally respected by Hindus. The Vedas depict a pantheon of deities in which each god and goddess has its own function in the terrestrial and celestial spheres. However, many Hindus, especially those informed by the sacred writings called the Upanishads (discussed below), believe that all things, including the various gods, originate from a single, eternal

Being. This principle, or power, is called Brahman (the Absolute, the Supreme Being); in fact, Brahman is often held as synonymous with absolute Truth. According to one philosophical view of the Hindu tradition, since Brahman is an abstract principle beyond all forms and qualities, and thus is ultimately incomprehensible to human minds, some aspirants choose an *ishtadeva* – a certain god, ideal, or divine incarnation – that appeals to their mind and emotions. Hindus worship the *ishtadeva*, or chosen ideal, as if it were Brahman. The *ishtadeva*, therefore, becomes the main object of their spiritual practices. Often, gurus, or spiritual teachers, suggest a certain ideal that seems to best fit the particular tendencies of an aspirant.[5] In that way, gurus, or those who have dedicated themselves solely to the spiritual life, may recommend a certain representation of Brahman that they believe will best facilitate an individual's spiritual growth and connection to the Supreme Being.

Underlying the concept of the *ishtadeva* is the idea (derived from the tradition of Vedanta, discussed below) that there are two ways of thinking about God – with qualities and attributes (referred to as *saguna brahman*) and without qualities and attributes (denoted as *nirguna brahman*). The former, *saguna brahman*, is equivalent to the *ishtadeva* – it is a way of viewing God, the Absolute, in a particular form and with particular qualities. The latter, *nirguna brahman*, is Brahman in its Infinite, Absolute and Ultimate sense, which transcends any possible image or finite conception. *Saguna brahman*, or God

Hindu interpretations of the nature of God, the Supreme Being, are diverse

with qualities and attributes, allows an aspirant to worship in a personal way, i.e. through devotion and prayer. On the other hand, *nirguna brahman* is the object of meditation for Hindu contemplatives, satisfying the tendency or disposition of philosophically oriented aspirants. In that way, *saguna brahman* and *nirguna brahman* can be understood as complementary, and are both considered suitable religious ideals. Thus, the Hindu religion is remarkably adaptable in that it can be practiced as non-theistic (or monistic), monotheistic, or polytheistic. It is, however, far more accurate to describe the relationship that most Hindus have with their religion as henotheism, the belief in a single Godhead that is worshiped through a variety of deities.

REINCARNATION AND *KARMA*

Hindus believe that all living things have souls and the form into which each soul incarnates, whether plant, animal, human, or celestial being, is directly determined by one's actions in previous lives, i.e. by *karma* or the law of cause and effect. The principle of *karma* was first formulated, in written form, in the sacred texts called the Upanishads. Specifically, *karma* means "willed activity" and implies that an agent of action is held responsible for the motivation and consequences of that action, including thoughts, words, deeds, and intentions.

Hindus believe that each soul accrues karmic propensities or subliminal habit tendencies (*samskaras* or *vasanas*) through many rebirths in conditioned reality or *samsara*. From this perspective, each soul is indefinitely reborn in conditioned reality until it attains *moksha* or unconditional freedom from the wheel of rebirth. Conditioned reality and the wheel of rebirth are synonymous, that is, both are ways of describing the reality of *samsara*. The basic impetus behind Hindu spirituality is the striving for *moksha*, the yearning to free oneself from ego-driven impulses, suffering, and separation from God. In the words of one scholar:

> To "free oneself" is equivalent to forcing another plane of existence, to appropriating another *mode of being* transcending the human condition. This is as much to say that, for India, not only is metaphysical knowledge translated into terms of *rupture* and *death* ("breaking" the human condition, one "dies" to all that was human); it also necessarily implies a consequence of a mystical nature: *rebirth to a nonconditioned mode of being*. And this is liberation, absolute freedom.[6]

DHARMA AND HINDU ETHICS

At the core of Hindu ethics and social order is the concept of *dharma*. The term has various levels of meaning and no single English equivalent. At the cosmic level, *dharma* refers to the unchanging universal law that decrees that every entity in the universe should behave in accordance with the laws applicable to its own particular nature. *Dharma* also signifies powers attained through the performance of *yajñas* (Vedic rituals and sacrifices), the right way of living, righteousness, law, religion, and duty. *Dharma* also entails virtues, such as truthfulness, charity, self-control, and non-violence. Beyond such universally acknowledged virtues, Hindu ethics consist of various duties and responsibilities in the religious, social, and familial spheres of life. According to Swami[7] Nikhilananda:

> Every normal [Hindu] person endowed with social consciousness has a threefold debt to discharge: his debts to the gods, to the rishis, and to the ancestors. His debt to the gods … is paid through worship and prayer. The debt to the rishis [the ancient seers who recorded the sacred Vedas] … is paid through regular study of the scriptures. The debt to the ancestors … is paid through propagation of children, ensuring the preservation of the line. With the blessings of the gods, the rishis, and the ancestors, one can cheerfully practice spiritual disciplines for the realisation of the highest good [Brahman], in which all worldly values find fulfillment.[8]

Besides the threefold sacred duty each Hindu owes to the gods, the *rishi*s, and the ancestors, there are other responsibilities such as those accorded to one's parents, teachers, spouse, children, and fellow creatures; these are conceived as sacred duties that are part and parcel of Hindu life.

The Four Goals of Life

The majority of Hindus who do not take up the life of a monk (*sannyasin* or *sadhu*) pursue four religiously accepted goals in life. These four goals are sensual pleasure (*kama*), material gain (*artha*), moral duty (*dharma*), and – the ultimate goal – to transcend conditioned reality and the cycle of rebirth (*moksha*). Idealized, these goals represent successive objectives of a single lifespan that progressively matures as the aspirant realizes the vanity of this world, and through self-determination, develops a longing for God. As evidenced by the four goals of

Hindu spirituality embraces the full spectrum of experience

life, Hindu spirituality embraces the full spectrum of experience, including sensuality, aesthetics, and the earning of money. The only requirement is that such experiences are pursued in accordance with *dharma*, or righteousness and duty, and that they are not viewed as ends in and of themselves, but within the context of a spiritual journey. In order to understand fully the sacred duties and responsibilities of Hindus, as well as the goals of Hindu life, it is important to view them from the context of the four successive stages of life, or *ashrama*s.

The Four Stages of Life

The four stages of life (*ashrama*s) provide culturally recognized time-periods in the lifespan. Each stage is imbued with different responsibilities and aims. The four stages are *brahmacarya*, *grihastha*, *vanaprastha*, and *sannyasa*. The first stage, *brahmacarya*, varies in duration but often lasts between the ages of eight and twenty-five. This stage, marking the transition from childhood to spiritual life, commences with an event called *upanayana* ("bringing near"). The *upanayana* is the second birth, or spiritual birth, of a Hindu, which ushers in the youth's new life under the tutelage of a guru. It is at this point that the youth enters religious life and thereby accepts the duties and responsibilities of *dharma*. This symbolic rebirth occurs when the guru invests the student with the sacred thread or *yajñoparita*. During this stage one lives as a student under the guidance of a teacher for about a decade or so. The relationship between the teacher and student is a spiritual apprenticeship. As such, the student offers services to the teacher while learning the Sanskrit language, sacred epics, and other holy scriptures. The stage often culminates when the teacher entrusts the student with one of the most essential and core ethical teachings in the Hindu tradition. This instructive teaching, taken from the *Taittriya Upanishad*, reads as follows:

> Speak the truth. Do your duty. Do not neglect the study of the scriptures. Do not cut the thread of progeny. Swerve not from truth.
> Deviate not from the path of good. Revere greatness.
> Let your mother be a god to you; let your father be a god to you;
> let your teacher be a god to you; let your guest also be a god to you.
> Do only such actions as are blameless. Always show reverence to the great.
> Whatever you give to others, give with love and reverence. Gifts must be given in abundance, with joy, humility, and compassion.
> If at any time there is any doubt with regard to right conduct,
> follow the practice of great souls, who are guileless, of good judgment
> and devoted to truth.
> Thus conduct yourself always. This is the injunction, this is the teaching, and this is the command of the scriptures.[9]

The second stage of a traditional Hindu life, *grihastha*, corresponds to the familial and occupational life of a householder. The householder stage entails such responsibilities as occupational work, marriage, and the rearing of children, which are fundamental to the accepted social order. These obligations, along with a householder's daily religious practices, such as scriptural study, honoring ancestors, and worshiping the gods, are viewed as more than mere duties: they are disciplines through which one can develop spiritual virtues. In that way, occupational, community, and family life are not disconnected from spiritual practice. They are a form of spiritual training that helps one transcend selfish concerns in favor of the welfare of others. When a householder's children mature, specifically with the birth of grandchildren or the graying of one's hair, the householder slowly begins to decrease his engagement in social and family life and increase study of scripture, meditation, and worship. This represents the lessening of worldly responsibilities in order to pursue what Hindus regard as ultimately more important, spiritual practice. The second stage is complete when the householder withdraws completely from society and enters the *vanaprastha* stage, often referred to as the "forest-dweller" stage. A forest dweller is a person who leaves society in favor of isolated and intense spiritual practice. The third stage, representing the transition to full renunciation, is fulfilled in the fourth stage, *sannyasa*. The *sannyasa* stage corresponds to monastic life and entails full-fledged renunciation of worldly concerns and desires. During the fourth stage, one's entire life is focused on the attainment of liberation. As such, Hindus regard non-attachment, abnegation of personal desires, meditative concentration, and renunciation as extremely important, and necessary, spiritual virtues.

It should be pointed out that traditionally the four stages were available only to the "twice-born" castes (Brahmins, Khasatriyas, and Vaishyas) and it was generally assumed to be confined to men (see below for a discussion of the caste system). Within that historical context, the stages provide a mechanism that orients and structures not only the individual lifespan, but the entire Hindu culture. They establish a path which enables one to engage the full range of human experiences through progressive, culturally accepted channels. The ritualization of daily life – informed by the concept of *dharma* – thereby allows for the inculcation of religious teachings and values at every phase of life. Thus, for the Hindu, life is a religious path, or *sadhana*, towards freedom, proximity to God, and Self-realization (meaning, God-realization). At each step one develops and deepens spiritual virtues necessary for the duties of each stage, such as non-attachment, compassion, generosity, self-control, and longing for God. Ultimately, one is led to complete renunciation of the pleasures and responsibilities of worldly life in the effort to realize God and to transcend the suffering of conditional existence. Traditionally, the stages are followed in sequence; however, exceptional adepts have been drawn to the most intense spiritual practice at early ages. Siddhartha Guatama (the historical Buddha), for example, became a *sannyasin* (member of the fourth stage) while he was a householder. Also, one of the greatest Hindu philosophers, Shankara (see below), renounced worldly life while he was a *brahmacarya* (member of the first stage). For *sadhus*, or monks, the duties associated with the life of a householder, including concern for material acquisition, money, sex, and family life, are viewed as obstacles that inhibit the actualization of the highest states of human consciousness.

SPIRITUAL PATHS TO LIBERATION

Within the Hindu religion there are four universally acknowledged spiritual paths that appeal to different personality tendencies. These four means of religious practice are (1) the path of knowledge or gnosis through philosophical investigation (namely, discrimination of the metaphysically real from the unreal) or *jñana yoga*; (2) the path of worship and devotion to God through love or *bhakti yoga*; (3) the path of selfless work as an offering to God or *karma yoga*; and (4) the psychosomatic path of meditative and physical exercises and disciplines, or *raja yoga* (the Raja Yoga system, as expounded by the sage Patañjali, is discussed below). These four general paths to God accommodate the dispositions of different people, and thereby offer different means of realizing God and achieving *moksha*.

Another prominent path to Self-realization within the Hindu religion is Tantra. The term *tantra* means "that by which knowledge is spread." Tantra is an important element in the Vajrayana (Tibetan) Buddhist tradition, and appears in many popular Hindu practices. Most scholars agree that both Buddhist and Hindu tantric practices were based on knowledge

Divali offering to the Ganga, India

which was preserved and transmitted by ascetic sages. Tantra emphasizes the guru–disciple relationship, initiation into a spiritual lineage, recitation of mantras (sacred and powerful verbal formulas), visualization techniques of meditation, and sexual symbolism that is imbued with cosmic meaning. In general, practitioners of Tantra utilize meditation techniques and identify themselves with a certain deity (an aspect of Ultimate Reality), such as Shiva, in order to exercise some measure of benefit from the cosmic power the deity represents. Different forms of *yoga* have developed based on tantric principles which are designed to cultivate dormant psychic energies. A common practice, for example, attempts to draw *kundalini* energy (energy that is believed to be coiled around the bottom of the spine) up the spinal column through various *chakra*s (energy centers) and into the crown of the head. Such esoteric yogic practices seek the transmutation of dormant, inner energies as a means of spiritual transformation.

THE *SHRUTI* SCRIPTURES

Shruti denotes a category of revealed scriptures which are the most sacred of the Hindu religion. The term *shruti*, meaning "that which is revealed or heard," refers to the revelatory visions both seen and heard by *rishi*s, the ancient seers of India who meditated in caves and forests and attained access to eternal truths. The *rishi*s, however, are not regarded as the authors of the *shruti* scriptures, but rather as those who discovered them through mystical visions and realizations. These revelatory hymns were transmitted orally but eventually were written down and preserved by the *brahmin*s (priests). The written Vedas, often regarded as the oldest religious scriptures of any "living" religion, consist of the *Rig Veda*, *Yajur Veda*, *Sama Veda*, and *Artharva Veda*. The collected corpus designated as the Vedas represents a revelation which has no particular beginning or end. Thus, some Hindus regard revelation as eternal and not limited to a certain number of books nor to a certain ethnicity, religion, or creed.

The four Vedas are permeated by four categories of writings: Mantras, Brahmanas, Aranyakas and Upanishads. The Mantras are hymns of invocation and praise to the gods. The Brahmanas explain the secret power of the Mantras in their mythic and ritual context. The Aranyakas explicate secretive and philosophical aspects of various rituals, usually performed by dedicated and secluded practitioners under the guidance of a teacher. The Upanishads, which are generally regarded as the most essential writings in the Hindu tradition, explain concepts such as the relationship between the self (*atman*) and the Supreme Being (Brahman). Upanishadic sections appear at the end of each Veda; when gathered together as one corpus, they are designated as the Upanishads.

Amongst the four books that comprise the Vedas, the *Rig Veda* is the oldest. It contains mainly hymns in praise of the various *deva*s (gods). The *Yajur Veda* incorporates some

hymns from the *Rig Veda* and includes procedural details for the performance of *yajña*s (sacrificial worship); one such sacrificial offering is performed during certain moon cycles; another is the ancient *soma* sacrifice (practitioners offer a seemingly hallucinogenic herb or fungus to the gods by digesting it). The *Sama Veda* contains mostly hymns and chants from the *Rig Veda*; the hymns, however, have been set to rhythmic melody. The singer of the hymns, given proper tonal resonance, is thought to achieve spiritual powers through recitation. The *Atharva Veda*, geared more toward household rituals rather than communal rites, contains a variety of philosophically inclined invocations, healing hymns, and formulas designed to ward off evil spirits.

The Upanishads

For many, the essence of the Hindu tradition is found in the Upanishads, which are contained in the concluding sections of the Vedas, and include the highest philosophical teachings recorded by the Vedic seers (*rishi*s). The Upanishads have served as a reservoir of inspiration for all later forms of Hindu philosophy. In general, the Upanishads can be understood as the esoteric aspect of Hindu sacred writings, in that they internalized the ritualistic injunctions of the Vedas and highlighted Vedic teachings on spiritual knowledge. The Upanishads are not so much concerned with rituals, spells, gods, and souls as with the metaphysical reality behind them – Brahman, the transcendent principle, ground, or support of all phenomenal things.

The philosophical essence of the Hindu tradition is recorded in the Upanishads

One interpretation of Upanishadic teachings holds that the true end or aim of Vedic religiosity (or Vedanta, literally meaning "the end of the Vedas") is to realize Brahman *within*. From this viewpoint, the Upanishads reject worship of cosmological gods and ritualistic religion, and instead teach inward purification, knowledge through introspection, and meditative realization of the divine principle within the "heart," understood symbolically as the seat of awareness or "city of Brahman." Notably, the scholar Karan Singh has summarized the essential teachings of the Hindu tradition, based on five basic concepts, all of which are found in the Upanishads:

> The first is the concept of Brahman, the unchanging undying reality that pervades the entire cosmos ... The second great insight of the Vedic seers was that, as the changing universe outside was pervaded by the Brahman, the changing world within man himself was based upon the undying Atman ... Having perceived the existence of the undying Brahman without and the undying Atman within, the great seers were able to

make the critical leap of realizing through their spiritual insight that the Atman and Brahman were essentially one … the fourth major tenet of Hinduism is that the supreme goal of life lies in spiritual realization whereby the individual becomes aware of the death-less Atman within him … The fifth concept which lies at the very heart of the Hindu way of life is that of karma, a concept that includes action, causality, and destiny.[10]

In sum, the Upanishads are centered on the relationship between Brahman and *atman*. Brahman is the Supreme Being that is infinite and eternal, transcendent and immanent. Dualistic Hindu schools understand *atman* (soul/self) to be dependent on, but different from, Brahman, while non-dualistic schools see no difference between the two. The latter view is often identified with the Upanishadic formula *tat tvam asi* (That Thou Art), which some ancient Hindu sages or seers regarded as the climax of the spiritual journey – the realization that one's essence (that is, beyond body and mind) is Brahman.

THE *SMRITI* SCRIPTURES

The *shruti* scriptures are completed by another type of scripture called *smriti*, meaning "that which is remembered." The *shruti* scriptures, which are eternal and authorless, consist of the Vedas, and are regarded as the principal Hindu holy texts because they are not of human origin. *Smriti*, or non-Vedic scriptures, on the other hand, are secondary because they are a recollection of, or further commentary on, the direct experiences recorded in the *shruti* scriptures. *Smriti* scriptures tend to concentrate on *dharma*, or moral law, and often address codes of conduct. One of the most famous *smriti* scriptures is *Manusmrti*, often translated as the "Laws of Manu." The Laws of Manu elaborate many concepts, including the philosophy behind the four goals of life (*arthas*), the four stages of life (*ashramas*), and the caste system. Included among the texts designated as *smriti* are two categories of scriptures called *Puranas* (meaning "having their origin in the distant past") and *Itihasas* or epic literature.

> The *shruti* scriptures are regarded as the principal Hindu holy texts because they were conveyed through direct revelatory experiences

The *Puranas* form the basis of popular, or mythological, Hindu beliefs and are based on legends and mythical stories about gods and divine incarnations (or *avatars*). The most well known *Purana* is the *Bhagavata Purana*, which describes the early life of Krishna. The *Puranas* are closely linked with another category of *smriti* scriptures known as *Itihasas* or epics. According to one scholar, "the two together [i.e. the *Puranas* and *Itihasas*] are known as the fifth Veda (*Pañcamo Vedah*). The aim of the *Puranas* is to broadcast religious knowledge and evoke religious devotion among the masses, through myths and stories, legends and chronicles of great national events."[11] The *Itihasas*, meaning "it happened thus," include the two great epics of India, the *Ramayana*, the story of Rama, and *Mahabharata*, the Great Story of the War of the Bharatas (Indians refer to themselves by the general term *bharatas*). In both texts, the god Vishnu manifests in human form: as Sri Rama in the *Ramayana* and as Sri Krishna in the *Mahabharata*. Both of these texts have exercised a profound and lasting influence upon Indian spiritual life, especially on the imagination of those who in the past were restricted from reading the Vedas due to caste prohibitions. In previous times, the Vedas were the exclusive right of the priestly caste (see below for further discussion on the caste system). The *Bhagavad-Gita* (meaning "the Song of the Lord"), which is regarded as the "Hindu Bible" by many non-Hindus, is part of the *Mahabharata*. Strictly speaking, then, the *Bhagavad-Gita* is not part of the *shruti*, i.e. the fundamental and most sacred scriptures, the Vedas. However, Hindus accept that the *Bhagavad-Gita* is divinely inspired and both practitioners and scholars believe that it succinctly expresses the essential aspects of the Hindu religion.

The *Bhagavad-Gita*

As indicated above, one brief section of the epic *Mahabharata* is a poem called *Bhagavad-Gita*, "the Song of the Lord." The *Bhagavad-Gita* has become one of the world's most influential sacred works. The poem begins at the start of a battle between two related families, the Pandavas and their cousins the Kauravas. It is during the outset of this battle that Arjuna, a warrior from the Pandava family, undergoes a moral crisis and refuses to fight his own relatives. The *Bhagavad-Gita* consists of a dialogue between Arjuna and his charioteer, Krishna, who urges him to fight in order to uphold *dharma*. Krishna, unbeknownst to Arjuna when the poem begins, is a divine incarnation, or *avatar*, of Vishnu (see below for a further discussion of Vishnu and the *avatars*). Arjuna later recognizes Krishna as an *avatar* but periodically forgets Krishna's divinity during their conversation. Some commentators suggest that this forgetfulness, or ignorance, is indicative of Arjuna's inability to sustain higher states of consciousness.

Confused by his predicament, Arjuna turns to Krishna for advice. Krishna first offers a provisional teaching by urging Arjuna to enter the battle because he is of the warrior caste and has a duty to fight; for if he does not fight, he will not only lose his status but fail to uphold the greater good, which is the defeat of the evil Kauravas. As their dialogue continues, the conversation between Arjuna and Krishna moves beyond Krishna's initial teaching, centered on duty and honor, and into a metaphysical discussion of Ultimate Reality, or Brahman. In order to grasp the reality of Brahman, Krishna reveals three spiritual paths: the path of devotion (*bhakti yoga*), the path of selfless work (*karma yoga*), and the path of knowledge (*jñana yoga*). By cultivating spiritual virtues through the path of self-less work, knowledge, or devotion – or through an integral combination of these paths into one way of life in accordance with one's individual tendencies and inner nature (or *swadharma*) – the aspirant can attain freedom beyond egoism.

The *Bhagavad-Gita* teaches that one must embrace the world with a spirit of non-attachment, avoiding lust, wrath, and greed while living a life based on the five cardinal virtues: purity, self-control, detachment, truth, and non-violence. Although action in the world normally leads to retribution (due to the law of cause and effect, i.e. *karma*), when there is no personal desire there is no karmic retribution, and hence all actions can be undertaken free from selfish desire and for the sake of God. In this way one is encouraged to engage in the world through work and action, but also to remain detached from the fruits of one's labors. When this is done, one's life becomes a sacrifice (*yajña*), or devotional offering to God. Ultimately, the *Bhagavad-Gita* is a masterful synthesis of Hindu religious thought. The diverse philosophical tapestry woven into it has spawned a rich tradition of commentaries from great Hindu teachers and sages. The *Bhagavad-Gita* unifies the Hindu philosophical systems and demonstrates the complementarity of the different Hindu *yoga*s.

THE VEDIC PERIOD

Scholars suggest that the ancient roots of the Hindu religion can be found in the interplay between the Dravidian tribes of India and Indo-Aryan migrants (see previous chapter for more on the Indo-Aryans). From this perspective, the Dravidian peoples inhabited the Indian subcontinent before the Aryans migrated to northern India from the Caucasus, possibly around 1500 B.C.E. It is believed that as the Aryan tribes became dominant, the Dravidians were pushed south. Linguists point out that Sanskrit, the sacred language of the Vedas, is part of the Indo-European family of languages, while languages prominent in southern India, such as Tamil, are of the Dravidian family (including Telugu, Malayalam, Kannada, etc.). From this viewpoint, the Aryan religion evolved into the Vedic–Hindu religion and eventually absorbed Dravidian culture. Proponents of an alternative perspective have suggested that the Aryans were not migrants from outside India but that they represented a cultural transformation of the Indus Valley civilization (Harappa and Mohenjo Daro).

Vedic religion centered on the performance of certain rituals that honored the gods (*deva*s) and preserved cosmic order or *rta*. The *deva*s, i.e. the various gods depicted in the Vedas, were the object of sacrificial offerings, or *yajña*s. In fact, it was believed that the *yajña*s kept the *deva*s alive; in exchange the *deva*s bestowed favor on humanity. The *yajña*s were performed according to instructions indicated in the Vedas. These rituals were followed with rigorous accuracy, for even the slightest deviation from such prescriptions could have dire repercussions. From the Vedic point of view, the *yajñas* "revealed such supernatural wisdom that they could not have been made [or invented] by any one but were self-existent. It came to be held that the hymns of the Vedas, as well as the sacrificial manuals, were without authorship; that they existed eternally, prescribing certain courses of ritualistic procedure for the attainment of particular advantages and prohibiting certain undesirable courses of action."[12] These rituals were performed by the *brahmins*, the elite priestly caste who were learned in the *yajñas*. The *brahmins* thus held the all-important position of performing the rituals needed to sustain the universe.

The Caste System

Most scholars believe that castes (*varnas*) were introduced to India by the Aryans, who used them as a means to maintain social and political dominance over the Dravidians. Aryans were lighter skinned than the Dravidians (*varna* means color). The caste system divided the populace into four classes, or castes. The highest castes, made up of well-educated priests (Brahmins), warriors and rulers (Khasatriyas), and ordinary tradesmen (Vaishyas), dominated the culture (these were known as the "twice-born" castes because they underwent the *upanayana* ceremony symbolizing spiritual rebirth). The fourth caste, the Shudra, was excluded from the traditional stages of life and relegated to hard labor. Outside the caste system altogether were

> **The caste system distributed societal roles to people based on their capacities and talents, not their social status**

the Harijans (untouchables), designated as such due to the unclean and polluted jobs available to them as outcasts to society. Modern India, however, has made "untouchability" illegal. Mahatma Gandhi (1869–1948), one of India's great reformers, interpreted the term "Harijan" as "children of God," instead of "untouchable," in his efforts to remove the stigma that surrounded the lower castes. The term Harijan, though coined by Gandhi, was later considered patronizing; the group has now adopted the title Dalit, meaning "the oppressed." In modern India, the government has instituted reforms to integrate and educate the lower castes, although many prejudices remain, and continue to inform patterns of interaction and social behavior.

The caste system, originally described in the Vedas, was imbued with cosmic importance. Each caste was believed to be a part of the body of the first Cosmic Person (Purusha). The Brahmins were the head, the Khasatriyas the arms, the Vaishyas the legs, and the Shudras the feet. Thus, the entire society consisted of one whole body; the welfare of one caste (or body part) therefore affected all castes (the whole body). The caste system was a very effective method of distributing labor; however, as some Indian thinkers have suggested, the system, like all aspects of conditioned reality (*samsara*), was susceptible to corruption and rigidity. Hindu thinkers now regard the prejudicial and rigid caste system as a corruption of an originally just and fair ordering of society based on the utilization of differing talents. From this perspective, some people are naturally disposed to pursue spiritual learning, some choose military service or political activity, others favor communications and commerce, while some are best suited for labor. The caste system, in its ideal form, distributed societal roles to people based on their capacities and talents, not their social status at birth. Within the Hindu worldview, however, one's disposition is thought to be determined by the law of cause and effect or *karma*; it is, therefore, appropriate to view the caste system from within a worldview that includes *karma* and rebirth (which implies the existence of innumerable lives directly influenced by accumulated karmic propensities). In this way, the caste system is a social aspect or byproduct of a just cosmic order. Over the centuries, many Hindu thinkers have struggled with the connection between *karma* and caste. One Indian philosopher has concluded:

> What matters most in my life is not my heredity; that only gives me my opportunity or my obstacle, my good or my bad material, and it has not by any means been shown that I draw all from that source. What matters supremely is what I make of my heredity and not what my heredity makes of me. The past of the world, bygone humanity, my ancestors are there in me; but still I myself am the artist of my self, my life, my actions.[13]

As the above quotation suggests, an aspirant can, regardless of caste, still pursue spiritual transformation and *moksha* (the most meaningful and ultimate pursuit from the Hindu perspective). Some Hindu saints, in fact, were from the lower castes, and came to be honored and revered even by *brahmins*.

THE EARLY (CLASSICAL) PERIOD

The Classical Period of the Hindu religion began around the sixth century B.C.E. At the dawn of the Classical Period, Siddhartha Gautama – the historical Buddha – began teaching an alternative spiritual path. At approximately the same time, if not slightly earlier, Mahavira, of the Jain tradition, was teaching another path to liberation. Mahavira, like the Buddha, spoke against excessive animal sacrifices and the caste system. One of the pivotal Jain teachings is the doctrine of *ahimsa*, or absolute non-violence against all living things. This doctrine has had a profound effect on the spirituality of India, and specifically it was a pivotal aspect of Mahatma Gandhi's philosophy and non-violent approach to social revolution. The nearly contemporaneous appearance of the Buddhist and Jain spiritual traditions indicates that there were other currents of religious expression in India apart from the Vedic approach. The appeal of Buddhist and Jain teachings partly explains why, during this period, the *brahmins* sought to retain their tradition by accommodating new movements. The Vedic religion thus developed the technique of absorbing practices and beliefs from the Buddhist and Jain traditions, and other traditions. Out of this fusion emerged a system that encompassed virtually every spiritual practice and caste and a great variety of gods and goddesses. Eventually, the old Vedic *deva*s were overshadowed by a powerful group of new deities, particularly the gods Brahma, Vishnu, and Shiva.

Brahma, Vishnu, Shiva, and the Great Goddess

The modern form of popular Hindu belief is structured around the following three deities: Brahma, the creative (or emanating) aspect of God; Vishnu, the sustaining or preserving aspect of God; and Shiva, the aspect of God that dissolves creation. Brahma, Vishnu, and Shiva are therefore a trinity (*trimurti*) that represents the essential aspects of the Supreme Being. The worship of Vishnu and Shiva, as well as their powerful consorts, spread throughout India during the classical period. The popular gods of local cults were regarded as aspects of Vishnu or Shiva. Under the syncretizing genius of the *brahmin* priests, the older substratum of Aryan principles was intertwined with the new importance of Vishnu and Shiva. Devotees of Shiva became known as Shaivites, while worshipers of Vishnu were called Vaishnavites. Within both the Vaishnava and Shaiva traditions there are numerous sub-sects of varying diversity. It should be noted that both of these traditions include tantric groups – which view a set of revelatory texts called *Tantras* as a supplement or alternative to the Vedas (and often these groups expound a radically different set of values than the brahminical Orthodoxy).

> **Brahma, Vishnu, and Shiva are a trinity that represents the essential aspects of the Supreme Being**

Vishnu is commonly worshiped through his incarnations or *avatar*s (most notably Sri Rama and Sri Krishna, both of whom are worshiped in India). The philosopher Sri Aurobindo, in his commentary on the *Bhagavad-Gita*, described the *avatar* as a "manifestation from above of that which we have to develop from below; it is the descent of God into that divine birth of the human being into which we mortal creatures must climb; it is the attracting divine example given by God to man in the very type and form and perfected model of our human existence."[14] Hindus hold that at least seven *avatar*s of Vishnu existed before Sri Krishna, and that others will appear.[15] Notably, many Hindus believe that the ninth *avatar* was the Buddha, who purged Hindu practices of animal sacrifice and other behaviors he found abhorrent. The tenth *avatar*, however, has not yet appeared, and is expected to be Kalki. Kalki Avatar will renew *dharma* at the end of this age (considered to be the Kali Yuga). The Kali Yuga is the most spiritually degraded age of the world cycle (or *mahayuga*) – which consists of four ages. It is interesting to note that some Hindus, at least in principle, interpret luminaries of non-Indian and non-Hindu origin as *avatar*-like incarnations, such as Jesus Christ.

Although Vishnu and Shiva are the most important gods in modern India, it should be noted that there is also an important goddess tradition. Veneration of female deities includes not only the consorts of Brahma, Shiva, and Vishnu – the goddesses Sarasvati, Parvati, and Lakshmi – but worship of Ultimate Reality in the form of the Divine Mother or Great Goddess (*devi*). The Hindu goddess tradition is thought by some scholars to have roots in the ancient (indigenous) Dravidian culture of India. In contemporary India, veneration of the Great Goddess is associated with Shaktism, or worship of Ultimate Reality as feminine energy (*shakti*) or in feminine aspects or manifestations (i.e. various goddesses). The most popular depiction of the Divine Mother is the goddess Durga. Durga is depicted in some puranic (or epic) literature as being more powerful than all the other gods, and is often identified with a variety of different regional goddesses. Interestingly, some representations of the Divine Mother, such as Kali (whose worship is popular in Bengal), include maternal, fertility, and destructive warlike qualities. This type of symbolism, often bewildering to outsiders, embodies the polarities of *samsara*. This symbolism also points to the transcendent source from which *samsara* emerges and into which it dissolves.

THE MIDDLE PERIOD

During the early part of the Middle Period, often called the Scholastic Period (*c*.300–1200 C.E.), great *acharya*s ("teachers," such as Shankara and Ramanuja) were active. It was during this period that classical Hindu philosophy, or scholasticism, emerged. The renaissance that occurred during the Middle Period, partly spawned by the challenge posed to traditionalist views by Buddhists and Jains, helped to bring about a Hindu revival (or an outpouring of religious thinking that turned toward the Vedas as an authority). This rise in Hindu philosophy blossomed into six main schools of thought or *darshana*s. Sometimes referred to as different schools of philosophy, *darshana*s are described by the scholar Diana Eck as "'points of view' which represent the varied phases of the truth viewed from different angles of vision."[16] The six *darshana*s are considered authentic systems of Hindu Orthodoxy, meaning that they accept the authority of the Vedas. The Buddhist and Jain traditions, which flourished during the Classical Period, are not considered Orthodox because they rejected the authoritative status of the Vedas and challenged the authority of the *brahmin* priests and other social norms. Sarvepalli Radhakrishnan, a scholar and former president of India, elaborated on what it means, as a Hindu, to accept the authority of the

Hindu temple. A typical feature of most temples is the presence of murtis *(statues)
of the Hindu deities to whom the temple is dedicated*

Vedas: "The acceptance of the Veda … does not mean either full agreement with all the doctrines of the Veda or admission of any belief in the existence of God. It means only a serious attempt to solve the ultimate mystery of existence; for even the infallibility of the Veda is not admitted by the [Orthodox Hindu] schools in the same sense."[17] In other words, the diversity of the six *darshana*s on theological issues is, oftentimes, substantial, and their emphasis and method of scriptural exegesis (or interpretation) varies – yet they are all accepted as authentic representations of Hindu religiosity. The six Orthodox *darshana*s are Nyaya, Vaiseshika, Samkhya, Purva-Mimamsa, Vedanta, and Yoga. The last two, Vedanta and Yoga, are discussed below.

Vedanta

The Upanishads, the *Bhagavad-Gita*, and the *Brahma Sutras* (which contain upanishadic philosophy in the form of aphorisms) constitute the foundational, authoritative texts of Vedantic philosophy (also known as Uttara Mimamsa). Great *acharya*s wrote commentaries (*bhasya*) on these texts; it is from these commentaries, or interpretations, that the different classical schools of Vedanta arose. In general, these schools place different emphasis on the relationship between the soul, the world, and the Ultimate Reality. However, all classical schools of Vedanta base their understanding in the sacred texts listed above, and all are united in their belief in the spiritual nature of existence, the divinity of the soul, and the ultimacy of Brahman.

Though there are different approaches within Vedanta (discussed below), some people identify the tradition with Advaita Vedanta, which is considered by many as Hindu philosophy par excellence. Similar to the Sufi path in Islam or the Zen Buddhist tradition, Advaita Vedanta is a mystical or esoteric path that typically requires the guidance of a teacher[18] (*guru*) and initiation (*diksha*) into a spiritual lineage or monastic tradition. The *advaita* (or non-dualistic) ideal was chiefly expounded by the great sage Shankara (*c.*788–820 C.E.), who is generally acknowledged to be the most influential Hindu philosopher from any period of Indian history. Considered by some to be a divine incarnation, Shankara systematized the essential insights of the Upanishads, or inward teachings of the *shruti* scriptures, into a rigorous philosophical and spiritual practice. In doing so he re-invigorated Hindu teachings across India and re-inspired faith in the Vedas (notably, the Upanishads) as the basis of religious authority. The spiritual path (*marga*) taught by Shankara is a jñanic yoga that seeks liberation (*moksha*) primarily through the acquisition of liberating gnosis (*jñana*). According to this path, people suffer because they mistakenly identify themselves with the body, mind (*manas*), and ego (*ahankara*). The mind, body, and phenomenal reality on the whole, however, are merely the passing (illusory) foreground of the one true reality – Brahman, the Self – which is never born and never dies and is unaffected by the passage of time. This reality, which is our essential identity, is the innermost subject of all experience – pure, impersonal consciousness (or *atman*). Only *atman*, which is none other than Brahman (the Supreme Reality), ultimately exists; everything else, including the world, heavens, gods, souls, etc., can be considered to exist from only a relative, or unenlightened, point of view.

The appearance of the relative or conventional world is generated through Brahman's concealing and projecting power (referred to as *maya*). Through this power the true nature of Brahman is concealed in a realm of illusory projections (also referred to as *maya*). In these projections *nirguna brahman* (Brahman without attributes) takes on the appearance of *saguna brahman* (Brahman with attributes) and the many things that constitute phenomenal reality. Thus, phenomenal reality is Ultimate Reality (or Brahman) misperceived. When misperception ceases, so does phenomenal reality – and along with it all forms of suffering and apparent multiplicity. Therefore, it is possible to achieve liberation from conventional reality. As ignorance (*avidya*) causes it to *appear*, so knowledge (*jñana*) causes it to *disappear*. At this stage of illumination, one realizes the non-duality of Brahman, the non-difference between the self and Brahman, and the non-reality of the phenomenal world. Shankara summarizes this teaching as follows: "*Brahman* is real: the world is an illusory appearance; the individual soul (jîva) is *Brahman* alone, not other."[19]

In order to attain non-dualistic Self-realization (or realization of *nirguna brahman*, the Absolute beyond names and forms) – which is the ultimate aim of Advaita Vedanta – Shankara taught that the seeker must accomplish the following prerequisites:

(1) discrimination between things permanent and transient, (2) renunciation of the enjoyment of fruits of action in this world and in the next, (3) the six treasures, as they are called, *viz* not allowing the mind to externalize, checking the external instruments of the sense organs … not thinking of things of the senses … ideal forbearance … constant practice to fix the mind in God … and faith … and (4) the intense desire to be free.[20]

If an aspirant is firmly established in the above spiritual requisites, Shankara holds he is capable of penetrating the illusory appearance of multiplicity (names and forms) and duality (subject–object thinking) through discrimination (*viveka*) and self-inquiry (*atma vichara*). Typically, this implies the inward practice known as *neti neti* ("not this, not this"), which entails a process of subjective investigation that negates everything which is not Self until the Self (which is the source of mind), is directly realized. Similarly, in accordance with the Upanishadic teaching that asserts "it is the Self that should be realized – should be heard of, reflected on, and meditated upon,"[21] Advaita Vedanta stresses three foundational spiritual practices (*sadhana*): listening (*sravana*) or hearing the Truth (from study of scripture or a guru); contemplating or analyzing (*manana*) the Truth; and introspectively meditating (*nididhyasana*) on the Truth. Other practices utilized in this tradition include recitation of mantras and meditation on the *mahavakya*s, or "great words," of the Upanishads: "Consciousness is *Brahman*, or *Prajnanam Brahma*";[22] "I am *Brahman*, or *Aham brahma asmi*";[23] "That thou art, or *Tat tvam asi*";[24] and "This *Atman* is *Brahman*, or *Ayam Atma Brahma*".[25]

Other interpretations, which differ from those of Shankara (and his followers) on certain philosophical issues, such as the relationship between the individual soul and Brahman, are found in other Vedantic schools. In the twelfth century, a Hindu saint and philosopher known as Ramanuja (1017–1137 C.E.) produced a system called Vishishtadvaita, or qualified non-dualism. Vishishtadvaita accepts that the soul and God are essentially one, but also teaches that an individual soul retains self-consciousness. Under Vishishtadvaita belief, the soul can exist in an eternal relationship with God. Later, Madhva (1199–1278 C.E.) opposed both the non-dualism of Shankara and qualified non-dualism of Ramanuja by purporting a concept called Dvaita (dualism). The Dvaita system introduced the concept of *bheda*, or difference, by positing that a fundamental distinction exists between any two elements: God and soul; one soul and another soul; God and matter; soul and matter; and one material thing and another. From this perspective, God, soul, and matter are ontologically distinct; however, God is considered independent while souls and matter are dependent on God. Thus, there is never a complete union with God, but rather souls exist in an eternal relationship with God, as lover and Beloved.

Yoga

The Sanskrit word *yoga* is derived from the root word *yuj*, meaning to join. Yoga, in its general and classical usage, implies a spiritual practice or technique for attaining *moksha* (liberation). Through it, a practitioner attempts "to *unify* the spirit, [and] to do away with the dispersion and automatism that characterizes profane consciousness. For the 'devotional' (mystical) schools of Yoga this 'unification,' of course, only precedes the true union, that of the human soul with God."[26] The philosophy of Yoga (*yoga-darshana*) is now associated with the Yoga Sutras, a collection of 195 aphorisms authored by the sage Patañjali, who lived in the second or third century of the Common Era. Patañjali was not the founder of Yoga per se, but rather he systematized preexisting philosophies, especially the metaphysical views of the Samkhya school, into a holistic (and theistic) spiritual path called Raja Yoga. Raja Yoga is accepted by Hindus as one of the major paths to achieving *moksha*.

> **At the foundation of Raja Yoga is a precept vital to all meditation practices – moral cultivation through strict ethical conduct**

The basic worldview associated with Patañjali's Raja Yoga is that humanity is engulfed in an ignorance that leads to suffering. Raja Yoga provides a way of life, as well as transformative disciplines, intended to transform consciousness and cultivate discriminatory powers. The development of spiritual discrimination allows practitioners to rid themselves of ignorance and free pure consciousness from its entanglement in nature. According to the scholar Mircea Eliade:

> The point of departure of Yoga meditation is concentration on a single object; whether this is a physical object (the space between the eyebrows, the tip of the nose, something luminous, etc.), or a thought (a metaphysical truth), or God (Īśvara) makes no difference. This determined and continuous concentration, called ekāgratā ("on a single point"), is obtained by integrating the psychomental flux (sarvārthatā, "variously directed, discontinuous, diffused attention") ... The immediate result of ekāgratā, concentration on a single point, is prompt and lucid censorship of all the distractions and automatisms that dominate – or, properly speaking, compose – profane consciousness.[27]

At the foundation of Raja Yoga is a precept vital to all meditation practices, namely, moral cultivation through strict ethical conduct. If one can live life morally and withdraw from the sensual world, one can progress on the Raja Yoga path through the practice of certain breathing, physical posture, and meditative techniques. As specified in Patañjali's Yoga Sutras, practitioners must master eight virtues: *yama* (restraint);[28] *niyama* (practice or observance);[29] *asana* (posture); *pranayama* (control of energy through restraint of breath); *pratyahara* (withdrawal of the senses); *dhavana* (concentration); *dhayana* (meditation); and *samadhi* (total absorption).

The eight aspects of Raja Yoga are reciprocal and provide a holistic way of life. The goal of Raja Yoga is the attainment of the unconditioned awareness or *samadhi*. Within the Raja Yoga system, the highest form of *samadhi* is synonymous with ultimate freedom through union with God. The overall spectrum of *samadhi* experiences reported by the great sages of India was explained by Swami Prabhavananda as follows:

> Samadhi is chiefly of two kinds: savikalpa, lower samadhi, and nirvikalpa, the higher kind. In the lower form of samadhi, there exists the sense of "I" as distinct though not separate from God, wherein is realized the personal aspect of God. God the Creator, God the Father, God the Mother, God the Friend, God the Beloved – any or all of these aspects of God may then be realized in their completeness. Nirvikalpa is the higher form of samadhi, wherein no sense of the separate ego is left, and there is realized the oneness of the self with God, the Impersonal. In that experience, there is neither I nor you, neither one nor many.[30]

What is commonly known as yoga, especially in the West, is really *hatha yoga*. *Hatha yoga* focuses on various *asana*s, or physical postures (one aspect of the full, eight-fold practice). Through proper training in yoga postures, one can obtain balance, stillness of mind, and concentration. In the Raja Yoga system designed by Patañjali, however, the other seven aspects are vital elements within a complete spiritual path that cannot be fragmented.

MOGUL INDIA

During the later portion of the Middle Period of Indian history (1200–1700 C.E.), the country was dominated by Islamic powers. Muslim invaders established the Delhi sultanate in 1206 and later the powerful Mogul dynasty, which ruled India from the fifteenth to the eighteenth centuries. The meeting point of the Islamic and Indian cultures featured both an inspiring religious exchange and persecution of Hindus by Muslim authorities. In particular, this period witnessed the rise of the *bhakti* spiritual path, which was greatly influenced by Muslim mystics (Sufis). One of the most significant figures in Indian history was Kabir (1440–1518). Kabir was influenced by both Sufi tradition and *bhakti yoga*, and he wrote inspiring poetry honoring both Muslims and Hindus as children of the same God. Kabir's inclusive message affected the founder of the Sikh faith, Guru Nanak (1469–1538). In fact, some of Kabir's poetry is included in the Sikh holy scripture, known as the *Adi Granth*.[31] The period of Mogul India was a time in which other prominent religious figures emerged, among them the female mystics Lallesvari (1317–1372) and Mirabai (1450–1512).

THE MODERN PERIOD

With the end of the Mogul period, India entered a Dark Age. The Portuguese navigator Vasco da Gama reached India in 1498. Shortly thereafter, the Portuguese navy invaded India and established Portuguese rule in certain coastal areas. Portuguese expansion aroused European political and commercial interest in India. The Dutch, the French, and the British all entered the fray, but it was the colonization by the British Empire during the eighteenth and nineteenth centuries that had the greatest impact on India. One Indian scholar concluded:

> By the time the British arrived in India, Hinduism had reached perhaps its lowest ebb. All sorts of superstitions and undesirable practices flourished in the name of religion … Widows were treated with great cruelty, female infanticide was rife in some castes, and compulsory immolation of widows was often enforced. Theologically also, the great Vedāntic truths that lay behind Hindu thought had been obscured by the jungle growth of superstition and corruption. The inspiration of the medieval saint-singers, while still prevalent, had begun to fade in the face of political turmoil and widespread anarchy that followed the collapse of Mughal power.[32]

India was subjected to oppression under foreign rule, but the country underwent a fantastic cultural–religious renaissance. Spiritual visionaries emerged to guide change and reform. India's cultural renewal, which revived Hindu pride, spirituality, and culture, helped inspire the Indian independence movement. In 1947, India attained independence from British rule.

The Brahmo Samaj and the Arya Samaj

In the modern period, a Hindu self-renewal and innovation movement was sparked by the thinker Ram Mohan Roy (1772–1883), among others. Roy was a scholar of religion, with knowledge of both Islam and Christianity. He believed that many of the ritualistic and seemingly polytheistic aspects of the Hindu tradition were a corruption of an original, ancient Hindu religion which remained preserved in the Upanishads. In 1828 Roy founded the Brahmo Samaj, a reformist and monotheistic Hindu group whose belief system focused on the existence of one formless and eternal God. As a reformer, Roy campaigned against the inequalities of the caste system that suffused everyday Hindu life; he also denounced the maltreatment of women.

Influenced by Roy, a reformer named Dayananda Sarasvati (1823–1883) denounced popular Hindu beliefs, such as those deriving from epic or puranic literature, and advocated a return to what he saw as the true and pure Vedic religion. Sarasvati believed in the impersonal God of the Upanishads and he criticized what he saw as "superstitious" Hindu traditions concerning *avatar*s, worship of God through images, pilgrimages, and tantric practices. Sarasvati's social teachings interpreted the caste system on more egalitarian grounds, and he argued for modernization and better treatment of women, and widows in particular. His reformation organized into a religious movement called the Arya Samaj, which promotes, through educational initiatives, a nationalistic return to an idealized Vedic Golden Age.

Sri Ramakrishna and Swami Vivekananda

The Hindu saint Ramakrishna (1834–1886) believed in a unified source of all religions. Sri Ramakrishna's child-like innocence, along with his simplicity and holiness, attracted and inspired many seekers of Truth. Those that gathered around Ramakrishna, in turn, created an energetic movement that helped revive the Hindu tradition. By the standards of today Sri Ramakrishna would be considered illiterate (he had only a basic level of schooling), but his teachings, often expressed in simple language and parables, contained the essence of Hindu spirituality. Sri Ramakrishna's admirers believe that he attained Truth not only by realizing the highest state of consciousness spoken of in the Hindu tradition, but also by practicing Christianity and Islam (specifically, Sufism). Based on his personal experiences, Sri Ramakrishna taught that all religions are paths to God. Sri Ramakrishna's teachings, recorded by his disciples, consist mostly of dialogues. To one devotee he said: "Do all your duties, but keep your mind on God. Live with all – with wife and children, father and mother – and serve them. Treat them as if they were very dear to you, but know in your heart of hearts that they do not belong to you."[33] Sri Ramakrishna taught that everyone is capable of realizing God: "The point is, to love God even as the mother loves her child, the chaste wife her husband, and the worldly man his wealth. Join together these three forces of love, these three powers of attraction, and direct them all to God. Then you will certainly see Him."[34]

Sri Ramakrishna's chief disciple was Swami Vivekananda (1863–1902). Swami Vivekananda consolidated and propagated the order of his master, Sri Ramakrishna, and shared Sri Ramakrishna's initiatives throughout India and abroad. Vivekananda is well known in the West for his address before the 1893 Parliament of World Religions in Chicago, where he represented the Hindu religion. His lectures illuminated the essence of Hindu philosophy as found in the Upanishads and Vedanta. Vivekananda reinvigorated Hindu philosophy at home and enlightened many Western scholars who had previously dismissed Indian philosophy as "primitive." Today, Sri Ramakrishna and Swami Vivekananda both enjoy a significant following among Hindus as well as among a number of Westerners. The Ramakrishna–Vivekananda Order is a promoter of the harmony of religions and emphasizes service to humanity through educational and social work.

Mahatma Gandhi

Mahatma Gandhi (1869–1948) was the chief architect of Indian independence from the British Empire, and therefore he is one of the great figures of Indian history. He also greatly influenced the modern practice of the Hindu religion.

Most influential of all, perhaps, were his teachings of *ahimsa* (non-violence). Furthermore, Gandhi was a social reformer who took a strong stand against the caste system, particularly the manner in which the "untouchables," or those at the bottom of the caste system, were treated. Gandhi's entire way of life, including his social ideas, were a practical application of his religious beliefs. Gandhi is often considered a karmic yogi in that his life and teaching exemplify a spiritual practice focused on selfless work in the world without attachment to the fruits of such labor.

> **Gandhi's entire way of life, including his social ideas, were a practical application of his religious beliefs**

Gandhi's passionate belief in justice and human equality greatly enhanced the ethical dimension of the modern Hindu experience. He was regarded as a *mahatma*, meaning a "great soul." Gandhi's leadership of the Indian independence movement was certainly a major political triumph, but perhaps more important was his ability to uphold religious values on a prodigious scale. Gandhi asserted:

> There is no such thing as "Gandhism," and I do not want to leave any sect after me. I do not claim to have originated any new principle or doctrine. I have simply tried in my own way to apply the eternal truths to our daily life and problems ... The opinions I have formed and the conclusions I have arrived at are not final. I may change them tomorrow. I have nothing new to teach the world. Truth and non-violence are as old as the hills. All I have done is to try experiments in both on as vast a scale as I could do. In doing so I have sometimes erred and learned by my errors. Life and its problems have thus become to me so many experiments in the practice of truth and non-violence. By instinct I have been truthful, but not non-violent ... In fact it was in the course of my pursuit of truth that I discovered non-violence.[35]

Gandhi was among the greatest in a series of Hindu "revivers" of the twentieth century. Along with others, he helped bring about a heightened awareness of Hindu identity. Gandhi also helped manage the rise of Hindu nationalism, and set an example that spurred the subsequent spread of the Hindu religion to the Western world. Other great Hindu revivers of the last century were Rabindranath Tagore (1861–1941), Sri Aurobindo (1872–1950), and Sri Ramana Maharshi (1879–1950).

RITES AND CELEBRATIONS

Puja

A common Hindu rite is the *puja*, or worship service. It can be performed either at home or at a temple; the only requirement is that the body of the believer be clean and their thoughts pure. Exact conformity to prescribed ritual is less important than a pure spirit of devotion. During a *puja* ceremony, an altar is usually arranged in a specific place which holds the image of the deity or *avatar* to which the adherent wishes to pray and offer devotion. In the home, the altar is a hallowed place where an aspect of God is displayed in one or more of its many forms. Each household has its own chosen deity, called the *ishtadeva*, whose representative image, in the form of a picture or statue, may be placed on the altar along with representations of other gods and their consorts. To perform the *puja*, a worshiper prostrates, recites from sacred writings or mantras, and offers food or flowers to the god.

A common misunderstanding among non-Hindus is that during a *puja* ceremony devotees worship idols. However, in India, images of God are not considered "idols." In other words, statues, pictures, or images of gods are not considered to exhaust or limit the transcendence or oneness of God (Brahman); however, the presence of God is considered to be in the image.[36] In fact, the central practice of popular Hindu religiosity is to worship by seeing; namely, to behold God, or an aspect of God, in a visible image. This most sacred visual experience is called *darshan*. In a similar way, *darshan* is also possible when beholding one's guru, a holy person, or a saint. *Darshan*, however, is primarily an act of worship at temples. It is common throughout India to witness hundreds of Hindus crowding into the inner sanctum of a temple in order to "take *darshan*," or catch a glimpse of the divine image represented by a statue of a particular deity or *avatar*. In most cases, priests (or *pujaris*) tend to the deities installed at temples according to a regular schedule. From early in the morning to late at night, *pujaris* perform the rites of awakening, clothing, and even singing to particular deities on specific days. In the great *pujas*, for example, the idol is greeted and asked about his journey, offered food, and given water for bathing. After several other steps, the attendants bid the deity goodbye. All actions taken by the presiding priest are done in a spirit of utmost reverence and veneration.

> The central practice of popular Hindu religiosity is to worship by seeing

Bhajans

Bhajans are a form of worship that can occur in places other than a temple. Friends and family may gather to sing devotional songs on a specific occasion or pray for the blessings of a particular deity. Similarly, worshipers may gather together to perform a *katha*, during which sacred verses from Hindu scriptures are recited. Believers benefit from hearing holy words which are selected according to a common theme chosen by the person hosting the event.

In addition to the *puja*, *bhajan*, and *katha*, Hindus have other ways to offer devotion to God. Special journeys, or pilgrimages, may be undertaken to holy places. Temples devoted to specific gods and historic sites associated with saints are among the places that Hindus may visit on pilgrimages. Many Hindus, for example, go on pilgrimage to places such as Varanasi (formerly known as Benares), India's most holy city, or to the Ganges, its most sacred river. Devotees believe that by bathing in the Holy Ganges, which personifies the goddess Ganga, they will be cleansed of karmic impurities.

Samskaras

There are over forty rites of passage, or *samskaras*,[37] revealed in the Vedas, of which only one-fourth are still practiced today. Participating in a *samskara* cultivates awareness of the sacred quality of life and the importance of one's place in the universe. From birth to burial, each significant change in a person's life is commemorated through a *samskara*. The first of these is the *namkara*, or naming ceremony. In the three highest castes, young male children are given a sacred thread, or *janeu*, to wear for the rest of their lives. This is done during the *upanayana* ceremony, a *samskara* that marks the beginning of a boy's spiritual life. He receives the *janeu* while reciting the *gayatri* mantra, a text taught to him by his father and a priest. The *gayatri* mantra is the most sacred of the Vedic mantras, which signifies the importance of this event. The next most important event in a person's life, according to the Vedas, is marriage. Marriage and the raising of a family are sacred duties. *Vivaha samskara* is the marriage sacrament.

THE HINDU CONCEPT OF TIME

The Hindu concept of time is based on repeating cycles. The basic unit in this cycle is called *yuga* (age or era). There are four *yuga*s occurring in the following order: Satya or Kreta Yuga (the Golden Age), the Treta Yuga (the Silver Age), the Dwaapara Yuga (the Copper Age) and Kali Yuga (the Black Age or the Age of Iron). A cycle of four *yuga*s constitute a *mahayuga* (about 4,320,000 years). A thousand *mahayuga*s constitutes a day in the life of Brahma, the creator god (representing the creative aspect of Brahman). At the end of Brahma's day, the world is submerged in *pralaya* (the great deluge). When a new day starts for Brahma, the *shristi* (the re-creation) and the various *yuga*s/*mahayuga*s begin again. The present age is the Kali Yuga within the twenty-eighth *mahayuga*. Hindus believe that a Kali Yuga represents the lowest decline in spiritual consciousness and righteousness out of any of the cycles.

CHAPTER SUMMARY

The *Rig Veda* records that "Truth is one; sages call it by different names."[38] This Vedic decree may provide the key to understanding the great diversity which exists within the Hindu religion. Some Hindus have an impersonal and abstract conception of the divine, while others view the divine as a personal God (in either male or female form); still others worship the Supreme Being by way of a variety of lesser deities. Underlying this diversity is the philosophical notion that Absolute Reality (Brahman) evades, in its totality, any particular representation. Brahman, however, can be worshiped through a deity or chosen ideal (*ishtadeva*). In this way, the Hindu religion offers and supports many forms of worship as well as different paths and yogic techniques for transforming consciousness and realizing God. The diversity inherent to the Hindu religion explains, in part, how the tradition was able to become the parent religion of the Buddhist, Jain, and Sikh religions. The religious diversity of India also allowed the Hindu tradition to revive and modify itself throughout history when it was confronted by internal and foreign challenges.

Three ways of orienting spiritual life within the Hindu tradition include the path of devotion (*bhakti yoga*), the path of selfless work (*karma yoga*), and the path of philosophical discrimination between the real and unreal (*jñana yoga*). A fourth way, which synthesizes various psycho-somatic practices, is called *raja yoga*. One Hindu thinker remarked that, "in the Hindu, reason saves the aspiring devotee from avoidable errors and pitfalls, work purifies his heart, meditation creates one-pointedness of mind, love gives him the urge to move forward, faith supports him with courage in the hour of despondency, and the grace of God bestows upon him the final fruit of liberation."[39] This kind of holistic spiritual practice permeates the life of a Hindu. It necessitates attention to ethical responsibilities and social duties while ultimately valu-

> **The Hindu religion can be understood as the application of three major ethical principles: truthfulness, self-control, and non-violence**

ing transcendence. From a practical point of view, the Hindu religion can be understood as the application of three major ethical principles: truthfulness (*satyam*), self-control (*brahmacharya*), and non-violence (*ahimsa*). For Hindus, "if God is Truth (satya), non-violence (ahimsā) is the way to realize him. 'If I were asked to define the Hindu creed', wrote Mahātmā Gandhi, 'I should simply say, search after Truth through non-violent means.'"[40]

Eighteenth-century stone statue of the Buddha

CHAPTER 7
THE BUDDHIST TRADITION

Whatever living beings there be: feeble or strong, tall, stout or medium, short, small or large, without exception; seen or unseen, those dwelling far or near, those who are born or those who are to be born, may all beings be happy!

Let none deceive another, not despise any person whatsoever in any place. Let him not wish any harm to another out of anger or ill-will.

Just as a mother would protect her only child at the risk of her own life, even so, let him cultivate a boundless heart toward all beings.

Let his thoughts of boundless love pervade the whole world: above, below and across without any obstruction, without any hatred, without any enmity.

Whether he stands, walks, sits or lies down, as long as he is awake, he should develop this mindfulness. This they say is the noblest living here.

Not falling into wrong views, being virtuous and endowed with insight, by discarding attachment to sense desires, never again is he reborn.[1]

– Buddha, *Metta Sutta*,
in the *Sutta-Nipata*

INTRODUCTION

The Buddhist spiritual tradition first emerged some 2,500 years ago in India. Those who consider themselves Buddhists base their spiritual practice on the teachings of Siddhartha Gautama, the historical Buddha. Since its inception the Buddhist tradition has demonstrated the ability to adapt itself in order to facilitate its message within different cultures. As the Buddhist path spread from its early roots near the Ganges Valley in India, throughout

Timeline

*c.*566-486 B.C.E.
Siddhartha Gautama, historical Buddha

*c.*483 B.C.E.
First Council at Rajagrha

*c.*380 B.C.E.
Second Council at Vaisali

3rd century B.C.E.
Theravada tradition ("Path of the Elders") emerges

272-232 B.C.E.
Reign of King Asoka

*c.*250 B.C.E.
Third Council at Pataliputra

2nd–1st century B.C.E.
Oral record of Buddha's teachings, as preserved by Theravada school, is put into writing

100 B.C.E.–200 C.E.
Mahayana Buddhist literature emerges, including *Perfection of Wisdom* sutras and *Lotus Sutra*

*c.*100 C.E.
Buddhist travelers first enter China

*c.*150–250 C.E.
Life of Buddhist sage Nagarjuna, founder of Madhyamika ("the Middle Way") school of Mahayana philosophy

India as a whole, and into neighboring Asian countries, it adapted to other cultures while demonstrating a continuity and essential unity of core beliefs derived from the teachings of the Buddha. The two major forms of the Buddhist tradition are the Theravada ("Path of the Elders") and the Mahayana ("Great Vehicle"). The Theravada tradition is prevalent in Sri Lanka, Myanmar, Thailand, Cambodia, and Laos. Mahayanists are found in countries such as China, Korea, Japan, Tibet, Mongolia, Nepal, Bhutan, and Vietnam. In recent decades, both Buddhist traditions have attracted a growing number of Western adherents, especially in Europe and the United States. Buddhists have also developed intriguing and fruitful dialogues with scientists and psychologists.

> **Hurt not others in ways that you yourself would find hurtful**
> *Udana-Varga 5:18*
> THE GOLDEN RULE

*c.*4–5th centuries C.E.
Nalanda, the great Buddhist University, established

*c.*5th century C.E.
Theravada monk Buddhaghosa compiles *Path to Purification*

*c.*460–534 C.E.
Life of first Cha'n/Zen patriarch, Bodhidharma

650 C.E.
Buddhist teachers first enter Tibet

The Buddhist religion has been a major influence on the spiritual and cultural life of South and East Asia. Only in the past century, due to the rise of communism and other ideologies, has Buddhist influence receded (for example, in China, Tibet, Mongolia, Vietnam, and North Korea). Some Buddhist communities have been persecuted by communist governments; such oppression has been particularly acute in Tibet, a traditional Buddhist country that was conquered by the People's Republic of China in 1950. In the wake of a failed anti-Chinese revolt which broke out in 1959, the young Tenzin Gyatso, the fourteenth Dalai Lama, who is both a Buddhist monk and Tibetan head of state, fled into exile in India where he was joined by a large number of Tibetans. Tibetan Buddhist teachers, or lamas, have since gained students worldwide and have increased the popularity and awareness of Buddhist teachings in Western countries. This situation is partly due to the Dalai Lama's eloquent teachings on altruistic ethics, peace, and justice (in 1989 he was awarded the Nobel Peace Prize).

THE THREE JEWELS

The word "Buddha" is derived from the Sanskrit word *buddhi*, meaning "to wake up." Accordingly, the word "Buddha" is a title which means "one who is awake" or "one who has awakened." The Buddha of this age was Siddhartha Gautama, an Indian prince who renounced a regal life and dedicated himself to spiritual practice. Siddhartha is not the only

Buddha, but rather is one in a line of many Buddhas who have appeared (and will appear) throughout the course of history to teach the path to truth, virtue, and, ultimately, enlightenment. The Buddha is sometimes referred to as "Bhagavan," meaning "Lord," in Buddhist scripture and literature. Specifically, in the Mahayana scriptures he is often called "Lord Buddha." In some cases, he is also known as the *tathagata*. According to the scholar Edward Conze, "the original meaning of the word 'Tathāgata' is no longer known. Later commentaries explain the term as composed of the two words 'Tathā,' 'Thus,' and the past participle 'āgata,' 'come,' or 'gata,' 'gone.' In other words, the Tathagata is one who has come or gone 'thus' i.e., as the other Tathagatas have come or gone."[2]

> The word "Buddha" is derived from the Sanskrit word *buddhi*, meaning "to wake up"

In general, Buddhists do not view the Buddha as a prophet or redeemer who delivered a revelation. Rather, the Buddha is viewed as the Supreme Teacher, or Physician, whose teachings help others achieve freedom and the cessation of suffering that he himself attained. Buddhist spiritual practice can therefore be understood as an effort to bring about an awakening in the present moment. Ultimately, awakening means the attainment of *nirvana*, which is liberation from *samsara* (the rebirth cycle of conditioned existence).

The indispensable aspects of the Buddhist religion are the Three Jewels, or Triple Gems. The Three Jewels are the Buddha, the *dharma*[3] (the teachings of the Buddha), and the *sangha* (the community of Buddhist practitioners). A Buddhist must have faith in all three of these dimensions of the Buddhist tradition. They form a complete spiritual system representing the very basis of the religion. As such, all Buddhists practice a procedure called *tisarana*, meaning "the taking of the Three Refuges." Taking refuge is a foundational practice, if not a minimum requirement, of anyone on the Buddhist path. The Three Refuges, usually recited daily by all Buddhists, are as follows:

> To the Buddha I go for refuge.
> To the *dharma* I go for refuge.
> To the *sangha* I go for refuge.

The First Refuge is an acknowledgement of trust in the Buddha as a source of wisdom and the exemplar of one who has achieved spiritual enlightenment. The Second Refuge reminds Buddhists that, although their spiritual teacher is no longer physically present, his teachings are the guide to *nirvana*. The Third Refuge, the *sangha*, can be understood to mean the monks, nuns, and laypeople who follow and uphold the *dharma* – but it is also any small supportive community that follows the teachings of the Buddha. In addition to reciting the Three Refuges on a regular basis, Mahayana Buddhists recite the four *bodhisattva* vows. For example, the four vows of the Zen tradition are as follows:

> All beings, without number, I vow to liberate.
> Endless blind passions I vow to uproot.
> Dharma gates, beyond measure, I vow to penetrate.
> The Great Way of Buddha I vow to attain.[4]

THE LIFE OF THE BUDDHA

In addition to its legendary and historical elements, the story of the Buddha's life is also didactic on account of the fact that it is an archetypical representation of the challenges and obstacles encountered on the spiritual path. The life story of the Buddha is didactic in that it provides the paradigm for Buddhist spiritual life. His followers believe that the Buddha lived many previous lives before his rebirth as Siddhartha Gautama. Siddhartha was born sometime between 626 and 560 B.C.E. into a princely family residing in the principality of Kapilavastu (located in the region of modern-day Nepal, a country to the northeast of India). The newborn child was given the name Siddhartha, meaning "he who has attained his goal."

Siddhartha's education in the arts and sciences befitted his status as the scion of a great ruling family. More than formal scholarly training, however, the youth was possessed of innate sagacity, benevolence, and integrity. An additional step in Siddhartha's rise to prominence came at age sixteen when he was married to the princess of a neighboring realm. With the birth of his son, called Rahula, Siddhartha seemed to be establishing the basis of an aristocratic family. Shortly after Rahula's birth, however, Siddhartha's life radically changed course and he was no longer content to play the role of pampered heir to a great clan. One day while traveling, Siddhartha underwent a transformative experience known to Buddhists as "The Four Passing Sights." Siddhartha observed first-hand, and in succession, the grim realities of life as manifested in a struggling elderly person, an agony-wracked sick man, and a burial ceremony filled with pathos. The Fourth Passing Sight Siddhartha beheld was that of a *shramana*, or ascetic holy man, who was journeying about in a state of tranquility. The counterpoise of suffering and contentment that Siddhartha witnessed made a deep impression on the young prince. After a period of intense and restless reflection, he determined that he would abandon his life of power and privilege, and instead take up the life of a *shramana*, or wandering ascetic. Although dramatic, Siddhartha's renunciation of the worldly life was hardly unique within the cultural milieu of his time and place. The *shramana*s were a prevalent aspect of Indian spiritual life during this period, and they were respected as

The life story of the Buddha is didactic in that it provides the paradigm for Buddhist spiritual life

spiritual teachers. Another prevalent and influential *shramana* of Siddhartha's day was Mahavira of the Jain tradition. *Shramana*s were wandering ascetics and charismatic teachers who were independent of the *brahmin*s, or priestly caste of the Brahminical religion – the precursor tradition of the modern Hindu tradition – and therefore they were not bound to rigid rules. The *shramana*s provided an alternative to the Brahminical religion and posed a threat to existing norms, such as the caste system, which were enforced by the *brahmin*s.

In six years spent as a *shramana* Siddhartha dedicated himself to intense spiritual practice. He sought out eminent teachers from the existing Indian tradition and learned and mastered a variety of meditation techniques. During his spiritual experimentations, he decided to adopt a severe ascetic lifestyle which bordered on self-mortification. This was an attempt to sever worldly desires, as other *shramana*s of that time were doing. Siddhartha pushed himself to the limits of endurance through fasting. Eventually he reached a state of severe malnutrition and debility. Physically spent, he realized that extreme self-denial did not bring about realization, but instead caused ill-health and reduced intellectual acumen. Siddhartha decided to abandon his ascetic practice, and was ridiculed by his ascetic companions for his decision to do so. After taking adequate sustenance and recovering from his ascetic practices, Siddhartha entered a grove in Bodh Gaya, sat at the foot of a bodhi tree, entered into meditation, and refused to move until he had attained ultimate enlightenment.

According to some traditions, during Siddhartha's meditation under the Bodhi Tree he was tempted by the evil deity Mara. The temptation symbolized Siddhartha's last inner struggle with the mental afflictions that arise due to ignorance about human identity and the nature of reality. Mara and his army of consorts (personifications of various fetters, or afflictions of the mind), however, failed to divert Siddhartha's attainment. Unmoved by Mara's tricks and temptations, Siddhartha reached down from his meditation seat and touched the earth. The earth quaked in recognition of Siddhartha's merit, thereby dispersing Mara and his consorts. After freeing himself from the evil of the mental afflictions, Siddhartha's state of awareness reached such a depth that he entered into the formless realm that is beyond the limitations usually associated with the space–time realm. According to tradition, during the "three watches of the night" Siddhartha saw all of his previous lives, the previous lives of others, and how these lives arise based on the consequential law of *karma*. According to some traditions, at the time of his enlightenment he uttered these words:

I have gone through many rounds of birth and death, looking in vain for the builder of this body. Heavy indeed is birth and death again and again! But now I have seen you, house-builder, you shall not build this house again. Its beams are broken; its dome is shattered: self-will is extinguished; nirvana is attained.[5]

(*Dhammapada*, 153–154)

Initially, unsure if anyone would understand his realization, Siddhartha, who came to be called "Buddha" or "the awakened one," remained in the forest for forty-nine days after attaining enlightenment. Out of compassion, the Buddha eventually decided to teach others the path of enlightenment. In an event known as the "turning of the wheel of *dharma*," he offered his first teaching. He passed these teachings to his old spiritual companions, the ascetic sages, who had previously ridiculed him for abandoning extreme fasting. The Buddha taught the ascetics a "middle path," which aimed at a balance between asceticism and indulgence. The Buddha also taught them the Four Noble Truths (see below), the foundation of the Buddhist worldview. These ascetics became the Buddha's first disciples and therefore formed the first *sangha* (or community following the spiritual path taught by the Buddha).

For more than four decades the Buddha journeyed far and wide, sharing his teachings. As a teacher, he addressed each student at their particular level of understanding, just as a physician adjusts the treatment for each patient. It is recorded that the Buddha returned to his family to teach them the path to liberation; he even ordained his son as a monk. He urged his students to turn away from worldly concerns and to pursue, above all else, spiritual practice. Unlike the existing Brahminical tradition in India, he admitted all people regardless of gender or caste (distinct and hierarchical social groupings) into his spiritual community. The Buddha's teaching, the Noble Eightfold Path, was called "Noble" (the English word for the Sanskrit *Aryan*) to indicate

> **For more than four decades the Buddha journeyed far and wide, sharing his teachings**

that one becomes Noble through actions and spiritual practice and not through heredity or social standing. In the *Sutta Nipata* the Buddha proclaimed: "I do not call a man a brahmin because of his mother or because of his breeding. Just because a man is entitled to be called 'Sir', it does not mean that he is free from habit and attachment. He who is free from attachment, he who is free from grasping is the person I call a brahmin."[6] The Buddha was not only delivering a new religious path based on his own experience of enlightenment, he was also a revolutionary reformer of the existing tradition that he himself had practiced as a wandering *shramana*.

The Buddha founded spiritual communities consisting of monks, nuns, and laypeople. He also established codes of conduct for each group of adherents. Near the end of his extraordinary life, his cadre of dedicated followers, the *sangha*, gathered together to receive his final instructions. The Buddha, however, did not choose a successor; rather, he enjoined his followers to turn to his teachings (the *dharma*) for guidance. This instruction was recorded in the Buddhist text *Digha Nikaya* (*sutta* 16:6.1), as follows:

> And the Lord said to Ānanda [his disciple]: "Ānanda, it may be that you will think: 'The Teacher's instruction has ceased, now we have no teacher!' It should not be seen like this, Ānanda, for what I have taught and explained to you as Dhamma and discipline will, at my passing, be your teacher."[7]

By his teachings, the Buddha oriented his followers toward personal experience and responsibility and not toward the establishment of an authoritative institution to carry on his teachings. In his last recorded utterance, he urged his followers to realize the impermanence of this life and to endeavor, above all else, for attainment of liberation (*Digha Nikaya* 16:6.7):

> Then the Lord said to the monks: "Now, monks, I declare to you: all conditioned things are of a nature to decay – strive on untiringly."[8]

EARLY BUDDHIST HISTORY AND THE THERAVADA TRADITION

A major development in the history of the Buddhist tradition occurred when King Asoka (pronounced "Ashoka"; r. *c*.272–232 B.C.E.) of the Maurya dynasty of India declared his allegiance to the teachings of the Buddha. Asoka, who had been instrumental in spreading the domain of the Maurya dynasty through violent conquest, became disillusioned with violence and war. Having discovered the teachings of the Buddha, he dedicated his life to *dharma*. He adopted the Buddhist principle of non-violence (*ahmisa*) and declared that peace would be his only method of conquest. When Asoka embraced the teachings of the Buddha, *dharma* was adopted throughout his territory. Subsequently, it spread throughout India and reached Sri Lanka, among other places. In addition to the great prestige that Asoka's patronage bestowed on the Buddhist community, on a practical level, Buddhist institutions, such as the network of monasteries, now enjoyed the support of state authorities. Furthermore, Asoka demonstrated his own commitment to the Buddhist path by personally sponsoring hospitals and animal shelters and by dispatching teachers to near and distant lands.

As early as a century after the Buddha's passing, variations began to develop in how different groups of monks interpreted his teaching. The Theravada tradition ("Path of the Elders") arose some time during the third century B.C.E. At that time, there was apparently a need for the elders to assert an authoritative representation of *dharma* in order to preserve the Buddha's teachings. The Theravada tradition holds that its scriptural corpus faithfully preserves the original teachings of the Buddha. The Theravada path also stresses the monastic ideal and the goal of individual liberation, or *arahat*-ship. An *arahat* is one who has perfected the virtues of a Buddha and has thus reached *nirvana*. As such, it is believed

Top: Buddhist stupa with prayer flags, Nepal
Bottom: Buddhist monks' daily offerings at Luang Phrabang, Laos

that an *arahat* is completely released from *samsara* at the moment of death, and will not incur a rebirth.

Shortly after the Buddha passed away, his disciples held an important assembly known as the First Council at Rajagrha. The purpose of the gathering was to establish matters of doctrine. During this assembly, the Buddha's two main stu-dents, Ananda and Upali, recited the teachings of the Buddha as they had heard them from the Buddha himself. This recita-tion formed the oral tradition of the Buddha's teachings, which was meticulously memorized and chanted by monks. Later, the oral tradition was written down and accepted as authoritative scripture by Theravadin monks around the first century B.C.E. In transcribing the teachings the monks used a colloquial Indian language called Pali and the scriptural corpus

> **A century after Buddha, variations began to develop in how different groups of monks interpreted his teaching**

thereby became known as the Pali Canon. Because the Pali Canon is composed of three sections – namely, the *Vinaya-Pitaka*, *Sutta-Pitaka*, and *Abhidhamma-Pitaka* – it is also known as the Tripitaka, or "Triple Basket." The *Vinaya-Pitaka*, meaning "Basket of Order," is an explanation of the monastic code and the formation of the Buddhist com-munity. The *Sutta-Pitaka*, or "Basket of Teachings," presents detailed accounts of the social, philosophical, and practical aspects of the Buddha's teaching. It should also be pointed out that the *Sutta-Pitaka* serves as the basis of the *Dhammapada*, a collection of verses viewed by many as the essence of the Buddhist religion. Notably, the *Dhammapada* was extremely popular amongst Buddhist monks as a handbook. For all Buddhists, the *Dhammapada* constitutes a sacred text. Finally, the third basket of the Pali Canon is the *Abhidhamma-Pitaka*, or "Basket of Higher Teaching," which is a comprehensive and schematic classification of various aspects of Buddhist philosophy and psychology.

THE MAHAYANA VEHICLE

Over the course of time, as the teachings of the Buddha gained greater currency amongst diverse groups of people, the *dharma* was adapted to meet different spiritual needs. Within the Hindu typology of spiritual tendencies, or personality types, there are three major kinds of aspirants: those of karmic, jñanic, and bhaktic dispositions. People of a karmic nature tend to focus on meritorious action in the world, those of a jñanic nature are more prone to philosophical thinking, while people of a bhaktic nature are devotional, preferring worship. The Mahayana Buddhist tradition developed aspects suited to all these types of people with-out compromising a worldview firmly rooted on the Buddha's core teachings. Mahayana Buddhists hold that their interpretations of the Buddha's teachings are found in embryonic form in the Pali Canon. Historically, practitioners of the Mahayana, the "great vehicle" or "greater vehicle," distinguish their beliefs from what they call the Hinayana (referring to the Theravada), meaning the "lesser vehicle." In that way, Mahayanists view their tradition as the esoteric and more advanced way of understanding the Buddha's message. In general, however, Buddhists from all schools believe that each branch of the Buddhist tradition offers a means or way toward *nirvana*.

The Mahayana Buddhist tradition arose sometime around 100 B.C.E., apparently as a revival of earlier Buddhist schools like the Mahasamghika. Mahayanists hold that their teachings were revealed through secret oral lineages, dreams, and meditative visions. As such, Mahayana *sutra*s (meaning "thread" or "book of instruction"), written in the language of Sanskrit, were said to be from the Buddha himself, although they were obviously written down at a much later date. In the Theravada tradition, the *arahat*s (enlightened monks) had, over time, attained a station of authority, even of superiority. It appears that some saw themselves as the sole interpreters of *dharma*, an attitude that may have bordered on elitism. One of the great innovations of the Mahayana perspective was to present the ideal of the *bodhisattva* ("enlightenment-being") as distinct from, and superior to, *arahat*-ship (which was the ultimate aim of Theravada practitioners). According to the Mahayana view, a *bodhisattva* reaches *nirvana* but defers parting from *samsara*, unlike the *arahat*, and chooses to be reborn in order to help others achieve realization. A *bodhisattva* vows to postpone leaving samsaric existence until all sentient beings are liberated. Thus the motivation of a *bodhisattva* is broadened to include the enlightenment of all sentient beings rather than just personal enlightenment. The *bodhisattva* ideal is powerfully represented in the following Mahayana saying:

> Can there be bliss when all that lives
>   must suffer?
> Shalt thou be saved and hear the whole
>   world cry?[9]

According to the Mahayana view, some *bodhisattva*s are celestial beings, or gods, from higher realms of existence, who can help aspirants attain enlightenment. These celestial *bodhisattva*s, who achieved great merit in previous lives, have the ability to transfer their merit to others. Thus the Mahayana school developed practices of worship, prayer, and devotion directed toward *bodhisattva*s. A classic Mahayana text that beautifully outlines the *bodhisattva* ideal is *A Guide to the Bodhisattva Way of Life* by Shantideva, a monk who lived during the eighth century C.E. in India.[10]

One Buddhist school that falls under the Mahayana umbrella, and which is well known in the West, is the tradition of Zen. The word "Zen" is a Japanese name which derives from the Chinese word *ch'an*, which is itself a translation of the Sanksrit term *dhayana*, meaning "meditation." According to legend, this Buddhist tradition was first transmitted to China (where it was known as Ch'an) by the monk Bodhidharma (*c.*460–534 C.E.) around 500 C.E. Notably, Bodhidharma achieved influence and fame in China among Taoists as well as Buddhists, and he is regarded as the First Patriarch of the Ch'an (or Zen) Buddhist tradition. It is recorded that Bodhidharma, after meditating for nine years while facing a wall, was asked by the Chinese emperor about the essence of Buddhism. He responded: "All things are empty, and there is nothing desirable or to be sought after."[11] Following the example of Bodhidharma, practitioners of Zen meditate as the chief means of achieving spiritual awakening. In Zen, a particular emphasis is placed on the transmission from teacher to student. In fact, the Zen tradition views itself as having a direct lineage, through teacher–student transmission, to the Buddha. Zen features a number of different techniques of meditation. A distinctive feature of the Zen tradition (particularly in the Rinzai school of Zen) is the use of *koan*s. A *koan* is a mental puzzle or paradox. A paradox is not solvable or logically comprehendible; thus the practitioner eventually discovers that it is fruitless to try to "solve" the puzzle by conventional rational inquiry. Through this process, the practitioner realizes that rationality will not yield enlightenment; therefore, he or she develops different ways of viewing the world that can lead to important insights. In addition to the *koan*, another technique typical of Zen is *zazen* (sitting meditation). During *zazen*, practitioners sit on *zafus*, traditional Zen meditation cushions, and usually dress in a traditional Zen robe with a belt while sitting in the cross-legged position. In *zazen* practice, heightened emphasis is placed on posture, which is strictly enforced by a *roshi*, or Zen master. The basic aim of *zazen* meditation is to allow thoughts to arise and disperse without grasping onto them or judging them.[12]

Sometime around 650 C.E. Mahayana Buddhist teachers first entered the region of Tibet. During the seventh century of the Common Era, the Tibetan king Trisong Detsen invited the Indian Buddhist Padmasambhava to spread Buddhist teachings in his realm. Revered by Tibetans as a supramundane sage, Padmasambhava, whose name means "born from lotus," is thought by them to have blessed the region, allowing *dharma* to take root. Padmasambhava's writings are considered spiritual classics by Tibetans, and it is thought that he concealed other works which were revealed later by Tibetan sages. By approximately 1000 C.E., the Buddhist religion was the dominant spiritual practice in Tibet. The Tibetan branch of the Mahayana Buddhist tradition is often regarded as its own distinct vehicle called the Vajrayana Buddhist tradition (or the Diamond Vehicle). The Tibetan tradition is unique in that it incorporates the most esoteric aspects of the Buddhist religion which were transmitted from the early tantric Buddhists of India. The Tibetan Buddhist path was influenced by the genius of the Tibetans, including their indigenous shamanic religion, the Bön tradition.

The Tibetans excelled at visualization techniques of meditation

The Tibetans also excelled at visualization techniques of meditation. One of the most important Mahayana Buddhist texts, and one first composed in Tibet, is the *Bardo Thodol*, or the Tibetan Book of the Dead. The *Bardo Thodol* consists of teachings on the afterlife.[13] The four schools, or orders, of the Tibetan Buddhist tradition are the Nyingma, the Kagyu, the Sakya, and the Geluk.[14]

DEPENDENT ORIGINATION AND THE THREE UNIVERSAL TRUTHS

One of the most important Buddhist concepts is *paticcasamuppada*, often translated as "dependent origination" or "interdependence." According to a scripture attributed to the Buddha himself, this principle, in compact form, was recorded as follows: "This being, that is; from the arising of this, that arises; this not being, that is not; from the cessation of this, that ceases."[15] The interdependent and causal understanding of reality, as indicated in the principle of *paticcasamuppada*, does not appeal to a mythic beginning or divine creation to explain reality; it does not suggest that there is a source, principle, or God which directs all events; nor does it, however, propose that reality is random. Instead, the Buddhist principle of *paticcasamuppada* purports that every event arises due to previous causes and conditions that are embedded within a complex matrix of events that extend back ad infinitum.

For Buddhists, the nature of this interdependent, conditioned reality is outlined in the Three Universal Truths. These are *anicca*, *anatta*, and *dukkha*. According to *anicca* (pronounced "anicha"), the nature of existence is impermanent and transient. *Anatta* means "selflessness," meaning that "selfhood" lacks a permanent, unchanging substratum (such as a soul). *Dukkha* refers to the inherent unsatisfactory nature of existence.

SELFLESSNESS

According to Buddhists, the "self" is merely a conception of (or imputation of an illusory idea upon) a variety of physical (bodily) and mental aggregates that are constantly changing and have no fundamental or eternal existence. The Five Aggregates (or *skandhas*) that make up the "self" are physical matter, physical sensations, perceptions, mental formations, and bits of consciousness. It is important to recall that during the time of the Buddha two extreme views were prevalent. One perspective held the personal self and the universe as eternal (*sassatavada*), while another perspective suggested that neither was eternal (*ucchedavada*). The path taught by the Buddha is a Middle Way between these two extremes. Thus, when Buddhists say that there is no "self," they do not mean that there is nothing. Rather, what is meant by *anatta* is that there is no inherent, permanent, independently existing entity called the personal self.

The Buddha's teaching regarding selflessness extends, however, beyond the personal self (or ego). According to the Buddhist perspective, the universe is also selfless, meaning it does not have an independent, unchanging substratum, but rather it is constantly changing, impermanent, and insubstantial, just like the selfhood of any person. In fact, according to Buddhist teachings ignorance of the nature of existence, including the self, leads to *dukkha* or suffering.

SUNYATA OR EMPTINESS

Buddhists often speak of two different levels of truth. One is conventional and exists for those who have not realized the real nature of reality. The other level, or ultimate truth, pertains to reality as it really is. This epistemological theory permeates the Buddhist worldview and often causes great confusion. The experience of reality as it (ultimately) is allows one to see the relative nature of conventional teachings; therefore, depending on how far one has progressed on the path, Buddhist teachings may mean different things to different people. The teaching of Emptiness, from the perspective of ultimate truth, suggests that all reality is Empty (*sunyata*), including *nirvana* and the teachings of the Buddha. According to this perspective, reality is not substantial – meaning that it does not exist as a singular, unchanging, independent thing – but rather is empty, lacks substratum, and only appears to be real due to ignorance and the reifying use of language. From this perspective, misleading use of linguistic constructs causes people to designate things, or objects, as existing beyond the transience of passing causes and conditions.

> **The teaching of Emptiness, from the perspective of ultimate truth, suggests that all reality is Empty**

Buddhists assert that nothing has an intrinsic reality of its own, but rather that all things exist in dependence on causes and conditions; all reality is Empty. Mahayana Buddhists refer to the quality of Emptiness as suchness (*tathata*), or buddha-nature (*buddhata*). According to this view, everything has a latent buddha-nature. This perspective found fruition in the concept of *tathagatagarbha*, which purports that all beings are potential buddhas, i.e. that each of us latently possesses, in embryonic form, all the virtues of a buddha. *Nirvana* can thus be viewed as an awakening of our suchness, or buddha-nature, which is covered by ignorance. It is asserted that the Buddhist path can remove the veil of ignorance that prevents us from realizing that we are really buddhas. According to the

Mahayana tradition, the experiential realization of one's buddha-nature is a spiritual transformation that enables a person to interact in the world with complete compassion and wisdom. The *bodhisattva*, who realizes ultimate reality, works within a dreamlike world to help others. But the *bodhisattva* is cognizant of the fact that, ultimately, there is no "person" who is helping "others." It should be pointed out that one of the most important thinkers of the Mahayana tradition, from whom much of the above discussion on Emptiness and the two levels of truth is drawn, was the Indian Buddhist philosopher Nagarjuna. Nagarjuna, a first-century C.E. Indian monk, was the founder of the Madhyamaka, or Middle Way, school of Buddhist philosophy. Madhyamaka serves as the formative and most important philosophy of the present-day Mahayana Buddhist tradition.[16]

THE FOUR NOBLE TRUTHS

The Four Noble Truths were the first teachings that the Buddha delivered after his enlightenment, and are his most important teachings. They are the framework for the entire Buddhist religion, and are accepted by all branches and denominations of the tradition. As the most essential teaching of the Buddha, the Four Noble Truths present the clearest path to enlightenment. The methodological approach that the Buddha utilized in exploring the Four Noble Truths is, in structure, the same methodology utilized by physicians in treating illnesses. In general terms, this approach entailed: (1) the diagnosis of an affliction; (2) the identification of the causes of the affliction; (3) the elimination of those causes; and (4) the administering of a holistic treatment. This methodology is logical, rational, and is an empirically testable process.

> **As the most essential teaching of the Buddha, the Four Noble Truths present the clearest path to enlightenment**

The First Noble Truth that the Buddha taught was the truth of suffering – all beings will necessarily endure suffering or unsatisfactory experiences (*dukkha*). Suffering is incurred during birth, aging, sickness, and death. Suffering arises when we desire things and cannot attain them; and even after we attain objects of desire we suffer in trying to keep them or experience them again. The Buddha's Second Noble Truth identifies the origin of suffering, which is desire (or grasping). Essentially, this grasping entails the ignorant reification of, and clinging to, a selfhood. Belief in a selfhood leads to grasping in general, for example onto other people, sensual pleasures, material objects, reputation, and so on. Because all things are impermanent and insubstantial, grasping leads, inevitably, to suffering. The Third Noble Truth is the truth of the cessation of suffering: one can

*Detail from the 200-year-old murals in Wat Pho,
the Temple of the Reclining Buddha, Bangkok*

eliminate suffering (*dukkha*) by eliminating its cause, i.e. grasping and desire. The "desire" referred to generally means selfish desires, including even the desire to have no desire. If one can eliminate attachment and desire, which also implies clinging onto a selfhood, one attains the cessation of *dukkha*.

The Fourth Noble Truth is the path that leads to the cessation of suffering. It outlines an integral way of life that facilitates spiritual transformation and the end of suffering. If the first, second, and third Noble Truths constitute the Buddha's diagnosis, i.e. of the universal condition of suffering, then the fourth Noble Truth is his treatment for the disease of suffering, i.e. a spiritual path and practice which leads to *nirvana*. The Noble Eightfold Path includes eight essential and reciprocal tenets of Buddhist spiritual practice:

1. Right Understanding. This refers to the need to acquire an experiential understanding of the Three Universal Truths and the Four Noble Truths. It also means that one must recognize the falsehoods and illusions of the world and the pernicious influence of grasping and selfish desire. Increasingly, one should regard reality with a compassionate mind freed from attachment.
2. Right Thought. This involves clearly understanding personal intentions and recognizing the true motives of one's own thoughts and actions. Right thought helps replace negative motives with wholesome ones.
3. Right Speech. This tenet prescribes disciplined speech and rejection of falsehoods, gossiping, idle talk, lies, and harsh words. Speech should be a source of compassion, kindness, and wisdom rather than a cause of suffering.
4. Right Action. As with speech, actions should be wholesome rather than harmful. Right Action involves adhering to the five ethical precepts (for lay practitioners) listed below.
5. Right Means of Livelihood. This involves following the principle of *ahimsa* (non-violence) when choosing an occupation. A Buddhist's profession should be in complete harmony with Buddhist ideals regarding spiritual development and the treatment of others.
6. Right Effort. By cultivating the aspiration to practice *dharma*, one can develop tendencies toward wholesome thoughts, words, and deeds rather than unwholesome states of mind.
7. Right Mindfulness. As a key attribute of the Eightfold Path, Right Mindfulness entails developing an attentive awareness of bodily and mental states, including sensations, feelings, and thoughts.
8. Right Concentration. This step teaches that the essential ingredients of mental concentration and insight are achieved through meditative practices. Ultimately, the

sword of gnosis developed through meditative insight severs ignorance and selfish desires at their root.

Collectively, the Four Noble Truths offer a way to overcome the mental afflictions that arise from the root causes of suffering (and samsaric existence in general): ignorance of the nature of existence; attachment to selfhood and selfish desires; and hatred. To be sure, the Buddhist perspective does not suggest that "life is suffering." Rather, suffering is a reality for those who have not fully awakened; suffering is, therefore, not intrinsic to life itself but is an affliction based in ignorance and selfish desire. Therefore, suffering can be overcome. The Buddha's teachings are, therefore, radically optimistic in suggesting that everyone has the potential to transcend all suffering and attain *nirvana*.

Some non-Buddhists have concluded that the Buddhist view of *dukkha* (suffering) implies that Buddhists are pessimists who reject the enjoyment of life. Buddhists, however, do not shun a life of enjoyment provided that such enjoyment constitutes a life of *dharma*, i.e. following an ethical code of conduct while developing meditative concentration, virtue, and wisdom. For Buddhists, a life based on *dharma* is the most enjoyable life possible, although some suffering is inevitable. Some Buddhists believe that *dharma* is found not in any particular creed, but rather, it is found wherever truth and virtue reside. It has been said by some Buddhist teachers that when *dharma* practice becomes enjoyable one is progressing on the Buddhist path. Given the Buddhist belief in *karma* and rebirth, many Buddhist laypersons live in society, have jobs and families, and devote themselves to compassionate action for the sake of others. From the Buddhist perspective, the attainment of positive karmic merit helps one attain the ultimate goal of *nirvana* in a future lifetime.

ETHICS

Buddhist teaching enjoins lay practitioners to uphold five ethical principles or precepts:

to refrain from harming living beings;
to refrain from taking what is not given;
to refrain from sexual misconduct;
to refrain from wrong speech;
to refrain from taking intoxicants, such as drugs or alcoholic beverages, which impair the mind.

The five precepts listed above constitute the core foundation of Buddhist living. Adhering to these principles is generally known in the *sangha* as taking the five vows (or the five precepts). These rules form a set of guidelines toward which individuals aspire. In many cases, lay practitioners supplement these five principles with others. In monastic communities, more than two hundred precepts govern different aspects of a monk or nun's daily life. As such, members of Buddhist monastic orders are held to higher standards of conduct than laypeople.

One of the most important Buddhist texts to address the issue of ethics is the *Dhammapada*, meaning "the path of virtue." In the *Dhammapada*, verse 183, the message of the Buddha is encapsulated in three simple counsels: to refrain from unwholesome acts; to remain committed to performing positive deeds; and to cultivate a pure mind. Various Buddhist texts describe wholesome and unwholesome actions. That which is unwholesome is referred to as a fetter. Fetters are negative habits of mind, such as attachment to material possessions, which bind individuals to the physical world. The ten fetters are: (1) self-illusion; (2) doubt; (3) indulgence in (wrong) rites, rituals and ceremonies; (4) attachment to sense desires; (5) ill-will; (6) attachment to forms; (7) attachment to the formless; (8) conceit; (9) restlessness; and (10) ignorance.[17] In following the Eightfold Path, the ten fetters can be broken and the virtues of a buddha attained. In fact, one way to view a buddha is as one who has perfected a set of virtues. According to the Buddhist worldview, it is necessary that one live many lives in order to cultivate virtues. Originally, the six virtues, called *paramitas* (typically translated as "perfections"), were considered to be the most essential. These Six Perfections are charity, or generosity (*dana*); ethical conduct (*sila*); patience (*ksanti*); vigor, or energy (*virya*); concentration (*samadhi*); and insight, or wisdom (*prajña*). As the Mahayana Buddhist tradition developed, this list was extended to ten in order to emphasize the ideal of *bodhisattva*-hood. These additional virtues include skillful means (*upaya-kausalya*); resolution, or determination (*pranidhana*); strength (*bala*); and knowledge (*jñana*).

> In monastic communities, more than two hundred precepts govern different aspects of a monk or nun's daily life

REBIRTH AND *KARMA*

Two essential Buddhist concepts, both fundamental to the existing Indian tradition with which the Buddha interacted, are rebirth and *karma*. *Karma*, in its general usage, can be interpreted as the law of cause and effect. Specifically, the word "*karma*" implies a volitional act which has consequences. The ripening of the consequences of karmic actions is *vipaka*. According to the Buddhist view, the present moment determines future moments based on our verbal, physical, and mental thoughts, actions, and intentions. Certain causes and conditions arise in the present moment which catalyze the ripening (*vipaka*) of past actions, thoughts, words, and intentions (*karma*). This is an eternal law relevant to the conditioned reality of *samsara*. The Buddhist view of cause and effect is not fatalistic; every moment provides the opportunity to direct the course of one's future. One Buddhist tradition records that, in response to a questioner who had asked about his future and past lives, the Buddha suggested that the best way to know one's past lives and future lives is to look at the present moment (which was determined by past states and is, in turn, determining future states).

If there is a "remainder" of *karma* which has not come to fruition or ripened, then rebirth occurs in order to exhaust the *karma*. However, there is no permanent, unchanging "self" or "soul" that is reincarnated; rather, *karma* determines the next life in the manner of a rock which, when thrown into a lake, causes waves that ripple outward. Just as each moment is dependent on the previous moment, each life (a consciousness which forms in the womb under certain psychosomatic conditions) is dependent on the karmic waves of previous lives. After death, due to ignorance, there is a momentum caused by sensual craving and mental grasping. One Buddhist scripture states: "It is this 'thirst' (craving, *tanhā*) which produces re-existence and re-becoming … and which is bound up with passionate greed … and which finds fresh delight now here and now there … namely, (1) thirst for sense-pleasures (*kāma-tanhā*), (2) thirst for existence and becoming (*bhava-tanhā*), and (3) thirst for non-existence (self-annihilation, *vibhava-tanhā*)."[18] Most Buddhists generally believe there are six categories of realms where rebirth can occur: the hell realm; the hungry ghost realm; the animal realm; the *asura* or titan realm; the human realm; and the celestial realm. Rebirth in a certain realm depends on karmic merit attained through previous lives. From this perspective, "gods" are celestial beings that, through many lifetimes, have attained great karmic merit and achieved rebirth in a celestial realm. These godly beings, however, like humans, are still operating under the law of cause and effect and therefore are not exempt from rebirth into lesser realms and forms. The human realm is regarded with great esteem because individuals can achieve enlightenment. In the lesser realms, however (such as the ghost and animal realms), one is too afflicted to reach enlightenment, and in celestial realms one is too complacent. Rebirth in the human realm is therefore extremely rare and precious, an opportunity not to be wasted. Given such a complex system of rebirth, Buddhists believe that it took Siddhartha Guatama many lifetimes, even eons, to finally attain buddhahood.

> **Just as each moment is dependent on the previous moment, each life is dependent on the karmic waves of previous lives**

THE NON-THEISTIC PERSPECTIVE OF THE BUDDHIST TRADITION

Some Hindus accept the Buddha as the ninth divine incarnation of Vishnu in this cycle of existence; however, the Buddha did not explicitly claim to be a divine incarnation or *avatar*. It does seem, though, that some of Buddha's early followers may have implicitly viewed him as a kind of divine sage. He was, for example, sometimes referred to as "Lord" by early Buddhists. One prevalent but misinformed view is that the Buddha was a nihilist. During Buddha's lifetime many views circulated in India regarding the existence and nature of

> **One prevalent but misinformed view is that the Buddha was a nihilist**

Ultimate Reality, including that of the Upanishads. The Buddha, when questioned by his followers about God and other metaphysical issues, did not answer, but instead remained silent. Some have interpreted this to mean that his answers would have been either beyond the level of understanding of the questioners or that he believed his answers would have simply caused confusion rather than helping. Many scholars agree that the Buddha's answers would have probably varied depending on the understanding of the questioner.

It should be noted that in all the teachings of the Buddha compiled in the Pali canon, which consists of a library of volumes, nowhere does he explicitly state that God either does or does not exist. The Buddha could have easily given an answer regarding the existence of God — or that ineffable Ultimate Reality which the term "God" connotes — if he had wished to do so (and the Buddha was clearly not afraid of challenging the status quo of the Brahminical religion). The Buddha, however, seems to have wanted his followers to avoid abstract concepts and dogma and to focus on eliminating the causes of suffering. Though it is widely held that Buddhist doctrines are not compatible with a "personal" God, one of the Buddha's recorded sayings, however, does speak of an "Unborn," which presents a challenging aspect of his teachings given other statements regarding the selflessness and impermanence of all things. This saying of the Buddha reads as follows: "There is, monks, an Unborn, Unbecome, Unmade, Uncompounded … If there were not this Unborn … then there would be no deliverance here visible from that which is born, become, made, compounded. But since there is this Unborn, Unbecome, Unmade, Uncompounded, therefore a deliverance is visible from that which is born, become, made, compounded."[19]

NIRVANA

Nirvana is an experience that transcends dualistic modes of thinking and the normal categories of thought. The nirvanic experience is ultimately inexpressible, and the Buddhist teachings try to avoid explaining it in conceptual terms (abstract concepts are viewed as obstacles or as a means rather than an end). Rather than objectifying concepts in the outside world, Buddhists tend to concentrate on cultivation within the subjective domain, aiming at transformative experiences. Because the attainment of *nirvana* is the ultimate soteriological aim of the Buddhist tradition, which all of its facets (such as the practice of ethics and the cultivation of meditative concentration and insight) seek to facilitate, the Buddhist practitioner works to transcend egoistic individuality, attachment, and selfish desires which are the main inhibitors of one's own buddha-nature. The attainment of *nirvana* was described by the Buddha as the extinguishing of the fires of attachment, desire, and hatred. It was also referred to as the

> **The attainment of *nirvana* is the extinguishing of the fires of attachment, desire, and hatred**

cessation of suffering and the highest bliss. In fact, some Buddhist masters have emphasized that there is no real ontological difference between the reality of *samsara* and *nirvana*; it is only that while in the grip of mental afflictions we fail to see *samsara* as *nirvana*.

MEDITATION PRACTICE

The cultivation of virtues and ethics (*sila*) serves as the foundation of Buddhist practice. Given a stable ethical foundation, Buddhists engage in meditation practice in order to deepen compassion, concentration, and wisdom. The most important states of mind, which are achievable through Buddhist meditation, are called the Four *brahma-viharas*, or the Four Divine Abodes. The first, *metta*, is extending universal love and goodwill to all beings. The second, *karuna*, is having compassion for all suffering beings. The third, *mudita*, is sympathetic joy or the sharing in the happiness of others. And the fourth, *uppekkha*, is maintaining equanimity despite the vicissitudes of life. These four states hold particular import for Mahayana Buddhists, who cultivate them in order to develop the disposition of a *bodhisattva*.

The category of Buddhist meditation practice called *samatha* is designed to enhance concentration, attentional stability, and vividness of the mind.[20] *Samatha* practice is also referred to as "tranquility meditation." One of the most authoritative texts dealing with *samatha* and other important meditation practices was compiled by the Theravada monk Buddhaghosa in his erudite *Path to Purification*, written in the fifth century C.E.[21] In general, during *samatha* practice one can find temporary release from mental afflictions by calming the mind and developing a one-pointed attention. A common practice of *samatha* is mindfulness of breathing, which focuses on the tactile sensations associated with breathing, i.e. the stomach, nostrils, etc. The practice may then advance to more subtle objects of meditation, such as those in the mental domain. *Samatha* meditation is utilized in all Buddhist traditions, although its techniques vary. In general, it is believed there are eight levels of absorptive concentration, or *jhanas*, which can be attained through *samatha* practice, the highest levels of which are in the formless realm, completely transcending dualistic reality. It is believed that on the path of *samatha* practice one will develop extraordinary mental capabilities and powers. The Buddha, however, warned that these powerful psychic abilities often serve as distractions on the path to enlightenment rather than as useful tools for eliminating suffering.

The Buddha discovered that the blissful states to which the highest levels of *samatha* practice can lead, although free from mental afflictions, are not *nirvana*. In order to eliminate suffering completely, mental afflictions must be uprooted at their source and not merely temporarily suspended through meditation. Accordingly, it is generally held that one must practice *vipassana* meditation, commonly referred to as "insight meditation," in order to uproot and destroy the causes of mental afflictions, namely ignorance, through the attainment of illuminating wisdom.[22] In that sense, *samatha* cultivates a refined attention which allows for a stable equilibrium from which one can investigate the nature of reality through *vipassana* techniques. If one attains a high level of *samatha* practice, the insights gained through *vipassana* can lead to transformation. In general, the goal of *vipassana* is the attainment of wisdom (*prajña*) – to experience reality as it truly is.

> **To eliminate suffering, mental afflictions must be uprooted at their source and not temporarily suspended through meditation**

Another common Buddhist meditation technique is called *metta*. This practice cultivates loving-kindness for all sentient beings. Visualization meditations, often concerned with the imaginative generation of a Buddha or a *mandala*, are most prominent in Tibetan Buddhist techniques. It should be noted that whatever approach is taken to Buddhist meditation, the cultivation of mindfulness (*sati*) is central. The Buddha's fundamental teaching on mindfulness is the *Satipatthana Sutta*, also called "The Establishment of Mindfulness." The Four Foundations of Mindfulness, which are common to all Buddhist traditions, are mindfulness of one's body, feelings, mental states, and mental objects.[23]

DOMESTIC AND COMMUNAL PRACTICES

Domestic forms of worship are typically performed daily, in the morning and evening, and may include recitation of mantras and prayers, study of scripture, and various techniques of meditation. At the outset, prostrations may be performed three times in honor of the Three Jewels: the Buddha, the *dharma*, and the *sangha*. In addition to denoting a form of respect, the practice of repetitive prostrations is a widespread psychosomatic discipline (practiced, for example, in Tibet) that seemingly provides a kind of integration of mind and body.

Not unlike Hindus and Jains, Buddhists view monastic life as the highest ideal, representing the optimal life for intense, spiritual training. In Buddhist communities laypeople believe it is a privilege to offer donations in support of those who have entered the monastery, and they commonly attend discourses given by monks and seek advice on aspects of the spiritual path. Temples are often maintained by monks and nuns, and are a central institution in the life of a Buddhist community. Larger temples include elaborate shrines, a public space for meditation and devotions, and other facili- ties. The burning of incense or candles and the giving of flow- ers, or other offerings, is a common sight at Buddhist shrines. Such practices are often interpreted as idol-worship by non-

Temples are a central institution in the life of a Buddhist community

Buddhists. In response to this incorrect conclusion, Piyadassi Thera, a Sri Lankan Buddhist monk of the Theravada school, explained the ideal behind such practices as follows:

> When a Buddhist offers flowers, or lights a lamp before the Buddha image or some sacred object, and ponders over the supreme qualities of the Buddha, he is not praying to anyone; these are not rites, rituals or acts of worship. The flowers that soon fade, and the flames that die down speak to him, and tell him of the impermanency (*anicca*) of all conditioned things. The image serves him as an object for concentration, for medita- tion; he gains inspiration and endeavors to emulate the qualities of the Master. Those who do not understand the significance of this simple offering hastily conclude: "This is idol worship." Nothing could be more untrue.[24]

RITES FOR THE DEAD

Although the role that Buddhist monks play in different ceremonies varies according to tradition and locality, they are, in general, not central to birth and marriage rites. In terms of rituals and observances related to death, however, participation by members of Buddhist monastic orders is considered essential. For Buddhists, the rebirth process that transpires after death makes this stage of the life cycle especially critical, and therefore it is a process that should be supervised by a trained monk. In experiencing the expiration of the physi- cal body, Buddhists hope to undergo a favorable rebirth – favorable being defined as one that advances rather than hinders the journey to *nirvana*.

When attending the mortally ill, Buddhist monks provide for the spiritual comfort of the dying. Specific acts undertaken at such a time vary according to different Buddhist tra- ditions. Tibetan monks typically read from the Tibetan Book of the Dead and then super- vise the ritual cremation of the deceased. Zen practices call for an extended, forty-nine-day series of services to be said in honor of the dead. The services consist of chants, appeals to the Buddha, and prayers for the departed person to receive succor. The family of the deceased presents gifts to the attending monks so that their relative will benefit from the merit earned. Similarly, in the Theravada school of the Buddhist tradition, the family of the departed provides a meal to the monks who have come to attend a dying person. In return, the monks comfort the sick, intone appropriate chants, and urge all those present to recollect the dying person's positive deeds.

CHAPTER SUMMARY

Although many religions present their beliefs in terms of tenets that must be accepted, the Buddhist tradition is somewhat different. A Buddhist is not faced with a fixed set of beliefs; ideally he or she is enjoined to examine personal experiences in light of the Buddha's teachings and to examine the Buddha's teaching in light of personal experiences. Ultimately, Buddhists strive to attain enlightenment and the example of the Buddha – both his life and teachings – serves as a guide. Buddhists, along with other sages from ancient India, developed advanced inner sciences, including

Many contemporary Buddhists live normal familial and occupational lives within society

methods of training the mind. The Buddhist way is not, however, merely about secluding oneself in meditation, although this is one aspect of the tradition. Illustrative of this fact, the Buddha himself, after attaining enlightenment, out of compassion, returned to society to teach others. Many contemporary Buddhists live normal familial and occupational lives within society, and strive, in their spiritual practice, to be fully present in each moment while acting compassionately toward all sentient beings.

Essentially, the Buddha's teachings are pragmatic; they discern the causes of suffering and offer a path to eliminate these causes in the here and now. The specific teaching which saturates and orients the way of life of all Buddhists is found in the fourth truth, i.e. the Noble Eightfold Path, of the Four Noble Truths. This Noble Eightfold Path is found in all Buddhist schools, which can be interpreted as different branches of the same tree. The Noble Eightfold Path is grouped into three major categories: *sila*, or ethical virtue (consisting of Right Speech, Right Action, and Right Livelihood); *samadhi*, or meditative concentration (consisting of Right Effort, Right Concentration, and Right Mindfulness); and *prajña*, or wisdom (consisting of Right Thought and Right Understanding). These three concepts – virtue, meditation, and wisdom – are reciprocal, and facilitate each other in support of one holistic way of life. They are, as it were, medicine for the three root causes of suffering: ignorance, greed, and hatred.

Carvings and sculptures found on the ancient Jain temples at Sametshikhar, Jharkhand, India

CHAPTER 8

THE JAIN TRADITION

May the sacred stream of amity flow forever in my heart. May the universe prosper – such is my cherished desire.

May my heart sing with ecstasy at the sight of the virtuous. And may my life be an offering at their feet.

May my heart bleed at the sight of the wretched, the cruel, the irreligious, and my tears of compassion flow from my eyes.

May I always be there to show the path to the pathless wanderers of life. Yet if they should not hearken to me, may I bide in patience.

May the spirit of goodwill enter all our hearts. May we all sing in chorus the immortal song of human concord.[1]

– Jain prayer

INTRODUCTION

There is no single body of sacred scriptures that unites all the religions that originate in India. The most influential scriptures of India, however, are the Vedas. The Vedas are the canonical scriptures of the six Orthodox Hindu schools of thought. The Jain religion, like the Buddhist, does not recognize the authority of the Vedas, as upheld by the *brahmins* (priests). For this reason, scholars classify the Jains as comprising a distinct religion which arose within the rich milieu of Indian spirituality. Although many foundational concepts of the Jain religion are in harmony with Hindu teachings, the Jain tradition, like the Buddhist tradition, has its own scriptural heritage. This heritage defines Jain principles and practices for the attainment of *moksha* – liberation from the cycle of life, death, and rebirth.

A man should wander about treating all creatures as he himself would like to be treated
Sutrakritanga 1.11.33
THE GOLDEN RULE

Timeline

*c.***4500–1500** B.C.E.
Pre-historical period: Jain tradition holds that first twenty-two *tirthankaras* of this cycle of time lived and taught

*c.***877–777** B.C.E.
Life of twenty-third *tirthankara*, Parsvabbnatha

*c.***599–527** B.C.E. Life of latest and twenty-fourth *tirthankara*, Mahavira

*c.***300** B.C.E.
Composition of *Kalpasutra*

*c.***150** B.C.E.
Kharvela, emperor of Kalinga (present day Orissa) in central-eastern India, becomes great patron of Jain tradition

*c.***79** C.E.
Split in Jain community, establishing the Svetambara and the Digambara

*c.***300** C.E.
Composition of *Tattvarthasutra*

*c.***350** C.E.
Western Ganga Dynasty in South India established, whose rulers patronized Jain religion

800–1000 C.E.
Royal patronage recedes in North India

1200–1800 C.E.
Lack of royal patronage and decline of influence

The Jain tradition takes its name from the Sanskrit root *ji*, meaning "to conquer." The word Jaina (usually pronounced without the final "a") is formed from this root, meaning "Followers of the Conquerors." The Conquerors are spiritual teachers revered by Jains because they conquered all forms of worldly attachment and, thereby, freed themselves from delusion and attained enlightenment. Persons who attain this liberation and teach others how to do so are referred to as *tirthankaras*, or "ford makers," meaning that they create a ford (or pathway) across *samsara* – the cycle of life, death, and rebirth and all the suffering and delusion it entails.

The Jains envision a universe in which innumerable beings are trapped in the cycle of rebirth. Those beings that attain a human birth have the unprecedented opportunity to learn from the teachings of the *tirthankaras*, to develop self-control, and to attain liberation. Jains believe that in the current phase of existence there have been twenty-four *tirthankaras*. The twenty-fourth of these is known as Mahavira ("The Great Hero"). Although Mahavira is not the founder of the Jain tradition, Jains inherit the wisdom of all previous *tirthankaras* through his teaching. Interestingly, Mahavira and the historical Buddha, Siddhartha Gautama, appeared in northern India at approximately the same time. Both of these religious teachers rejected aspects of the Brahminical religion (the precursor tradition of the modern Hindu religion), including the rigid caste system, the authority of both the Vedas and the *brahmins*, and the slaughter of animals for sacrificial purposes.

Mahavira is an honorific title given to Vardhamana Jnatrputraby by his followers. Vardhamana was born in 599 B.C.E. in Kundagrama, near modern Patna (a city in northeast India). His father was a chief and member of the warrior caste, and Vardhamana had a privileged upbringing and education. Jains believe that Vardhamana's father and mother were followers of Parsva, the twenty-third *tirthankara*, who is said to have lived approximately 250 years before Vardhamana. At the age of thirty, Vardhamana, turning away from the fame, fortune, and power that was his inheritance, renounced worldly concerns in order to dedicate himself to spiritual disciplines. He adopted the practices of extreme asceticism, meditation, fasting, and a vow of silence. According to tradition, after twelve years he conquered the afflictions of ego, pride, anger, and delusion and attained enlightenment. In the *Kalpasutra*, a sacred Jain text, it is recorded:

When the venerable ascetic Mahāvīra had become a Jina and Saint, he was a Liberated One, omniscient and comprehending all objects; he knew and saw all conditions of the world, of gods, men and demons: whence they come, whither they go, whether they are born as men or animals or become gods or beings in purgatory, the ideas, the thoughts of their minds, the food, doings, desires, the open and secret deeds of all the living beings in the world; he the Saint, for whom there is no secret, knew and saw all conditions of all living beings in the world, what they thought, spoke, or did at any moment.[2]

For the next thirty years Mahavira traveled throughout India as a spiritual teacher. He passed away at the age of seventy-three after having attained *moksha*.

PRINCIPLES OF THE JAIN TRADITION

The Many-sidedness of Truth

One of the foundational principles of the Jain tradition is that truth is many-sided. This doctrine is similar to the Middle Way of Mahayana Buddhist philosophy as elaborated by the Buddhist thinker Nagarjuna in the fifth century C.E. According to the Jain view, reality is multifaceted (*anekantavada*) and, therefore, no entity can be completely described without ascribing to it what appear to be mutually exclusive or contradictory properties. The concept of many-sidedness leads to the idea of qualified assertion (*syadvada*), under which statements are qualified by the phrase "in some respects." Thus, there are seven qualified assertions which, although apparently contradictory, can all be stated simultaneously:

> in some respects it is;
> in some respects it is not;
> in some respects it both is and is not;
> in some respects it is indescribable;
> in some respects it is and it is indescribable;
> in some respects it is not and it is indescribable;
> in some respects it both is and is not and is indescribable.

The scholar Hiralal Jain illustrates this principle as follows:

> A man is the father, and is not the father, and is both – are perfectly intelligible statements, if one understands the point of view from which they are made. In relation to a particular boy he is the father; in relation to another boy he is not the father; in relation to both the boys taken together he is the father and is not the father. Since both the ideas cannot be conveyed in words at the same time, he may be called indescribable; still he is the father and is indescribable; and so on.[3]

Due to the many relationships that the man has with other things, he possesses seemingly contradictory properties. Likewise, because there are innumerable vantage points from which to characterize the nature of Ultimate Reality and many equally authentic relationships that a knower may have to the same object of knowledge, Ultimate Reality cannot be fully encompassed in a single description that remains consistent. Thus, the true identity of any existing entity necessarily eludes a final characterization that states completely what the entity "really" is and, instead, requires alternative interpretations.

Recognition of the multifaceted nature of reality has the important consequence of fostering an open-ended attitude toward religious plurality. Utilizing *syadvada*, the principle of qualified assertion, it is easy to acknowledge the value of alternative religions and worldviews and to see them as complementary rather than as competitors. This enables one to accept them all as different but equally authentic ways of orienting one's life toward the sacred. In Jain scripture it is said: "All the doctrines are right in their own respective spheres – but if they encroach upon the province of other doctrines and try to refute their views, they are wrong. A man who holds the view of the cumulative character of truth never says that a particular view is right or that a particular view is wrong."[4]

The idea of many-sidedness was one of the Jain doctrines that made a particularly strong impact on Mahatma Gandhi – perhaps the best-known modern Hindu sage – who grew up in an area of India where Jains are prevalent. Concerning the failure to appreciate the many-sidedness of truth, Gandhi wrote:

> We are all thinking of the Unthinkable, describing the Indescribable, seeking to know the Unknown, and that is why our speech falters, is inadequate and even often contradictory ... And that is why all of us with one voice call one God differently as Paramatma, Ishwara, Shiva, Vishnu, Rama, Allah, Khuda, Dada Hormuzda, Jehova, God, and an infinite variety of names.[5]

Jiva and *Ajiva*: The Animate and Inanimate

According to the Jain worldview, the universe contains two fundamentally distinct elements: the living or sentient (*jiva*) and the non-living or non-sentient (*ajiva*). The latter category includes the corporeal, or physical, universe and its atomic constituents. The corporeal universe is composed of atoms (*paramanu*s) and aggregates of atoms (*skandha*), and is referred to as "the great aggregate" (*mahaskandha*). The atomic constituents that underlie all corporeal processes of change are themselves unchanging, uncreated, and everlasting. The motion of the constituents through space causes them to rearrange and form new aggregates, producing phenomenal changes in the corporeal world.

According to the Jain worldview, the universe contains two fundamentally distinct elements: the living or sentient and the non-living or non-sentient

The category of *jiva*s (living souls or sentient beings) includes human beings, animals, insects, plants, microscopic life-forms, and even earth, air, fire, and water. *Jiva*s are associated with the consciousness, or life principle, of living beings. According to the scholar

Depiction of a tirthankara at a Jain temple in Pawapuri, Bihar, India

S. N. Dasgupta: "The principle of life is entirely distinct from the body, and it is most erroneous to think that life is either the product or the property of the body. It is on account of this life-principle that the body appears to be living. This principle is the soul."[6]

Jains have developed a complex theory of life based on the classification of *jivas* according to the number of sensory faculties they possess. Members of the lowest class (exemplified by plants) possess only one sensory faculty, that of touch. The members of the next-highest class (exemplified by worms) possess two sensory faculties, touch and taste. Vertebrates possess five sensory faculties; those of touch, taste, sight, hearing, and smell. Lastly, the higher animals, including human beings, possess five sense organs plus an inner sense organ called *manas*, the faculty of rational intelligence.

This scheme of classification categorizes sentient beings based on their means of sensing the corporeal universe. In their essential nature, however, all sentient beings (all *jivas* or living souls) are alike; each is an uncreated and everlasting independent existence possessing infinite knowledge. Yet living souls fail to realize their nature, for "from beginningless time" they have been in a state of delusion that alienates them from the inherent qualities of the soul. The source of this delusion is the soul's association with a body, through which it senses the corporeal universe. More precisely, sense experience leads to passions – such as anger, greed, lust, pride, and hate – which cause the soul to accrue *karma*. In turn, *karma* clouds the soul's view of itself and the nature of reality.

Karma and the Delusions of Incarnation

Almost all religions originating in India share a belief in *karma*. In general, *karma* is understood as the law of cause and effect; namely, past thoughts, deeds, intentions, and words determine one's future state of being, including one's propensities, caste in society, and even the realm of one's birth (for example, the realm of the gods versus the realms of hell). The law of *karma* dictates that one's thoughts and actions will either imprison the soul within the cycle of birth, death, and rebirth (*samsara*), or they will lead the soul to liberation from *samsara* (*moksha*) and all of its misery and delusion. Interestingly, the Jains conceive of *karma* as a physical substance. This substance is very subtle and cannot be perceived with the senses, but it gathers around the soul causing karmic stains (*lesyas*) which tinge the soul and distort its understanding. This distortion ensnares the soul's perception in conditioned reality and inhibits its awareness of Unconditioned Reality.

Almost all religions originating in India share a belief in *karma*

Karmic stains do not destroy the soul, but they block the soul's awareness of its own pure and perfect nature. This situation is analogous to the presence of smoke before a mirror: the smoke is reflected on the surface of the mirror without altering the actual nature of the mirror itself. A verse from a Jain scripture states that the term *lesya* denotes "the alteration produced on the soul, just as on a crystal by the presence of black things."[7] A discussion of *lesya*s can be found in the thirty-fourth book of the Jain *sutra* entitled *Uttaradhyayana* ("Book of Later Instructions"). According to this book, different kinds of *lesya* have different colors that indicate varying levels of spiritual development. These are the karmic stains reflected in the soul. As for the *karma* itself, the same Jain *sutra* lists eight types:

> karma that obstructs right knowledge;
> karma that obstructs right faith;
> karma that leads to experiencing pleasure and pain;
> karma that leads to delusion;
> karma that determines the length of (incarnated) life;
> karma that determines the name or individuality of the embodied soul;
> karma that determines the soul's gotra [family ancestry];
> karma that prevents the soul's entrance on the path to eternal bliss.[8]

Each form of *karma* is created through the passions and desires that impinge on the soul because of its incarnation. The soul seeks relief from the miseries of incarnation by satisfying the very desires responsible for creating its *karma*, thereby leading to the soul's imprisonment in *samsara*. Thus, *karma* is both the cause and the effect of the desires binding the soul to the delusion of incarnation. The *Uttaradhyayana* states: "As a crane is produced from an egg, and the egg is produced from a crane, so they call desire the origin of delusion, and delusion the origin of desire."[9] The Jain path to *moksha* involves cleansing the soul of *karma* through ascetic practices and meditation. Such ascetic practices are believed to create a form of body heat known as *tapas*, which burns away one's *karma*. "As a bird covered with dust removes the grey powder by shaking itself," the *sutra* says, "so a worthy and austere Brahmana, who does penance, annihilates his Karma."[10]

The Uncreated Cosmos

As discussed above, in the Jain worldview the universe is composed of living souls and non-living corporeal atoms (the *jiva* and the *ajiva*), and these entities are all uncreated. Thus, Jains believe that there was no first act of creation: although atoms may form new aggregates and souls may attain liberation from *samsara*, everything has simply always existed and was never newly created. As there is no creation, so there is no creator. Like other religions originating in India, the Jain worldview posits the existence of cosmic cycles comprising different ages (*yuga*s) – ages of expansion and ages of contraction. The cycle of existence is now in its age of contraction. The cyclic expansion and contraction of the universe is beginningless as well as endless. In contrast to other religions originating in India, however, Jain belief does not posit the existence of a Supreme Being lying behind this cyclic process (such as *brahman* in the Hindu religion). For Jains, there is no supreme *jiva*. Nevertheless, it would, perhaps, be a mistake to conclude that Jains are "atheistic." Although the universe is uncreated, it is sacred. Although there is no supreme *jiva*, there are infinitely many *jiva*s, and each is divine and should be revered as such. For this reason, Jains hold firmly to one of the central practices of their tradition, that of *ahimsa* (usually translated as "non-violence").

PRACTICES OF THE JAIN TRADITION

Ahimsa: Non-violence and Reverence for All Living Beings

The Jain doctrine that all living souls are divine harmonizes with the Jain principle of *ahimsa* ("non-violence" or "doing no harm"). *Ahimsa* teaches that, although some violent actions may be unavoidable, violence should be eliminated as much as possible. According to the Jain way, a practitioner must transform and purify his or her mind in order to eliminate harmful thoughts and inner qualities (such as desire for revenge and jealousy). A Jain practitioner is also enjoined to skillfully regulate his or her speech (eliminating lying and verbal abuse) to insure that all words are non-violent. Non-violent thoughts and words are coupled with non-violent actions to form the basis of a compassionate life. Accordingly, Jains adhere to a strict vegetarian diet. They see the killing and eating of animals as a form of violence that disregards the intrinsic sacredness of other beings; therefore, they believe it is abhorrent. Some Jains even cover their faces with cloths to avoid inhaling microscopic beings. Practicing *ahimsa* means that

> **The Jain doctrine that all living souls are divine harmonizes with the Jain principle of *ahimsa***

Jains steer clear of certain professions and occupations because they cause harm (*himsa*) to other living beings. The restrictions inherent in *ahimsa*, which prevent Jains from pursuing violent actions and occupations, are motivated by a positive, unconditional love for the world and everything living in it. In this way, appreciation for the sacredness of all beings serves as the basis of a non-violent way of life.

In order to cultivate the principle of *ahimsa*, the Jain tradition (like the Buddhist tradition) has developed an elaborate code of ethics and moral guidelines. Violent actions are classified into four groups: (1) accidental; (2) occupational; (3) protective; and (4) intentional. In the first category are injuries to small living beings resulting from everyday activities such as cooking, walking, and bathing. The second category consists of actions such as a soldier killing an enemy in battle or a farmer tilling the land. In the third category are acts of self-defense. Finally, the most repugnant form of violence is the intentional killing of other living beings. We read in *Acarangasutra* 4.25–26: "One should not injure, subjugate, enslave, torment, or kill any animal, living being, organism, or sentient being. This doctrine of nonviolence is immaculate, immutable, and eternal. Just as suffering is painful to you, in the same way it is painful, disquieting, and terrifying to all animals, living beings, organisms, and sentient beings."[11]

The Three Jewels and Five Vows

According to the *Tattvartha Sutra*, Right Faith, Right Knowledge, and Right Conduct – the Three Jewels – constitute the path to liberation. Right Faith is belief in the teachings of the twenty-four *tirthankara*s (the ford-makers, or spiritual teachers, such as Mahavira). Right Knowledge is an understanding of their teachings. Right Conduct is turning these teachings into practice. As has been noted, different forms of karmic delusion obstruct the qualities of Right Faith and Right Knowledge. Thus, practicing the teachings and staying on the path to liberation requires great self-discipline.

Practicing Jain teachings involves adhering to five vows, in imitation of Mahavira's "Great Renunciation." Most Jains identify five auspicious moments (*panch kalyanaka*s) in the life of Mahavira: conception, birth, renunciation, enlightenment, and final liberation (death). The pivotal event occurred when Mahavira committed himself to five vows: nonviolence (*ahimsa*); commitment to truth (*satya*); a life devoid of stealing (*asteya*); sexual abstinence (*brahmacarya*); and non-attachment or non-possession (*aparigraha*). Mahavira's motivation for committing himself to the last vow is succinctly expressed in the following verse from the *Uttaradhyayana*: "Misery ceases on the absence of delusion, delusion ceases on the absence of desire, desire ceases on the absence of greed, greed ceases on the absence of property."[12]

Daily life for Jains is based on the principle of simplicity. A simple life entails the avoidance of violent actions, luxuries, sensual indulgences, and material possessions. Following the example of Mahavira, Jains do not seek fame, fortune, or worldly power, but instead favor a life based on spiritual exercises and austerities such as fasting, self-restraint, and meditation. Daily spiritual practice includes veneration of the *tirthankara*s, revering and learning from gurus (spiritual teachers), offering charity, such as food, to mendicants and the poor, and practicing the five vows. Jains especially extol the cultivation of virtues such as compassion, humility, and forgiveness. Ultimately, the Jain lifestyle pursues an ascetic ideal as the ultimate spiritual practice capable of purifying the soul of negative *karma*.

Ritual Fasting

The Jain tradition emphasizes the spiritual discipline of fasting. In the Buddhist tradition, fasting is discouraged, and many Hindus consider the practice optional rather than obligatory. In contrast, Jain lay and mendicant communities consider fasting as integral to spiritual purification, and so they routinely abstain from food and water. Recall that Jains believe that the soul's attachment to the body leads to desires and that these desires lead to the accumulation of *karma*, the source of the soul's delusion. The function of ritual fasting is to reduce one's attachment to the body by mastering the body's needs and desires. In some cases, fasting is carried on to the point of death. As the contemporary scholar Padmanabh Jaini states, there are four situations in which fasting to death (*sallekhana*) is permitted:

> **Since physical death is inevitable, it does not frighten the Jains**

> (1) *upsarga*, an unavoidable calamity (for example, captivity by an enemy) that makes keeping one's vows impossible; (2) *durbhiksā*, a great famine, during which there is no way to obtain acceptable food, much less to do so in the proper manner; (3) *jarā*, old age, defined by the onset of such problems as blindness, inability to walk without help, or senility, any of which make one likely to fall away from his *vratas* [restraints, vows]; (4) *nihpratikārā rujā*, a terminal illness from which death is imminent.[13]

Since physical death is inevitable, it does not frighten the Jains. Instead, Jains developed spiritual techniques, used under specific conditions, to spiritually facilitate the dying process.

CHAPTER SUMMARY

The Jain tradition derives its beliefs from the lives and teachings of twenty-four *tirthankaras*, or spiritual teachers, who created a path for transcending *samsara* (the cycle of birth, death, and rebirth). The last of these was "the Great Hero," Mahavira. The Jain practitioner follows Mahavira's teachings in the hope of attaining *moksha*, or liberation from the cycle of birth, death, and rebirth in conditioned reality.

According to the Jain conception of the cosmos, infinitely many souls (*jivas*) and lifeless atoms (*ajivas*) have existed throughout beginningless time. Souls are incarnated in aggregates of lifeless atoms, e.g. plant and animal bodies. This incarnation causes a variety of passions that delude and distract the soul. If proper steps are taken, it is possible for the soul to end its delusion and attain realization of its true nature, thus acquiring perfect knowledge, perfect perception, and permanent bliss. As Hiralal Jain succinctly states: "The

Jaina philosophy might be summed up in one sentence. The living and the non-living, by coming into contact with each other, forge certain energies which bring about birth, death, and various experiences of life; this process could be stopped, and the energies already forged destroyed, by a course of discipline leading to salvation."[14]

The steps that must be taken to attain the realization of one's true nature require self-discipline and living a deeply compassionate life of non-violence, honesty, simplicity, austerity, and the renunciation of possessions. Although the Jain religion is relatively small numerically (with roughly six to ten million adherents), Jain teachings have greatly influenced Indian spiritual life. The Hindu tradition, for example, absorbed many Jain teachings, particularly the teaching of *ahimsa* (non-violence). *Ahimsa* was a central element in the philosophy of Mahatma Gandhi, and today it plays a major role in social causes such as the environmental and animal rights movements.

The Temple of Heaven, Beijing

CHAPTER 9

THE TEACHINGS OF LAO TZU

See, all things howsoever they flourish
Return to the root from which they grew.
This return to the root is called Quietness;
Quietness is called submission to Fate;
What has submitted to Fate has become part of
    the always-so.
To know the always-so is to be Illumined;
Not to know it, means to go blindly to
    disaster.[1]

        – Lao Tzu, *Tao Te Ching*, Chapter 16

INTRODUCTION

Almost nothing is known about the life of Lao Tzu. Even his name is not known with certainty. Throughout the ages he has been referred to as Lao Tzu, which simply means "the Old Fellow," or "the Grand Old Master." According to tradition he was the founder of the Taoist spiritual philosophy.

    It is thought that Lao Tzu was born sometime around 604 B.C.E. However, the earliest historical record concerning his life is dated some five hundred years later. Begun by Ssu-ma T'an (d. 110 B.C.E.), and completed by his son, Ssu-ma Ch'ien (145–90 B.C.E.), the *Shih Chi*, or Records of the Historian, is an extensive history of China which was written around 100 B.C.E. In the *Shih Chi* it is said that Lao Tzu was a native of the state of Ch'u, located in the southern part of the modern-day Hunan province, and that he served as the archivist of the Chou court. Signs of the decline of the Chou royal house prompted Lao Tzu

> **Regard your neighbor's gain as your own gain, and your neighbor's loss as your own loss**
> *T'ai Shang Kan Ying P'ien*
> **THE GOLDEN RULE**

Timeline

*c.*1700 B.C.E.
Lost ancient texts on Tao composed

*c.*1100 B.C.E.
I Ching (Book of Changes) composed

*c.*604 B.C.E.
Lao Tzu born (date highly contested)

4th century B.C.E.
Life of Taoist sage Chuang Tzu

*c.*100 B.C.E.
Shih Chi or Records of the Historian completed

*c.*3rd century C.E.
The Book of Lieh-Tzu, classic Taoist text, written

5–8th century C.E.
Emergence of Cha'n (or Zen) Buddhist movement in China

to leave for the West. Legend says that when he reached the Han-ku Pass, a gatekeeper asked him to write a record of his philosophy. Lao Tzu granted the gatekeeper's wish and in three days produced the *Tao Te Ching* ("The Way and its Power"), a work composed of eighty-one short chapters, totaling around five thousand characters. He then disappeared and was never heard from again. He left behind nothing but the five thousand characters of this document: no commentary, no explanation, no organization, and no followers.

This anecdote is nearly all the biographical information that exists about Lao Tzu, and historians generally consider the story to be more legendary than factual. Arthur Waley, a scholar of Chinese history and philosophy, writes in the closing section of his introduction to the *Tao Te Ching*:

> The reader may at this point well ask why I have all this time [after ninety nine pages of introduction] said nothing about the author of the book [the *Tao Tê Ching*]. The reason is a simple yet cogent one. There is nothing to say. We do not know and it is unlikely that we shall ever know who wrote the Tao Tê Ching.[2]

Despite Lao Tzu's uncertain identity, the teachings attributed to him affected the philosophical, cultural, and political life of China for thousands of years. Taoist influence was maintained by a number of sages who carried on the philosophical tradition originated by Lao Tzu. The most influential of these sages was Chuang Tzu, who lived sometime during the fourth century B.C.E. Chuang Tzu clarified and commented upon the teachings of Lao Tzu through a series of philosophical inquiries that address various subjects such as language, art, ceremonies, and metaphysics.

Because they form the core of the Taoist tradition, this chapter is focused on the insights of Lao Tzu. However, it should be noted that, over the course of time, Lao Tzu's teaching developed into two strands – a Taoist religion and a Taoist school of spiritual philosophy – each of which had a profound impact on other traditions. The Taoist religion emerged in China around the second century of the Common Era. One of the principal aims of its adherents is freedom from death. Although inspired by the teachings of Lao Tzu, the Taoist religion includes many aspects that were not directly handed down by the master himself (such as an organized priesthood, a pantheon of gods, and various rituals). In contrast, the original sages of the philosophical school had no codified set of rules or doctrines,

Lao Tzu's teaching developed into two strands – a Taoist religion and a Taoist school of spiritual philosophy

as found, for instance, in the Buddhist and Confucian traditions. Instead, they dedicated themselves to direct experience of mystical unity and harmony with the endless flow of events. In carrying this out they drew on the existing Chinese concept of a "way" (*tao*), referring to a method or discipline, and added to it the idea of the Way (the Tao) – the transcendent principle in accordance with which all oppositions are harmonized and all multiplicity is unified (discussed further below).

Taoist insights into the Way did eventually influence both the Buddhist and Confucian traditions, and were integral to the development of the Ch'an or Zen Buddhist movement (in the seventh and eighth centuries of the Common Era) and the Neo-Confucian movement (in the eleventh).[3] The Taoist emphasis on transcending the confines of language and conceptual thinking had particular influence on Ch'an Buddhist teachings. For instance, the opening lines of the *Tao Te Ching* underscore this fundamental aspect of Lao Tzu's philosophy: "The Tao (Way) that can be told of is not the eternal Tao; The name that can be named is not the eternal name."[4] A similar message is presented in the writings of the great Taoist sage Chuang Tzu:

> The fish trap exists because of the fish; once you've gotten the fish, you can forget the trap. The rabbit snare exists because of the rabbit; once you've gotten the rabbit, you can forget the snare. Words exist because of meaning; once you've gotten the meaning, you can forget the words. Where can I find a man who has forgotten words so I can have a word with him?[5]

The Ch'an school of Buddhist philosophy turned the forgetting of words and the transcendence of conceptual thought into central features of its spiritual practices. The essence of Ch'an teachings was summarized by the Buddhist monk Bodhidharma (*fl.* 460–534 C.E.), referred to as the first patriarch in China of Ch'an (Zen), in these lines:

> Outside teaching; apart from tradition.
> Not founded on words and letters.
> Pointing directly to the human mind.
> Seeing into one's nature and attaining Buddhahood.[6]

THE DEVELOPMENT OF TAOIST PHILOSOPHY

The Taoist tradition is unlike many other spiritual traditions in that its central and founding text, the *Tao Te Ching*, does not contain a historical narrative or an account of any individual or family. Nevertheless, like all spiritual traditions, religions, and philosophies, the Taoist tradition emerged in the midst of specific conditions and events. In particular, such external factors as social and political conditions, the presence of contrasting viewpoints (especially that of the Confucians), and the influence of existing traditions all had an impact on the formulation of the Taoist philosophy.

Social and Political Conditions

Spiritually impoverished social conditions (such as those involving hypocritical religious authorities, political corruption, the loss of traditional wisdom through poor education, war, and social instability) often directly or indirectly provoke radical social change, inspire renewed religious yearning, and reinvigorate intellectual activity. The Taoist tradition emerged amid such collapsing social conditions. As noted, it is said that Lao Tzu left the Chou court, in which he was serving as an official, in response to signs of irreversible political deterioration. Regardless of uncertainties concerning Lao Tzu's life, China's history in the centuries before the Common Era was fraught with strife among the various Chinese states. Thus, it is highly probable that the *Tao Te Ching* was written at a time of social and political turmoil. Lao Tzu's attitude toward such conditions was that, in the long run, only Nature could restore order and good governance. In chapter 29 of his work, Lao Tzu writes:

> Do you think you can take the universe and improve it?
> I do not think it can be done.
> The Universe is sacred.
> You cannot improve it.
> If you try to change it, you will ruin it.
> If you try to hold it, you will lose it.[7]

Here, Lao Tzu suggests that lasting order is established by following the Way of Nature and not by formulating strict rules of social interaction and subsequently inculcating them among citizens. This approach sets the Taoist tradition apart from a complementary Chinese tradition, the Confucian.

Contrasting Viewpoints

Although the Taoist tradition took form in the presence of many alternative philosophies and worldviews, historically the Confucian tradition has served as its most influential counterpart. The Taoist and Confucian traditions contrast sharply in many respects. For instance, they differ in regard to their principal concerns in that the Confucian tradition generally addresses guidelines for acting and living virtuously for the benefit of society as a whole. The Taoist tradition, on the other hand, is more focused on mystical illumination.

Furthermore, Lao Tzu stressed the idea that illumination acquired from the Way is a spontaneous source of social order. He claimed that the need for formulating rules of social conduct only arises when individuals have lost touch with the Way. In chapter 18, Lao Tzu writes:

> Great Tao rejected:
> Benevolence and righteousness appear.
> Learning and knowledge professed:
> Great hypocrites spring up.
> Family relations forgotten:
> Filial piety and affection arise.
> The nation disordered:
> Patriots come forth.[8]

In each of these couplets, something natural is lost and something artificial and contrived comes forward to take its place. From the Taoist viewpoint, rules and regulations as formulated in the teachings of Confucius fall into the latter category.

It should be emphasized that, although differences between the Taoist and Confucian philosophies have played a role in their history, these differences must not be exaggerated. These two teachings often harmoniously complemented one another. The relationship between the Confucian and Taoist traditions demonstrates how China was one of the few cultures that fostered the peaceful coexistence of differing religions (and Buddhist *dharma* also flourished in China along with the Taoist and Confucian traditions).

By defining themselves in contrast to each other, the Confucian and Taoist traditions depend upon one another, and together they constitute a more complete and multifaceted worldview. Thus, their differences can be conceived as drawing them together rather than pushing them apart. In fact, the inner components of Taoist and Confucian philosophy were intertwined, for instance, by the thinker Lui I-ming in his late eighteenth-century commentary on the *I Ching*, an ancient work from which both Lao Tzu and Confucius drew inspiration.

The Influence of Existing Traditions

The *I Ching* (Book of Changes) is thought to have been composed by the founders of the Chou dynasty around 1100 B.C.E. The *I Ching* influenced virtually all subsequent Chinese religion and philosophy. It is one of the oldest surviving texts concerning the concept of Tao. Other ancient texts on Tao are believed to have been written as early as the Shang-Yin dynasty, around 1700 B.C.E., but they are now lost. In addition to the *I Ching*, three foundational Taoist texts have survived – namely *Tao Te Ching*, *Chuang-Tzu*, and *The Book of Lieh-tzu*. These works provide ethical, political, and social, as well as spiritual, insight into the significance of life and existence as a whole. At the center of these insights is the concept of the Tao.

Literally, the word *tao* (pronounced "dow") refers to a road, path, or way. It can also signify a method of performing a task, an art, a science, a principle, or a doctrine. Its ideogram in the Chinese language is a combination of two characters, one meaning "going forward" and the other meaning "head." Such an image does not capture the meaning of "Tao," but it serves as a suggestive basis for the imagination through which the meaning of this profound word may be better understood. Thus, one way to read the ideogram for "Tao" is "leading and the path it creates."[9]

Through his poetry, which was often paradoxical, Lao Tzu draws our attention toward a transcendent and ultimately inconceivable Tao hidden within all things. Its presence is felt everywhere, and yet it is nowhere to be found. As one ancient text elaborates:

[The Tao] is close at hand, stands indeed at our very side; yet is intangible, a thing that by reaching for cannot be got. Remote it seems as the furthest limits of the Infinite. Yet it is not far off; everyday we use its power. For Tao (i.e. the Way of the Vital Spirit) fills our whole frames, yet man cannot keep track of it. It goes, yet has not departed. It comes, yet is not here. It is muted, makes no note that can be heard, yet all of a sudden we find that it is there in the mind. It is dim and dark, showing no outward form, yet in a great stream it flowed into us at our birth.[10]

According to Lao Tzu, in yielding to the motion of this hidden Way and following the path that it mysteriously creates we return to the Source from which all things grow and find illumination. It is through this process that we return to the state of the "Uncarved Block" (see below for further discussion on this concept).

The Tao which Lao Tzu addresses is ultimately transcendent. Because it is transcendent, it is inconceivable. Because it is inconceivable, it is inexpressible. But what, then, is Taoist philosophy? If the Tao is ultimately transcendent, inconceivable, and inexpressible, how can Taoist philosophy be anything but a reverent silence before this transcendent mystery?

According to a long tradition of Chinese philosophy, there are three realms in which Tao is present: the realms of heaven, earth, and humanity. The *I Ching*, according to an ancient commentator, combines a Tao of heaven, a Tao of earth, and a Tao of humanity into one philosophy.[11] Another ancient commentator explains the Tao of these three realms in this way: "[The ancient holy sages] determined the tao of heaven and called it the dark and the light. They determined the tao of the earth and called it the yielding and the firm. They determined the tao of man and called it love and rectitude."[12] According to the *I Ching* and commentators on this work, heaven, earth, and human life are parallel with one another since independent entities are formed in each of these realms by combining and balancing contrasting qualities (dark and light, yielding and firm, love and

Statue of Lao Tzu, the founder of Taoism, in Xian, China

rectitude). In each realm, Tao is the combining and balancing principle which unites these qualities in an ever-changing and dynamic equilibrium.

Lao Tzu's philosophy encompasses these manifestations of Tao (in heaven, earth, and the life of human beings), and looks to an unmanifest Tao hidden behind them. Lao Tzu writes, "The ways of men are conditioned by those of earth. The ways of earth, by those of heaven. The ways of heaven by those of Tao, and the ways of Tao by the Self-so [the unconditioned]."[13] Thus, Taoist philosophy addresses a Tao immanent in Nature (in heaven and earth), a Tao immanent in the life of human beings, and the Tao as it is in itself, unconditioned and unmanifest. Because of these varying forms of Tao, Taoist philosophy is more than a meditative silence in the face of the transcendent. It also involves concepts and principles through which one gains insight into the Tao. By meditating on these concepts and principles, the Taoist sage both merges into the immanent Way and dissolves into the silence of the transcendent.

CONCEPTS AND PRINCIPLES OF THE TAOIST TRADITION

Yin–Yang Duality

One principle at the center of virtually all Chinese religion and philosophy is that of yin–yang duality. This principle originated in ancient Chinese religion and was absorbed into the Taoist tradition. The terms *yin* and *yang* refer to dark and light, respectively. Their ideograms are "the cloudy, overcast" and "banners waving in the sun."[14] Yin and yang represent a more general kind of dualism between mutually opposing qualities; for instance, such dualities as male and female, light and shadow, positive and negative, and even contrasting periods of history or points of view. As scholar J. C. Cooper observes, Taoist and Confucian philosophy serve as a case in point:

> The two indigenous religions of China were in themselves yin-yang forces in the life of the people and helped to maintain it in balance. Taoism supplied the creative, artistic and mystic element, while Confucianism was responsible for the social order, decorum and ritual. Taoism is based on rhythm and flux, on the natural, the unconventional, the freedom-loving detachment from worldly things and its product is the poet, the artist, the metaphysician, the mystic, together with all that is laughter-loving and light-hearted. Confucianism is concerned with the stable order, the formal, the conventional and the practical administration of worldly affairs; the one idealistic, the other realistic, but together the perfect combination offsetting and correcting each other and preventing too unconstrained an informalism on the one side or too arid and rigid a classicism on the other.[15]

The significance of the principle of yin–yang duality is that, according to Chinese philosophy, each thing or situation is composed of contrasting elements that are in mutual opposition and yet – because of this very opposition – become harmonized into a completed whole. By interacting, contrasting qualities limit each other and coalesce together in a single, relatively stable "something" – an object, a situation, a historical epoch, unified within itself and differentiated from other objects, other situations, or other historical epochs. This co-mingling of contrary qualities is a process of differentiation which creates "the ten thousand things": the multiplicity of individuated entities which collectively constitute the phenomenal world. Lao Tzu writes:

> Tao gave birth to the One; the One gave birth successively to two things, three things, up to ten thousand [or indefinitely many]. These ten thousand creatures cannot turn their backs to the shade without having sun on their bellies [that is, each is a combination of contrary qualities], and it is on this blending of the breaths that their harmony depends.[16]

Any island of relative stability providing for such differentiated existence, any blending which balances opposites into a unified whole, eventually succumbs to other influences and its own impermanence, and passes away into the endless flow of change.

Tao and Te: The Way and its Power

As discussed above, Tao is at once the transcendent principle beyond all duality and the immanent principle that balances and regulates the flow of interaction between the yin and yang. This leads to another ancient principle adopted into the Taoist tradition, namely *te* (power). The ideogram for this term is composed of three parts: "going forward," "straight," and "heart."[17] It represents the natural inborn power that one acquires from the Way. This is not a power for dominating and defeating opposition. Rather, it is the power of harmonizing with the Way and thus transcending opposition altogether.

Taoist writings often employ the analogy of flowing water. In order to actualize *te*, one should "flow" like water by adapting to conditions without resistance and by peacefully settling into the lowest, most inconspicuous, and unassuming places. By adopting this path, one becomes peacefully unified with nature and spontaneously draws others into harmony with the Way. In chapter 66, Lao Tzu says:

How did the great rivers and seas get their kingship over the hundred lesser
    streams?
Through the merit of being lower than they; that was how they got their kingship.
Therefore the Sage
In order to be above the people
Must speak as though he were lower than the people.
In order to guide them
He must put himself behind them.
Only thus can the Sage be on top and the people not be crushed by his weight.
Only thus can he guide, and the people not be led into harm.
Indeed in this way everything under heaven will be glad to be pushed by him and will
    not find his guidance irksome.
This he does by not striving; and because he does not strive, none can contend with
    him.[18]

Wu-wei: Taking No Action

The practice of yielding to the ongoing motion of the Way was developed into a uniquely
Taoist principle called *wu-wei*. As we have discussed, the concepts of Tao, *te*, and yin–yang
duality were discussed in China before the time of Lao Tzu; in some forms, they are
explained in the teachings of Confucius and other sages such as Mo Tzu and Hsün Tzu.
Wu-wei, however, is a unique contribution of the Taoist tradition. The term has been
translated from Chinese as "non-interference," "letting go," "pure effectiveness," "taking
no action," and "inaction." According to this principle, the existence of yin–yang oppositions calls not for action but for acceptance, not for resistance but for acquiescence. The
contemporary Chinese scholar Liu Xiaogan has written:

Wu-wei is, rather, a concept or idea that is used to negate or restrict human action. In
other words, wu-wei means the cancellation or limitation of human behavior, particularly social activities. There are a number of gradations in the Taoist theories of wu-wei:
wu-wei as nonbehavior or doing nothing; wu-wei as taking as little action as possible;
wu-wei as taking action spontaneously; wu-wei as a passive or pliable attitude toward
society; wu-wei as waiting for the spontaneous transformation of things; and wu-wei as
taking action according to objective conditions and the nature of things, namely, acting
naturally.[19]

Many people consider the practice of *wu-wei* objectionable because they believe its practitioners seek self-knowledge while neglecting the collective responsibility of contributing to the welfare of the community at large. In the *Tao Te Ching*, Lao Tzu denies that *wu-wei* entails such irresponsibility and states, to the contrary, that it represents the only means by which one can create enduring benefits for others. He writes that, by attaining self-knowledge through *wu-wei*, "the Sage is all the time in the most perfect way helping men, he certainly does not turn his back on men."[20]

But how does the sage help others by taking no action? By withdrawing from the manifold of opposites, the realm of yin–yang duality, the sage spontaneously draws others toward the transcendence of opposition. When the sage withdraws from duality, other beings flow into the emptiness thus created, like water flowing into the space from which a stone has been removed. Flowing in this way, others are spontaneously brought into harmony with the Tao. Chapter 2 of the *Tao Te Ching* illustrates these ideas:

> It is because every one under Heaven recognizes beauty as beauty, that the idea of ugliness exists.
> And equally if every one recognized virtue as virtue, this would merely create fresh conceptions of wickedness.
> For truly Being and Not-being grow out of one another;
> Difficult and easy complete one another.
> Long and short test one another;
> High and low determine one another…
> Front and back give sequence to one another.[21]

In other words, the action or existence of a given yin–yang quality always reinforces and accompanies its opposite, just as there cannot be a northern mountainside without a southern mountainside, or the inside of a circle without an outside. Therefore, whatever action is taken in this realm necessarily perpetuates opposition. Chapter 2 continues:

> Therefore the Sage relies on actionless activity.
> Carries on wordless teaching.
> But the myriad creatures are worked upon by him; he does not disown them.
> He rears them, but does not lay claim to them,
> Controls them, but does not lean upon them,
> Achieves his aim, but does not call attention to what he does;
> And for the very reason that he does not call attention to what he does
> He is not ejected from fruition of what he has done.[22]

It was through such "inactivity," Lao Tzu believed, that the ancient rulers governed the state effectively. It is clear, then, that by "taking no action," Lao Tzu does not mean sitting still and doing nothing (although this is certainly a form of *wu-wei*). Practicing *wu-wei* simply means "submitting to fate" by ceasing to act as one entity in opposition to any other, thus yielding to the motion of the Tao. Because this motion transcends all opposition, to flow with this motion is "pure effectiveness." As mentioned above, attaining this effectiveness is not a form of domination, but one of acceptance. In acquiring this effectiveness, one does not take possession of the Tao but gives oneself over to its motion. To the question of "whether one can possess the Way," the Taoist sage responds in the *Book of Lieh-tzu* as follows:

Your own body is not your possession … It is the shape lent to you by heaven and earth. Your life is not your possession; it is harmony between your forces, granted for a time by heaven and earth. Your nature and destiny are not your possessions; they are the course laid down for you by heaven and earth. Your children and grandchildren are not your possessions; heaven and earth lend them to you to cast off from your body as an insect sheds its skin. Therefore you travel without knowing where you go, stay without knowing what you cling to, are fed without knowing how. You are the breath of heaven and earth which goes to and fro; how can you ever possess it?[23]

Thus, the Taoist Way reveals the paradoxical equivalence between "doing nothing" and "pure effectiveness." It emphasizes "the usefulness of what is not," as in the following passage from the *Tao Te Ching*:

We put thirty spokes together and call it a wheel;
But it is on the space where there is nothing that the
usefulness of the wheel depends.
We turn clay to make a vessel;
But it is on the space where there is nothing that the
usefulness of the vessel depends.
We pierce doors and windows to make a house;
And it is on these spaces where there is nothing that the
usefulness of the house depends.
Therefore just as we take advantage of what is, we should
recognize the usefulness of what is not.[24]

The Uncarved Block

Social activity is not the only domain to which *wu-wei* applies. It is also applicable to physical activities such as the martial arts and to functions of the mind. With this aspect of *wu-wei*, we have reached the threshold of the reverent silence discussed previously. The mind performs activities such as differentiating one thing from another (including differentiating oneself from other things), drawing conceptual distinctions, making judgments such as "this is true" and "that is false," "this is right" and "that is wrong." When the practice of *wu-wei* is applied to these activities, one's consciousness is no longer entangled within them, but is set free to merge with the Way. When this happens, one no longer observes the world of phenomena with mental activities. Rather, one observes the unity of existence from a vantage point of complete inner silence.

Entering into this state of inner silence is referred to as "getting into the bird-cage without setting the birds off singing." As Arthur Waley notes, there is a pun involved in this statement because the Chinese term *fan* means both "bird-cage" and "return," while the term *ming* means both "sing" and "name."[25] Thus, in applying *wu-wei* in this way, one returns to the state of unity that underlies the differentiation among things, represented by naming and categorizing. This underlying state is the Uncarved Block, the primal unity of all Being, the "always-so."

CHAPTER SUMMARY

The central text of the Taoist tradition is the *Tao Te Ching*, a short collection of terse, enigmatic verses which provide intimations of a realm into which language cannot penetrate: the transcendent state of the unnameable Tao. Little is known of its author, but tradition assigns him the name Lao Tzu, "the Grand Old Master." The tradition founded by Lao Tzu drew upon elements of ancient Chinese religion and philosophy, such as yin–yang duality and the Ways of heaven, earth, and human life. Certain Taoist concepts were defined in contrast with existing viewpoints, such as the Confucian perspective and its emphasis on ritual and social order. With respect to the principle of yin–yang duality, which pervades all Chinese philosophy and religion, it is important to emphasize that the duality of the yin and the yang should not necessarily be taken to imply a clash of warring opposites struggling to eliminate one another. Rather, the principle of yin and yang expresses the fact that opposing polarities are inseparable from one another and together form a unified whole, as the front-side and back-side of an object

> **The duality of the yin and the yang should not be taken to imply a clash of warring opposites**

necessarily accompany one another and together constitute the object as a whole. Lao Tzu's teaching points to the Tao, which is the unifying principle that both transcends these polar opposites and brings them together, balancing them in a harmonious whole.

The Taoist tradition refined inherited influences into a unique realization of the transcendental unity of all being, and influenced later traditions such as the Ch'an Buddhist and Neo-Confucian schools. In addition to mystical elements, the Taoist teachings penetrated into the political domain with principles concerning the effective ways of governance. The central Taoist insight in this regard is that the ruler ought to become inconspicuous in order to lead others to the Way. This view was contrasted with that of the Confucian tradition, which stressed the ruler's prominence as a master of ritual and adherence to the ways of the ancient sages. In some respects the Taoist and Confucian traditions were polar opposites of one another. One legendary tale describes an occasion on which Lao Tzu and Confucius purportedly met one another and discussed their philosophies, after which Confucius remarked:

> I know a bird can fly; I know a fish can swim; I know animals can run. Creatures that run can be caught in nets; those that swim can be caught in wicker traps; those that fly can be hit by arrows. But the dragon is beyond my knowledge; it ascends into heaven on the clouds and the wind. Today I have seen Lao Tzu, and he is like the dragon![26]

Scholars parade on Confucius' birthday, China

CHAPTER 10

THE TEACHINGS OF CONFUCIUS

The Master said: "Shen! My teaching contains one all-pervading principle." "Yes," replied Tsêng Tzu. When the Master had left the room the disciples asked, "What did he mean?" Tsêng Tzu replied, "Our Master's teaching is simply this: Conscientiousness to self and consideration for others."[1]

– The Analects of Confucius, IV.15

Timeline

551–479 B.C.E.
Life of Confucius
*c.*390–305 B.C.E.
Meng Tzu (Mencius)
206 B.C.E.–**220** C.E.
Han Dynasty
960–1279 C.E.
Sung Dynasty
2nd century B.C.E.
Confucius' philosophy
   becomes state religion
   of China
11th century C.E.
Neo-Confucian
   movement
1949 C.E.
Communist revolution in
   China after which
   Confucius' philosophy
   disregarded

INTRODUCTION

No one has had a greater influence on Chinese culture than Confucius. Nevertheless, Confucius himself claimed that there was nothing original in his teachings: "I have 'transmitted what was taught to me without making up anything of my own.' I have been faithful to and loved the Ancients."[2] Confucius believed that the Ancients were Divine Sages of unparalleled wisdom and virtue and, therefore, he felt that his primary duty was to restore the wisdom of the Ancients and re-establish their virtue in himself and his contemporaries. Specifically, he hoped to communicate the inherited teachings to the state's rulers so that they could reform and govern society properly. As part of his efforts, Confucius "reanimated" the old wisdom by demonstrating its relevance to the conditions of his own time. He said, "He who by reanimating the Old can gain knowledge of the New is fit to be a teacher."[3] By renewing the wisdom of the Ancients, Confucius came to be called the "First Teacher" of China, "not that there were no teachers before him," Huston Smith explains, "but because he stands first in rank."[4]

> **Try your best to treat others as you would wish to be treated yourself, and you will find that this is the shortest way to goodness**
> *Mencius VII.A.4*
> **THE GOLDEN RULE**

According to most accounts, Confucius (Kung Fu-tzu or "Kung the Master") was born during the twenty-second year of the reign of Duke Hsiang (551 B.C.E.) in the Chinese state of Lu (modern-day Shandong Province). It is likely that his ancestors were aristocrats from the state of Sung who were forced to migrate to Lu because of hostile political conditions in Sung. Confucius' father was a soldier in the Lu military who died when Confucius was very young, leaving his mother to raise him on her own. The hardships of his early years forced Confucius to take various menial jobs, which gave him a deep sense of connection with common people.

Confucius married at the age of eighteen or nineteen and later had two children, a son and a daughter. In his twenties, he held various minor government positions, established himself as a tutor, studied ancient systems of governance, and served in Lu as a manager of state granaries and an overseer of public fields. By the time he reached his thirties, he is said to have mastered the six arts – li (ritual), music, archery, charioteering, calligraphy, and arithmetic. He was also knowledgeable in classical traditions such as poetry and history.

In his late forties and early fifties, Confucius held other government positions. He began as a magistrate and eventually rose to the post of minister of justice. But when he realized that other ministers were not interested in implementing needed social reforms, he resigned at the age of fifty-six and left in search of another state where his ideas could be put into practice. For the next fourteen years Confucius traveled widely, discussing his ideas with students and bureaucratic officials.

In 484 B.C.E., when Confucius was approaching the age of seventy, he returned to Lu. That same year his son died. Two years later, his greatest disciple, Yen Hui, died. Three years after the death of Yen Hui, in 479 B.C.E., the master himself died at the age of seventy-three. Reflecting on the course of his life, Confucius once remarked: "At the age of fifteen I set my heart on learning. At thirty I was established. At forty I was unwavering. At fifty I knew the order of Heaven [the Transcendent]. At sixty I listened receptively. At seventy I followed my heart's desire without going too far."[5]

Confucius had inspired disciples and through them his teachings eventually influenced the cultural, religious, and political life across a wide arc of Asia. By the second century B.C.E., Confucius' philosophy had become the state religion of China, which it remained until 1949 when it was abolished by the newly established Communist government.

THE TEXTS OF THE CONFUCIAN TRADITION

Confucius' teachings are contained in the Wu Ching ("The Five Classics") and the Ssu Shu ("The Four Books"), collectively referred to as the "Confucian Classics." Much of the material in the Five Classics predates Confucius. He edited and commented on earlier works in an effort to preserve and reanimate ancient Chinese culture. It is believed that only one of the Five Classics, the *Ch'un Ch'u* ("Book of Springs and Autumns"), was written by Confucius himself. This work is a history of the state of Lu from 776 to 442 B.C.E. The others are: the *I Ching* ("Book of Changes"), which establishes an elaborate philosophy of change and presents a method of divination based on the yin–yang principle; the *Shu Ching* ("Book of History"), which contains royal chronicles, narratives, and decrees; the *Shi Ching* ("Book of Songs"), on love, rituals, family life, and government; and the *Li Chi* ("Book of Rites"), which describes the rituals and ceremonies of ancient China.

The Four Books (or *Ssu Shu*) were compiled by Neo-Confucian philosophers of the Sung dynasty (960–1279 C.E.). Two of them record and comment on the sayings of Confucius. The *Lun Yu* ("The Analects" or "Collected Sayings") is perhaps the most influential of the Four Books. It is a collection of discourses and sayings of Confucius compiled by his disciples after his death. The *Meng Tzu Shu* ("The Book of Mencius") is a work by the second most important figure in the Confucian tradition, Meng Tzu or Mencius (*c.*390–305 B.C.E.). This work emphasizes the Confucian concepts of filial piety and human goodness. The two remaining books were extracted from the Five Classics (from the *Li Chi*). They are the *Ta Hsuah* ("The Great Learning"), which is a very short course on learning to be a person of the highest virtue and establishing order in society, and the *Chung Yung* ("The Doctrine of the Mean"), which addresses the importance of moderation for achieving harmony. The *Ta Hsuah* and the Chung Yung complement one another in that the former addresses social and political matters, while the latter examines philosophy and metaphysics.

Today Confucian texts constitute an important part of the spiritual heritage of China and of humanity in general

This body of Confucian literature (the Five Classics and Four Books) had a profound and enduring influence on Chinese culture. For centuries, students were required to memorize this literature, and government examinations intensely tested applicants on their knowledge of these works. Today these Confucian texts constitute an important part of the spiritual heritage of China and of humanity in general.

GOODNESS AND SOCIAL ORDER

The backdrop to Confucian teachings includes a number of fundamental elements such as belief in Fate or Providence (*ming*), belief in spirits or lesser gods, and the practice of filial piety. In ancient Chinese religion there existed a long-standing belief that the universe is governed by a "Supreme Ruler" (known as Shang Ti). In order to secure prosperity throughout the land, each year during the winter solstice the emperor sacrificed a red-brown calf in an elaborate ceremony before reading a tablet called "The Supreme Ruler (Shang Ti) of Imperial Heaven." By Confucius' time the term T'ien (Heaven) had been introduced to refer to an all-encompassing, transcendent power that determines all elements of existence. This concept came to play a very important part in Confucian philosophy (for instance, see the discussion of the Mandate of Heaven later in this chapter). Thus, the humanistic attitude of the Confucian philosophy (with its doctrine that "the measure of man is man") is balanced by belief in a transcendent Supreme Power. The secondary gods, known as *shen*, were believed to govern local fortunes and were identified with objects and scenes in nature. In time, they were divided into two classes, good and evil. In addition to secondary gods, the ancient Chinese also believed in the spirits of departed ancestors. The practice of ancestor worship was one of the most deeply rooted traditions within Chinese religion. It reinforced the importance of unity within the family, community, and society. The teachings of Confucius perpetuate this tradition with their focus on filial piety (discussed later in this chapter).

One concern that underlies all elements of Confucian teachings is the task of embodying humanity in the individual. As Tu Wei-ming, one of the foremost authorities on Confucian thought, explains: "The fundamental concern of the Confucian tradition is learning to be human. The focus is not on the human in contrast with nature or with Heaven but the human that seeks harmony with nature and mutuality with Heaven."[6] From the Confucian perspective, the embodiment of humanity in the individual entails not only harmony with Heaven (the Transcendent) and nature, but a balanced social order as well. This is because an individual's humanity and his or her social relationships are inextricably linked. Indeed, the very word for "humanity" (*jen*) is written by combining the characters for "man" and "two," suggesting people living together in a social group or, as Wing-tsit Chan suggests, "man in society."[7] Thus, the establishment of humanity in the individual and order in the state are interconnected challenges that must be confronted together. When these goals are fulfilled, culture flourishes and the Way of Human Life is united with the Ways of Heaven and Earth.[8]

> **"The fundamental concern of the Confucian tradition is learning to be human"**

Interestingly, Confucius refused to provide an explicit definition of *jen* (translated both as "Humanity" and as "Goodness"). Instead, he often discussed its outward manifestations without disclosing its inner nature. His disciple Tzu-kung said: "Our Master's views concerning culture and the outward insignia of goodness, we are permitted to hear; but about Man's nature and the ways of Heaven he will not tell us anything at all."[9] Similarly, when asked if a particular disciple or ruler possessed Goodness, Confucius would acknowledge some virtue of the individual in question and conclude: "But whether he is Good, I do not know."[10]

Confucius' concern as a teacher was not simply to formulate a definition of Goodness and present it to his students. Rather, he sought to engage his students in a form of moral training that would facilitate their attainment of Goodness. Both his refusal to define Goodness explicitly and his insistence on discussing its outward manifestations rather than its inner nature served this aim. On the one hand, his refusal to define Goodness left his students with tantalizing clues that stimulated sincere investigations into the nature of Goodness. On the other hand, his insistence on discussing the outward signs of Goodness (which are made manifest in culture and ritual) was derived from his belief that mastery of these outward expressions is the foundation for developing the inner qualities of Goodness.

Yen Hui, one of Confucius' favorite disciples, confirmed his Master's pedagogical effectiveness:

> The more I strain my gaze upwards towards [Goodness], the higher it soars. The deeper I bore down into it, the harder it becomes. I see it in front; but suddenly it is behind. Step by step the Master skillfully lures one on. He has broadened me with culture and restrained me with ritual. Even if I wanted to stop [searching for the Good and practicing its outward expressions], I could not.[11]

The Master's method was itself a message, and Yen Hui understood it: one must find out what Goodness is through one's own inner struggle and through mastering its outward expressions in actual practice.

THE OUTWARD MANIFESTATIONS OF GOODNESS

In spite of the fact that Confucius did not explicitly define Goodness, the outlines of such a definition do exist in the corpus of Confucian classics. Moreover, although he placed great emphasis on the outward expressions of Goodness, Confucius was not under the illusion that there is nothing more to Goodness than what is found in these expressions. He stressed the importance of rituals and codes of conduct, but he did not do so at the expense of an inner, spiritual way of life. For instance, he said, "A man who is not Good [and so does not have the appropriate attitudes and inner qualities], what can he have to do with ritual?"[12] In other words, the enactment of a ritual depends upon the existence of corresponding inner attitudes (such as loyalty and good faith). Rituals are only spiritually effective if they are animated by a corresponding inner disposition. Thus, the enactment of ritual, when accompanied by proper inner attitudes, is a discipline which can bring about spiritual transformation. "He who can himself submit to ritual," Confucius said, "is Good."[13] It is also important to note that the Chinese term *li*, translated as "ritual," has a

Statue of Confucius at a temple in Shanghai, China

variety of connotations that cannot be captured by any single English word. As the Chinese scholar Lin Yutang noted: "On one extreme, it [*li*] means 'ritual', 'propriety'; in a generalized sense, it simply means 'good manners'; in its highest philosophical sense, it means an ideal social order with everything in its place."[14]

In addition to ritual practices, Confucius considered education to be integral to developing good character. The form of education with which he was primarily concerned was moral education, a process that transforms the student's character. Confucius believed that moral education is a lifelong process that contributes significantly to the well-being and the fundamental equality of society as a whole, thus transcending social classes: "Where there is education," he said, "there are no classes."[15] Further, he taught that the pursuit of wisdom is not a simple intellectual exercise; rather, acquired knowledge should be employed for the cultivation of the primary virtues (such as humanity, justice, and courtesy). Awareness of the limitations of intellectual

> **Moral education is a lifelong process that contributes to the well-being and the equality of society as a whole**

knowledge is captured in the Chinese character *hsin*, which is sometimes translated as "heart–mind," indicating both an "intellectual awareness and moral awakening."[16] Additionally, Confucius advised, one must understand the limits of one's knowledge, for, he said, "to know what you know and know what you don't know is the characteristic of one who knows."[17] Another essential aspect of education is the love of learning, about which Confucius said:

> Love of Goodness without love of learning degenerates into silliness. Love of wisdom without love of learning degenerates into utter lack of principle. Love of keeping promises without love of learning degenerates into villainy. Love of uprightness without love of learning degenerates into harshness. Love of courage without love of learning degenerates into turbulence. Love of courage without love of learning degenerates into mere recklessness.[18]

Thus, education and the development of good character go hand in hand. Confucius refers to the gradual development of good character as the "piling up of moral force (*te*)."[19] He explains: "By 'piling up of moral force' is meant taking loyalty and good faith as one's guiding principles [that is, as the inner attitudes that guide one's outward actions], and migrating to places where right prevails."[20] By enacting the ancient rituals and observing the codes of conduct, one develops moral force and good character. Therefore, when Confucius was asked about the way of good people, he replied, "If you do not walk in their footsteps, you do not gain access to their abode."[21]

THE *CHUN-TZU* AND THE DOCTRINE OF THE MEAN

In the Confucian tradition "good character" is sometimes interpreted as a state of inner versatility which allows a person to assume an attitude that is appropriate to the situation at hand, and thus to act accordingly. This conception is epitomized by the image of the cultured, or superior, person (the *chun-tzu*). The term *chun-tzu* literally means "son of a ruler." As a member of the upper class, the son of a ruler was expected to adhere to high standards of morality, and so the term (often translated as "superior man") came to mean a cultured, or cultivated, person in general. The subject of the *chun-tzu*'s inward versatility runs through the whole of the *I Ching*. This ancient text is one of the Five Classics of the Confucian tradition. It is believed that Confucius himself composed commentaries on this work. There is no doubt, however, that he had high regard for the *I Ching*. Near the end of his life he said: "Give me a few years to finish the study of the *Book of Changes*, then I hope I shall be able to be free from making serious mistakes (or errors of judgment)."[22]

The Chinese term *I*, translated as "change" in this classic's title, can also be translated as "versatility." The scholars Rudolf Ritsema and Stephen Karcher explain: "Though often translated as change or changes, *I* is neither orderly change – the change of the seasons, for example – nor the change of one thing into another, like water changing into ice or a caterpillar changing into a butterfly."[23] According to Ritsema and Karcher, *I* is unpredictable, unfathomable, sudden change. Therefore, it presents the possibility of unexpected trouble. The superior person's inward versatility enables him or her to respond effortlessly to such unpredictable changes in the most appropriate way.

It is a basic idea of the *I Ching*'s philosophy that, as Richard Wilhelm says, "Each situation demands the action proper to it. In every situation, there is a right and a wrong course of action."[24] The *I Ching* contains countless descriptions of how the *chun-tzu*'s versatility expresses itself in taking the right course of action. However, the *I Ching* is not simply a book of changes; it is the Oracle of Changes. The Oracle is consulted to gain insight into the ideal course of action when responding to some problematic situation. The wisdom of the Oracle is called upon by a technique of divination that involves tossing yarrow stalks or coins. Based on the pattern into which the stalks or coins fall, the Oracle interprets the situation as a particular arrangement of yin–yang oppositions. The Oracle reveals a way of seeing or assessing a situation from the perspective of the superior person, and discloses which course of action the superior person takes in such a situation. By internalizing this "image" of the superior person and choosing a course of action that exemplifies the versatility of good character, one nurtures the innate moral force and develops the inner qualities of good character.

The idea that the superior person's action is always suited to the situation at hand is more explicitly formulated as the "Doctrine of the Mean." This posits that good character is a mean between the extremes of excess and deficiency. "The superior [person]," Confucius said, "*embodies* the course of the Mean."[25] According to the Neo-Confucian classic *Chung Sung* ("The Doctrine of the Mean"), the superior person, or person of good character, is one who avoids excess and deficiency, exercising moderation by following the "Middle Way." Thus, he or she neither goes too far nor fails to go far enough, but exhibits a proportionate response to whatever situation is at hand.[26] Take, for example, the virtue of courage. In dangerous situations, the courageous are neither crippled with fear nor absolutely fearless to the extent of recklessness or incautiousness. Rather, the courageous person responds with a level of caution appropriate to the situation. To err on the side of excessive fear is cowardice, and a deficiency of fear – altogether

> The Oracle is consulted to gain insight into the ideal course of action when responding to some problematic situation

lacking in caution – is recklessness. Likewise, the person of good character is one whose responses are suited to circumstances in all respects. In praise of this way, Confucius said, "How transcendent is the moral power (*te*) of the Middle [Way]! That it is rarely found among the common people is a fact long admitted."[27]

According to Confucius, adherence to the Middle Way instills the five attributes of a fully realized person. These five qualities are: "respectfulness, magnanimity, truthfulness, acuity, and generosity."[28] One can best enact the proportionate response (or Middle Way) in any given moment, Confucius believed, by modeling oneself after the ancient ideal of the *chun-tzu* and consulting the Oracle of Change. It is important to note, however, that the moderation advocated by the Doctrine of the Mean does not imply an indiscriminate restraint or curtailing of all intense emotions. Generally, the Doctrine of the Mean does not assert that whatever is halfway between two opposites is more worthy of choice than the opposites. Midway between the opposites of pleasure and pain is the insensate; midway between the opposites of joy and sorrow is the passionless. But these opposites are not extremes of excess and deficiency (that is, they are not examples of "too much" or "not enough" of something); thus their middle points are not favored by the Middle Way. For example, when Confucius witnessed a production of the Succession (a mimetic dance depicting the actions of a legendary emperor), his response was not a restrained moment of mild pleasure. He was overwhelmed by the beauty of the dance to such a degree that for three months thereafter he reportedly sensed no flavor in anything he ate. Confucius said, "I did not picture to myself that any such music existed which could reach such perfection as this."[29] Because the occasion was not merely a lackluster performance, Confucius' response was in no way insipid or emotionless; his response was not midway between pleasure and pain, but instead was intensely emotional. Presumably, his response was neither more nor less emotional than the performance warranted and, hence, it was in accordance with the Middle Way. Another example that illustrates the same point is Confucius' response to the death of his favorite disciple, Yen Hui: "When Yen Hui died the Master wailed without restraint. His followers said, Master, you are wailing without restraint! He said, Am I doing so? Well, if any man's death could justify abandoned wailing, it would surely be this man's!"[30]

Again, Confucius' response was extreme without being in excess of what was called for; the extremity of the response was proportionate to the extremity of the situation. Intense behavior such as this is not uncommon among awakened spiritual teachers; it exemplifies their mindfulness — that great ability to be completely present and attentive in each moment and thus completely free to respond from the depth of one's being.

THE ESSENTIAL NATURE OF GOODNESS

According to the *Chung Sung*, "Humanity (*jen*) is [the distinguishing characteristic of] man, and the greatest application of it is in being affectionate toward relatives."[31] Such affection is referred to as "filial piety." "Men of filial piety," the *Chung Sung* reports, "are those who skillfully carry out the wishes of their forefathers and skillfully carry forward their undertakings."[32] It is clear from this that the filial piety that Confucius saw as defining Humanity is not simply sentimental kindness or affection. Rather, it is a form of kindness and affection that is expressed in respectful, responsible, and intelligent action that perpetuates the wisdom and virtue of one's ancestors. If this form of action and attitude prevail, culture and society flourish. For this reason, Confucius makes conscientiousness to self and consideration for others the all-pervading principles of his doctrine; these are the central threads running through his teaching.[33]

Following this thread through the outer and inner aspects of Goodness leads us back to where our discussion of Confucius' teachings began: back, that is, to the idea that an individual's Humanity and his or her social relationships are inextricably meshed. Given this view of human nature, it is not surprising to find the Golden Rule embedded in the teachings of Confucius: "Do not do to others what you would not like yourself."[34] The Golden Rule is elaborated in the Confucian book called *The Great Learning*:

What a man dislikes in his superiors, let him not show it in dealing with his inferiors; what he dislikes in those in front of him, let him not show it in preceding those who are behind; what he dislikes in those behind him, let him not show it in following those in front of him; what he dislikes in those on the right, let him not apply it to those on the left; and what he dislikes in those on the left, let him not apply it to those on the right.[35]

Studying Confucius' philosophy of human nature can stimulate fidelity to the Golden Rule. Confucius' philosophy teaches that the very essence of being human involves maintaining affectionate relationships with others. Therefore, the members of society are inextricably linked together in one essence. Adherence to the Golden Rule not only sustains the well-being of society, but preserves the integrity of a person's own Humanity. To violate another is to compromise your own Humanity.

SOCIAL ORDER AND THE MANDATE OF HEAVEN

The Confucian tradition is deeply concerned with balance, order, and harmony in society. Society is based on five fundamental relationships. It is notable that family life plays an important part in the foundations of society as a whole, since three of these five relationships fall within the household. The Doctrine of the Mean states:

> There are five universal ways [in human relations], and the way by which they are practiced is three. The five are those governing the relationship between ruler and minister, between father and son, between husband and wife, between elder and younger brothers, and those in the intercourse between friends. These five are universal paths in the world. Wisdom, humility, and courage, these three are the universal virtues.[36]

In order to establish a society in which individuals flourish harmoniously, society must be governed by the power of moral example ("moral force," *te*), not by the power of physical force. The ruler's moral force earns the Mandate of Heaven (*t'ien-ming*). This Mandate alone entitles the emperor (or any leader) to rule. Should the emperor fail to uphold morality, his right to rule is forfeited. As the ancient *Book of History* explains, "The Mandate of Heaven is not easily [preserved] … Those who have lost the mandate did so because they could not practice and carry on the reverence and brilliant virtue of their forefathers."[37] Rulers who lost the Mandate of Heaven were thus deficient in filial piety. With respect to the significance of the ruler's moral force, the Doctrine of the Mean states: "Therefore the Way of the ruler is rooted in his own personal life and has its evidence [in the following] of the common people … Therefore every move he makes becomes the way of the world, every act of his becomes the model of the world, and every word he utters becomes the pattern of the world."[38] Without moral force, there cannot be effective governance; with moral force, governance is natural and effective.

The Confucian tradition is deeply concerned with balance, order, and harmony in society

Therefore, moral force is not only necessary for effective governance, it is also sufficient for effective governance: "If a man (the ruler) can for one day master himself and return to propriety [that is, ritual (*li*)]," Confucius said, "all under heaven will return to humanity."[39] From Confucius' point of view, the brilliant illumination of virtue shown by the Ancients inspired virtue in the people. The role of the ruler is to display virtue in his own life and thereby inspire this quality in his people. The radiant Humanity of the Ancients evokes the Humanity (*jen*) within each individual human being. The ruler's function is to present Humanity at its best to the people. By doing so, he draws forth from each citizen an ideal realization of humanity from which a perfectly harmonious society emerges.

As described in *The Great Learning*, good governance consists of three aspects: manifesting the clear character of humanity; loving the people; and abiding in the highest good.[40] The text then describes how wise rulership leads to peace in the world:

> The ancients who wished to manifest their clear character to the world would first bring order to their states. Those who wished to bring order to their states would first regulate their families. Those who wished to regulate their families would first cultivate their personal lives. Those who wished to cultivate their personal lives would first rectify their minds. Those who wished to rectify their minds would first make their wills sincere. Those who wished to make their wills sincere would first extend their knowledge. The extension of knowledge consists in the investigation of things. When things are investigated, knowledge is extended; when knowledge is extended, the will becomes sincere; when the will becomes sincere, the mind is rectified; when the mind is rectified, the personal life is cultivated; when the personal life is cultivated, the family will be regulated; when the family is regulated, the state will be in order; and when the state is in order, there will be peace throughout the world.[41]

CHAPTER SUMMARY

The central concerns of the Confucian tradition are the establishment of Goodness, or Humanity (*jen*), in the individual and the establishment of balance, order, and harmony in society as a whole. These objectives are achieved together or not at all. Critical to their attainment is the development of good character. Good character is an enduring condition of balance between extremes. This quality endows a person with the versatility to adapt to the unexpected, doing so in a way called for by the circumstances. Standards for what constitute appropriate responses in a situation are represented in the rites and rituals of the Ancients, the pronouncements of the Oracle, and the image of the *chun-tzu*. By internalizing such images and guiding one's actions accordingly, one attains good character. Thus, Confucius' concern with the outward manifestations of Goodness was a component of his quest to instill good character in his students.

Confucius is often referred to as the First Teacher of China; he is also revered as one of the great teachers of humanity. In spite of the greatness he achieved, Confucius was a very humble person. He said:

> There are four things in the moral life of man, not one of which I have been able to carry out in my life. To serve my father as I would expect my son to serve me: that I have not been able to do. To serve my sovereign as I would expect a minister under me to serve me: that I have not been able to do. To act towards my elder brothers as I would expect my younger brother to act towards me: that I have not been able to do. To be the first to behave towards friends as I would expect them to behave towards me: that I have not been able to do.[42]

Confucius saw his life's mission as reviving the teachings of the Ancients. His disciples learned that the wisdom of the Ancients could bring forth the ideal human being in each of them. According to Confucius, being human necessitates involvement in society. Displaying the essence of humanity requires responsible and respectful interaction with others. Confucius embodied this principle in his actions as a teacher. He described his willingness to teach by saying: "Do I regard myself as a possessor of wisdom? Far from it. But if even a simple peasant comes in all sincerity and asks me a question, I am ready to thrash the matter out, with all its pros and cons, to the very end."[43]

Furthermore, Confucius made no claim to being a Divine Sage. He said that he was a lover of wisdom and a teacher. Addressing this question, he said, "As to being a Divine Sage or even a Good Man, far be it from me to make any such claim. As for unwearying effort to learn and unflagging patience in teaching others, those are merits that I do not hesitate to claim."[44]

Itsukushima Shrine, Japan

CHAPTER 11
THE SHINTO TRADITION

It is hard to describe;
It is impossible to name it.
One only senses
the presence of a mysterious kami.[1]

– The *Man'yoshu*

INTRODUCTION

The name "Shinto" consists of the prefix *shin*, a synonym for *kami* – meaning the sacred – and the suffix *to*, derived from the Chinese *tao* (indicating the Way articulated in Chinese religious philosophy). The Japanese people typically refer to the Shinto tradition as *kami-no-michi* ("the way of the *kami*"). The first recorded use of the name Shinto was in the sixth century of the Common Era, after the Buddhist tradition had entered Japan. The name was apparently used to distinguish "the way of the *kami*" from "the way of the Buddha" (or *butsudo*). Thus, before the diffusion of Buddhist *dharma* in Japan there was no particular name for what is now called "Shinto"; rather, in light of an influx of foreign religious thinking the name was employed in reference to preexistent Japanese practices.

Modern scholars note that what is now referred to as the Shinto religion represents a spiritual tradition that was influenced by other religious movements, including the Taoist, Confucian, and Mahayana Buddhist traditions, which entered Japan from China and Korea. Some scholars, therefore, question the extent to which Shinto, as a cumulative tradition, can be viewed as simply the "indigenous" religion of Japan. As one scholar has observed, "The blending of Japanese and foreign elements into one great national tradition is the

> **Be charitable to all beings; love is the representative of God**
> *Ko-ji-ki Hachiman Kasuga*
> **THE GOLDEN RULE**

Timeline

*c.*660 C.E.
Jimmu Temmo, first (legendary) emperor of Japan

7–8th century C.E.
Man'yoshu compiled

712 C.E.
Kojiki compiled

*c.*720 C.E.
Nihonshoki compiled

1635–1703 C.E.
Tachibana Mitsuyoshi

1730–1803 C.E.
Motoori Norinaga

1776–1843 C.E.
Hirante Atsutane

1868–1912 C.E.
Meiji period

1945 C.E.
Japanese government and Shinto identity separated

19–20th centuries C.E.
New religious movements, influenced by Shinto, arise in Japan

distinctive contribution of Shinto."[2] That the Shinto tradition has transformed, and been transformed by, other traditions is demonstrated by Shinto's ability to coexist peacefully alongside other religious movements. In fact, being more of a spiritual orientation than a theological creed, Shinto allows outside religious beliefs to mix with, or to be superimposed on, what may be considered an underlying Shinto disposition. The late High Priest of the Tsubakai Grand Shrine, Yukitaka Yamamoto, identified the spiritual impulse of Shinto religiosity with *kannagara*[3] – defined, in part, as the "spontaneous awareness of the Divine that can be found in any culture." [4] Yukitaka Yamamoto elaborated on the inner meaning of *kannagara* – what he called a "non-exclusive principle of universalism" – as follows:

> In a sense, kannagara refers to the underlying basis of spirituality common to all religions … Kannagara has to do with spirit, and with bringing the spirit of man and his activities into line with the spirit of Great Nature [Daishizen].
>
> The Spirit of Great Nature may be a flower, may be the beauty of mountains, the pure snow, the soft rains or the gentle breeze. Kannagara means being in communion with these forms of beauty and so with the highest level of experiences of life. When people respond to the silent and provocative beauty of the natural order, they are aware of kannagara. When they respond in a similar way, by following ways "according to the kami," they are expressing kannagara in their lives. They are living according to the natural flow of the universe and will benefit and develop by so doing.[5]

This chapter illuminates "the way of the *kami*," including its recognition of a sacred cosmos and its commitment to living in accord with this sacrality. It does not provide an exhaustive socio-historical treatment of the many Shinto schools of thought. Instead, the focus here is on salient features of the Shinto worldview that have demonstrated continuity over time and which offer insight into how Shintoists understand existence and engage reality. In so doing, the chapter heeds the advice of the Japanese scholar Muraoka Tsunetsugo, who noted: "If we were to concentrate on the individual qualities of each form of Shinto, it would be difficult, if not impossible, to identify the special characteristics of Shinto as a whole."[6] As a start, the unique diversity of Japanese religion – so important to how religion is understood in Japan – will be discussed.

RELIGION IN JAPAN

In Japan, the majority of people participate in religiously oriented practices and festivals; many, however, do not identify themselves as adherents of a particular "religion" (*shukyo*). Initially, non-Japanese scholars who studied the religions of Japan were perplexed when many of their Japanese contacts denied affiliation with a particular "religion," yet actively participated in religious activities. In part, this phenomenon relates to the connotations associated with the word *shukyo*. The scholar Ian Reader has noted:

> The Japanese word generally used in surveys and elsewhere to denote 'religion' is shūkyo, a word made up of two ideograms, shū, meaning sect or denomination, and kyo, teaching or doctrine. It is a derived word that came into prominence in the nineteenth century as a result of Japanese encounters with the West and particularly with Christian missionaries, to denote a concept and view of religion commonplace in the realms of nineteenth-century Christian theology but at that time not found in Japan, of religion as a specific, belief-framed entity. The term shūkyo thus, in origin at least, implies a separation of that which is religious from other aspects of society and culture, and contains implications of belief and commitment to one order or movement – something that has not been traditionally a common factor in Japanese religious behavior and something that tends to exclude many of the phenomena involved in the Japanese religious process. When tied to questions of belief it ["religion" or *shukyo*] does conjure up notions of narrow commitment to a particular teaching to the implicit exclusion and denial of others – something which goes against the general complementary nature of the Japanese religious tradition.[7]

Religious identity among the Japanese tends to be fluid; it is foreign to Japanese thinking to conceptualize one's religious orientation in terms of a doctrinal standpoint set against other religious viewpoints. In Japan, as also represented in Chinese yin–yang philosophy, there is a tendency to see the complementarity of so-called opposites rather than their duality. Relationships between things are, therefore, not conceived under an either/or premise. Hence, religions are not necessarily viewed as mutually exclusive or mutually negating.

Many Japanese people participate in more than one religious tradition. Illustrative of this fact is the way in which variant religious beliefs and practices peacefully converge and enrich one another in Japan. For example, the Shinto tradition's affirmative and positive view of life in this world is closely related to the Japanese experience of seeing the divine in nature. Nevertheless, the Neo-Confucian tradition of China was instrumental in shaping Japan, including its political, educational, and civil service structures. Taoist religious ideals also of Chinese origin, such as concern for certain auspicious days in the calendar year, are evident throughout Japanese popular culture. Such Taoist influences, stemming from the religious or popular Taoist tradition, are manifested alongside the general longstanding shamanic strand of Japanese religious history. This shamanic strand depicts a multi-dimensional world inhabited by spirits and includes practices such as divination and exorcisms.[8] Much of the intellectual

Religious identity among the Japanese tends to be fluid

world of Japan is, however, dominated by the Mahayana Buddhist tradition which entered Japan as early as the sixth century of the Common Era. Originally from India, but entering Japan by way of China and Korea, the Buddhist outlook, as it has taken distinctive shape in Japan, is central to the way Japanese people relate to many ultimate concerns, especially death and the afterlife. The drawing of sharp divisions between the religions of Japan, as seen in Japanese popular culture, can therefore be somewhat artificial. This is especially the case because religious practice in Japan is related to both locality (participation in one's local Shinto shrine) and family tradition (participation in a certain Buddhist school based on hereditary tradition). With respect to the religious diversity of Japan, the scholars Robert Ellwood and Richard Pilgrim have observed the following:

> Perhaps it is best to consider the various [religious paths or] ways [such as Shinto or "the way of the gods," *butsudo* or "the way of the buddhas," *onmyodo* or the Taoist "way of the ying and yang," and *judo* or the Confucian "way of the gentleman"] as strands within a larger rope called "Japanese religion" or the "Japanese way" – a rope that extends from prehistoric time up to this very day. The rope is not everywhere and always the same. The strands change and shift along its length, and the rope is flexible and changing. Nonetheless it is identifiable as the Japanese way. In fact, some have argued that this rope is itself the fundamental religion of Japan, and the strands that make it up are so many support systems to a larger religion called nihondo, the "way of Japan." Such an appeal to an overarching "civil religion" has some merit, but it can easily be overemphasized to the exclusion of the unique importance and specificity of the distinctive ways as particular religious modes of life.[9]

THE SHINTO WORLDVIEW

The Shinto tradition did not arise from the experience of a certain historical founder, nor does it have a corpus of scripture understood as inerrant revelation. Instead, it is rooted in the multi-sided spirituality of the ancient Japanese people, representing a coalescence of variant strands of religiosity that includes animism, shamanism, ancestor worship, and agricultural rites. The spiritual message of Shinto may be universal, but as a historical and organized tradition it is inextricably linked to the people and nation of Japan – including Japan's unique history and its natural landscape (which is often imbued with divine attributes).[10] One scholar, in fact, has remarked: "There is a significant sense in which virtually every Japanese, no matter his personal profession, may be said to be Shintoist."[11] This spiritual unity exists in spite of the fact that, geographically, Japan is a conglomerate of distinct islands – such as Hokkaido, Honshu, Shikoku, and Kyushu – on the eastern coast of Asia in the western Pacific Ocean.

Inhabitants of the Japanese archipelago live in a majestic surrounding that includes forests, mountains, volcanoes, and rivers. The region incurs frequent rains, and has a long history of natural disasters such as earthquakes and typhoons.

Just as desert life influenced the Jewish and Islamic world-views, the powerful environment of the Japanese islands – which were regarded as an earthly paradise – undoubtedly played an important role in shaping Shinto religiosity. In fact, Shinto spirituality tends not to look beyond the phenomenal world to find the sacredness of true reality – it posits an indwelling, or immanent presence, of the divine within nature. Rather than looking toward a future paradisal state or culminating point in history, Shinto suggests that the present moment is the most auspicious of all moments; it is an eternal moment (*naka-ima*). Shinto embraces the universe as it is; it does not seek liberation from this world. Instead, as the Shinto priestess Akiko Kobayashi has stated, "Shinto … [is] a spiritual approach to nature and as a religion … [it teaches] … attainment of self-control and consequent self purification and final salvation of human beings in and through … nature."[12] In the Shinto tradition, therefore, divine revelation is not predominantly found in scripture or history but in nature.

> **In the Shinto tradition, divine revelation is not predominantly found in scripture or history but in nature**

It is important to clarify what the terms "nature" or "natural world" signify within the Shinto context. Nature, from the Shinto perspective, can be understood as a sacred cosmos – a view holding that nature is a divine process. In that sense, nature – or existence – is not the product of mere randomness, neither is it generally viewed as the result of a transcendent Creator. Viewing nature as a process, the Shinto path emphasizes the need to maintain a harmonious relationship with the spiritual ecology that is the universe. This outlook holds that all things are interconnected, that a life guided by spiritual principles entails securing the mutually beneficent coexistence of all beings, and that spiritual reality is responsive to human actions, including religious ritual and invocation.

It should be noted that the Shinto perspective does not hold the fundamental reality of the "natural world" to be physical matter. Rather, the Shinto worldview is spiritual and animistic – it sees all things as permeated with spiritual vitality and animated by divine powers. The Japanese scholar Ueda Kenji noted:

> The Japanese had no word to indicate sheer "matter" (busshitsu) in the Western sense. As intimated by the term mono no ke [lit., the "aura of a thing"; a spectre], even the word mono [thing] was thought to refer to a kind of spiritual being (reiteki na sonzai). Namely, all things were conceived of as spiritual existence, which existed in a relationship of mutual effect on human beings, and those which possessed particularly awesome agency were the tama[13] [spirit] revered as kami.[14]

In English translations, the term *kami* is sometimes rendered as "powers," "gods," "deities," "spirits," "superior beings," "the divine," or "the sacred." Like other religious ideals of Asian or Indian origin – including the religious principles of Tao or *dharma* – there is no English equivalent of *kami*. In many ways, *kami* encompasses notions associated with all the aforementioned English terms, but it is not exhausted by any of them; in fact, *kami* connotes something mysterious that goes beyond all concepts. The Shinto scholar Sokyo Ono pointed out that Shintoists "are aware of the kami intuitively at the depth of their consciousness and communicate with the kami directly without having formed the kami-idea conceptually or theologically."[15] A time-honored, provisional definition of *kami* was offered by the Shinto thinker Motoori Norinaga (1730–1801 C.E.) – who is held by many to be the greatest scholastic thinker of the tradition. Norinaga concluded the following:

> Generally, kami denotes, in the first place, the divine beings of heaven and earth that appear in the ancient texts and also the enshrined spirits that are revered in the nation's jinga [shrine]; furthermore, among other beings, not only human but also animate and inanimate beings such as birds, beasts, trees, grass, seas, mountains, and the like. Any form of being whatsoever which possesses some unique and eminent quality, and is awe inspiring, may be called kami.[16]
>
> Furthermore, [in ancient Shinto texts] we can find frequent instances of rocks, stumps of trees, and leaves of plants speaking. All these were kami. It is not that the spirit of the sea or the mountains is referred to as kami. The sea or the mountain itself is considered a kami, because it possesses the property of inspiring wonder and awe in those who observe it.[17]

In general, a Shintoist's relationship with the *kami* is experiential and qualitative, and not philosophical or based on faith in doctrine; namely, the *kami* are felt or sensed within nature – to different degrees in different places.[18] Thus, anything that possesses a numinous, awe-inspiring quality may be interpreted as *kami*. Mythological texts of the Shinto tradition purport the existence of an innumerable number of *kami*. The myriad *kami*, however, act in concert to form a cosmic harmony. In that sense, emphasis is placed not on a monistic divine unity, but on a divine plurality that functions harmoniously.[19] The diverse ways in which a Shintoist can relate to the *kami* – a notion that eludes rigid definition – is undoubtedly an important element in the general religious tolerance inherent to the tradition. In regard to this point, one scholar has observed:

> [A] … reason for the indefinable nature of kami is that it simply does not matter. As the most important aspect [in the Shinto tradition] is direct communication with the divine, the individual emotional experience of the worshipper, which will, in any case, differ

from person to person, there is really no point in insisting upon a precise description of the divine. Thus the appearance of kami can vary to suit the needs of the worshipper. Farmers will pray to kami protecting the harvest and to kami of the locality. Merchants and tradesmen have their own kami. A very personal kind of protection is given by the ancestral kami. They are worshipped at the family altar and in return they have the duty to protect the house and its inhabitants.[20]

The *kami* are not conceived as wholly good in a moralistic way; rather, they are, from humanity's perspective, experienced as both malevolent and benevolent. This viewpoint can be understood within the wide spectrum of human experiences incurred while living within a mysterious, unpredictable universe. Awe-inspiring *kami* may, therefore, range from a beautiful sunset to a fatal earthquake. From this way of seeing things, what many people conceptualize as "good and evil" is imputed on a divine process that ultimately transcends human comprehension. Although some of the powers and unseen forces of the Shinto universe might be considered harmful, overall the Shinto viewpoint is over-whelmingly positive; namely, Shinto embraces the universe as a sacred cosmos – derived from the *kami* – and understands humanity's life within it to be a blessing deserving of grat-itude (*kansha*). As the following poem by the Japanese emperor Go-Fushimi (r. 1298–1301 C.E.) suggests, all the modalities of nature are inherently good and are consequences of the *kami*:

> Even that shape, even those plants
> Are perfect;
> The mind of the kami –
> As always, full of life.[21]

The importance of direct, qualitative experience in the Shinto tradition – over and above thoughts and words – is found in the religious function afforded to aesthetics and the phys-ical senses within Shinto spirituality. The Shinto scholar Motoori Norinaga identified an aesthetic principle – *mono no aware* – that he surmised represented not only the distinctive Shinto way of life, but also the distinguishing characteristic of the Japanese people. *Mono no aware* entails a way of sensitively engaging the world while remaining attentive to the "stimulating or affecting significance"[22] of things or events – it implies an awareness of "the mutual empathy of all natural phenomena."[23] Thus, an intuitive sensitivity that is capable of being moved to tears by the sight of an exceptionally beautiful flower represents, according to Motoori, the true, uninhibited spiritual nature of humankind. This intense recognition of beauty is not without acknowledgment of its ultimate impermanence – in fact, it is the transience of beauty that seemingly increases its pre-ciousness. Motoori suggested that the human heart, when not sullied with sociological roles or moralistic dogmas, is essentially "tender, like words uttered by a woman or a child."[24] This Shinto ideal – and the poetic way of life it entails – embodies the archetypal feminine and is distinct from other models of living, such as those represented by the ascetic monk, rationalistic scholar, or stoic warrior.

In the Shinto model of living, the whole of life is considered to be a spiritual experience. This view derives from the fact that, according to the Shinto perspective, human beings are descendants of the divine *kami* and, therefore, possess an essentially divine nature. As the scholar Jean Herbert explains, humanity and the *kami* "share one and the same divine blood, which flows through animals, plants, minerals, and all other things in Nature."[25] Some human beings are, in fact, revered as *kami* after their death and are honored as such by their familial descendants. Nevertheless, the essential unity of humankind and the *kami* does not prevent an imperfect humanity from committing transgressions against the way of nature (synonymous with the way of the *kami*). In such cases – amid the tribulations of daily life – humanity encounters polluting (*tsumi*) elements that require purification to restore and renew one's essential *kami*-nature. Such purification practices, pivotal to the inner life of Shintoists, include the spiritual discipline of *misogi harai* – purificatory immersion in a cold sea, river, or cascading waterfall. The scholar Stuart D. B. Picken describes *misogi harai* when practiced under a free-flowing waterfall – a discipline honed at the Tsubakai Grand Shrine in Mie Prefecture – as follows:

> **In the Shinto model of living, the whole of life is considered to be a spiritual experience**

> There is ultimate authenticity in the act of standing under the fall and being immersed in nature itself. You will not know where your physical existence ends and the flow of the fall begins. For that moment, you and nature, daishizen, the cosmos, are one. Misogi simultaneously creates the awareness and satisfies the longing of the hungry to feel and experience nature in a way that assures and confirms that we are rooted in its life and processes. Standing under the fall, we are a part of that process, for that time, an indistinguishable element of it returning to the source of life itself, living water.[26]

The practice of *misogi* invigorates the vital force that permeates the body, mind, and spirit; it promotes spiritual renewal and aims to bring the practitioner into harmony with nature. Shinto practices seek the removal of egotistic and physiological impurities that obscure the effulgence of one's latent *kami*-nature.

The view that there is an immanent divine, or enlightened, nature intrinsic to human beings and ever present throughout the cosmos is central to the teachings of the Mahayana

Buddhist tradition, which transformed the civilization of Japan, as it did Tibet, with its well-developed system of philosophy, monastic practice, spiritual disciplines, and arts. It has been suggested by scholars that the Buddha was first perceived within Japan as a foreign *kami*, but it was not long before Japan's indigenous *kami*-centered religious practices were engulfed by the more encompassing and philosophical Buddhist worldview – which inclusively accepted the *kami* as protectors of *bodhisattva*s or as *deva*s (or gods) that have, through many lives, attained birth in the highest karmically determined realm of existence, i.e. a celestial realm, but have, nevertheless, not yet attained *nirvana* (i.e. liberation from the laws of *samsara* or conditioned reality). Other schools of thought viewed certain *kami* as signifying the same ultimate Truth as connoted by the (symbolic) Buddhas of the Mahayana tradition. In later periods, especially during the seventeenth to twentieth centuries, a Shinto revival sparked the return of the *kami* understood as independent of the Buddhist worldview. During this period, ethnocentric and nationalistic thinkers criticized syncretic identifications across the two religions and championed Shinto as the unique Japanese spiritual tradition. In any case, the Buddhist and Shinto religions of Japan have enriched each other and persist side by side to this very day, and their syncretic coexistence was instrumental in the formation of Japanese culture and spirituality.

It is important to note that regardless of debates among competing schools of Shinto thought, Mahayana Buddhist teachings, like those of the Neo-Confucian tradition, were instrumental in the developmental maturation of Shinto. In fact, principles that stem from these traditions were absorbed and applied within a Shinto context and were influential in later Shinto views that posit an ultimate *kami* essence and an inner *kami*-nature.[27] Paralleling Mahayana motivations, for some Shinto adherents to walk in the way of the *kami* is to strive toward actualizing one's *kami* potential. From this point of view, the aspirant must live a life that reflects his or her divine progenitor – a life of correctness and uprightness. The Shinto thinker Tachibana Mitsuyoshi (1635–1703 C.E.) commented on such an ethical life as follows:

What is truly upright is what flows out from our innermost self as a result of sincerity shown by observing the will of the kami. This sincerity must be practiced even in the least significant of the activities of life. Courtesy and ritual in the absence of sincerity and honesty is without significance …

In the affairs of daily life … the rectification of the mind is important. This enables us to derive great pleasure from doing good deeds. It will be to no avail if you are merely motivated by the desire to have some reward from the kami. We must simply believe that to love the good and to act honestly is the fundamental condition for being human. We should not be negligent for even a moment.[28]

Top: The Shinto Tsubaki Grand Shrine in Suzuka, Mie Prefecture, Japan
Bottom: A Shinto altar inside the Tsubaki Grand Shrine

It is held that through the spiritual path of Shinto, one is capable of attaining a "bright heart" or "pure heart." An individual with a pure heart is in harmony with nature and, thereby, can be intuitively led to the proper course of action – that which is representative of the will of the *kami* – in ever-changing circumstances. Rather than adherence to commandments or laws, ethics and behavior in Shinto are determined by the flow of the moment. Life-directing spiritual values, such as honesty, gratitude (*kansha*), purity of mind, and sincerity of heart (*makoto-no-kokoro*) are therefore the very fabric of religious life.

THE HISTORICAL EMERGENCE OF SHINTO

Scholars suggest that a variety of different ethnic groups migrated to the Japanese archipelago; the convergence of these variant ethnic streams was an important part in the formation of the multifaceted religion and culture of Japan. The thinker Joseph J. Spae commented: "Cultural aspects of Japanese religiosity are notoriously difficult to assess and isolate. In the case of Shinto, the reason is clear: Shinto is not primarily an institutional religion; it is a polymorphous, diffused religion."[29] In part, scholars attribute the wide-ranging ancient religious practices of Japan – out of which modern Shinto was partly derived – to the amalgamation of foreign cosmologies and local beliefs that occurred over the course of Japanese history.

Around the first century of the Common Era, the development of irrigation techniques transformed the dispersed, hunting and gathering lifestyle of the ancient Japanese to clan-based patterns centered on the cultivation of rice. Rice cultivation allowed for increased populations and required systematic cooperation among large groups of people. Agriculture not only revolutionized the sociological structure of ancient Japan, it also inculcated a sense of gratitude (*kansha*) toward the life-giving forces of nature and an appreciation of the interdependency of life. For example, the cultivation of rice requires the combination of a number of different, interrelated elements – weather, seeds, material, and labor – if it is to bear the life-sustaining grain that became the staple food of Japan and the basis of its economy. Uesugi Chisato, chief priest of the Suwa Shinto Shrine, noted that "farmers sometimes talk about the roots of the rice plant, *ne*, as having 'breath' (*ne no iki*) ... Rice is alive, it's breathing out there in the field, and because of its life-giving properties to those early communities, it was considered divine, with a Kami dwelling within it."[30] Notably, the ancient Japanese honored the seasonal sowing and harvesting of rice cultivation with sacred rituals and festivals. These ancient celebrations are, in fact, an important part of the fundamental, communal nature of Shinto spirituality that thrives to the present day at Shinto shrines (*jinga*) across Japan (see below for further discussion of Shinto shrines or "Shrine Shinto").

According to the Shinto priestess Akiko Kobayashi, "The yearly work cycle and prayers for a good harvest extend from planting and germination of the rice shoots to harvesting the crops. The religious culture and customs built around this … celebration of rice cultivation can be designated as the origin of Shinto religion."[31]

If community and ritual in ancient Japan were rooted in the emergence of an agricultural way of life, it was the mysterious, awe-inspiring *kami* that provided the unifying component among ancient Japan's complex religious milieu. In ancient Japan, the *kami* played an important role as "tutelary deities" (*uji-gami*) – or protective benefactors – of the Japanese clans or lineage groups (*uji*). The clans of ancient Japan were the basic social units of Japanese society; the socio-political role, geographical location, and mode of sustenance of each clan shaped the worldview of its members. One clan in particular – the Yamato (which was also the old name of Japan) – rose to political prominence. The scholar Joseph Kitawaga explained the socio-religious dynamics of the ancient Japanese clan society, including the role of the Yamato, as follows:

Each uji [clan] was not only a social, economic, political, and often military unit but also a unity of religious solidarity centering around its progenitor/tutelary kami (uji-gami), who was usually attended by the chieftain of the uji. In a sense, sharing the same kami was more important than blood relations. In the event that a certain uji should be subjugated by another, the uji-bito [tutelary *kami*] of the former group were incorporated into the structure of the latter, whereas the kami of the former was sometimes venerated as an auxiliary kami of the latter uji. Among all the uji groups … the most powerful was the uji which claimed solar ancestry [namely, the Yamato clan]; it also excelled in military affairs. In the course of time the chieftains of this uji [the Yamato] gradually solidified their influence over other uji chieftains and received the kingly title [*tenno*, meaning "heavenly king"] from China by paying tribute to the Chinese imperial court. They began to assume royal prerogatives … conferring court titles (kabane) on other prominent uji chieftains, granting sacred seed at spring festivals, and establishing sacred sites for various kami as well as regulating rituals for them.[32]

With the ascendancy of the Yamato – from which the long line of Japanese emperors claim lineage – the various clans were consolidated under imperial rule. At the order of the Yamato imperial court, the mythological texts *Kojiki* ("Records of Ancient Matters") and *Nihonshoki* ("Chronicles of Japan") were written. These texts serve, in part, as records of the mythic events that occurred during the "age of the *kami*" – representing an amalgamation of preexistent Japanese mythic oral traditions (as interpreted from the Yamato clan's perspective). The first of these texts, the *Kojiki*, was compiled around

682 C.E., and the second, the *Nihonshoki*, around 720 C.E. Although they are not accepted as canonical scriptures, both texts have, throughout Shinto history, served as a wellspring of inspiration, spawning variant Shinto interpretations that have provided innovative ways of grasping meaning within a changing world. The *Kojiki* and *Nihonshoki* were also important in providing a common religious heritage for the nascent Japanese nation.

It should be noted that the cultural center of Asia during this period was China. Just as European countries imbibed the legacy of ancient Greece during the Middle Ages of Europe, China served as the major cultural and intellectual paradigm for neighboring Asian countries. Notably, the presence of Chinese thought, including the yin–yang cosmology and the theory of the five elements (metal, wood, water, fire, and earth), are evident in both the *Kojiki* and *Nihonshoki*. These texts were, in fact, the first books written in the Japanese language. Although spoken Japanese is not related to Chinese, written Japanese developed by recording Japanese words using Chinese characters phonetically. Thus, within the *Kojiki* and *Nihonshoki*, Chinese categories of thought were utilized to record indigenous Japanese traditions and mythic narratives.[33] In studying the *Kojiki* and *Nihonshoki* it is important to take into consideration the following observation by the scholar H. Byron Earhart:

> The Kojiki and Nihongi [or *Nihonshoki*] have often been considered the watershed of myth from which all later Japanese religion (particularly Shinto) is derived. This general notion is inadequate, however. In the first place, these scriptures reflect both political and religious motives for unifying Japan. They were compiled by the court elite and did not necessarily mirror the faith of the country at large. In the second place, there is probably no such thing as a foundational myth in Japanese religion. For the Japanese there is neither one sacred myth nor one set of sacred scriptures.[34]

Nevertheless, as the earliest mythological writing of the Shinto tradition, the *Kojiki* and *Nihonshoki* are invaluable for understanding both the Shinto religion and the history of Japan. The myths – which demonstrate similarities with the ancient European mythologies of the Celtic, Nordic, and Greco-Roman peoples – explain that both the universe and, in particular, the Japanese islands, are of divine descent – a sacred space – and that humanity, and most notably the Japanese people, are of divine lineage. It is also in these texts that the mythic happenings of sacred time – the "age of the *kami*" – are documented. These events function as divine models that inform patterns of Shinto behavior and ritual. Reenactments of these mythic events were understood to affect both personal and cosmic renewal. Joseph Kitagawa commented:

That is to say, people in the early period of Japan, like their counterparts in other parts of the world, took it for granted that they or their ancestors had learned all the necessary knowledge and techniques regarding social behavior and practical matters from the world of the *kami*. This world was far away from, and yet closely related to, their world, such that the success or failure of their daily work, to say nothing of the meaning of the whole of life, was interpreted in religious terms.[35]

THE AGE OF THE *KAMI*

According to the *Kojiki*, in the mythic beginning there was a spontaneous emergence of three *kami* amidst the dark primordial ether. The three *kami* that emerged, in succession, were the Master of the August Center of Heaven (Ame-no-minakushi), the August Producing *Kami* (Takami-musubi-no-kami), and the Divine Producing *Kami* (Kami-musubi-no-kami). The latter two *kami* – sometimes called the *kami* of birth and growth – have the Japanese word *musubi* in their names. The scholar Floyd Hiatt Ross noted that "the word *musubi* … comes from *musubu*, which means to grow, to tie, to bind. This involves the idea of a power immanent in nature; in other words, creative evolution."[36] Some interpreters have viewed this power-of-becoming as the agent of evolutionary growth behind the entire cosmos. After the appearance of the first three creative *kami*, mentioned above, two more *kami* spontaneously sprang forth from a reed shoot that emerged from the drifting, oil-like earth. The exact nature of how or why the first five *kami*, collectively regarded as the *kami* of the High Plain of Heaven (*Takamhara*), appeared, and reportedly disappeared, is not indicated. The mysteriousness is, in fact, part and parcel of the nature of the divine processes themselves. To be sure, there is no distinct creation; rather, the *kami* arise without progenitors and their intrinsic, generating powers catalyze a creative movement toward greater complexity – in other words, an indefinite existence gradually evolves toward an ordered and harmonious cosmos.

> It was the mysterious, awe-inspiring *kami* that provided the unifying component among ancient Japan's complex religious milieu

The *Kojiki* depicts the formation of the cosmos through the spontaneous emergence of (opposite) pairs of *kami*. This process apparently entails the harmonizing, binding, or uniting of opposites – seemingly the forces, or principles, that are constituents of the very matrix of the universe. After ten such *kami* arise (five pairs), two of the most important *kami* emerge: the Male-Who-Invites (Izanagi-no-mikoto) and the Female-Who-Invites (Izanami-no-mikoto) – hereafter referred to by their shortened Japanese names Izanagi and Izanami. This divine couple – the primal parents – were asked by the heavenly *kami* to coagulate and solidify the drifting land. They were given a jeweled spear and, while standing on the Floating Bridge of Heaven, plunged the spear into the murky waters below and stirred. The brine that dripped from the tip of the spear as it was removed formed an island. After descending to the island they noticed their bodily differences and their desire for union. After receiving proper divination instructions from the heavenly *kami*, they made love and begot the islands of Japan and the *kami* that dwell therein (such as the wind-*kami*, sea-*kami*, mountain-*kami*, tree-*kami*, etc.). Thus, these *kami* are not symbolic representations but literally the natural phenomena and landscape. In that way, nature inspires awe and wonder and is translucent to the divine mystery of the *kami*.

When Izanami was giving birth to the Fire Generating *Kami*, she was badly burned. Due to the severe burns, Izanami died and descended to the underworld (Yomi-no-kami), indicating that the *kami* are generally considered "finite gods" lacking complete omniscience and omnipotence. Out of anger, a weeping Izanagi cut the Fire Generating *Kami* into pieces and descended to the underworld in search of Izanami. When he found her in the underworld Izanami appealed to him not to cast his eyes upon her. Izanagi, however, grew impatient and defied her request. When Izanagi finally did gaze at her he beheld a hideous sight – a maggot-infested, decomposing body.

> **Nature inspires awe and wonder and is translucent to the divine mystery of the *kami***

Feeling shamed by this action, Izanami sent spirits to chase after Izanagi who, fleeing, barely escaped from his pursuers. Izanami then pushed an immense rock across the threshold separating the land of the living from that of the dead and threatened to kill a thousand beings every day if he returned. To emphasize the futility of her threat, Izanagi replied that he would simply cause fifteen hundred to be born each day. Shinto thinkers identify this exchange as the primary mythological background to the fundamental, life-affirming optimism of Shinto. Namely, although death is identified with pollution, the power of life is greater than that of death. This may shed light on why there is so little speculative thought concerning death and the afterlife in Shinto religiosity – for Shintoists, life in this world is central.

Izanagi, having ventured beyond a safe, normative boundary into the polluted region of the underworld, was exposed to defilements. The *Kojiki* records that after Izanagi returned, he bathed in the Tachibana River to remove the impurities (*tsumi*). The mythic action of Izanagi's bathing is the paradigm for the ritual lustration, or purificatory bathing, known as *misogi* – a central spiritual practice of the Shinto tradition, discussed above. While Izanagi washed his face, three *kami* appeared: from his left eye arose the *kami* of the sun, Amaterasu-o-kami (hereafter referred to by the shortened Japanese name Amaterasu); from his right eye came the *kami* of the moon, Tsuki-yomi-no-mikoto; and from his nose came the *kami* of storms, Susano-no-mikoto (hereafter referred to by the shortened Japanese name Susano). The most important of these three *kami* were Susano and the "solar goddess" Amaterasu.

Susano, a trickster of sorts, performed a variety of unruly deeds that wreaked havoc and offended other *kami*. In response to such chaotic behavior, Amaterasu hid herself within a cave-like abode, causing the cosmos to fall into darkness – a motif found in the religious myths of neighboring peoples as well. The heavenly *kami* consulted each other and attempted to lure Amaterasu out by lighting a fire, reciting magical incantations, and waving a sacred tree (*sakaki*), beads, and other symbolic items. As part of the continued effort to induce the return of Amaterasu, a *kami* named Ame-no-Uzume performed a shamanic dance to the laughing and clapping delight of the other *kami*. The commotion of the promiscuous dance sparked the interest of Amaterasu, who peeked out to see what the gleeful uproar was about. Amaterasu was lured out of the rock dwelling when she became mesmerized by her own image reflected in a mirror before her. The world was thus renewed and the life-giving light of the sun restored. Scholars suggest that the actions performed by the *kami* to lure Amaterasu out of the cave represent ancient Japanese shamanic practices of exorcism, divination, and trance. In fact, the comical dance of Ame-no-Uzume functions as an archetypal representation of a variety of different Japanese religious and artistic dance performances known as *kagura*. Such dances remain prevalent in Japan to the present day in the imperial court, at local villages, and among shamanic mediums, as well as in dramas and other musical performances.

Later in the *Kojiki*, after unruly *kami* residing in the earthly realm were subdued, Amaterasu sent her grandson, Ninigi – by divine command – to rule over the Japanese islands. Amaterasu gave Ninigi three sacred objects – a string of jewels, a mirror, and a sword. Amaterasu decreed: "This mirror – have [it with you] as my spirit, and worship it just as you would worship in my very presence."[37] The mirror, jewels, and sword are, in fact, important symbolic objects that became the imperial regalia of the Yamato court and remain, to the present day, signs of imperial authority. The thirteenth-century Shinto thinker Kitabatake Chikafusa interpreted the inner meaning of the three imperial regalia as follows:

> The Mirror harbors nothing within itself. As it reflects all phenomena without a selfish heart, there is never an instance when the forms of right and wrong, or good and evil, fail to show up. Its virtue consists in responding to these forms as they come. This is the basic source of correctness and uprightness. The virtue of the Jewel includes gentleness, peace, goodness, and obedience. These are the basic sources of compassion. The virtue of the Sword includes strength, benefit, resolution, and decisiveness. These are the basic sources of wisdom. Unless these three qualities are combined in people, it will be truly difficult for the world to be put right.[38]

According to Shinto mythology, after seven divine generations the first (legendary) emperor of Japan – Jimmu Temmo (*c.*660 C.E.) – gained ascendancy and inherited the three sacred objects. Each new emperor was bequeathed the sacred objects in a coronation ritual regarded as an authentication of the emperor's especially privileged station as a direct descendant of Amaterasu.

Amaterasu, who was the protective *kami* of the Yamato clan, became the chief *kami* of Japan.[39] In the mythological text *Nihonshoki* it is recorded that Amaterasu declared: "The province of Ise, whose divine winds blow, is washed by successive waves from the Eternal Land. It is a secluded and beautiful place, and I wish to dwell here."[40] In fact, the shrine built at Ise in Mie prefecture is the most important Shinto shrine, and pilgrimage to its hallowed grounds is common. A fourteenth-century pilgrim reported on his pilgrimage experience as follows:

It is quite customary for us neither to bring any offerings to the Goddess nor to carry rosaries … In short, we have nothing special wherewith to recommend ourselves in petitioning her Divinity. This is the true signification of inner purity. Washing oneself in the sea water, and being cleansed of the bodily filth – this is outer purity. Being pure in mind and body, our soul is at one with the Divine, and divinity in humanity thus realized, there remains no desire unsatisfied – there is no occasion for further petition or prayer to the Goddess. This is the true esoteric meaning of worshipping the Sun Goddess at the Ise Shrine. Being thus enlightened by the Shinto priest of the shrine, I was overwhelmed with a sense of pious joy, and burst into tears of gratitude.[41]

Thousands of Shinto shrines emerged honoring *kami* in nature (natural phenomena), *kami* that were held as special benefactors, *kami* featured in the mythological texts, and others. Many of these shrines were supported by the imperial clan, which had, by the seventh century of the Common Era, issued an edict that specified details regarding the performance of Shinto rituals and festivals. In that sense, the folk-spiritual traditions of ancient Japan inherited by what is now called "Shinto" – including *kami* worship, animism, concern for purification, shamanism, and reverence for ancestors – took a more organized form with the propagation of shrines and festivals under imperial direction.

SHRINE SHINTO (JINJA SHINTO)

In ancient Japan certain areas of nature were felt to manifest an intense vitality. These sacred spaces – believed to have a special proclivity to manifest a *kami* – were signified with pebbles, stones, or by a rope which marked off the numinous and spiritually potent area. Over time shrines were built at such places and shamanistic divination and rituals were performed. The scholar John K. Nelson observed:

> [Shrines] gave early societies a center around which to orient and integrate their civil, social, administrative, and ethical affairs. This place was the absolute reality, the "localized sacred," which transcended, yet at the same time manifested itself in, the world. With a tree at its far end for the Kami to alight upon and invest with their numinous power, it was here that the community gained access, via the petitions and summonings of the head priest and shamans, to the blessings and protection they needed for their crops and villages.[42]

Currently there are over eighty thousand shrines operational across Japan – six hundred of which maintain a full-time staff.[43] Shrines not only provide a link to Japan's traditional past, they offer a safe haven for spiritual renewal and purification in an increasingly industrial nation. Most shrines are connected to the Association of Shinto Shrines (Jinga Honcho) which allocates funds, upholds the qualifications of priests, and serves other organizational functions. The activities of the many shrines, however, are colored by local custom, and tend to focus their devotional attention on local *kami*. Chief Priest Uesugi of the Suwa Shrine in Nagasaki contextualized the worship of local *kami* as being "points of access to the more encompassing powers of Amaterasu."[44] Commonly, worshipers visit shrines to pray for divine protection, to offer thanks for blessings received, to participate in a cultural and communal aspect of Japanese society, and to receive oracles and protective amulets. Typically, visits to shrines are emphasized during transitional periods of life, such as shortly after birth, throughout childhood (such as at the ages of three, five, and seven), during school entrance exams, or at the time of marriage.

There are over eighty thousand shrines operational across Japan

Shrine buildings and grounds are intentionally simplistic, and are intended to demonstrate continuity and harmony with nature. Modern shrines are known for their characteristic *torii* – or wooden archway – under which a practitioner must pass to gain entrance to the sacred premises. One then proceeds to a purificatory basin to wash one's hands and mouth to purify the outer and inner being. Similar to worship performed at one's home at a private *kami* altar (*kamidana*), a worshiper faces the shrine, claps twice, bows twice, and recites a prayer or petitions divine favor. During shrine services, ceremonial procedures are led by trained priests, and may feature purification, adoration, offerings of food to the *kami*, music, dance, and liturgical prayers (*norito*). After this more structured ceremonial atmosphere – which emphasizes carefully enacted ritual movements – a more festive feast ensues. Notably, the eating of the food offerings and the drinking of sake (rice wine) are considered sacraments through which an aspirant can commune with the *kami*.

An important aspect of Japanese communal identity transpires through lively and colorful Shinto festivals known as *matsuri*. Such festivals – which are traditionally believed to entertain and induce the presence of *kami* – may include activities such as sake drinking, horse racing, sumo wrestling, archery, and parades. At important annual festivals associated with the agricultural calendar a procession may be enacted in which energetic worshipers carry a *kami* palanquin (*mikoshi*) on their shoulders in a grand, even seemingly chaotic, scene that transcends normative roles and conduct. The scholar Yanagawa Keiichi suggested that "a *matsuri* involves taking the conscious states received through the senses, namely sensual experience, and indulging it, or using it to the greatest possible limits, without begrudging or restricting it in any way."[45] In that sense, exhaustive bodily exertion and sensual excitation, resembling shamanistic practices, is experienced in the hope of achieving a sort of ecstatic communion with the *kami*. Such intense experiences are in accord with Shinto's basic affirmation of life in this world, including the essential goodness of nature and the bodily senses.

THE MEIJI PERIOD AND MODERN JAPAN

As noted above, from the Shinto perspective human beings – and the Japanese people in particular – are understood to be divine descendants of the *kami*; the Japanese emperors, however, were viewed as having a direct lineage to the solar deity Amaterasu. Thus, the emperors were thought to manifest the inborn *kami* nature – present within all humanity – to a more potent degree. The emperor was therefore regarded as best suited to steer the nation in accord with the will of the *kami*. In that sense, the prosperity of the nation depended on the emperor's spiritual competence as a sacred leader or high priest. Although there has been longstanding concern for aligning rulership with ethical and spiritual principles in Japan, during most periods of Japanese history the emperor held little political power beyond figurehead status. Notably, however, in the late nineteenth century, during the Meiji period (1868–1912 C.E.), the emperor became the focal point of a nationalistic, modernizing movement. After the failure of the Tokugawa feudal regime, imperial rule was restored and statecraft returned to the religious polity of ancient times. Inspired, in part, by a scholastic Shinto revival and the

> The prosperity of the nation depended on the emperor's spiritual competence as a sacred leader

perceived imperialistic motivations of Western countries, Japanese thinkers saw Shinto as the basis of Japan's culture and internal solidarity. A rapid process of industrialization and militarization ensued, which utilized Shinto as an identity-preserving link that honored tradition amidst social change. By governmental initiative, hostile lines were drawn separating the Shinto and Buddhist traditions, which had existed in amalgamative sects, and without sharp distinction, for centuries. Shinto rituals, myths, and symbols were regarded as the basis of indigenous Japanese culture and therefore taken over and transformed into "State Shinto" – in the form of the Department of Shinto. Shinto practices were reinterpreted as civic duties, and participation in "State Shinto" was required by law regardless of personal religious affiliation or disposition. Shinto priests were subordinated to governmental orders and dissenters were silenced. From the Meiji period to the tragedy that was World War II, the politicized State Shinto – which highlighted Japanese ethnocentrism – was indoctrinated in schools. This resulted in a sort of "cult of the Emperor" that left many misunderstandings regarding the spirituality of Shinto across the world. After the war, State Shinto was officially abolished, and replaced with the constitutional protection of religious freedom and the separation of government funds and religion. In practice, however, aspects of the two remain intertwined. This complicated relationship – viewed by some as intrinsic to Japanese culture – has sparked controversy; for example, the emperor technically remains the supreme priest of many traditional Shinto shrines in Japan.

It is important to note that during the nineteenth and twentieth century new religious movements arose in Japan, inspired by shamanistic leaders. Although these traditions generally accept premises of a Shinto or Buddhist worldview, as well as demonstrating influences from Western culture and Christianity, they regard themselves as independent religions (although they are sometimes referred to as Shinto-derived sects). Many such traditions flourished, and spread with great popularity, during the social crisis and disillusionment of the post-World War II period. These new religious movements, however, remain an important force within the religious diversity of modern Japan.

Women have played an important role as founders of some of the new religions

Although an in-depth discussion of these various traditions surpasses the scope of this chapter, many of these movements are, in general, of a messianic and monotheistic nature, centering on charismatic leadership, revelation, salvation, prophecy, and a centralized form of organization. In general they stem from miraculous revelatory experiences of particular founders (some of whom are regarded as "living *kami*") and tend to speak to the realities of a new age. Interestingly, women have played an important role as founders of some of the new religions – a testament to the traditional role of women as shamans in ancient Japan. Other features emphasized by the new religions include the attainment of spiritual powers, techniques of spiritual purification, healing through the channeling of spiritual energy, and communion with *kami*.

CHAPTER SUMMARY

As a cumulative tradition Shinto represents both continuity and change. On the one hand, it has preserved the basis of ancient Japanese spirituality – with roots in shamanism, *kami* worship, agricultural rites, and concern for purification – while on the other, it has peacefully adapted to, and assimilated, foreign religious beliefs and practices stemming from the Taoist, Confucian, and Mahayana Buddhist traditions. Notably, Shinto has neither a particular founder nor a set of texts viewed as canonical scriptures – although the mythological writings found in the *Kojiki* and *Nihonshoki* are held as sacred traditions linked to Japanese history, identity, and nationalism. At its foundation the Shinto tradition is guided by the life-directing values of sincerity, purity of heart, and gratitude.

Shinto posits a vitalistic, sacred cosmos permeated by a plurality of harmoniously functioning divine *kami* – which are predominantly recognized within nature and in anything awe-inspiring. Shinto's religious approach to nature has, in fact, drawn increasing attention from modern ecological movements which look toward the natural environment as a source of meaning and sacredness. Over and above theology or moralistic doctrine, communion with nature and direct experience of the multifarious *kami* in daily life is central to Shinto spirituality. As the mythologist Joseph Campbell noted, "Shinto, at root, is a religion not of sermons but of awe: which is a sentiment that may or may not produce words, but in either case goes beyond them. Not a 'grasp of the conception of spirit,' but a sense of its ubiquity, is the proper end of Shinto."[46]

The Western or Wailing Wall, Jerusalem

CHAPTER 12

THE JEWISH FAITH

Hear, O Israel! The LORD is our God, the LORD alone. You shall love the LORD your God with all your heart and with all your soul and with all your might. Take to heart these instructions with which I charge you this day. Impress them upon your children. Recite them when you stay at home and when you are away, when you lie down and when you get up. Bind them as a sign on your hand and let them serve as a symbol on your forehead; inscribe them on the doorposts of your house and on your gates.

– Deuteronomy 6:4–9

INTRODUCTION

The Hebrews, whose descendants are the Jewish people, were originally a nomadic Semitic tribe. They coexisted with other Semitic tribes, as well as the Sumerians, in the region of Mesopotamia.[1] As herders who worshiped their own Supreme God, the Israelites were unlike other Mesopotamian peoples, who

> **You shall love your neighbor as yourself**
> *Leviticus 19:18*
> THE GOLDEN RULE

worshiped common gods (such as Ishtar, Marduk, and Baal). The distinctive worship of the early Israelites was influenced by their mentality as wandering desert people: God could be worshiped from any locality, and religious practice was not tied to fixed temples or landmarks. The Hebrews eventually settled in Canaan (Palestine) and adopted an agricultural lifestyle. Their belief in one Supreme God became a point of tension with neighboring tribes who worshiped the Mesopotamian gods. Over time,

Timeline

19th century B.C.E.
Abraham
14th century B.C.E.
Moses
*c.*1021–1000 B.C.E.
Saul, the first king
*c.*1040–970 B.C.E.
David, the second king
965–928 B.C.E.
Solomon
8th–2nd centuries B.C.E.
Hebrew scriptures written
722 B.C.E.
Jews expelled
7–6th centuries B.C.E.
Jeremiah
640–609 B.C.E.
Reign of King Josiah of Judah
586 B.C.E.
Fall of Jerusalem
586–536 B.C.E.
The Exile
164 B.C.E. Maccabean revolt
63 B.C.E.
Jerusalem falls to Pompey
*c.*20 B.C.E.–50 C.E.
Philo of Alexandria
66 C.E. Roman authority in Judea challenged
70 C.E.
Romans plunder Jerusalem
73 C.E.
"Rabbinic tradition" begins
*c.*450 C.E.
Palestinian (or Jerusalem) Talmud completed

the Israelite perspective was shaped by unfavorable contact with, and even subjugation to, powerful kingdoms of the region, including the Egyptians, Canaanites, Philistines, Assyrians, Babylonians, Persians, Greeks, and Romans. Amid hostile conditions, including forced migrations and persecution, the Hebrew people have consistently responded creatively to harsh socio-political challenges, renewed their commitment to spirituality, and preserved their tradition.

The Jewish understanding of God was influenced by the teachings of prophets, or those who speak on behalf of God. Beginning with the patriarch Abraham, the prophets instructed the Israelites in moral learning, especially the importance of justice. The prophets play a major role in the history of the Jewish religion; they spoke with a towering authority that eclipsed even the decrees of the political leaders of their day. In some instances, they were harbingers of doom, warning the Jewish people when they strayed too far from God's love and laws. In other instances, they fortified the faith of the Hebrew people during times of especially harsh suffering or national catastrophe. They were, in fact, conduits through which God is believed to have intervened in the unfoldment of history.

Over the long history of the Jewish faith, many terms have been used to describe the Jewish people and the major components of their religion. The etymological and historical background of these terms was explained by the scholar David Ariel:

*c.*550 C.E.
Babylonian Talmud completed
882–942 C.E.
Sa'adiah ben Joseph, known as Sa'adiah Gaon
1040–1105 C.E.
Rabbi Solomon ben Isaac, known as the Rashi
*c.*1080–1141 C.E.
Yehudah Halevi
1135–1204 C.E.
Moses Maimonides
*c.*1260–1340 C.E.
Bahya ibn Pakuda
*c.*1280 C.E.
The *Zohar* written under likely authorship of Moses De Leon
1522–1572 C.E.
Moses Cordovero
1700–1760 C.E.
Israel ben Eliezer, also known as the Baal Shem Tov
1939–1945 C.E.
The Holocaust
1948 C.E.
The founding of the state of Israel

The terms "Judaism" and "Jew" are first used around the beginning of the first millennium C.E. There is no word in the Bible for what we call Judaism; the religion is variously referred to as the "teachings" (Torah), "commandments" (mitzvot), and "laws" (hukkim or mishpatim). In the Torah, the Jewish people are called Hebrews (ivrim) and Israel (yisrael). Ivrim refers to the migration of Abraham and his clan from the Tigris-Euphrates region to the land of Canaan. The word yisrael literally means "you have striven with beings divine" and refers to the acquired name of the patriarch Jacob, who wrestled with the mysterious figure at Peniel (Genesis 32:29). Both the people and the homeland came to be known by this name, Israel. Following the establishment of the kingdom of Judah during the First Temple period, Judeans were called yehudim, which was soon translated as Jews.[2]

The religion of the Hebrews began when Abraham proclaimed a covenant between God and the Hebrews. The sacred scriptures of the Jewish religion record how "God put Abraham to the test. He said to him, 'Abraham,' and he answered, 'Here I am.'" (Genesis 22:1). The covenant declared by Abraham was confirmed when the prophet Moses read from the book of the covenant and the people of Israel responded: "All that the LORD has spoken we will faithfully do!" (Exodus 24:7). The acceptance of the covenant, a pledge of allegiance to God as the Creator and sole authority, has given the Jewish people a purposeful quest. In turn, God enjoins His chosen people to uphold a life of morality, faith, and sacrifice.

> **History, from the Jewish perspective, is saturated with divine purpose**

History, from the Jewish perspective, is saturated with divine purpose. The Jews drew moral and spiritual lessons from their socio-political circumstances. Some of these circumstances entailed divine intervention and even chastisement. Given how the Jewish people emphasized the religious meaning of history, it is no surprise that the Israelites carefully preserved their history in a series of sacred texts. Jewish texts document the gradual evolution of their relationship with God, and their transformation from a loose grouping of tribes into a cohesive nation whose social structure and identity were based on divinely ordained laws.

GENESIS

Genesis, the first book of the *Tanakh* (or Jewish Bible), describes important tenets of the Jewish worldview (these are also central to the Christian and Islamic faiths). What is labeled as the "Old Testament" by Christians is substantially the same as the Jewish *Tanakh*, though the order of the texts is arranged differently. Some translations of the book of Genesis open with the phrase "In the beginning," an indication that the narrative addresses a prehistory or primordial time. Many scholars agree that parables and stories of a mythic type, like those found in the book of Genesis, should not be read as if they are historical accounts. From this perspective, mythic literature conveys tiered levels of meaning through didactic stories rather than literal facts. The book of Genesis has helped the Jewish people find meaningful answers to fundamental questions of existence for thousands of years. As a creation story, it sheds light on the Israelite religious consciousness (a monotheistic belief in one God, free will, providence, divine intervention, destiny, prophecy, prayer, sacrifice), sociological consciousness (the importance of procreation, parental genealogy, marriage, burial rites, food and health customs), and political consciousness (concern for justice, law, fair trade, currency, kingdoms, property).

God, the all-powerful Creator, plays a central role in the book of Genesis. In Genesis we read, "When God began to create heaven and earth – the earth being unformed and void, with darkness over the surface of the deep and a wind from God sweeping over the water – God said, 'Let there be light'; and there was light" (Genesis 1:1–3). God then separated the light from the darkness, water from water (to create the sky above), and drew forth the land; God was pleased and, according to Genesis, "saw that it was good." From the Jewish perspective, nature is viewed as a creation of God that is wholly good. According to the book of Genesis, God established day and night, which "serve as signs for the set times – the days and the years" (Genesis 1:14). Accordingly, the Jewish worldview entails a linear conception of time (as opposed to a cyclical view), a perspective which blossomed into a rich tradition informed by past achievements and tribulations, the importance of present action, and hope for the future. Genesis (1:27–28) describes how after creating all of the animals on the planet, God then created humankind:

> **Genesis contains religious principles, myths, motifs, and symbols that have informed the religious consciousness of the Jewish faith**

> God said, "Let us make man in our image, after our likeness. They shall rule the fish of the sea, the birds of the sky, the cattle, the whole earth, and all the creeping things that creep on earth." And God created man in His image, in the image of God He created him; male and female He created them. God blessed them and God said to them, "Be fertile and increase, fill the earth and master it; and rule the fish of the sea, the birds of the sky, and all the living things that creep."

Thus, according to Genesis, humankind, both male and female, were created together as equals in the image of God, and have been given dominion over both nature and the animals.

Chapter 2 of Genesis records an alternative story concerning the creation of humankind: in this version, God created Adam, the first human, and placed him in the paradise of the Garden of Eden. In order that Adam, a man, would not be alone, God created the first woman, named Eve, from the rib of Adam. Genesis 2:24 reads, "Hence a man leaves his father and mother and clings to his wife, so that they become one flesh." For Jews, the union of man and woman is thereby a sanctified relationship. Genesis then describes how Adam and Eve are expelled from the Garden of Eden. They are apparently tricked by a serpent into eating the fruit of the forbidden tree in disobedience to God's command. By eating this fruit, they attained knowledge of good and evil. Some students of the Bible emphasize Adam and Eve's disobedience of God as the reason for their expulsion from Eden; others stress their failure to take responsibility for their actions when confronted by God about the incident (Adam blames Eve, and Eve blames the serpent). Adam and Eve, the primordial father and mother of all humanity, are punished by God, expelled from Eden (interpreted by some as a fall from unity into duality), and forced to live mortal lives. According to the scriptures, God decrees that Eve, as punishment, will be ruled by Adam and must suffer the pangs of childbearing; Adam is forced into performing hard labor. Didactically, the story of Adam and Eve presents the human species as one family.

The book of Genesis contains a treasury of religious principles, myths, motifs, and symbols that have informed the religious consciousness of the Jewish, Christian, and Islamic faiths. As a holy text, Genesis is imbued with divine mystery, and each reading of the scripture can shed new light on its spiritual meaning. Genesis also includes important (mythological) stories, such as those concerning Cain and Abel, the Tower of Babel, and the story of Noah and the Great Flood. Significantly, stories concerning a Great Flood were common throughout Mesopotamia; one such story, of particular interest to Bible scholars, was found in a pre-biblical Babylonian text called the *Epic of Gilgamesh*.[3] The book of Genesis also includes the story of Abraham and his sons, the patriarchs of the Jewish people.

ABRAHAM

Abraham lived in the Mesopotamian town of Ur (located in modern Iraq) during the nineteenth century B.C.E. While traveling from Ur to another city named Haran, Abraham was instructed by God to guide his kinsmen to a different region filled with spiritual bounties. This epiphany prompted Abraham to reject ancestor worship and idolatry, the traditional religion of his people, and dedicate his life to serving El Shaddai ("God Almighty"). Genesis (12:1–3) describes Abraham's commission from El Shaddai:

The LORD said to Abraham,
  "Go forth from your native land and from your father's house to the land that I will
     show you.
  I will make of you a great nation,
  And I will bless you;
  I will make your name great,
  And you shall be a blessing.
  I will bless those who bless you
  And curse him that curses you;
  And all the families of the earth
  Shall bless themselves by you."

Energized by his faith in God and determined to spread the message of the new faith, Abraham began preaching a new religion. His complete rejection of familiar beliefs and forms of worship, however, was not welcomed among some influential circles of his people. Only one of Abraham's nephews, Lot, pledged to follow the new faith. Having been spurned by his tribe, Abraham followed God's command and took his wife, Sarah, to live in the "Promised Land," which according to Jewish scripture (Genesis 13:15–16) was a bountiful country: "For I give all the land that you see to you and your offspring forever. I will make your offspring as the dust of the earth, so that if one can count the dust of the earth, then your offspring too can be counted."

Such pronouncements by God puzzled Abraham because he had no offspring; Sarah, his wife, was unable to bear children. Still, Abraham did not waver in his absolute faith in God's promises. A terrible shortage of food caused by famine compelled Abraham and Sarah to move to Egypt. In Egypt, Sarah urged Abraham to marry Hagar, her Egyptian maidservant, so that he could at last have an infant. Abraham agreed, took Hagar as his second wife, and soon Hagar had a son who was named Ishmael ("God hears"). According to Genesis (17:1, 4–8), God concluded a covenant with Abraham when the prophet was ninety-nine years old:

I am El Shaddai [God Almighty]. Walk in My ways and be blameless … this is My covenant with you: You shall be the father of a multitude of nations … for I make you the father of a multitude of nations. I will make you exceedingly fertile, and make nations of you; and kings shall come forth from you. I will maintain My covenant between Me and you, and your offspring to come, as an everlasting covenant throughout the ages, to be God to you and to your offspring to come. I assign the land you sojourn in to you and your offspring to come, all the land of Canaan, as an everlasting holding. I will be their God.

God promised Abraham that his ninety-two-year-old wife, Sarah, would soon have a child. Delighted, Abraham and Sarah named their new baby Isaac ("laughter"). In the story of Genesis, God intermittently assures Abraham that his offspring will continue to receive divinely inspired good fortune. For Jewish believers, God's recurring pledge to Abraham is representative of His covenant with the Jewish people and is a sure guarantee that they will uniquely benefit from the Almighty's grace. Abraham is a figure of critical importance for Jews, Christians, and Muslims alike. While none is formally named after Abraham, all three faiths are, in a significant way, animated by his profound faith in, and obedience to, God's commandments, and they are often referred to together as the "Abrahamic religions."

Each Jewish patriarch and prophet is unique, but Abraham, as the original patriarch of the Jewish people, is imbued with a special status. He was severely tested by God when he was asked to offer his own son, Isaac, as a sacrifice (Genesis 22:1–19). In another story, Abraham confronted God and challenged His plan to destroy the innocent along with the guilty in the cities of Sodom and Gomorrah (Genesis 18:25). These two accounts underscore the profound religious principles that have animated the Jewish worldview. The first incident demonstrates willingness to sacrifice, while the second event underscores a readiness to challenge even divine decrees if they violate one's conscience. In terms of genealogy (which is heavily stressed

> **For Jewish believers, God's recurring pledge to Abraham is representative of His covenant with the Jewish people**

in the Hebrew scriptures), Abraham is of central importance because Jews trace their origins to Abraham's son Isaac, and through Isaac's son Jacob (and Jacob's twelve sons). Jacob, after wrestling with an angelic being (Genesis 32:23–31), was blessed with the name Israel (the Jewish people are often referred to as Israelites). One of Jacob's sons, Joseph, was separated from him at an early age, and later became an interpreter of the pharaoh's dreams in Egypt. In a remarkable turn of events, Jacob (Israel) and his other sons migrated to Egypt and were reunited with Joseph.

MOSES

Moses is a central and transformational figure in the Jewish faith. When he was a baby, the daughter of the pharaoh of Egypt discovered him in a basket floating down the Nile River. Childless, the pharaoh's daughter took the baby as her own, gave him the name Moses, adopted him into the royal family, and raised him as an Egyptian prince. This unusual circumstance came about through a series of events. In the 1300s B.C.E., the pharaoh concluded that the large community of Israelites he ruled over threatened his power. In order to reduce the Israelite population, the pharaoh decreed that all newborn males should be killed by drowning. Desperate to save her baby, the mother of Moses placed him in a basket and hid him among reeds growing along the Nile. The river's current then carried the basket downstream, where the pharaoh's daughter discovered it. Even before God appointed him as a prophet to the Israelites, Moses' character, like that of Abraham, was marked by profound spiritual qualities. According to the Torah, as he matured he tried, whenever possible, to assist the Israelites in their struggle against the cruelty and persecution they faced at the hands of the Egyptians. Moses was a natural leader, possessing a brilliant intellect and driven by deep compassion and a desire for justice. Eventually, he left Egypt and lived as a shepherd in Midian, a region now comprising the Sinai Peninsula, southern Israel, and parts of Jordan. It was in Midian that Moses received God's revelation.

As an adult, Moses' spiritual mission commenced when an angel appeared to him within a burning bush while he was on Mount Sinai (also known as Mount Horeb). From the bush, Moses heard God calling aloud to him, commanding him to liberate the Israelites from their Egyptian oppressors and lead them to safety and peace in the land of Canaan. According to Exodus 3:2–6:

> An angel of the LORD appeared to him in a blazing fire out of a bush. He gazed, and there was a bush all aflame, yet the bush was not consumed. Moses said, "I must turn aside to look at this marvelous sight; why doesn't the bush burn up?" When the LORD saw that he had turned aside to look, God called to him out of the bush: "Moses! Moses!" He answered, "Here I am." And He said, "Do not come closer. Remove your sandals from your feet, for the place on which you stand is holy ground. I am," He said, "the God of your father, the God of Abraham, the God of Isaac, and the God of Jacob." And Moses hid his face, for he was afraid to look at God.

In order to obey the commandments he had received from God, Moses had to return to Egypt and overcome the obstreperous pharaoh, who refused to free his Israelite slaves. According to scripture, it was only after God afflicted the Egyptians with a series of ten plagues that the pharaoh liberated the Israelites, who quickly escaped from Egypt under the leadership of Moses. This great migration of the Israelites from Egypt is known as the Exodus. In the course of their journey to freedom, Moses led the Israelites to Sinai, where he had formerly lived. Upon their arrival there, a covenant was made between God and the Israelites, and the moral code known as the Ten Commandments was revealed. Moses

Moses' spiritual mission commenced when an angel appeared to him within a burning bush while he was on Mount Sinai

conveyed this revelation to the Israelites as part of the covenant. Having received the Commandments, the Israelites continued their journey under the leadership of Moses. The great suffering experienced during the Exodus, however, undermined the self-reliance and confidence of the former slaves, and provoked a brief rebellion against Moses. To punish the Israelites for their insolence, God prolonged their journey to the Promised Land. As the years passed, a series of spiritual and physical trials taught a new generation of Jews to obey the laws and Covenant revealed by God to Moses. Finally, after forty years of wandering in the wilderness, the Jews entered the Promised Land, Canaan. By then, Moses had died.

Through the agency of Moses, the promise given to Abraham by God was fulfilled: the children of Abraham were now a multitude, peacefully inhabiting the Promised Land. The culture and spirituality of the new Jewish civilization uplifted not only the Jews themselves but also, over the ensuing centuries, the moral life of other cultures. In fulfilling the

God-given mission of leading the Israelites to Canaan, Moses not only liberated his people from terrible oppression, he also ushered in a powerful civilization based on a divine revelation.

THE TORAH

Throughout the ages, Jews have been known as a People of the Book because study of their sacred texts constitutes an essential part of Jewish life. The basic scripture of the Jewish faith is the Hebrew Bible, known as *Tanakh*. The word is an abbreviation derived from the first letters of the Hebrew words *Torah* (Law), *Nevi'im* (Prophets), and *Ketuvim* (Writings), the library of texts that collectively form the *Tanakh*. The texts include writings of different literary genres, and should be interpreted accordingly. Some books, for exam-

> **Throughout the ages, Jews have been known as a People of the Book**

ple, are closely tied to socio-political developments and offer a form of interpretive history, while other books are inspired poetry. The authors of the Hebrew scriptures, many of whom are unknown, also utilized parables, proverbs, riddles, fables, allegories, hymns, and other forms of expression to convey meaning (all of which are difficult to capture in translation).

The Hebrew scriptures were written between the eighth and second centuries B.C.E.; scholars believe that much of the material was redacted over time. It is important to understand that Christians and Muslims affirm the revelations from God by the Jewish prophets; in fact, the Jewish religion serves as the parent religion of both the Christian and Islamic faiths. The Christian and Islamic faiths view themselves as a continuation of the prophetic line begun with the creation of Adam and the proclamation of the Jewish prophets. Notably, Christians hold the Jewish Torah (the books of Genesis, Exodus, Leviticus, Numbers, and Deuteronomy) as the first five books of the Christian Bible, also known as the Pentateuch. Jews, however, usually refer to the Torah in reference to the whole of their scriptures; in that way Jews recognize both the Written Torah (which is not only the first five books but also the whole of the *Tanakh*) and the Oral Torah (orally transmitted interpretations of Jewish law which were later written down by rabbis, or trained Jewish teachers). For the Jews, the Torah is "one exceptional manifestation of an eternal process of hearing God's commanding presence."[4]

The centrality of the Torah in the Jewish experience can be discerned by the way it is integrated into everyday life. The book of Deuteronomy, for example, contains a passage (6:4–5) that is known as the Shema. The Shema is periodically recited as an affirmation of the Jewish belief in one God. The words of the verse are first learned by a Jewish child

Top: Synagogue in Trencin, Slovakia
Bottom: Synagogue in London, 1809

and the last uttered by a Jew before passing from this earthly life: "Hear, O Israel! The LORD is our God, the LORD alone. You shall love the LORD your God with all your heart and with all your soul and with all your might."

Deuteronomy (5:7–21) records the Ten Commandments received by Moses in Sinai. The ethical and moral importance of the Ten Commandments transcends the Jewish community. The Ten Commandments, for example, form the basis of Christian ethical teachings and are the basis of much modern law. The Commandments, revealed to Moses by God, are as follows:

> You shall have no other gods besides Me.
> You shall not make for yourself a sculptured image, any likeness of what is in the heavens above, or on the earth below, or in the waters below the earth.
> You shall not swear falsely by the name of the LORD your God.
> Observe the Sabbath day and keep it holy.
> Honor your father and your mother.
> You shall not murder.
> You shall not commit adultery.
> You shall not steal.
> You shall not bear false witness against your neighbor.
> You shall not covet your neighbor's wife.

Jewish law, also called Halakhah, includes prohibitions, practices, rituals, and customs. Halakhah orients and structures the life of a Jewish practitioner. It includes the written law, consisting of 613 individual *mitzvot* ("commandments") which are upheld by traditional Jewish believers. Non-Jews are enjoined to observe seven universal, or Noahide, commandments in order to gain God's favor. The seven Noahide commandments are: "(1) recognition of the rule of law in society; (2) the prohibitions against idolatry, (3) against blaspheming God, (4) against murder, (5) against sexual impropriety, (6) against theft, and (7) against cannibalizing animals, that is, ripping a limb from a living animal for food. Jewish tradition maintains that a Gentile [a non-Jew] who observes the seven Noahide commandments is equal in God's eyes to a Jew who observes the entire Torah."[5] It is clear that the Jewish concept of being "the chosen people" does not refer to a special superiority inherent to an ethnicity or tribe. Rather, the chosen people are held to a higher degree of moral accountability by God. Jewish tradition records that God offered the Torah to other peoples, but only the Israelites accepted its burden of responsibility.

HISTORY

The Biblical Period

The following historical survey of Jewish life in the biblical period is based primarily on the narrative found within the *Tanakh* itself. When Moses passed away, Joshua assumed leadership of the Jews. After their settlement of Canaan, the Jews underwent major social changes. No longer wanderers in a harsh wilderness, the Israelites adopted a sedentary, farming lifestyle. Numerous regional temples were established as centers of Jewish religious life. In a sense, the local temples were substitutes for the Ark of the Covenant, the conveyance that housed the stones inscribed with the terms of the covenant. The Jews brought the Ark with them during their forty-year journey to the Promised Land. With the settlement of the Promised Land and the establishment of temples of worship, an order of priests emerged. Among other duties, priests were assigned custodial duties over holy sanctuaries. In addition, priests and other learned figures began writing a Hebrew canon, thus preserving Jewish literature for the ages.

When the Israelites arrived in Canaan, they retained their ancient internal division of twelve separate tribes. Both the Bible and non-biblical historical evidence suggest that from 1200 to 1000 B.C.E. the Jewish people developed new institutions that reflected their growing political unity, a unity that supplemented and reinforced the traditional religious and social unity of the Israelites. Prominent figures known as "judges," for example, commanded Israelite troops when they took the field against foreign armies. Over the course of time, the Jews founded a monarchy, with its capital in Jerusalem, with Saul (*c.*1021–1000 B.C.E.) as the first king of Israel. However, it was the second king of Israel, David (*c.*1040–970 B.C.E.), who has been cited as the ultimate exemplar of correct governmental rule combined with total fidelity to the laws of God. David and his son and successor, the wise Solomon, oversaw a golden age of Israelite culture. King Solomon is primarily known and remembered for his wisdom (writings attributed to him appear in the *Ketuvim* section of the *Tanakh*) and for having built the First Temple in Jerusalem. The prosperity of the David–Solomon era is captured in the chapters of the Bible, such as the Psalms, that preserve their actions and even, according to some interpretations, their very words. But the unity achieved by the Israelites in the time of King David and King Solomon did not endure for long.

Following the death of Solomon, political disputes split the Israelites into a northern kingdom with ten tribes called Israel and a southern kingdom with two tribes known as Judah. This situation arose because the northern tribes were angry over tax burdens and other grievances and petitioned the new king, Solomon's son Rehoboam, for relief. Rehoboam haughtily refused to make any concessions, and so the dissident tribes broke away from his rule and formed their own kingdom.

In reaction to political chaos and a notable decline in religious belief, a series of teachers, later known as great prophets, called upon the Israelites to forsake their corrupt ways and return to the pious life ordained by God. The activities and messages of the prophets who appeared in the northern kingdom of Israel were mirrored by prophets who proclaimed their teachings in the southern realm of Judah. The southern prophets included Isaiah, Jeremiah, and second Isaiah. Like Hosea, the prophets of the south cautioned that to ignore the sacred covenant with God was to invite internal degeneracy and external invasion. Then, in 722 B.C.E., the mighty and fearsome Assyrian army overran and destroyed the northern kingdom of Israel. To consolidate control over the newly captured land, the Assyrians expelled the Jews of the northern kingdom; the ten tribes of the north became known as the "Ten Lost Tribes of Israel." By the time of the prophet Jeremiah (seventh and sixth centuries B.C.E.), the kingdom of Judah was battered by threats that eventually led to its total collapse.

Jeremiah's teachings emphasized the importance of morality in the life of the individual. During the long rule of King Josiah of Judah (640–609 B.C.E.), concepts and teachings of the prophets came to be accepted by a broad range of Jewish scholars and religious leaders. In effect, a new consensus regarding the Jewish religion emerged. Articles of faith included the following: pagan traditions and practices should not be incorporated into the Jewish religion; personal, national, and spiritual well-being were founded on fidelity to the sacred covenant with God; the Israelites were a people chosen by God to receive His special graces. The auguries and edifications of the prophets, despite the influence they attained in later generations, did not save the Israelites from ruin. In 586 B.C.E., Babylonian invaders captured territories of the southern kingdom of Judah. In the denouement of the conquest, the capital, Jerusalem, was sacked. Along with the city, Jerusalem's Temple, the most holy Jewish house of worship, was demolished. Afterwards, the population of Judah was forcibly relocated to the enemy's heartland, Mesopotamia. During this period of "Babylonian captivity," a new religious spirit and commitment to God took hold among the Israelites. As in the past, prophets and messengers from God appeared among the people, urging them to place their hopes for redemption in the limitless powers of God.

According to the book of Isaiah, the suffering visited upon the Israelites was an instrument employed by God to purge them of their sins. In this way, God communicated to His people that they must remain faithful, strictly obey the laws, and never take His favor for granted. Such a theological explication of their plight allowed Jewish believers to maintain their identity in captivity, bound them to their religious traditions, and made them eager to revive both their faith and their nation so as to make both worthy of God's special dispensation. Having been spiritually readied for the reestablishment of their nation by Ezekiel's prophecy, Jewish exiles in Babylonia experienced a remarkable turn of fortune that, for them, confirmed the reality of God's power, love, righteousness, and forgiveness.

In 539 B.C.E., the ruler of the Persian Empire, Cyrus the Great, defeated the Babylonian army in battle. Throughout his growing empire Cyrus permitted religious diversity. In line with this policy, he issued a decree allowing the Jews in Babylonian captivity to return to their homeland. Thus, the Israelites were granted a measure of self-rule in what became the Persian province of Yehud (Judah). Later, Cyrus again affirmed his policy of religious toleration by allowing the Jews to rebuild their Temple at Jerusalem. For the Jews who had returned from exile, these developments were nothing less than miraculous, and truly confirmed the greatness of God.

The Post-Exilic Period

Rebuilding the Jerusalem Temple was of paramount importance to the Jews when they returned from exile. At first, they constructed an altar where the old Temple had stood. During his brief ministry, the prophet Haggai continually urged the people to maximize their efforts to construct a new Temple. Along with their main Temple in Jerusalem, the revitalized Jewish community also constructed a number of smaller synagogues, or houses of worship. The rebirth of the Jewish faith was manifested not only in the building program, but also in an expansion of the priestly orders, the flourishing of religious scholarship, and a general flowering of Jewish literature.

Whenever practicable, the Persian Empire under Cyrus and his successors maintained a policy of ruling conquered provinces indirectly, through locally appointed governors. In conformity with this technique of imperial rule, under the emperor Darius I (522–486 B.C.E.) the governor of the Persian province of Yehud (Judah) was the Israelite Zerubbabel, a descendant of King David. Protecting the Jewish religion and culture was essential to preserving Jewish identity because a restoration of a truly independent Israelite polity proved impossible. Despite the ardent wishes of Jewish patriots, who sought to reestablish an independent Jewish kingdom under the rule of a descendant of King David, Jewish territories fell under the sway of successive waves of foreign conquerors. After the waning of Persian power came Greek colonizers. When Alexander of Macedonia (more commonly known as Alexander the Great) overthrew the Persian Empire and established control over its territories (including Jewish lands in *c*.331 B.C.E.), the spread of Greek culture, or Hellenism, occurred. Thus, for an extended period of time (*c*.331–142 B.C.E.) the Israelites were directly exposed to the great influence of Greek thought and culture. After the political dominance of the Greeks, the fearsome Romans came into power and annexed Jewish lands, lording over them as a province of their empire.

Jewish philosophical thought, creative arts, judicature, theology, and religious practices were profoundly shaped by Hellenism. Scholars, for example, studied sacred Hebrew texts by employing techniques developed by Greek thinkers. One of the most respected Jewish philosophers was Philo of Alexandria (*c.*20 B.C.E.–50 C.E.), who also influenced later Christian and Islamic thinkers. Philo, whose works were preserved by the Christian Church in their original Greek, was a major force in Western philos-ophy until the seventeenth century. Influenced particularly by Stoics and Platonists, Philo integrated Greek philosophy and Jewish spirituality. He saw God as transcendent and beyond all human notions, and deemed many aspects of Jewish scripture as allegorical and metaphorical. Notwithstanding an emergent philosophical creativity, over-all Hellenistic influences on the Israelites were far from benign. According to the scripture known as 1 Maccabees, in

Jewish philosophical thought, creative arts, judicature, theology, and religious practices were profoundly shaped by Hellenism

167 B.C.E. the Seleucid ruler Antiochus Epiphanes passed a series of laws compelling Jews to adopt Greek religious practices. In a brazen act of cultural imperialism, even the most sacred house of worship, the Temple of Jerusalem, was forced to adhere to foreign religious rituals.

The Rabbinic Tradition

Not surprisingly, the period of Hellenistic ascendancy in Jewish history led to a reaction against foreign ideas, power, and culture. Violent opposition to Hellenistic religious and political authority occurred during the Maccabean revolt against Seleucid rule in the sec-ond century B.C.E. The rebellion began under the leadership of Judas, called "Maccabeus" (meaning "hammer-like"), around 164 B.C.E. Judas inflicted a series of military defeats on the Seleucids. He temporarily liberated the Temple of Jerusalem, and expelled its foreign custodians. Judas was later killed in battle, and his successors, Jonathan and after him Simon, continued the Maccabean rebellion by skillful military and diplomatic maneuvers. Around 142 B.C.E., Simon led the Maccabees to triumph when he forced the Seleucids to withdraw from Jerusalem and compelled them to recognize Judah's independence. At the same time as the Maccabees were fighting the Seleucid armies, a parallel intellectual revolt against Hellenistic thought was arising among conservative Jewish scholars, who founded a new social movement. The leaders of this new movement, the Pharisees (spiritual lead-ers) and their successors, the rabbis (teachers), upheld fundamental Jewish beliefs and pro-moted the conscientious observance of Jewish law in daily life as an essential spiritual duty. Other Jewish scholars, known as lay scribes or lawyers, also advocated a return to strict observance of the laws. These scholars venerated Jewish traditions enshrined in the Torah as the only means of preserving the favor of God and the covenant with Him. The strengthening of the spiritual leadership of the Jewish community was important because the political independence attained by Judah in 142 B.C.E. endured for less than a century. Although the Jewish people had, during the struggle against the Seleucids, looked favorably upon the Romans as distant but powerful allies of the Maccabees, in 63 B.C.E. Jerusalem fell to Roman legions under the command of Pompey the Great. Jewish territories became part of the Roman province of Syria.

Important elements of Jewish society never accepted Roman rule, and Judea was known as a hotbed of anti–Roman sedition. Messianic hopes flourished among Jews during this period, and it was within this combustible atmosphere that the itinerant preacher called Jesus of Nazareth, proclaimed by some as the promised Messiah, was tried and executed by authority of the Roman governor, Pontius Pilate. During this time period others figures were declared messiahs, including Judas the Galilean and Simeon Bar Kokhba. Bar Kokhba led a revolt against the Romans in 135 C.E. and was accepted as the Messiah by Rabbi Akiva, a renowned Jewish sage. In general, messianic movements were sustained by both political and religious aspirations, including the restoration of an autonomous Jewish kingdom and the establishment of God's kingdom on Earth. Some Jewish sects thought that the Messiah would be a priest, others a king, and still others a prophet and herald of the last days. According to the scholar David Ariel:

> Real expectation of the coming of the Messiah has been fundamental to postbiblical Judaism. The idea is too deeply rooted and too powerful not to erupt occasionally into messianic movements. There has also been a deep bias against the belief that the Messiah has arrived. Jewish messianism is best understood as an unrealizable promise, a dream unfulfilled. It is ironic that Judaism devotes so much attention to the conditions and circumstances of messianism, but is loath to declare the arrival of a Messiah. Thus, Jewish messianism is both the theory of messianism and the history of false messiahs and messianic disappointments.[6]

Throughout the long history of the Jewish religion, many figures have proclaimed themselves to be the Messiah, including Moses of Crete (fifth century C.E.), Serenus of Syria (eighth century C.E.), Abu Isa of Ispahan (eighth century C.E.), David Alroy of Baghdad (twelfth century C.E.), Abulafia of Messina (thirteenth century C.E.), Asher Lemmlein of Istria (fifteenth century C.E.), David Reubeni (sixteenth century C.E.), and Solomon Molcho (sixteenth century C.E.).[7] Another widely known case is that of Sabbatai Zevi, whose messianic claim swept through territories controlled by the Ottoman Empire in the seventeenth century.

In the years after the execution of Jesus, Roman authority in Judea was effectively challenged by the Zealots, a fanatical band of Jewish rebels who in 66 C.E. seized the formidable mountaintop fortress of Masada and held it as their base of operations (the Zealots occupied Masada until 73 C.E., but committed mass suicide when the besieging Romans finally overran the fortress). The Zealot occupation of Masada was part of a general uprising that compelled the Romans, who were weakened by an internal civil war, to evacuate Jerusalem. In 70 C.E., however, the Roman army returned with a vengeance when legions under the command of Titus, son of the emperor Vespasian, recaptured Jerusalem after a bloody siege. Determined to check further rebellion, Titus allowed his troops to plunder Jerusalem, ordered the destruction of the Temple, and decreed the forcible expulsion of the Jews from Judea. The fall of Jerusalem signaled a dramatic turning point in Jewish history that would determine the evolution of the community for almost two millennia. The Jews were cast into a vast Diaspora, or a mass of scattered communities. In the Diaspora, as during the previous Babylonian captivity, Jewish spiritual leaders played a central role in preserving and upholding Jewish identity.

The destruction of the Temple and the elimination of the regular priestly functions that had been conducted there left a vacuum in the religious life of the Israelites. This vacuum was soon filled by worship services held in local synagogues and conducted by rabbis. The pattern of Jewish religious life based on the synagogue, therefore, became known as the "rabbinic tradition." To furnish guidance to believers, rabbis developed a system of textual exposition focused on the Torah. The interpretations and analyses of rabbis, whose insight and wisdom were regarded as superlative, were recognized as having value for future generations. Therefore, the work of rabbis was carefully recorded and collected in a large text known as the Talmud, meaning "the learning." There are two categories of texts in the Talmud: the first, the Mishnah, is a series of analyses of the Jewish laws that were preserved in oral traditions; the second, the Gemara, is a collection of commentaries on the Mishnah. There are two versions of the Talmud. The first version is the Palestinian (or Jerusalem) Talmud, completed around 450 C.E. The second version of the Talmud, the Babylonian Talmud, was completed around 550 C.E. The Babylonian Talmud is significantly larger, and is usually accepted as the more authoritative version. The historical development of the Mishnah is illustrative of the religious life of the Israelites before and after the Roman conquest. Its origin dates to about the end of the first century B.C.E. At that time, legal disputes that could not be resolved by reference to verses or principles of the Torah were systematically referred to experts on Jewish law. Decisions by these legal specialists were gradually recorded and collected by the Pharisees. Following the Roman conquest of 70 C.E. and the resulting collapse of Jewish religious, political, and social structures, the Mishnah gained importance as a source of guidance. Rabbis throughout the Diaspora referred to the Mishnah in their efforts to provide spiritual guidance to their local communities.

By 200 C.E., rabbis had systematically expanded the Mishnah, producing a detailed, comprehensive written text. The written version consisted of six broad sections dealing

> **The pattern of Jewish religious life based on the synagogue became known as the "rabbinic tradition"**

with all major facets of life as conceived in the rabbinic tradition, including religious rituals; personal and civil laws; personal rights in all classes of society; the religious calendar; economic and agricultural issues; and the Sabbath. The principles, laws, and ethical guidelines of the Talmud deal with virtually every aspect of Jewish life. Thus, the Talmud has served as the foundation upon which a cohesive Jewish society has been preserved since the beginning of the Diaspora. The Talmud embodies a worldview that is generally positive. It describes a universe full of goodness and suffused with the bounties of God freely available to all those who follow God's teachings. The Talmud prescribes, in detail, the proper actions to take in any situation so as to avoid harm and promote goodness.

The Middle Ages

During the medieval period (fifth to fifteenth centuries), the Jewish community adopted and adapted theological concepts and scholarly techniques first developed by Greek and Islamic thinkers. Gradually, the Jews created a new philosophy of life and religion. One of the great philosophers of this period was Sa'adiah ben Joseph (882–942), known as Sa'adiah Gaon ("Gaon" is an honorific title given to leaders of Jewish academies). Sa'adiah was born in Egypt and eventually settled in Iraq. As a proponent of both rationality and faith, he produced many classic works including *The Book of Doctrines and Beliefs*. Another important figure was Rabbi Solomon ben Isaac, known as the Rashi (1040–1105). Rashi is credited as one of the greatest commentators on the Torah and Talmud. His life is associated with miraculous stories and his synagogue, in western Germany, remains a place of pilgrimage for Jews.

The preeminent Jewish sage of the Middle Ages was Moses Maimonides (1135–1204). Maimonides was born in the city of Cordoba in Spain, but during his youth his family was forced to flee that country to escape a wave of anti-Semitic persecutions carried out by fanatical Muslims known as Almohads (a dynasty based in Morocco). Maimonides eventually settled in Cairo, where he became a famous Talmudic scholar and renowned medical doctor. In an impressive feat of synthesis achieved through systematic analysis, he distilled the essence of the Jewish religion into thirteen simple, yet profound, principles. While theologians have since debated the truth, accuracy, and nature of his codification, Maimonides' conception was nevertheless influential and, eventually, most Jews accepted his ideas as authoritative. His thirteen principles were:

1. The existence of God, the Creator;
2. The absolute unity of God;
3. God's incorporeality;
4. The eternality of God;

5. The obligation to worship God alone;
6. The truth of the teachings of the prophets;
7. The superiority of the prophecy of Moses;
8. The Torah is God's revelation to Moses;
9. The immutability of the Torah;
10. God's omniscience;
11. Reward and punishment according to one's deeds;
12. The coming of the Messiah;
13. The resurrection of the dead.

Maimonides' most influential and well-known philosophical work was *The Guide of the Perplexed*, originally composed in Arabic under the title *Dalalat al-Ha'irin*. In this philosophical masterpiece, Maimonides explained the meaning of various biblical terms (distinguishing between literal and spiritual meanings), offered proofs of the existence of God, argued that the world was created by God (opposing the doctrine of the eternality of the world), and expounded on miracles, prophecy, free will, and Jewish law. Maimonides was influenced by the philosophy of Aristotle, and the works of Muslim commentators on Aristotle. A central aspect of Maimonides' contribution to Jewish philosophy, and to Western philosophy in general, was his synthesis of Aristotelian rationality and Jewish religious ideals. Maimonides' great legal code, the *Mishneh Torah*, is a codification of the Oral Torah and is organized in a clear and decisive manner; the work is accepted by all Jews as authoritative.

Another Jewish figure of Spanish origin, Bahya ibn Pakuda (*c.*1260–1340), composed an influential treatise entitled *Duties of the Heart*. In this work, Bahya argued that daily rituals, observances, and actions had no intrinsic spiritual worth. Rather, he believed that deeds were imbued with spiritual value only if they were performed in a spirit of true devotion and love for God. He strongly advocated detachment from worldly desires; an ascetic way of life; conscientious examination of thoughts, motives, and deeds; solitary contemplation; and communion with God. Although *Duties of the Heart* presented a great challenge to its readers, the book became popular in the rapidly changing world of the European Renaissance. Bahya, like Maimonides, emphasized the believer's personal relationship with God as the true focus of the religious life.

A third prominent personality of the medieval period was Yehudah Halevi (1080–1141). Halevi, like Maimonides and Bahya, was of Spanish origin, and he is widely regarded as one of the greatest Hebrew poets. He saw the suffering that the Israelites experienced throughout history as a mysterious part of God's love. Through this mystery of love, the seeming contradiction between the status of the Israelites as a chosen people and their centuries-long persecution is reconciled. Halevi's poetry was an expression of an ancient tradition of Jewish mysticism that, like other streams of the Jewish tradition, evolved through many stages.

It should be noted that Jewish migrations, voluntary and compulsory, have led to regional distinctiveness in Jewish spirituality. Ashkenazi (German or North European Jews) was a term which referred to those Israelites who lived near the Rhine River in Germany. Eventually, the Ashkenazi Jews comprised the overwhelming majority of Jewish practitioners worldwide. The Ashkenazi included the Jews of countries stretching from France to Russia. Their descendants constitute the majority of Jews living in Israel and the United States. The Sephardi (Spanish or South European, North African, and Middle Eastern) Jews were originally the Jews of Spain who were later dispersed by the expulsion of 1492. The Ashkenazi and Sephardi Jews developed distinctive practices and cultural patterns which informed their way of life. The Yiddish language, for example, was prevalent among Ashkenazi Jews, while the Ladino and Spanish languages were used by many Sephardi Jews. Although some tensions have existed between Ashkenazis and Sephardis, solidarity movements have gained influence in modern times. The internal diversity of the Jewish religion continues to enrich the tapestry of modern Jewish culture.

> **The internal diversity of the Jewish religion continues to enrich the tapestry of modern Jewish culture**

The Early Modern Period

The Hasidic movement, which was dedicated to the reform and revitalization of the Jewish community, arose within the context of the persecution and rejection experienced by Jews throughout the Diaspora. Unlike the decentralized rabbinic tradition that was based on the community synagogue, the Hasidim ("pious ones") were drawn to the leadership of an individual, the *zaddik*, a man of perfect righteousness. Hasidim, influenced by the Jewish mysticism of Kabbalah (discussed below), believed that such a blessed figure had the ability to achieve a unique spiritual union with God, and could act as an intermediary through whom God's benedictions were transmitted. Hasidim first emerged in Eastern Europe under the leadership of the charismatic mystic Israel ben Eliezer (1700–1760), who became known as the Baal Shem Tov. Possessing miraculous powers (according to his followers), and experiencing states of transcendence and religious ecstasy, he attracted a group of disciples who joined him in living a life of devotion, meditation, and prayer.

Baal shem in Hebrew means "master of the Name," and "*tov*" means "good." The Baal Shem Tov, often referred to as Besht, was born in Ukraine and is regarded as the founder of the Hasidic tradition. Many of his interpretations, recorded by his disciples, were not accepted by traditionalists. Over time, however, as the Hasidic movement spread

A Cohen performs the Priestly Blessing ceremony (Birkat Kohanim) during Passover at the Western Wall, Jerusalem

throughout Eastern Europe, the Besht was honored and revered as a true sage. In particular, Hasidic practice focuses on transformation and immediate experience of the divine. According to tradition, the Besht concluded, "We say, 'God of Abraham, God of Isaac and God of Jacob'; we do not say 'God of Abraham, Isaac and Jacob,' so that you may be told: Isaac and Jacob did not rely on Abraham's tradition, but they themselves searched for the Divine."[8] The Hasidic way was one of purity, and the movement contributed many figures that manifested this ideal to a superlative degree. Hasidim emanated a fervent love for God and humanity and cultivated higher states of consciousness in the hope of experiencing the immediacy of the divine presence within all creation. Through prayer and contemplation, the Hasidic movement stimulated a renewal of deep piety. Indeed, Hasidic ideas on devotion were widely adopted by many believers throughout the Jewish community. Traditional rabbis, however, rejected the emphasis that Hasidim placed on blessed figures who acted as conduits between God and the people. This conception of humanity's relationship with God, many rabbis warned, made the community dependent on one mystical leader who constituted the sole authority by virtue of his intimate relationship with God.

Hasidic movements represent the esoteric dimension of the Jewish faith. They have developed techniques of advanced spiritual development and have served as conduits through which the essence of the Jewish religion has been conveyed to the global religious community. Notably, the Hasidic perspective influenced two of the most important and well-known modern Jewish thinkers, Martin Buber (1878–1965) and Abraham Joshua Heschel (1907–1972). Furthermore, Hasidic communities have produced many unique and charismatic spiritual leaders, including Rabbi Nachman of Bretzlov (1772–1810), a great-grandson of the Baal Shem Tov; Rabbi Shneur Zalman of Liadi (1745–1813), the founder of Habad Hasidism, who authored the systematic law of the Habad known as the *Tanya*; and Rabbi Menachem Mendel Schneerson (1902–1994), the highly regarded and socially active Rebbe (a Hasidic honorific title meaning "teacher" in Yiddish) of the Habad–Lubavitch movement.

The Jewish Faith in the Modern World

The rising tempo of scientific and intellectual investigations that occurred in the 1600s led to a great transformation of European life in the following century, a period historians call the Enlightenment or the Age of Reason. Within the freer atmosphere of the Enlightenment, the orthodox Jewish tradition underwent a revitalization. The new liberties allowed a strengthening and confirmation of the values, ideals, and historical identity that had been kept in the shadows. A contemporary but contrary development was the rise of the Reform movement, a new concept of Jewish life that sought to reconcile modernity and tradition. The Reform movement sought a balance between progressive change and continuity, between integration and equality with the Gentiles and preservation of a distinct Jewish consciousness. The Reform movement created a new worship ceremony based on the church services of Germany. Reform Jews abandoned the goal of creating a national homeland in Zion (the Promised Land) and rejected laws against associating with Gentiles. In addition to the emergence of the Reform and Orthodox traditions, the Conservative movement (sometimes referred to as Masorti, "traditional") has maintained Jewish tradition while adapting the law to modern demands. The Conservative perspective has become a popular and meaningful way for contemporary Jews to embrace their religion in the modern age, especially in countries such as the United States. The Reconstructionist movement, which is based on the inclusive viewpoint of Mordecai Kaplan (1881–1903), envisions the Jewish faith as an evolving community in motion. Reconstructionists emphasize a progressive or evolutionary point of view, an approach that distinguishes them from the more traditional aspects of Orthodox practice.

The Orthodox and Reform branches of the Jewish faith, in the early twentieth century, were somewhat overshadowed by the Zionist movement. The hope of returning to the Promised Land, Zion, has inspired Jews ever since the beginning of the Diaspora following the second destruction of the Jerusalem Temple by the Romans in 70 C.E. The Zionist dream began to take shape as a reality when the Jewish Hungarian journalist Theodore Herzl (1860–1904), through his writings calling for the creation of a Jewish state in Palestine, encouraged Jewish people to work towards that goal. Herzl's ideas received widespread consideration among influential Jews because, in his day, strong currents of anti-Semitism were manifested in most European countries. According to Herzl, the return of the Jewish people to their ancient homeland was not merely a political or social goal, it was in fulfillment of the messianic tradition.

Herzl's activities led to the first Zionist World Congress, which convened in Basle, Switzerland, in 1897. A decade later, amidst the diplomatic maneuvering and deal-making of World War I, a momentous development occurred when British foreign secretary Lord Balfour publicly declared Britain's support for the establishment of a Jewish homeland in Palestine. At the time, Palestine was under the control of the Ottoman Empire, a World War I ally of imperial Germany, Britain's antagonist. For the British, the Balfour Declaration was an expedient measure designed to undermine their enemy's strategic position. Because of the Declaration, however, the Zionist movement received the official recognition and sanction of Britain, the world's preeminent Great Power.

After World War II, when the scale and scope of the Holocaust – the Nazi genocide perpetrated against Jews and other groups – became known, people were horrified and sympathetic to its victims. Postwar statements by Zionist activists, some of whom were survivors of Nazi-run extermination camps, claimed that the Jews had a moral right to a national homeland in Palestine. This view gained adherents among the international community, especially in Western Europe and North America. It was within this context that the state of Israel was officially proclaimed in 1948. Thus, the extermination of Jews by the Nazis and the establishment of the modern state of Israel are the two most significant events in twentieth-century Jewish history.

THE COVENANT

For the Jewish people, the idea of a covenant with God is a hallowed tenet and a fundamental pillar of their religion. In certain aspects, God's covenant with the Israelites shares the attributes of a standard legal contract such as a mutual commitment to fulfill responsibilities. However, unlike a legal contract, the covenant was believed to have been divinely ordained, and its provisions were not negotiated and revised through a process of bargaining; rather, it was granted by the sole initiative of God. According to Jewish scripture, covenants between God and the Israelites were concluded at various junctures in Jewish history.

The first covenant is described in the book of Genesis. God promised Noah that he and his family would survive the Great Flood and that no similar cataclysm will ever again come to pass. In a second covenant, God pledged to Abraham that his progeny would dwell in the Promised Land and there build a formidable dominion. God communicated a third covenant – designating the Israelites as His chosen people – to Moses when the prophet was atop Mount Sinai. Shortly thereafter, God revealed through Moses the laws known as the Ten Commandments (the book of Deuteronomy characterizes the Commandments as an essential component of the covenant between the Israelites and God). The book of 1 Chronicles depicts the conclusion of a fourth covenant. On this occasion, God proclaimed that King David's successors would forever be drawn from his line. By recalling that David began life as a humble shepherd, God prompted the King, and by implication all of Israel, to remember that greatness depends upon His power and blessing.

> **For the Jewish people, the idea of a covenant with God is a fundamental pillar of their religion**

THE ONE GOD

Another pillar of the Jewish faith is the belief that there is only one God, the Creator. The reality of God's authority, power, and will is, according to the Jewish perspective, witnessed in God's acts which are designed to protect His chosen people. God alone sent the prophets Abraham and Moses; God alone saved the Israelites from slavery in Egypt; and God alone allowed them to reach the Promised Land and to build a flourishing civilization based on His divine commandments. For Jewish people of faith, these are not mere accidents of history, but measures of divine will that demonstrate not only the existence of God, but also His continuous presence among, and guidance of, the Jewish people. The language of the Talmud often depicts God in terms that personify the Divine: God is the father to His children; He contemplates the scriptures; He dons a prayer cloth; He ministers to the sick and lays to rest

> **The reality of God's authority, power, and will is witnessed in acts which are designed to protect His chosen people**

those who have passed away. In particular, the metaphor of God as father consistently appears in Jewish texts. Yet the Jewish belief system clearly does not see God as a being of this Earth; rather, God is conceived of as the supreme one whose nature and power are beyond the limited understanding of mortals. It is precisely this restricted capacity for comprehension that necessitates the representation of God by means of metaphors and allegories.

JEWISH MYSTICISM

One early expression of Jewish mysticism, referred to as "merkabah mysticism," focused upon contemplation of Ezekiel's vision of God's chariot (*merkabah*). This mystical discipline was practiced by the sage Johanan ben Zakkai at least as early as the first century C.E., and may have also been practiced by Saul (who became St. Paul of the Christian tradition). Toward the other end of the historical spectrum, elements of Jewish mysticism are also found in the modern Hasidic movement (described above). But the most influential of all the Jewish mystical movements is called Kabbalah (also written as Cabala, Cabbala, or Cabbalah). The Kabbalah first emerged in France, and attained great influence in thirteenth-century Spain. At that time, the movement was dedicated to a revival

> **The most influential of all the Jewish mystical movements is called Kabbalah**

of the teachings attributed to Moses and the sages of earlier times. For practitioners of Kabbalah, called kabbalists or *mekubbalim*, all letters, numbers, and words contained in Jewish scripture encompass hidden meanings that can be revealed by means of theosophical deciphering techniques. Kabbalists believe that such mystical methods of explicating scripture reveal the essential qualities of God and insights into the unity of all existence. For this reason, the Kabbalah is also referred to as "the Hidden Wisdom." According to the scholar Daniel Matt, "The Hebrew word *kabbalah* means 'receiving' or 'that which has been received.' On the one hand, Kabbalah refers to tradition, ancient wisdom received and treasured from the past. On the other hand, if one is truly receptive, wisdom appears spontaneously, unprecedented, taking you by surprise."[9] Jewish mysticism, however, did not begin with Kabbalah; the prophets were mystical in that they embodied the archetype to which the mystics aspired. But a prophet, as one who speaks on God's behalf, is more than a mystic.

The primary kabbalistic text is the *Zohar* (meaning "Book of Splendor"), which was probably written by the Spanish mystic Moses de Leon around 1280 C.E. The Holy *Zohar* is an analysis of the Torah written in Aramaic. It offers an interpretation of the ethereal and material worlds and the relationship between God and humankind. The author of the *Zohar* refers to God as En (Ein) Sof (meaning "That Which is Without Limit" or "the Infinite"), and describes Him as a transcendent being and wellspring of the *sefirot*, or ten supreme attributes. The *sefirot* include aspects such as justice, understanding, wisdom, kindness, and intelligence. While the qualities associated with the *sefirot* are manifested in the physical plane of existence, their source, the En Sof, is inscrutable to mortal faculties. The author of the *Zohar* developed a complex theology in which the spiritual world of the En Sof and the material world of human beings mysteriously interact and communicate via mediatory planes of existence.

For its practitioners, the Kabbalah offers a pathway whereby individuals can spiritually journey to the very presence of the Divine. Furthermore, this contact with the Divine can allow the *shekhinah* ("presence of God") to permeate the material world and vanquish evil. One of the most important kabbalistic perspectives, and one that has had lasting influence on modern Jewish spirituality, was developed by Isaac ben Solomon Luria (1534–1572), a student of the prolific Kabbalist Moses Cordovero (1522–1572). The esoteric perspective developed by Luria posited that En Sof, the Infinite Godhead, "withdrew Itself from Itself" in an act of cosmic contraction. By this mysterious action, a cosmic void was created into which divine light emanated (the definitive act of creation). But the vessels through which the light of En Sof emanated ruptured (the so-called "breaking of the vessels"), which marked the origin of evil. Some of these sparks of divine light, unable to return to the Infinite Source from which they emanated, became submerged in materiality. One scholar, expounding on Luria's philosophy, has noted:

> The human task is to liberate, or raise, these sparks, to restore them to divinity. This process of tiqqun (repair or mending) is accomplished through living a life of holiness. All human actions either promote or impede tiqqun, thus hastening or delaying the arrival of the Messiah. In a sense, the Messiah is fashioned by our ethical and spiritual activity. Luria's teaching resonates with one of Franz Kafka's paradoxical sayings: "The Messiah will come only when he is no longer necessary; he will come only on the day after his arrival."[10]

According to Luria, humanity has the crucial, messianic responsibility of repairing or mending (*tikkun*) the world to its original unity. From this perspective, cosmic restoration is the ultimate aim of all human action (as well as the inner meaning of history). The ideal of *tikkun* has been absorbed into modern Jewish spirituality; Jewish believers can play a role in mending the world through many different channels, including social, environmental, and political initiatives.

THE SYNAGOGUE

By the time of the second destruction of the Jerusalem Temple in 70 C.E., houses of worship existed in many localities throughout Jewish lands. Such a house of worship was called a synagogue, meaning "gathering." According to Jewish traditions, as few as ten male adults could come together and constitute their own synagogue, also known as *minyan*. Women attended synagogues as onlookers, not as active participants in the services. Although they could hear and witness synagogue services, women were physically separated from the men by barriers. In modern times, the tradition of segregating the sexes within synagogues is preserved in Orthodox congregations; typically, women and children are seated in an upstairs area from which they can view the services taking place below. In ancient times, devotees attending a synagogue were expected to wash their feet prior to entering, usually at a fountain that was designated for this purpose. Once inside, worshipers remained barefooted and, because there were few places to sit, remained standing during the devotions. The synagogues were more than places where devotional services were performed periodically. Synagogues were, and are, important temples of study and learning. In synagogues the young are taught the tenets and practices of their faith, and the learned gather to study scripture, exchange interpretations, and conduct debate. Since the time when the Jews were cast into the Diaspora, the preservation of the Jewish faith has depended upon written texts. For this reason, synagogues always promoted literacy. In the modern world, many Jews rely on synagogues to provide their children with Hebrew language lessons and instruction in sacred texts. Historically and today, the synagogues are central to Jewish religious life and cultural identity.

> **Historically and today, the synagogues are central to Jewish religious life and cultural identity**

THE HOME

In addition to the synagogue, another institution that plays an important role in the preservation of Jewish culture and traditions is the home. In the Orthodox tradition, daily prayer for men involves a ritual laying of the *tefillin*, a pair of small black boxes made of leather, which are fastened to the body by leather thongs. Each contains a paper upon which is inscribed the Shema (Deuteronomy 6:4–5), the Jewish affirmation of faith. The laying of the *tefillin* involves several steps: first, the worshiper covers his head with a yarmulke, a small skullcap; second, he drapes a *tallith* (a prayer shawl and symbol reminding the believer to be obedient to God), over his shoulders; third, he winds one of the *tefillin* around his forehead and the other around the biceps of his left arm. The home of an observant Jewish family contains many symbols of spiritual concepts and religious rituals. On the front door of the house, and on all interior doors except entrances to bathrooms, is affixed a small receptacle containing a scroll of the Shema. This scroll is called a *mezuzah*. The *mezuzah* reminds all who see it that God is ever present and that devotion to God's laws must be unwavering.

RITES AND CELEBRATIONS

In the Jewish faith, rituals have played a critical role by preserving Jewish tradition and history, both of which play a central role in Jewish culture and identity. Religious rituals have been meticulously preserved for thousands of years, and continue to orient Jewish daily life. The following section describes some of the major traditional rituals. It must be understood, however, that actual observance of these rituals can vary greatly.

Rites of Passage

By tradition, any child born to a Jewish mother is considered to be Jewish. According to practices prescribed by scripture, eight days after birth a male baby is given his name and is circumcised. Later, a critical rite of passage occurs for boys at age thirteen (the Bar Mitzvah) and for girls at age twelve (the Bat Mitzvah). After extensive preparation, the young person attains maturity during the Bar Mitzvah or Bat Mitzvah ceremony.

Following this symbolic passage into adulthood, the next major rite of passage is marriage. The marriage union is an especially important institution in the Jewish faith because the scriptures place an obligation on Jews to procreate. From the sacred union of man and woman a new family is created, thus ensuring that a new generation will come to serve God's will. A wedding takes place in a synagogue with a rabbi presiding and a minimum of two witnesses. During the rite, prayers are said, a marriage document is read aloud, and the groom places a ring on the bride's finger. At the close of the ceremony, a glass is placed on the floor and stepped upon, causing it to break. The shattering of the glass is taken as a symbol of the smashing of the Temple in Jerusalem by the Romans.

One of the most important ceremonies in the Jewish faith concerns burying the dead. The body of a Jewish believer who has passed away is interred as soon as possible after death. Following the passing, a one-week period of mourning commences during which friends and relatives honor the memory of the departed. Today, some Jews stipulate in their will that their body should be brought to Israel for interment in the Promised Land. In other instances, the link between Jews and Israel is manifested when soil from the Holy Land is scattered atop the casket prior to its burial.

Calendar and Festivals

Traditionally, the Jewish people date their calendar from the creation of the world as depicted in the book of Genesis. Specifically, 3760 B.C.E. is accepted as the date of the creation of Adam, and serves as the first year of the calendar (years numerically advance from this date, prefaced with AM, meaning *anno mundi* or years of the world since creation). The Jewish calendar is lunar, with each month beginning at the appearance of the new moon. This lunar calendar is maintained in synchronization with the seasons and the solar year by the addition of an extra month in the leap year, which occurs approximately every three years (or more exactly, seven times during a nineteen-year interval according to pre-determined calculations).

The Jewish calendar opens with a two-day New Year celebration called Rosh Hashanah (meaning "beginning of the year"). Rosh Hashanah (which generally occurs in late September or early October) is a time of happiness and festivity, but it is also a deeply spiritual event when sins are recalled and God's forgiveness is solicited. During Rosh Hashanah, congregants assemble at their synagogue to the sound of a *shofar*, an instrument of ancient origin that is fashioned from a ram's horn. Yom Kippur (or "Day of Atonement") occurs ten days after Rosh Hashanah. Yom Kippur is the day on which Jews atone for their sins and, as such, it is the holiest observance of the

> **In the Jewish faith, rituals have played a critical role by preserving Jewish tradition and history**

Jewish calendar. When gathered in their synagogues, they hold solemn remembrances of the ancient ceremony in which the senior priest entered the Jerusalem Temple on Yom Kippur. Five days after Yom Kippur, Jews celebrate Sukkoth (also called Sukkot), or the Feast of Tabernacles. The celebrations of Sukkoth, Passover, and Shavuoth are called the Pilgrimage Festivals; they contain strong agricultural roots and are celebrations of thanksgiving for the bounty of harvest and for beneficence of the earth. Sukkoth is a sacred commemoration of the escape from ancient Egypt (the Exodus). The festival of Simchat Torah occurs at the end of Sukkoth. It is a major observance which celebrates the reading cycle of the sacred Torah, and is characterized by joyous processions, singing, and dancing.

Hanukkah (meaning "dedication"), also called the Festival of Lights, occurs eight weeks after the Feast of Tabernacles. During Hanukkah, the Jews memorialize the recapture and rededication of the Temple of Jerusalem by the Maccabees after its occupation and debasement by the Seleucids in the second century B.C.E. Hanukkah celebrations are centered on the menorah, a candlestick with seven branches.

Purim (meaning "lots"), also called the Feast of Lots, memorializes an event depicted in the book of Esther. According to Jewish scripture, in the fifth century B.C.E. corrupt authorities of the Persian Empire planned to massacre the Jews. Haman, the official planning the bloodbath, selected the date on which the killing was to begin by drawing lots. Haman's plot was foiled, however, through the bravery and astuteness of the heroine Esther. During Purim celebrations, the book of Esther is read aloud in synagogues, and congregants take an active part in the ceremony by cheering or denouncing the various characters in the story.

Following the Feast of Lots by one month is the weeklong celebration of Passover, also called Pesach. Passover commemorates the miraculous escape of the Jews from Egypt under the divinely inspired leadership of Moses. Passover observances commence with the preparation of a distinctive meal called the Seder. During the Seder and for the whole period of Passover, a special unleavened bread, called matzah, is consumed. The Haggadah, the story of the Exodus as related in Jewish scripture, is read aloud. Like other Jewish rituals the Seder plays an important social function by emphasizing the centrality of family.

Shavuoth (Pentecost), also called the Feast of Weeks, occurs seven weeks after Passover. During Shavuoth the book of Ruth, which tells the story of how the ancient Israelites conducted harvests, is read in synagogues. The purpose of this holiday is to celebrate God's gift of the Ten Commandments through His prophet, Moses. One month and one week after Shavuoth observances, Jews begin a three-week period during which they recollect, with tremendous sadness, the two occasions on which the Temple of Jerusalem was demolished by the enemies of Israel (in 586 B.C.E. by the Babylonians and in 70 C.E. by the Romans).

The traditional calendar of Jewish rites and celebrations closes with a one-month interval dedicated to penitence and spiritual devotions; these measures are undertaken to prepare believers for the commencement of a new cycle of worship which the New Year brings. In the modern era, the classical calendar of holidays outlined above has been supplemented by additional sacramental occasions. Holocaust Day (*Yom ha-Shoah*), for example, was inaugurated soon after World War II to commemorate and mourn the millions of Jews killed by the Nazis during the war.

In terms of the weekly cycle of devotions, the Jewish Shabbat (or Sabbath), the day of prayer and rest, begins at sundown on Friday and lasts through sundown on Saturday. Shabbat observances commence when a member of the family, usually the mother, lights special candles just before dusk on Friday. The Shabbat marks God's day of rest following the Creation. It also celebrates the Exodus from Egypt. On the Shabbat, observant Jews gather together with their family members for prayers and readings of scripture. A special meal is prepared, which includes a type of bread known as *challah*. In addition to private prayer sessions and readings of scripture, congregational services also take place at synagogues.

CHAPTER SUMMARY

Following the example of Abraham, the Hebrews answered the call of God and, as God's chosen people, have sought to exemplify commitment, sacrifice, service, and moral conduct. Amidst a polytheistic environment, Abraham, the father of the Jewish people, established a monotheistic conception of God. The descendants of Abraham, committed to the realization of God's oneness and power, came to understand God as the Creator of heaven and earth. The covenant secured between Abraham and God guaranteed a special destiny for Jews as redeemers of humankind. The Jewish prophet Moses, who lived around the 1300s B.C.E., was chosen by God to receive the Ten Commandments – those revealed laws that raised the moral consciousness and social order of the age and subsequent ages.

Emphasizing deed over creed and focusing more on this world and this life than on life after death, Jews strive above all else to be faithful to God. As a people who have endured unprecedented persecution, the Jews keenly discern the spiritual value of sacrifice and suffering. Often negative socio-political conditions have been interpreted as tribulations leading to spiritual renewal. By contemplating and questioning their destiny and sacred teachings, the Jewish people have demonstrated a commitment to searching for meaning and Truth. The modern Jewish thinker Martin Buber proclaimed: "Man should not ask what the meaning of his life is, but rather he must recognize that it is he who is asked. Each man is questioned by life and he can only answer to life by answering for his own life."[11] This search for meaning has allowed new interpretations of tradition to emerge through modern forms of religious expression. Accordingly, in recent times, the Jewish religion has experienced one of its most creative phases. Different strands of interpretation have arisen, including Orthodox, Conservative, Reform, and Reconstructionist. Although Jewish practice varies, the essence of the tradition, as confirmed by Rabbi Hillel (c.first century B.C.E.–first century C.E.), remains unchanged. According to tradition, the eminent Rabbi Shammai (c. 50 B.C.E.–30 C.E.) was asked by a non-believer to explain the Torah while standing on one foot. Angered by the effrontery of the request, the rabbi sent the man away. The questioner then confronted Rabbi Hillel and repeated his query: "It was then that Hillel, in order to define Jewish law in one sentence, coined his most famous dictum: 'Do not unto others that which you would not have them do unto you. That is the entire Torah; the rest is commentary. Now go and study.'"[12]

> **As a people who have endured unprecedented persecution, the Jews keenly discern the spiritual value of sacrifice and suffering**

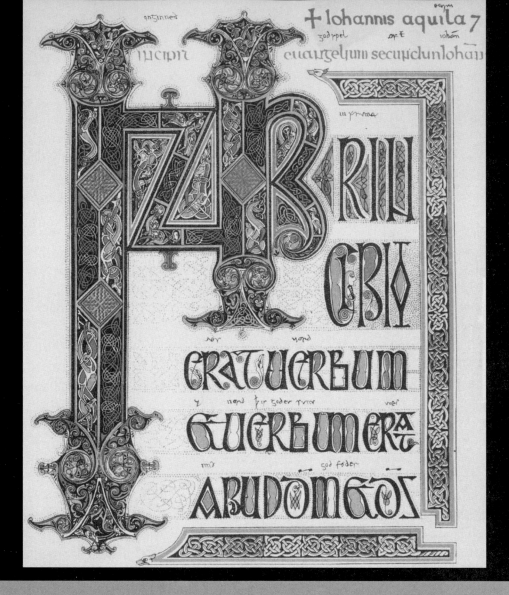

Title page of the illuminated Latin manuscript of St. John's Gospel from the Lindisfarne Gospels

CHAPTER 13
THE CHRISTIAN FAITH

Our Father which art in heaven, Hallowed be thy
name.

Thy kingdom come. Thy will be done in earth, as
it is in heaven.

Give us this day our daily bread.

And forgive us our debts, as we forgive our
debtors.

And lead us not into temptation, but deliver us
from evil:

For thine is the kingdom, and the power, and the
glory, for ever. A'-men

– Matthew 6:9–13

INTRODUCTION

The Christian faith, or Christianity, is named after Jesus of
Nazareth, who was called Christ (or *Christos*) by his later
followers. *Christ* is the Greek
word for the Hebrew term
moshiach (rendered in English
as "Messiah"). "Messiah"
translates into English as
"Anointed One," and refers to
the method by which the kings
of Israel received a blessing from the Jewish high priest.
"Messiah" was also the name given to the expected messenger of God, or savior, who would fulfill the prophecies
of the Jewish scriptures and lead the people of the Jewish
faith into a sanctified age. The Greeks and Romans applied
the term "Christian" to any follower of Christ. The development of the Christian tradition has spawned a variety of
denominations and, in turn, numerous churches. Despite
the great diversity and many interpretative differences, at
the most fundamental level, being Christian means affirming the reality of God, the utter centrality of Jesus, and the
central importance of the Bible.[1]

> **Treat others as
> you would wish to
> be treated**
> *Matthew 7:12*
> **THE GOLDEN RULE**

Timeline

*c.*6 B.C.E.
Birth of Jesus

*c.*36 C.E.
Crucifixion of Jesus

*c.*49–62 C.E.
St. Paul's letters to the
Churches

*c.*64–67 C.E.
Martyrdoms of St. Paul
and St. Peter

70 C.E.
Romans plunder Jerusalem

*c.*107 C.E.
Martyrdom of St. Ignatius
of Antioch

*c.*150–215 C.E.
St. Clement of Alexandria

*c.*160–225 C.E.
Tertullian

*c.*165 C.E.
Martyrdoms of St. Polycarp
and St. Justin Martyr

*c.*186–254 C.E.
Origen

*c.*250–356 C.E.
St. Anthony of Egypt

312 C.E.
Emperor Constantine I
implements policies
favorable to Christians

325 C.E.
Nicene Creed formulated

354–430 C.E
St. Augustine

431 C.E.
Council of Ephesus

When Jesus was born, the Holy Land was a troubled land seething with discontent. The armies (legions) of the expanding Roman Empire had captured Jerusalem in 63 B.C.E., about sixty years before Jesus was born. Eventually, the conquered Jewish territories were incorporated into the Roman Empire as part of the province of Syria. A local commander appointed by the Roman emperor ruled over Jewish lands, which the Romans called Judea. Instituting a standard technique of imperial rule, the Romans attempted to co-opt preexisting Jewish institutions to serve Roman interests. In this regard, the Romans supported a Jewish monarchy in Judea that was under the control of a succession of kings named Herod. Despite the façade of Jewish authority represented by the Herods, many Jews were never reconciled to the Roman occupation of their homeland. Bitter resentment against Roman soldiers, officials, and their local Jewish collaborators took many forms. Some Jews joined the ranks of the Zealots, a group that passionately fought against the Romans. Others rejected Rome by embracing their own religious faith and fervently prayed for the coming of a Messiah. For some, the foretold Messiah was a great spiritual teacher who would reinvigorate Jewish religious life and thereby bring forth the bounty of God's favor. Others believed that the Messiah was a great soldier of God who would lead a holy war against the hated Romans and restore an independent Jewish kingdom. In anticipation of the coming of the Messiah, numerous small sects sprang up; some of these were under the leadership of charismatic figures who claimed to be the Messiah. As this brief survey demonstrates, a threatening environment of occupation, sedition, and religious ferment formed the background of Jesus' brief thirty-year or so life and even briefer public ministry (which lasted only about three years).

Historical information on first-century Judea is derived from a variety of sources, including Roman literature, Jewish texts, and archeological evidence. Accounts written by Josephus Flavius, a historian who lived from about 37 to 95 C.E., describe the strife-filled history of

451 C.E.
Council of Chalcedon
c.480–547
St. Benedict of Nursia
1054 C.E.
Great schism separates the Christian community in Europe into the Eastern Orthodox and Roman Catholic Churches
1095–1291 C.E.
The Crusades
1181–1226 C.E.
St. Francis of Assisi
c.1184 C.E.
First medieval Inquisition begins to suppress heresy
c.1225–1274 C.E.
Thomas Aquinas
c.1260–1327 C.E.
Meister Eckhart
1401–1464 C.E.
St. Nicholas of Cusa
1483–1546 C.E.
Martin Luther
1509–1547 C.E.
Reign of King Henry VIII
1509–1564 C.E.
John Calvin
1542–1591 C.E. St. John of the Cross
1869 C.E. First Vatican Council
1906–1945 C.E.
Dietrich Bonhoeffer
1960s C.E.
Second Vatican Council

Roman–Jewish relations during this period.[2] The most important sources on Jesus, however, are the first four books of the New Testament of the Bible: Matthew, Mark, Luke, and John. These books are called the Gospels (*gospel* is a Greek word meaning "good news"), and taken together they form a biography describing the life, death, and resurrection of Jesus.

JESUS IN THE GOSPELS

According to Gospel accounts, the archangel Gabriel visited Jesus' mother, Mary (Miriam in Hebrew), and announced to her that her child would be the Messiah. Shortly thereafter, Mary married Joseph, a carpenter from Galilee. Jesus, miraculously conceived by Mary (who was a virgin) through the power of the Holy Spirit, lived with his mother and Joseph in Galilee. Jesus received the same formal religious training that all young Jews did, and hence he made frequent trips to the local synagogue with Joseph. Even as a boy, Jesus' wisdom and insight aroused the attention of noted Jewish scholars, and by the time he was twelve Jesus would visit the Temple in Jerusalem to witness and participate in learned religious discussions.

As a young man, Jesus was associated with the movement led by John the Baptist, a prophet delivering sermons in the area of the Jordan Valley along the banks of the Jordan River. John proclaimed to his growing flock of disciples that the Messiah would soon come, and prepared his followers for this event by baptizing them in the waters of the Jordan as an act of repentance. One day Jesus himself came to John seeking baptism. At the moment of his baptism, Christians believe that the Holy Spirit settled on Jesus. John the Baptist understood this to be a sign that Jesus was the Messiah that he, John, had foretold was coming. Sometime after he baptized Jesus, John, who was seen as a threat to the political stability of the region, was arrested by troops loyal to the Roman collaborator King Herod. Herod's wife, Herodias, and her daughter, Salome, connived to have John executed, and the death sentence was carried out on the order of the king.

Biblical accounts relate how, after commencing his ministry, Jesus went into the desert for a period of forty days and nights. While undergoing the physical rigors of desert life and fasting, he experienced a great spiritual test during which he endured and overcame a succession of temptations proposed by Satan (a Hebrew word meaning "adversary," *al-Shaytan* in Arabic). Satan is the malevolent being that Christians believe is the embodiment of evil and the primary source of humanity's suffering. Following this significant retreat into the desert, Jesus returned to spread his teachings. He taught his followers that the coming of the "Kingdom of God" (or "Kingdom of Heaven") was at hand, and urged them to prepare themselves by responding to his ministry, affirming the dominion of God, and by living in accordance with God's prescriptions. He instructed those who wished to attain grace to free themselves of avarice, self-indulgence, desire, conceit, and hostility. Jesus attracted a wide circle of devotees, from whom twelve formed his disciples or apostles. These men formed a trustworthy band of followers who accompanied Jesus on his travels and who were instructed to dedicate their entire lives to the service of God. Jesus also became well known throughout the region as a healer and miracle worker, with numerous stories of curing both physical and spiritual illnesses.

Some among the established priestly authorities of the region viewed the movement that surrounded Jesus with grave concern. Particularly troubling to certain priests and community leaders was the bold way in which he disregarded accepted social norms, such as the strict ordering of society into different groups – for example, the rich and the poor. According to Jesus, the favored aspirants to the Kingdom of God were the outcasts of society, the marginalized, and the poor: "For it is easier for a camel to go through a needle's eye, than for a rich man to enter into the kingdom of God" (Luke 18:25). Jesus claimed adherents from across the social spectrum; women, who were confined to a low social status during this period, were uplifted within Jesus' revolutionary, spiritual movement. Additionally, those who answered Jesus' call included well-known sinners such as prostitutes, as well as the despised tax collectors. Jesus declared, "Judge not, that ye be not judged. For with what judgment ye judge, ye shall be judged: and with what measure ye mete, it shall be measured to you again" (Matthew 7:1–2). Despite the scandal and controversy such attitudes provoked among the larger community, Jesus and his followers received all people openly and with love. A very dramatic example of how Jesus rejected prevailing practices occurred when he visited the Temple in Jerusalem. Furious at the sight of moneychangers doing business on its grounds, Jesus overturned their tables and expelled them from the building. Christians later interpreted this story to mean that Jesus had been sent to purge God's house, the Temple, and by extension the larger community of faith.

Along with the religious leaders, civil authorities in Judea became concerned about the activities of Jesus and his disciples. The officers and officials who reported to King Herod took note of Jesus' growing popularity, and feared that the wandering teacher might encourage his flock to join a rebellion against Herod and the Roman emperor. In the prevailing atmosphere of subversion and repression, any challenge to the authority of King Herod or the Romans was dealt with harshly. Eventually, anxiety over Jesus led to his arrest, trial, and crucifixion, just as he had foretold.

Theologically, the crucifixion of Jesus represents an act of the utmost significance for Christians. It not only exemplifies God's compassion and love for humanity, through the sacrifice of His son, but the path to redemption. Furthermore, the story of Jesus' own willingness to sacrifice himself continues to capture the minds and hearts of people across the globe. Jesus' acceptance of his execution, and his expressions of love and forgiveness for his persecutors, mark the culmination of his earthly ministry. Christians believe that three days after his crucifixion, death, and burial Jesus was raised by God in an act called the Resurrection; through the Resurrection, they believe that Jesus' spiritual significance, or his eternal life, is unending and his heavenly character is confirmed.

THE EARLY JESUS MOVEMENT

During the time of Jesus a variety of Jewish sects existed, including the Pharisees, Sadducees, Zealots, and Essenes. Thus, the Jesus movement, which proclaimed Jesus as the promised Messiah of the Hebrew scriptures, emerged as one sect among many. From the beginning, Christian thinkers struggled with how their tradition was both related to and distinct from the Jewish faith. After the Crucifixion of Jesus, stories surrounding his empty tomb and his miraculous reappearances set in motion an animated movement led by Jesus' apostles (or disciples). In order to follow the evolution, consolidation, and development of this movement, it is best to examine two of the most important early Christians, Peter and Paul.

After the Crucifixion, Peter, along with other disciples, returned to Galilee. One must imagine the confusion and dismay that Jesus' disciples experienced following his death on the cross. Their disappointment, however, did not last long. According to Gospel accounts, a resurrected Jesus appeared to many of his disciples, most of whom did not recognize him initially. He ate with them, and is reported to have walked through closed doors. According to the Gospels, forty days after his first post-Crucifixion appearance before Mary Magdalene, Jesus blessed his disciples and ascended to heaven. His disciples, led by Peter, then set out for Jerusalem to prepare the people of Israel for redemption. According to the New Testament (Matthew 16:13–20), Peter was the preeminent apostle, chosen by Jesus himself to establish a new church. As described in the New Testament (Acts 2:1–4), an extraordinary event transpired in Jerusalem when the apostles were celebrating the Jewish festival of Pentecost:

The story of Jesus' willingness to sacrifice himself continues to capture the minds and hearts of people across the globe

And when the day of Pentecost was fully come, they were all with one accord in one place. And suddenly there came a sound from heaven as of a rushing mighty wind, and it filled all the house where they were sitting. And there appeared unto them cloven tongues like as of fire, and it sat upon each of them. And they were all filled with the Holy Ghost, and began to speak with other tongues, as the Spirit gave them utterance.

For Christians, this scene depicts the Holy Spirit anointing the twelve disciples (Matthias replaced Judas, who betrayed Jesus to those who arrested him), an act which signaled the dawn of salvation based in a new covenant with God. For Christians, the establishment of the Church was a divine rather than a human act. Initially, the followers of Jesus in Jerusalem continued to participate in Jewish spiritual life centered on the Synagogue. After the apparent imprisonment of Peter by Roman authorities, James assumed leadership of the Christian movement (this James was the younger brother of Jesus and should not be confused with the apostle James, the son of Zebedee, who was martyred *c.*46). Although James, or "James the Just" as he was sometimes called, is rarely mentioned in the Gospels, he became the leader of the Christian community of Jerusalem. Elsewhere, Paul (or Saul as he was then called), unknown to the disciples and the family of Jesus, was emerging as a powerful advocate of the Jesus movement.

Before becoming a devotee of Jesus, Paul was a member of a Jewish sect known as the Pharisees. The Pharisees were noted for their inflexible adherence to traditional Jewish observances and interpretations. When the community of Jesus' followers became larger and better known, Paul actively participated in efforts to eradicate the movement. One day, however, while traveling to the city of Damascus on a mission to arrest Christians in that city, Paul experienced a vision of the Resurrected Jesus (Acts 9:1–19) that led to his spiritual transformation and conversion to the new faith. Paul, who had never met Jesus, was not so much concerned with the historical Jesus (the Jesus of the flesh) but rather the risen Jesus of the Spirit (2 Corinthians 5:16). Paul brought the message of Jesus, as he understood it, to the Hellenistic Gentiles (non-Jews), and was particularly successful amongst those referred to as "God-fearers" (or Gentiles who were sympathetic to the monotheism of the Jewish worldview but who did not participate in Jewish rites).

Like many early Christians, Paul anticipated the imminent return of Jesus and the Kingdom of God. It appears that he expected, at least early in his missionary career, that Jesus would return to judge the world within his own lifetime (1 Thessalonians 4:16–18). Paul, who believed himself a conduit of the will of God (1 Galatians 1, 2 Galatians 2, etc.), was adamant that Jesus' message was universal and that faith in the resurrected Christ was the criterion for salvation by way of divine grace. From his perspective, often called Pauline theology, Christians did not need to follow Jewish law because Jesus Christ, the Son of God, had ushered in a new era of the Holy Spirit that abrogated and superseded the Jewish dispensation. The Pauline interpretation, however, differed somewhat from other early Christian perspectives. Paul's letter to the Galatians, preserved in the New Testament as an epistle, is particularly helpful in identifying interpretive differences within the mainstream Christian movement.

The early Church in Jerusalem, as founded by Peter and subsequently directed by James, remained closely tied to Jewish rites and customs. Scholars suggest that the Church was similar in organization and ritual practice to Essene communities of the same period (communal and apocalyptic Jewish sects such as the one at Qumran). Members of the Church at Jerusalem searched through the Hebrew scriptures (or the "Old Testament") and interpreted certain passages as prophecies that foretold the life of Jesus. Converts to the Christian movement at Jerusalem, mostly by way of the missionary work of Peter, consisted mainly of Aramaic-speaking Jews, some of whom had been followers of John the Baptist. In contrast, Paul was converting many Gentile communities (such as those in Galatia and Corinth) to the Christian faith without requiring converts to observe Jewish law (including, for example, circumcision). On the other hand, circumcision, an obligatory Jewish rite established as the mark of the covenant between Abraham and God, seems to have been upheld as a required rite of passage for Christians in Jerusalem.

> **The early Church in Jerusalem remained closely tied to Jewish rites and customs**

A meeting, referred to as the Apostolic Council, was held between Paul and the three central figures of the Jerusalem Christian community – James, Peter, and John – around the year 48. According to Paul (Galatians 2:7–10), an agreement was reached that confirmed the legitimacy of Paul's work, namely the conversion of Gentiles to Christianity independent of Jewish law. However, Paul reports that the agreement of the Apostolic Council was not upheld by Peter when he went to the city of Antioch. This led to a direct confrontation between Paul and Peter (Galatians 2:11–14), in which Paul asserted authority and reprimanded Peter. A clear difference existed between Paul and his interpretation, which attracted Hellenistic Gentiles, from that of Peter's interpretation, which, like that of other apostles, remained embedded within a Judaic context. The majority of converts to the Jesus movement, however, were brought in by Paul and his companions (such as Barnabas). These converts consisted mainly of Hellenistic Gentiles and not Jews. Thus, at this early time, the future direction of the Jesus movement was established not as a sect of the Jewish religion, but as a universal religion offering salvation to all.

After the Crucifixion, the followers of Jesus were able to move about and congregate, with relatively little harassment by Roman authorities. This freedom, however, was short-lived. The Roman emperor Nero (r. 54–68) blamed the Christians, and even more so the Jews, for a terrible fire that broke out in Rome in 64.[3] Heightened tensions between Rome and the Jewish community, animated by Nero's policy of persecution, resulted in a Jewish rebellion led by the Zealots. The Jewish–Roman War (66–73) ended in the plunder of Jerusalem by Roman soldiers, including the destruction of the Temple. This marked an important period both in Christian and Jewish history. It appears that the Christian community of Jerusalem made a conscious decision to break with Jewish nationalism by remaining neutral in the Jewish–Roman War. The Christians of Jerusalem apparently fled before the city fell in the year 70. In contrast, other Jewish sects, such as the Essenes, fought against Rome. After the destruction of Jerusalem, the cultural and religious center of the Jewish world, the Christian movement entered a new era as its center shifted to the Greco-Roman world.

Gnostics and Marcionites

The spiritual impulse released by the figure and teachings of Jesus spawned religious movements throughout the region, and varying perspectives emerged as a result of different points of view. This diversity of interpretation is not surprising given that the Gospels depict Jesus' own disciples as struggling to grasp the meaning and sublimity of his parables and aphorisms. As recorded in the New Testament, Jesus himself proclaimed, "Therefore speak I to them in parables: because they seeing see not; and hearing they hear not, neither do they understand" (Matthew 13:13). It should be noted that although a mainstream Church emerged which was connected to Jesus' disciples and family, the wider Jesus movement consisted of many spiritual groups that were influenced by the teachings of Jesus. One important group of early Christians was the Gnostics (whose name derives from *gnosis*, a Greek word meaning knowledge).

Scholars disagree as to the nature of the Gnostic movement before the appearance of Jesus. There is no doubt, however, that the Gnostics adopted Jesus' teachings as a central part of their worldview. Christian communities, influenced by the Gnostic perspective, were led by teachers such as Basilides and Valentinus, both of the second century of the Common Era. The Gnostics claimed that they authoritatively represented the teachings of Jesus. They maintained their own schools, spiritual communities, and gospels that differed from those of the New Testament.

Viewing the material world as a spiritual imprisonment, Gnostics emphasized redemptive self-knowledge rather than salvation through faith. They regarded inward reflection as the essence of spirituality, echoing Jesus' words "For, behold, the kingdom of God is within you" (Luke 17:20–21). Gnostic communities, with their complex philosophies and cosmologies, rich in allegory, were spread throughout the Roman Empire, from Gaul to Alexandria. The Gnostics, however, were viewed as heretical by the mainstream Christian Church. A contemporary remnant of the Gnostic movement is the Mandeans, a small religious community living in southern Iraq and southwestern Iran.[4] Interestingly, the Mandeans revere John the Baptist, and he features prominently in their holy writings. Some scholars believe that the Mandeans, who practice the rite of baptism, are the descendants of John the Baptist's original disciples (possibly they are the Sabeans referred to in the Qur'an, the Holy Book of Islam).

Another Christian community that emerged in the early years of the Jesus movement was formed by Marcion (d. *c.*160). He rejected the totality of the Hebrew tradition and accepted only the letters of Paul and some of the Gospel of Luke. The followers of Marcion flourished in Syria and Mesopotamia, and apparently became major rivals to the mainstream Church. As such, they were the subject of many intellectual attacks written by such authors as Irenaeus and Tertullian. Scholars suggest that some Marcionite groups may have been absorbed into the Manichaean religion, which was established by the Persian prophet Mani (d. 276). For its part, the Manichaean tradition grew into a movement of such influence that, for a time, it appeared that it might displace the Catholic Church.[5]

EARLY CHRISTIANITY IN THE GRECO-ROMAN WORLD

The intolerant policy inaugurated by the emperor Nero toward Christians and Jews lasted, in varying degrees of severity, until the time of Constantine the Great (r. 306–337). During Nero's reign, James, Peter, and Paul were martyred. During this period, the emperor of Rome was imbued with divine attributes, although this status was conferred more by official propaganda than by any real conviction on the part of the populace. Christians, who met secretly in the catacombs of Rome, refused to make offerings to the emperor (such as the burning of incense), which was one way that Roman authorities identified them. In general, if Christians who were arrested recanted their belief in Christ they would be set free.

> **Martyrs became the object of veneration amongst many Christians, and their grave sites became places of pilgrimage**

The Christians, however, overwhelmingly embraced martyrdom rather than denouncing their faith. Martyrs became the object of veneration amongst many Christians, and their grave sites became places of pilgrimage. St. Ignatius of Antioch (d. *c.*107) is one of the most famous martyrs of early Christian history, particularly because of the letters he wrote while he was held prisoner and awaiting execution. In a letter to his Christian brethren in Rome, he implored them not to interfere by trying to obtain a pardon on his behalf. His martyrdom, he said, was the culmination of his life, his sacrifice to God, and his way to Jesus Christ:

> It is not men that I want you to gratify, but God, just as you habitually do. I shall never have a better chance than this of getting to God; and you on your part will never have a finer piece of work to your credit, if only you will keep your lips sealed. For by staying silent and letting me alone, you can turn me into an intelligible utterance of God; but if your affections are only concerned with my poor human life, then I become a

mere meaningless cry once more. This favour only I beg of you: suffer me to be a liba-
tion poured out to God, while there is still an altar ready for me … For good does not
reside in what our eyes can see; the fact that Jesus Christ is now within the Father is
why we perceive Him so much more clearly. For the work we have to do is no affair
of persuasive speaking; Christianity lies in achieving greatness in the face of the world's
hatred.[6]

In various cities of the Roman Empire, including Rome, Christians were executed during
great public spectacles; sometimes, they were burned alive as human torches or thrown
into pits to be devoured by lions. As one scholar observed: "The early Christians were rev-
olutionaries of the Spirit, heralds of the last judgment and the coming transformation; they
had to be ready for martyrdom at any moment."[7] Persecution was, however, sporadic.
Christian communities were able to spread, and gained considerable numbers of converts.
It was during the third century, an unstable period in Roman history, that Christian communities were viewed as a serious threat to Roman authority. During the reigns of the
emperors Decius (r. 249–251), Valerian (r. 253–260), and Diocletian (r. 284–305), severe
persecution became the policy throughout the empire.

Because Christ did not return immediately as the earliest Christians had expected, the
movement needed an organizational structure. Hence, the ecclesiastical order of bishops,
priests, and deacons emerged. Churches were led by bishops, who held authoritative
weight among the greater community of a given city or region. Initiation to the Christian
way was through baptism. Weekly religious services, held on Sundays, culminated in the
Eucharist (a reenactment of the communal meal, the Last Supper, shared by Jesus and his
twelve disciples). Christian integration into the Greco-Roman world shifted Christian
missionary work away from the Jews and the Hebrew scriptures and to Gentiles of the
Hellenistic religions. Prevalent Greco-Roman religions of the first century of the
Common Era, each offering different forms of spirituality, included the mystery cult of Isis,
Orphism, Mithraism, the Bacchics, and others. The rich philosophical climate of the time
period included Pythagoreans, Aristotelians, Neoplatonists (such as Ammonius Saccas,
Plotinus, and Porphyry), Stoics (such as Seneca and the emperor Marcus Aurelius), as well
as the Jewish philosopher Philo of Alexandria (c.20 B.C.E.–50 C.E.), whose allegorical interpretations of Hebrew scriptures included an important articulation of the Greek philosophical concept of the *logos*.

Some Christian thinkers, such as Tertullian (c.160–225), declared heretical all
Hellenistic forms of philosophy and religiosity. Other Christian contemplatives, however,
such as Clement of Alexandria (c.150–c.215), Justin Martyr (c.100–165), and Origen
(c.185–254), embraced a more universal outlook. They articulated Christian compatibility,

even continuity, with the Hellenistic religious systems. One modern Christian scholar has observed:

> According to Eusebius [the bishop of Caesarea], for example, Christianity is the restoration of the religion of the patriarchal age … and St. Augustine himself writes: "That which today is called Christian religion existed also among the Ancients and has never ceased to exist from the origin of the human race until the time when Christ Himself assumed human form and men began to call Christian the true religion which already existed beforehand."
>
> In these early stages … there was much in Christian form and practice that was reminiscent of the initiates or the esoterism of the ancient mysteries like those at Eleusis … Origen talks of faith being useful for the masses, and further says that the intelligent are more congenial to God than the unintelligent. He explicitly speaks of secret doctrines that can be taught only to the initiated. Clement of Alexandria says the same thing, and such a secret (and oral) tradition is referred to by St. Cyril of Alexandria, St. Gregory of Nazianzen, Dionysios the Areopagite, and many others. Unless one is automatically prevented by prejudice, one has to recognize that in its essential form Christianity is an initiatory religion that is in many ways similar to the mystery religions of the pre-Christian world.[8]

St. Justin Martyr and other Christian thinkers who were learned in Hellenistic philosophies of the period developed a universalistic perspective within the Christian worldview. Justin, an eminent Christian teacher, was influenced by the Hellenistic philosophical concept of *logos spermatikos*. He viewed the *logos* as the generative and rational Power of God, identified as Wisdom (*sophia*) and supremely manifested in Christ the Son. Justin saw Hellenistic systems of thought as partaking in Wisdom (through reason), and thus, albeit indirectly, in Christ, the source of all Wisdom. For if the Word was the source of all things, then all things (in different degrees) partake of the Word, including pagan philosophers. In the Gospel of John (1:1–4) it is written: "In the beginning was the Word [*logos*], and the Word was with God, and the Word was God. The same was in the beginning with God. All things were made by him; and without him was not any thing made that was made. In him was life; and the life was the light of men."

Constantine and the Nicene Creed

One of the most significant events in the history of Christianity occurred early in the fourth century of the Common Era, when persecution of Christians in the Roman Empire was stopped. In the year 312, the emperor Constantine (r. 306–337) defeated his rival, Maxentius, and occupied Rome with an army whose ranks contained many Christians.

St. Paul's Cathedral, London

Afterwards, Constantine implemented policies favorable to Christians (such as a decree issued in 313 on religious tolerance known as the Edict of Milan). Constantine built a new city on the site of Byzantium and named it Constantinople (now Istanbul), which became a center of the Christian faith. With the help of Constantine, Church bishops held a council that drafted an authoritative creed of Christian beliefs, especially as they pertained to the station and life of Jesus Christ. This creed, called the Nicene Creed (formulated in 325), became the standard definition of Christian doctrine, and all bishops who dissented from the final formulation of the text were banished. Shortly before his death, Constantine embraced Christianity and underwent baptism.

The Nicene Creed was of particular importance because a plethora of Christian interpretations existed during this period. Indeed, no system of theology had emerged as the orthodox version. A Church that was not unified could not perpetuate itself. In 380 Christianity became the official state religion of the Roman Empire by the order of Emperor Theodosius. Further points of dogma were established at ecumenical gatherings such as the Council of Ephesus in 431 and the Council of Chalcedon in 451. The Council of Chalcedon named the bishops of the major cities of the Roman Empire (including Constantinople, Antioch, Alexandria, Jerusalem, and Rome) as patriarchs. Today, the patriarch of Constantinople is the spiritual leader of the Eastern Orthodox Church, while the patriarch of Rome is now known as the Pope of the Roman Catholic Church.

> **In 380 Christianity became the official state religion of the Roman Empire**

The alliance forged in 312 between Christians and Constantine, and the formulation of the Nicene Creed in 325, were seminal events in the evolution of the Church. The nascent Catholic Church was able to consolidate the Jesus movement by emphasizing an authoritative creed and ecclesiastical hierarchy; all other interpretations were deemed as heresy. Christianity's movement through the Roman Empire led to the destruction or Christianization of pagan schools, shrines, and temples; Christian festivals, such as Easter and Christmas, became publicly observed holidays. In a remarkable turn of events, what started as a small, persecuted, apocalyptic Jewish sect became Christendom, a spiritual empire striving for the collective salvation of humanity through the erection of the Kingdom of God on Earth.

CHRISTIAN CONTEMPLATIVES

With the support of officials of the Roman Empire starting around the fourth century, Christian missionaries were sent far and wide. They won converts in places such as Ethiopia, Syria, North Africa, Asia Minor, Mesopotamia, India, Persia, Germany, Britain, and Ireland. This outward expansion of the Church was complemented by the inner development of Church philosophy and spiritual practice. The internal evolution of the Church can be traced through the works of important Christian figures. Such writings distill the essence of Christian tradition, learning, and spiritual practice. One of the most influential of the early Church thinkers was Augustine of Hippo (354–430), later known as St. Augustine.

As the bishop of Hippo (a city located in modern-day Algeria), Augustine wrote major treatises including *The Confessions*, *The Trinity*, and *The City of God* – which have influenced Catholic doctrine and are regarded as classics of Christian thought. Before his conversion to Christianity in 386, St. Augustine subscribed to the Manichaean religion (or Manichaeism); he also exhibited a philosophical disposition greatly informed by Platonic philosophy. Following his conversion experience (depicted in his book *Confessions*), Augustine took up the cause of defending the Christian faith against pagan religions and philosophies. Regarded by some as

> **The internal evolution of the Church can be traced through the works of important Christian figures**

the Father of the Catholic Church, St. Augustine's theological viewpoints, such as his belief in free will and salvation through grace, became formative aspects of Church doctrine. In particular, his concept of Original Sin (humanity's inherently sinful nature stemming from the fall of Adam) became an essential tenet of the Catholic worldview. In his book *The Enchiridion on Faith, Hope, and Love*, written sometime around 420, Augustine writes:

> What I shall now say is what I have also often said in several places in my shorter works: there are two reasons why we sin, either because we do not see what we ought to do, or because we do not do what we know ought to be done: the first of these evils comes from ignorance, the second from weakness. We should fight against both of them. But we cannot win without divine help.[9]

As the Christian church developed, a significant spiritual movement known as monasticism emerged. Monasticism was the practice of retreating from society in order to concentrate on spiritual practice. The figure usually cited as the archetype of Christian hermitage is St. Anthony of Egypt (*c.*250–356). Anthony, who according to legend performed various miracles, retreated to the desert to cultivate spiritual virtues and purity. Others soon followed his example by entering the desert to practice in solitude. Around 320, St. Pachomius founded several monasteries near the Upper Nile in Egypt where Christians lived together as monks. In the year 530, in the central Italian region of Monte Cassino, the monk Benedict of Nursia (*c.*480–547), who was influenced by the work of St. Pachomius, founded a monastic community that became known as the Benedictine order. Benedict (later St. Benedict) and his order had a profound influence on the development and practice of Christian monasticism. Benedict formulated guidelines prescribing how the monks of his community were to live, work, pray, and serve society. His detailed guidelines, known as the *Rule of Saint Benedict*, consist of seventy-three chapters. Benedict's teachings emphasize obedience, humility, and discipline.

According to St. Benedict, life in the monastery should consist of communal living, i.e. all possessions are held in common. Daily routines should be supervised by an elected abbot who is a superior and experienced practitioner. In his teaching on the qualities of an abbot, St. Benedict says that "the abbot should always observe the Apostle's recommendation in which he says: use argument, appeal, reproof (2 Tim. 4:2)."[10] Benedict's goal was to nurture a way of living that gave free rein to the expression of Christian beliefs, and he and his monks became renowned for their service to God and humanity at large. In addition, the monasteries founded by the Benedictine order made great contributions to scholarship, the arts, and the economy. Benedictine monks were responsible for important advances in the study of religion, techniques of scientific inquiry, and improved farming methods. Inspired in part by the Benedictine order, monasteries throughout the Christian world were responsible for bringing the fruits of modern advancement to peoples on the periphery of Europe who had not benefited from Roman civilization.

Another important figure in the history of the Church is St. Francis of Assisi (1181–1226), founder of the Franciscan order. After a conversion experience, Francis left a societal position of great privilege and wealth and took up a life of poverty. He devoted himself to the care of lepers, building churches, and spreading the message of the Gospels through preaching. In a book attributed to St. Francis, entitled *Little Flowers of St. Francis*, he spoke to flowers, birds, rivers, and nature as a whole, imbuing the reader with a sense of gratitude to God:

My little bird sisters, you owe much to God your Creator, and you must always and everywhere praise Him, because He has given you freedom to fly anywhere – also He has given you a double and triple covering, and your colorful and pretty clothing, and your food is ready without your working for it, and your singing that was taught to you by the Creator, and your numbers that have been multiplied by the blessing of God … And you are also indebted to Him for the realm of the air which He assigned to you. Moreover, you neither sow nor reap, yet God nourishes you, and He gives you the rivers and springs to drink from. He gives you high mountains and hills, rocks and crags as refuges, and lofty trees in which to make your nests. And although you do not know how to spin or sew, God gives you and your little ones the clothing which you need. So the Creator loves you very much, since He gives you so many good things. Therefore, my little bird sisters, be careful not to be ungrateful, but strive always to praise God.[11]

It is not surprising that many regard St. Francis as the patron saint of the environmental movement. Renowned for his remarkable purity, he is the object of many legends and remains one of the most popular and appealing saints in Christian history. In general, St. Francis emphasized a simple lifestyle of poverty rather than spiritual advancement through intellectual learning.

CHRISTENDOM

Centuries after the first monks founded monasteries on the marches of Europe, a series of military campaigns were undertaken known as the Crusades. (The word "crusade" is derived from the Latin *cruciata*, meaning "those who wear a cross.") The Crusaders were believers enlisted by the Church – or by secular authorities acting under Church sanction – to wage war. Early Crusader campaigns were mounted to defend Christian lands from attack and to take back the Holy Land from the Muslims who had conquered it. In the eleventh century such defensive wars were fought in Spain and Sicily, both of which were threatened by Muslim armies. Internally, Crusader campaigns were fought in the thirteenth century against heretics (Christians who dissented from the Church) and apostates (Christians who had left the Church). The Crusades did lead to certain positive developments, such as increased cultural, scientific, and trading contacts between the East and West. Yet the bitter fruit of conflict that is the major legacy of the Crusades continues to perpetuate misunderstandings between Christians and Muslims even today.

In 1054, a pivotal event in the history of the Christian Church occurred. In that year, the Roman Catholic Pope, Leo IX, publicly denounced the Orthodox patriarch of Constantinople. This discord originated in the 400s when Christians in the eastern Roman Empire (based in Constantinople) distanced themselves from the western part of the Church (which was centered in Rome). Consequently, each branch of the church effectively maintained an independent structure with its own doctrines, rituals, and clergy. The western community came to be called the Catholic ("universal") Church, and the eastern community the Orthodox ("right-thinking") Church.

Even after the split with the Eastern Church was officially confirmed, theological debates and dissension continued within the Catholic Church. Disagreements among Catholics became so heated that in the thirteenth century Pope Gregory IX established a tribunal called the Inquisition to investigate and correct deviance from Church doctrines. At first, the Inquisition favored methods of reasoned persuasion. Later, however, some leaders of the Inquisition, called Inquisitors, resorted to acts of brutal violence, including the torture and execution of heretics and apostates. Thus, the Inquisition itself fell victim to corruption and became notorious for its abuse of power, use of torture, and oppression of Catholic dissidents and Jews.

Although the central Church authorities in Rome sometimes attempted to curb the excesses of certain prominent Inquisitors, many Catholics were deeply troubled by the Inquisition. Over the centuries, other Church practices also caused controversy. The selling of indulgences, for example, led many pious believers to oppose the hierarchy of the Catholic Church. Indulgences took different forms, but in the late eleventh century "plenary indulgences" became commonplace. In exchange for specific acts of service, such as joining a Crusade, an individual was granted a plenary indulgence that set aside all forms of punishment for sins. Eventually, such plenary indulgences were sold for specific sums of money; some members of clergy actually became full-time "salesmen" who traveled from town-to-town peddling indulgences. Such practices deeply offended reformers such as the German priest Martin Luther (1483–1546). In the year 1517 Luther publicly declared his wholehearted opposition to the sale of indulgences, a practice that he described as an affront to the spirit and teachings of Jesus.

In propagating his "ninety-five theses" attacking a variety of Church practices and doctrines, Luther launched a movement that quickly attracted the allegiance of Christians throughout Germany and neighboring lands – a movement that became known as the Protestant Reformation. Under the influence of the Reformation, the Catholic Church experienced another schism between those Christians who remained loyal to the authorities in Rome and adherents of **Religious wars broke out and threatened to destroy European civilization** the new, independent Protestant Churches. Having broken with Rome, Protestants fell into further doctrinal disputes. Sectarian rivalries, intolerance, and persecution occurred throughout Europe. Religious wars, or wars with a religious component, broke out and threatened to destroy European civilization. Although the Protestant Churches are too numerous to describe in detail, their main branches (see below) have great influence in the Christian community worldwide. Today, the various Protestant denominations collectively claim about 500 million adherents.

A brief description of some of the major churches will help clarify the status of the main branches of the Christian faith. What follows is an illustrative rather than a comprehensive treatment.

THE ROMAN CATHOLIC CHURCH

Catholics view the apostle Peter as the founder of the Catholic Church (sometimes called the Church of Rome). The Catholic Church is numerically the largest and most geographically widespread branch of Christianity in the world. The head of the Catholic Church is the

Bishop of Rome, or Pope (from the Greek word for "Father"), who in a sense is the successor of St. Peter. As the senior clergyman of the Catholic Church, the Pope oversees a worldwide clerical order comprising cardinals, archbishops, bishops, priests, monks, and nuns. Among Catholics, the Pope possesses a unique quality: unlike any other priest, he enjoys the attribute of infallibility when upholding a doctrine of faith or morality. The Pope exercises infallible guidance only when he specifically invokes this principle, and such infallibility does not apply to non-doctrinal spheres such as economics or politics. Catholics believe that the Holy Spirit imbues the Church as a whole with infallibility. In addition to the Pope, an ecumenical council (a meeting attended by the Pope and all the bishops) can, acting as a collective, invoke the attribute of infallibility. Catholics believe that only God is infallible in the full sense of immunity from error; however, they believe that the Church was empowered with this attribute by Christ and that it can be exercised by Church officials, if only in a limited sense.

The Catholic Church is numerically the largest and most geographically widespread branch of Christianity in the world

The foundation of Catholic philosophy was provided by Thomas Aquinas (*c.*1225–1274), who was the most important philosophical mind of the Catholic tradition, and was declared a Doctor of the Church in 1567. Aquinas synthesized Christian beliefs with the dominant system of science and philosophy of his age, the philosophy of Aristotle. In general, he held the view that reason and faith were compatible aspects of the same spiritual journey (i.e. that reason is trustworthy given the premise of faith). Aquinas believed that the existence of God is discernible through nature and reason alone, but that salvation is attained only through revelation. His corpus of writings addresses many aspects of philosophy and spirituality. As the most prolific thinker of the Middle Ages, Aquinas' works are regarded as classics of Western thought by Christians and non-Christians alike.

Although the Church is an ancient institution that traces its origin to the very founding of the Christian community, it has periodically attempted to adjust itself to societal changes. In the early 1960s, for example, the Church convened the Second Vatican Council, which redefined the Catholic Church as consisting of a community of believers rather than a hierarchy of priests and laity. The Second Vatican Council also refined the Church's message by acknowledging the social conditions of modernity. In 1968, the Roman Catholic bishops of Latin America met in Colombia to study the effects of the Second Vatican Council. They were particularly concerned with what they saw as the exploitation of the peoples of Latin American and Africa by industrialized societies. Some of the bishops advocated a shift in the role of theology away from abstraction in favor of pragmatic action. Reformers viewed theology as a means to raise the political, social, and economic status of the poor, oppressed, and marginalized peoples of the world – a position they said was rooted in the life of Jesus himself. This dynamic and controversial movement is known as Liberation Theology.[12]

Through an abundance of remarkable spiritual adepts, honored as saints, the Catholic Church has made distinct and significant contributions to the entire world. Saints have amplified the message of the Bible through their interpretations, teachings, and, most importantly, the quality of their lives. The honorific title of "saint" is bestowed by the Catholic Church upon extraordinary Christians after death. The inward essence of Christianity is exemplified by the saints, many of whom have offered guidelines on how to lead a spiritual life. One example, out of many, can be found in the writings of the Spanish mystic St. John of the Cross

> **Through saints, the Catholic Church has made distinct and significant contributions to the entire world**

(1542–1591). In one of his lesser-known works, *The Sayings of Light and Love*, St. John of the Cross describes how to live a spiritual life through Christ:

> The further you withdraw from earthly things the closer you approach heavenly things and the more you find in God.
> Whoever knows how to die in all will have life in all.
> Abandon evil, do good, and seek peace [Ps. 34:14].
> Anyone who complains or grumbles is not perfect, nor even a good Christian.
> The humble are those who hide in their own nothingness and know how to abandon themselves to God.
> The meek are those who know how to suffer their neighbor and themselves.
> If you desire to be perfect, sell your will, give it to the poor in spirit, come to Christ in meekness and humility, and follow him to Calvary and sepulcher.
> Those who trust in themselves are worse than the devil.
> Those who do not love their neighbor abhor God.
> Anyone who does things lukewarmly is close to falling.
> Whoever flees prayer flees all that is good.
> Conquering the tongue is better than fasting on bread and water.
> Suffering for God is better than working miracles.
> Oh, what blessings we will enjoy in the vision of the Most Blessed Trinity!
> Do not be suspicious of your brother, for you will lose purity of heart.
> As for trials, the more the better.
> What does anyone know who doesn't know how to suffer for Christ?[13]

St. John of the Cross, along with St. Teresa of Avila (1567–1582), reformed the Carmelite order, one of the most influential and respected Catholic monastic orders. Other lofty spiritual figures of the Catholic tradition include St. Bernard of Clairvaux (1091–1153), Julian of Norwich (c.1342–after 1413), St. Nicholas of Cusa (1401–1464), and St. Francis of Sales (1567–1622).

THE EASTERN ORTHODOX CHURCH

The Eastern Orthodox Church is a grouping of self-governing but reciprocally accredited Christian churches that trace their lineage back to Jesus' disciples, especially Paul. The Church comprises some twenty Churches, including those established at the Council of Chalcedon in 451, such as Constantinople, Alexandria, Antioch, and Jerusalem, and later the Churches of the Eastern European countries and Russia. These Churches are among the oldest in Christendom, and include the National Church of Armenia, which was the first country to become an officially Christian state in 301. Additionally, the Eastern Orthodox Church is connected to Churches established in both Japan and China.

Despite its break with the Catholic Church, the Orthodox Church adheres to a similar set of tenets and rituals, although its rites have their own particular form. Significantly, the clergy of the Orthodox Church does not recognize the authority of the Catholic Pope, and its major dignitary is the patriarch of Constantinople. Unlike Catholic priests, Orthodox clergy are permitted to marry. There have been a number of attempts to achieve reconciliation between the Catholic and Orthodox churches, but none have been successful. Dialogue continues, however, and Pope John Paul II (1920–2005) had been keenly interested in improving relations between the two communities. In addition to the Eastern Orthodox tradition, an even older Oriental Orthodox Church exists. The Oriental Orthodox community consists of five independent Churches, including an Ethiopian Church.

> **Despite its break with the Catholic Church, the Orthodox Church adheres to a similar set of tenets and rituals**

THE PROTESTANT CHURCHES

The Lutheran Church

The Lutheran Church originated in the reformist activities of the German priest Martin Luther, some of whose ideas were presented earlier in the chapter. Luther's forceful opposition to the Catholic Church led to a movement known as Lutheranism, although he himself rejected use of that term. The Lutheran branch of Protestant activity gained its strongest support in northern Germany and northern Europe generally. In accord with

Luther's teachings, Lutherans emphasize study of biblical scripture and salvation through faith as the true path to redemption. Although retaining some Catholic rituals, the Lutherans modified important aspects of Catholic doctrine (see the discussion of the sacrament of communion below). Many eminent Christians of the Lutheran perspective emerged as powerful forces in the history and development of Christian thought. For example, a young Lutheran pastor, Dietrich Bonhoeffer (1906–1945), was instrumental in an underground movement which opposed the Nazi regime in Germany. He was imprisoned and executed by the Nazis shortly before the end of World War II. In his work *The Cost of Discipleship*, Bonhoeffer discussed the relationship between Christian suffering and discipleship:

> To endure the cross is not a tragedy; it is the suffering which is the fruit of an exclusive allegiance to Jesus Christ. When it comes, it is not an accident, but a necessity. It is not the sort of suffering which is inseparable from this mortal life, but the suffering which is an essential part of the specifically Christian life. It is not suffering per se but suffering-and-rejection, and not rejection for any cause or conviction of our own, but rejection for the sake of Christ. If our Christianity has ceased to be serious about discipleship, if we have watered down the gospel into emotional uplift which makes no costly demands and which fails to distinguish between natural and Christian existence, then we cannot help regarding the cross as an ordinary everyday calamity, as one of the trials and tribulations of life. We have forgotten that the cross means rejection and shame as well as suffering.[14]

As an erudite Christian thinker, Bonhoeffer addressed many issues pertinent to modern Christians, such as the rise of atheism. Other influential works by Bonhoeffer include *Ethics and Letters* and *Papers from Prison*. These works have become the impetus for progressive and socially engaged Christian movements.

Calvinism

In addition to Martin Luther, another prominent Protestant leader was the French religious scholar John Calvin (1509–1564). Originally a student of law and theology, Calvin had a spiritual awakening and dedicated himself to the cause of the Protestant Reformation. Applying the techniques of inquiry he learned as a scholar, Calvin worked to document and organize Protestant writings and thought. He was opposed to the power of the Pope and the Catholic hierarchy, and upheld a principle known as predestination, the belief that God grants special favor to those persons He knows will achieve salvation. Banished from various jurisdictions by both Catholic and Protestant authorities, Calvin eventually settled in Geneva, Switzerland, where he sought to establish a system of rule based on religious law. Calvinism had a profound influence on the Protestant movement throughout Europe. One of the main Protestant Churches founded on Calvinist beliefs is the Presbyterian Church. Like Lutherans, Presbyterians emphasize the importance of the Bible as a guide to salvation. Keith Ward, a contemporary Protestant theologian, writes:

> The church is for Protestants always the product of personal faith. Its teachings must always be subordinate to the Biblical revelation, and its practices must always be judged by whether or not they build up the fruits of the Spirit – of joy, patience, peace, faith, and hope (Galatians 5:22) – in the hearts of believers. This is clearly a very different picture of the church from the traditional Catholic picture of a priestly, authoritative, centralized, and sacramental institution, so much so that some people have regarded Catholicism and Protestantism as different religions.[15]

The Church of England

Christianity in Britain traces its origins to the early Celtic Christian community that emerged in the northern reaches of the Roman Empire. Under Roman influence, Christianity was brought to the British Isles in the fourth century. In the following century, however, invading pagan armies nearly eliminated the Christian presence in England. Sent on a mission to reestablish the Catholic Church in Britain, St. Augustine founded a Christian mission at the town of Canterbury in southern England in the year 597. From this base, Augustine supervised the reintroduction of Christianity throughout England and reestablished ties to central Church authorities in Rome. In the course of the following centuries, however, English monarchs periodically clashed with the Church hierarchy over the proper relationship between kingly authority and papal authority.

English monarchs clashed with the Church hierarchy over the proper relationship between kingly authority and papal authority

When the Protestant Reformation began challenging the Pope's supremacy in continental Europe, the powerful English king Henry VIII (r. 1509–1547) rallied to the defense of the Catholic Church. Henry, who was trained in theology, authored a discourse against the teachings of the Protestant reformer Martin Luther. In appreciation, Pope Leo X designated Henry as "Defender of the Faith." Later, however, Henry broke with the Pope and declared himself to be the head of an independent Church of England. Henry implemented a variety of anti-Catholic measures in his realm, including the confiscation of Catholic properties and the imprisonment and execution of prominent Catholic leaders.

Although Henry VIII established the institutional independence of the Anglican Church from the Catholic Church, the two branches continued to share many core beliefs and ceremonies. The religious leader of the Anglican Church is the archbishop of Canterbury. The archbishop is the senior cleric of the worldwide Anglican Church, but he does not hold the same formal authority that is enjoyed by the Pope within the Catholic Church. Reflecting its institutional origins, the British monarch is designated as the leader, or "Supreme Governor," of the Anglican Church. Perhaps the best-known contemporary figure in the Anglican Church is Desmond Tutu, the former archbishop of Cape Town in South Africa, who received the Nobel Peace Prize in 1984.

GLOBAL DIFFUSION OF CHRISTIANITY

Over the centuries, the Christians of Europe evolved into a highly diverse, and sometimes extremely contentious, community of believers. But even before European missionaries were active, the Christian Church spread far beyond the borders of Europe and the Holy Land, some of the oldest Christian Churches being those of Armenia, Ethiopia, Malabar (South India), and the Assyrian/Nestorian Church. These churches, and the Nestorians in particular, took Christianity to India, Central Asia, and as far as China, Korea, and possibly Japan long before the European missionaries reached there. By extending throughout the world, the Christian Church influenced, and was in turn influenced by, numerous non-European cultures. The process of cultural interaction is exemplified by the penetration of Christians into Africa. Both Catholic and Protestant missionaries actively sought converts among African populations. In some cases, European missionaries tried to reconcile Christian customs and traditional African spiritual practices. In addition, some African converts to Christianity founded independent Churches distinguished by their use of ancestral music, dance, and symbols in their rites. Thus, the modern successors to the first African Churches continue to express the message of the Christian Gospel within an African spiritual and cultural context. A similar process of intercultural blending has occurred in many other parts of the world. The Protestant and Catholic Churches of Europe and North America have been influenced by their geographic spread in another way that is likely to have profound significance: an increasing number of clergy are recruited from countries that are part of the non-European, non-North American developing world.

While the Catholic and Protestant Churches each have their historical roots in Europe, an additional Christian Church was founded much later in America – the Mormon

> Over the centuries, the Christians of Europe evolved into a highly diverse, and sometimes extremely contentious, community of believers

Statue of St. Peter at the Vatican in Rome, Italy

Church or the Church of Jesus Christ of Latter-Day Saints. According to the Mormons, in 1822 an angel revealed the location of certain gold tablets to Joseph Smith (1805–1844), founder of the Latter-Day Saints movement. In 1833 Smith published a translation of these tablets as the *Book of Mormon*. It states that lost tribes of Israel journeyed to America, whose last surviving individuals were Mormon and his son Moroni. The gold tablets uncovered by Smith were written by Mormon and buried near Palmyra, New York, by his son in the year 438. Among other unique doctrines, the book states that after his Resurrection Jesus was present in America.

BELIEFS

The earliest followers of Christ, who taught the Good News, did more than share Jesus' ethical or social teachings; instead, they were transformed by the spiritual presence of Christ. The divine virtues exhibited by Jesus during his lifetime, such as compassion, forgiveness, and humility, became amplified and universally available by way of the Resurrection. No longer restricted to a particular time and place, the Risen Christ is a universal presence active in the world through the Holy Spirit. The experience of the Holy Spirit is often described as a joyful, ever-present love that has the power to transform and regenerate a believer's consciousness beyond the limitations of material and self-centered concerns. In fact, the message of God's infinite compassion and love, and our need to partake in and share that love with others, is considered by many observers as the central message of Christ. In the Christian scriptures, St. Paul (1 Corinthians 13:4–7) provided the most comprehensive and universal definition of the divine love (translated as "charity") of the Risen Christ:

> Charity suffereth long, and is kind; charity envieth not; charity vaunteth not itself, is not puffed up, Doth not behave itself unseemly, seeketh not her own, is not easily provoked, thinketh no evil; Rejoiceth not in iniquity, but rejoiceth in the truth; Beareth all things, believeth all things, hopeth all things, endureth all things.

A central aspect of Jesus' teachings is the Kingdom of Heaven. This kingdom cannot be attained except through spirituality. It is, therefore, a metaphor for living a spiritual life. Such a life entails change from profane consciousness to perception of God's ever-present kingdom. Christians taught that salvation was possible for all people, regardless of their station in society – an inclusive perspective at odds with the elitism of many Greco-Roman religions. Christians interpreted Christ as universalizing the covenant(s) established between God and the Jewish prophets, making them available to all people regardless of race or ethnicity. Three distinctive tenets have distinguished Christianity from the other Abrahamic traditions (namely, the Jewish and Islamic faiths): the doctrines of Incarnation (the belief that Jesus was God incarnate), Atonement (the reconciliation of humanity to God through the sacrificial crucifixion of Jesus), and the Trinity (the belief that the Godhead manifests in three aspects: the Father, the Son, and the Holy Spirit).

The Sermon on the Mount, found in the Gospel of Matthew, contains the essence of Jesus' ethical teachings. These were not presented as unattainable ideals but as practical guidance for conducting a person's daily affairs according to spiritual principles. The Sermon on the Mount is among the most important and well-known passages of the Gospels. A key point made in this sermon is known as the Golden Rule: "Therefore all things whatsoever ye would that men should do to you, do ye even so to them: for this is the law and the prophets" (Matthew 7:12). The love Jesus advocated, which spread rapidly among his early followers, was a love that knew no bounds, for it was not limited by material considerations, social circumstances, or cultural traditions. Through an inner transformation of the self, this love became a practical reality upheld by believers.

> Jesus was also a reformer who spoke out against the corruption prevalent in his time

Jesus was not only a religious teacher, he was also a reformer who spoke out against the corruption prevalent in his time. He taught a radical scheme of values informed by a divine vision of reality. He stressed God's compassion, and extended this compassion through an inclusive love for all people, even sinners. In a set of verses known as the Beatitudes delivered in his Sermon on the Mount (Matthew 5:3–10), Jesus affirmed that God's blessings can be obtained by renouncing the material life and embracing the spiritual qualities of humility, meekness, kindness, and mercy:

Blessed are the poor in spirit: for theirs is the kingdom of heaven. Blessed are they that mourn: for they shall be comforted. Blessed are the meek: for they shall inherit the earth. Blessed are they which do hunger and thirst after righteousness: for they shall be filled. Blessed are the merciful: for they shall obtain mercy. Blessed are the pure in heart: for they shall see God. Blessed are the peacemakers: for they shall be called the children of God. Blessed are they which are persecuted for righteousness' sake: for theirs is the kingdom of heaven.

THE NATURE OF JESUS

Christians have always debated the central questions of Jesus' nature, mission, and relationship to God. The Nicene Creed (formulated in the year 325) represents the first authoritative summation of the essential beliefs of the Christian Church, including the station of Jesus. The section of the Creed that addresses the nature of Jesus reads in part:

> We believe in one Lord, Jesus Christ,
> the only Son of God,
> eternally begotten of the Father,
> God from God, Light from Light,
> true God from true God,
> begotten, not made, one in Being with the Father.
> Through him all things were made.
> For us men and for our salvation
> he came down from heaven:
> by the power of the Holy Spirit
> he was born of the Virgin Mary, and became man.[16]

In the Nicene Creed, Jesus is described as being united with God and fully identified with Him. At the same time, Jesus is also the Son of God, and his purpose in taking human form is to teach humanity, guide it, correct its errors, and sacrifice himself to redeem all of humanity. The Nicene Creed describes the nature of divinity as a Trinity consisting of God the Father, Jesus the Son, and the Holy Spirit. The elements of the Trinity are inseparable aspects of one divine reality, and each element can be understood only in the context of the

Jesus sacrificed himself in an act of atonement for humanity's sins

other two. Another aspect of faith addressed by the Creed is the relationship between humanity and God. Humanity is regarded as innately sinful, errant, and disobedient. All humanity has struggled through life weighted down by an oppressive burden of sin, causing harm and destruction. But by recognizing the sacrifice of Jesus and by accepting his teachings, humanity's sins are forgiven, and believers can attain eternal life. Jesus sacrificed himself in an act of atonement for humanity's sins. Through Jesus' sacrifice, humanity is able to enter the kingdom of heaven.

Like the earliest followers of Christ, modern Christians differ from one another in the way they interpret Jesus and his teachings. However, Christians generally are united in accepting the soteriological power of belief in Christ. Nevertheless, belief alone is often seen as insufficient for producing the transformation that would bring salvation. As Reverend Jim Wallis, an Evangelical social activist and founding member of the Sojourner Community, suggests:

> When someone is converted to Christ, he or she does not receive an automatic pass to celestial bliss but is called to take up a cross and follow in obedience the one who fed the hungry, healed the sick, was a friend to all manner of men and women, most identified with the poor, the oppressed, the weak, and broken, blessed the peacemakers, and was executed as a political criminal and subversive. This is the Christ of the New Testament. There is no other. Preaching another Christ, serving another Christ, worshipping another Christ, is paying homage to an idol who is the incarnation of humankind rather than the incarnation of God.[17]

To be sure, the interpretation of scripture greatly affects a believer's approach to Christian life, as well as attitudes toward other religions. Contemporary Christian theologians such as John Hick, Raimon Panikkar, W. C. Smith, Paul Knitter, and Hans Küng, to name but a few, have developed Christian theologies that are inclusive in nature. These approaches have paved the way for universalistic Christian perspectives, which are accommodating and respectful of other religions.

GOD

Christians believe that God is the sole creator of existence, and has authority, knowledge, and power that are transcendent. He is regarded as a personal God, meaning that He is not an inanimate force, but the living Father of each and every soul. According to the doctrine of the Trinity, God is One but is manifested in three ways: as the Father, the Son, and the Holy Spirit. Regarding the Christian view of God, the Greek Orthodox thinker Philip Sherrard offered the following insight:

> Its central message is that God, in manifesting Himself, becomes "other" than Himself and makes Himself His own symbol without any lapse from His essential reality in the process. It is this expression of the non-manifest in the manifest, of the absolute in the contingent, of eternity in time, of the One in the many, that overcomes dualistic conceptions of the relationship between God and the world. And this surpassing of such conceptions has its counterpart in the surpassing of the barrier between the esoteric and the exoteric.[18]

Many Christian mystics have attempted to grasp the reality of God through a philosophical approach known as apophatic theology or *via negativa*. This approach suggests that the way to God is by negation; in other words, one can only posit what God is not rather than what God is (since God is ultimately beyond human conception and language). This way of conceiving God entered early Christian thinking by way of the Neoplatonic tradition and the Jewish philosopher Philo. It was especially developed in a Christian context by St. Gregory of Nyssa (*c*.330–*c*.395) and Dionysius the Areopagite (*c*.500). St. Gregory of Nyssa observed:

> The simplicity of the True Faith assumes God to be that which He is, namely, incapable of being grasped by any term, or any idea, or any other device of our apprehension, remaining beyond the reach not only of the human but of the angelic and all supramundane intelligence, unthinkable, unutterable, above all expression in words, having but one name that can represent his proper nature, the single name being "Above Every Name."[19]

The Catholic philosopher St. Thomas Aquinas also approached an understanding of God through negation. Aquinas suggested: "The chief way to consider the divine essence is the way of negation, for by its immensity the divine essence transcends every form attained by our intellect … But by *knowing what it is not* we get some knowledge of it, and the more things we are able to deny of it, the nearer we come to knowing it."[20]

THE HOLY SPIRIT

Christians believe that the Holy Spirit originates in God. Jesus, the human manifestation of God, was miraculously born to Mary by the power of the Holy Spirit. Through the Holy Spirit, believers are empowered to follow the example of Jesus and to maintain a relationship with God. Many Christian mystics believe that through the power of the Holy Spirit, communion with God can be achieved. Meister Eckhart (*c*.1260–1327), a thirteenth-century Dominican theologian and perhaps the greatest of the many notable German mystics, declared in one of his sermons:

> You must know that this is in reality one and the same thing – to know God and to be known by God, to see God and to be seen by God. In knowing and seeing God we know and see that He makes us know and see. And just as the luminous air is not different from the fact of illuminating, for it illumines because it is luminous, so do we know by being known, and because He makes us know.[21]

It should be noted that many of Eckhart's teachings, along with those of other Christian mystics, were not always accepted by Church authorities. However, many spiritual figures that were silenced by Church authorities were later, after their deaths, recognized, honored, and even revered by the Church.

SCRIPTURE

Christians believe that the Gospels and the other books that comprise the New Testament are united with what they call the "Old Testament" (the Hebrew scriptures), and that both sets of scripture are sacred. Over the centuries, differences have arisen among Christians as to the nature of the Bible. Nowhere in the Bible does the text explicitly claim to be the infallible word of God. Some Christians, however, believe that the Bible is a direct, literal revelation. Other Christians hold that the Bible includes both inspired teachings as well as literary forms composed by human authors. Given the importance of the Bible for all Christians, it must be understood that not all Christians agree on what constitutes the "Old Testament" and the "New Testament." The Old Testament of the Roman Catholic Bible includes books that other Christians call the Apocrypha, or "Hidden Things." Protestant Bibles, notably the King James version, do not include the Apocrypha. With respect to the New Testament, the Roman Catholic and Protestant Bibles both contain twenty-seven books. The Syrian Church's Peshitta Bible, however, has twenty-two books, and the Ethiopian Church recognizes a New Testament with thirty-five. Both the Syrian and Ethiopian Churches trace their history to the fourth or fifth century of the Common Era.[22] (The discussion that follows addresses the version of the New Testament with twenty-seven books which is common to most Christian Churches.)

> **Nowhere in the Bible does the text explicitly claim to be the infallible word of God**

The Gospels are accounts of Jesus' life and teachings which are attributed to the saints Matthew, Mark, Luke, and John. It is uncertain, however, whether these saints were the actual authors of the texts credited to them, or if they are of unknown authorship. Authoritative names were later allotted to the Gospels by unidentified members of the early Church. The Gospel of St. John stands apart from the others in that it includes a deeper, possibly Gnostic-influenced discussion of the meaning of Jesus' life and teachings. John portrays Jesus as God's word (*logos*) – a transcendent, spiritual, and creative power that was made flesh.

The New Testament includes thirteen letters, or epistles, said to be written by St. Paul. Paul offers a vital interpretation of Jesus which laid the foundation of Christian theology. Paul's letters, however, rarely quote Jesus; this is probably so because Paul never heard Jesus speak, but came to know the Resurrected Jesus (or Jesus of the Spirit) through a visionary experience. Paul's perspective, especially his emphasis on salvation through faith, greatly influenced Christian thinkers such as St. Augustine, Martin Luther, and John Calvin. In addition to the writings of Paul, other epistles are attributed to James, Peter, John, and Jude.

The twenty-seventh book of the New Testament is called the book of Revelation. Thought to have been composed sometime around the year 90, Revelation is an apocalyptic text consisting of prophetic visions which describe battles between good and evil with the eventual victory of God. It is a poetic and complex text suffused with symbolic language. The numerical scheme embedded in the book of Revelation is quite complex; the number seven is a recurring theme, as in seven churches and seven seals. Making frequent references to the Hebrew scriptures, the author of Revelation was clearly steeped in previous apocalyptic writings. In general, Revelation heralds the return of Christ and the establishment of God's Kingdom on Earth. Because of the book's allusive and cryptic style, it has been reinterpreted periodically throughout history.

Because Jesus did not write any texts himself, his sayings and parables were preserved as an oral tradition. Jesus most likely preached in the Aramaic language; the New Testament Gospels, however, were written in Greek. Therefore, the original, non-translated words of Jesus are not known. According to scholars, the Gospels in the New Testament were written at different times from approximately forty to one hundred years after the events they describe. The Gospel of John was written last, sometime around the year 100. In fact, some scholars have concluded that all of the Gospels were written by people who had never actually met Jesus.

> **Because Jesus did not write any texts himself, his sayings and parables were preserved as an oral tradition**

The fact that the early Christian community did not immediately produce written texts is often attributed to their belief in an imminent return of Jesus. They felt no need to write anything down, but instead prepared themselves for the coming of the Kingdom of God. Scholars have suggested that the narrative Gospels of Mark, Matthew, and Luke–Acts (the Synoptic Gospels) were written in some kind of coordinated fashion. Specifically, it seems likely that Mark (which was written around the year 65) served as a source document for the authors of Matthew and Luke–Acts (both of which were written around the year 90). Given the overlapping portions of the texts, many experts infer that the authors of Matthew and Luke utilized the same source for Jesus' parables and aphorisms. Scholars have labeled this source "Q" (an abbreviation for the German word *Quelle*, meaning "source"). The existence of a source document like the proposed Q is only a theory.

The criteria used to validate the canonical scriptures that were included in the New Testament is somewhat vague. Thus, exactly why some gospels and epistles entered the collection of books known as the New Testament and why similar writings of the same period were excluded from it remains unclear. An ancient text, similar in structure to the proposed Q document, was unearthed near Nag Hammadi in the Upper Nile region of Egypt in 1945. It contains many sayings of Jesus, some of which differ from those found in the New Testament. Within this Gnostic corpus of writings, later labeled as the Nag Hammadi library, was the Coptic Gospel of Thomas. This gospel included aphorisms, parables, and pithy sayings of Jesus. Scholars have concluded that the Gospel of Thomas dates to around 60 to 70 C.E. Unlike the New Testament Gospels, this work does not provide details of the life of Jesus; instead, it is a collection of mostly mystical sayings. Two examples follow:

His disciples said to him, "When will the kingdom come?"

[Jesus said,] "It will not come by waiting for it. It will not be a matter of saying 'here it is' or 'there it is'. Rather, the kingdom of the father is spread out upon the earth, and men do not see it."[23]

When you come to know yourselves, then you will become known, and you will realize that it is you who are the sons of the living father. But if you will not know yourselves, you dwell in poverty and it is you who are that poverty.[24]

PRAYER

As noted, it is common for Christians to engage in solitary prayer as part of daily spiritual practice. Prayer is regarded as a form of direct communication with God. Prayer is also an act of spiritual renewal and strengthening of faith. A modern advocate of interreligious dialogue, the Trappist monk and prominent Catholic Thomas Merton (1915–1968), elucidated the significance of prayer as a universal technique of spiritual development. Merton wrote:

All religious traditions have ways of integrating the senses, on their own level, into higher forms of prayer. The greatest mystical literature speaks not only of "darkness" and "unknowing" but also, and almost in the same breath, of an extraordinary flowering of "spiritual senses" and aesthetic awareness underlying and interpreting the higher and more direct union with God "beyond experience."[25]

Prayer is one of the main methods Christians utilize to expand spiritual perception and move closer to God. One of the most important Christian prayers, which later became known as the Lord's Prayer, is attributed to Jesus himself (it is quoted at the opening of this chapter).

Although the Lord's Prayer is a way for believers to summon God's grace, Christians often address their prayers to Jesus. Furthermore, Catholics believe that Mary (the mother of Jesus), as well as the saints, respond to prayer by interceding on behalf of believers.

William Johnston, a contemporary Jesuit priest (a religious order within the Catholic Church), described the different ways that Christians approach Jesus through prayer:

> You can think about Jesus
> You can pray to Jesus
> You can pray through Jesus
> You can pray with Jesus
> You can imitate and follow Jesus
> You can allow Jesus to pray within you.[26]

Similarly, in the Orthodox tradition many techniques for spiritual development have been derived from the teachings of the Fathers and the saints of the early Church. These teachings are known as the *Philokalia* (meaning "love of what is beautiful"), a collection of discourses and texts written between the fourth and fifteenth centuries. The *Philokalia* was compiled in the eighteenth century by two Greek Monks, St. Nikodimos of the Holy Mountain of Athos (1749–1809) and St. Makarios of Corinth (1731–1803). In the nineteenth century a Russian pilgrim, carrying a copy of the Bible and a Russian translation of the *Philokalia*, endeavored to learn the spiritual practice of

It is common for Christians to engage in solitary prayer as part of daily spiritual practice

constant prayer. The pilgrim's journeys were recounted in the spiritual classic known as *The Way of a Pilgrim*. The foundational teaching of this book is based on a meditation called the Jesus Prayer: "Lord Jesus Christ, Son of God, have mercy on me."[27] This meditation, common among Orthodox monks of monasteries on Mount Athos, entails the constant repetition of the Jesus Prayer in combination with certain breathing techniques which are intended to open the heart to the Mystery of God.

MAJOR FESTIVALS

Despite denominational and cultural differentiation, most Christians celebrate a set of core observances that mark important episodes in the life of Jesus. Advent is a four-week period before Christmas during which Christians prepare to celebrate the birth of Jesus with prayer and special church services. It is also a time to reflect on the anticipated Second Coming of Christ. As part of Advent observances, Christians of different denominations may fast, light candles, or seek forgiveness of sin by performing acts of contrition.

Christmas, the second most important Christian holy day, celebrates the birth of Jesus and the incarnation of the divine in human form. As the celebration of the birth of Jesus,

Christmas has special importance to all Christians. Symbols mark the spiritual significance of the event; for example, gifts are exchanged in remembrance of God's gift of Jesus to redeem all peoples of their sins.

Lent is a forty-day term of fasting and repentance observed by the Eastern Orthodox and Roman Catholic churches, as well as by some Protestant denominations. The self-denial that Christians practice during Lent recalls the forty days Jesus spent alone in the wilderness. During Lent, Christians solemnly recall the sacrifices Jesus made for humanity and exert a special effort to do penance. The purpose of Lenten observances is to approach the standard of holiness and spirituality that was set by Jesus.

Easter, sometimes called the Feast of the Resurrection of Christ, or Pascha (from the Greek word "passover"), was the first and remains the most important Christian observance. Easter is an occasion for Christians to mark the Resurrection of Christ. Christians believe that with his Resurrection, Jesus rose from the dead and affirmed that his ministry was everlasting. The Feast of Ascension occurs forty days after Easter. Ascension celebrates Jesus' ascent to heaven to join his Father following his Resurrection. Christians interpret Jesus' Ascension as the end of his physical presence on the earth, but he is eternally present by the work of the Holy Spirit.

SACRAMENTS

According to the Catholic Church, the sacraments are rituals that help believers benefit from the grace of God. The actual form of these rituals has evolved over the course of the Catholic Church's history, but they are derived from the Bible. The Roman Catholic and Orthodox churches recognize and observe seven sacraments: Eucharist (mass, holy communion); penance (confession, reconciliation); ordination (holy orders); anointing of the sick (extreme unction); baptism; confirmation; and marriage. Most Protestant churches recognize only the sacraments of baptism and Eucharist as having been prescribed by Jesus. Paul Tillich, one of the most influential Protestant theologians of the twentieth century, writes:

> A sacrament is a visible, sensuous sign instituted by God as a medicament in which under the cover of a visible thing the power of God is hiddenly working. The basic ideas are: divine institution, visible sign, medicament (the medical symbol is very important), the hidden power of God under the cover of the sensuous reality. A sacrament is valid if it has a material substance, a form, that is, the words by which it is instituted, and the intention of the minister to do what the church intends to do.[28]

The Eucharist – a Greek word meaning "thanksgiving" – is the most important Christian ritual. The Eucharist celebration renews a believer's spiritual bond with Christ by recreating the Last Supper that Jesus shared with his disciples. More than a reenactment, the Eucharist becomes, in spiritual terms, the living reality of the Last Supper. Catholics believe that through a mystery of faith, also called "transubstantiation," the substance of the bread and wine used in the ritual is transformed into the substance of the flesh and blood of Christ, even while they retain their original appearance. Although Protestants do not accept transubstantiation, they regard the bread and wine as powerful symbols that embody spiritual realities.

New believers are inducted into Christian Churches by means of the sacrament of baptism (derived from the Greek word *baptein*, "to immerse"). Baptizing a believer can be carried out in different ways, such as total immersion in a river or lake, or by pouring a quantity of water on the initiate's head. The process of baptism represents the entry of a disciple into the Kingdom of God. Various Christian Churches prescribe different ages at which the baptism rite should be performed. Whenever possible, for example, the Catholic Church encourages infant baptism (converts, of course, can be baptized at any time in their life). In contrast, many Protestant denominations,

Catholics believe that the bread and wine is transformed into the flesh and blood of Christ

most notably the Baptist Church, practice adult baptism so that believers can consciously make a choice whether or not to enter the church in response to Jesus' call. Some Churches that practice infant baptism, such as the Catholic Church, also have a ceremony for adolescents called confirmation. During confirmation, a youth declares his or her commitment to the Church and its teachings.

Although the Catholic Church holds marriage to be a sacrament, in the Protestant community marriage signifies the relationship between Christ and the Church – notably, the Church is referred to as Christ's bride. For many Christians, marriage is symbolic of God's complete and unconditional love for humanity. It is difficult, however, to come to a conclusive understanding of the Christian view of divorce based on the scriptures. The writings attributed to Matthew (5:31) and Paul (1 Corinthians 7:10–15) permit divorce in certain circumstances (in the case of adultery), but in the writings attributed to Mark (10, 11, 12) divorce is forbidden. As a result of these differences, various Churches hold differing positions on the permissibility of divorce.

AFTERLIFE AND FUNERAL RITES

For Christians, the physical life of earthly existence is merely a prelude to the eternal life that follows in the hereafter. In the Resurrection and Ascension of Jesus, Christians find evidence that the human soul is eternal. Christians believe that each individual soul is judged according to the kind of life lived on the material plane; those who followed the path of Jesus, forgiving others and doing good works, are granted entry into the heavenly Kingdom of God. The souls of evildoers, in contrast, are cast into Hell. In a third category are those souls who enter what is called purgatory, an in-between state wherein the soul is cleansed before entry into heaven is permitted. There are, however, diverse interpretations of Hell amongst Christians, and different views on the necessary conditions for entering Heaven. The Christian mystic Emmanuel Swedenborg (1688–1722) was a renowned Swedish scientist who developed a remarkable visionary faculty and influenced many people, such as the English poet William Blake (1757–1827). Swedenborg concluded:

> **There are diverse interpretations of Hell amongst Christians, and different views on the necessary conditions for entering Heaven**

> People who know what makes heaven can know that Gentiles are saved just as Christians are. For heaven is within us, and we enter heaven if we have heaven within us. Heaven in us is to acknowledge the Divine and to be led by the Divine … It is recognized that Gentiles lead just as moral lives as Christians do many of them, more moral lives … Anyone who lives a moral life for the sake of the Divine is being led by the Divine.[29]

CALENDAR

In Christian practice, years are numbered in relation to the birth of Jesus. Until recently, any year from the period before the birth of Jesus was identified as B.C. (Before Christ), and any year after his birth was A.D. (Anno Domini, or "the year of the Lord" in Latin) With the secularization of Western society, modern sensibilities have discouraged such overtly religious references. According to modern convention, years from before the birth of Jesus are referred to as B.C.E. (Before the Common Era), while years since the birth of Jesus are C.E. (Common Era). Because Christianity arose during the ascendancy of the Roman Empire, Christian communities, and later the Catholic Church, followed the Julian calendar, which was originally designed by the Roman general and statesman Julius Caesar in 46 B.C.E. Although the Julian calendar is based on a solar system, the astronomical calculations that went into its formation were not sufficiently accurate to prevent the gradual loss of synchronization with the sun's movements and the seasons. Even with a leap year of 366 days, the definition of 365-and-a-quarter days led to the loss of ten days by the year 1582 C.E. In that year, Pope Gregory XIII issued a revised system of reckoning dates that eventually became known in his honor as the Gregorian calendar. While most Christians use the Gregorian calendar, many Orthodox churches still use the Julian calendar, or a revised Julian calendar.

CHAPTER SUMMARY

Christian worship has evolved over time, and has become one of the most diverse and widespread (as well as numerically the largest) of the world religions. As a tradition that emerged from within the context of the Jewish faith, Christianity interprets the historical figure of Jesus as the promised Messiah. Jesus lived during the reign of Herod the Great, probably between 6 or 7 B.C.E. and 36 C.E., in the region of modern-day Palestine (consisting then of Galilee and Judea). After his baptism by John the Baptist, a Jewish prophetic figure who was beheaded by King Herod, Jesus began his short career of public ministry. As a charismatic teacher and healer, he attracted large crowds of people, and some became his disciples. Jesus proclaimed not only the presence of God's Kingdom in the world but also its future coming. He spoke out against religious and social corruption. As a teacher of selfless compassion, he extended love to everyone regardless of social barriers. He welcomed into his fold marginalized people, including women, the sick, prostitutes, and the poor.

In Jerusalem, Jesus spoke out against the Temple authorities, and was executed by order of the Roman procurator Pontius Pilate. Jesus' followers said that he reappeared after his death; and in responding to the Resurrection, his disciples arose reinvigorated to preach the Good News. The Resurrection confirmed for believers the divine nature of Jesus. For Christians, the Risen Christ transcended time and place as a universal presence through whom the love of God could flow to all people. Indeed, for Christians, God is love (1 John 4:8). Christians believe that all people can be transformed by divine love, and hence they can transcend egoistic desires and selfish aspirations. The Christian Church saw Jesus as a divine savior, the Son of God who sacrificed himself to insure the redemption of all humanity. The doctrine of the Trinity is central to most Christian theologies, teaching that God, essentially one, is manifestly three aspects: the Father, the Son, and the Holy Spirit. Christ is the incarnation of the Infinite in the finite and the ultimate exemplar of divine virtues such as love, forgiveness, and humility. Although many interpretations and forms of Christianity exist, Jesus remains of central importance to them all.

Although many interpretations and forms of Christianity exist, Jesus remains of central importance to them all

Illustrated pages from a 300-year-old Turkish Qur'an

CHAPTER 14
THE FAITH OF ISLAM

Al-Fatihah

In the Name of Allah, the Compassionate, the
  Merciful

Praise be to Allah, the Lord of the Worlds,

The Compassionate, the Merciful,

Master of the Day of Judgement,

Only You do we worship, and only You do we
  implore for help.

Lead us to the right path,

The path of those You have favoured

Not those who have incurred Your wrath or have
  gone astray.

— Qur'an 1:1–7[1]

INTRODUCTION

Islam is the religion founded by the Prophet Muhammad
(also written as Mohammad). The word "Islam" means
"submission to the will of
God," and the word "Muslim"
means "one who has submitted
oneself to the will of God."
Individuals enter the Islamic
faith by reciting the *shahadah*,
a declaration of belief: "There
is no god but God and
Muhammad is His Messenger."
The Arabic word for God,
Allah, is the preferred term used
throughout the Muslim community. Some Western writers have incorrectly called followers of Islam
"Muhammadans." This term is misleading, for it implies
that the believer worships Muhammad, whereas Muslims
regard Muhammad as God's servant (*'abd*) and messenger
(*rasul*), and worship only the one God.

> **Not one of you is
> a believer until
> he desires for his
> brother that
> which he desires
> for himself**
> *Forty Hadith of
> an-Nawawi 13*
> **THE GOLDEN RULE**

Timeline

570 C.E.
Muhammad born

610 C.E.
First declared revelation
  received by
  Muhammad

622 C.E.
The Hijra. Muslims
  migrate to Medina.
  Islamic calendar begins

630 C.E.
Muhammad leads conquest
  of Mecca

632 C.E.
Death of Muhammad

632–634 C.E.
Abu Bakr succeeds the
  Prophet as first caliph
  of Islam

634–644 C.E.
'Umar, second caliph

644–656 C.E.
'Uthman, third caliph,
  under whom the
  authorized version of
  the Holy Qur'an was
  compiled

656–661 C.E.
'Ali, fourth and last of
  Orthodox caliphate

657 C.E.
Battle at Siffin

661 C.E.
'Ali assassinated

661–750 C.E.
Umayyad dynasty

Many countries of the Middle East are Muslim, a reality consistent with the fact that the religion was founded in Arabia, the heart of the region. Westerners often mistakenly believe that all Arabs are Muslim and that all Muslims are Arab. The peoples of the Middle East, however, are not all Arabs; they include numerous ethnic groups, many of whom speak languages other than Arabic and follow religions other than Islam. Second, the faith of Islam is not limited to the Middle East. Rather, it has continued to spread since its earliest years beyond the region into Africa, and then to the Mediterranean lands, Central Asia, the Indian subcontinent, Europe, China, Indonesia, the Philippines, and now to the Americas. Simply put, "Arab" refers to a culture and ethnicity, while "Muslim" refers to a religion.

HISTORY

The Prophet Muhammad

Muhammad was born in Mecca, Arabia, in the year 570 C.E. His parents died when he was a small child, and at first he was adopted and raised by his grandfather, Abdul Muttalib. When his grandfather died soon thereafter, he was adopted by his uncle, Abu Talib. Abu Talib had children of his own and, although he was not wealthy, he nevertheless welcomed Muhammad into his family. Already in his youth Muhammad's personality was distinguished by unusual spiritual qualities, deep compassion for the elderly and the sick, gentleness, kindness, piety, and humility. These exceptional qualities earned him recognition by his peers as he grew to young adulthood. Muhammad demonstrated such trustworthiness that he became known by the name al-Amin, meaning "the Trustworthy" or "the Truthful."

Muhammad's life revolved around household tasks and his duties as a member of his uncle's merchant caravan that traveled between the city of Mecca and Syria. At some point in his early twenties, his outstanding character and his good work on the caravan came to the attention of a

680 C.E.
Martyrdom of Husayn, 'Ali's son, at battle of Karbala
711–718 C.E.
Muslim armies conquer Spain and Portugal
732 C.E.
Battle of Tours (or Poitiers)
750–1258 C.E.
Abbasid dynasty
922 C.E.
Execution of Sufi mystic Mansur al-Hallaj in Baghdad
c.980–1037 C.E.
Ibn Sina (Avicenna in Latin)
1126–1198 C.E.
Ibn Rushd (Averroes in Latin)
1058–1111 C.E.
Abu Hamid al-Ghazali
1165–1240 C.E.
Muhyi-al-Din ibn-al-'Arabi
1095–1291 C.E. The Crusades
1191 C.E.
Execution of Sufi mystic Suhrawardi in Aleppo
c.1207–1273 C.E.
Jalaluddin Rumi
1220 C.E.
Mongol invasion of Central Asia begins
1290–1924 C.E.
Ottoman caliphate

wealthy, middle-aged widow of Mecca named Khadijah. She employed Muhammad as a trading agent. Muhammad increased Khadijah's profits year after year, and performed his duties with great skill and integrity. Muhammad and Khadijah married when he was twenty-five and she was forty. Khadijah had been twice widowed and already had children, but these unconventional circumstances did not influence the marriage, which proved joyful and fulfilling. Muhammad and Khadijah had a number of children together; although the sons died in infancy, the daughters reached maturity and married. The only descendants of Muhammad to survive were the children of his daughter Fatimah, who was married to Muhammad's cousin 'Ali ibn Abi Talib (subsequently referred to as 'Ali). Fatimah's sons, Hasan and Husayn, are the forefathers of all the descendants of Muhammad.

Muhammad's spiritual nature continued to develop as he grew older. He eventually reached a point where his soul became restless and dissatisfied with human society and material concerns, and in order to regain some sense of harmony in his life he periodically withdrew to the desert outside Mecca. He retreated to a cave, known as Hira, and devoted himself, day and night, to meditation, fasting, and spiritual communion to purify his heart. During one of these retreats, when Muhammad was forty years old, he suddenly found himself surrounded by a brilliant light. In the midst of that light a mystic figure, the archangel Gabriel, appeared before him and gave him the following command: "Iqra," meaning "recite" or "read." Muhammad, who had never received any formal education and was illiterate, fearfully replied that he could not obey the command. The archangel continued (Q 96:1–5):

> Read, in the Name of your Lord, Who created:
> He created man from a clot.
> Read, by your Most Generous Lord,
> Who taught by the pen.
> He taught man what he did not know.

Muhammad obeyed, reciting the words he had heard, whereon the angel disappeared. Muhammad had received the divine call from God, and felt burdened by so weighty a mission. This event is known as *laylat al-qadr*, meaning "the Night of Power"; it was the first of many revelations from God to Muhammad. He returned to Mecca and informed Khadijah of what had transpired and of his trepidation about the event.

Despite his fears, Muhammad began to preach in public about the oneness of God. He called on people to cease worshiping idols and to worship only the one God. The first person who believed in the new faith was his wife, Khadijah. Gradually, his followers grew in number, and as they multiplied they faced increasing opposition and persecution. By 622, the community of Muslims was forced to leave Mecca by the established powers in that city, and they fled for safety to the city of Medina. Far from being ruined, the young Muslim community was strengthened far beyond its original state because the citizens of Medina welcomed and embraced the faith of Islam. The flight to Medina, known as the *hijrah* (Hegira in English), was a turning point in the fortunes of the infant religion; for this reason the Muslim calendar dates from the year 622, and Muslim years are designated A.H., meaning *Anno Hegira*.

Over the next ten years, Muhammad's stature and following steadily grew. When the Muslims first arrived in Medina most of them were homeless and poor, having been forced to leave behind almost all their possessions in Mecca. But the Medinans gave the Muslims warm hospitality and sheltered them in their own homes. The central concern of Muhammad was not the material wealth of Muslims but their faith in God. Gradually, he organized the Muslim community by creating institutions to serve its spiritual and social needs. In Medina, Muhammad established the first mosque, or Islamic house of worship, and prescribed that prayers should be recited at regular times during the day. He created a constitution that remains the foundation of Muslim civilization; it specifies individual responsibilities and safeguards the rights of all members of the community without discrimination based on race, sex, class, or tribe. Non–Muslims are to be treated with respect. For Muhammad, all people were the servants of God and as such deserved equal treatment. Eventually, all the Arab tribes were united under Muhammad's spiritual and political leadership.

> **Cleansed of materialism, corruption, and idol-worship, Mecca was designated by Muhammad as the holiest city in Islam**

Aware that the new religion was winning converts and consolidating its position, the Meccans conducted raids against Medina that increasingly turned into full-scale battles. The Meccans also attacked families residing in their city who had Muslim relatives in Medina and seized their possessions. These conflicts escalated until Muhammad led an army of ten thousand warriors against Mecca in 630 (8 A.H.). As soon as Muhammad appeared before Mecca with his army, the Meccans surrendered. A triumphant Muhammad destroyed the idols but, consistent with his character, he treated the Meccans with compassion and forgiveness. As a result, almost all of the Meccans converted to Islam and gave their allegiance to Muhammad. Cleansed of materialism, corruption, and idol-worship, Mecca was designated by Muhammad as the holiest city in Islam and a place of pilgrimage.

Following the conquest of Mecca and its conversion to Islam, Muhammad returned to Medina in 630. Realizing that his earthly life was coming to an end, he returned once again to Mecca on pilgrimage in 632. A large number of Muhammad's followers accompanied him. During the course of his pilgrimage, Muhammad preached a sermon to the inhabitants of Mecca, calling on them to submit to the one true God, to obey the ordinances of the Qur'an (the recorded revelation received by Muhammad), and to live together in peace. After his return to Medina, Muhammad continued teaching the word of God, but before long he fell ill and died. For all Muslims, Muhammad, God's servant and messenger, is the most important figure in history.

Islam after the Prophet

Following the death of Muhammad, a series of four prominent believers, and close companions of the Prophet, served as his successors; these successors were called *khalifah* (in English, caliph). These caliphs were Abu Bakr al-Siddiq, 'Umar ibn al-Khattab, 'Uthman ibn 'Affan, and 'Ali ibn Abi Talib. In the early period of Abu Bakr's caliphate (r. 632–634), certain Arab tribes, which had been united by Muhammad, sought to regain independence in the aftermath of the Prophet's passing. These rebellious tribes were particularly discontented by the Islamic system of taxation. Abu Bakr, through military conquest, subdued the rebel tribes and preserved the federation established by Muhammad. He also expanded the domain of the Islamic state to eastern Arabia. Abu Bakr was succeeded by 'Umar (r. 634–644), who is often regarded as the architect of the Islamic Empire. 'Umar formed an elite military to facilitate expansion and conquest. Under 'Umar's direction, the Islamic conquests reaped financial benefit by establishing garrisons and imposing taxes. Jews and Christians were the "Peoples of the Book" who enjoyed protected status. Muhammad had taught that Jews and Christians were followers of older written revelations, and they were thus regarded as "People of the Book," who enjoyed protected status under Islamic law.

During 'Umar's caliphate the Islamic state launched successful military campaigns that spread the rule of the caliph to Damascus, Egypt, and Persia. After 'Umar's assassination in 644, 'Uthman (r. 644–656) became caliph, and continued 'Umar's policy of military expansion. An important event in Islamic history, propagated under the direction of 'Uthman, was the creation of an authoritative version of the Qur'an. The formation of this text, and the subsequent destruction of all Qur'anic traditions that were not deemed authentic, created uniformity and made the Qur'an available to everyone. 'Uthman, however, came under criticism for nepotism in economic policies and for failing to follow the Prophet's example; he was murdered while reading the Qur'an in 655. 'Uthman's successor, 'Ali, was the son of the Prophet's uncle Abu Talib and the husband of the Prophet's youngest daughter, Fatimah.

'Ali had been well respected by the Prophet, and was renowned throughout the Islamic world for his piety and knowledge of the Qur'an. His lectures, sermons, and letters were important Islamic writings of the period, and were preserved in the *Nahjul Balagha* ("Peak of Eloquence"). By the time 'Ali ascended to the caliphate, Muslim communities were engulfed in dissension; various groups vied for power over the rapidly expanding empire. One such group was an alliance of Meccan elites, which was defeated by 'Ali. A more serious threat arose when the politically astute governor of Syria, Mu'awiyah, challenged 'Ali. Mu'awiyah had been appointed to the governorship of Syria by 'Umar, the second caliph. Mu'awiyah demanded that 'Ali produce the murderers of 'Uthman or be counted as an accomplice. In fact, Mu'awiyah was positioning himself to become caliph. In the famous battle at Siffin (657), Mu'awiyah's Syrian army placed copies of the Qur'an on top of their swords and requested a resolution of the dispute through arbitration. 'Ali accepted, but the mediation ultimately favored Mu'awiyah. A faction of 'Ali's followers, who were opposed to and angered by the arbitration, broke with 'Ali and became known as Kharijites (seceders). In 661, a Kharijite murdered 'Ali while he was in a mosque in Kufa (present-day Iraq). 'Ali was subsequently buried in Najaf (present-day Iraq), where his tomb is the site of a major shrine.

After the death of 'Ali, Mu'awiyah established the Umayyad dynasty, and became its first caliph. Those Muslims who gave their allegiance to the first four caliphs and the Umayyad dynasty (661–750), and its successor, the Abbasid dynasty (750–1258), became known as Sunni Muslims (derived from the word *sunnah*, meaning "the way of the Prophet"). A significant minority of Muslims, however, believed that the rightful caliphal lineage was through 'Ali (the cousin and son-in-law of the Prophet). They considered Hasan and Husayn, the sons of 'Ali and the only descendants of Muhammad, to be the rightful successors. Husayn refused to give his allegiance to the second caliph of the Umayyad dynasty, Yazid I, whom he viewed as unqualified for the station of *khalifa*. Husayn was killed, along with other members of the Prophet's family, in a battle at Karbala (a holy city in present-day Iraq) in 680 (61 A.H.). Thereafter, the followers of 'Ali's family disassociated themselves from the Sunnis and eventually became known as Shi'is. Shi'is grew apart from Sunnis, not only on the question of caliphate succession, but also with regard to important doctrinal and practical aspects of Islam. The Kharijites, the faction that broke from 'Ali due to his decision to accept arbitration in his dispute with Mu'awiyah, rejected the legitimacy of both 'Ali and Mu'awiyah (and thus the legitimacy of both the Shi'i and Sunni branches). The Kharijites are known as Ibadis today and persist in small numbers, representing the third branch of Islam, in addition to the Sunni and Shi'i.

The Shi'i branch of Islam, the second largest in terms of adherents, considers the Sunni caliphate to be a tyranny which attempted to block the proper succession of Imams through the lineage of the Prophet Muhammad. The Shi'is believe that Imams, like the *khalifa*, are divinely ordained leaders who possess secret knowledge based on a lineage of succession, or chain of transmission, which is traced back to the Prophet himself. Imams, therefore, are capable of directing the destiny of human civilization through divine guidance. Shi'is believe that the first Imam was 'Ali, followed by his two sons Hasan and Husayn. According to the majority Shi'i perspective – the Ithna 'Ashariyyah (or Twelvers) – the twelfth Imam, Muhammad al-Mahdi (b. 868), disappeared as a child. It is believed, however, that this Imam, subsequently called the Hidden Imam (also known as the Mahdi or Qa'im) went into spiritual occultation (*ghaybah*), and will one day return as an eschatological savior. From this perspective, the title Imam refers to one of the twelve hereditary successors of the Prophet Muhammad from 'Ali to Muhammad al-Mahdi. There are, however, other Shi'i perspectives which differ from the majority view (i.e. that of the Ithna 'Ashariyyah) on issues of Imam succession. These other groups include the Zaydis (or Fivers) and Isma'ilis (or Seveners) – who spawned the Druzes. These groups, which consist of a relatively small number of adherents, have developed a variety of important esoteric doctrines and practices.

After the period of the first four caliphs and the confusion that followed the death of 'Ali, the Islamic Empire was expanded by the Umayyad dynasty. The empire, with its capital city in Damascus, included, at its peak, a wide expanse from North Africa and Spain to Central Asia and India. In fact, the Umayyad Empire nearly conquered Europe, but they were defeated at the battle of Tours or Poitiers (732 C.E.) in modern-day France by a Frankish army. The battle is regarded by Muslims as a *balat al-shuhada'* (pavement of martyrs). Shortly thereafter, the Umayyad dynasty was unseated from within and a new dynasty, the Abbasids, took power. Under the Abbasid dynasty the artistic and intellectual achievements of the Muslim world attained unprecedented heights. Muslim authorities, as patrons of the arts, founded the first modern institutions of higher education in Baghdad, Cairo, and Cordoba, each attracting distinguished scholars from foreign lands. The capital city, Baghdad, became a flourishing city in which aesthetic, scientific, and philosophical Islamic endeavors attained unparalleled achievements. For example, Muslim physicians developed techniques that far advanced the medical field, and Muslim scientists built the first telescope.

Islamic learning greatly benefited from both Greek philosophy and Indian wisdom. The Arabic language, consecrated by Islam as the tongue of revelation, had become one of the principal languages of learning. Its precision made it an ideal instrument for assimilating and transmitting the accumulated knowledge of a wide variety of cultures. In fact, Muslims preserved the works of the ancient Greek philosophers, such as Plato and Aristotle, which were later reintroduced to European Christendom during the Renaissance through Arabic translations.[2] Some of the most important Muslim thinkers of this period include al-Kindi (d. *c.*873) and al-Farabi (d. 950). Notably, the erudite works of such philosophers as Ibn Sina, or Avicenna in Latin (d. 1037), and Ibn Rushd, or Averroes in Latin (d. 1198), exercised a lasting influence in the realm of learning, being of especial importance in the medieval debates between the Muslim, Jewish, and Christian traditions.

Islamic learning greatly benefited from both Greek philosophy and Indian wisdom

Challenges to Islam and the Fall of the Abbasid Dynasty

A series of wars (1095–1291), called the Crusades by Christian Europe, engulfed Islam and Christianity in a conflict that left many misunderstandings between the two religions. They did, however, open the way for a pivotal exchange of ideas between the Islamic and Christian civilizations. The Crusades also bore witness, in 1192, to a historic act of peace-making – the epic and humane truce concluded between the two great and legendary figures Salah al-Din, or Saladin, and Richard I of England (Richard Coeur de Lion, or Richard the Lionheart).

Another serious challenge to Islamic civilization was posed by the Mongol invasion of Central Asia and Asia Minor, which began around 1220. The Mongols ended the reign of the last Abbasid caliph and destroyed many of the smaller realms that had emerged during the Abbasid caliphate as a result of internal strife. Among the regimes overrun and brutally conquered by the Mongols was the Saljuq Empire of Persia, which had been home to a vibrant Sufi presence and a Persian cultural revival that had flourished once set free from Arab (i.e. Abbasid) dominance. In addition to Persia, the Mongols conquered Central Asia, Iraq, and Palestine, ravaging the eastern lands of the Islamic world. Eventually, Mongol dominion stretched as far as the northwest regions of India, where it continued for several hundred years. In the wake of the Mongol conquests, the map of the Islamic world was redrawn and new dynasties emerged. In Persia, for example, various kingdoms were established; later, in the sixteenth century, the Safavids of Persia established a Shi'i dynasty that transformed Persia (present-day Iran) into a major power. However, it was the Ottoman dynasty of Asia Minor that became the most powerful modern Islamic empire. In fact, Ottoman rule reached as far as central Europe. The Ottoman Empire lasted for many centuries, finally disintegrating in the aftermath of World War I.

From its origin in Arabia, Islam spread to lands such as India, Pakistan, China, Afghanistan, Malaysia, and Indonesia (where Muslims constitute the majority of the population). To the west, it reached as far as Spain and even southern France, as well as the Balkans and the Danube regions of Eastern Europe. Proclaimed by a number of charismatic figures, the faith was embraced in many areas of Africa, where a variety of Islamic kingdoms were established. Today, Islam is practiced throughout the world, including in the United States and Europe.

THE DIVINE LAW (*AL-SHARI'AH*)

The Islamic faith is rooted in a divine law, referred to as the *shari'ah* (the literal meaning of which is "the broad" or "the wide path," generally referred to as the Sacred Law of

Holy Ka'bah, Mecca

Islam). This law orders, organizes, and orients the life of all Muslims. Apart from Shi'i and Ibadi interpretations, there are four Sunni schools of *shari'ah*: Hanafite, Hanbalite, Malikite, and Shafi'ite. In addition to the primary source, the Qur'an, interpretation of *shari'ah* relies on *hadith* (the sayings of the Prophet), *ijma'* (consensus of the learned of the Islamic community, or *'ulama*), and *qiyas* (philosophical reasoning through analogy). These sources are not given equal weight by the different schools of interpretation. *Ijma'* and *qiyas*, in particular, are not universally accepted. Each school emphasizes aspects of interpretation; local social conditions and customs also play a role. The interpretative schools still coexist, and no single, uniform approach has emerged. The Prophet Muhammad himself concluded: "Difference of opinion in my community is a sign of Divine mercy."[3]

> **The Prophet Muhammad himself concluded: "Difference of opinion in my community is a sign of Divine mercy"**

ISLAMIC SCRIPTURE

The Qur'an

Muslims believe that the Qur'an is the word of God, revealed through the archangel Gabriel to Muhammad. Muhammad heard the revelations and recited them to his companions. During the reign of the third caliph, 'Uthman, the various verses spoken by Muhammad were collected, authenticated, and put into book form in the Qur'an. Muslims believe that the Qur'an is significantly different from the Bible because it is considered to be the direct word of God collected and preserved as a single book. From this perspective, the Qur'an is not subject to the errors stemming from an oral tradition, human authors, or the process of translation. Muslims believe that the Qur'an can never be translated adequately because its Arabic is not only the highest form of the language, but it is also the direct word of God. Thus, the sanctity of the Qur'anic text is necessarily lost when it is translated into another language by the agency of the human mind. The Qur'an is always recited in the original Arabic, the language in which it was revealed; translations are designated as mere "interpretations." The Qur'an is divided into 114 *surahs*, or chapters. The first *surah*, the *Fatihah* (quoted at the opening of this chapter), is often regarded as the essential message of the Qur'an, and is recited at least five times a day. It is important to note that the Qur'an consists of revelations received and recited by Muhammad over a twenty-two-year period (610–632), some of which are best understood in the context of the time and place of revelation. Qur'anic chapters are not organized chronologically or thematically; instead, they are organized by chapter length (with, in general, the longest chapters at the beginning and the shortest at the end). Many scholars distinguish between the revelations given to Muhammad during the Meccan period and those received later, in Medina. According to traditional accounts, such as that given by Hisham ibn 'Urwa (d. *c.*763), the Meccan Revelations are concerned with past events, and describe the relationship between God and humanity. In contrast, the Medinan Revelations focus on the public and private ethics necessary for community building. In general, most versions of the Qur'an include introductory and reference information indicating when each *surah* was revealed.

The Qur'an is not regarded as a static record of the past, but as a book whose value and truth continually unfold and serve as a link between humanity and God. Muslims regard the Qur'an as a miracle (*mu'jizah*), a divine disclosure which provides the way for understanding the will of God and His purpose for humanity. The Qur'an is very clear that believers must choose their religious faith based on personal religious motives; faith can never be imposed by force: "There is no compulsion in religion; true guidance has become distinct from error. Thus he who disbelieves in the Devil and believes in Allah grasps the firmest handle that will never break. Allah is the All-hearing, All-knowing" (Q 2:256).

> **In short, the Qur'an is a rich treasure of detailed instructions from God**

Traditionally, embracing Islam as a faith has consisted of accepting that there is only one true God and that Muhammad was His Messenger. Islam, however, like all religions, is more than a creed – it is a way of life. The Qur'an, for example, offers a clear definition of what constitutes a "righteous" person (Q 2:177):

> Righteousness is not to turn your faces towards the East and the West; the righteous is he who believes in Allah, the Last Day, the angels, the Book and the Prophets; who gives of his money, in spite of loving it, to the near of kin, the orphans, the needy, the wayfarers and the beggars, and for the freeing of slaves; who performs the prayers and pays the alms-tax. Such are also those who keep their pledges once they have made them, and endure patiently privation, affliction and in times of fighting. Those are the truthful and the God-fearing.

In short, the Qur'an is a rich treasure of detailed instructions from God. These instructions form the core beliefs of Islam. Guidance is found throughout the text; therefore, each reader must make a complete and careful study of the Qur'an. A set of commandments similar to the Ten Commandments received by the Prophet Moses can be found in the Qur'an (Q 17:22–32):

Do not set up another god with Allah, lest you be despised and forsaken. Your Lord has decreed that you worship none but Him and to be kind to your parents. If either of them or both reach old age with you, do not say to them "Fie," nor tell them off, but say to them kind words. And lower to them the wing of humility out of mercy and say: "Lord, have mercy on them, as they took care of me when I was a child." Your Lord knows best what is in your hearts. If you are righteous, He is All-Forgiving to those who repent. And give the kinsman his due, and to the destitute and the wayfarer, and do not squander your wealth wastefully. Surely the spendthrifts are the brothers of the devils; and the Devil is ever ungrateful to his Lord. But if you turn away from them, seeking a mercy you expect from your Lord, then speak to them kindly. Do not keep your hand chained to your neck, nor spread it out fully, lest you sit around condemned and reduced to poverty. Surely your Lord gives generously to whom He pleases, and He gives sparingly [to whom He pleases]. He knows and observes His servants well. Do not kill your children for fear of poverty. We will provide for you and for them. To kill them is a great sin. Do not draw near adultery; it is an abomination and an evil way.

Hadith

The Qur'an, as the Word of God, is the most sacred text of Islam. The recorded sayings and actions of Muhammad, called *hadith* (traditions), are also regarded as sacred sources of spiritual guidance. Like all oral traditions, the *hadith* are subject to disputes over their authenticity. Such debates led classical Islamic scholars to assemble authentic sayings of the Prophet. The Islamic scholar Muhammad ibn Isma'il al-Bukhari (d. 870), for example, researched, classified, and selected *hadith* from across the Islamic world. Other scholars contemporary to al-Bukhari produced similar collections of the Prophet's sayings. These books, including al-Bukhari's, are often referred to as the Six Correct Books. These six collections are canonical sources of *hadith* for Sunni Muslims. The Shi'is, however, use different collections of *hadith*, although there are significant similarities in Shi'i and Sunni traditions. One distinction is that Shi'is regard the sayings of the Imams as a type of *hadith* which provide authoritative explication of the Prophet's teachings. In general, the Sufis, or mystics of Islam, give the sayings of the Prophet, referred to as *hadith qudsi* ("sacred sayings"), a similar station to those in the Qur'an since, they believe, God is talking through Muhammad in both situations.

RELIGIOUS BELIEFS AND PRACTICES

God

The most important of Muhammad's teachings is that there is only one God, and that God alone should be worshiped. Muhammad undertook his mission in a culture where the people worshiped a vast array of idols. Pre-Islamic Arabs had no concept of monotheism except when they came into contact with the Christian and Jewish faiths. To reject idol-atrous beliefs and worship in favor of one all-powerful and all-knowing God was a radical change. This new belief in divine unity, called *tawhid*, is expressed in the primary word (*kalimah*) of Islam: "There is no god but God" (*la ilaha illa Allah*). God the all-powerful is unique; no other power (*ilah*) can compare to Him. Therefore, God alone is worthy of humanity's devotion. It is important to note that all the chapters of the Qur'an except one begin with the phrase "In the name of God, the Compassionate and the Merciful." As the scholar Huston Smith has noted, "God's compassion and mercy are cited 192 times in the Koran, as against 17 references to his wrath and vengeance."[4]

> **To reject idolatrous beliefs and worship in favor of one all-powerful and all-knowing God was a radical change**

For Muslims, God, the Ultimate Reality, the One, is both the Manifest (al-Zahir) and the Hidden (al-Batin). He is both transcendent and immanent; He is beyond all human conception and categories of thought and yet He is closer "than the jugular vein" (Q 50:16). 'Ali, the cousin and close companion of the Prophet Muhammad, described the nature of God as follows:

> Praise be to Allāh Who lies inside all hidden things, and towards Whom all open things guide. He cannot be seen by the eye of an onlooker, but the eye which does not see Him cannot deny Him while the mind that proves His existence cannot perceive Him. He is so high in sublimity that nothing can be more sublime than He, while in near-ness, He is so near that no one can be nearer than He. But his sublimity does not put Him at a distance from anything of His creation, nor does His nearness bring them on equal level to Him. He has not informed (human) wit about the limits of His qualities. Nevertheless, He has not prevented it from securing essential knowledge of Him. So he is such that all signs of existence stand witness for Him till the denying mind also believes in Him. Allāh is sublime beyond what is described by those who liken Him to things or those who deny Him.[5]

According to Islamic philosophy, knowledge of God is gained through His names, which manifest His Essence. The Ninety-Nine Beautiful Names of God, derived from the Qur'an and *hadith*, are the realities through which God reveals Himself. The names of God, divided into names of mercy and names of majesty, are theophanies that comprise existence and all that is within existence. From this perspective, it is by recognizing and experiencing the names of God that the seeker of God is attracted to His Unity.

Allah is the Greatest name of God, for it designates the Unknowable Essence which is God. The Beautiful Names are attributes of that Essence. It is important to note that God's attributes are not limited to "the Ninety-Nine Names of God," but rather Muslim tradition holds these names as the most beautiful divine attributes. The following is a translation of the most beautiful names of God based on a portion of Abu Hamid al-Ghazali's treatise entitled *al-Maqsad al-Asna* (in some instances two or more names appear together because their complementarity or oppositeness contributes to the overall expression of the fuller meaning of the name in the original Arabic context):

God, Allah; The Merciful and the Compassionate One, Al-Rahman, Al-Rahim; The King, Al-Malik; The Most Holy One, Al-Quddus; The Sound One, Al-Salam; (the Peace), The Author of Safety and Security, Al-Mu'min; The Protector and Guardian, Al-Muhaymin; The Incomparable and Unparalleled One, Al-'Aziz; The One Who Compels His Creatures to Do as He Wills, Al-Jabbar; The One Supreme in Pride and Greatness, Al-Mutakabbir; The Creator, Al-Khaliq; The Maker, Al-Bari'; The Fashioner, Al-Musawwir; The Very Forgiving One, Al-Ghaffar; The Dominating One, Al-Qahhar; The One Who Gives Freely, without Thoughts of Compensation, Al-Wahhab; The One Who Provides All Sustenance, Al-Razzaq; He Who Opens All Things, Al-Fattah; The Omniscient One, Al-'Alim; The One Who Withholds and Provides the Means of Subsistence as He Wills, Al-Qabid, Al-Basit; The One Who Abases the Unbeliever and Exalts the Believer, Al-Khafid, Al-Rafi'; The One Who Raises to Honor and Abases, Al-Mu'izz, Al-Mudhill; The All-Hearing One, Al-Sami'; The All-Seeing One, Al-Basir; The Arbiter, Al-Hakam; The Just One, Al-'Adl; The Subtle One, Al-Latif; The All-Cognizant One, Al-Khabir; The Non-Precipitate and Forbearing One, Al-Halim; The Great One, Al-'Azim; The Most Forgiving One, Al-Ghafur; The One Who Expresses Thankfulness by Rewarding Bounteously, Al-Shakur; The Most High One, Al-'Ali; The Grand One, Al-Kabir; The Preserver, Al-Hafiz; He Who is Cognizant and Capable of Providing His Creation With Everything It Needs, Al-Muqit; He Who Satisfies the Needs of All Creation, Al-Hasib; The Sublime One, Al-Jalil; The Selflessly Generous One, Al-Karim; The One Who Watches All, Al-Raqib; The One Who Responds to Every Need, Al-Mujib; The One Whose Capacity is Limitless, Al-Wasi'; The Ultimately Wise One, Al-Hakim; The Objectively Loving One, Al-Wadud; The Most Glorious One, Al-Majid; The Quickener, Al-Ba'ith; The One Who Witnesses and Knows Everything Manifest, Al-Shahid; The Real One, Al-Haqq; The Ultimate and Faithful Trustee, Al-Wakil; The Perfectly Strong and Firm One, Al-Qawi, Al-Matin; The Patron, Al-Waliy; The Ultimately Praiseworthy One, Al-Hamid; The Absolute Reckoner, Al-Muhsi; The Originator and Restorer, Al-Mubdi',

Al-Mu'id; The One Responsible For Both Life and Death, Al-Muhyi, Al-Mumit; The Absolutely Percipient One, Al-Hayy; The Self-Subsisting One, Al-Qayyum; He Who Has No Needs, Al-Wajid; The Glorified One, Al-Majid; He Who is Uniquely One, Al-Ahad; He To Whom One Turns In Every Exigency, Al-Samad; He Who Acts, Or Does Not Act, As He Pleases, Al-Qadir, Al-Muqtadir; The One Who Causes Men To Be Both Near To And Distant From Him, Al-Muqaddim, Al-Mu'akhkhir; He Who Is Both First and Last, Al-Awwal, Al-Akhir; The Manifest and Hidden One, Al-Zahir, Al-Batin; The Dutiful One, Al-Barr; He Who Constantly Turns Man To Repentance, at-Tawwab; The Avenger, Al-Muntaqim; The One Who Erases Sin, Al-'Afuw; The Very Indulgent One, Al-Ra'uf; Malik Al-Mulk, The One Who Has Perfect Power Over His Kingdom; Al-Muta'ali (the Exalted); The One Possessed of Majesty and Honor, Dhu al-Jalal wa al-'Ikram; He Who Has Charge Over All, Al-Wali; The Highly-Exalted One, Al-Muta'ali; The Ultimately Equitable One, Al-Muqsit; He Who Combines All Things in the Universe to Accomplish His Purpose, Al-Jami'; The Rich, The Enriching One, Al-Ghani, Al-Mughni; He Who Repels Those Things Detrimental To His Creation, Al-Mani'; He Who Is Responsible For Both Good and Evil, Al-Darr, Al-Nafi'; The Light, Al-Nur; The Guide, Al-Hadi; The Matchless, Unequaled One, Al-Badi'; The Everlasting One, Al-Baqi; The Inheritor, Al-Warith; The Absolutely Judicious Guide, Al-Rashid; He Who Times All Things Perfectly, Al-Sabur.[6]

Islam teaches that God controls all things in the universe, no matter how vast or minute. In Arabic, this divine mastery is called *qada wa qadar*, meaning "the measure" of God's decree. Any extant thing, any event, and any process in creation is known by God and is controlled by Him, no matter how insignificant it may seem to humans. Thus, nothing occurs by chance; there are no accidents of nature. Even death itself is the result of God's command, and comes to each person at a time and place, and in a manner, ordained by God. While belief in *qada wa qadar* provides believers with a profound consciousness of the ever-present power of God, it does not sanction the belief that individuals are not responsible for their own actions. On the contrary, because God alone knows the destiny of each person the individual must exert every effort to fulfill his or her spiritual and social duties. They will be judged according to the effort they have made. If individuals fulfill their duties, they can rest assured that whatever befalls them is the will of God and hence must be accepted with patience and faith.

Dhikr

An important aspect of Islam is the sacred duty to remember God, known in Arabic as *dhikr* (a word which also implies recitation). By the practice of *dhikr*, the spiritual bond between a believer and God is not only renewed, it is also strengthened; the more *dhikr* is practiced, the more the relationship deepens. The celebrated Sufi poet Jalaluddin Rumi said of *dhikr*: "There is one thing in this world that must never be forgotten. If you were to forget everything else, but did not forget that, then there would be no cause to worry; whereas if you performed and remembered and did not forget anything else, but forgot that one thing, then you would have done nothing whatsoever."[7] *Dhikr* becomes a transformative process when a believer invokes with deep reverence, verbally or mentally, any of the Ninety-Nine Names of God. These names, revealed to Muhammad, possess surpassing sacredness, and have a creative power that helps believers attain greater spiritual understanding, nearness to God, and peace through submission to Him. As a daily practice, Muslims often recite the names of God on the Muslim rosary (*subhah*).

The Prophets of God

The Qur'an delivered a universal message that explicitly accepts preceding revelations given to Moses, the Hebrew prophets, and Jesus. In a *hadith* the Prophet Muhammad states that, in the past, God sent humanity 124,000 prophets to teach the same path of truth – Islam (that is, acceptance of the Unity of God and the need to surrender to God). The word for "prophet" in Islam, *nabi*, is not applied to one who foretells the future. Rather, "prophet" carries the broader meaning of one who informs others of the Truth. A prophet is characterized by sanctity, piety, and nearness to God. Most of all, a prophet is a divine messenger. Prophets share the message of God far and wide and guide people to obey divine precepts. The Qur'an (Q 4:136) records: "O believers, believe in Allah and His Messenger and in the Book which He revealed to His Messenger, and the Book which He revealed before. Whoever disbelieves in Allah, His Angels, His Books, His Prophets and the Last Day has gone far astray."

The Qur'an mentions a number of prophets before Muhammad, who are major figures in the Hebrew and Christian scriptures: Adam (Adam); Noah (Nuh); Abraham (Ibrahim); Ishmael (Isma'il); Isaac (Ishaq); Jacob (Ya'qub); Joseph (Yusuf); Moses (Musa); David (Da'ud); Solomon (Suleyman); John the Baptist (Yahya); and Jesus ('Isa). There is also mention of prophets not in the Bible, such as Hud and Salih. Notably, the Qur'an states that Muhammad is "the Seal of the Prophets," which is generally understood to mean that Muhammad is the culmination of this long line of prophets from God to humanity.

The Qur'an clearly recognizes the existence and sanctity of previous prophets and revelatory books; in fact, it suggests that each nation has, at some point, received a Messenger from God. In the Qur'an, previous religions of divine origin are mentioned, such as the religions of the Hebrews, Sabaeans, and Christians. Followers of those three faiths are explicitly recognized as constituting "Peoples of the Book." Some Islamic thinkers have extended this list to include other world religions (especially given the *hadith* tradition stated above which decrees the existence of 124,000 previous Messengers of God). The universality of the Qur'an's message was particularly grasped by the Sufis, who often wrote poetry extolling figures such as Abraham and Jesus as exemplars of divine virtues. The mystic and theologian Muhyi al-Din ibn al-'Arabi (1165–1240), whose book *Bezels of Wisdom*[8] is one of the most authoritative writings among Sufis, captured the inner meaning of the Qur'an's universal message in the following poem:

> My heart has become capable of every form: it is a pasture for gazelles and a convent for Christian monks,
> And a temple for idols and the pilgrim's Ka'ba and the tables of Tora and the book of the Koran.
> I follow the religion of Love: whatever way Love's camels take, that is my religion and my faith.[9]

Angels and *Jinn*

Muhammad taught that angels are beings free of sin who influence the lives of humans, although they themselves exist in a spiritual realm. The primary role of angels is to fulfill commands of God, both in the physical life of humanity and after death. After people die, angels give God an account of each soul's life. Another category of beings mentioned in the Qur'an are the *jinn*, which is the origin of the English word "genie." Unlike angels, *jinn* exist in association with the physical world, and they can interact directly with human beings. Like humans, *jinn* possess a free will, which some use for good and others for evil.

The Day of Judgment

The Qur'an contains many references to the creation of the human race, its resurrection after death, and its judgment by God. According to Islamic teaching, each individual is born with a sense of right and wrong, is endowed with free will to choose between them, and is held responsible for the choices made when tested by God. When God judges the soul after death, those who have done good are rewarded and those who have committed evil are punished. Some scholars believe that this doctrine of responsibility is, in part, counterbalanced by a concept of pre-Islamic origin that posits the existence of fate or predestination. Predestination in Islam is typically understood to mean that God has measured out and foreordained the span of every person's life, their portion of good or ill fortune, and whether they will follow the straight path or not.

In the Qur'an, life after death and the idea of resurrection on the Day of Judgment (*yawm-al-qiyamah*) are of great importance. According to the Qur'an, at the end of time God will resurrect the bodies of all the dead and reunite each with its soul; all will then be judged by God and rewarded or punished according to past fidelity to the teachings of God. Those who obeyed divine laws will be rewarded with entry into Paradise, an existence filled with countless joys. Believers, therefore, see death and the afterlife in a positive light. For example, one account of what Muslims believe will occur after death is that the soul passes through several stages: the first stage is *barzakh*, a condition of waiting (although there is no time or space) until God decrees the Day of Judgment and the resurrection of souls. On Judgment Day, the souls of the dead, reunited with their physical bodies, stand together with the living in the presence of God. Everyone is assigned a judgment by God according to their earthly deeds. According to the Qur'an, "Had Allah pleased, He would have made you a single nation, but He leads whom He pleases astray and guides whom He pleases. And you will surely be questioned about what you did" (Q 16:93). From this perspective, everything is known to God, the All-knowing and All-powerful. One should, therefore, live in humility, strive toward righteousness, and avoid judging others, for only God knows best.

Jihad

In recent years, the concept of *jihad* has become a subject of widespread discussion and, often, confusion. The word *jihad* means "exertion" or "striving in the cause of God." In Islam there are two categories of *jihad*. The greater *jihad* denotes the spiritual battle with evil that occurs within oneself; the lesser *jihad* is the defense of Islam against aggressive forces. The Prophet Muhammad specifically qualified the lesser *jihad* as a defensive stance which must not harm innocent people; neither can *jihad* be undertaken for the purpose of converting people to Islam. The Qur'an is clear that there can never be compulsion in religion (Q 2:256), and therefore conversion by force or coercion is prohibited.

Marriage and Relations between the Sexes

In Muslim societies, young people are generally separated by sex in all situations. Secondary schools, and sometimes universities, are single sex. Separation by gender is practiced to ensure that modesty and chastity – central principles in Islam – are strictly observed. Marriages are arranged not through direct social contact between males and females but by designated intermediaries, most often parents. In Islam, married women enjoy inherent rights independent of their husbands. Married women possess their own property and wealth, and retain full control over its disposition. Islamic teachings do not

Whirling dervishes from the Sufi tradition in Istanbul, Turkey

stipulate that Muslim women are restricted to working at home; however, a husband must give his consent if his wife wishes to work outside the home. Islamic marriage is based on an ideal of mutual respect, love, and kindness between husband and wife.

Some Muslim men practice polygamy (having two or more wives), but the majority have only one spouse. The Qur'an permits men to have up to four wives, but only if special conditions apply. A husband must treat each wife equally in terms of equity and affection. Some Muslims interpret these conditions to mean that polygamy is not acceptable because it is impossible, as the Qur'an declares, for an imperfect man to act with perfect justice and equity.

THE FIVE PILLARS OF ISLAM

The Islamic way of life rests on fundamental practices known as the Five Pillars, each of which is a means for the glorification of God and the purification of the individual Muslim. The purpose of the Five Pillars is to strengthen the religious life of believers, to bring them closer to God, to deepen their understanding of spiritual virtues, and to reinforce the bonds that unite the Muslim community. In offering glory to God, believers benefit themselves and their community. Yet God remains above all human efforts to express thanks and praise, and no expression, however sanctified and lofty, can ever attain His realm. Each of the Five Pillars of Islam is specified in the Qur'an. Because they are divinely ordained, their observance is obligatory for all Muslims. It is the responsibility of every Muslim community to establish the institutions necessary for the fulfillment of these duties. Muslims carry out their obligations in the manner that Muhammad himself performed them.

The First Pillar is the declaration of faith, or *shahadah*: "Ashhadu 'an la ilaha illa Allah wa ashhadu 'anna Muhammadan rasul Allah." The verse says that there is no god but the one true God, and that Muhammad is His messenger. This is recited by all those who wish to give allegiance to God. The verse is not merely a statement by which a new religious identity is established; it has a creative spiritual power that cleanses the soul of allegiance or devotion to any other object of worship. Conversion to Islam, therefore, is really a process of transformation and of commitment to live a new and liberated life.

The Second Pillar, prayer (*salat*), is prescribed for every believer at five specified times each day: dawn, noon, afternoon, sunset, and night. The purpose of prayer, which consists of reciting verses from the Qur'an, is to place remembrance of God at the forefront of the believer's consciousness. Prayer strengthens awareness of the omnipresence of God, and counteracts the distracting forces of daily life and its many concerns. Through prayer, the true reality of God and His teachings permeate and inspire the believer's actions, giving him a clear vision and purpose. Prayers are not only recitations of scripture, they also involve gestures and bodily movements such as standing, raising one's hands toward heaven, prostrating, and bowing. These movements, together with reciting scripture, express a believer's complete dedication of body and soul to the worship of God.

When offering prayers, Muslims always face toward Mecca, the holiest place in the Islamic world. Before praying, each believer performs ablutions (*wudu*) to insure that his body and clothing are ritually clean. The obligation to say prayers begins at around age twelve, but learning the requisite practices starts as early as age seven. While prayers may be conducted in any clean place, whether at home, work, or outdoors, congregational prayers held in a mosque are preferred. At such community gatherings, believers stand shoulder to shoulder and move as one when performing the gestures of each prayer. This communal experience reinforces spiritual unity and a sense of equality before God.

During the ninth month of the Islamic calendar, called Ramadan (the month in which Muhammad received his first revelation of the Qur'an), Muslims observe the Third Pillar by fasting during daylight hours and by abstaining from sexual relations. During Ramadan, believers attempt to avoid evil thoughts, words, and actions; they also seek to control negative emotions and restrain base passions. Particular attention is devoted to the poor during the Muslim holy month. The daily fast begins after a pre-dawn meal called *suhur* and ends at sunset with a meal called *iftar*. The fast is an exercise that is meant to strengthen self-discipline, heighten spiritual awareness, and promote com-

> **In the course of Ramadan, Muslims experience a heightened sense of spirituality**

passion for the poor. Through hunger and thirst, it encourages believers to be detached from the powerful forces and appetites inherent in material life. The fast attracts believers to the spiritual world described in the Qur'an. In the course of Ramadan, Muslims experience a heightened sense of spirituality. During Ramadan, a sixth daily prayer, called *tarawih*, is recited each night, either individually or in congregation. As the end of Ramadan approaches, the number of devotional observances increases. According to the *sunnah* – traditions describing the Prophet's own actions – over the course of the month the Prophet recited the entire Qur'an. Many Muslims, therefore, recite the Qur'an in an effort to follow the Prophet's example as closely as possible. A night of particularly fervent devotions commemorates the first revelation received by Muhammad, *laylat al-qadr*. *Laylat al-qadr* is one of the last ten days of the month, and occurs at the apex of Ramadan observances.

Islam recognizes the needs of the poor and the spiritual necessity of giving on their behalf through the institution of *zakat*, the Fourth Pillar. Although the Arabic word *zakat* has no exact English equivalent, it is often understood to signify "poor-tax" or "poor-due." But a more accurate rendering is "purification," for the act of giving *zakat* performs another function in addition to rendering assistance: the act of giving the needy a percentage of one's wealth purifies the remaining wealth and helps detach the donor from the material world. The believer, in sacrificing for others according to God's decree, draws away from himself and moves nearer to God. The act of giving has a powerful and direct effect on the donor's spiritual development. But *zakat* need not be a direct donation: it can also consist of indirect donations for the construction of community institutions such as mosques, schools, and hospitals. Donations can also be made to individuals rendering service to the community. As a divinely ordained institution, *zakat* uplifts the poor, strengthens spirituality through sacrifice, and preserves the dignity of both the giver and the recipient. Feelings of inferiority and superiority are not generated by *zakat*, for Islam teaches that all wealth belongs to God and that He is the source of all riches. Those who contribute to the poor do so in recognition that all resources derive from God's bounty, and so the fortunate have an obligation to assist others generously.[10]

The Fifth Pillar of Islam is the *hajj*, a pilgrimage to Mecca undertaken at least once in a believer's lifetime. The *hajj* is obligatory only for those who can afford the journey and still provide for their family during their absence. It is an opportunity to express devotion and submission to God more completely than at any other time. It calls for total dedication to the rituals and prayers of the pilgrimage without distraction. Muslims undertake the *hajj* from the eighth through the thirteenth day of the twelfth Islamic month, Dhu 'l-Hijjah. Muslims travel from all over the world to Mecca, and in the course of their journey they follow traditions originating with Muhammad himself. These traditions are known as *ihram* (consecration). Under *ihram*, Muslims forsake the trappings of their normal life and adopt an attitude of sanctity and selflessness. Aspects of individuality such as distinctive dress are eliminated. Instead, all pilgrims wear simple clothing specific to the *hajj* symbolizing the oneness of believers and their humility before God.

> **Pilgrimage confirms belief, deepens faith, and broadens a believer's vision of the worldwide Islamic community**

The focal point of the *hajj* is the most holy place in the Islamic world, the Ka'bah in Mecca, also known as the "Sacred House." A large, cube-shaped structure built of massive stones, the Ka'bah is draped in finely woven black cloth on which verses of the Qur'an are embroidered in gold. The Qur'an states that the Ka'bah was first built by Adam and then rebuilt by Ibrahim (Abraham) and his son Isma'il. Thus, the Ka'bah was the first house dedicated to the worship of God. The Ka'bah is the point to which all Muslims around the world turn in prayer five times daily. It symbolizes the unity of the spiritual direction of a Muslim's life. The first duty of pilgrims is to circumambulate the Ka'bah seven times counterclockwise with an attitude of love and devotion. Thereafter, pilgrims perform a variety of other rituals and symbolic gestures. For every Muslim, the *hajj* is the holiest and most cherished time in life. Pilgrimage confirms belief, deepens faith, and broadens a believer's vision of the worldwide Islamic community. Pilgrims from all corners of the earth, speaking hundreds of different languages and representing diverse cultures, are visibly united as one community within the holiest sanctuary.

Although the Five Pillars of Islam permeate the structure of Muslim life, many phrases from the Qur'an are commonplace in everyday language, thus imbuing daily experiences with a sense of sacredness and remembrance of God. Many of these phrases have entered into common vernacular in Islamic lands and, from there, have transited into other languages. Such common expressions include *bismillah* ("In the name of God").

THE SUFI TRADITION

The Divine Law or *shari'ah* is complemented by the *tariqah*, which is an inner path traveled only by the few. *Tariqah* (which corresponds to the practice of Islamic mysticism, or Sufism) combines the outward discipline of the *shari'ah* with inward disciplines utilized to transform consciousness in order to experience the presence of the Divine. The *shari'ah* can be regarded as indispensable for all Muslims, while Sufis consider that the *tariqah* consists of additional disciplines utilized by advanced practitioners.

The Sufi perspective is essentially mystical, and this mysticism distinguishes it from the more literal and legalistic schools of Qur'anic interpretation. In general, a Sufi (in Muslim countries a Sufi is actually known as a *faqir* or a *darvish*) seeks intimate knowledge and direct experience of God. Although there is no single approach to the Sufi way, also known as *tasawwuf*, Sufis view themselves as pilgrims advancing on a path (*tariqah*) through states and stages of spiritual maturation – the ultimate aim of which is reunion with God. The longing for reunion with God, the Origin, the Truth (*haqq*), is the central impetus of the Sufi path. The path is interpreted as culminating in *fana* (annihilation of human attributes, the ego) and *baqa* (perpetual existence in the blessed presence of God). Within the Sufi tradition, two principles are often emphasized, *wahdat al-wujud*, or the Transcendent Unity of Being, and *al-insan al-kamil*, the Universal or Perfect Human.

The etymology of the word "Sufi," as well as the origins of Sufi practice, has been debated. Some suggest that the word is derived from the root *suf* (wool) and thus refers to the fact that many Sufis wore clothes made of wool. Others have argued that the word comes from *safa*, meaning purity. Regardless of the etymology of the word, to be a Sufi means to live a particular way of life and to attain a higher level of consciousness. Early Muslim authorities have provided elaborate definitions of what it means to be a Sufi; for example:

> Sufism is entry into exemplary behavior and departure from unworthy behavior.
> Sufism means that God makes you die to yourself and makes you live in him.
> The Sufi is single in essence; nothing changes him, nor does he change anything.
> The sign of the sincere Sufi is that he feels poor when he has wealth, is humble when
>   he has power, and is hidden when he has fame.
> Sufism means that you own nothing and are owned by nothing.
> Sufism means entrusting the soul to God most high for whatever he wishes.[11]

Sufis view their movement as rooted in the emulation of the sayings and actions of the Prophet. In that way, the first Sufis are often thought to have been faithful companions of the Prophet, who were characterized by expressions of piousness, humility, and love of God. From this viewpoint, as the Islamic Empire grew, Muslim society was transformed from a group of simple desert people into the state-oriented, luxurious civilization of the caliphate. Organized Sufi movements, or orders, may have therefore developed as part of a yearning for the simple religious lifestyle of the early followers of Muhammad.

Sufism means that you own nothing and are owned by nothing

Two tendencies were prevalent among traditional Sufi orders: the Ecstatic and the Sober. Early practitioners of the Ecstatic form, concentrated in Khorasan (eastern regions of Iran), included such masters as Bistami (d. 875) who were known to attain trance-like states of union with God. This form of Sufi spirituality, which is still practiced in Iran and India, has produced a remarkable tradition of poetry that exhibits an intimate love of God. In the western area of the Islamic world (mainly Iraq, Syria, Egypt, and North Africa), Sufis such as al-Junayd (c.870–950) tended to be more moderate in their outward expressions, and became known for their masterful philosophical treatises. Over time, the Sufi way of life, with its emphasis on direct experience and symbolic interpretations of the Qur'an, was denounced as heresy by many political and legal Islamic authorities. In certain areas of the Islamic world, the Sufi movement was barely tolerated, and even persecuted.

The negative view of Sufis held by mainstream Muslims was reversed, in large measure, by the life and teachings of the philosopher-mystic Abu Hamid al-Ghazali (d. 1111). Born in Tus, a city in the northeastern part of Iran, al-Ghazali was an eminent professor and the foremost Muslim scholar of his day. Many thought of him as the greatest Islamic authority since the Prophet Muhammad. Al-Ghazali, however, underwent a monumental personal crisis; he concluded that his erudite intellectual knowledge and accolades did not equate to nearness to God. He decided to leave his academic post and become a Sufi in order to complement his knowledge of the outward practices (*shari'ah*) with inward practices (*tariqah*). After ten years of intense spiritual practice, al-Ghazali returned to the public eye to produce major treatises such as *The Revival of Religious Sciences*, *Niche of the Lamp*, and *The Incoherence of the Philosophers*. Together, these works provided a systematic presentation of the Sufi tradition. Furthermore, al-Ghazali demonstrated how the Sufi path was based in the Qur'an and on the Tradition of the Prophet. Many Sufis, for example, cite the following Qur'anic passage (24:35):

> Allah is the Light of the heavens and the earth. His Light is like a niche in which there is a lamp, the lamp is in a glass, the glass is like a glittering star. It is kindled from a blessed olive tree, neither of the East nor the West. Its oil will always shine, even if no fire has touched it. Light upon light, Allah guides to His Light whomever He pleases and gives the examples to mankind. Allah has knowledge of everything.

Al-Ghazali became an "ambassador" and teacher of the esoteric dimension of Islam. He argued that reason was inadequate and ultimately a distraction in the religious quest; instead, he insisted that revelation, faith, and, ultimately, mystical illumination were essential. Al-Ghazali upheld the importance of direct mystical experience, and suggested that true spiritual transformation is that which carries over into daily life by ethical and moral conduct. His authoritative writings did much to validate the Sufi perspective among the wider Islamic community.

Sufi orders are hierarchical; the highest station is that of the Sufi master (a *shaykh* or *pir*), one who has completed all phases of the path and who can now guide aspirants along the way. To assist the operation of the order the *shaykh* often assigns experienced practitioners certain advisory and administrative duties. Each Sufi order maintains somewhat distinctive rules and customs as well as different techniques of spiritual awakening. There is, however, a common framework which orients and unites all Sufis. In general, this framework consists of obeying the *shari'ah* (the Law); walking on the *tariqah* (the esoteric path) under the guidance of an authentic teacher; reaching or "tasting" the *haqiqah* (the Truth of Existence); and finally, living in *ma'rifah* (Gnosis) – that is, having transformed one's awareness, one then lives with full wisdom of the true nature of Reality. Sufis emphasize the necessity of a teacher as well as the need to receive initiation into an order. Initiation into a Sufi order represents an entrance into an esoteric lineage, or chain of transmission, which is traced back to the Prophet Muhammad.

All Sufi practice entails intense devotion above and beyond outward austerities. Specifically, Sufis practice an ethic of courtesy, generosity, and polite manners (*adab*), simple living, contemplation, meditation, and remembrance and recitation of the Names of God. One important and distinctive contribution of the Sufi tradition to Islam has been its utilization of the arts for spiritual transformation. Sufis are well known for their inspired poetry, the practice of *sama'* (performing and listening to music as a technique for drawing near to God) and rhythmic movements (such as the whirling dance of the Mevlevi Sufi order). All of these expressions are performed as techniques for opening the heart and transforming the personality. Some of the greatest and most celebrated Muslim sages were Sufis, including the mystic philosopher Muhyi al-Din ibn-'Arabi, known as the *al-shaykh al-akbar* (the grand master), the poet Jalaluddin Rumi (*c*.1207–1273), and Arabia's most important woman poet, Rabi'ah al-'Adawiyyah (*c*.713–801). Another important Sufi, the philosopher Suhrawardi (1154–1191), established the Ishraqi

> **The most important contribution of the Sufi tradition to Islam has been its utilization of the arts for spiritual transformation**

or Illuminationist school in Persia, which synthesized Islamic philosophy with the mystical teachings of the ancient Persians (Zoroastrians) and Greeks. Some notable scientists were Sufis as well, including Ibn Sina (980–1037). Ibn Sina's medical textbooks and interpretations of Aristotle were utilized throughout Europe during the Middle Ages.

Sufis have established many houses of worship around the world, and their writings and lifestyle have attracted many people to Islam and its spiritual practices. Sufi orders are also known for their philanthropic work in local communities.

RITES AND CELEBRATIONS

Festivals and Holy Days

The two most important Muslim festivals are 'Id al-Fitr, which marks the end of the Ramadan fast, and 'Id al-Adha, the feast of sacrifice during the *hajj*. The Arabic word *'id*, which in Islam means "festival," derives from an earlier etymological meaning "returning at regular intervals."

At the end of the Ramadan fast a new moon appears. Muslims often go outdoors to search the sky for its appearance. When it is sighted, 'Id al-Fitr, a three-day celebration, begins, during which workplaces and schools remain closed. On the first day of the holiday, people cleanse themselves with a bath, put on new clothing, eat a simple breakfast, and go out to join the crowds gathering at mosques to offer prayers of thanksgiving. Gifts and cards are exchanged, contributions to the poor are given, and visits are made to cemeteries in remembrance of deceased relatives and friends. The highlight of the day is the midday feast, the first daytime meal since the beginning of Ramadan thirty days before.

'Id al-Adha is the most important festival in the Islamic calendar. It celebrates the climax of the *hajj*, and occurs two months after the end of Ramadan. During 'Id al-Adha, pilgrims recall Ibrahim's submission to the will of God by overcoming the devil's temptations and agreeing to sacrifice his son, Isma'il. Besides 'Id al-Fitr and 'Id al-Adha, Muslims observe six other holy days. The birthday of Muhammad is celebrated on *mawlid al-nabi*. The first occasion on which Muhammad received a revelation from God, *laylat al-qadr*, is celebrated on one of the last ten nights of Ramadan. However, it usually is held on the twenty-seventh day of the month. When

> **'Id al-Adha is the most important festival in the Islamic calendar**

Muhammad and his followers faced the most severe opposition and persecution, God granted him the privilege of ascending from Jerusalem through the seven heavens and attaining His presence, an event known as the Night Journey. This miraculous journey, known as *laylat al-mi'raj*, is celebrated as evidence of the divine origin of Muhammad's authority and as the source of the five daily prayers.

The night of the full moon before the start of Ramadan is known as *laylat al-bara'at*. Following the *sunnah*, the way of the Prophet, many Muslims spend the night praying, studying sacred texts, and reciting the Qur'an.

'Ashura, which is the tenth day of Muharram, the first month of the Islamic year, is celebrated for several reasons. In pre-Islamic society, this day was traditionally observed as a day of fasting. Among Jews, it was observed as the Day of Atonement, when sacrifices were offered as penance for sins. For Muslims, 'Ashura is remembered as the day when Noah and his family were able to leave the Ark and return to land following the Great Flood, and also as the day when God saved Moses from the pharaoh of Egypt. To Shi'is, 'Ashura commemorates the martyrdom of Husayn at the battle of Karbala. Though it is not obligatory, some Muslims fast on 'Ashura, and eat a specially prepared meal at night. The month of Muharram as a whole is regarded as holy because it was during that period that Muhammad and his followers fled Mecca and resettled in Medina. That event, the *hijrah*, is recognized as the establishment of the Muslim community, the *ummah*.

Shi'i Muslims hold 'Ali, the cousin and son-in-law of the Prophet, in high, if not supramundane, esteem. Shi'is, in fact, believe that the Prophet Muhammad appointed 'Ali as his successor, and so he is regarded as the first Imam of the Shi'i tradition. Shi'is commemorate the day that the Prophet declared 'Ali as his successor on Ghadir Khum, or 17 Dhu 'l-Hijja. Shi'is also honor the birthday and martyrdom of 'Ali and, in general, the birthdays of all the twelve Imams.

Rites of Passage

When a child is born it is formally welcomed into the *ummah* by the head of the family, who whispers in the baby's right ear the Islamic call to prayer, the *adhan*. Thus the first word heard by the infant is Allah. He then whispers in the left ear the command to worship, or *iqamah*. A second ritual follows, called *tahnik*, during which the oldest relative present places a morsel of sugar, honey, or date in the baby's mouth as a symbol that the child will have a sweet disposition and be kind and obedient. The ritual concludes with prayers offered on behalf of the infant and the family.

A naming ceremony, called *'aqiqah*, is held seven days after the baby's birth, and is attended by relatives and friends of the family. In addition to naming the child, several other rituals are also conducted. A donation is set aside for the poor, the amount of which is determined by cutting the baby's hair, weighing it, and apportioning the same weight in gold or silver. If the child is a boy, circumcision is performed, although some boys are not circumcised until months or years later. Rituals related to birth and infancy are not universal, but rather vary among the different cultures of the Muslim world.

When it is known that a Muslim is near death, his friends and relatives gather at his bedside. He expresses his desire for their forgiveness and the forgiveness of God for all sins that he may have committed. The last word he utters before dying is the name of God, Allah, just as the first word he heard after birth was Allah. Since the physical body plays a vital role in the Resurrection, cremation of the dead is forbidden in Islam. The washing of the body (*ghusl*) and prayers for the deceased are completed as soon as possible after death. The washing and preparation of the body may take place at a mosque or in a home. Traditionally, Muslims do not use coffins for burial. The body is anointed with perfumes or spices and is wrapped in sheets of white cloth (three sheets are used for a male, and five for a female). The treatment and preparation of the body is the same for all Muslims regardless of the social status of the deceased. The typical Muslim funeral is simple and inexpensive. The body is carried to the cemetery rather than transported by vehicle, and it is buried in the earth facing in the direction of Mecca. The following verse of the Qur'an is recited by the people gathered at the cemetery as the body is lowered into the grave: "From it We have created you, and into it We shall return you, and from it We shall raise you a second time" (Q 20:55). Expressions of grief and mourning occur for no longer than three days. Widows, however, mourn for up to four months and ten days, during which time they are not to remarry. The family of a dead person has responsibility for honoring any of the deceased's outstanding financial debts.

CALENDAR

The Muslim calendar originated in 622 with the *hijrah*, Muhammad's flight to Medina and his inauguration of the Muslim community. The calendar follows a lunar system, and has twenty-nine or thirty days per month. The lunar year is never intercalated to synchronize with the solar calendar, although occasionally an intercalary day may be added to the last month of the year to make that month thirty days long. Because the lunar year of 354 days is out of phase with the solar year (being more than eleven days shorter), the dates of Islamic festivals are continually changing relative to the solar calendar. Such a change in the date of festivals from year to year is particularly important with regard to Ramadan, the month of the fast. Ramadan sometimes falls in the summer season when days are longer and hotter, and the fast is consequently more arduous; but it can also fall in seasons with very long or very short days in regions near the poles. Besides Ramadan, the two most import-ant Islamic months are Muharram, the first month of the year, and Dhu 'l-Hijjah, the last month during which the *hajj* takes place. Although the moon plays the central role in the calendar, prayer times are determined by the position of the sun, as are periods of fasting.

CHAPTER SUMMARY

The religious consciousness of Islam is centered on belief in the Unity of God, the Day of Judgment, and the existence of God's prophets, angels, and revelatory books. From the Muslim perspective, the revelation delivered through the Prophet Muhammad, the exem-plar of all spiritual virtues, was the final dispensation in a succession of prophets, all of whom taught a primal religion which was renewed through messengers sent by God. The prophets taught righteousness, justice, and the unity of God. Although Muhammad is a prophet, he is of peripheral importance when compared to the Qur'an. In Islam the Qur'an is central: it is the Word of God, a theophany which in the original Arabic is unsurpassable in holiness. The spiritual impulse released by the Qur'anic revelation animated the rapid unification of a scattered, tribal, and desert people into an advanced and thriving Islamic Empire.

For Muslims, God, the Merciful, the Compassionate, is the Creator of all existence and the Ruler of the Day of Judgment. Daily life for Muslims, as structured by the Five Pillars of religious practice, is permeated by the awareness of the majesty and mercy of God. God is worshipped as the Ultimate Reality. For Sufis, Muslims with intense yearning for reunion with the divine, God is not only the Ultimate Reality but the only Reality. In short, the life of a Muslim, as the word "Islam" implies, is the inner peace attained through submission to the will of God.

The Golden Temple at Amritsar, India

CHAPTER 15
THE SIKH FAITH

There is one Supreme Being, the Eternal Reality. He is the Creator, without fear and devoid of enmity. He is immortal, never incarnated, self-existent, known by grace through the Guru.[1]

– Guru Nanak

INTRODUCTION

The passage cited above is known as the Mul Mantra – the "basic sacred formula" of the Sikh religion. The words are those of Guru Nanak (1469–1539 C.E.) and the Sikh scripture, the *Adi Granth* ("First Anthology"), begins with them. This mantra is part of a larger poem called the *Japji* ("Recitation"), which is recited by devout Sikhs every morning at dawn.

> **Treat others as thou wouldst be treated thyself**
> *Adi Granth*
> **THE GOLDEN RULE**

Adherents of the Sikh faith thus remind themselves daily of the Eternal Reality and the Guru, through whom Sikhs approach this Reality. The term "Sikh" is derived from the Sanskrit word *sishya*, meaning "a learner" or "a disciple," signifying that Sikhs are those who dedicate themselves to learning and practicing *gurmat*, the doctrines and spiritual disciplines of the Gurus. Sikhs acknowledge only one ultimate Guru, and that is God, the True Teacher (*satguru*). Sikhs also recognize ten human Gurus. Their teachings represent the embodiment of God's Word. Following Guru Nanak, spiritual leadership passed successively from one Guru to another until Guru Gobind Singh (1666–1708), the tenth Sikh Guru, appointed the *Adi Granth* as his spiritual successor.[2]

GURU NANAK AND THE ORIGINS OF THE SIKH FAITH

Guru Nanak was born in the Punjab region of northern India in 1469. Members of his family were orthodox Hindus, and in all likelihood Nanak was raised in this

Timeline

1469–1539 C.E.
Life of Sikh faith founder, Guru Nanak

1538 C.E.
Guru Nanak chooses Lehna, later known as Guru Angad, as successor

1601 C.E.
Guru Arjan completes *Adi Granth* (or *Guru Granth Sahib*)

1604 C.E.
The holy Harmandir, also known as the Golden Temple, completed in present-day Amritsar, India

1666 C.E.
City of Amritsar founded by Guru Tegh Bahadur

1699 C.E.
Khalsa order instituted by Guru Gobind Singh

1704 C.E.
Adi Granth (or *Guru Granth Sahib*) finalized and end of Sikh lineage of personal Gurus announced by Guru Gobind Singh

1708 C.E.
Guru Gobind Singh assassinated

1711 C.E.
Collection of Guru Gobind Singh's writings, known as *Dasam Granth*, completed and regarded as sacred text

tradition as well. He was educated at a traditional school (a *madrasa*), where he learned Sanskrit, Persian, and Arabic. At age twelve or thirteen, he was married, and later had two sons. As a young adult, and with the help of his brother-in-law, he became an accountant. Spirituality, however, was always foremost in his thoughts. From a very early age Nanak was filled with spiritual yearning, and spent much of his time singing devotional hymns. Sometime around 1490, Nanak befriended a Muslim musician named Mardana, who accompanied his singing on the *rebec* (a three-stringed instrument similar to a violin). Nanak and Mardana remained lifelong friends. Mardana not only traveled extensively with Nanak, accompanying his hymns with music, but also became Nanak's first disciple.

Over the course of his early years, Nanak was in close association with both Hindu and Muslim sages. The juxtaposition of the Hindu and Islamic traditions in the Punjab region played a critical role in the origin and development of the Sikh faith. Although Nanak certainly learned from these traditions and was inspired by them, by the time of his young adulthood he had become disillusioned with their practices. The tradition that Nanak founded was more clearly rooted in the teachings of the *sant*s ("mendicants"), who advocated *bhakti* (devotional worship). The teachings of some *sant*s, such as Namdev (b. 1270 C.E.), Ravidas (*c.*1414–1526 C.E.), and Kabir (d. 1518 C.E.), are included in the *Adi Granth*. Of these three, Kabir exerted a particularly significant influence within the *sant* movement. He was a student of Ramanand (*c.*1360–1470 C.E.), a Hindu religious reformer, and was admired by Hindus and Muslims alike. The details of his early life are uncertain, but he grew into an outspoken religious sage. Like other *sant*s, Kabir stressed non-orthodox principles and rejected the caste system, idol worship, and excessive pre-occupation with ritual. In place of these outward forms the *sant*s took the inward path of *bhakti*.

The notion of *bhakti* originates in the Hindu tradition. That tradition distinguishes at least three ways to liberation: liberation through action (*karma yoga*); liberation through knowledge (*jñana yoga*); and liberation through devotion (*bhakti yoga*). These three techniques are distinguished and exalted, for instance, in the sacred poem titled the *Bhagavad-Gita*. Both the *sant* teachings and the Sikh tradition that emerged from them favor the way of *bhakti* over the others. For this reason, much of Guru Nanak's teaching came in the form of devotional hymns, sung to Mardana's musical accompaniment. Most of these hymns were composed by Nanak, but others were written by Sufi and *bhakti* poets. Indeed, the five fundamental Sikh observances originated from within the *bhakti* perspective: *gan*, singing the praises of God; *dan*, the giving of charity without preference or discrimination; *ashnan*, self-purification by means of bathing in the morning; *sewa*, service to humanity; and *simran*, chanting of and meditation upon the name of God, and the offering of prayers to God.

As mentioned above, the Sikh tradition emerged in the context of three religious currents – the Hindu tradition, the Islamic religion, and the *sant* movement. For Sikhs, however, Guru Nanak's teaching was neither a synthesis of the first two nor a mere extension of the third. Instead, it resulted from a profound experience of transformation in which he was instructed by God to sing God's praises. One morning, following his usual practice, Nanak went bathing in the river near his home. He did not return as usual, but disappeared for three days and nights. His family assumed that he had drowned. When he finally did return home, he said nothing at all. On the fourth day he proclaimed: "There is neither Hindu nor Mussulman [Muslim] so whose path shall I follow? I shall follow God's path. God is neither Hindu nor Mussulman and the path I follow is God's."[3] This was the first statement of Guru Nanak's teaching. Its message was carried on from the first Sikh Guru to the last, Guru Gobind Singh, who declared:

> **The Sikh tradition emerged in the context of the Hindu tradition, the Islamic religion, and the *sant* movement**

Hindus and Muslims are one.
The same Reality is the Creator and Preserver of all;
Know no distinctions between them.
The monastery and the mosque are the same;
So are the Hindu worship and the Muslim prayer.
Humans are all one![4]

Shortly after his mystical experience, Guru Nanak gave away his possessions and embarked on a series of extended travels to spread his message. He was accompanied by Mardana, who continued to provide music for Nanak's hymns. Nanak traveled across the Indian subcontinent, and reportedly journeyed as far as Mecca in Arabia. These travels are the source of some enlightening anecdotes that illustrate Guru Nanak's simultaneous respect for the wisdom of other traditions and his insistence that true religion transcends the outward rituals of these traditions. On one occasion, for example, Guru Nanak began singing a hymn while he was amongst a crowd of Hindus bathing in the Ganges, the holy river. When some Hindus were drawn to Nanak's music, a priest overlooking the scene called out and reprimanded them, saying: "Time is running out, and you have yet to take your bath. Let not this opportunity slip away, lest your sins should remain unwashed." Guru Nanak replied, "By bathing the body, how does one wash away one's sins? How will the

> **"By bathing, how does one wash away one's sins? How will the impurity of the heart be cleansed by it?"**

impurity of the heart be cleansed by it?" He carried on, singing: "They are truly pure in whose heart dwells the Lord."[5] According to another tale, when Guru Nanak journeyed to Mecca he fell asleep in the mosque with his feet pointing towards the Ka'bah, which Muslims hold to be the most sacred shrine. When he was scolded for adopting this "sinful posture," he replied: "Please turn my legs in the direction in which God does not exist."[6]

THE SUCCESSION OF SIKH GURUS AND THE DEVELOPMENT OF THE SIKH FAITH

After many years of travel, Guru Nanak returned to the Punjab, and continued teaching until his death, sometime around 1539. Many Sikhs expected that before Guru Nanak passed away he would appoint one of his sons as his successor. Instead, he appointed a recent convert named Lehna as his heir. According to tradition, while Guru Nanak, his two sons, and Lehna were traveling they encountered something that resembled a corpse wrapped in a sheet. When Guru Nanak asked the others who would eat the unidentified item, Lehna affirmed his readiness to comply if it was the will of Guru Nanak. Lehna then uncovered the wrapping and found a tray of sacred food. Lehna would not eat the food until Guru Nanak and his two sons had their portion. Touched by this generous act, Guru Nanak said:

> Lehna, you were blessed with the sacred food because you could share it with others. If the people use the wealth bestowed on them by God for themselves alone or for treasuring it, it is like a corpse. But if they decide to share it with others, it becomes sacred food. You have known the secret. You are my image.[7]

Guru Nanak then designated Lehna as the second Guru of the Sikh tradition; he changed Lehna's name to Guru Angad (meaning "limb") to signify that, as the second Guru, Lehna was inseparable from Guru Nanak.

As previously noted, the succession of Gurus spanned from Guru Nanak to the tenth Guru, Guru Gobind Singh, who named the *Adi Granth* his spiritual successor (for this reason, the Sikh scripture is also referred to as *Guru Granth Sahib*). The compilation of the *Adi Granth*, undertaken by the fifth Sikh Guru, Guru Arjan, was no less significant in Sikh history than its appointment as Guru. By Guru Arjan's time, Sikh followers needed a definitive scriptural basis for their tradition. Guru Arjan supplied such a text. This sacred text, the *Adi Granth*, contains hymns of the Sikh Gurus and of many Hindu and Muslim sages. Guru Arjan's second significant act was initiating a tithe tax (*daswandh*), which provided revenue for the construction of many buildings, including a number of sacred pools and temples (or *gurdwara*s). During this period, the Golden Temple was constructed in Amritsar (400 km northwest of Delhi), and it remains the most sacred house of worship of the Sikh religion.

During the leadership of the tenth Guru, Gobind Singh, the Sikh faith entered a militant phase in response to hostile invasions carried out by various Hindu kings and the Muslim forces known as the Moguls. Guru Gobind Singh's father, the ninth Guru, Guru Tegh Bahadur (1621–1675), was martyred in Delhi by the order of the Mogul emperor Aurangzeb. As a consequence, Gobind Singh instituted military discipline and training within the Sikh community. During this period the Sikhs grew in economic and political power. Among the Sikhs an order of purified soldier-saints, referred to as the *khalsa*, emerged. Those initiated into the *khalsa* are recognized by five outward signs known as *kakkar*, or "the five K's": *kes* (uncut hair and beard, signifying devotion to the Sikh faith); *kanga* (a comb holding the hair in place); *kachh* (knee-length breeches, suggesting discipline and chastity); *kara* (a steel bracelet symbolizing commitment to the Guru and to performing good deeds with the hands); and *kirpan* (a saber, an indication of fearlessness, self-reliance, and dedication to justice).

Guru Gobind Singh introduced the writings of his father, Guru Tegh Bahadur, into the *Adi Granth*. Shortly before his death, he proclaimed that the spiritual authority of the Sikh faith would reside in this expanded version of the *Adi Granth*, which contains roughly six thousand hymns. The number of hymns attributed to each Guru is as follows: Guru Nanak, 974; Guru Angad, 62; Guru Amar Das, 907; Guru Ram Das, 679; Guru Arjan Dev, 2218; and Guru Tegh Bahadur, 115. In addition, the *Adi Granth* includes contributions that originated with Hindu *sant*s and Sufis, including 541 hymns attributed to Kabir. Guru Gobind Singh wrote many poetic verses in Persian and Sanskrit, as well as Punjabi. He did not, however, include any of his own writings in the *Adi Granth*. After his death, a Sikh known as Bhai Mani Singh organized the writings of the last Guru into a work known as the *Dasam*.

It should be emphasized that the Sikh tradition places great emphasis on the role of the Guru. The *Adi Granth* states:

> A thousand moons might rise
> A thousand suns might shine
> Yet all that outer brightness
> Would leave the inner world in
> darkness
> If it had not the benign Guru's light.[8]

Top: Sikhs lighting candles on the anniversary of Guru Gobind Singh
Bottom: The Amrit Ceremony with the five holy ones

Sikhs do not, however, worship their Gurus. They believe that God transcends all names and forms and, as stated in the Mul Mantra, God is never incarnated. Thus, they do not believe that Gurus (or any other persons) are *avatars* or incarnations of God. Furthermore, while the Sikh Gurus respected and derived inspiration from the Vedas and the Qur'an (the Hindu and Muslim holy books, respectively), they denied the absolute authority of both texts, believing them to embody sacred wisdom but not final revelations. Additionally, Sikhs rejected the caste system, gender inequalities, and idol worship. Instead, they sought to turn their learner-disciples toward an inner religion. As recorded in the *Adi Granth*:

Religion does not lie in patched garments and a staff, or in smearing the body with ashes. Religion does not lie in suspending large rings from split ears, in shaving the head or blowing a conch shell. To live uncontaminated amid worldly temptations is to find the secret of religion. It does not consist of empty words: he is religious who regards all men as equals.[9]

Another verse of the Sikh scriptures declares:

Why dost thou go to search for Him
In lonely forest groves?
Like the fragrance that envelops a flower,
The Supreme Lord permeates the universe,
But is not confined by it …
Seek Him within thyself.
Truly, He abides in thee.[10]

THE TEACHINGS OF THE GURUS

Sikh Ethics: Fulfilling One's Duties

An important feature of Sikh teachings is the extent to which they integrate conditions of ordinary life into religious practice. Unlike other Indian traditions that hold renunciation as the culmination of spiritual practice, the Sikh faith considers involvement in the affairs of ordinary life to be essential. This is emphatically expressed in Guru Nanak's statement that "Truth is higher than all, but higher still is true living."[11]

Thus, it is mandatory for Sikhs to contribute to the welfare of their community, to deal with the challenges of family life, and to be involved with worldly affairs. As the *Guru Granth Sahib (Adi Granth)* states, "One who lives by earning through hard work, then gives some of it away in charity, knows the way to God."[12]

However, it would be a mistake to conclude that the Sikh doctrine is "materialistic" or "worldly" in its principal focus. Like other Indian sages, Guru Nanak believed that the material world is an illusion (*maya*), and that God is the only Ultimate Reality. But Guru Nanak did not believe that the material world is merely an illusion. Rather, he describes it as "the place where men are confronted with duty,"[13] suggesting that life serves a spiritual function. In particular, during this life we are faced with duality, and must discern what is truly valuable from what is not. Our duty is to honor the former over the latter, and fulfilling that duty is part of attaining spiritual liberation. In Guru Nanak's understanding, then, the principal effect of succumbing to the illusions of *maya* is not simply that one fails to know what is truly real, but that one fails to value what is truly worthy of being valued. Thus, the Gurus declared that one must earnestly face responsibilities in the material world without allowing one's values to be drawn away from God by the attractions of this world. Therefore, the Sikh ethos is often defined simply in three guidelines of action: (1) to work hard to earn an honest living; (2) to share what one earns with those who are needy; and (3) to remember the Lord by reciting His name.

> **It is mandatory for Sikhs to contribute to the welfare of their community and to be involved with worldly affairs**

The Nature of God

One pronouncement on the nature of God is repeated more frequently and with greater finality than any other statement on God in the Sikh tradition: *Ik Onkar* – "God is one." This formulation has tremendous significance in the Sikh religion. It is the first declaration found in the Mul Mantra (the "basic sacred formula" of the Sikh faith which is quoted at the opening of this chapter) and in the *Adi Granth*. The term *Ik* represents the numeral "1." The word *Onkar* (also *Omkara* or *Oankar*) is etymologically derived from the Sanskrit *Om* (the sacred monosyllable of the Hindu tradition) and designates God as Ultimate Reality. Thus, *Ik Onkar* refers to God as the singular divine Reality other than which there is nothing. *Ik Onkar* is called the *bij* mantra or "seed formula," because it is the seed from which the complete realization of God originates.

In the Sikh worldview, God has both a manifest and an unmanifest nature. In His unmanifest aspect, God is formless (*nirankar*) and without qualities (*nirguna*). He is an invisible (*alakh*), timeless Being (*akal purakh*). The vehicle through which He becomes manifest, thereby creating and sustaining the universe, is the reverberation (*pranava*) of a divine Sound Current (*shabad* or *sabda*). This Sound Current is God's Word or Name (*naam*), which is "both the message and the messenger of Truth, the revelation and the revealer of Ultimate Reality. It is the Primal Guru, the Enlightener. It is what we can know of the Unknowable One Who pervades all existence and is beyond existence."[14]

Through *naam*, God issues His Command or expresses His Will (*hukam*). In this way, God acquires a manifest aspect in which He is the repository of all qualities (*saguna*). In this manifest form, God is referred to by terms such as the True Teacher (*satguru*), the First Teacher (*adiguru*), and the Wonderful Teacher (*vahiguru*). Throughout the first half of the seventeenth century, Sikh history went through a militant phase during which God was also metaphorically called "all steel" (*sarab loh*) and was symbolized by a divine sword (*bhagauti*). Guru Nanak described God's act of creation as follows:

It was all dark billions of years ago.
There was no earth, no heaven except God's supreme order [*hukam*].
There was no day or night, neither the moon or the sun – God
    meditated in a void.
There was no eating, no talking, neither air nor water.
No one was created, no one died; none came, no one went.
There were no continents, no nether world,
Nor were there seven seas; there was no water in the rivers.
There was neither heaven, nor any tortoise underneath the earth.
With His order [*hukam*], the world was created.
It is maintained without any support.
He created Brahman, Vishnu, and Siva.
He created also the love of Maya.
Only a few were blessed with His word [*naam* or *shabad*].
But He watched and ruled over all.
He set going this world and the other world.
And became Himself manifest.
It is the true Guru alone who gives this understanding.
Says Nanak, those who are truthful live in eternal bliss,
They are blessed with the recitation of God's name.[15]

The divine Sound Current, or Word, is indescribable and unfathomable; it can only be experienced directly. It is through the Guru's grace that one gains this experience. Under the guidance of the Guru, one is trained in the meditative practice of *naam simran*, repetition (or remembrance) of the Divine Name (or Word). Guru Amar Das said, "The pathway to God is revealed by the Guru, a meeting which God decrees. God knows the pathways which lead us to him, The Order [*hukam*] his Word has revealed."[16] Guru Arjan compared the Divine Word to a blind man's staff: with a staff, the blind man finds his way; with the Divine Word, the believer finds his way to God.[17]

Turning Toward the Divine

Sikhs work toward God-realization by becoming attuned to the Divine Sound Current. Doing so entails submission to God's Will (*hukam*) and the dissolution of one's ego, or "I-am-ness" (*haumai*). "I-am-ness," or egotism, is an obstruction hindering the experience of the Divine. Impulses and inclinations toward gratifying desires must yield to the Divine Will. As Guru Nanak proclaims in the *Japji*,

> Through ritual purity [God] can never be known though one cleanse oneself a hundred thousand times. Silent reflection will never reveal him though one dwell absorbed in deepest meditation. Though one gather vast riches the hunger remains, no cunning will help in the hereafter. How is Truth to be attained, how the veil of falsehood torn aside? Nanak, thus it is written: Submit to God's Order [*hukam*], walk in its way.[18]

As Guru Nanak states elsewhere, "He conquers the world who conquers self."[19] A similar (although perhaps not identical) idea of relinquishing one's desires in favor of submission to the Will of God is prevalent in the Islamic and Christian traditions.

In the Sikh tradition, a person who has aligned himself with the Will of God and the teachings of the Gurus is referred to as a *gurmukh*, one who has turned his face toward God or the Guru. Such a person always has God and the teachings of the Guru in his or her thoughts. This condition contrasts with that of the *manmukh*, the self-centered person. Such a person focuses on himself or herself at all times, and is absorbed in his or her own ego. As a consequence, he or she strays from spiritual liberation and succumbs to the "five sins": lust, anger, greed, attachment, and pride.

Turning away from the ego and toward the Divine oneness of all Being involves passing through various stages, or "realms" (*khand*s). These are described in the *Japji* as follows: First, in the Realm of Duty (Dharam Khand) the devotee is confronted with the need to discern the noble from the ignoble and to act accordingly. Second, in the Realm of Knowledge (Gian Khand) the devotee gains understanding of Divine knowledge. Third, in the Realm of Beauty (Saram Khand) the devotee acquires Divine intuition and true wisdom. Fourth, in the Realm of Divine Grace (Karam Khand) the devotee is released

> **Egotism is an obstruction hindering the experience of the Divine**

from *maya* and absorbed into the Divine Name or Sound Current. The Divine Name thus becomes enshrined within the devotee's heart and mind. Such a person is referred to as a *jivamukta*, or one who has been liberated while living. Finally, in the Realm of Truth (Sach Khand) the devotee is dissolved into God, the Formless One. Sikhs describe this final passage into union with God as a passage through the "Tenth Gate" (*dasam dwar*).[20] The

Tenth Gate is a spiritual opening through which one can unite with the divine oneness of Ultimate Reality – God.

CHAPTER SUMMARY

Today there are roughly fourteen million Sikhs in India, most of them living in the Punjab, which has been divided between India and Pakistan for more than half a century (although most Sikhs live on the Indian side of the border). However, Sikhs are found in many other parts of the world, the largest community outside of India being in Britain. Contemporary Sikhs carry on many of the traditions initiated by the Gurus. One notable example is that of the communal kitchen (*langar*), which originated with Guru Nanak. These are places where free meals are provided to all, regardless of social or religious background. This practice harmonizes with two core principles of the Sikh faith: that it is incumbent on the Sikh to fulfill social responsibilities and contribute to the community; and that the "community" is not restricted according to religious or social background, but extends to all humanity.

The Sikh faith originated at a time of religious reformation in northern India and grew alongside the Hindu and Muslim traditions. From its very inception the Sikh community respected other traditions and absorbed much of their wisdom. At the same time, Sikhs stressed that true religion transcends the names and images that any specific tradition assigns to God, the Formless One. Differences between images are the consequences of time and place, but God is eternal and pervades the whole of creation. Beginning with the message of Guru Nanak, the teachings of the Sikh Gurus were unique in that they turned away from the external forms of any one tradition and sought the internal reality represented by all religions.

Sikh Gurus taught their disciples not to renounce the duties of everyday life, but to confront them with virtue and dignity. The virtues of the Realm of Duty are not the completion of spiritual life; they are the basis of an ascent through various stages or Realms of spiritual progress. Paramount in this ascent through the Realms (*khand*s) is remembrance of God (*naam simran*). The transformation symbolized by this "ascent" is one of turning one's face toward God and the teachings of the Gurus, submitting to God's Will (*hukam*), and leaving behind "I-am-ness" (*haumai*). This transformation leads to passage through the "Tenth Gate" to the Divine singularity of Ultimate Reality, out of which all forms are created. As Guru Nanak states in the *Japji*, "As light dawns from darkness and returns to it again, so does all proceed from God, its source and final destination."[21]

> **Sikhs stress that true religion transcends the names and images that any specific tradition assigns to God**

The Shrine of the Bab, Mount Carmel, Haifa, the second holiest Baha'i shrine

CHAPTER 16
THE BAHA'I FAITH

I bear witness, O my God, that Thou hast created me to know Thee and to worship Thee. I testify, at this moment, to my powerlessness and to Thy might, to my poverty and to Thy wealth. There is none other God but Thee. The Help in Peril, the Self-Subsisting.[1]

— Baha'u'llah

INTRODUCTION

The Baha'i Faith originated in Iran (Persia) in the mid-nineteenth century. Its Founder is Baha'u'llah (1817–1892), a title signifying "the Glory of God" in Arabic. His followers, known as Baha'is, believe that Baha'u'llah is the most recent of the divine messengers sent by God, including Abraham, Krishna, Moses, Zoroaster, Buddha, Jesus, and Muhammad. Furthermore, Baha'is regard Baha'u'llah as the Promised One of the world's great faiths who is destined to usher in a long-awaited age of peace.

Baha'u'llah teaches that the central aim of his religion is to bring about the unity of the human race. Three central principles of Baha'i teachings lie at the foundation of the unity that Baha'u'llah describes. The first is the belief that there is one God, who is the creator of all life and the source of inspiration to all the world's peoples and faiths. The second principle upholds the belief in

> **Desire not for anyone the things that ye would not desire for yourselves**
> *Baha'u'llah*
> **THE GOLDEN RULE**

the oneness of the entire human race. The third asserts that all of the world's great religions and their founders are divine in origin, and reflect one continuous faith that is renewed from age to age. In one of his writings, Baha'u'llah states:

Timeline

1753–1825 C.E.
Shaykh Ahmad-i-Ahsa'i

1817–1892 C.E.
Baha'u'llah (Mirza Husayn-'Ali)

1819–1850 C.E.
The Báb (Siyyid 'Ali-Muhammad) founder of Babi religion, and forerunner of Baha'i Faith

1844–1921 C.E.
'Abdu'l-Baha ('Abbas Effendi)

1853 C.E.
Baha'u'llah exiled to Baghdad under Nasiri'd-Din Shah

1863 C.E.
Baha'u'llah makes first public declaration that he was the promised Manifestation of God

1868 C.E.
Ottoman caliph Sultan 'Abdu'l-'Aziz banishes Baha'u'llah to Akka (Palestine)

1897–1957 C.E.
Shoghi Effendi, appointed in 1921 as Guardian of Baha'i Faith by 'Abdu'l-Baha; lays foundation of Baha'i administrative order

My object is none other than the betterment of the world and the tranquility of its peoples. The well-being of mankind, its peace and security, are unattainable unless and until its unity is firmly established. This unity can never be achieved so long as the counsels which the Pen of the Most High hath revealed are suffered to pass unheeded.[2]

1911–1913 C.E.
'Abdu'l-Baha travels to the West
1963 C.E.
Universal House of Justice elected as supreme governing and administrative body of Baha'i community worldwide

Baha'u'llah's revelation was preceded by the emergence of another religion, the Babi Faith, founded by Siyyid 'Ali-Muhammad (1819–1850). Siyyid 'Ali-Muhammad took for himself the title "the Bab," meaning "Gate" in Arabic, and signifying that his mission was to prepare the world for the coming of someone far greater than himself. Baha'is regard the Bab both as a divine messenger and the forerunner of Baha'u'llah.

Baha'u'llah's teachings explicitly safeguard his religion from division into different sects and branches. In his writings, Baha'u'llah has left clear instructions regarding both successorship in, and administration of, the community of believers after his passing. He appointed his eldest son, 'Abdu'l-Baha, as the center of his faith and the interpreter of his teachings, and established what Baha'is refer to as the Covenant of Baha'u'llah. The Covenant of Baha'u'llah forbids ideological and theological differences to legitimize the formation of sects and factions. Through the Covenant, Baha'u'llah has laid the foundation for the maintenance of unity within the Baha'i community.

Baha'u'llah's writings, numbering some one hundred volumes, are filled with instructions and guidance that inform his followers of their purpose and responsibilities as individuals in relation to their creator and as members of society. As such, Baha'u'llah has instructed his followers to carry out certain responsibilities, which include prayer, meditation, reading of sacred texts, fasting, contributing to society through an occupation, and teaching his faith to others. His writings also address, at length, issues regarding the functioning of society and the development of institutions that will operate in the context of an emerging global civilization.

This chapter will cover significant elements of the history of the Baha'i Faith, its major principles and teachings, and features of its administration and laws.

THE BAB

The Bab lived amidst the milieu of heightened religious expectations in Iran that the Promised One of Shi'i Islam – the Qa'im or Mahdi – was soon to come. The turn of the century witnessed the emergence of a new branch of Islamic theology, named the Shaykhi school, founded by Shaykh Ahmad-i-Ahsa'i (1753–1825). Followers of this theological movement were preparing themselves for the imminent arrival of the Qa'im. After the passing of Shaykh Ahmad-i-Ahsa'i and his successor, the followers of the Shaykhi school were instructed to disperse across Persia to find the Promised One. On 23 May 1844, a meeting took place between the young merchant Siyyid 'Ali-Muhammad and a devoted and prominent member of the Shaykhi school, Mulla Husayn-i-Bushrui. During the course of that interaction, the young merchant declared that he was the Promised One and took for himself the title of the Bab. Mulla Husayn-i-Bushrui became the first of the followers of the Bab, named Babis. Thus, a new chapter in religious history was opened.

The Bab was born in Persia in 1819 to a family that traced its origins to the Prophet Muhammad. His father died soon after his birth, and he was raised under the care of his maternal uncle. From a young age, he exhibited signs of an extraordinary, innate knowledge and a distinguished character. Early accounts of his life note the indelible impression he made on those who met him; he was known for his purity, integrity, and dignity. These qualities likewise characterized his work as a merchant in the port city of Bushehr, where he followed his occupation as a young man.

The Bab was twenty-five years of age when he declared himself to be the Qa'im to Mulla Husayn-i-Bushrui. On that momentous occasion, the Bab instructed his first disciple to keep the news of his revelation a secret, explaining that through prayers, dreams, and visions, seventeen others would spontaneously and independently find the Bab and recognize his station. As prophesied, seventeen others did indeed find him independently. Those first eighteen followers were given the title "Letters of the Living," and were given specific instructions by the Bab to spread out across the land and teach the new faith to others. Mulla Husayn was assigned a unique mission, to travel northward to Tehran, the capital city, and deliver the message of the Bab to the home of a special personage. Referring to the mission he had assigned to Mulla Husayn, the Bab instructed him with the following words:

> Beseech almighty Providence that He may graciously enable you to attain, in that capital, the seat of true sovereignty, and to enter the mansion of the Beloved. A secret lies hidden in that city. When made manifest, it shall turn the earth into paradise. My hope is that you may partake of its grace and recognize its splendor.[3]

Mulla Husayn successfully delivered the Bab's message to Baha'u'llah, who immediately embraced the teachings of the Bab and became one of the most devout and prominent followers of the new religion.

The Bab's ministry endured six intense and dramatic years that would witness the great influence and rapid spread of his teachings across Iran as well as waves of persecution of the Bab and his followers. The preeminent theme of the Bab's message was the promise of the imminent arrival of a messenger of God far greater than the Bab himself. The Bab referred to this prophetic figure as "Him whom God shall make manifest." Furthermore, the Bab claimed to bring a new set of laws and a new message distinct from, and fulfilling the religion of, Islam. His message had wide appeal and spread rapidly, gaining tens of thousands of new adherents and attracting the concern of the religious leaders of the time. In a very short period after the declaration of the Bab, resistance to his movement grew intense.

> **His message gained tens of thousands of new adherents and attracted the concern of the religious leaders of the time**

The Letters of the Living and the early followers of the Bab endured persecution and torture, and many were killed. Exiled to remote mountain prisons, the Bab suffered at the hands of the religious authorities, who viewed his teachings as heretical and dangerous. Despite the hopes of the authorities that his exile would suppress the momentum of his movement, the Bab's teachings continued to exercise influence over his followers and to attract new adherents. In 1850, the Bab was taken to the city of Tabriz, where he and a companion were executed by a firing squad. The martyrdom of the Bab at the hands of his executioners holds great significance for Baha'is, who commemorate it each year as a holy day.

According to historical accounts, the night before his death the Bab was joyful, believing that his mission was accomplished. The following morning, as he was dictating final instructions to one of his companions, the guards appeared and demanded he accompany them to the place of execution. He replied: "Not until I have said to him all those things that I wish to say can any earthly power silence Me. Though all the world be armed against Me, yet shall they be powerless to deter Me from fulfilling, to the last word, My intention."[4] Along with a young companion, the Bab was taken and suspended by ropes against the wall of the barracks square in the city, while thousands of onlookers crowded the rooftops to view the spectacle. A regiment of 750 soldiers took aim and fired. When the dense cloud of gun smoke cleared

> **The night before his death the Bab was joyful, believing that his mission was accomplished**

a great shout went up from the crowd. The Bab was nowhere to be seen, and his young companion stood alone in the square, unharmed, the ropes lying in shreds on the ground. After a frantic search for him, he was found sitting in his prison cell finishing the instructions that he had been dictating prior to being summoned to his execution. As a result of this event, the leader of the regiment refused to carry out the order to execute the Bab, and a second regiment had to be brought in. The second attempt succeeded in carrying out the sentence. At noon, the Bab and his companion were executed.

The Bab revealed many works during his six-year ministry. The *Persian Bayan* is considered the foundational text of his faith, and consists of the laws and precepts of his religion. The Bab's commentary on the *surah* of Joseph, one of the chapters of the Qur'an, is considered by Baha'is to be his most important work because it prophesizes the coming of Baha'u'llah. Baha'is regard the Bab's brief and dramatic ministry as a significant period in religious history and as a preparatory phase for the revelation of Baha'u'llah.

BAHA'U'LLAH

Baha'u'llah was born Mirza Husayn-'Ali, in Tehran, Persia, in 1817, to one of the distinguished families of the nobility. As a child, he was known for his unusual wisdom, and people marveled at his knowledge. Yet, like the Bab, he never attended any school and learned only the minimal skills of reading and writing expected of men in the upper ranks of society. Such were his abilities that at the age of seven he represented his father in a property dispute at the court of the shah and won the case. His early adulthood was characterized by commitment to serving the downtrodden and dispossessed of society, and he was popularly known as the "Father of the Poor." It was during that period of his life that Baha'u'llah was offered a high position in the court of the shah but refused the opportunity for advancement in society to dedicate himself to the service of the poor.

After reading a scroll of the Bab's writings, which had been delivered to him by Mulla Husayn – the first to recognize the Bab – Baha'u'llah immediately accepted the newly born faith, and became one of its most prominent figures. Almost immediately after his acceptance of the Babi religion, Baha'u'llah began to endure suffering and persecutions.

Two years after the Bab was executed, a storm engulfed the young Babi Faith. In an unbalanced state of mind, and distraught with anger and grief over the death of their leader, two young Babis attempted to assassinate the shah. Although their act was in opposition to the teachings of the Bab and to the behavior of their fellow believers, it triggered a terrible wave of persecution against the Babis throughout Persia. Baha'u'llah was seized and forced to walk in chains, barefoot and bareheaded in the fierce midsummer sun, from his country home outside Tehran to a subterranean dungeon in the city. The road along which he walked was lined with fanatical mobs that ridiculed and abused him. When he finally reached the black, unventilated pit, which was ankle-deep in filth and populated by murderers and thieves, his feet were placed in stocks, and huge chains were fixed

Two years after the Bab was executed, a storm engulfed the young Babi Faith

around his neck. In this damp, vermin-infested hole he spent four months, all the while maintaining the spirits of his fellow prisoners by teaching them to chant prayers. It was here that Baha'u'llah received the first intimations of his revelation. Later he described his experience:

> One night, in a dream, these exalted words were heard on every side: "Verily, We shall render Thee victorious by Thyself and by Thy Pen. Grieve Thou not for that which hath befallen Thee, neither be Thou afraid, for Thou art in safety. Erelong will God raise up the treasures of the earth – men who will aid Thee through Thyself and through Thy Name, wherewith God hath revived the hearts of such as have recognized Him."[5]

Another ten years were to pass before Baha'u'llah would announce himself as "Him Whom God shall make manifest," but the knowledge of his revelation had come to light in the darkest of circumstances, while in that infamous prison.

Those who had ordered Baha'u'llah's imprisonment found no evidence to prove that he had been an accomplice in the irresponsible attempt on the shah's life. The Russian minister to the shah's court exerted his influence, and Baha'u'llah was released from prison, whereupon he was stripped of all his wealth and, along with his family and companions, was expelled from Persia.

After a harrowing journey lasting three months through high mountains in the dead of winter, Baha'u'llah and his family arrived in Baghdad in 1853. Thus began the first of four exiles that took him further and further away from his homeland. In Baghdad, Baha'u'llah began to revitalize the Babi community, whose morale had been devastated by the martyrdom of the Bab, the attempt on the life of the shah, and the subsequent persecutions. The success of his efforts, and the great esteem in which he was held by believers and citizens of Baghdad alike, aroused the jealousy of his half-brother, Mirza Yahya, who was also a prominent Babi. In 1854, to avoid becoming a cause of discord among the Babis, Baha'u'llah withdrew to the mountains of Kurdistan, where he spent much of his time in seclusion. Later, he was persuaded to reside in the town of Sulaymaniyyih, famous as a seat of learning.

Immediately after his return from Sulaymaniyyih in 1856, Kurdish mystics and scholars traveled to Baghdad to visit him. They were in the vanguard of many leaders, government officials, and eminent personages who increasingly sought counsel from Baha'u'llah. Babis from all over Persia began to flock to Baghdad to visit Baha'u'llah, and would return to their homeland with stories of his great spirit. By personal example and written exhortations, Baha'u'llah was at last able to achieve the moral rejuvenation of the Babi community, and to bring the behavior of the Babis into accord with the teachings set down by the Bab. The Babi Faith was disassociated from all political activity, emphasizing

A calligraphic rendering of the phrase, "In the Name of God, the Glorious, the Most Glorious One" in Arabic by the prominent Baha'i calligrapher, Mishkin-Qalam (d. 1912)

non-violence and strict obedience to law and authority. Love rather than hatred, and forgiveness rather than retaliation, were the virtues taught by Baha'u'llah. His presence uplifted the spirits of all those around him and created a sense of peace in the Babi community. Baha'u'llah inspired his companions with universal ideals and instilled in them new hope for a better world. As the prestige of the Babi community rose to new heights, the enemies of the Babi Faith exerted greater efforts to conspire against Baha'u'llah, even organizing assassination attempts. Persistent misrepresentation of Baha'u'llah and the Babi community resulted in his being banished yet again. This time Sultan 'Abdu'l-'Aziz ordered him to move from Baghdad to Constantinople (now known as Istanbul), the capital of the Ottoman Empire.

Before embarking on this second exile, Baha'u'llah and his companions went to a garden outside the city of Baghdad. In 1863, in this beautiful garden and surrounded by a small group of his followers, Baha'u'llah made his first public declaration that he was the promised Manifestation of God, "Him Whom God shall make manifest" foretold by the Bab. Baha'u'llah remained with his family and companions for a period of twelve days in the garden, known as the Garden of Ridvan (Paradise). Many Babis went to the garden to hear his teachings and exhortations. Those who accepted the declaration of Baha'u'llah became known as Baha'is.

In Istanbul, the machinations of Baha'u'llah's enemies continued apace, and before the completion of even four months in that city he was ordered once again to move with his followers to Adrianople (now known as Edirne), where he would settle for over four years.

In Edirne, Baha'u'llah began revealing Tablets in which he proclaimed his revelation to kings, rulers, religious authorities, and other leaders of society. In one of his writings, Baha'u'llah proclaims:

> O KINGS of the earth! We see you increasing every year your expenditures, and laying the burden thereof on your subjects. This, verily, is wholly and grossly unjust. Fear the sighs and tears of this Wronged One, and lay not excessive burdens on your peoples. Do not rob them to rear palaces for yourselves; nay rather choose for them that which ye choose for yourselves. Thus We unfold to your eyes that which profiteth you, if ye but perceive. Your people are your treasures. Beware lest your rule violate the commandments of God, and ye deliver your wards to the hands of the robber. By them ye rule, by their means ye subsist, by their aid ye conquer. Yet, how disdainfully ye look upon them! How strange, how very strange! …
>
> O Rulers of the earth! Be reconciled among yourselves, that ye may need no more armaments save in a measure to safeguard your territories and dominions. Beware lest ye disregard the counsel of the All-Knowing, the Faithful.

> Be united, O Kings of the earth, for thereby will the tempest of discord be stilled amongst you, and your people find rest, if ye be of them that comprehend. Should any one among you take up arms against another, rise ye all against him, for this is naught but manifest justice.[6]

In 1868, Sultan 'Abdu'l-'Aziz, who was alarmed by Baha'u'llah's rising prestige, once again banished him, this time to the notorious, vermin-infested prison-city of Akka in the Ottoman province of Syria. Baha'u'llah and his companions were placed in the citadel, which was being used as a prison, and local people were not permitted to associate with them. Months later, one of his beloved sons, Mirza Mihdi, died after a fall from the prison roof where he had been reciting prayers. After two years in the citadel, Baha'u'llah and his companions were moved to other quarters elsewhere in the city, yet they were still required to remain within Akka's walls.

Baha'u'llah's exile and imprisonment did not hinder the spread of his faith. Angered by the reports about Baha'u'llah brought back by returning pilgrims, the Islamic religious leaders and members of the public in Persia committed atrocities against the Baha'i community in that country. On many occasions, Baha'u'llah asked his followers to be patient and tolerant. In one well-known epistle, Baha'u'llah exhorts his followers thus:

> Be generous in prosperity, and thankful in adversity. Be worthy of the trust of thy neighbour, and look upon him with a bright and friendly face. Be a treasure to the poor, an admonisher to the rich, an answerer of the cry of the needy, a preserver of the sanctity of thy pledge. Be fair in thy judgment, and guarded in thy speech. Be unjust to no man, and show all meekness to all men. Be as a lamp unto them that walk in darkness, a joy to the sorrowful, a sea for the thirsty, a haven for the distressed, an upholder and defender of the victim of oppression. Let integrity and uprightness distinguish all thine acts. Be a home for the stranger, a balm to the suffering, a tower of strength for the fugitive. Be eyes to the blind, and a guiding light unto the feet of the erring. Be an ornament to the countenance of truth, a crown to the brow of fidelity, a pillar of the temple of righteousness, a breath of life to the body of mankind, an ensign of the hosts of justice, a luminary above the horizon of virtue, a dew to the soil of the human heart, an ark on the ocean of knowledge, a sun in the heaven of bounty, a gem on the diadem of wisdom, a shining light in the firmament of thy generation, a fruit upon the tree of humility.[7]

Baha'u'llah visited Haifa four times in the remaining years of his life and, while in that city, pitched his tent on Mount Carmel. He pointed out to 'Abdu'l-Baha where the remains of the Bab should be buried and a majestic shrine built over them. Baha'u'llah's earthly life ended in 1892. Baha'u'llah left a treasury of writings which are of immense importance to Baha'is. Most of his laws and ordinances are contained in the *Kitab-i-Aqdas* ("The Most Holy Book"), which he revealed in Akka. While in Edirne, he had addressed a series of Tablets to the monarchs and rulers of the world announcing his revelation and calling on them to heed his message of unity. In his second most important work, the *Kitab-i-Iqan* ("The Book of Certitude"), revealed in Baghdad before his public declaration, Baha'u'llah elucidates on the meanings of significant passages

> **Baha'u'llah left a treasury of writings which are of immense importance to Baha'is**

and concepts in the Bible and the Qur'an. *Kalimat-i-Maknunih* ("The Hidden Words"), the greatest of his ethical writings, and *Haft Vadi* ("The Seven Valleys"), his greatest mystical work, were also revealed in Baghdad. In all, his collected writings number some one hundred volumes in authenticated written form. From the Baha'i perspective, Baha'u'llah's unique revelation does not obscure or contradict his essential oneness with the founders of previous world religions. Baha'is believe that his revelation, however, is more intense than former revelations because this is the day of humanity's maturity. Baha'u'llah wrote: "That which hath been made manifest in this preëminent, this most exalted Revelation, stands unparalleled in the annals of the past, nor will future ages witness its like."[8]

'ABDU'L-BAHA

Baha'u'llah left clear instructions regarding to whom his followers should turn after his death. He appointed in writing his eldest son, 'Abbas Effendi, as the Center of his Covenant. 'Abbas Effendi (1844–1921) had been a constant companion and devoted follower of his father from childhood, and had endured the hardships of exile and imprisonment with him. He took for himself the title by which he is most commonly known, 'Abdu'l-Baha ("The Servant of Baha"). Baha'u'llah bestowed upon 'Abdu'l-Baha a high station. While he is not considered a messenger or Manifestation of God, he is regarded by Baha'is as the perfect exemplar of the teachings of his father and infallible in his guidance, as conveyed through his talks and writings. 'Abdu'l-Baha conveyed through his unique station the substance and spirit of the Baha'i message over the course of his life.

'Abdu'l-Baha was born on the night of the declaration of the Bab. At the age of nine, his father was imprisoned in Tehran, and 'Abdu'l-Baha witnessed firsthand the suffering of his father in prison and the loss of his family's wealth and estate at the hands of the religious authorities. He and his family were subjected to cruelties by violent mobs, and their home was ransacked and destroyed. 'Abdu'l-Baha accompanied his father on his exiles and remained a loyal and most reliable companion. During his years as a young adult, he served his father in many capacities, and devoted his life to serving the poor and destitute of society. He acted as his father's representative on many occasions, and became his chief steward.

During his ministry 'Abdu'l-Baha vastly expanded the borders of the Baha'i community, visiting several countries in Asia, Europe, North America, and Egypt in Africa. For many years he had been virtually confined to the Akka region as a political prisoner of the Ottoman sultan. But with the Young Turk rebellion in 1908, the Ottoman Empire's political prisoners were released, 'Abdu'l-Baha among them. His first goal was to visit the West in order to spread his father's teachings. From 1911 to 1913, he traveled and taught the new faith to the people of the West, speaking at diverse religious and civil establishments throughout Europe, Canada, and the United States. During those momentous meetings, 'Abdu'l-Baha spoke often about the harmony of religion and also the need for racial reconciliation. He visited the poor areas of the cities to which he traveled, demonstrating great concern and compassion for the oppressed and the needy.

'Abdu'l-Baha's most important writings include his *Will and Testament* – which appointed his grandson, Shoghi Effendi, as Guardian of the Baha'i Faith and interpreter of the teachings of Baha'u'llah, and also provided numerous elucidations of the general administrative principles set down by Baha'u'llah for the organization of the Baha'i community – and *Tablets of the Divine Plan*, which provides guidance for the growth and spread of the Baha'i community throughout the world. Along with the Bab and Baha'u'llah, 'Abdu'l-Baha is considered by Baha'is to be one of the three Central Figures of the Baha'i Faith. His unique function and station preserved the Baha'i community from division into factions, and guided that community to develop its capacity and to more fully realize the

> **'Abdu'l-Baha witnessed the growth of the Baha'i Faith from a small religious community into a faith active in five continents**

vision enshrined in the teachings of Baha'u'llah. The ministry of 'Abdu'l-Baha witnessed the growth of the Baha'i Faith from a small religious community limited to a few locations in Asia and Africa into a faith active in five continents, while preserving its unity and integrity.

SHOGHI EFFENDI

'Abdu'l-Baha died in 1921, stating in his *Will and Testament* that he was to be succeeded by his eldest grandson, Shoghi Effendi (1897–1957), whom he named the Guardian of the Baha'i faith. Shoghi Effendi's first task was to develop more fully the Baha'i administrative system specified in the writings of Baha'u'llah and 'Abdu'l–Baha. Simultaneously, he produced the first authoritative English translations of many of the major writings of Baha'u'llah and 'Abdu'l-Baha, which prepared the way for the translation of Baha'i texts into many other languages. Shoghi Effendi worked to establish a firm foundation for the Baha'i Faith to be recognized as an independent religion. He also began to work toward the implementation of the Baha'i system of administration and governance. According to the specific provisions of Baha'u'llah and 'Abdu'l-Baha, and using the American Baha'i community as a prototype for other national communities, he nurtured the development of administrative bodies, known as Local and National Spiritual Assemblies, which serve as channels for the spread of the Baha'i teachings and spirit. Through the establishment of such Spiritual Assemblies, Shoghi Effendi set in motion the means necessary for the subsequent election of what was ordained by Baha'u'llah in the *Kitab-i-Aqdas* as the supreme governing body of the Baha'i Faith, the Universal House of Justice. The Universal House of Justice, which is elected every five years at an international convention, gives spiritual guidance to and directs the administrative activities of the worldwide Baha'i community. By 1957, the year when Shoghi Effendi died in London, the Baha'i Faith was well established throughout the world. Despite sporadic episodes of persecution, particularly in Iran, and numerous other obstacles, Shoghi Effendi's ministry as

> By 1957, the Baha'i Faith was well established throughout the world

the Guardian was characterized by rapid growth and consolidation. The Universal House of Justice, which was first elected in 1963, is now the supreme governing body of the Baha'i community and has its headquarters at the Baha'i World Centre on Mount Carmel in Haifa, Israel.

PRINCIPLES OF THE BAHA'I FAITH

Manifestations of God

Central to the Baha'i Faith is the concept of divine revelation. Baha'is believe that God is revealed to humanity in the same way that the sun is revealed in a mirror. God is like the sun, and His divine messengers are like mirrors: God is unknowable, infinite, inaccessible, and beyond the comprehension of the human intellect and soul. In other words, He is the "Unknowable Essence." Just as the sun cannot approach the earth, so too God cannot reveal His very essence to humankind, for an infinitely transcendent Being could not possibly be understood in finite terms. Therefore, God reveals Himself by means of His Manifestations, who are not the essence of God but rather His creation, yet who perfectly reflect all the attributes of God – His power, majesty, authority – just as a flawless mirror reflects the light and heat of the sun. While the mirror is not the sun, the sun is perfectly reflected in the mirror.

Similarly, although the Manifestations of God are mere creatures in relation to God, to the world of humanity they represent God in that they are the perfect reflection of God's attributes and will. The Bab and Baha'u'llah both are regarded by Baha'is as Manifestations of God, as are Abraham, Krishna, Moses, Zoroaster, Buddha, Jesus, and Muhammad. Furthermore, Baha'is uphold that there have been Manifestations of God whose names have with the passage of time been forgotten.

Progressive Revelation

In the *Kitab-i-Iqan* and other writings, Baha'u'llah gives to humanity a broad vision of the evolution of civilization and the role played by religion in that process. He states that all civilizations are the fruits of the word of God as revealed by a divine messenger. History has repeatedly witnessed the appearance of a divine messenger, the growth of his religion, the founding of a society on the principles and laws of that religion, and the subsequent flourishing of institutions, skills, sciences, and arts. Eventually, the civilization forgets the spiritual origins of its vitality, becomes blinded to spiritual truth, increasingly worships material goals, and eventually declines and collapses in disasters of its own making. Subsequently, another messenger appears with a new message to remedy the ills of the new era, and new progress results.

Baha'u'llah explains that all the prophets and messengers are divine teachers sent by one God. The Manifestations teach the same spiritual truths – love of God, love of humanity, service, and the Golden Rule. All the religions are therefore one in their essence and in their origin. Baha'u'llah differentiates between transient and eternal elements of religion. Transient (or non-essential) aspects of religion, such as their unique social laws, pass away with the changes and chances of time, whereas the universal truths embodied in religion are renewed with the coming of every new faith. It is the transient elements that have often been the cause of conflict and misunderstanding between religions. Baha'u'llah's teachings aim to reiterate the universal truths embodied in all the great faith traditions of the world, and thereby to establish their unity. The principle of the oneness of religion was explained by Baha'u'llah: "These principles and laws, these firmly-established and mighty systems, have proceeded from one Source and are the rays of one Light. That they differ one from another is to be attributed to the varying requirements of the ages in which they were promulgated."[9]

> **Baha'u'llah's teachings aim to reiterate the universal truths embodied in all the great faith traditions of the world**

Furthermore, Baha'u'llah explains that divine revelation is a continuous and progressive process that guides humanity in the context of an ever-advancing civilization. As humanity has moved from primarily tribal identities, to city-states and then nation-states, allegiances have broadened to incorporate larger groups of people. Baha'u'llah elucidates that the next stage of social evolution is the formation of a global civilization, where individuals will regard themselves as members of one race and citizens of one homeland. Within this framework, religions have served as the primary impulse for the advancement of societies. Thus, from a Baha'i perspective, religions have been part of one unfolding faith of God. Each religion fulfills a previous one and prepares people for a subsequent messenger of God.

Divine guidance does not end with the Baha'i Faith; rather, the revelations of the Bab and Baha'u'llah will be succeeded in ages to come by further outpourings of the word of God according to the needs of humanity in those times. Baha'is believe that God has always sent messengers to humanity in the past, and will always do so in the future.

The Oneness of Humanity

The foundational teaching of Baha'u'llah is that humanity is one and that the long-awaited era of peace and unity promised in many of the world's traditions is now within the reach of humankind. Thus, many of Baha'u'llah's exhortations and teachings address the subject of the oneness of humanity and counsel his followers and all people to arise to a global consciousness and a higher standard of human behavior: "Ye are the fruits of one tree, and the leaves of one branch. Deal ye one with another with the utmost love and harmony, with friendliness and fellowship ... So powerful is the light of unity that it can illuminate the whole earth."[10]

This sense of the oneness of humanity, according to Baha'i teachings, supersedes and replaces the contemporary, narrow definition of nationalism. Baha'u'llah said: "It is not for him to pride himself who loveth his own country, but rather for him who loveth the whole world. The earth is but one country, and mankind its citizens."[11]

The Baha'i scriptures are filled with analogies from nature to elucidate the concept of unity that Baha'u'llah envisioned. Furthermore, they clarify that unity should not be mistaken for uniformity; rather, unity must be achieved while maintaining and indeed valuing the diversity of the human family. 'Abdu'l-Baha gives the example of two gardens, one wherein all the flowers and plants are of the same color, and another whose blossoms are of different colors and shapes. The second garden, he teaches, is enhanced by the rich variations of color and form and is therefore preferable. He concludes that the diversity of races, cultures, and traditions in the world enhance the beauty and richness of humanity, and should be sources of celebration, not conflict.

Top: The Baha'i House of Worship in New Delhi, India
Bottom: A choir performs inside the Baha'i House of Worship, New Delhi

The Lesser Peace and the Most Great Peace

The revelations of the Bab and Baha'u'llah claim to usher in a new era in world history, a period in which humanity will live in harmony and will flourish. Baha'u'llah taught that this promised era of peace would be achieved though various stages of development. One of the significant stages of development would be marked by the establishment of political unity in the world. Baha'u'llah calls this stage the Lesser Peace, which will be achieved through the formation of a world parliament. The ultimate goal to which Baha'is aspire, however, is what Baha'u'llah calls the Most Great Peace, which will come about in the distant future. The Lesser Peace spoken of in the Baha'i writings precedes the Most Great Peace, and is a world civilization motivated by political and economic expediency – essentially material forces. The Most Great Peace is a world civilization inspired by true spirituality and universal love, a civilization that is the fruit of the balance between science and religion, the material and the spiritual, and a civilization that has overcome prejudice and superstition. Baha'u'llah says:

> **The revelations claim to usher in a new era, in which humanity will live in harmony and will flourish**

> O Children of Men:
>
> Know ye not why we created you all from the same dust? That no one should exalt himself over the other. Ponder at all times in your hearts how ye were created. Since We have created you all from one same substance it is incumbent on you to be even as one soul, to walk with the same feet, eat with the same mouth and dwell in the same land, that from your inmost being, by your deeds and actions, the signs of oneness and the essence of detachment may be made manifest.[12]

In general, Baha'is view the process of globalization as dictated by the evolution of human civilization, regarding it as the inevitable outcome of the gradual maturing of humanity as a whole. Shoghi Effendi, the Guardian of the Baha'i Faith, outlined the following essential preconditions for the establishment of a viable global system, which he called "a world commonwealth":

> The unity of the human race, as envisaged by Bahá'u'lláh, implies the establishment of **a world commonwealth** in which all nations, races, creeds, and classes are closely and permanently united and in which the autonomy of its state members and the personal freedom and initiative of the individuals that compose them are definitely and completely safeguarded. This commonwealth must, as far as we can visualize it, consist of **a world legislature**, whose members will, as the trustees of the whole of mankind, ultimately

control the entire resources of all the component nations, and will enact such laws as shall be required to regulate the life, satisfy the needs, and adjust the relationships of all races and peoples. **A world executive**, backed by an international Force, will carry out the decisions arrived at, and apply the laws enacted by, this world legislature, and will safeguard the organic unity of the whole commonwealth. **A world tribunal** will adjudicate and deliver its compulsory and final verdict in all and any disputes that may arise between the various elements constituting this universal system. **A mechanism of world intercommunication** will be devised, embracing the whole planet, freed from national hindrances and restrictions, and functioning with marvelous swiftness and perfect regularity. **A world metropolis** will act as the nerve center of a world civilization, the focus towards which the unifying forces of life will converge and from which its energizing influences will radiate. **A world language** will either be invented or chosen from among the existing languages and will be taught in the schools of all the federated nations as an auxiliary to their mother tongue. **A world script, a world literature, a uniform and universal system of currency, of weights and measures**, will simplify and facilitate intercourse and understanding among the nations and races of mankind. In such a world society, science and religion, the two most potent forces in human life, will be reconciled, will co-operate, and will harmoniously develop. **The press** will, under such a system, while giving full scope to the expression of the diversified views and convictions of mankind, cease to be mischievously manipulated by vested interests, whether private or public, and will be liberated from the influence of contending governments and peoples. **The economic resources of the world** will be organized, its sources of raw materials will be tapped and fully utilized, its markets will be co-ordinated and developed, and the distribution of its products will be equitably regulated.

National rivalries, hatred, and intrigues will cease, and racial animosity and prejudice will be replaced by racial amity, understanding, and co-operation. The causes of religious strife will be permanently removed, economic barriers and restrictions will be completely abolished, and the inordinate distinction between classes will be obliterated. Destitution on the one hand, and gross accumulation of ownership on the other, will disappear. The enormous energy dissipated and wasted on war, whether economic or political, will be consecrated to such ends as will extend the range of human inventions and technical development, to the increase of the productivity of mankind, to the extermination of disease, to the extension of scientific research, to the raising of the standard of physical health, to the sharpening and refinement of the human brain, to the exploitation of the unused and unsuspected resources of the planet, to the prolongation of human life, and to the furtherance of any other agency that can stimulate the intellectual, the moral, and spiritual life of the entire human race.

> **A world federal system**, ruling the whole earth and exercising unchallengeable authority over its unimaginably vast resources, blending and embodying the ideals of both the East and the West, liberated from the curse of war and its miseries, and bent on the exploitation of all the available sources of energy on the surface of the planet, a system in which Force is made the servant of Justice, whose life is sustained by its universal recognition of one God and by its allegiance to one common Revelation – such is the goal towards which humanity, impelled by the unifying forces of life, is moving.[13]

From the Baha'i point of view, this vision of a global society should not evoke the specter of worldwide uniformity imposed by a centralized, totalitarian power. Instead, Baha'is suggest that a diverse world affords the optimal conditions for all to realize their highest potential through independent intellectual, spiritual, and aesthetic endeavors.

The Covenant of Baha'u'llah

In the Baha'i Faith there is a relationship, known as the Covenant of Baha'u'llah, between the Manifestation of God and his followers. In its simplest sense, this Covenant consists of Baha'u'llah's instructions to his followers – written in his own hand near the end of his life – that after him all should turn to 'Abdu'l-Baha for guidance. 'Abdu'l-Baha became the head of the Baha'i Faith, the sole interpreter of Baha'u'llah's revelation, and the foundation upon which the future development of his father's faith was to be laid.

For Baha'is, this Covenant is not merely a pact or agreement, but a spiritual power that maintains the unity of the Baha'i community and will usher in the unity of the entire planet. Baha'u'llah designated 'Abdu'l-Baha not only as his chosen successor, but as the Center of his Covenant. There is no priesthood or clergy in the Baha'i Faith; in their place stands the directly appointed chain of authority reaching from the Bab to Baha'u'llah, 'Abdu'l-Baha, Shoghi Effendi, and the Universal House of Justice, which is the democratically elected international governing body of the Baha'i community.

Education

The Baha'i Faith lays particular stress on education, and regards it as a compulsory provision of its teachings. Wherever possible, Baha'is educate their children to the highest standards, and promote education throughout the world. If resources are limited, they believe that priority in education should go to girls and women. When women are educated, they are equipped to educate their children, thereby eliminating the root source of the ignorance that plays so great a role in the rise and perpetuation of prejudice and war. When it comes to other aspects of life, the Baha'is believe in the equality of men and women. 'Abdu'l-Baha says:

> The world in the past has been ruled by force and man has dominated over woman by reason of his more forceful and aggressive qualities both of body and mind. But the balance is already shifting; force is losing its dominance, and mental alertness, intuition, and the spiritual qualities of love and service, in which woman is strong, are gaining ascendancy. Hence the new age will be an age less masculine and more permeated with the feminine ideals, or, to speak more exactly, will be an age in which the masculine and feminine elements of civilization will be more evenly balanced.[14]

Baha'i educational philosophy aims not solely at the development of the mind, but at creating a harmony between intellectual learning (science, religion, the arts, physical development, etc.), spiritual awareness, and craftsmanship. The ultimate goal of Baha'i education is the realization of the full potential that lies within the reality of the human being. Baha'u'llah stated: "Regard man as a mine rich in gems of inestimable value. Education can, alone, cause it to reveal its treasures, and enable mankind to benefit therefrom."[15]

Baha'u'llah taught that religion and science are in harmony with each other, and that true religion and true science have never contradicted each other but are complementary aspects of one truth. Religion and science, according to Baha'i teachings, are necessary for the development and transformation of modern humanity, and are the two most potent forces in the world of existence. 'Abdu'l-Baha stated: "Religion and science are the two wings upon which man's intelligence can soar into the heights, with which the human soul can progress. It is not possible to fly with one wing alone!"[16]

In another passage, 'Abdu'l-Baha states that because truth (or reality) is one, it is not possible that something can be scientifically false and at the same time religiously true:

> If religious beliefs and opinions are found contrary to the standards of science, they are mere superstitions and imaginations; for the antithesis of knowledge is ignorance, and the child of ignorance is superstition. Unquestionably there must be agreement between true religion and science. If a question be found contrary to reason, faith and belief in it are impossible, and there is no outcome but wavering and vacillation.[17]

Another important aspect of Baha'i education is the principle of the independent investigation of truth. All young Baha'is are encouraged to study and search for truth. 'Abdu'l-Baha says: "The fact that we imagine ourselves to be right and everybody else wrong is the greatest of all obstacles in the path towards unity, and unity is necessary if we would reach truth, for truth is *one*."[18]

Spiritual Refinement and the Afterlife

Baha'is understand humanity's relationship to life as analogous to the nurturing relationship that the embryo has in the womb during the embryonic stages. 'Abdu'l-Baha explained: "The development and growth of man on this earth, until he reached his present perfection, resembled the growth and development of the embryo in the womb of the mother: by degrees it passed from condition to condition, from form to form, from one shape to another, for this is according to the requirement of the universal system and Divine Law."[19] Life in all its stages and manifestations, whether of joy or pain, is ultimately a preparation and training for the soul's coming life in the immortal world.

Each individual's effort to cultivate and exemplify the divine attributes – love, purity, humility, selflessness, truthfulness, and wisdom – acts as a polish for the mirror that is the soul. This is a process of spiritual refinement, or the actualizing of one's latent spiritual potential. This refinement process is the way in which one moves closer to God, and it is through this process that the dust, or ephemeral attachment, is removed from the mirror of the soul until it perfectly reflects the Divine light. 'Abdu'l-Baha proclaimed: "Behold how the light of the sun illuminates the world of matter: even so doth the Divine Light shed its rays in the kingdom of the soul."[20] From this perspective, the human body, which decays, is of an entirely different realm than the immortal soul. The soul is thought to have no parts and it is believed to be an eternal element that is limitless and indivisible, unlike its corresponding temporary vessel.

An important aspect of Baha'i education is the principle of the independent investigation of truth

Baha'i scriptures posit that there are endless worlds of God beyond this earthly one, and that souls continue to progress throughout these worlds, approaching ever nearer to God. This progression toward the Divine necessitates that the soul identifies itself with its spiritual potentialities, rather than the material animalistic qualities of this transitory realm. For a Baha'i, life is not disdained; instead, it is embraced as the means of acquiring the virtues necessary to move closer to God.

BAHA'I ADMINISTRATION

The Baha'i Faith is organized by means of a system of administration outlined in the *Kitab-i-Aqdas* and the *Will and Testament of 'Abdu'l-Baha*. The Baha'i administration functions with two branches: elected institutions and appointed institutions.

Elected Institutions

Wherever the number of adult Baha'is in a locality equals or exceeds nine, a nine-member Local Spiritual Assembly is formed. If the number exceeds nine, the Assembly is elected annually by secret ballot. When sufficient Local Spiritual Assemblies are formed in a country, the Baha'is in each region of that country – for example, in each state – elect from among themselves delegates to a yearly national Baha'i convention. At this convention, the delegates elect from among all the Baha'is in the country a nine-member National Spiritual Assembly. While the Local Spiritual Assembly governs the affairs of the Baha'i community at the local level, the National Spiritual Assembly performs the same function at the national level. The members of all the National Spiritual Assemblies in the Baha'i world, in turn, serve as delegates to an international Baha'i convention that is held every five years at the Baha'i World Centre to elect the nine members of the Universal House of Justice. The Universal House of Justice is the highest administrative body that governs the affairs of the Baha'i community at the global level. In Baha'i elections there is no electioneering, campaigning, or nominations. Secret ballots are cast in an atmosphere of prayerful meditation. The aim is for each elector, without prior discussion or propaganda, to freely and individually elect an institution constituted of the most excellent, capable, and spiritually mature believers.

> **The Universal House of Justice is the administrative body that governs the affairs of the community at the global level**

Spiritual Assemblies and the Universal House of Justice reach decisions not through impassioned debate amongst the members, but by means of consultation. Consultation, 'Abdu'l-Baha explained, requires that each member fully and frankly offer his or her opinion about the matter at hand, while remaining detached from that opinion so as to see the wisdom of any other viewpoint. Decisions reached through unanimity are preferred, but, if necessary, votes are taken and the majority decision is accepted. As soon as a decision is reached, there is no dissenting voice; rather, all members of the Assembly support the decision for the sake of unity. Even if the decision is wrong, 'Abdu'l-Baha explains that through unity differences will be reconciled and divisive dissent will be avoided. During the ministry of 'Abdu'l-Baha, embryonic Local and National Assemblies were formed in regions of the Middle East and the West. In the early 1920s, under the Guardianship of

Shoghi Effendi, the first Local and National Assemblies were elected according to the provisions laid down by Baha'u'llah and 'Abdu'l-Baha. Today, Local and National Spiritual Assemblies are found in nearly every country in the world.

The Universal House of Justice was first elected in 1963. The Universal House of Justice exercises legislative and judicial functions, passing laws on subjects not specifically dealt with in the writings of Baha'u'llah. Baha'is are encouraged to seek assistance and guidance regarding community and personal matters from their Local Spiritual Assembly. Any problems that cannot be resolved at the local level may be referred to the National Spiritual Assembly and, on final appeal, to the Universal House of Justice.

The twin cities of Haifa and Akka, in whose environs Baha'u'llah spent the last years of his life, are regarded by Baha'is everywhere as their spiritual and administrative World Centre. Thus, the Baha'i World Centre incorporates the sacred shrines of the three Central Figures of the Faith: the Forerunner, the Bab; the Founder, Baha'u'llah; and the Center of His Covenant, 'Abdu'l-Baha (1844–1921) – as well as the Seat of the Supreme Governing Body of the Baha'i community, the Universal House of Justice.

Appointed Institutions

The appointed arm of the Baha'i administration is designed to nurture and protect the growth and development of the Baha'i community. The first people in Baha'i history to serve in this capacity were known as Hands of the Cause of God. The Hands of the Cause are outstanding individual believers who were appointed by the Head of the Baha'i Faith – the first Hands of the Cause were appointed by Baha'u'llah – to render extraordinary service in the propagation and protection of the Baha'i Faith. The Universal House of Justice ruled that no further Hands of the Cause could be appointed after the death of the Guardian (1957), as the House of Justice was not given the authority to do so in the writings of Baha'u'llah. The Universal House of Justice has, therefore, perpetuated certain functions of the Hands of the Cause by creating a new institution of appointed Continental Boards of Counselors, who serve a five-year renewable term in a specific continental region. Counselors themselves appoint Auxiliary Board members to aid them in their work at a regional level, and the Auxiliary Board members appoint assistants. These appointed officers aid the Local and National Assemblies in carrying out their work, serve as advisers to the Assemblies and individuals alike, and assist in the identification of new goals that should be adopted for the advancement of the Baha'i Faith. They belong to the "learned" of the Baha'i Faith, yet are, like all the other believers, subject to the authority of the Assemblies and the Universal House of Justice. The elected institutions and the institution of the Hands of the Cause were ordained by Baha'u'llah and 'Abdu'l-Baha in the *Kitab-i-Aqdas* and the *Will and Testament of 'Abdu'l-Baha*.

PRACTICES OF THE BAHA'I FAITH

Prayer

The Bab, Baha'u'llah, and 'Abdu'l-Baha revealed many hundreds of prayers for different purposes and occasions. The most important of these are the daily obligatory prayers revealed by Baha'u'llah, of which there are three: the long; the medium; and the short. The individual believer is free to choose which of these prayers he will recite, but Baha'u'llah enjoins each Baha'i to recite one of them every day. Baha'u'llah enjoins Baha'is to study his Tablets and other writings each morning and evening. The length of study or the amount of writings covered in the period of study is, he states, not important; what is important is the spirit in which the activity is undertaken. He also encourages believers to meditate on the word of God. The Baha'i writings do not prescribe any particular style or method of meditation, but leave such choices to the individual believer. The Obligatory Prayer is directed towards the Most Holy Spot in the Baha'i world, the Shrine of Baha'u'llah in Akka, Israel. The prayer for the dead is another obligatory prayer, and is the only obligatory prayer that is said communally; otherwise the daily obligatory prayers are regarded as a private obligation and practice. The prayers were originally revealed by the Bab, Baha'u'llah, and 'Abdu'l-Baha in Arabic, Persian, and Turkish, but today many of them have been translated, and are recited in approximately eight hundred different languages around the world.

Fasting and Pilgrimage

A period of fasting is observed by Baha'is during the Baha'i month of 'Ala (signifying "loftiness" in Arabic), which lasts for nineteen days, from 2 to 20 March. During this time, Baha'is refrain from eating and drinking between sunrise and sunset. People who are ill, traveling, over the age of seventy or under the age of fifteen, and women who are pregnant or nursing a child are exempt from the Fast. The Baha'i teachings explain that the purpose of fasting is to cleanse and purify the soul from attachments to the material world, and to strengthen its bond to God. Immediately following the Fast is the festival of Naw-Ruz, the Baha'i New Year celebration. Just as spring is the renewal of the natural world, so too the Fast brings cleansing and renewal to the soul. Thereafter the soul is refreshed and strengthened to enter another year of work, service, and spiritual development.

> **The purpose of fasting is to cleanse and purify the soul from attachments to the material world**

To complete the obligation of pilgrimage as prescribed by Baha'u'llah, a believer must visit the House of Baha'u'llah in Baghdad, and that of the Bab in Shiraz once in a lifetime.

However, pilgrimage to these sites has not been possible in recent decades. Baha'i pilgrims also make pilgrimage to the Shrine of Baha'u'llah in Bahji and the Shrine of the Bab in Haifa.

Marriage

In the *Kitab-i-Aqdas* Baha'u'llah states: "Enter into wedlock, O people, that ye may bring forth one who will make mention of Me amid My servants."[21] Thus Baha'u'llah encourages Baha'is to marry, and affirms that the chief purposes of marriage are unity and the perpetuation of the human race. He taught that man and woman must become both spiritually and physically united so that their unity may be eternal. To promote unity in the family, he ordained that before marrying a Baha'i must obtain the consent of all living parents. The Baha'i marriage ceremony is very simple; the only ritual is that the bride and groom recite in turn, before two witnesses, the following verse prescribed in the *Kitab-i-Aqdas*: "We will all, verily, abide by the Will of God."[22] Baha'u'llah strongly discouraged divorce. However, he made provision in his laws that divorce is permissible if irreconcilable resentment or antipathy arises between a couple. A Baha'i couple wishing to divorce must first consult a Local Spiritual Assembly, and must separate for one year to allow any possible reunion to occur. Thereafter, should no reconciliation take place, the divorce may proceed.

THE *MASHRIQU'L-ADHKAR*

The *mashriqu'l-adhkar* is the Baha'i House of Worship, and its name means "dawning place of the mention of God." It is a nine-sided, domed building dedicated to the worship of God. Institutions such as orphanages, retirement homes, hospitals, colleges, and universities open to people of all religions and all nations are to be built around it, demonstrating the unity of worship to God and service to humanity. To date, there are seven *mashriqu'l-adhkar*s in the world: one each in the United States, Uganda, Australia, Germany, Panama, Samoa, and India. An eighth *mashriqu'l-adhkar* is currently under construction in Chile. As most local Baha'i communities are not yet able to build a House of Worship, for the present these local communities worship in their administrative buildings, a rented or owned Baha'i center, or in private homes; in the future, however, each local Baha'i community will have its own *mashriqu'l-adhkar*. The

> There are seven *mashriqu'l-adhkar*s in the world: one each in the United States, Uganda, Australia, Germany, Panama, Samoa, and India

mashriqu'l-adhkar symbolizes the Baha'i teachings of peace, harmony, and unity, and is open to people of all faiths and all backgrounds for meditation and prayer.

CALENDAR

In his writings the Bab ordained a new calendar, composed of nineteen months in a year, each month having nineteen days. The remaining four days (or five in leap years) required to complete the solar year were termed by him the *Ayyam-i-Ha* (or Intercalary Days), a time when Baha'is prepare for the Fast, give gifts, visit friends and neighbors, and offer charity and hospitality. Each Baha'i month is named after one of the attributes of God, as is each of the days of the seven-day week. Baha'is assemble on the first day of each of the nineteen months in the Baha'i calendar for a communal, devotional meeting called the Nineteen Day Feast. The Feast is the heart of local Baha'i activity, and consists of three parts: the first part is called the devotional or spiritual portion and consists of the reciting of Baha'i prayers, meditations and tablets, and sacred texts of other religions; the second is called the administrative or consultative portion, in which Baha'i community affairs are discussed; the third is the social portion, in which refreshments are served while the Baha'is socialize.

CHAPTER SUMMARY

The founder of the Baha'i Faith is Baha'u'llah. He revealed some one hundred volumes of sacred writings, foremost of which are the *Kitab-i-Aqdas*, the Most Holy Book (his book of laws) and the *Kitab-i-Iqan*, the Book of Certitude. For the last forty years of his life he was a prisoner and in exile, during which time he spread his teachings by means of his writings. His chief message is that humanity has reached an age of maturity that will find its fruition, first in a political unity, and ultimately in a spiritually enlightened world civilization. The concept of progressive revelation, which states that all the divine religions are stages in a progressive unfoldment of one spiritual truth from one God, is central to the Baha'i concept of unity. Thus, the three basic teachings of Baha'u'llah are that there is but one God; all the religions are one; and humanity is one. The Covenant of Baha'u'llah guarantees the preservation of unity in the Baha'i community and serves as the basis for the eventual spiritualization of humanity. The leadership of the Baha'i community now rests with the

Humanity has reached an age of maturity that will find its fruition in a spiritually enlightened world civilization

institutions of the Baha'i administrative order, which were ordained by Baha'u'llah and his chosen successor, 'Abdu'l-Baha. Baha'i worship centers around prayer, fasting, the Nineteen Day Feast, and the observance of spiritual and social laws found in Baha'u'llah's writings. Today the Baha'i Faith is established in all parts of the world.

The characteristic doctrines of Baha'i beliefs are succinctly described by Shoghi Effendi, the Guardian of the Baha'i Faith, as follows:

The Bahá'í Faith upholds the unity of God, recognizes the unity of His Prophets, and inculcates the principle of the oneness and wholeness of the entire human race. It proclaims the necessity and the inevitability of the unification of mankind ... enjoins upon its followers the primary duty of an unfettered search after truth, condemns all manner of prejudice and superstition, declares the purpose of religion to be the promotion of amity and concord, proclaims its essential harmony with science, and recognizes it as the foremost agency for the pacification and the orderly progress of human society. It unequivocally maintains the principle of equal rights, opportunities, and privileges for men and women, insists on compulsory education, eliminates extremes of poverty and wealth, abolishes the institution of priesthood, prohibits slavery, asceticism, mendicancy, and monasticism, prescribes monogamy, discourages divorce, emphasizes the necessity of strict obedience to one's government, exalts any work performed in the spirit of service to the level of worship, urges either the creation or the selection of an auxiliary international language, and delineates the outlines of those institutions that must establish and perpetuate the general peace of mankind.[23]

ENDNOTES

FOREWORD

1. See the introduction below.
2. See Mircea Eliade, *Shamanism: Archaic Techniques of Ecstasy*, trans. Willard R. Trask (Princeton: Princeton University Press, 1964), 107.

INTRODUCTION

1. Albert Einstein, *Ideas and Opinions* (New York: Crown, 1954), 11.
2. See Paul Tillich, *Theology of Culture*, ed. Robert C. Kimball (New York: Oxford University Press, repr. 1966).
3. Ludwig Wittgenstein, *Tractatus Logico-Philosophicus*, trans. D. F. Pears and B. F. McGuinness (Atlantic Highlands, NJ: Humanties Press International, 1961), 73 (emphasis in the original). Wittgenstein goes on to say: "We feel that even when all *possible* scientific questions have been answered, the problems of life remain completely untouched. Of course there are then no questions left [that can be answered in words], and this itself is the answer." In this case, the mystical, that which cannot be put into words, "*makes itself manifest.*"
4. Edwin Markham, "A Conversation with Edwin Markham: On the Poet As Teacher," in *The Arena*, New York, December 1902 (available at http://www.english.uiuc.edu/maps/poets/ m_r/markham/interview.htm).
5. Abraham Joshua Heschel, *God in Search of Man: A Philosophy of Judaism* (New York: Farrar, Straus, & Giroux, 1957), 46 (emphasis added).
6. Einstein, *Ideas and Opinions*, 11.
7. Albert Einstein, *The Quotable Einstein*, comp. and ed. A. Calaprice (Princeton: Princeton University Press, 1996), 199.
8. Sri Aurobindo, *The Life Divine* (Pondicherry: Sri Aurobindo Ashram, repr. 2001), 760.
9. The historian Arnold Toynbee viewed religion as the animating force behind all traditional cultures. Through his historical studies, Toynbee came to believe that all world religions share a common essence. He viewed the differences to be non-essential accretions relevant to time, place, and socio-cultural conditions. Toynbee observed that "religions are historical institutions; and they have been making a transit through Space-Time in which, at every point-moment in their trajectory, they have been encountering the local and temporary circumstances of human life ... These accidental accretions are the price that the permanently and universally valid essence of a higher religion has to pay for communicating its message to the members of a particular society in a particular stage of this society's history ... If the essence

of a religion did not compromise with local and temporary circumstances by 'turning in' to them, it would never reach any audience at all; for, in every human society, the permanent and universal counsels and truths are overlaid by one of those local and temporary culture patterns." See Arnold Toynbee, *An Historian's Approach to Religion* (New York: Oxford University Press, 1956), 265–266.

10. Wilfred Cantwell Smith, "Theology of the World's Religious History," in *Toward a Universal Theology of Religion*, ed. Leonard Swidler (New York: Orbis Books, 1987), 59.

11. "Religion has given birth to all that is essential in society … We have established the fact that the fundamental categories of thought, and consequently of science, are of religious origin … In summing up, then, it may be said that nearly all the great institutions have been born in religion": Émile Durkheim, *The Elementary Forms of the Religious Life*, trans. Joseph Swain (Glencoe: Free Press, 1912), 48.

12. John Hick, *Problems of Religious Pluralism* (London: Macmillan, 1985), 39.

13. In theistic religions the prevalent focus is on a personal conception of Ultimate Reality (sometimes mediated by a divine Messenger, Incarnation, or Avatar); however, it is also acknowledged that God is Infinite, Transcendent, beyond human conception, and thus unknowable in essence. In general, the unknowable aspect of God, or the conception of Ultimate Reality as the Absolute or Transcendent, is emphasized by contemplatives and mystics who lean toward philosophical thinking (for example, the Vedantists of the Hindu tradition, the mystics of Christianity, the Sufis of Islam, or the Kabbalists of the Jewish faith).

14. Conditioned reality is referred to in different ways within the religious traditions. For example, Plato called it the realm of "becoming," Taoists designate it as the "ten thousand things," Sufis "*al-dhahir*" (the manifest), and religions native to India denote it as *samsara* or *maya*.

15. Some esoteric perspectives, such as some Mahayana Buddhist teachings, do not view conditioned reality as ultimately distinguished from Unconditioned Reality. In such cases, enlightenment is required to see, to stay with Buddhist terminology, *samsara* (conditioned reality) as *nirvana* (Unconditioned Reality). The distinction, although not ontological, nevertheless suggests an analogous dissimilarity, albeit the emphasis is placed on one's state of being.

16. See Huston Smith, *Beyond the Postmodern Mind*, 3rd ed. (Wheaton, Ill: Theosophical Publishing House, 2003), 43–69.

17. Some scholars include ideologies such as Marxism, nationalism, and scientism in their presentation of religion – which is essentially a discussion of worldviews. Study of these secular ideologies is necessary to grasp the different viewpoints of the peoples of the world. Although these ideologies resemble organized religion in certain respects, this book does not treat them as "religions" in the traditional sense. Moreover, they are not representative of what has been termed here the spiritual heritage of the human race. For a discussion of both religious and secular ideologies as worldviews see Ninian Smart, *Worldviews* (New York: Charles Scribner's Sons, 1983).

18. Frederick J. Streng, Charles L. Lloyd, Jr., and Jay T. Allen, eds., *Ways of Being Religious: Readings for a New Approach to Religion* (Englewood Cliffs: Prentice-Hall, 1973), 6.

19. This discussion of religion as a path or way is, in part, indebted to Leonard Swidler and Paul Mojzes, *The Study of Religion in an Age of Global Dialogue* (Philadelphia: Temple University Press, 2000), 8–10.

20. James Duerlinger, "Religion, its Disciplines, and their Relation to Ultimate Reality," in *Ultimate Reality and Spiritual Discipline*, ed. James Duerlinger (New York: Paragon House, 1984), 48.

21. According to Lama Govinda, "Religion and exact science both seek after truth, and they can both exist side by side without contradiction or hindering each other. This does not mean that the two can be fused into one, or that their statements must always agree. Their differences are based, not so much on the objects of their consideration or their aims, as on their *method* of consideration. The research method of science goes outward from within, that of spiritual investigation goes inward from outward. And each can only achieve the highest results by following its own laws": Lama Anagarika Govinda, *Buddhist Reflections* (York Beach, Me.: Samuel Wiser, 1991), 19.

22. Jesine Andresen and Robert K. C. Forman, "Methodological Pluralism in the Study of Religion: How the Study of Consciousness and Mapping Spiritual Experiences Can Reshape Religious Methodology," *Journal of Consciousness Studies*, 7, 11–12, 2000, 7.

23. Philip Novak, "The Dynamics of Attention in Spiritual Discipline," in Duerlinger, *Ultimate Reality and Spiritual Discipline*, 84.

24. The term "numinous" was coined by the scholar Rudolf Otto. See chapter 1, "Spiritual Traditions of the First Peoples" in this book for further discussion of Otto's thought. For a classic study of religious experience, see William James, *The Varieties of Religious Experience* (New York: Random House, 1936).

25. The term "profane" is derived from the Latin words *pro* and *fanum* (meaning "outside the temple").

26. Hendrik M. Vroon, "Can Religious Experience Be Shared? Introduction to the Theme 'Sharing Religious Experience,'" in *On Sharing Religious Experience*, ed. Jerald D. Gort, Hendrik M. Vroon, Rein Fernhout, and Anton Wessels (Grand Rapids, Mich.: William B. Eerdmans, 1992), 6.

27. The psychologist Abraham Maslow suggested that such foundational religious experiences represent the intrinsic core or essence of a religion. Maslow referred to these experiences as "peak experiences." He posited that all peak experiences have a common essence and that the world religions, therefore, have a common essence. See Abraham Maslow, *Religions, Values, and Peak-Experiences* (Columbus: Ohio State University Press, 1964), 20–29.

28. Mahatma Gandhi, quoted in Diana Eck, *Encountering God: A Spiritual Journey from Bozeman to Banaras* (Boston: Beacon Press, 1993), 219.

29. Raimundo Panikkar, "The Invisible Harmony: A Universal Theory of Religion or a Cosmic Confidence in Reality," in *Towards a Universal Theology of Religion*, ed. Leonard Swidler (Maryknoll, NY: Orbis Books, 1987), 138.

30. See J. Samuel Preus, *Explaining Religion* (Atlanta: Scholars Press, 1996).

31. See Swidler and Mojzes, *The Study of Religion*, 96.

32. See Daniel L. Pals, *Seven Theories of Religion* (New York: Oxford University Press, 1996).

33. Mircea Eliade, *Patterns in Comparative Religion*, trans. Rosemary Sheed, introd. John Clifford Holt (Lincoln: University of Nebraska, repr. 1996), xvii.

34. Friedrich Schleiermacher, quoted in Gustav Mensching, *Tolerance and Truth in Religion*, trans. Hans-J. Klimkeit (University, Ala.: University of Alabama Press, 1971), 160.

35. Ninian Smart, *The Religious Experience of Mankind*, 3rd ed. (New York: Charles Scribner's Sons, 1984), 3.

36. Wilfred Cantwell Smith, "Comparative Religion – Whither and Why?" in *The History of Religions: Essays in Methodology*, ed. M. Eliade and J. M. Kitagawa (Chicago: University of Chicago Press, 1959), 34.

37. Masao Abe, "The End of World Religion," *The Eastern Buddhist*, 13, 1980, 38.

38. Ervin Laszlo, *You Can Change the World* (Clun: Positive News, 2002), 80.

39. Martin Luther King Jr., *A Call to Conscience: The Landmark Speeches of Dr. Martin Luther King Jr.*, ed. Clay Carson and Kris Shepard (New York: Warner Books, 2001), 160–161.

40. According to Thich Nhat Hanh, "the word inter-be should be in the dictionary. We have to inter-be with every other thing. This sheet of paper is, because everything else is": Thich Nhat Hanh, *Peace is Every Step* (New York: Bantam Books, 1991), 96.

41. Abraham Joshua Heschel, "No Religion Is an Island," in *No Religion Is an Island*, ed. Harold Kasimow and Byron Sherwin (Maryknoll, NY: Orbis Books, 1991), 6.

42. Swidler and Mojzes, *The Study of Religion*, 87.

43. See Ashok K. Gangadean, "Awakening Global Consciousness," *Kosmos – An Integral Approach to Global Awakening*, 3, Spring/Summer 2004.

44. M. K. Gandhi, introduction to Allama Sir Abdullah al-Mamun al-Suhrawardy, *The Sayings of Muhammad* (London: John Murray, 1941; repr., Boston: Charles E. Tuttle Company, 1992), 7 (page citation is to the reprint edition).

45. Eck, *Encountering God*, 174. Professor Diana Eck is the director of the Pluralism Project at Harvard University, an initiative dedicated to helping Americans to positively experience religious diversity. See http://www.pluralism.org for additional information and resources.

46. Hans Küng, *Global Responsibility: In Search of a New Global Ethic* (New York: Crossroad, 1991), 78.

47. See, for example, John Hick and Hasan Askari, eds., *The Experience of Religious Diversity* (Aldershot: Gower, 1985).

48. Many scholars view a religion as consisting of two levels: the exoteric and the esoteric. The exoteric, or outer level, anchors adherents within a spiritual orientation and structures and disciplines a believer's life based on moral precepts, participation in a community, ceremonies, rites, and rituals. On the other hand, the esoteric, or inner, dimension signifies the metaphysical or sapiental knowledge attained through spiritual practices (such as prayer, meditation, etc.) which are preserved in the contemplative lineages of each religion. From this perspective, the exoteric and esoteric dimensions are considered to be reciprocal and equally important aspects of any religious path.

49. See Mehrdad Massoudi, "A Spherical Model of Spirituality: A Pluralistic Perspective on World's Religions," *Journal of Ecumenical Studies*, 41, June 2004, 341–354.

50. The scholar Stephen Batchelor noted that a "constant threat to the vitality of religion is the tendency to raise its conceptual and symbolic framework to ultimacy, and then to concern one-self only with its structural forms instead of the inner meaning to which these structural features refer": Stephen Batchelor, *Alone with Others* (New York: Grove Press, 1983), 41.

51. Hasan Askari, "Within and Beyond the Experience of Religious Diversity," in Hick and Askari, eds., *The Experience of Religious Diversity*, 218.

52. Eck, *Encountering God*, 191, 192, 193, 196, 197.

53. John Hick, *Problems of Religious Diversity* (London: Macmillan, 1985), 36–37.

54. See Wilfred Cantwell Smith, *The Meaning and End of Religion* (Minneapolis: Fortress Press, 1991).

55. Hick, *Problems of Religious Diversity*, 29.

56. For a discussion of "faith" and "cumulative tradition" see Smith, *The Meaning and End of Religion*.

57. An insight offered by the philosopher Immanuel Kant may prove helpful. For Kant, "phe-nomenon" indicates an empirical object of experience that is subject to space-time and the cat-egories of logic. On the other hand, "noumenon" signifies a transcendent object that is beyond sensory experience and is unknowable as a thing-in-itself. "Noumenon" is therefore indicative of how a thing (or Ultimte Reality, Truth) truly is in-itself (beyond space-time and the sub-jective conception of it). In this case, Truth, as it is refered to in its ultimate sense, is transcen-dent and beyond the full grasp of the human mind and therefore uncontainable within one particular worldview, although surely an expression of Truth may be found within that world-view. John Hick took special notice of Kant's realization in terms of its import for a pluralist view of religions (a perspective that is similar to Vedantic strands of Hindu philosophy). From this point of view, Hick suggested that "the Gods are divine personae through whom the Ultimate is experienced as personal within certain strands of human history. The non-theistic Absolutes represent other ways in which the Ultimate is experienced within yet other strands of religious life. The Ultimate or Real in itself is, however, beyond all human categories, so that for human thought it has to be described as both personal and non-personal": See John Hick, "Religious Diversity as Challenge and Promise," in Hick and Askari, eds., *The Experience of Religious Diversity*, 19–20.

58. Raimundo Panikkar, "The Myth of Pluralism: The Tower of Babel – a Meditation on Non-Violence," *Cross Currents*, 29, 1979, 226.

59. The scholar Marco Pallis concluded that "a judgment is inadequate insofar as it claims to judge the whole absolutely from a particular standpoint likewise treated as absolute; this is the error of 'dogmatism,' that is, of an abusive stretching of relative formulations that are true as far as they go. A judgment is valid, however, insofar as, starting out from criteria duly recognized to be relative, it judges a phenomenon whose relative limits are likewise recognized. Given that one is vigilantly heedful of those conditions, a judgment can be perfectly exact, to the point of being called 'relatively absolute' within its proper context": Marco Pallis, *A Buddhist Spectrum* (London: George Allen & Unwin, 1980), 7.

60. The scholar Frithjof Schuon noted that "every expressed truth necessarily assumes a form, that

of its expression, and it is metaphysically impossible that any form should possess a unique value to the exclusion of other forms; for a form, by definition, cannot be unique and exclusive, that is to say, it cannot be the only possible expression of what it expresses. Form implies specification or distinction, and the specific is only conceivable as a modality of a 'species,' that is to say, of a category that includes a combination of analogous modalities": Frithjof Schuon, *The Transcendent Unity of Religions*, 2nd ed. (Wheaton, Ill.: Theosophical Publishing House, 1993), 18.

61. Eck, *Encountering God*, 196.

62. Pope John Paul II, under whose ministry numerous Catholic initiatives for interreligious dialogue were undertaken, offered the following profound observation that "there is basis for dialogue and *for the growth of unity*, a growth that should occur at the same rate at which we are able to overcome our divisions – divisions that to a great degree result from the idea that one can have a monopoly on truth": John Paul II, *Crossing the Threshold of Hope* (New York: Alfred A. Knopf, 1994), 147. In this passage the Pope is describing the need for intra-Christian dialogue. However, if the Pope's point is generalized from the particular to the universal, from the intra-Christian to the interreligious context, it has great import for the attitude needed to pursue unity on a global scale.

63. Francis Cardinal Arinze, *Religions for Peace* (New York: Doubleday, 2002), xiii.

64. Hans Küng, "A New Paradigm for International Relations? Reflections on September 11, 2001," *GHI Bulletin*, 31, Fall 2002, 15.

65. Since the first meeting in 1893, the Parliament of World's Religions has reconvened in 1993 in Chicago, 1999 in Cape Town, and 2004 in Barcelona. The Council for a Parliament of World's Religions promotes interreligious harmony and cooperative endeavors. For more information and resources, see http://www.cpwr.org.

66. Max Müller, *The Essential Max Muller: On Language, Mythology, and Religion*, ed. Jon R. Stone (New York: Palgrave Macmillan, 2002), 348.

67. Swami Vivekananda, *Vivekananda: The Yogas and Other Works*, rev. ed., ed. Swami Nikhilananda (New York: Ramakrishna-Vivekananda Center, repr. 1996), 183.

68. Some interfaith organizations include the Temple of Understanding, the International Association for Religious Freedom, the World Council of Religions for Peace, the United Religions Initiative, the World Congress of Faiths, and the World Council of Religious Leaders.

69. Donald J. Puchala, "The 1995 John W. Holmes Memorial Lecture" (available at http://yale.edu/acuns/publications/95_Holmes_Lecture.html, accessed 1 May 2003). Puchala is summarizing the views of the modern philosopher Martha Nussbaum.

70. Homer A. Jack, ed., *Religion for Peace: Proceedings of the Kyoto Conference on Religion and Peace* (New Delhi: Gandhi Peace Foundation, 1973), ix.

71. See the Parliament of World's Religions, *Declaration Toward a Global Ethic* (available at http://www.cpwr.org/resource/global_ethic.htm).

72. Ibid.

73. See the Declaration of Human Rights in *The United Nations and Human Rights* (New York: United Nations, 1984), 242. Also see Article 18 of the International Covenant on Civil and Political Rights.

74. Leonard Swidler, John B. Cobb, Jr., Paul F. Knitter, and Monica K. Hellwig, *Death or Dialogue? From the Age of Monologue to the Age of Dialogue* (Philadelphia: Trinity Press, 1990), i.

75. See the website of the Tanenbaum Center for Interreligious Understanding (available at http://www.tanenbaum.org/resources/golden_rule.asp, accessed 30 October 2003). The mission of the Tanenbaum Center is to diffuse violent action and rhetoric perpetrated in the name of religion.

76. As the scholar A. K. Coomaraswamy has noted, "Tolerance, then, is a merely negative virtue, demanding not sacrifice of spiritual pride and involving no abrogation of our sense of superiority; it can be commended only in so far as it means that we shall refrain from hating or persecuting others who differ or seem to differ from ourselves in habit or belief. Tolerance still allows us to pity those who differ from ourselves, and are consequently to be pitied! ... Tolerance, carried further, implies indifference, and becomes intolerable": A. K. Coomaraswamy, *The Bugbear of Literacy* (Bedfont: Perennial Books, 1979), 52.

77. Johann Wolfgang von Goethe, *Maxims and Reflections*, trans. E. Stopp (New York: Penguin Books, 1998), 116. Goethe, like other nineteenth-century European poets, was spiritually enriched by contact with religious writings from beyond his native culture. He encountered in the writings of Hafiz, a Persian Muslim from the fourteenth century, a kindred spirit whom he called his "twin." The growing exchange between East and West, evident in Goethe's inspired translation of Hafiz, marked a significant shift in human consciousness toward a planetary perspective capable of elevating patterns of religious and philosophical thought beyond religious and nationalistic exclusivism.

78. The philosopher Martha Nussbaum has noted that "the first step of understanding the world from the point of view of the other is essential to any responsible act of judgment": Martha Nussbaum, *Cultivating Humanity: A Classical Defense of Reform in Liberal Education* (Cambridge, Mass.: Harvard University Press, 1997), 11.

79. Huston Smith, *The World's Religions* (New York: HarperCollins, 1991), 11.

80. When addressing a conference on dialogue between the religions, Thomas Merton, a pioneer of modern interreligious initiatives, offered the following insight: "My dear brothers, we are already one but we imagine that we are not. What we have to recover is our original unity. What we have to be is what we already are": Thomas Merton, quoted in Marcus Braybrooke, *Pilgrimage of Hope: One Hundred Years of Global Interfaith Dialogue* (New York: Crossroad, 1992), 113.

81. According to the philosopher Masao Abe, "interfaith dialogue must be concerned with the mutual transformation of the religions involved. Then and only then will a deep and expansive human spirituality be opened up before each of the world's religions": Masao Abe, *Buddhism and Interfaith Dialogue*, ed. Steven Heine (Honolulu: University of Hawaii Press, 1995), 5.

82. J. A. Buehrens and F. Church, *A Chosen Faith: An Introduction to Unitarian Universalism*, rev. ed. (Boston: Beacon Press, 1998), 101.

83. For an explication of dialogue as spiritual practice see John N. Ferrer, "Dialogical Inquiry as Spiritual Practice," *Tikkun*, 18, January/February 2003.

84. Raimundo Panikkar, *Myth, Faith and Hermeneutics: Cross-Cultural Studies* (New York: Paulist Press, 1980), 243.

85. See Swidler and Mojzes, *The Study of Religion*, 166–167.

86. The scholar Abraham Heschel has observed: "Awe is more than an emotion; it is a way of understanding, insight into a meaning greater than ourselves. The beginning of awe is wonder, and the beginning of wisdom is awe … What we cannot comprehend by analysis, we become aware of in awe": Heschel, *God in Search of Man*, 74.

87. S. Suzuki, *Zen Mind, Beginner's Mind* (New York: Weatherhill, 1983), 21.

88. David Bohm and F. D. Peat, *Science, Order and Creativity* (London: Routledge, 1989), 241. Also see David Bohm, *On Dialogue* (London: Routledge, 1996).

89. Mahatma Gandhi, quoted in Glyn Richards, *The Philosophy of Gandhi* (Calcutta: Rupa Paperback, 1991), 51.

90. Leonard Swidler, "The Decalogue Dialogue: Ground Rules for Interreligious Studies," *Journal of Ecumenical Studies*, 20, 1, Winter 1983; April 1984 revision, 1–4, reprinted by permission of the *Journal of Ecumenical Studies*. For more information on the *Journal of Ecumenical Studies*, one of the premier academic journals on religion, including cross-cultural understanding and interreligious dialogue, see http://ecumene.org/jes/.

91. S. Radhakrishnan, *Eastern Religion and Western Thought* (New York: Oxford University Press, 1959), viii.

92. The scholar Wilfred Cantwell Smith has observed that "human development has reached a point where we must construct some kind of world order, or we perish": Wilfred Cantwell Smith, *The Faith of Other Men* (New York: Harper & Row, 1972), 100.

CHAPTER 1

1. Black Elk, quoted in J. G. Neihardt, *Black Elk Speaks* (Lincoln: University of Nebraska Press, repr. 1961), 42–43.

2. C. G. Jung, quoted in C. S. Hall and V. J. Nordby, *A Primer of Jungian Psychology* (New York: New American Library, 1973), 39.

3. Mircea Eliade, *Yoga: Immortality and Freedom*, 2nd ed., trans. Willard R. Trask (Princeton: Princeton University Press, 1970), xii–xiv.

4. E. Bolaji Idowu, *African Traditional Religion* (New York: Orbis Books, 1973), 135.

5. Geoffrey Parrinder, *African Traditional Religion* (Westport, CT: Greenwood Press, 1976), 34.

6. E. E. Evans-Pritchard, *Nuer Religion* (Oxford: Clarendon Press, 1956), 51–52.

7. Black Elk, quoted in Joseph Epes Brown, *The Sacred Pipe: Black Elk's Account of the Seven Rites of the Oglala Sioux* (New York: Viking Penguin, 1971), 115.

8. Ninian Smart and Richard D. Hecht, eds., *Sacred Texts of the World: A Universal Anthology* (New York: Crossroad, repr. 2001), 349.

9. Joseph Campbell, *Myths to Live By* (New York: Bantam Books, repr. 1973), 89–90.

10. Ananda Coomaraswamy, quoted in Joseph Epes Brown, *The Spiritual Legacy of the American Indian* (New York: Crossroad, 1982), 84.

11. Frithjof Schuon, *The Essential Writings of Frithjof Schuon*, ed. Seyyed Hossein Nasr (New York: Amity House, 1986), 181.

12. See Mircea Eliade, *The Sacred and Profane*, trans. Willard R. Trask (New York: Harcourt, Brace & World, 1959), chapter 2.

13. Evan Zuesse, *Ritual Cosmos: The Sanctification of Life in African Religions* (Athens: Ohio University Press, 1979), 242.

14. Smith, *The World's Religions*, 367.

15. Rudolf Otto, *The Idea of the Holy* (Oxford: Oxford University Press, repr. 1958), 4.

16. Eliade, *The Sacred and Profane*, 12–13.

17. R. H. Codrington, *The Melanesians: Studies in Their Anthropology and Folk Lore* (New York: Dover, repr. 1972), 118–119 n1.

18. Parrinder, *African Traditional Religion*, 21–22 (emphasis added).

19. Eliade, *The Sacred and Profane*, 11–12.

20. Joseph Epes Brown, "The Spiritual Legacy of the American Indian," *Studies in Comparative Religion*, 14, Winter/Spring 1980, 27.

21. Frithjof Schuon, *The Feathered Sun* (Bloomington: World Wisdom Books, 1990), 6.

22. Solon T. Kimball, Introduction, in Arnold van Gennep, *The Rites of Passage* (Chicago: University of Chicago Press, repr. 1960), xvii–xviii.

23. See van Gennep, *Rites of Passage*.

24. The word "liminal" is etymologically derived from the Latin word *limen*, meaning "threshold."

25. See Sam Gill, *Native American Religious Action: A Performance Approach to Religion* (Columbia: University of South Carolina Press, 1987), 58–75.

26. See ibid. for a detailed description and first-hand accounts of *kachina* dancing, *kachina* cult initiation, and Powamu ceremony. The account that follows is based on the scholarship of Professor Gill.

27. Ibid., 69–70.

28. Ibid., 70.

29. Joseph Epes Brown, "Modes of Contemplation through Actions: North American Indians," *Main Currents in Modern Thought*, 30, November/December 1973, 62.

30. Quoted in Richard Erdoes and Alfonso Ortiz, eds., *American Indian Myths and Legends* (New York: Pantheon Books, 1984), 72.

31. See Robert Ellwood, *Mysticism and Religion*, 2nd ed. (New York: Seven Bridges Press, 1999), 57–58.

32. Eliade, *Shamanism*, 5.

33. Transpersonal indicates a state of consciousness beyond the ordinary, personal, or ego functioning of the psyche. Psychiatrist and scholar Bruce W. Scotton noted that "an account of a mystical, ineffable experience that brought about improved functioning for the experiencer would be an account of a transpersonal experience": Bruce W. Scotton, "Introduction and Definition of Transpersonal Psychology," in *Textbook of Transpersonal Psychiatry and Psychology*, ed. Bruce W. Scotton, Allan B. Chinen, and John R. Battista (New York: Basic Books, 1996), 4. Also see Robert Walsh, "Shamanism and Healing," in ibid., 96–103.

34. See Stephen Larsen, *The Mythic Imagination* (New York: Bantam Books, 1990), 95–118.

35. Francois Petitpierre, quoted in Huston Smith, *Forgotten Truth* (San Francisco: HarperCollins, repr. 1992), 42 n9.

36. Parrinder, *African Traditional Religion*, 10.

37. Jamake Highwater, *The Primal Mind* (New York: Harper & Row, 1981), 75.

CHAPTER 2

1. *Codex Matritensis*, quoted in Miguel León-Portilla, ed., *Native Mesoamerican Spirituality* (New York: Paulist Press, 1980), 186–187.

2. See chapter 1 above, "The Spiritual Traditions of the First Peoples," for more on shamans and shamanic religious traditions.

3. The first three of these codices are named after the cities where they are presently located, while the fourth is so-called because it was first exhibited at the Grolier Club in New York City in 1971. Although the Grolier Codex is now generally regarded as an authentic Maya codex, it should be noted that some scholars, such as J. Eric S. Thompson, have argued that it is not an authentic Maya codex but a modern forgery.

4. Dennis Tedlock, *Popol Vuh: The Definitive Edition of the Mayan Book of the Dawn of Life and the Glories of the Gods and Kings* (New York: Simon & Schuster, 1996), 65.

5. Ibid., 67.

6. Ibid., 69.

7. Ibid., 32.

8. Miguel León-Portilla, *Time and Reality in the Thought of the Maya*, 2nd ed., enlarged, trans. Charles L. Boilès, Fernando Horcasitas, and Miguel León-Portilla (Norman: University of Oklahoma Press, 1988), 33.

9. Miguel León-Portilla and Earl Shorris, *In the Language of Kings: An Anthology of Mesoamerican Literature – Pre-Columbian to the Present* (New York: W. W. Norton & Company, 2001), 400.

10. Davíd Carrasco, *Religions of Mesoamerica: Cosmovision and Ceremonial Centers* (New York: Harper & Row, 1990), 100.

11. The image of the cosmos as comprising three regions conjoined by a central axis, depicted as the World Tree, is reminiscent of many shamanic cosmologies. See Eliade, *Shamanism*, chapter 8.

12. *Florentine Codex*, Book 3, Chapter 14, quoted in León-Portilla, ed., *Native Mesoamerican Spirituality*, 167.

13. *Florentine Codex*, Book 3, Chapter 3, quoted in ibid., 151.

14. Although scholars recognize the name "Aztec" as an inappropriate substitute for "Mexica," it is customary to follow the entrenched usage of the former.

15. Enrique Florescano, *The Myth of Quetzalcoatl*, trans. Lysa Hochroth (Baltimore: Johns Hopkins University Press, 1999), 1.

16. Guilhem Olivier, "Tezcatlipoca," trans. Susan Romanosky, in *The Oxford Encyclopedia of Mesoamerican Cultures: The Civilizations of Mexico and Central America*, ed. Davíd Carrasco (New York: Oxford University Press, 2001), vol. 3, 218.

17. Miguel León-Portilla, "The Aztec Gods – How Many?," in *Circa 1492: Art in the Age of*

Exploration, ed. Jay A. Levenson (New Haven: Yale University Press for the National Gallery of Art, 1991), 508.

18. Miguel León-Portilla, *Aztec Thought and Culture: A Study of the Ancient Nahuatl Mind*, trans. Jack Emory Davis (Norman: University of Oklahoma Press, repr. 1990), 183.

19. From *The Destruction of the Jaguar: Poems from the Books of Chilam Balam*, trans. Christopher Sawyer-Lauçanno (San Francisco: City Lights Books, 1987), 7–8.

20. Ibid., 19.

CHAPTER 3

1. The Book of the Dead, quoted in R. T. Rundle Clark, *Myth and Symbol in Ancient Egypt* (London: Thames & Hudson, 1959), 79.

2. Frithjof Schuon, *The Essential Writings of Frithjof Schuon*, ed. Seyyed Hossein Nasr (New York: Amity House, 1986), 178.

3. The image of a world covered with primordial waters is a perennial motif. Similar images are found within later creation stories from other societies. See, for example, the *Rig Veda* (10.129), the Greek poet Homer (*Iliad*, Book XIV, lines 200–203), the Torah/Bible (Genesis 1:1–6), and the *Enuma Elish* (the Babylonian creation myth).

4. Pyramid Text, quoted in Clark, *Myth and Symbol*, 51.

5. H. Frankfort, *Ancient Egyptian Religion* (New York: Columbia University Press, 1948), 53.

6. John A. Wilson, "Egypt," in *The Intellectual Adventure of Ancient Man*, ed. H. Frankfort, H. A. Frankfort, J. A. Wilson, T. Jacobsen, and W. A. Irwin (Chicago: University of Chicago Press, 1946), 64–65.

7. Jan Assmann, *The Search for God in Ancient Egypt*, trans. David Lorton (New York: Cornell University Press, 2001), 4.

8. Ian Shaw, quoted in *The Oxford History of Ancient Egypt*, ed. Ian Shaw (Oxford: Oxford University Press, 2000), 7–8.

9. Clark, *Myth and Symbol*, 141.

10. See chapter 4 below, "The Religious Traditions of Ancient Greece," for an elaboration on Plotinus' theological philosophy.

11. Plotinus, quoted in Pierre Hadot, *Plotinus or the Simplicity of Vision*, trans. Michael Chase (Chicago: University of Chicago Press, 1993), 40.

12. The philosopher Marsilo Ficino (1433–1499 C.E.), an ordained Catholic priest, translated the *Corpus Hermeticum* – the mystical tradition attributed to Hermes Trismegistus, a prophet figure identified with the Egyptian god Thoth and the Greek god Hermes – from Greek into Latin. Although Hermes Trismegistus was considered a contemporary of Moses, later it was suggested that the extant writings attributed to him were written around the first century of the Common Era. These philosophical and alchemical writings helped to spawn a rich movement within Christianity during the Italian Renaissance. This movement propounded a belief in an Ancient Theology or Perennial Wisdom that had been passed down through various World Teachers, such as the Persian prophet Zoroaster (Zarathustra), Moses, Hermes

Trismegistus, Orpheus, Pythagoras, Plato, and, most prominently, Jesus. Hermes Trismegistus was also known in the Islamic tradition as the "father of philosophers" and was identified with the Prophet Idrís, known as Enoch in the Hebrew scriptures.

13. See chapter 4 below, "The Religious Traditions of Ancient Greece," for a discussion of Isis during the Hellenistic period.

14. See *The Book of the Dead*, trans. E. A. Wallis Budge (Secaucus, NJ: University Books, 1960). The Book of Going Forth by Day was buried with the deceased, and served as a guidebook for the afterlife. It was first called The Book of the Dead by tomb-robbers.

15. Incidentally, the process of mummification was very expensive, and therefore was not always affordable. In later periods, pictures or statues of the deceased, rather than a mummified corpse, were believed to be sufficient.

16. See chapter 4 below, "The Religious Traditions of Ancient Greece," for more on the cult of Asklepios.

17. Eliade, *The Sacred and Profane*, 77.

18. The Papyrus of Ani (from The Book of the Dead): see Smart and Hecht, eds., *Sacred Texts of the World*, 37.

19. Akhenaton's *Great Hymn to Aten* (from the Tomb of Amarna): see ibid., 12–13.

20. See chapter 4 below, "The Religious Traditions of Ancient Greece," for more on the Greek gods and Hellenistic religiosity.

21. See chapter 13 below, "The Christian Faith," for a discussion of monasticism and Gnosticism.

22. Clark, *Myth and Symbol*, 263.

CHAPTER 4

1. Euripides, *The Trojan Women*, lines 884–888, in *The Complete Greek Drama*, vol. 1, ed. Whitney J. Oates and Eugene O'Neill, trans. Gilbert Murray (New York: Random House, 1938), 992.

2. Arnold Toynbee, *A Study of History*, vol. 12: *Reconsiderations* (London: Oxford University Press, 1961), 273.

3. Aristotle, *Nicomachean Ethics*, line 1097b11, in *Aristotle: Nicomachean Ethics*, trans. Joe Sachs (Newburyport, Mass.: Focus Publishing, 2002).

4. Wilfred Cantwell Smith, "Philosophia as One of the Religious Traditions of Mankind," unpublished paper, quoted in Huston Smith, "Western Philosophy as a Great Religion," in *Transcendence and the Sacred*, ed. Alan M. Olson and Leroy S. Rouner (Notre Dame, Ind.: University of Notre Dame Press, 1981), 19.

5. Scholars have seriously questioned the historicity of these figures, particularly Homer. It is possible that the works attributed to these authors were produced by a composite of poets.

6. Accordingly, psychologists and mythologists, such as those who study Depth Psychology, have emphasized the psychological import of symbolic and archetypal interpretations of the Greek gods and myths. These researchers believe that the symbolism of Greek mythology, and mythology in general, can provide insight into the conscious and unconscious energies of the

human psyche (the word "psyche" is derived from the Greek *psuche*, meaning "spirit" or "soul").

7. Hesiod, *Works and Days*, lines 252–278, in Hesiod, *Works and Days and Theogony*, trans. Stanley Lombardo, intro. Robert Lamberton (Indianapolis: Hackett, 1993), 30.

8. Herodotus, *Histories*, Book 1, line 91, in Herodotus, *The Histories*, trans. Aubrey De Sélincourt, introd. John Marincola (New York: Penguin Books, repr. 1996), 38.

9. See Ovid, *Metamorphoses*, trans. A. D. Melville, introd. E. J. Kenney (Oxford: Oxford University Press, repr. 1998).

10. Herodotus, *Histories*, Book 1, line 207, in *The Histories*, 81.

11. Sophocles, *Antigone*, line 505, in Sophocles, *The Three Theban Plays*, trans. Robert Fagles (New York: Penguin, 1984), 82.

12. Marcus Tullius Cicero, quoted in Robert Flacelière, *Greek Oracles*, trans. Douglas Garman (London: Elek Books, 1965), 1.

13. See Fragment 15 in *The Complete Works of Aristotle*, vol. 2, ed. Jonathan Barnes (Princeton: Princeton University Press, 1984), 2392.

14. Walter Burkert, *Ancient Mystery Cults* (Cambridge, Mass.: Harvard University Press, repr. 1987), 8.

15. Diane Rayor, *The Homeric Hymns: A Translation, with Introduction and Notes* (Berkeley: University of California Press, 2004), 33.

16. Friedrich Nietzsche, *The Birth of Tragedy*, trans. Clifton P. Fadiman (New York: Dover, repr. 1995), 4.

17. It is interesting to note that the ancient Greek word for "body" (*soma*) was closely related to a word meaning "tomb" (*sema*). In fact, Plato discusses the possibility that the term *soma* was actually derived from *sema* by the Orphic poets. See Plato's *Cratylus*, 400c. Further discussions can be found in W. K. C. Guthrie's *Orpheus and Greek Religion* (Princeton: Princeton University Press, repr. 1993), 156–157.

18. Werner Heisenberg, quoted in *Quantum Questions*, ed. Ken Wilber (Boston: Shambhala, 1985), 57.

19. For example, scholars believe that Pythagorean doctrines influenced Kabbalah, the Jewish mysticism.

20. John Burnet, *Greek Philosophy: Thales to Plato* (London: Macmillan, repr. 1962), 12.

21. See Werner Jaeger, *The Theology of the Early Greek Philosophers* (Oxford: Oxford University Press, repr. 1952), 1–17.

22. Ibid., 2.

23. James Lesher, *The Greek Philosophers: Selected Greek Texts from the Presocratics, Plato, and Aristotle, with Introduction, Notes, and Commentary* (London: Bristol Classical Press/Duckworth, 1998), 21–22.

24. Stanley Lombardo, *Parmenides and Empedocles: The Fragments in Verse Translation* (San Francisco: Grey Fox Press, repr. 1982), 4.

25. In the case of the Milesian "physicists," their philosophy was the impetus behind the materialistic atomism of Democritus (d. *c*.370 B.C.E.), who, like Leucippus before him, proposed that

all things were composed of tiny invisible particles, or "atoms." The view of the atomists was elucidated by the Greek Epicurus (341–270 B.C.E.) and the Roman Lucretius (*c.*96–55 B.C.E.). The atomist viewpoint was the precursor of the mechanistic physics of the eighteenth and nineteenth centuries.

26. In fact, pre-Socratic thought remains influential in modern times. For example, the philosophy of Heraclitus had a strong effect on the Swiss psychologist Carl Gustav Jung (1875–1961); the ontological concept of Being in Parmenides' philosophy influenced the metaphysics of the German philosopher Martin Heidegger (1889–1976); and Empedocles' cosmic cycles of Love and Strife inspired the Irish poet W. B. Yeats (1865–1939), as evinced by his occult masterpiece, *A Vision*.

27. Herodotus traced Demeter to the Egyptian goddess Isis, Dionysus to Osiris, and Zeus to Amon-Ra. Throughout antiquity Greek thinkers, especially the philosophers, spoke of the Egyptians as sages, and seem to have been thoroughly fascinated with Egyptian culture and civilization. Many Greek philosophers are believed to have traveled to Egypt, including Thales, Pythagoras, Plato, and others.

28. Plato, *Crito*, line 49B, in *Plato: The Collected Dialogues*, ed. Edith Hamilton and Huntington Cairns (Princeton: Princeton University Press, 1961), 34.

29. Plato, *Apology*, line 41D, in *Plato: Complete Works*, ed. John Cooper (Indianapolis: Hackett, 1997), 36.

30. Alfred North Whitehead, *Process and Reality* (New York: Free Press, repr. 1979), 39.

31. Quoted in *The Symposium of Plato: The Shelley Translation*, ed. David K. O'Connor (South Bend, Ind.: St. Augustine's Press, 2002), xliii.

32. Samuel Taylor Coleridge, *Spiritual Writings: Selected Proems and Prose*, introd. Robert Van de Weyer (London: HarperCollins, 1997), 88.

33. Jaeger, *Theology*, 4.

34. Plato, *Timaeus*, 90a–c, in Francis M. Cornford, *Plato's Cosmology: The Timaeus of Plato* (Indianapolis: Hackett, repr. 1997), 353–354.

35. Plato, *Meno*, lines 81C–D, in *Plato: Complete Works*, 880.

36. Aristotle, *Nicomachean Ethics*, line 1098a16, in *Great Books of the Western World: The Works of Aristotle*, vol. 2, ed. Robert Maynard Hutchins (Chicago: Encyclopaedia Britannica, 1952), 343.

37. Jaeger, *Theology*, 5.

38. See ibid., pp. 1–17.

39. Aristotle, *Metaphysics*, line 1074b34, in *Great Books of the Western World: The Works of Aristotle*, vol. 1, 605.

40. Aristotle, *Eudemian Ethics*, line 1249b17, in *The Complete Works of Aristotle*, vol. 2, 1981.

41. Religious diversity in the Greco-Roman–Egyptian world, especially during the early period of the Common Era, encouraged a lively debate between Greek philosophers, followers of various mystery religions, Jews, Gnostics, and Christians. Some thinkers discerned the commonalities between Greek philosophy and the Abrahamic religions. This trend was evident in the late second century when the Syrian-born Platonist Numenius of Apamea concluded: "What is Plato but Moses in Greek form?" Contrary to the syncretic approach, numerous treatises were

written to refute other traditions. Despite opposing views, the philosophy of Aristotle emerged as the dominant philosophical–scientific approach of both Judaic–Christian Europeans and Islamic intellectuals for centuries; however, Platonism and Neoplatonism remained a constant influence, especially among mystics and poets.

42. Apuleius, *The Golden Ass* (*The Transformation of Lucius*), trans. Robert Graves (New York: Noonday Press, repr. 1992), 264–265.

43. See Plato, *Republic*, Book X, line 613A.

44. See Plato, *Phaedo*, line 64A.

45. *Neoplatonic Saints: The Lives of Plotinus and Proclus by their Students*, trans. and introd. Mark Edwards (Liverpool: Liverpool University Press, 2000), 44.

46. E. R. Dodds, quoted in *Select Passages Illustrating Neoplatonism*, trans. and introd. E. R. Dodds (Chicago: Ares, repr. 1979), 10.

47. Ibid., 15.

48. Friedrich Schiller, *On the Aesthetic Education of Man: In a Series of Lectures*, trans. and introd. Elizabeth Wilkinson and L. A. Willoughby (Oxford: Oxford University Press, repr. 1982), 31.

49. W. H. Auden, *Forewords and Afterwords* (New York: Random House, 1973), 32 (emphasis in original).

CHAPTER 5

1. Yasna 60.5, quoted in Andrew Wilson, *World Scripture: A Comparative Anthology of Sacred Texts* (New York: Paragon House, 1991), 198.

2. Mary Boyce, *Zoroastrians: Their Religious Beliefs and Practices* (London: Routledge & Kegan Paul, 1987), 29.

3. Karl Jaspers, *Way to Wisdom: An Introduction to Philosophy*, trans. Ralph Manheim (London: Yale University Press, 1954), 98.

4. Karen Armstrong, *The Great Transformation* (New York: Alfred A. Knopf, 2006), xiii–xiv.

5. Ibid., xii–xiii.

6. Mary Boyce, *Zoroastrianism: Its Antiquity and Constant Vigour* (Costa Mesa: Mazda, 1992), 53.

7. Curiously, the Indo-Aryan tradition developed along different lines in Vedic India; notably, for non-Zoroastrians in India the *daeva*s (*deva*s) are held to be holy while it is the *ahura*s (*asura*s) that are considered evil. Indra was also revered as the High God, and it is he who is most praised in the *Rig Veda*.

8. Boyce, *Zoroastrians: Their Religious Beliefs and Practices*, 18.

9. See Joseph Campbell, *The Hero with a Thousand Faces*, 2nd ed. (Princeton: Princeton University Press, repr. 1973).

10. Yasna 31.8, quoted in Farhang Mehr, *The Zoroastrian Tradition* (Costa Mesa: Mazda, 2003), 29.

11. See Mary Boyce, ed. and trans., *Textual Sources for the Study of Zoroastrianism* (Chicago: University of Chicago Press, repr. 1990), 104–105.

12. See Piloo Nanavutty, *The Parsis* (New Delhi: National Book Trust, 1977).

13. The five Gathas are: *Ahunavaiti*, or the Gatha of Free Choice (Yasna 28–34); *Ushtavaiti*, or the Gatha of Bliss (Yasna 43–46); *Spenta Mainyu*, or the Gatha of the Holy Spirit (Yasna 47–50); *Vohu Khashathra*, or the Gatha of Sovereignty (Yasna 51); and *Vahishtoishti*, or the Gatha of the Highest Wish (Yasna 53).

14. Mehr, *The Zoroastrian Tradition*, 30.

15. Yasna 31.7, quoted in *The Gathas of Zarathushtra*, trans. Piloo Nanavutty (Middletown, NJ: Grantha Corporation, 1999), 84.

16. As stated earlier, *asha* (Sanskrit, *rta*) was the principle of cosmic order found in the Indo-Aryan tradition; it is now deified as an Amesha Spenta and theologically identified with the will of God.

17. Cyrus R. Pangborn, *Zoroastrianism: A Beleaguered Faith* (New Delhi: Vikas, 1982), 17.

18. Yasna 30.5, quoted in Boyce, *Textual Sources for the Study of Zoroastrianism*, 35. Also see Yasna 45.2.

19. Mircea Eliade, *A History of Religious Ideas*, vol. 1, trans. Willard R. Trask (Chicago: University of Chicago Press, 1978), 310.

20. Yasna 30.2, quoted in *The Gathas of Zarathushtra*, 78.

21. Yasna 43.5, quoted in ibid., 110.

22. Similarly, religions of India uphold the notion of a cosmic law, or *dharma*, as well as a law of moral cause and effect or *karma*.

23. Yasna 48.2, quoted in ibid., 137.

24. Mehr, *The Zoroastrian Tradition*, 142.

25. For more on Mithraism see Franz Cumont, *The Mysteries of Mithra*, trans. Thomas J. McCormack (New York: Dover, 1956).

26. See Hans-Joachim Klimkeit, *Gnosis on the Silk Road* (New York: HarperCollins, 1993).

27. Mircea Eliade and Ioan P. Couliano, *The Eliade Guide to World Religions* (New York: HarperCollins, 1991), 99.

28. Wilfred Cantwell Smith, *The Meaning and End of Religion* (Minneapolis: Fortress Press, 1991), 95.

29. Seyyed Hossein Nasr, *Religion and the Order of Nature* (New York: Oxford University Press, 1996), 49. For more on this and related mystical issues see Henry Corbin, *Spiritual Body and Celestial Earth: From Mazdean Iran to Shī'ite Iran*, trans. Nancy Pearson (Princeton: Princeton University Press, 1977).

30. Eliade, *A History of Religious Ideas*, vol. 1, 302.

31. Richard C. Foltz, *Spirituality in the Land of the Noble: How Iran Shaped the World's Religions* (Oxford: Oneworld, 2004), 49.

32. See *The Pythagorean Sourcebook and Library*, trans. Kenneth Sylvan Guthrie (Grand Rapids: Phanes Press, 1987), 131.

33. Rabindranath Tagore, *The Religion of Man* (London: Unwin Hyman, repr. 1988), 47.

34. See *The Zend Avesta of Zarathustra*, trans. Edmond Bordeaux Szekely (n.p.: International Biogenic Society, 1990), 37.

CHAPTER 6

1. Swami Prabhavananda, *The Spiritual Heritage of India*, 3rd ed. (Hollywood: Vedanta Press, repr. 1980), 23.

2. Octavio Paz, *In Light of India* (Orlando: Harcourt Brace & Company, 1998), 37.

3. A. L. Basham, *The Origins and Development of Classical Hinduism* (Boston: Beacon Press, 1989), 22–24.

4. *Rig Veda* 10.129, quoted in Basham, *Classical Hinduism*, 23.

5. Since ancient times, Hindu scriptures have emphasized the importance of teachers. In the *Mundaka Upanishad*, for example, two essential qualifications of a guru are specified: He must be *shrotriya*, one who is learned in the scriptures; and *brahmanistha*, one who is established and grounded in *brahman*. The word "guru" means "dispeller of darkness." In many schools within the Hindu tradition and in the popular forms of practice, gurus are indispensable.

6. Mircea Eliade, *Yoga: Immortality and Freedom*, 2nd ed., trans. Willard R. Trask (Princeton: Princeton University Press, 1970), 4.

7. "Swami" is an honorific title given to Hindu spiritual teachers.

8. Swami Nikhilananda, *Hinduism: Its Meaning for the Liberation of the Spirit* (Madras: Sri Ramakrishna Math, 1968), 69.

9. *Taittriya Upanishad*, I.xi, quoted in Prabhavananda, *Spiritual Heritage*, 65.

10. Karan Singh, *Essays on Hinduism* (Chattanooga: Insights Press, 1998), 4–6.

11. T. M. P. Mahadevan, *Outlines of Hinduism* (Bombay: Chetana, repr. 1984), 35.

12. S. N. Dasgupta, *Hindu Mysticism* (Delhi: Motilal Banarsidass, repr. 1983), 7.

13. Sri Aurobindo, *The Essential Writings of Sri Aurobindo*, ed. P. Heehs (New Delhi: Oxford University Press, 1998), 254.

14. Sri Aurobindo, *The Message of the Gita*, ed. Anilbaran Roy (Pondicherry: Sri Aurobindo Ashram, repr. 1999), 73.

15. The following are eight of the *avatar*s of Vishnu: Matsya, the fish upon whose back all humanity was saved during the time of the great flood; Kurma, the great tortoise who bestowed *amritam*, the nectar of immortality, on the *deva*s so that they could defeat the *asura*s; Varaha, the boar who rescued Mother Earth, Bhoomidevi, from the evil demon Hiranyaksha; Narasimha, the half-man and half-lion, who saved the world from the wrath of the evil demon Hiranyakashipu, Hiranyaksha's brother; Vamana, the dwarf *brahmin* who saves the righteous and kills the vain king of the *asura*s; Parashurama, the forest dweller who wielded an ax that destroyed all the evil Khasatriyas and evil king Arjuna; Rama, the prince who vanquished the evil king Ravana of Lanka; and Krishna, the king who advised the five Pandavas against their evil cousins, the Kauravas.

16. Diana Eck, *Darśan: Seeing the Divine Image in India*, 2nd ed. (Chambersburg, Pa.: Anima Books, repr. 1985), 10.

17. Radhakrishnan, *Indian Philosophy*, vol. 2, 2nd ed. (London: George Allen & Unwin Ltd., 1971), 20.

18. See Mehrdad Massoudi, "On the Qualities of a Teacher and a Student: An Eastern Perspective Based on Buddhism, Vedanta, and Sufism," *Intercultural Education*, 13 (2002), 137–155.

19. Shankara, quoted in Mahadevan, *Outlines of Hinduism*, 141.

20. *Brahmasutrabhasya* I,1,1. *Brahma Sutras: According to Sri Sankara*, trans. and introd. Swami Vireswarananda (Calcutta: Advaita Ashrama, repr. 2005), 20.

21. *Brihadaranyaka Upanishad*, II, iv.5, *The Upanishads: A New Translation*, vol. 3, trans. and introd. Swami Nikhilananda (New York: Ramakrishna-Vivekananda Center, repr. 1990), 176.

22. See *Aitareya Upanishad*, 3.3.

23. See *Brihadaranyaka Upanishad*, 1.4.

24. See *Chandogya Upanishad*, 6.8.

25. See *Mandukya Upanishad*, 1.2.

26. Eliade, *Yoga*, 5 (emphasis in original).

27. Ibid., 47.

28. There are four *yamas* (restraints): (i) *ahimsa* (non-violence or non-injury); (ii) *satya* (truthfulness); (iii) *asteya* (non-stealing); (iv) *brahmacarya* (continence and self-control); and (v) *aparigraha* (freedom from avarice).

29. There are also five *niyamas* (observances): (i) *sauca* (cleanliness or purity); (ii) *santosa* (contentment); (iii) *tapas* (religious fervor and austerity); (iv) *svadhyaya* (study of one's self and the sacred scriptures); and (v) *Isvara pranidhana* (surrender of the self to God).

30. Swami Prabhavananda, *Religion in Practice* (Hollywood: Vedanta Press, repr. 1969), 110–111 (emphasis in the original).

31. See chapter 15 below, "The Sikh Faith."

32. Singh, *Essays on Hinduism*, 26.

33. Sri Ramakrishna, *The Gospel of Sri Ramakrishna*, abridged ed., trans., and intro. Swami Nikhilananda (New York: Ramakrishna-Vivekananda Center, repr. 1988), 127.

34. Ibid., 130.

35. K. L. Klostermaier, *Hindu Writings: A Short Introduction to the Major Sources* (Oxford: Oneworld, 2000), 138.

36. See Eck, *Darsán*.

37. The term *samskaras* also indicates the karmic impressions, trace memories, or tendencies acquired from previous lives that, in part, form the habits and propensities of one's current life.

38. *Rig Veda* I, 164:46.

39. Nikhilananda, *Hinduism*, 20–21.

40. Mahadevan, *Outlines of Hinduism*, 26.

CHAPTER 7

1. *Sutta-Nipata*, trans. H. Saddhatissa (London: Curzon Press, 1985), 15–16.

2. Edward Conze, *Buddhism: Its Essence and Development* (New York: Harper & Row, repr. 1975), 36.

3. The term "*dharma*" has many meanings depending on the context. *Dharma*, as denoted in the

Three Jewels, refers to the teachings of the Buddha. In other contexts it may mean cosmic law, morality, primary particles of existence, and ultimate truth (reality as it really is).

4. Roshi P. Kapleau, *The Three Pillars of Zen* (New York: Anchor Books, 1980), 177.

5. *The Dhammapada*, trans. Eknath Easwaran (Petaluma, Calif.: Nilgiri Press, repr. 1987), 116–117.

6. *Sutta-Nipata*, 72.

7. *Digha-Nikaya*, trans. M. Walshe as *The Long Discourses of the Buddha* in *Thus Have I Heard* (Boston: Wisdom, 1995), 269–270.

8. Ibid., 270.

9. Quoted by Edward Conze in "Buddhism: The Mahayana," in *Encyclopedia of the World's Religions*, ed. R. C. Zaehner (New York: Barnes & Noble, repr. 1997), 302.

10. See Śāntideva, *A Guide to the Bodhisattva Way of Life*, trans. Vesna A. Wallace and B. Alan Wallace (Ithaca, NY: Snow Lion, 1997).

11. Conze, *Buddhism*, 132.

12. For more on the Zen tradition see Kapleau, *The Three Pillars of Zen*.

13. See *The Tibetan Book of Living and Dying*, trans. Sogyal Rinpoche, ed. Patrick Gaffney and Andrew Harvey (New York: HarperCollins, 1992).

14. For an introduction to the Tibetan tradition see B. Alan Wallace, *Tibetan Buddhism From the Ground Up* (Boston: Wisdom, 1993).

15. *The Udāna*, trans. John D. Ireland (Kandy: Buddhist Publication Society, 1990), 13.

16. See David J. Kalupahana, *Nāgārjuna: The Philosophy of the Middle Way* (New York: State University of New York Press, 1986).

17. See, for example, Piyadassi Thera, *The Buddha's Ancient Path* (Kandy: Buddhist Publication Society, repr. 1987).

18. W. Rahula, *What the Buddha Taught* (New York: Grove Press, 1974), 29.

19. Udana 8.3 quoted in Introduction to *Digha-Nikaya*, 29.

20. For a discussion of *samatha* meditation see B. Alan Wallace, *Boundless Heart: The Four Immeasurables*, ed. Zara Houshmand (New York: Snow Lion, 1999), 31–84.

21. See *Vissudhimaga* (The Path to Purification), trans. Bhikkhu Nanamoli (Kandi: Buddhist Publication Society, 1991).

22. For example, see Joseph Goldstein, *Insight Meditation* (Boston: Shambhala, 1994).

23. For example, see Bhante G. Gunaratana, *Mindfulness in Plain English* (Boston: Wisdom, 1993).

24. Piyadassi Thera, *Buddha's Ancient Path*, 32.

CHAPTER 8

1. Joel Beversluis, ed., *Sourcebook of the World's Religions* (Novato, Calif.: New World Library, 2000), 79.

2. *Kalpasutra*, quoted in Smart and Hecht, eds., *Sacred Texts of the World*, 279.

3. Hiralal Jain, "Jainism: Its History, Principles, and Precepts," in *The Cultural Heritage of India*, vol. 1 (Calcutta: Ramakrishna Mission, Institute of Culture, repr. 2001), 406.

4. *Siddhasena Sanmatitarka* 1.28, quoted in Wilson, ed., *World Scripture*, 39–40.

5. M. K. Gandhi, *The Moral and Political Writings of Mahatma Gandhi*, ed. Raghavan Iyer (Clarendon: Oxford University Press, 1986–1987), vol. 2, p. 20.

6. Surendranath Dasgupta, *A History of Indian Philosophy*, vol. 1 (Delhi: Motilal Banarsidass, repr. 1992), 188.

7. From the *Avakuri*, in F. Max Muller, ed., *Sacred Books of the East*, vol. 45, *Jaina Sutras*, book 2 (Delhi: Motilal Banarsidass, repr. 1980), 196 n2.

8. See *Uttaradhyayana* XXXIII, *Jaina Sutras*, 192–193.

9. *Uttaradhyayana* XXXII.6, ibid., 185.

10. *Sutrakritanga* Book I.2, Chapter 1.15, ibid., 252.

11. Quoted in Wilson, ed., *World Scripture*, 208.

12. *Uttaradhyayana* XXXII.8, in *Jaina Sutras*, 185.

13. P. S. Jaini, *The Jaina Path of Purification* (Delhi: Motilal Banarsidass Publishers, repr. 1990), 229.

14. Jain, "Jainism," 403.

CHAPTER 9

1. Translated by Arthur Waley in *The Way and Its Power: A Study of the* Tao Te Ching *and Its Place in Chinese Thought* (New York: Grove Weidenfeld, 1958), 162.

2. Ibid., 99.

3. Ch'an is more popularly known by its Japanese name, Zen. The word Zen ultimately derives from the Sanskrit word *dhyana*, meaning "meditation" or "absorption."

4. Translated by Wing-Tsit Chan in *A Source Book in Chinese Philosophy* (Princeton: Princeton University Press, 1963), 139.

5. Translated by Burton Watson in *Chuang Tzu: Basic Writings* (New York: Columbia University Press, 1964), 140.

6. Quoted in Alan Watts, *The Way of Zen* (New York: Vintage Books, 1957), 88. For further reading on Bodhidharma, see Jeffrey L. Broughton, *The Bodhidharma Anthology: The Earliest Records of Zen* (Berkeley: University of California Press, 1999).

7. Translated by G. F. Feng and J. English in *Tao Te Ching* (New York: Vintage Books, repr. 1989), chapter 29, 31.

8. Translated by Stephen Addiss and Stanley Lombardo in *Lao-Tzu: Tao Te Ching* (Indianapolis: Hackett, 1993), 18.

9. Rudolf Ritsema and Stephen Karcher, *I Ching: The Classic Chinese Oracle of Change* (Rockport, Mass.; Element Books, 1994), 28.

10. Kuan Tzu, quoted in Waley, *The Way and Its Power*, 48–49.

11. *The I Ching or Book of Changes. The Richard Wilhelm Translation Rendered into English by Cary F. Baynes*, 3rd ed. (Princeton: Princeton University Press, 1967), 351–352.

12. Ibid., 264.

13. *Tao Te Ching*, chapter 25, in Waley, *The Way and Its Power*, 174.

14. See *The I Ching or Book of Changes*, lvi.
15. J. C. Cooper, *Taoism: The Way of the Mystic* (Wellingborough: Aquarian Press, repr. 1990), 35.
16. *Tao Te Ching*, chapter 42, in Waley, *The Way and Its Power*, 195.
17. See Ritsema and Karcher, *I Ching*, 29.
18. Waley, *The Way and Its Power*, 224.
19. Liu Xiaogan, "Taoism," in *Our Religions*, ed. Arvind Sharma (New York: HarperCollins, 1995), 243.
20. *Tao Te Ching*, chapter 27, in Waley, *The Way and Its Power*, 177.
21. Ibid., 143.
22. Ibid.
23. Lieh Tzu, *The Book of Lieh-tzu*, trans. A. C. Graham (New York: Columbia University Press, repr. 1990), 29.
24. *Tao Te Ching*, chapter 11, quoted in Waley, *The Way and Its Power*, 155.
25. Ibid., 45.
26. Smith, *The World's Religions*, 197.

CHAPTER 10

1. William Edward Soothil, *The Analects of Confucius*, 2nd ed. (New York: Paragon Book Reprint Corp., 1968), 237.
2. *The Analects*, VII.1, trans. Arthur Waley in *The Analects of Confucius* (New York: Vintage Books, 1938), 123.
3. *The Analects*, II.11, in ibid., 90.
4. Smith, *The World's Religions*, 154.
5. *The Analects*, II.4, in *The Essential Confucius*, trans. Thomas Cleary (Edison, NJ: Castle Books, 1992), 115.
6. Tu Wei-ming, "Confucianism," in Sharma, ed., *Our Religions*, 141.
7. Chan, *A Source Book in Chinese Philosophy*, 789.
8. See *The Doctrine of the Mean*, Chapter 22, trans. Wing-Tsit Chan, in ibid., pp. 107–108.
9. *The Analects*, V.12, in Waley, *Analects*, 110. See also *Analects*, XII.1–3.
10. See, for example, *The Analects*, V.7.
11. *The Analects*, IX.10, in Waley, *Analects*, 140.
12. *The Analects*, III.3, in ibid., 94.
13. *The Analects*, XII.1, in ibid., 162.
14. Lin Yutang, *The Wisdom of Confucius* (New York: Modern Library, repr. 1966), 13–14.
15. Quoted in *Essential Confucius*, 2.
16. Tu Wei-ming, *Confucian Thought: Selfhood as Creative Transformation* (Albany: State University of New York Press, 1985), 174.
17. Ibid., 178.
18. *The Analects*, XVII.8, in Waley, *Analects*, 211.
19. See the discussion of *te* (power, moral force) in chapter 9 above.
20. *The Analects*, XII.10, in Waley, *Analects*, 165.

21. *The Analects*, XI.20, in *Essential Confucius*, 107.

22. Lin, *Wisdom of Confucius*, 163.

23. Ritsema and Karcher, *I Ching*, 9.

24. *The I Ching or Book of Changes*, liii.

25. From *The Doctrine of the Mean*, trans. Alfred Doeblin in *The Living Thoughts of Confucius* (Greenwich, Conn.: Fawcett Books, 1959), 65.

26. It is noteworthy that around the same time that Confucius was teaching the Doctrine of the Mean in China, thinkers in ancient Greece, such as Socrates, Plato, and, most notably, Aristotle, were teaching a similar doctrine. Incidentally, on account of the profusion of wisdom during this era, the philosopher Karl Jaspers referred to this period in history as the "Axial Period," a turning point in the development of civilization. Furthermore, just as the Doctrine of the Mean influenced the heirs of Confucius' teachings in the "East," so this same doctrine influenced the inheritors of the Greek formulation in the "West." However, while the *histories* of these teachings were initially divided by time and place, their source transcends such divisions since they are expressions of the spiritual yearning common to all humanity.

27. *The Analects*, VI.27, in Waley, *Analects*, 121–122. A parallel passage is found in *The Doctrine of the Mean*, Chapter 3 (translated in Chan, *A Source Book in Chinese Philosophy*, 99).

28. *The Analects*, XVII.6, in *Essential Confucius*, 4.

29. *The Analects*, VII.13, in Waley, *Analects*, 125.

30. *The Analects*, XI.9, in ibid., 154–55.

31. *The Doctrine of the Mean*, Chapter 20, in Chan, *A Source Book in Chinese Philosophy*, 104 (brackets in the original).

32. *The Doctrine of the Mean*, Chapter 19, in ibid., 103.

33. See the epigraph at the beginning of this chapter.

34. *The Analects*, XII.2, in Waley, *Analects*, 162. See also *The Doctrine of the Mean*, Chapter 13, in Chan, *A Source Book in Chinese Philosophy*, 101.

35. Chan, *A Source Book in Chinese Philosophy*, 92.

36. From *The Doctrine of the Mean* in ibid., 105.

37. Ibid., 7 (brackets in the original).

38. Ibid., 111 (brackets in the original).

39. *The Analects*, XII.1, in ibid., 38.

40. Ibid., 86.

41. Ibid.

42. Lin, *Wisdom of Confucius*, 110.

43. *The Analects*, IX.7, in Waley, *Analects*, 140.

44. *The Analects*, VII.33, in ibid., 130.

CHAPTER 11

1. The *Man'yoshu*, quoted in *Great Asian Religions: An Anthology*, ed. Wing-tsit Chan, Isma'īl Rāgī al Fārūqī, Joseph M. Kitagawa, and P. T. Raju (London: Macmillan, 1969), 239. The *Man'yoshu*

("Collection of Myriad Leaves"), dated to the late seventh and eighth centuries of the Common Era, is the earliest anthology of Japanese poetry. It is considered by many Shinto scholars as the most authentic representation of Japanese spirituality bereft of foreign influences.

2. Byron H. Earhart, *Japanese Religion: Unity and Diversity*, 3rd ed. (Belmont, Calif.: Wadsworth, 1982), 29.

3. *Kannagara*, in its various connotations and meanings, is also used as another name for the Shinto religion in Japan. In general, the term signifies the movements, actions, and gestures that designate a life in accord with the way of the divine *kami*. See the glossary in Stuart D. Picken, *Shinto Meditations for Revering the Earth* (Berkeley: Stone Bridge Press, 2002).

4. Yukitaka Yamamoto, *Kami No Michi: The Way of the Kami* (Stockton, Calif.: Tsubaki America Publications, 1987), 73.

5. Ibid., 74–75.

6. Muraoka Tsunetsugo, *Studies in Shinto Thought*, trans. Delmer M. Brown and James T. Araki (Tokyo: Ministry of Education, 1964), 11.

7. Ian Reader, *Religion in Contemporary Japan* (Honolulu: University of Hawaii Press, 1991), 13–14.

8. An existent remnant of the shamanic substratum of Japanese religion is represented by the Yamabushi or Shugendo mountain ascetics. The Yamabushi are an esoteric order that draws from Taoist, Shinto, and Mahayana Buddhist practices. For an interesting account of a Yamabushi ceremony see Joseph Campbell, *Sake & Satori: Asian Journals – Japan*, ed. David Kudler (Novato, Calif.: New World Library, 2002), 119–125.

9. Robert S. Ellwood and Richard Pilgrim, *Japanese Religion* (Englewood Cliffs: Prentice-Hall, 1985), 3.

10. For example, the mountains of Japan, especially Mount Fuji, have traditionally been viewed as *kami*. Mount Fuji, in fact, is the central object of devotion for some Shinto sects (some of which were influenced by the Mahayana Buddhist tradition).

11. H. Neill McFarland, *The Rush Hour of the Gods: A Study of New Religious Movements in Japan* (New York: Macmillan, 1967), 20.

12. Akiko Kobayashi, "Shintoism: Nature's Own Religion," *Journal of Dharma*, 26, January–March 2001, 90. Notably, Akiko Kobayashi is the former priestess of the Meiji Shinto shrine in Tokyo and the current priestess of the Shinto shrine in Goryo, Japan.

13. *Tama*, meaning spirit or soul, was understood as the animating force within living beings and objects. Disembodied *tama*s, some beneficent and others malevolent, were forces to be reckoned with in the here and now. Such spiritual entities were thought to be influenced and subdued through religious rituals and practices.

14. Ueda Kenji, quoted in Norman Havens, "Immanent Legitimation: Reflections on the *Kami* Concept," in *Kami*, ed. Inoue Nobutaka, trans. Norman Havens (Tokyo: Kokugakuin University, Institute for Japanese Culture and Classics, 1988), 233.

15. Sokyo Ono, *Shinto: The Kami Way* (Rutland, Vt.: Charles E. Tuttle, 1962), 8.

16. Motoori Norinaga, quoted in Stuart D. Picken, *Sourcebook in Shinto: Selected Documents* (Westport: Praeger, 2004), 200.

17. Ibid., 201.

18. Many scholars have considered the descriptive term "numinous," which was coined by the scholar Rudolf Otto, to be valuable in enabling one to approach the qualitative religiosity of the Shinto tradition. See chapter 1 above, "The Spiritual Traditions of the First Peoples," for more on numinous experiences.

19. Traditionally, the phrase "the will of the *kami*" is not understood to indicate the will of a single sovereign God that rules over all things, but rather is representative of a consensus between many divine *kami* or cosmic processes. From the point of view of some Shinto thinkers, human life is a microcosm of the divine cosmos and ought to be patterned after the harmonious and consultative way of interaction and ruling exhibited by the many *kami*. It should be noted, however, that although Shinto, strictly speaking, is not a monotheistic religion there have been Shinto viewpoints, including those stemming from Buddhist and Confucian amalgamative schools, which are akin to monotheistic perspectives. Notably, some Shinto thinkers, such as Hirata Atsutane (1776–1843), who posited a trinitarian doctrine of *kami* unity influenced by Catholicism, have held monotheistic viewpoints. Also, during the nineteenth and twentieth centuries new Shinto-derived religious groups emerged led by charismatic leaders (so-called "Sect Shinto"), some of which are considered independent monotheistic religions.

20. Beatrice M. Bodart-Bailey, "Religion and Society in the Shinto Perspective," *Journal of Dharma*, 9, January–March 1984, 72.

21. Emperor Go-Fushimi, quoted in Picken, *Sourcebook*, 41.

22. Shigeru Matsumoto, *Motoori Norinaga* (Cambridge, Mass.: Harvard University Press, 1970), 45.

23. Floyd Hiatt Ross, *Shinto: The Way of Japan* (Westport: Greenwood Press, repr. 1983), 126.

24. Motoori Norinaga, quoted in Matsumoto, *Motoori Norinaga*, 50.

25. Jean Herbert, quoted in Bodart-Bailey, "Religion and Society in the Shinto Perspective," 70.

26. Picken, *Sourcebook*, 357.

27. The Buddhist master Kukai or Kobo Daishi (774–835 C.E.), founder of the Shingon Buddhist order, explained: "All beings possessing form or mind necessarily have the Buddha-Nature. Buddha-Nature and Essence pervade the entire Realm of Essence and are not separate." Kukai, quoted in Alan G. Grapard, "Flying Mountains and Walkers of Emptiness: Toward a Definition of Sacred Space in Japanese Religion," *History of Religions*, 21, February 1982, 203.

28. Tachibana Mitsuyoshi, quoted in Picken, *Sourcebook*, 168–169.

29. Joseph J. Spae, quoted in ibid., 302.

30. Uesugi Chisato, quoted in John K. Nelson, *A Year in the Life of a Shinto Shrine* (Seattle: University of Washington Press, 1996), 184.

31. Kobayashi, "Shintoism: Nature's Own Religion," 89.

32. Joseph Kitawaga, *On Understanding Japanese Religion* (Princeton: Princeton University Press, 1987), 50–51.

33. It is interesting to note that before the first recorded Japanese use of the (Chinese-derived) word "Shinto" the term was employed in the culturally influential, sacred text of China known as the *I Ching*: "shen-tao," from which the word Shinto is derived, is found in the passage under the hexagram "kuan" (contemplate) and signifies the divine way or the law of Heaven and Earth. See Muraoka, *Studies in Shinto Thought*, 3.

34. Earhart, *Japanese Religion*, 30.
35. Kitagawa, *On Understanding Japanese Religion*, 142.
36. Ross, *Shinto: The Way of Japan*, 20.
37. *Kojiki,* Book 1, Chapter 39, line 3, in *Kojiki*, trans. Donald L. Philippi (Tokyo: University of Tokyo Press, 1968), 140.
38. Kitabatake Chikafusa, quoted in Muraoka, *Studies in Shinto Thought*, 39.
39. In later periods, when esoteric or tantric Mahayana Buddhist schools held sway over Japan – such as the Shingon tradition – Amaterasu was identified as the Buddha Mahavairochana Tathagata (or Dainichi Nyorai). Buddha Mahavairochana is the visualized, symbolic Buddha that represents the Buddha-body (*dharmakaya*) or the undifferentiated nature of all appearance from which all buddhas and *bodhisattva*s proceed. The Buddha Mahavairochana provides a representational ideal of a truth beyond words that, through *mudra*s (gestures), mantras, and devotionally oriented practices, is accessed and engaged directly via the visualizations of a tantric practitioner. Associated with the heavenly shining sun, Amaterasu was naturally akin to Buddha Mahavairochana, whose name means sun-like "illuminator" in its original Sanskrit form.
40. Chan et al., eds., *Great Asian Religions*, 240.
41. Saka Shibutsu, quoted in Ross, *Shinto: The Way of Japan*, 100.
42. Nelson, *A Year in the Life*, 45.
43. John K. Nelson, *Enduring Identities: The Guise of Shinto in Contemporary Japan* (Honolulu: University of Hawaii Press, 2000), 8.
44. Chief Priest Uesugi, quoted in Nelson, *A Year in the Life*, 29.
45. Yanagawa Keiichi, "The Sensation of *Matsuri*," in *Matsuri: Festivals and Rite in Japanese Life: Contemporary Papers on Japanese Religion*, ed. Inoue Nobutaka, trans. Norman Havens (Tokyo: Kokugakuin University, Institute for Japanese Culture and Classics, 1988), 12.
46. Joseph Campbell, *The Masks of God: Oriental Mythology* (New York: Penguin Books, repr. 1979), 476.

CHAPTER 12

1. For a discussion of ancient Mesopotamia see Karen Rhea Nemet-Nejat, *Daily Life in Ancient Mesopotamia* (Westport: Greenwood Press, 1998).
2. David S. Ariel, *What Do Jews Believe?* (New York: Schocken Books, 1995), 110.
3. See *The Epic of Gilgamesh*, intro. and trans. by Maureen Gallery Kovacs (Stanford: Stanford University Press, 1989).
4. Ariel, *What Do Jews Believe?*, 136.
5. Ibid., 128.
6. Ibid., 237.
7. See Abraham Joshua Heschel, *Israel: An Echo of Eternity* (Woodstock, Vt.: Jewish Lights, 1995), 74.
8. Quoted in Martin Buber, *On Judaism*, ed. N. N. Glatzer (New York: Schocken Books, repr. 1995), 81.

9. Daniel C. Matt, *The Essential Kabbalah: The Heart of Jewish Mysticism* (Edison, NJ: Castle Books, 1997), 1.

10. Ibid., 15.

11. Martin Buber, *Hasidism and Modern Man* (New York: Harper, 1958), 140.

12. Rabbi Adin Steinsaltz, *The Essential Talmud* (New York: Basic Books, 1976), 26.

CHAPTER 13

1. See Marcus J. Borg, *The Heart of Christianity: Rediscovering a Life of Faith* (New York: HarperCollins, 2003).

2. From this point forward all dates refer to the Common Era unless otherwise noted.

3. Some historians believe that Nero was responsible for starting the fire, or for deliberately making it worse.

4. See Edmondo Lupieri, *The Mandeans: The Last Gnostics*, trans. Charles Hindley (Grand Rapids: William B. Eerdmans Publishing Company, 2002).

5. See chapter 5 above, on the Zoroastrian religion, for more on the Manichaean tradition.

6. *Early Christian Writings*, trans. Maxwell Staniforth (Harmondsworth: Penguin, repr. 1982), 103–104.

7. E. Arnold, *The Early Christians*, 4th ed. (Farmington, Pa.: The Plough Publishing House, 1997), 20.

8. Philip Sherrard, *Christianity: Lineaments of a Sacred Tradition* (Brookline, Mass.: Holy Cross Orthodox Press, 1998), 29.

9. St. Augustine, *The Augustine Catechism*, ed. J. E. Rotelle (Hyde Park, NY: New City Press, 1999), 103.

10. St. Benedict, *The Rule of Saint Benedict* (New York: Random House, 1998), 9–10.

11. St. Francis of Assisi, *Omnibus of Sources*, ed. M. A. Habig (Chicago: Franciscan Herald Press, 1973), 1336.

12. See G. Gutierrez, *A Theology of Liberation* (Maryknoll, NY: Orbis, 1998).

13. St. John of the Cross, *The Collected Works of St. John of the Cross*, rev. ed., trans. K. Kavanaugh and O. Rodriguez (Washington, DC: ICS Publications, 1991), 97.

14. Dietrich Bonhoeffer, *The Cost of Discipleship* (New York: Macmillan, repr. 1963), 98.

15. Keith Ward, *Christianity: A Short Introduction* (Oxford: Oneworld, 2000), 100.

16. The Nicene Creed, quoted in *The HarperCollins Encyclopedia of Catholicism*, ed. Richard P. McBrien (New York: HarperCollins, 1995), 917.

17. Jim Wallis, *Agenda for Biblical People* (New York: Harper & Row, 1976), 32.

18. Sherrard, *Christianity*, 31.

19. St. Gregory of Nyssa, quoted in John Hick, *An Interpretation of Religion* (New Haven: Yale University Press, 1989), 238.

20. Thomas Aquinas, *An Aquinas Reader*, ed. Mary Clark (New York: Doubleday, 1972), 139 (emphasis in the original).

21. Meister Eckhart, *Sermons and Treatises*, vol. 1, ed. and trans. M. Walshe (Shaftesbury: Element Books, 1991), 63.

22. See Robert Funk, *Honest to Jesus* (New York: HarperCollins, 1996), 115.

23. *The Nag Hammadi Library*, ed. James M. Robinson (New York: HarperCollins, 1990), 138.

24. Ibid., 126.

25. Thomas Merton, *Contemplative Prayer* (New York: Doubleday Dell, 1996), 85.

26. William Johnston, *Being in Love: A Practical Guide to Christian Prayer* (New York: Fordham University Press, 1999), 76.

27. See, for example, *The Philokalia*, vol. 1, ed. and trans. G. E. H. Palmer, P. Sherrard, and K. Ware (London: Faber & Faber, 1983), 363.

28. Paul Tillich, *A History of Christian Thought*, ed. Carl E. Burton (New York: Simon & Schuster, 1968), 156.

29. Emmanuel Swedenborg, "Heaven and Hell," quoted in George F. Dole, ed., *A Thoughtful Soul: Reflections from Swedenborg* (West Chester, Pa.: Swedenborg Foundation, 1995), 48.

CHAPTER 14

1. Subsequently, references to the Holy Qur'an will be indicated by use of the letter "Q," followed by chapter and verse numbers.

2. For example, many Islamic thinkers were strongly influenced by Greek philosophy, especially Aristotle. Plato and the Neoplatonists were also extensively translated into Arabic and had a profound effect on Islamic philosophy and mysticism. Muhyi-al-Din ibn al-'Arabi, often considered the greatest metaphysical Sufi thinker, was later surnamed "the Son of Plato." Neoplatonism was familiar to the Islamic world through the misidentified "Theology of Aristotle," which was in fact selections from the writings of the Neoplatonists Plotinus and Proclus. Ibn-Rushd, the Hispano-Arab rationalist philosopher from Cordoba, was held in great esteem by Jewish and Christian thinkers for his interpretive works on Aristotle. In fact, Ibn Rushd was known as "the commentator," while Aristotle held the title of "the master." Ibn Rushd's philosophical treatises, exalted for their scientific rationalism, became an integral part of the philosophical curricula of leading European universities.

3. *Hadith*, quoted in Annemarie Schimmel, *Islam: An Introduction* (Albany: State University of New York Press, 1992), 61.

4. Huston Smith, *Islam: A Concise Introduction* (New York: HarperCollins, 2001), 236.

5. Imam 'Ali ibn Abu Talib, *Nahjul Balagha: Peak of Eloquence*, 4th ed., trans. Sayed 'Ali Reza (New York: Tahrike Tarsile Qur'an, repr. 2000), 181.

6. The list of the most beautiful Names of God, including the English translations, is derived from Robert Sade, *The Ninety-Nine Names of God* (Ibadan: Daystar Press, 1970).

7. Jalaluddin Rumi, *Discourses of Rumi*, trans. A. J. Arberry (Richmond: Curzon Press, 1993), 35.

8. See Ibn al-'Arabi, *The Bezels of Wisdom*, trans. and introd. R. W. J. Austin (New York: Paulist Press, 1980).

9. Ibn al-'Arabi, *Tarjuman al-Ashwaq: A Collection of Mystical Odes*, ed. and trans. R. Nicholson (London: Theosophical Publishing House, 1978), 67.

10. A second form of contribution to the poor is *sadaqah*, which, unlike *zakat*, is purely voluntary. *Sadaqah* is considered a meritorious way of demonstrating compassion. A third financial institution in Islam is known as the *jizyah*, a tax applied in medieval times to non-Muslims who shared the benefits given by the Islamic state such as community services, internal security, and protection from external enemies. Unlike Muslim men, non-Muslim males were not obliged to serve in the military; instead, they were required to pay the *jizyah* tax.

11. "The Qushayrian Treatise," quoted in C. W. Ernst, *The Shambhala Guide to Sufism* (Boston: Shambhala, 1997), 23.

CHAPTER 15

1. *Japji*, composed by Guru Nanak, trans. W. H. McLeod in *Textual Sources for the Study of Sikhism* (Manchester: Manchester University Press, 1984), 86.

2. The ten Sikh Gurus are Guru Nanak Dev (1469–1539), Guru Angad Dev (1504–1552), Guru Amar Das (1479–1574), Guru Ram Das (1534–1581), Guru Arjan Dev (1563–1606), Guru Hargobind (1595–1644), Guru Har Rai (1630–1661), Guru Harkrishan (1656–1664), Guru Tegh Bahadur (1621–1675), and Guru Gobind Singh (1666–1708).

3. Guru Nanak, quoted in W. O. Cole and P. Singh Sambhi, *The Sikhs: Their Religious Beliefs and Practices* (London: Routledge & Kegan Paul, repr. 1985), 145.

4. Guru Gobind Singh, "Akal Ustat," quoted in N. G. K. Singh, *The Name of my Beloved: Verses of the Sikh Gurus* (New York: Harper San Francisco, 1995), 8.

5. See J. R. Puri, *Guru Nanak: His Mystic Teachings* (Amritsar: Radha Soami Satsang Beas, 1982), 25.

6. Ibid., 32.

7. Guru Nanak, quoted in K. S. Duggal, *Sikh Gurus: Their Lives and Teachings* (Honesdale, Pa.: Himalayan International Institute, 1987), 31.

8. *Adi Granth*, p. 463, quoted in Eleanor M. Nesbitt, "Sikhism,"in Zaehner, ed., *Encyclopedia of the World's Religions*, 419.

9. *Adi Granth*, p. 730, quoted in Cole and Sambhi, *The Sikhs*, 150.

10. This free verse translation, and other additions to this chapter, were generously provided to the authors by Dr. Amarjit Singh of the University of Maryland.

11. *Adi Granth*, p. 62, quoted in Singh, *My Beloved*, 9.

12. Translated by Charanjit K. AjitSingh in *The Wisdom of Sikhism* (Oxford: Oneworld, 2001), 113.

13. McLeod, *Textual Sources*, 92.

14. Singh, *My Beloved*, 5.

15. Guru Nanak, quoted in Duggal, *Sikh Gurus*, 24–25.

16. From the *Adi Granth*, quoted in McLeod, *Textual Sources*, 46.

17. See Kirpal Singh, *Naam or Word* (Bowling Green, Va.: Sawan Kirpal Publications, 1981), 36.

18. Translated by McLeod in *Textual Sources*, 86.

19. Ibid., 91.

20. The *Bhagavad-Gita*, for instance, refers to the physical body as a "nine-gated city" on account of the nine passages leading out of the body. See *Bhagavad-Gita* 5.13 in *The Bhagavad Gita and its Message*, trans. Sri Aurobindo (Twin Lakes, Wis.: Lotus Press, 1995), 93.
21. McLeod, *Textual Sources*, 57.

CHAPTER 16

1. Bahá'u'lláh, *Prayers and Meditations by Bahá'u'lláh* (Wilmette. Ill.: Bahá'í Publishing Trust, 1987), 314.
2. Bahá'u'lláh, *Gleanings from the Writings of Bahá'u'lláh* (London: Bahá'í Publishing Trust, 1949), 286.
3. The Bab, quoted in Shoghi Effendi, *The Dawnbreakers* (London: Bahá'í Publishing Trust, 1953), 87.
4. Ibid., 373.
5. Bahá'u'lláh, *Epistle to the Son of the Wolf* (Wilmette, Ill.: Bahá'í Publishing Trust, 1988), 21.
6. Bahá'u'lláh, *Proclamation of Bahá'u'lláh* (Wilmette, Ill.: Bahá'í Publishing Trust, 1978), 122.
7. Ibid., 284.
8. Shoghi Effendi, *The World Order of Bahá'u'lláh*, 2nd rev. ed. (Wilmette, Ill.: Bahá'í Publishing Trust, 1974), 167.
9. Bahá'u'lláh, *Gleanings*, 286.
10. Ibid., 287.
11. Ibid., 249.
12. Bahá'u'lláh, *The Hidden Words*, centenary edition (London: Nightingale Books, 1992), 20.
13. Shoghi Effendi, *Guidance for Today and Tomorrow: A Selection of Writings of Shoghi Effendi* (London: Bahá'í Publishing Trust, 1953), 167–169.
14. J. E. Esslemont, *Bahá'u'lláh and the New Era*, 4th rev. ed. (Wilmette, Ill.: Bahá'í Publishing Trust, 1980), 149.
15. Bahá'u'lláh, *Gleanings*, 259.
16. 'Abdu'l-Bahá, *Paris Talks: Addresses Given by 'Abdu'l-Bahá in Paris in 1911–1912*, 10th ed. (London: Bahá'í Publishing Trust, 1961), 143.
17. 'Abdu'l-Bahá, *The Promulgation of Universal Peace*, 2nd ed. (Wilmette, Ill.: Bahá'í Publishing Trust, 1982), 181.
18. 'Abdu'l-Bahá, *Paris Talks*, 136.
19. Abdu'l-Bahá, *Some Answered Questions*, trans. Laura Clifford Barney (Wilmette, Ill.: Bahá'í Publishing Trust, 1981), 300.
20. 'Abdu'l-Bahá, *Paris Talks*, 85.
21. Bahá'u'lláh, *The Kitáb-i-Aqdas, The Most Holy Book* (Haifa: Bahá'í World Centre, 1992), 41.
22. Ibid., 105.
23. Shoghi Effendi, *Guidance for Today and Tomorrow*, 3–4.

BIBLIOGRAPHY

THE RELIGIOUS TRADITIONS OF THE FIRST PEOPLES

Works Cited

Brown, Joseph Epes. "Modes of Contemplation through Actions: North American Indians," *Main Currents in Modern Thought*, 30 (November/December 1973): 58–63.

——. *The Sacred Pipe: Black Elk's Account of the Seven Rites of the Oglala Sioux*. New York: Viking Penguin, 1971.

——. "The Spiritual Legacy of the American Indian," *Studies in Comparative Religion*, 14 (Winter/Spring 1980): 18–33.

——. *The Spiritual Legacy of the American Indian*. New York: Crossroad, 1982.

Campbell, Joseph. *Myths to Live By*. New York: Bantam Books, 1973.

Codrington, R. H. *The Melanesians: Studies in their Anthropology and Folk Lore*. New York: Dover, 1972.

Eliade, Mircea. *The Sacred and Profane*, trans. Willard R. Trask. New York: Harcourt, Brace & World, 1959.

——. *Shamanism: Archaic Guide to Ecstasy*, trans. Willard R. Trask. New York: Bollingen Foundation, 1964.

——. *Yoga: Immortality and Freedom*, trans. Willard R. Trask. Princeton: Princeton University Press, 1970.

Ellwood, Robert. *Mysticism and Religion*, 2nd ed. New York: Seven Bridges Press, 1999.

Erdoes, Richard, and Alfonso Ortiz, eds. *American Indian Myths and Legends*. New York: Pantheon Books, 1984.

Evans-Pritchard, E. E. *Nuer Religion*. Oxford: Clarendon Press, 1956.

Gill, Sam. *Native American Religious Action: A Performance Approach to Religion*. Columbia: University of South Carolina Press, 1987.

Hall, Calvin S., and Vernon J. Nordby. *A Primer of Jungian Psychology*. New York: New American Library, 1973.

Highwater, Jamake. *The Primal Mind*. New York: Harper & Row, 1981.

Idowu, Bolaji E. *African Traditional Religion*. New York: Orbis Books, 1973.

Larsen, Stephen. *The Mythic Imagination*. New York: Bantam Books, 1990.

Neihardt, John G. *Black Elk Speaks*. Lincoln: University of Nebraska Press, repr. 1961.

Otto, Rudolf. *The Idea of the Holy*. Oxford: Oxford University Press, repr. 1958.

Parrinder, Geoffrey. *African Traditional Religion*. Westport: Greenwood Press, repr. 1976.

Schuon, Frithjof. *The Essential Writings of Frithjof Schuon*, ed. Seyyed Hossein Nasr. New York: Amity House, 1986.

——. *The Feathered Sun*. Bloomington: World Wisdom Books, 1990.

Scotton, Bruce W., Allan B. Chinen, and John R. Battista, eds. *Textbook of Transpersonal Psychiatry and Psychology*. New York: Basic Books, 1996.

Smart, Ninian, and Richard D. Hecht. *Sacred Texts: A Universal Anthology*. New York: Crossroad, repr. 2001.

Smith, Huston. *Forgotten Truth*. San Francisco: HarperCollins, repr. 1992.

——. *The World's Religions*. New York: HarperCollins, repr. 1991.

van Gennep, Arnold. *The Rites of Passage*. Chicago: University of Chicago Press, repr. 1960.

Zuesse, Evan. *Ritual Cosmos: The Sanctification of Life in African Religion*. Athens: Ohio University Press, 1979.

Additional Reading

Campbell, Joseph. *The Hero with a Thousand Faces*. Princeton: Princeton University Press, 1973.

——. *Primitive Mythology*. New York: Penguin Books, repr. 1987.

Eliade, Mircea. *Patterns in Comparative Religion*, trans. Rosemary Sheed. Lincoln: University of Nebraska Press, repr. 1996.

——. *Rites and Symbols of Initiation*. New York: Harper & Row, 1965.

Evans-Pritchard, E. E. *Theories of Primitive Religion*. London: Oxford University Press, 1965.

Gill, Sam D. *Native American Religions*. Belmont, Calif.: Wadsworth, 1982.

King, Noel. *African Cosmos: An Introduction to Religion in Africa*. Belmont, Calif.: Wadsworth, 1986.

Lévi-Strauss, Claude. *The Savage Mind*. Chicago: University of Chicago Press, 1965.

Radin, Paul. *Primitive Man as Philosopher*. New York: Dover, repr. 1957.

Zahan, Dominique. *The Religion, Spirituality, and Thought of Traditional Africa*. Chicago: University of Chicago Press, repr. 1979.

THE RELIGIOUS TRADITIONS OF MESOAMERICA

Works Cited

Carrasco, Davíd. *Religions of Mesoamerica: Cosmovision and Ceremonial Centers*. New York: Harper & Row, 1990.

Carrasco, Davíd, ed. *The Oxford Encyclopedia of Mesoamerican Cultures: The Civilizations of Mexico and Central America*. New York: Oxford University Press, 2001.

The Destruction of the Jaguar: Poems from the Books of Chilam Balam, trans. Christopher Sawyer-Lauçanno. San Francisco: City Lights Books, 1987.

Eliade, Mircea. *Shamanism: Archaic Techniques of Ecstasy*, trans. Willard R. Trask. Princeton: Princeton University Press, 1972.

Florescano, Enrique. *The Myth of Quetzalcoatl*, trans. Lysa Hochroth. Baltimore: Johns Hopkins University Press, 1999.

León-Portilla, Miguel. *Aztec Thought and Culture: A Study of the Ancient Nahuatl Mind*, trans. Jack Emory Davis. Norman: University of Oklahoma Press, repr. 1990.

——. *Time and Reality in the Thought of the Maya*, 2nd ed. enlarged, trans. Charles L. Boilès, Fernando Horcasitas, and Miguel León-Portilla. Norman: University of Oklahoma Press, 1988.

León-Portilla, Miguel, ed. *Native Mesoamerican Spirituality*. New York: Paulist Press, 1980.

León-Portilla, Miguel, and Earl Shorris, eds. *In the Language of Kings: An Anthology of Mesoamerican Literature – Pre-Columbian to the Present*. New York: W. W. Norton & Company, 2001.

Levenson, Jay A., ed. *Circa 1492: Art in the Age of Exploration*. New Haven: Yale University Press for the National Gallery of Art, 1991.

Tedlock, Dennis. *Popol Vuh: The Definitive Edition of the Mayan Book of the Dawn of Life and the Glories of Gods and Kings*, rev. ed. New York: Simon & Schuster, 1996.

Further Reading

Christenson, Allen J. *Popol Vuh: The Sacred Book of the Maya*. New York: O Books, 2003.

Morley, Sylvanus Griswold. *An Introduction to the Study of the Maya Hieroglyphs*. New York: Dover, repr. 1975.

Schele, Linda, and David Freidel. *A Forest of Kings: The Untold Story of the Ancient Maya*. New York: William Morrow & Company, 1990.

Thompson, J. Eric. S. *Maya History and Religion*. Norman: University of Oklahoma Press, 1970.

THE RELIGIOUS TRADITIONS OF ANCIENT EGYPT

Works Cited

Assmann, Jan. *The Search for God in Ancient Egypt*, trans. David Lorton. New York: Cornell University Press, 2001.

The Book of the Dead, trans. E. A. Wallis Budge. Secaucus, NJ: University Books, 1960.

Clark, R. T. Rundle. *Myth and Symbol in Ancient Egypt*. London: Thames & Hudson, 1959.

Eliade, Mircea. *The Sacred and Profane*, trans. Willard R. Trask. New York: Harcourt, Brace & World, 1959.

Frankfort, H. *Ancient Egyptian Religion*. New York: Columbia University Press, 1948.

Frankfort, H., H. A. Frankfort, J. A. Wilson, T. Jacobsen, and W. A. Irwin, eds. *The Intellectual Adventure of Ancient Man*. Chicago: University of Chicago Press, 1946.

Hadot, Pierre. *Plotinus or the Simplicity of Vision*, trans. Michael Chase. Chicago: University of Chicago Press, 1993.

Schuon, Frithjof. *The Essential Writings of Frithjof Schuon*, ed. Seyyed Hossein Nasr. New York: Amity House, 1986.

Shaw, Ian, ed. *The Oxford History of Ancient Egypt*. Oxford: Oxford University Press, 2000.

Smart, Ninian, and Richard D. Hecht, eds. *Sacred Texts of the World: A Universal Anthology*. New York: Crossroads, 2001.

Additional Reading

Boylan, Patrick. *Thoth: The Hermes of Egypt*. Chicago: Ares, repr. 1987.

Breasted, James Henry. *Development of Religion and Thought in Ancient Egypt*. New York: Charles Scribner's Sons, 1912.

The Egyptian Heaven and Hell, trans E. A. Wallis Budge. Mineola, NY: Dover, repr. 1996.

Eliade, Mircea. *A History of Religious Ideas*, vol. 2. Chicago: University of Chicago Press, repr. 1978.

Lamy, Lucie. *Egyptian Mysteries*. London: Thames & Hudson, repr. 1997.

Quirke, Stephen. *Ancient Egyptian Religion*. New York: Dover, repr. 1995.

Shafer, Byron E. *Religion in Ancient Egypt*. Ithaca: Cornell University Press, 1991.

THE RELIGIOUS TRADITIONS OF ANCIENT GREECE

Works Cited

Apuleius. *The Golden Ass (The Transformation of Lucius)*, trans. Robert Graves. New York: Noonday Press, repr. 1992.

Aristotle. *The Complete Works of Aristotle*, vols. 1 and 2, ed. Jonathan Barnes. Princeton: Princeton University Press, 1984.

——. *Great Books of the Western World: The Works of Aristotle*, vols. 1 and 2, ed. Robert Maynard Hutchins. Chicago: Encyclopaedia Britannica, 1952.

——. *Aristotle: Nicomachean Ethics*, trans. Joe Sachs. Newburyport, Mass.: Focus Publishing, 2002.

Auden, W. H. *Forewords and Afterwords*. New York: Random House, 1973.

Burkert, Walter. *Ancient Mystery Cults*. Cambridge, Mass.: Harvard University Press, repr. 1987.

Burnet, John. *Greek Philosophy: Thales to Plato*. London: Macmillan, repr. 1962.

Coleridge, Samuel Taylor. *Spiritual Writings: Selected Poems and Prose*, introd. Robert Van de Weyer. London: HarperCollins, 1997.

Cornford, Francis M. *Plato's Cosmology: The Timaeus of Plato*. Indianapolis: Hackett, repr. 1997.

Dodds, E. R. *Select Passages Illustrating Neoplatonism*. Chicago: Ares, repr. 1979.

Edwards, Mark. *Neoplatonic Saints: The Lives of Plotinus and Proclus by their Students*. Liverpool: Liverpool University Press, 2000.

Flaceliere, Robert. *Greek Oracles*, trans. Douglas Garman. London: Elek Books, 1965.

Guthrie, W. K. C. *Orpheus and Greek Religion*. Princeton: Princeton University Press, repr. 1993.

Herodotus. *The Histories*, trans. Aubrey De Sélincourt, introd. John Marincola. New York: Penguin Books, repr. 1996.

Hesiod. *Works and Days and Theogony*, trans. Stanley Lombardo and introd. Robert Lamberton. Indianapolis: Hackett, 1993.

Jaeger, Werner. *The Theology of the Early Greek Philosophers*. Oxford: Oxford University Press, repr. 1952.

Lesher, James. *The Greek Philosophers: Selected Greek Texts from the Presocratics, Plato, and Aristotle, with Introduction, Notes, and Commentary*. London: Bristol Classical Press/Duckworth, 1998.

Lombardo, Stanley. *Parmenides and Empedocles: The Fragments in Verse Translation*. San Francisco: Grey Fox Press, repr. 1982.

Nietzsche, Friedrich. *The Birth of Tragedy*, trans. Clifton P. Fadiman. New York: Dover, repr. 1995.

Oates, Whitney J. and Eugene O'Neill, eds. *The Complete Greek Drama*, trans. Gilbert Murray, vols. 1 and 2. New York: Random House, 1938.

Olson, Alan M., and Leroy S. Rouner, eds. *Transcendence and the Sacred*. Notre Dame, Ind.: University of Notre Dame Press, 1981.

Ovid. *Metamorphoses*, trans. A. D. Melville, introd. E. J. Kenney. Oxford: Oxford University Press, repr. 1998.

Plato. *The Collected Dialogues*, ed. Edith Hamilton and Huntington Cairns. Princeton: Princeton University Press, 1961.

——. *Complete Works*, ed. John M. Cooper. Indianapolis: Hackett, 1997.

——. *The Symposium of Plato: The Shelley Translation*, ed. David K. O'Connor. South Bend, Ind.: St. Augustine's Press, 2002.

Rayor, Diane. *The Homeric Hymns: A Translation, with Introduction and Notes*. Berkeley: University of California Press, 2004.

Schiller, Friedrich. *On the Aesthetic Education of Man: In a Series of Lectures*, trans. and introd. Elizabeth Wilkinson and L. A. Willoughby. Oxford: Oxford University Press, repr. 1982.

Sophocles. *The Three Theban Plays*, trans. Robert Fagles. New York: Penguin Books, 1984.

Toynbee, Arnold. *A Study of History*, vol. 12: *Reconsiderations*. London: Oxford University Press, 1961.

Wilber, Ken, ed. *Quantum Questions*. Boston: Shambhala, 1985.

Whitehead, Alfred North. *Process and Reality*. New York: Free Press, repr. 1979.

Additional Reading

Angus, S. *The Mystery Religions*. New York: Dover, 1975.

Dodds, E. R. *The Greeks and the Irrational*. Boston: Beacon, 1957.

Homer. *Iliad*, trans. Stanley Lombardo. Indianapolis: Hackett, 1997.

——. *Odyssey*, trans. Stanley Lombardo, intro. Sheila Murnaghan. Indianapolis: Hackett, 2000.

Kirk, G. S., J. E. Raven and Malcolm Schofield, *The Presocratic Philosophers: A Critical History with a Selection of Texts*, 2nd ed. Cambridge: Cambridge University Press, 2002.

Plotinus. *Great Books of the Western World: The Six Enneads*. Chicago: Encyclopaedia Britannica, 1952.

THE ZOROASTRIAN FAITH

Works Cited

Armstrong, Karen. *The Great Transformation*. New York: Alfred A. Knopf, 2006.

Boyce, Mary. *Zoroastrianism: Its Antiquity and Constant Vigour*. Costa Mesa: Mazda, 1992.

———. *Zoroastrians: Their Religious Beliefs and Practices*. London: Routledge & Kegan Paul, 1987.

Boyce, Mary, ed. and trans. *Textual Sources for the Study of Zoroastrianism*. Chicago: University of Chicago Press, repr. 1987.

Campbell, Joseph. *The Hero with a Thousand Faces*, 2nd ed. Princeton: Princeton University Press, repr. 1973.

Cumont, Franz. *The Mysteries of Mithra*, trans. Thomas J. McCormack. New York: Dover, 1956.

Eliade, Mircea. *A History of Religious Ideas*, vol. 1, trans. Willard R. Trask. Chicago: University of Chicago Press, 1978.

Eliade, Mircea, and Ioan P. Couliano. *The Eliade Guide to World Religions*. New York: HarperCollins, 1991.

Foltz, Richard. *Spirituality in the Land of the Noble: How Iran Shaped the World's Religions*. Oxford: Oneworld, 2004.

The Gathas of Zarathushtra, trans. and commentary Piloo Nanavutty. Middletown, NJ: Grantha, 1999.

Jaspers, Karl. *Way to Wisdom: An Introduction to Philosophy*, trans. Ralph Manheim. London: Yale University Press, 1954.

Klimkeit, Hans-Joachim. *Gnosis on the Silk Road*. New York: HarperCollins, 1993.

Mehr, Farhang. *The Zoroastrian Tradition*. Costa Mesa: Mazda, 2003.

Nanavutty, Piloo. *The Parsis*. New Delhi: National Book Trust, 1977.

Nasr, Seyyed Hossein. *Religion and the Order of Nature*. New York: Oxford University Press, 1996.

Pangborn, Cyrus R. *Zoroastrianism: A Beleaguered Faith*. New Delhi: Vikas, 1982.

The Pythagorean Sourcebook and Library, trans. Kenneth Sylvan Guthrie. Grand Rapids: Phanes Press, 1987.

Smith, Wilfred Cantwell. *The Meaning and End of Religion*. Minneapolis: Fortress Press, 1991.

Tagore, Rabindranath. *The Religion of Man*. London: Unwin Hyman, repr. 1988.

Wilson, Andrew. *World Scripture: A Comparative Anthology of Sacred Texts*. New York: Paragon House, 1991.

The Zend Avesta of Zarathustra, trans. Edmond Bordeaux Szekely. n.p.: International Biogenic Society, 1990.

Additional Reading

Barr, James. "The Question of Religious Influence: The Case of Zoroastrianism, Judaism, and Christianity," *Journal of the American Academy of Religion*, 53, 2 (June 1985): 201–235.

Corbin, Henry. *Spiritual Body and Celestial Earth: From Mazdean Iran to Shī'ite Iran*, trans. Nancy Pearson. Princeton: Princeton University Press, 1977.

Dhalla, M. N. *History of Zoroastrianism*. New York: Oxford University Press, 1938.

Duchesne, Guillemin J. *The Hymns of Zarathustra*. Boston: Charles E. Tuttle, 1992.

Mehta, P. D. *Zarathustra: The Transcendental Vision*. Shaftesbury: Element Books, 1985.

Nigosian, S. A. *The Zoroastrian Faith*. Montreal: McGill-Queen's University Press, 1993.

Randeria, J. D. *The Parsi Mind*. New Delhi: Munshiran Manohazlal, 1993.

Razavi, M. A. *Suhrawardi and the School of Illumination*. Richmond: Curzon Press, 1997.

Rivetna, Roshan, ed. *The Legacy of Zarathustra: An Introduction to the Religion, History, and Culture of the Zarathushtis (Zoroastrians)*. Hinsdale, Ill.: Federation of the Zoroastrian Associations of North America, 2002.

Taraposewala, I. J. S. *The Religion of Zarathustra*. Tehran: Sazman-e-Faravahar, 1980.

Zaehner, R. C. *The Dawn and Twilight of Zoroastrianism*. London: Weidenfeld & Nicolson, 1961.

THE HINDU TRADITION

Works Cited

Aurobindo, Sri. *The Essential Writings of Sri Aurobindo*, ed. P. Heehs. New Delhi: Oxford University Press, 1998.

——. *The Message of the Gita*, ed. Anilbaran Roy. Pondicherry: Sri Aurobindo Ashram, repr. 1999.

Basham, A. L. *The Origins and Development of Classical Hinduism*. Boston: Beacon, 1989.

Brahma Sutras: According to Sri Sankara, trans. and introd. Swami Vireswarananda. Calcutta: Advaita Ashrama, repr. 2005.

Dasgupta, S. N. *Hindu Mysticism*. Delhi: Motilal Banarsidass, repr. 1983.

Eck, Diana L. *Darśan: Seeing the Divine Image in India*, 2nd ed. Chambersburg, Pa.: Anima Books, repr. 1985.

Eliade, Mircea. *Yoga: Immortality and Freedom*, trans. Willard R. Trask. Princeton: Princeton University Press, 1970.

Klostermaier, K. L. *Hindu Writings: A Short Introduction to the Major Sources*. Oxford: Oneworld, 2000.

Mahadevan, T. M. P. *Outlines of Hinduism*. Bombay: Chetana, repr. 1984.

Massoudi, Mehrdad. "On the Qualities of a Teacher and a Student: An Eastern Perspective Based on Buddhism, Vedanta, and Sufism," *Intercultural Education*, 13 (2002): 137–155.

Nikhilananda, Swami. *Hinduism: Its Meaning for the Liberation of the Spirit*. Madras: Sri Ramakrishna Math, 1968.

Paz, Octavio. *In Light of India*. Orlando: Harcourt Brace & Company, 1998.

Prabhavananda, Swami. *Religion in Practice*. Hollywood: Vedanta Press, repr. 1969.

——. *The Spiritual Heritage of India*. Hollywood: Vedanta Press, repr. 1980.

Radhakrishnan, S. *Indian Philosophy*, vol. 2, 2nd ed. London: George Allen & Unwin, 1971.

Ramakrishna, Sri. *The Gospel of Sri Ramakrishna*, abridged ed., trans. and introd. Swami Nikhilananda. New York: Ramakrishna-Vivekananda Center, repr. 1988.

Singh, Karan. *Essays on Hinduism*. Chattanooga: Insights Press, 1998.

The Upanishads, trans. Eknath Easwaran. Petaluma, Calif.: Nilgiri Press, repr. 1988.

The Upanishads: A New Translation, vol. 3, trans. and introd. Swami Nikhilananda. New York: Ramakrishna-Vivekananda Center, repr. 1990.

Additional Reading

The Bhagavad Gita trans. and introd. Swami Nikhilananda. New York: Ramakrishna-Vivekananda Center, repr. 1987.

Brockington, J. L. *The Sacred Thread*. Edinburgh: Edinburgh University Press, 1996.

Chinmayananda, Swami. *Self-Unfoldment*. Percy, Calif.: Chinmaya, 1994.

——. *Talks on Shankara's* Vivekachoodamani. Bombay: Central Chinmaya Mission Trust, repr. 1993.

The Cultural Heritage of India, vols. 1–4. Calcutta: Ramakrishna Mission Institute of Culture, repr. 2001.

Dasgupta, S. N. *A History of Indian Philosophy*, vols. 1–5. Delhi: Motilal Banarsidass, repr. 1992.

Embree, A. T., ed. *The Hindu Tradition*. New York: Random House, 1972.

Feuerstein, George. *Teachings of Yoga*. Boston: Shambhala, 1997.

Gandhi, M. K. *All Men are Brothers*, comp. and ed. K. Kripalani. New York: Continuum, 1988.

Iyengar, B. K. S. *Light on the Yoga Sutras of Patanjali*. n.p.: Thorsons, 2003.

Nikhilananda, Swami. *Man in Search of Immortality: Testimonials from the Hindu Scriptures*. London: Allen & Unwin, 1968.

Radhakrishnan, S. and C. A. Moore, eds. *A Sourcebook in Indian Philosophy*. Princeton: Princeton University Press, 1957.

Sivananda, Swami. *All About Hinduism*. Shivanandangar: Divine Life Society, 1988.

Torwesten, Hans. *Vedanta: Heart of Hinduism*. New York: Grove Press, 1991.

Zimmer, H. *Philosophies of India*, ed. Joseph Campbell. Princeton: Princeton University Press, 1969.

THE BUDDHIST TRADITION

Works Cited

Conze, Edward. *Buddhism: Its Essence and Development*. New York: Harper & Row, repr. 1975.

The Dhammapada, trans. Eknath Easwaran. Petaluma, Calif.: Nilgiri Press, repr. 1987.

Digha-Nikaya, trans. M. Walshe as *The Long Discourses of the Buddha* in *Thus Have I Heard*. Boston: Wisdom, 1995.

Goldstein, Joseph. *Insight Meditation*. Boston: Shambhala, 1994.

Gunaratana, Bhante G. *Mindfulness in Plain English*. Boston: Wisdom, 1993.

Kalupahana, David J. *Nāgārjuna: The Philosophy of the Middle Way*. New York: State University of New York Press, 1986.

Kapleau, Roshi P. *The Three Pillars of Zen*. New York: Anchor Books, 1980.

Piyadassi Thera. *The Buddha's Ancient Path*. Kandy: Buddhist Publication Society, repr. 1987.

Rahula, W. *What the Buddha Taught*. New York: Grove Press, 1974.

Śāntideva, *A Guide to the Bodhisattva Way of Life*, trans. Vesna A. Wallace and B. Alan Wallace. Ithaca, NY: Snow Lion, 1997.

The Sutta-Nipata, trans. H. Saddhatissa. London: Curzon Press, 1985.

The Tibetan Book of Living and Dying, ed. Patrick Gaffney and Andrew Harvey, trans. Sogyal Rinpoche. New York: HarperCollins, 1992.

The Udāna, trans. John D. Ireland. Kandy: Buddhist Publication Society, 1990.

Vissudhimaga (The Path to Purification), trans. Bhikkhu Nanamoli. Kandy: Buddhist Publication Society, 1991.

Wallace, B. Alan. *Boundless Heart: The Four Immeasurables*, ed. Zara Houshmand. New York: Snow Lion, 1999.

———. *Tibetan Buddhism From the Ground Up*. Boston: Wisdom, 1993.

Additional Reading

Abe, M. *Zen and Western Thought*, ed. W. R. La Fleur. Honolulu: University of Hawaii Press, 1989.

Achaan Chah. *A Still Forest Pool*, ed. J. Kornfield and P. Breiter. Wheaton, Ill.: Quest, 1985.

Buddhadāsa, Bhikkhu. *Mindfulness with Breathing: A Manual for Serious Beginners*, trans. Santikaro Bhikkhu. Boston: Wisdom, 1997.

Chodron, Thubten. *Open Heart, Clear Mind*. Ithaca, NY: Snow Lion, 1991.

Dalai Lama, XIV. *The Meaning of Life from a Buddhist Perspective*. Boston: Wisdom, 1992.

Dogen. *Moon in a Dewdrop*, ed. K. Tanahashi. San Francisco: North Point Press, 1990.

Govinda, Lama A. *A Living Buddhism for the West*. Boston: Shambhala, 1990.

Harvey, P. *An Introduction to Buddhism*. Cambridge: Cambridge University Press, 1990.

Middle Length Discourses of the Buddha (*Majjhima Nikaya*), trans. Bhikkhu Nanamoli and Bhikkhu Bodhi. Boston: Wisdom, 1995.

Morreale, D., ed. *The Complete Guide to Buddhist America*. Boston: Shambhala, 1998.

Ross, N. W. *Buddhism: A Way of Life and Thought*. New York: Vintage Books, 1981.

Sangharakshita, Ven. *A Survey of Buddhism*, 7th ed. Moseley: Windhorse, 1993.

Snelling, J. *The Buddhist Handbook*. London: Rider, 1987.

Suzuki, D. T. *An Introduction to Zen Buddhism*. New York: Grove Press, 1964.

THE JAIN TRADITION

Works Cited

Beversluis, Joel. *Sourcebook of the World's Religions*. Novato, Calif.: New World Library, 2000.

The Cultural Heritage of India, vol. 1. Calcutta: Ramakrishna Mission, Institute of Culture, repr. 2001.

Dasgupta, S. *A History of Indian Philosophy*, vol. 1. Delhi: Motilal Banarsidass, repr. 1992.

Gandhi, M. K. *The Moral and Political Writings of Mahatma Gandhi*, vol. 2, ed. Raghavan Iyer. Oxford: Clarendon Press, 1986–1987.

Jaini, P. S. *The Jaina Path of Purification*. Delhi: Motilal Banarsidass, repr. 1990.

Muller, F. Max, ed. *Sacred Books of the East*, vol. 45: *Jaina Sutras*, book 2. Delhi: Motilal Banarsidass, repr. 1980.

Smart, Ninian, and Richard D. Hecht., eds. *Sacred Texts of the World: A Universal Anthology*. New York: Crossroads, 2001.

Wilson, Andrew. *World Scripture: A Comparative Anthology of Sacred Texts*. New York: Paragon House, 1991.

Additional Reading

Altman, N. *The Nonviolent Revolution*. Shaftesbury: Element Books, 1988.

Bhattacharyya, N. N. *Jain Philosophy: Historical Outline*. New Delhi: Munshiram Manoharlal, 1976.

Chapple, C. K. *Nonviolence to Animals, Earth, and Self in Asian Traditions*. Albany: State University of New York Press, 1993.

Chitrabhanu, Gurudev Shree. *Realize What You Are: The Dynamics of Jain Meditation*. New York: Dodd, Mead, & Company, 1978.

——. *Twelve Facets of Reality: The Jain Path to Freedom*. New York: Dodd, Mead, & Company, 1980.

Dundas, P. *The Jains*. London: Routledge, 1992.

Kumar, Satish. *No Destination: A Resurgence Book*. Totnes: Green Books, 1992.

Prabhavananda, Swami. *The Spiritual Heritage of India*, 3rd ed.. Hollywood: Vendanta Press, 1980.

Sushil Kumarji Maharaj, Acharya. *Song of the Soul*. Blairstown, NJ: Siddhachalam, 1987.

That Which Is: Tattvarth Sutra, trans. N. Tatia. San Francisco: HarperCollins, 1994.

Tobias, M. *Life Force: The World of Jainism*. Berkeley: Berkeley Humanities Press, 1991.

Weeraperuma, S. *Major Religions of India*. Bombay: Chetana, 1985.

Zaehner, R. C., ed. *Encyclopedia of the World's Religions*. New York: Barnes & Noble, 1997.

THE TEACHINGS OF LAO TZU

Works Cited

Addiss, S., and S. Lombardo. *Tao Te Ching*. Indianapolis: Hackett, 1993.

Broughton, Jeffrey L. *The Bodhidharma Anthology: The Earliest Records of Zen*. Berkeley: University of California Press, 1999.

Chan, Wing-Tsit. *A Source Book in Chinese Philosophy*. Princeton: Princeton University Press, 1963.

Cooper, J. C. *Taoism: The Way of the Mystic*. Wellingborough: Aquarian Press, repr. 1990.

Feng, G. F., and J. English. *Tao Te Ching*. New York: Vintage Books, repr. 1989.

The I Ching or Book of Changes: The Richard Wilhem Translation rendered into English By Cary F. Baynes, 3rd ed. Princeton: Princeton University Press, 1967.

Lieh Tzu. *The Book of Lieh-tzu*, trans. A. C. Graham. New York: Columbia University Press, repr. 1990.

Ritsema, Rudolf, and Stephen Karcher. *I Ching: The Classic Chinese Oracle of Change*. Rockport, Mass.: Element Books, 1994.

Sharma, Arvind, ed. *Our Religions*. New York: HarperCollins, 1995.

Smith, Huston. *The World's Religions*. New York: HarperCollins, 1991.

Waley, Arthur. *The Way and its Power: A Study of the* Tao Te Ching *and its Place in Chinese Thought*. New York: Grove Weidenfeld, 1958.

Watson, Burton. *Chuang Tzu: Basic Writings*. New York: Columbia University Press, 1964.

Watts, Alan. *The Way of Zen*. New York: Vintage Books, 1957.

Additional Reading

Chuang Tzu. *The Complete Works of Chuang Tzu*, trans. B. Watson. New York: Columbia University Press, 1968.

Cleary, Thomas. *The Essential Tao*. Edison, NJ: Castle Books, 1998.

Lao Tzu. *Tao Te Ching: A New English Version*, trans. S. Mitchell. New York: Harper & Row, 1988.

Lin, Yutang. *The Importance of Living*. New York: William Morrow & Company, repr. 1965.

——. *The Wisdom of Laotse*. New York: Random, repr. 1976.

Liu, I. M. *Awakening to the Tao*, trans. Thomas Cleary. Boston: Shambhala, 1988.

Wei, H. *The Guiding Light of Lao Tzu*. Wheaton, Ill.: Theosophical Publishing House, 1982.

THE TEACHINGS OF CONFUCIUS

Works Cited

Chan, Wing-Tsit. *A Source Book in Chinese Philosophy*. Princeton: Princeton University Press, 1963.

The Essential Confucius, trans. Thomas Cleary. Edison, NJ: Castle Books, 1992.

Doeblin, Alfred. *Living Thoughts of Confucius*. Greenwich, Conn.: Fawcett Books, 1959.

The I Ching or Book of Changes. The Richard Wilhelm Translation Rendered into English by Cary F. Baynes, trans. Richard Wilhelm, 3rd ed. Princeton: Princeton University Press, 1967.

Lin Yutang. *The Wisdom of Confucius*. New York: Modern Library, repr. 1966.

Ritsema, Rudolf, and Stephen Karcher. *I Ching: The Classic Chinese Oracle of Change*. Rockport, Mass.: Element Books, 1994.

Sharma, Arvind, ed. *Our Religions*. New York: HarperCollins, 1995.

Smith, Huston. *The World's Religions*. New York: HarperCollins, 1991.

Soothil, William Edward. *The Analects of Confucius*, 2nd ed. New York: Paragon Book Reprint Corp., 1968.

Waley, Arthur. *The Analects of Confucius*. New York: Vintage Books, 1938.

Wei-ming, Tu. *Confucian Thought: Selfhood as Creative Transformation*. Albany: State University of New York Press, 1985.

Additional Reading

Bahm, A. J. *The Heart of Confucius*. Fremont, Calif.: Jain Publishing Company, repr. 1992.

Fingarette, H. *Confucius: The Secular as Sacred*. New York: Harper & Row, 1972.

Koller, John M. *Oriental Philosophies*, 2nd ed. New York: Charles Scribner's Sons, repr. 1985.

Mencius (Meng Tzu). *Mencius*, trans. D. Hilton. Washington, DC: Counterpoint, 1998.

——. *Mencius*, trans. D. C. Lau. New York: Penguin Books, repr. 1984.

Overmyer, D. L. *Religions of China*. New York: Harper, 1986.

THE SHINTO TRADITION

Works Cited

Bodart-Bailey, Beatrice M. "Religion and Society in the Shinto Perspective," *Journal of Dharma*, 9 (January–March 1984): 68–76.

Campbell, Joseph. *The Masks of God: Oriental Mythology*. New York: Penguin Books, repr. 1979.

——. *Sake & Satori: Asian Journals – Japan*, ed. David Kudler. Novato, Calif.: New World Library, 2002.

Chan, Wing-tsit, Isma'īl Rāgī al Fārūqī, Joseph M. Kitagawa, and P. T. Raju, eds. *Great Asian Religions: An Anthology*. London: Macmillan, 1969.

Earhart, H. Byron. *Japanese Religion: Unity and Diversity*, 3rd ed. Belmont, Calif.: Wadsworth, 1982.

Ellwood, Robert S., and Richard Pilgrim. *Japanese Religion*. Englewood Cliffs: Prentice-Hall, 1985.

Grapard, Alan G. "Flying Mountains and Walkers of Emptiness: Toward a Definition of Sacred Space in Japanese Religion," *History of Religions*, 21 (February 1982): 195–221.

Kitagawa, Joseph. *On Understanding Japanese Religion*. Princeton: Princeton University Press, 1987.

Kobayashi, Akiko. "Shintoism: Nature's Own Religion," *Journal of Dharma*, 26 (January–March 2001): 87–95.

Kojiki, trans. Donald L. Philippi. Tokyo: University of Tokyo Press, 1968.

Matsumoto, Shigeru. *Motoori Norinaga*. Cambridge, Mass.: Harvard University Press, 1970.

Matsuri: Festivals and Rite in Japanese Life: Contemporary Papers on Japanese Religion, ed. Inoue Nobutaka, trans. Norman Havens. Tokyo: Kokugakuin University, Institute for Japanese Culture and Classics, 1988.

McFarland, H. Neill. *The Rush Hour of the Gods: A Study of New Religious Movements in Japan*. New York: Macmillan, 1967.

Muraoka, Tsunetsugo. *Studies in Shinto Thought*, trans. Delmer M. Brown and James T. Araki. Tokyo: Ministry of Education, 1964.

Nelson, John K. *Enduring Identities: The Guise of Shinto in Contemporary Japan*. Honolulu: University of Hawaii Press, 2000.

——. *A Year in the Life of a Shinto Shrine*. Seattle: University of Washington Press, 1996.

Nobutaka, Inoue, ed. *Kami*, trans. Norman Havens. Tokyo: Kokugakuin University, Institute for Japanese Culture and Classics, 1988.

Ono, Sokyo. *Shinto: The Kami Way*, 2nd ed. Rutland, Vt.: Charles E. Tuttle, 1962.

Picken, Stuart D. *Shinto Meditations for Revering the Earth*. Berkeley: Stone Bridge Press, 2002.

Picken, Stuart D., ed. *Sourcebook in Shinto: Selected Documents*. Westport: Praeger, 2004.

Reader, Ian. *Religion in Contemporary Japan*. Honolulu: University of Hawaii Press, 1991.

Ross, Floyd Hiatt. *Shinto: The Way of Japan*. Westport: Greenwood Press, repr. 1983.

Yamamoto, Yukitaka. *Kami no Michi: The Way of the Kami*. Stockton, Calif.: Tsubaki America Publications, 1987.

Additional Reading

Blacker, Carmen. *The Catalpa Bow: A Study of Shamanistic Practices in Japan*. London: George Allen & Unwin, repr. 1986.

Bocking, Brian. *A Popular Dictionary of Shinto*. Chicago: NTC Publishing Group, repr. 1997.

Ellwood, Robert S. *An Invitation to Japanese Civilization*. Belmont, Calif.: Wadsworth, 1980.

Hori, Ichiro. *Folk Religion in Japan*. Chicago: Chicago University Press, 1968.

Nihongi: Chronicles of Japan from the Earliest Times to A.D. 697, trans. W. G. Aston. London: George Allen & Unwin, repr. 1956.

Picken, Stuart D. *Essentials of Shinto: An Analytical Guide to Principal Teachings*. Westport: Greenwood Press, 1994.

——. "Religiosity and Irreligiosity in Japan: Aspects of mu-shukyo," *Japanese Religions*, 11 (December 1979): 51–72.

Smith, Robert J. *Ancestor Worship in Contemporary Japan*. Stanford: Stanford University Press, 1974.

THE JEWISH FAITH

Works Cited

Ariel, David S. *What Do Jews Believe?* New York: Schocken, 1995.

Buber, Martin. *Hasidism and Modern Man*. New York: Harper, 1958.

——. *On Judaism*, ed. N. N. Glatzer. New York: Schocken, repr. 1995.

The Epic of Gilgamesh, intro. and trans. by Maureen Gallery Kovacs. Stanford: Stanford University Press, 1989.

Heschel, Abraham Joshua. *Israel: An Echo of Eternity*. Woodstock, Vt.: Jewish Lights, 1995.

Matt, Daniel C. *The Essential Kabbalah: The Heart of Jewish Mysticism*. Edison, NJ: Castle Books, 1997.

Nemet-Nejat, Karen Rhea. *Daily Life in Ancient Mesopotamia*. Westport: Greenwood Press, 1998.

Steinsaltz, Rabbi Adin. *The Essential Talmud*. New York: Basic Books, 1976.

Tanakh: The Holy Scriptures. Philadelphia: Jewish Publication Society, 1985.

Additional Reading

Bachya ben Joseph ibn Paquda. *Duties of the Heart*, Hebrew–English ed., vols. 1 and 2, trans. D. Haberman. Nanuet, NY: Feldheim, 1999.

Borowitz, Eugene B. *Liberal Judaism*. New York: Union of American Hebrew Congregations (UAHC), 1984.

Cohn-Sherbok, Lavinia and Dan. *A Short History of Judaism*. Oxford: Oneworld, 1994.

De Lange, N. R. M. *An Introduction to Judaism*. Cambridge: Cambridge University Press, 2000.

Green, Rabbi Arthur. *Seek My Face, Speak My Name: A Contemporary Jewish Theology*. Northvale, NJ: Jason Aronson, 1994.

Heschel, Rabbi Abraham Joshua. *God in Search of Man: A Philosophy of Judaism*. New York: Farrar, Straus & Giroux, 1957.

——. *Man is Not Alone: A Philosophy of Religion*. New York: Farrar, Straus & Giroux, 1951.

Holtz, Barry W., ed. *Back to the Sources: Reading the Classic Jewish Texts*. New York: Simon & Schuster, 1984.

Jacobs, Louis. *Jewish Values*. Hartford, Conn.: Hartmore House, 1969.

Kaplan, Rabbi Aryeh. *The Light Beyond: Adventures in Hassidic Thought*. New York: Maznaim, 1981.

Kaplan, Mordecai M. *Judaism as a Civilization*. New York: Schocken, 1967.

Maimonides, Moses. *The Guide of the Perplexed*, trans. Schlomo Pines. Chicago: Chicago University Press, 1963.

Prager, D., and J. Telushkin. *The Nine Questions People Ask about Judaism*. New York: Simon & Schuster, 1981.

Sacks, Rabbi Jonathan. *To Heal a Fractured World: The Ethics of Responsibility*. New York: Schocken Books, 2005.

Schneerson, Rabbi M. M. *Toward a Meaningful Life*, adapted by Simon Jacobson. New York: William Morrow & Company, 1995.

Scholem, Gershom. *Major Trends in Jewish Mysticism*. New York: Schocken, 1941.

Solomon, Norman. *Judaism: A Very Short Introduction*. Oxford: Oxford University Press, 1996.

Soloveitchik, Rabbi Joseph B. *Halakhic Man*. Philadelphia: Jewish Publication Society, 1983.

Steinberg, Rabbi Milton. *Basic Judaism*. Orlando: Harcourt Brace & Company, 1975.

Telushkin, Joseph. *Jewish Wisdom*. New York: William Morrow, 1994.

Twerski, Rabbi Abraham J. *Wisdom Each Day*. New York: Mesorah Publications, 2000.

Wolpe, Rabbi David J. *Why Be Jewish?* New York: Henry Hold & Company, 1995.

THE CHRISTIAN FAITH

Works Cited

Aquinas, Thomas. *An Aquinas Reader*, ed. Mary Clark. New York: Doubleday, 1972.

Arnold, Eberhard. *The Early Christians*, 4th ed. Farmington, Pa.: The Plough Publishing House, 1997.

St. Augustine. *The Augustine Catechism*, ed. J. E. Rotelle. Hyde Park, NY: New City Press, 1999.

St. Benedict. *The Rule of Saint Benedict*. New York: Random House, 1998.

Holy Bible: The King James Version. Nashville, Tenn.: Thomas Nelson, 1984.

Bonhoeffer, Dietrich. *The Cost of Discipleship*. New York: Macmillan, repr. 1963.

Borg, Marcus J. *The Heart of Christianity: Rediscovering a Life of Faith*. New York: HarperCollins, 2003.

Dole, George F., ed. *A Thoughtful Soul: Reflections from Swedenborg*. West Chester, Pa.: Swedenborg Foundation, 1995.

Early Christian Writings, trans. Maxwell Staniforth. Harmondsworth: Penguin, repr. 1982.

Eckhart, Meister. *Sermons and Treatises*, vol. 1, ed. and trans. M. Walshe. Shaftesbury: Element, 1991.

St. Francis of Assisi. *Omnibus of Sources*, ed. M. A. Habig. Chicago: Franciscan Herald Press, 1973.

Funk, Robert W. *Honest to Jesus*. New York: HarperCollins, 1996.

Gutierrez, G. *A Theology of Liberation*. Maryknoll, NY: Orbis, 1998.

Hick, J. *An Interpretation of Religion*. New Haven: Yale University Press, 1989.

St. John of the Cross. *The Collected Works of St. John of the Cross*, rev. ed., trans. K. Kavanaugh and O. Rodriguez. Washington, DC: ICS Publications, 1991.

Johnston, William. *Being in Love: A Practical Guide to Christian Prayer*. New York: Fordham University Press, 1999.

Lupieri, Edmondo. *The Mandeans: The Last Gnostics*, trans. Charles Hindley. Grand Rapids: William B. Eerdmans Publishing Company, 2002.

McBrien, R. P., ed. *The HarperCollins Encyclopedia of Catholicism*. New York: HarperCollins, 1995.

Merton, Thomas. *Contemplative Prayer*. New York: Doubleday Dell, 1996.

The Nag Hammadi Library, ed. James M. Robinson. New York: HarperCollins, 1990.

The Philokalia, vol. 1, ed. and trans. G. E. H. Palmer, P. Sherrard, and K. Ware. London: Faber & Faber, 1983.

Sherrard, Philip. *Christianity: Lineaments of a Sacred Tradition*. Brookline, Mass.: Holy Cross Orthodox Press, 1998.

Tillich, Paul. *A History of Christian Thought*, ed. Carl E. Burton. New York: Simon & Schuster, 1968.

Wallis, Jim. *Agenda for Biblical People*. New York: Harper & Row, 1976.

Ward, Keith. *Christianity: A Short Introduction*. Oxford: Oneworld, 2000.

Additional Reading

Holy Bible: With the Apocryphal/Deuterocanonical Books: NRSV, New Revised Standard Version. New York: Harper Bibles, 2007.

Borg, Marcus J. *On Reading the Bible Again for the First Time*. New York: HarperCollins, 1992.

Crossman, John Dominic. *Jesus: A Revolutionary Biography*. New York: HarperCollins, 1995.

Edwards, David L. *Christianity: The First Two Thousand Years*. Maryknoll, NY: Orbis, 1997.

Frend, W. H. C. *The Early Church*. Minneapolis: Fortress Press, repr. 1991.

Hick, John, and Paul F. Knitter, eds. *The Myth of Christian Uniqueness*. Maryknoll, NY: Orbis, 1987.

King, Ursula. *Christian Mystics*. New York: Simon & Schuster Editions, 1998.

Knitter, P. *No Other Names? A Critical Survey of Christian Attitudes Towards World Religions*. Maryknoll, NY: Orbis, 1985.

The New American Bible: Translated from the Original Languages with Critical Use of All the Ancient Sources: With the Revised Book of Psalms and the Revised New Testament, trans. Confraternity of Christian Doctrine, Catholic Church, and United States Catholic Conference. Iowa Falls: World Bible Publishers, n.d.

Pelikan, Jaroslav. *Jesus Through the Centuries*. New Haven: Yale University Press, 1985.

Romero, Oscar. *The Violence of Love*. Farmington, Pa.: The Plough Publishing House, 1998.

Spong, John Shelby. *Why Christianity Must Change or Die*. New York: HarperCollins, 1999.

Thurman, Howard. *Jesus and the Disinherited*. Boston: Beacon, 1996.

Tutu, Desmond. *No Future Without Forgiveness*. New York: Random House, 1999.

Ware, T. *The Orthodox Church*. New York: Penguin, 1997.

THE FAITH OF ISLAM
Works Cited

'Ali, Imam ibn Abu Talib. *Nahjul Balagha: Peak of Eloquence*, 4th ed., trans. Sayed 'Ali Reza. New York: Tahrike Tarsile Qur'an, repr. 2000.

Ibn al-'Arabi. *The Bezels of Wisdom*, trans. and introd. R. W. J. Austin. New York: Paulist Press, 1980.

——. *Tarjuman al-Ashwaq: A Collection of Mystical Odes*, ed. and trans. R. Nicholson. London: Theosophical Publishing House, 1978.

Ernst, C. W. *The Shambhala Guide to Sufism*. Boston: Shambhala, 1997.

An Interpretation of the Qur'an, trans. Majid Fakhry. Reading: Garnet Publishing, 2000.

Rumi, Jalaluddin. *Discourses of Rumi*, trans. A. J. Arberry. Richmond: Curzon Press, 1993.

Sade, Robert. *The Ninety-Nine Names of God*. Ibadan: Daystar Press, 1970.

Schimmel, A. *Islam: An Introduction*. Albany: State University of New York Press, 1992.

Smith, Huston. *Islam: A Concise Introduction*. New York: HarperCollins, 2001.

Additional Reading

Asad, Muhammad. *The Message of the Qur'an: The Full Account of the Revealed Arabic Text Accompanied by Parallel Translation*. Bitton: Book Foundation, 2003.

Cragg, K., and R. M. Speight. *The House of Islam*, 3rd ed. Belmont, Calif.: Wadsworth, 1988.

Esack, Farid. *On Being a Muslim*. Oxford: Oneworld, 1999.

Frager, Robert, and James Fadiman. *Essential Sufism*. Edison, NJ: Castle Books, repr. 1998.

Lewis, Bernard. *Islam and the West*. New York: Oxford University Press, 1993.

Lings, Martin. *Muhammad: His Life Based on the Earliest Sources*. Rochester, Vt.: Inner Traditions International, 1983.

Muzaffer, Ozak al-Jerrahi. *Irshad: Wisdom of a Sufi Master*. Westport: Pir, 1988.

Nasr, Seyyed Husayn. *Ideals and Realities of Islam*, 2nd ed. London: Unwin Paperbacks, 1988.

——. *Knowledge and the Sacred*. Albany: State University of New York Press, 1989.

——. *Science and Civilization in Islam*. New York: Barnes & Noble, 1992.

Nicholson, R. A. *The Mystics of Islam*. London: Arkana, 1989.

Nurbakhsh, J. *In the Tavern of Ruin*. New York: Khanigahi Nimatullahi, 1978.

Rahman, F. *Islam*, 2nd ed. Chicago: University of Chicago Press, 1974.

Rauf, Imam Feisal Abdul. *What's Right with Islam*. New York: HarperCollins, 2004.

Schimmel, A. *Mystical Dimensions of Islam*. Chapel Hill: University of North Carolina Press, 1975.

Schuon, F. *Christianity/Islam: Essays on Esoteric Ecumenicism*. Bloomington: World Wisdom Books, 1985.

——. *Understanding Islam*. Bloomington: World Wisdom Books, 1994.

Smith, Margaret. *Rabi'a*. Oxford: Oneworld, 1994.

——. *Readings from the Mystics of Islam*. Westport: Pir, 1994.

Trimingham, J. S. *The Sufi Orders in Islam*. New York: Oxford University Press, 1998.

THE SIKH FAITH

Works Cited

The Bhagavad Gita and its Message, trans. Sri Aurobindo. Twin Lakes, Wis.: Lotus Press, 1995.

Cole, W. O. and P. Singh Sambhi. *The Sikhs: Their Religious Beliefs and Practices*. London: Routledge & Kegan Paul, repr. 1985.

Duggal, K. S. *Sikh Gurus: Their Lives and Teachings*. Honesdale, Pa.: Himalayan International Institute, 1987.

McLeod, W. H. *Textual Sources for the Study of Sikhism*. Manchester: Manchester University Press, 1984.

Nesbitt, Eleanor M. "Sikhism," in R. C. Zaehner, ed., *Encyclopedia of the World's Religions*, New York: Barnes & Noble, 1997, pp. 408–37.

Puri, J. R. *Guru Nanak: His Mystic Teachings*. Amritsar: Radha Soami Satsang Beas, 1982.

Singh, Kirpal. *Naam or Word*. Bowling Green, Va.: Sawan Kirpal Publications, 1981.

Singh, N. G. K. *The Name of My Beloved: Verses of the Sikh Gurus*. New York: Harper San Francisco, 1995.

The Wisdom of Sikhism, trans. Charanjit K. Ajit Singh. Oxford: Oneworld, 2001.

Additional Reading

The Cultural Heritage of India, vol. 4. Calcutta: Ramakrishna Mission Institute of Calcutta, repr. 2001.

Dass, Nirmal. *Songs of Kabir from the Adi Granth*. Albany: State University of New York Press, 1991.

——. *Songs of the Saints from the Adi Granth*. Albany: State University of New York Press, 2000.

Duggal, K. S. *The Sikh People: Yesterday and Today*. New Delhi: UBS Publishers' Distributors, 1995.

Sethi, V. K. *Kabir: The Weaver of God's Name*. Amritsar: Radha Soami Satsang Beas, 1984.

Singh, Darshan. *The Secret of Secrets*. Bowling Green, Va.: Sawan Kirpal Publications, 1983.

Singh, Kirpal. *The Crown of Life*. Bowling Green, Va.: Sawan Kirpal Publications, 1980.

——. *Godman*. Anaheim, Calif.: Ruhani Satsang, 1989.

——. *Prayer: Its Nature and Technique*. Bowling Green, Va.: Sawan Kirpal Publications, 1981.

Singh, Patwant. *The Sikhs*. London: John Murray, 1999.

THE BAHA'I FAITH

Works Cited

'Abdu'l-Bahá. *Paris Talks: Addresses given by 'Abdu'l-Bahá in Paris in 1911–1912*, 10th ed. London: Bahá'í Publishing Trust, 1961.

——. *The Promulgation of Universal Peace*, 2nd ed. Wilmette, Ill.: Bahá'í Publishing Trust, 1982.

——. *Some Answered Questions*, trans. Laura Clifford Barney. Wilmette, Ill.: Bahá'í Publishing Trust, 1981.

Bahá'u'lláh. *Epistle to the Son of the Wolf*. Wilmette, Ill.: Bahá'í Publishing Trust, 1988.

——. *Gleanings from the Writings of Bahá'u'lláh*. London: Bahá'í Publishing Trust, 1949.

——. *The Hidden Words*, centenary ed. London: Nightingale Books, 1992.

——. *The Kitáb-i-Aqdas, The Most Holy Book*. Haifa: Bahá'í World Centre, 1992.

——. *Prayers and Meditations by Bahá'u'lláh*. Wilmette, Ill.: Bahá'í Publishing Trust, 1987.

——. *Proclamation of Bahá'u'lláh*. Wilmette, Ill.: Bahá'í Publishing Trust, 1978.

Effendi, Shoghi. *The Dawnbreakers*. London: Bahá'í Publishing Trust, 1953.

——. *Guidance for Today and Tomorrow: A Selection of the Writings of Shoghi Effendi*. London: Bahá'í Publishing Trust, 1953.

——. *The World Order of Bahá'u'lláh*, 2nd rev. ed. Wilmette, Ill.: Bahá'í Publishing Trust, 1974.

Esslemont, J. E. *Bahá'u'lláh and the New Era*, 4th rev. ed. Wilmette, Ill.: Bahá'í Publishing Trust, 1980.

Additional Reading

'Abdu'l-Bahá. *Selections from the Writings of 'Abdu'l-Bahá*, comp. Research Department of the Universal House of Justice. Haifa: Bahá'í World Centre, 1978.

——. *The Will and Testament of 'Abdu'l-Bahá*, 2nd ed. Wilmette, Ill.: Bahá'í Publishing Trust, 1971.

The Báb. *Selections from the Writings of the Báb*. Haifa: Bahá'í World Centre, 1976.

Bahá'u'lláh. *The Kitáb-i-Íqán; The Book of Certitude*, 3rd ed. London: Bahá'í Publishing Trust, 1982.

Effendi, Shoghi. *The Advent of Divine Justice*, 3rd ed. Wilmette, Ill.: Bahá'í Publishing Trust, 1969.

——. *God Passes By*, 3rd ed. Wilmette, Ill.: Bahá'í Publishing Trust, 1974.

Ferraby, J. *All Things Made New*. London: Bahá'í Publishing Trust, 1974.

Hatcher, W. S., and J. D. Martin. *The Bahá'í Faith: The Emerging Global Religion*. New York: Harper & Row, 1985.

Taherzadeh, A., ed. *The Revelation of Bahá'u'lláh*, vols. 1–4. Oxford: George Ronald, 1986.

INDEX